CONFESSIONS OF A GUERRILLA WRITER

Books by Dan E. Moldea

The Hoffa Wars:
Teamsters, Rebels, Politicians, and the Mob
1978

The Hunting of Cain:
A True Story of Money, Greed, and Fratricide
1983

Dark Victory:
Ronald Reagan, MCA, and the Mob
1986

Interference:
How Organized Crime Influences Professional Football
1989

The Killing of Robert F. Kennedy:
An Investigation of Motive, Means, and Opportunity
1995

Evidence Dismissed:
The Inside Story of the Police Investigation of O. J. Simpson
(with Tom Lange and Philip Vannatter)
1997

A Washington Tragedy:
How the Death of Vincent Foster Ignited a Political Firestorm
1998

Confessions of a Guerrilla Writer:
Adventures in the Jungles of Crime, Politics, and Journalism
2013

Hollywood Confidential:
A True Story of Wiretapping, Friendship, and Betrayal
2018

Money, Politics, and Corruption in U.S. Higher Education:
The Stories of Whistleblowers
2020

Confessions of a Guerrilla Writer

*Adventures in the Jungles of
Crime, Politics, and Journalism*

Third Edition

Dan E. Moldea

MOLDEA.COM
Washington, D.C.

Copyright © 2013, 2015, 2020 by Dan E. Moldea

Moldea.com

All rights reserved
Printed in the United States

Portions of this book have appeared in Dan Moldea's previous books and articles, as well as on his website, *www.moldea.com*, where updates about this work will appear.

Library of Congress Cataloging-in-Publication Data

Moldea, Dan E., 1950-

Confessions of a Guerrilla Writer / by Dan E. Moldea

1. Moldea, Dan E.—Crime. 2. Politics. 3. Journalism.

ISBN-13: 978-1-7350984-0-1

Third Edition

To Marsha Moldea

Betty Lee (Clark) and Mary Ann (Guzik) Andrews

Barbara Allyne Bennet and Father Nick

Jack, Joe, Jim, Mary Frances (Chenier) and Jean Craciun

Eugenia Marie, Joe and Tom Craciun

John and Diane Kisbac

Becky (Scoarste) and Dennis Moldovan

James Romosca

Jane (Salanty) and Sam Romosca

CONTENTS

PREFACE: On taking it · xv

PROLOGUE: Chasing a ghost · xxi

PART ONE: Entering the fray · 1
   1. Kent State · 3
   2. Surviving the revolution · 8
   3. Into the real world · 12
   4. Running for office · 15
   5. On selling out · 20
   6. Becoming a writer · 26
   7. Set up in Chicago · 28
   8. Jimmy Hoffa disappears · 32
   9. At the Red Fox · 35
  10. The goon squad · 40
  11. The Local 299 violence · 43
  12. Manitoulin Island · 47
  13. A guerrilla writer in New York · 50
  14. The man in the black Cadillac · 54

PART TWO: The Teamsters & the Mafia · · · · · · · · · · · · · · · · 61
  15. Dealing with the FBI · 63
  16. Back to Detroit · 65
  17. The Hoffa Reward Fund · 70
  18. A surprise witness at the grand jury · · · · · · · · · · · · · · · · 74
  19. The payoff man · 78
  20. Brother in The Bond · 81
  21. Confronting McMaster · 85
  22. "Jimmy ran off to Brazil with a black go-go dancer" · · · · · · · · 92
  23. Calling Sally Bugs at Local 560 · · · · · · · · · · · · · · · · · · · 97
  24. My lunch with Hoffa's alleged killers · · · · · · · · · · · · · · · · 99
  25. Death threat · 104
  26. The contract · 107
  27. To Washington · 110

PART THREE: Hoffa, Marcello & Trafficante · · · · · · · · · · · · · · · · 113
  28. "Who is Frank Sheeran?" · 115
  29. "To do two things at once is to do neither" · · · · · · · · · · · 117
  30. The Hoffex Memo · 120
  31. The killing of the President · 121
  32. "I think my dad knew Jack Ruby" · · · · · · · · · · · · · · · · 125
  33. Findings · 127
  34. Brill and S & S get tough · 130
  35. Briguglio and I get whacked · 132
  36. Paddington to the rescue · 135
  37. The New York Times creates me · · · · · · · · · · · · · · · · · 137
  38. Yes, we have no Central Sanitation · · · · · · · · · · · · · · · 141
  39. The U.S. House Assassinations Committee · · · · · · · · · · 145
  40. Helping TDU and PROD make peace · · · · · · · · · · · · · 149
  41. "The mob did it. It's a historical fact." · · · · · · · · · · · · · 153
  42. The Paddington bankruptcy · 155
  43. Fear causes indecision · 157

PART FOUR: Ronald Reagan & MCA · · · · · · · · · · · · · · · · · · · 159
  44. Reagan courting Teamsters · 161
  45. The Institute for Policy Studies · · · · · · · · · · · · · · · · · · 163
  46. The CIA and the Mafia again? · · · · · · · · · · · · · · · · · · 167
  47. Writers' rights · 170
  48. The American Writers Congress · · · · · · · · · · · · · · · · · 173
  49. The Milo murder · 178
  50. Paying respects · 183
  51. Subpoenaed · 185
  52. Going back East · 190
  53. The Wall Street Journal settles · · · · · · · · · · · · · · · · · · 193
  54. Reagan and the Hollywood Mafia · · · · · · · · · · · · · · · · 194
  55. Finding gold in Los Angeles · 197
  56. William Morris Agency, Viking Press · · · · · · · · · · · · · · 202
  57. Korshak gets a pass · 204
  58. Political Isolation · 207
  59. Bad timing · 210
  60. Trouble with the New York Times · · · · · · · · · · · · · · · · 214

PART FIVE: The NFL & the Mafia · 221
  61. The Frontline broadcast · 223
  62. Investigating professional football · · · · · · · · · · · · · · · · 225
  63. Game fixing in the NFL · 228

64. Rosenbloom was not murdered · 231
65. Predicting the media's reaction · · · · · · · · · · · · · · · · · · 232
66. Pre-publication · 236
67. "A troublesome book" · 239
68. Looking for fights · 241
69. Debating an empty chair · 244
70. A secret meeting in Las Vegas · 246
71. "We have to destroy you now" · · · · · · · · · · · · · · · · · · · 248
72. A sudden problem · 250
73. The review in the New York Times · · · · · · · · · · · · · · · · 252
74. Pigs and sausages · 254
75. Combat on Nightline · 258
76. A game of chicken · 262
77. "I'll give you a good fight!" · 266

PART SIX: Moldea v. New York Times · · · · · · · · · · · · · · · · · **269**
78. At war with the New York Times · · · · · · · · · · · · · · · · · · 271
79. Joe Browne and Gerald Eskenazi · · · · · · · · · · · · · · · · · 274
80. Cooke v. Washingtonian · 278
81. A slow judge makes a fast decision · · · · · · · · · · · · · · · · 283
82. The U.S. Court of Appeals · 287
83. "Reversed and remanded" · 290
84. "Beyond a Bad Review" · 293
85. Kenneth Starr and The World Amicus · · · · · · · · · · · · · · 295
86. An unprecedented reversal: Moldea II · · · · · · · · · · · · · 298
87. The Simmons-Starr debate · 303
88. The Supreme Court says "no" · 308
89. Alien Ink · 310
90. The Washington Post and the FBI informant · · · · · · · · · · · 314

PART SEVEN: From RFK to OJ · **317**
91. An appearance of conspiracy · 319
92. Releasing the LAPD's files · 323
93. Interviewing the cops · 325
94. The suicide of Greg Stone · 328
95. Back in the game · 331
96. Getting to Sirhan · 335
97. Doubts · 339
98. Confronting Sirhan · 341
99. When wisdom comes late · 346
100. Bad photograph, great review · · · · · · · · · · · · · · · · · · · 350

    101. Old problems become a new reality · · · · · · · · · · · · · · · · · 358
    102. The O. J. Simpson case · 362
    103. Working with Lange and Vannatter · · · · · · · · · · · · · · · · · 366
    104. Mark Fuhrman's lies and delusions · · · · · · · · · · · · · · · · · 370
    105. Back on the defensive · 373

PART EIGHT: The road to impeachment · · · · · · · · · · · · · · · · · · · **379**
    106. From Fuhrman to Foster · 381
    107. The odd couple · 384
    108. Help from an unexpected source · · · · · · · · · · · · · · · · · · · 387
    109. The Foster crime scene · 391
    110. Creating a political firestorm · 394
    111. Regnery's pro-Clinton book · 397
    112. The Lewinsky scandal · 401
    113. The OIC leaks · 405
    114. Openly taking sides · 407
    115. The secret tapes · 411
    116. Heresy · 418

PART NINE: The Flynt Project ·**421**
    117. Exposing hypocrisy · 423
    118. Trying to remove the President · 426
    119. I become Larry Flynt's investigator · · · · · · · · · · · · · · · · · 428
    120. Targeting Clinton's critics · 431
    121. The Flynt team's first meeting · 433
    122. Going after the House Speaker · 435
    123. The bombshell · 442
    124. Livingston resigns · 447
    125. At play in the fields of scandal · 450
    126. "The rule of law" · 452
    127. Abortion and aftermath · 456
    128. Geraldo sandbags Flynt · 458
    129. Barr overplays his hand · 460
    130. "Who got Bob Livingston?" · 464
    131. Newsweek outs me · 468
    132. The right-wing media reacts · 472
    133. Flynt nearly dies · 478
    134. The Byrd resolution · 479
    135. Light my fire · 482

PART TEN: Intermezzo · 485
136. Buried alive by the Jello Left · 487
137. Collateral damage · 493
138. Caucus of One · 500
139. When I'm 64 · 505

PART ELEVEN: The D.C. Madam · 509
140. Cowboy and Lightfoot · 511
141. "Are you two working together?" · 516
142. "So tell me about David Vitter" · 524
143. Morals of a Muckraker · 532
144. "Are you okay?" · 535
145. Suicide before prison · 541
146. Opposition research · 549

PART TWELVE: Hoffa redux · 553
147. Frank Sheeran's conflicting confessions · 555
148. Not a distinction without a difference · 562
149. "They're digging at a farm in Wixom" · 568
150. "It's going to be a great day tomorrow" · 576
151. Brother Moscato and the Jersey City landfill · 582
152. "Picardo basically had it right" · 588

PART THIRTEEN: Intermezzo II · 593
153. "Remember where you heard it first" · 595
154. RFK Jr. calls to discuss his father's murder · 599
155. Working to save an ex-KGB officer · 612
156. On reversions, wiretappers and whistleblowers · 617

PART FOURTEEN: Hoffa redux II · 621
157. Three-act drama, different characters in each act · 623
158. Murder, oil drum, Gateway truck, Jersey City · 628
159. Great cinema, bad history · 634
160. "This is where my dad buried Jimmy Hoffa" · 641
161. "Frank, are you okay?" · 647

EPILOGUE: So far . . . · 651

Endnotes · 653

**I came into this game for the action, the excitement.
Go anywhere; travel light.
Get in, get out—wherever there's trouble.
A man alone.**

> Harry Tuttle,
> from Terry Gilliam's *Brazil*

PREFACE:

On taking it

For most of my adult life, I worked as a fiercely independent investigative journalist who had concentrated, for the most part, on investigations of organized crime—a really stupid way to make a living. During my turbulent career—which has now yielded eight true-crime books—I was widely known as one of the most relentless freelance reporters in America.

But, refusing to take a punch without fighting back, I made nearly as many enemies as friends, burning as many bridges as I had built. Along with my probes of the Mafia, I had taken on such powerful institutions as the Teamsters Union, the National Football League, the National Rifle Association, the Los Angeles Police Department, MCA, the Reagan White House, the FBI and the Department of Justice, the legal and illegal gambling communities, the *New York Times*, the *Wall Street Journal*, the *Washington Post*, Kenneth Starr and the Office of the Independent Counsel, and both the political left and right wings, as well as a variety of politicians, white-collar criminals, and murderers.

Although my career-long obsession revolves around the 1975 disappearance of former Teamsters president Jimmy Hoffa, I was the first reporter to present the case that Hoffa—along with Carlos Marcello, the boss of the New Orleans Mafia, and Santo Trafficante, the Mafia boss of Tampa—had arranged and executed the murder of President John Kennedy in 1963, "a straight mob hit."

A year after I revealed this in my 1978 book, *The Hoffa Wars*, the U.S. House Select Committee on Assassinations released its final report, insisting that Hoffa, Marcello and Trafficante had the "motive, means and opportunity" to kill the President. The chief counsel of the committee flatly stated, "The mob did it. It's a historical fact."

My subsequent news-breaking books about the contract killing of an Ohio businessman (1983), the Mafia's penetration of Hollywood and the corruption of Ronald Reagan (1986), and the influence of organized crime in professional football (1989) were equally controversial but also led to wider investigations.

With regard to my 1995 book about the 1968 murder of Senator Robert Kennedy, I did conclude that the LAPD had arrested the right man. However, because of all the police errors, the existing evidence gave critics of the official investigation, like me, ample opportunity to claim that the senator had been killed by a conspiracy. In the end, twenty-seven years later, I solved that case—because, for the first time, I explained what the LAPD could not: Why the crime-scene evidence had given the illusion that two guns had been fired—when, in fact, Sirhan Sirhan, whom I interviewed extensively, had acted alone.

I later wrote equally solid books, concluding that football star O. J. Simpson had also acted alone when he allegedly killed his ex-wife and a friend of hers in 1994 and that Deputy White House Counsel Vincent Foster had acted alone when he committed suicide in 1993. I published those books in 1997 and 1998, respectively. The O. J. book, which I co-authored with the two lead LAPD detectives in the case, was a national bestseller.

In addition, in 2018, I published a book about the Anthony Pellicano wiretapping scandal in Hollywood, which became a major RICO federal-conspiracy case. And, in 2020, I released my tenth book, featuring the stories of whistleblowers and their heroic work while fighting corruption in higher education.

In what many considered an act of journalistic heresy—apart from my 1990-1994 landmark libel suit against the *New York Times*, the newspaper that created, destroyed, and then resurrected me—I served as Larry Flynt's lead investigator for eight weeks during his highly publicized crusade to expose President Bill Clinton's enemies who had conflicting standards of private behavior for public officials: one for those they like, and another for those they don't like.

Specifically, my work for Flynt led to the dramatic resignation of U.S. House Speaker-designate Bob Livingston on December 19, 1998—the climactic moment that derailed Republican dreams and schemes to remove the President from office.

For this, I make no apology. However, my work for Flynt represented a career-altering experience. After years as an independent investigative

PREFACE: ON TAKING IT

journalist, I began working as an independent investigative consultant who specialized on opposition research against the radical right of the Republican Party, which, to me, had become as dangerous and nefarious as the Mafia.

Nine years later, I discovered the phone number of U.S. Senator David Vitter (R-Louisiana), another right-wing hypocrite, in the private telephone records of Deborah Jeane Palfrey, the so-called "D.C. Madam" with whom I had worked on a book about her life and times prior to her tragic suicide in 2008.

Meantime, as a favor to a friend, a former CIA case officer, I tried to help spring a KGB agent from a Russian prison. That KGB agent, whose life was in danger, was responsible for exposing Robert Hanssen, a top official in the FBI, as a Russian spy.

Yet, despite the chronic chaos and combat that has marked my career, I have worked hard to establish a solid reputation as an honest, careful, and thorough journalist, author, and investigator. I have never missed a deadline. I have never misquoted a source. I have never taken an off-the-record quote and placed it on the record. I have never revealed a confidential source without permission from the source. Also, no one has ever sued me for any reason for anything contained in any of my previous seven books.

Joe the Boss of my own operation, I receive no weekly paycheck, no expense account, no paid vacations, and no pension or welfare plans. I will not get a gold watch when I retire. Because I never had any real business sense, I have spent most of my career overcommitted and underfinanced. And never having any real institutional protection, I have been nearly killed on no fewer than six different occasions. Inasmuch as I am neither naturally courageous nor trained to be brave, I have battled primal fear in any number of situations, trying not to freeze up.

Through all of this, I have become a very tough guy—not because I can dish it out, but because I can take it.

The following story is not simply a series of unconnected anecdotes and vignettes. It is an interconnected succession of events in which one adventure leads to the next, with high-and-low-profile characters who weave in and out of the overall plot.

Also, on a higher level, this is a contemporary history of five decades of crime, politics, and journalism—and many of the news-making events that have occurred during this fascinating period—as seen through the eyes of a fiercely independent man who has taken some hard licks but survived to tell this story.

As with all of my previous works, everything in this book has been extensively fact-checked with the documentation on file. Whenever possible, I used the databases of the *New York Times*, the *Washington Post*, and the *Los Angeles Times*—along with other authoritative sources—as the final arbiters when discrepancies arose over the spellings of proper names. In addition, I have given many of my sources the opportunity to approve their quoted words, as well as the option to amend and expand upon them. Further, I asked several experts on some of the specific areas of this book to read those portions of my manuscript to ensure their accuracy and fairness.

In short, I have always worked hard to get my facts straight. However, I do make mistakes, and I am more than willing to atone for them. When informed, I will immediately list provable errors on an errata sheet on my website, *www.moldea.com*, and I promise to make any and all necessary corrections in future editions of this book as quickly as possible.

Further, I have attempted to be as scrupulous as possible to credit those reporters and authors who broke major news stories about the events discussed in this book. Their cited works are contained either in the main text or in the endnotes.

Significantly, along with all of the newly published material, this book also contains an anthology of some of my earlier writings, including but not limited to those works in which I appeared as a first-person character. Just to be clear, I own the copyrights to that selected collection reprinted in this book.

Finally, as part of my independent-operator thing, I never pitched this particular book project to any publisher in or out of the publishing industry in New York. More than anything I've ever written, I wanted this book to be exactly what I wanted it to be—although I do apologize for not having an index in this edition.

I would like to thank my personal attorney and "big brother," Roger C. Simmons, and his "of counsel," Susan Eisner, of Frederick, Maryland, and one of my oldest and most trusted friends, George L. Farris of Akron, Ohio, who has been the Moldea-family attorney for over thirty years.

Also, I want to express appreciation to my literary agent, Alice Martell of New York, and my lecture-booking agents, Jodi Solomon and Bill Fargo of Jodi Solomon Speakers in Boston. In addition, I want to extend my

PREFACE: ON TAKING IT

deepest gratitude to the late Mrs. Nancy Nolte of Boulder, Colorado—my long-time writing coach and editor to whom I had dedicated two of my previous books, along with trusted friends and advisors Jeff Goldberg, Jon Oberg, and Kristina Rebelo, as well as Thomson von Stein and the Charlotte von Stein Charitable Trust.

And I send my love, gratitude, and respect to my late Mother, the former "Mary Christmas," who died in December 2018, as well as to Mimi, for all of her love and support during the past thirty-two years.

Dan E. Moldea
Washington, D.C.
Third Edition
May 15, 2020

PROLOGUE:

Chasing a ghost

The man promised to deliver Jimmy Hoffa's dead body to me, gift-wrapped in a 55-gallon drum.

Yet, while sitting alone in my black 2007 Jeep Liberty at our prearranged meeting place in the rear parking lot of a Mobil station just off an empty country road in Hartland Township about an hour northwest of Detroit, all that went through my mind was how many federal, state, and local laws I was about to violate if this actually happened. However, regardless of the consequences, if Hoffa's remains were really offered to me, I was going to accept them.

It was the hot and sunny late afternoon of August 20, 2009—thirty-four years after the ex-Teamsters boss disappeared on July 30, 1975. A young freelance writer back then, I had started my investigations of Hoffa and Teamsters eight months before he vanished. Hoffa's still-unsolved murder had been my obsession ever since, even after the 1978 publication of my book, *The Hoffa Wars*.

Knowing the Hoffa case as well as any journalist, I recognized the good leads from the bad and had received dozens over the years. But the stunning detail that a Michigan man—"AH," as I called him—provided in the summer of 2009 had really grabbed me. Inasmuch as AH, a convicted scam artist, was simultaneously cooperating with the FBI and had nothing to gain by conning me, I decided to play out this drama, primarily because he had once worked for former Detroit Teamster leader Rolland McMaster, a top suspect in Hoffa's disappearance. Aside from Hoffa, McMaster, who had died in October 2007, was the principal character of my 1978 book. I had spent years investigating him and openly alleged that he had played a role in the disposal of Hoffa's body.

In May 2006, the FBI had launched a well-publicized search for Hoffa's body at a farm in Wixom, Michigan, excavating a portion of the property, destroying and then rebuilding a large barn in the process. In July 1975, that farm was owned by McMaster.

Although the FBI did not find Hoffa, the *New York Times* quoted an FBI spokesperson who "was convinced that Mr. Hoffa's body had been buried on the farm, and there was 'no indication that it has been moved.'"

During my 2009 adventure, AH admitted to me that he was trying to plea-bargain his way out of state criminal charges that were pending against him, hoping that his information about Hoffa could help get him out of trouble. With McMaster now dead, AH said that he no longer feared for his safety and had agreed to talk.

When the FBI special agent with whom AH was cooperating asked me what I thought, I replied with some amusement but a considerable amount of curiosity that AH's cooperation with the bureau made him semi-believable, even though I still viewed his story as a million-to-one shot.

Lying to me was one thing, but lying to the FBI was something else.

AH recalled that he had worked as McMaster's driver in July and August 1975 and was instructed to pick him up at a local restaurant—the Wheat & Rye on Middlebelt Road, just south of I-94—a few days after Hoffa disappeared. Also along for the ride were two other alleged co-conspirators, whom he named. Both were other top suspects in the murder, named by the FBI.

Continuing his story, AH explained that he took the three men to another McMaster farm just off U.S. 23 in Fenton—about twelve miles from the site of the 2006 excavation—where he saw a 55-gallon drum on a paneled pickup truck just outside the barn. Inside this barn was a backhoe which had already been used to dig a hole. He added that McMaster had said with some exasperation, "This is the last goddamn time we're moving this son of a bitch."

AH told me that, as a reward for his role in Hoffa's disappearance, McMaster received a hidden interest in a Las Vegas hotel/casino.

From the outset, I often repeated to AH that I would not engage in any illegal activities, including the act of criminal trespass. However, my interest piqued when AH drew a floor plan of the barn where he claimed Hoffa's body was buried and actually placed a circle at what he insisted was the specific location of Hoffa's grave.

He wasn't talking about a major excavation. Instead, he was saying that he knew the exact spot for a simple dig within a nine-square-foot area. In addition, he said that he was acquainted with the farm's caretaker who would give him permission to enter the property.

AH even allowed me to repeat anything he said to the FBI agent, adding that he never saw Hoffa's body—only the 55-gallon drum which the conspirators used as his coffin. The barn and the surrounding farm, AH said, was now owned by McMaster's brother-in-law, Stanton Barr, who had served as McMaster's alibi on the day Hoffa vanished.

Pat Clawson of Flint, a trusted friend and a licensed private investigator, had volunteered to watch my back since this drama began nearly two weeks earlier. During the interim, I had tolerated the con man's constant abuse, rejecting no fewer than three shakedown attempts and shrugging off his numerous threats to have me killed. Further, I had caught him in numerous contradictions and even flat-out lies.

But he wasn't asking me to do anything, except to receive Hoffa's body.

There was one major complication. AH also alleged that he had possession of tape-recorded conversations among the actual co-conspirators in the Hoffa murder—before and after the killing. And, of course, I wanted them.

When he finally gave the half-dozen cassette tapes to me, they were sealed in plastic and inserted in a black-vinyl pouch. That was when the threats began. He warned that if I opened the plastic before receiving Hoffa's body, I would be killed.

Upon receiving the tapes and for my own legal protection, I filled out a standard chain-of-custody form, noting the transfer—even though I could see through the plastic that no fewer than three of the tapes appeared to be pre-recorded country-western music cassettes.

When AH threatened me the first time, I trembled—even though I have been threatened on numerous occasions during my career. After that, I was nothing more than amused with his bluster. Once again, all he had to do was be right about one thing. And all I had to do was keep my motel room for another day or two.

When he demanded money from me, I told him that the sky was the limit if he delivered Hoffa's body, and I would help him get everything he ever wanted. Even though I remained completely skeptical throughout, I did fantasize about my own reward and how I could parlay this exclusive story into a matter for history, as well as my own personal vindication after years of frustrating investigation of the Hoffa case.

AH told me that he and his team would bring a ground-radar detector and the backhoe on a flatbed trailer to the farm. He said that the entire operation would take about two hours. Meantime, I was instructed to wait for delivery at the Mobil station, which was just a few hundred yards away from the farm.

AH gave me the rules for the dig, scheduled for 5:00 P.M. on Thursday, August 20, saying:

> 1. I was to wait in my car until the flatbed trailer carrying the 55-gallon drum arrived at the Mobil station. When AH got out of the truck, I could leave my car, climb onto the flatbed and take pictures of the barrel as well as its contents—and even take a DNA sample. He said that the top would already be off.
>
> 2. He said that my associate, Pat Clawson, could not go near the flatbed. If he did, he would be shot. However, as AH and his men worked in the barn, Clawson would be permitted to videotape the unfolding events from a position across the street from the farm.
>
> 3. AH said that he would give me the videotape his own team would make of the dig inside the barn before they pulled away from the Mobil station.
>
> 4. After I finished photographing the barrel and its contents, he said he planned to take everything to an officer with the Michigan State Police, *a woman named Robin*, with whom he appeared to have some connection.
>
> 5. He added that I could call anyone I want after they pulled away. I told him that my first call would be to the FBI special agent assigned to this case.

On the day of the dig, I continued to believe that this was a wild-goose chase, and that AH wasn't even going to show up.

After eating a late lunch, I went to the Mobil station where Clawson and I had agreed to meet at 4:30. While I waited for Clawson who was a few minutes late, I filled my tank with gas and bought a couple of bottles of spring water and a small bag of Fritos at an adjoining mini-mart. Then, I drove my car to the back of the station and into a large parking lot as AH had directed.

At 4:45, my cell phone rang. It was AH who asked me if I was at the Mobil station. I replied that I was. AH said that he and his men were running a half hour behind schedule, adding that they would be coming

PROLOGUE: CHASING A GHOST

from the west. They would arrive at 5:30. He further said that he and his men had already placed some equipment at the farm, adding that everyone who lived and worked there was gone for the afternoon.

Within minutes after ending my call with AH, Clawson drove into the gas station and parked next to me. When he climbed out of his car, I told him that I had just heard from AH who said that he and his team were en route.

At that point, we didn't know what to believe. But we did know that something was about to happen.

Even though he remained as skeptical as I, Clawson had photocopied a section of Michigan law, which discussed unauthorized excavations for dead bodies that included stiff penalties for the principals as well as their accomplices. He suggested that we call a local law-enforcement agency and make them generally aware of what we were doing.

Agreeing to talk about that option, I got into Clawson's car, and we drove to the farm.

When we arrived, we saw two horses running free in a pasture. And we clearly saw an older, silver-haired man wearing a blue shirt in the barn. I assumed that this was either the farm's owner or its caretaker. However, AH had just told me a few minutes earlier that no one would be on the property.

As Clawson scouted for his best position to set up his video camera across the road from the farm, I suddenly feared that we had been set up. I suspected that a trap had been set for me when I returned to the Mobil station alone which would result in the theft of my car—or that I would be jumped and beaten.

With the two of us still deciding to move forward, Clawson dropped me off at the gas station. Then he returned to his surveillance location.

At or about 5:15 P.M., a Livingston County sheriff's car pulled into the parking lot and stopped next to my car.

I said to myself, "This can't be for me."

The deputy sheriff, Pete Hairston, stepped out of his car and asked me for some identification. Without saying a word, I pulled out my wallet and gave him my Washington, D.C., driver's license.

I then believed that Clawson had gone ahead and called the county sheriff's office and tipped them off as to what was happening.

As the deputy began to question me about what I was doing in Michigan, another squad car pulled up. This one was from the Michigan

State Police. A woman officer, Trooper Karla Aguzzi, climbed out of her car and approached the deputy and me.

Hairston again asked me what I was doing in their state.

I replied that I was visiting friends.

"Where do they live?"

"Flint."

"What's their address?"

"I don't know their address. I just have directions on how to get there."

"What are their names?"

"Look," I said, "what's this all about?"

"We received a call that a person driving a 2007 black Jeep Liberty with D.C. tags was parked in this lot and behaving suspiciously."

"Suspiciously?" I laughed. "I'm a customer. I bought gas and made a purchase in the mini-mart. I have the receipts in my pocket."

Trooper Aguzzi asked me if I would empty my pockets.

I took off my sleeveless, multi-pocketed, dark-gray photographer's vest and handed it to her.

The deputy also asked if he could search my car. I told him that, if he told me what this was about, I would probably have no objection.

The trooper put my vest on the hood of the deputy's car and examined its contents, which included my spiral-bound "Reporter's Note Book."

The deputy asked me to identify my friends in Flint.

When I asked why this was necessary, he repeated his question with what appeared to be restrained anger.

"I'm here visiting a friend of mine who used to live in Washington, Pat Clawson, who now lives in Flint."

"And who are you waiting for here?"

"I'm waiting for Pat."

"Where is he now?"

"Like I said, I'm waiting for him."

After going through my pockets, the trooper returned to the deputy and me. The deputy then left us and went to his car where he immediately started talking on his radio and punching in information on his dashboard computer.

With both police cars pointed at me, I assumed that I was being filmed by their dashboard cameras.

While the deputy continued to check me out in his squad car, I leaned back against the front of my car while the trooper kept her distance

PROLOGUE: CHASING A GHOST

from me. When I stood up and took a step forward, she put her right hand on the service revolver in her holster and barked, "Step back, sir!"

She didn't pull her gun, but, at that point, I knew that this was something very serious. I was certain that if I didn't step back—which I did immediately—she would have drawn her weapon.

Shortly after that, a third police officer arrived, Trooper Rich Chaffee, also of the Michigan State Police.

Upon his arrival and with the return of Deputy Hairston, Trooper Aguzzi got in her car and drove away.

Chaffee then, quite literally, got in my face and demanded to know what I was doing there.

At that point, I told him that I was a journalist who was working on a story.

He asked me, "What story?"

"Do I have to say?"

Hairston told me, "We received a call out of Detroit that a man in a black Jeep with D.C. tags was carrying a load of cocaine, along with a large amount of cash."

As he said that, a fourth police car pulled up. The officer in this car stepped out, along with his large drug-sniffing dog.

My heart almost fell into my stomach—now knowing that I had been totally set up but in a different way than I had earlier suspected.

Hairston continued, "May we search your car?"

At that point, my mind focused on the black-vinyl pouch that conman AH had given me with the sealed tapes inside. Standing by my word, I still had not opened it, but I now suspected that the package contained illegal drugs, and that I was about to be busted.

Hairston growled, "Do you have any guns or drugs in your car?"

I replied that I did not.

"Once again, sir, may we search your car?"

Believing that I would be arrested as soon as the pouch was discovered, I asked to speak with an attorney.

Hairston replied, "You said before that you had no problem if we searched your car."

"Sir, I'm a good guy. I'm not a bad guy. I'm a journalist who's working on a story. Pat Clawson is a licensed private investigator who is helping me with that story. I was standing here waiting for him."

Upon hearing that I wanted an attorney, Trooper Chaffee pulled Deputy Hairston off to the side out of my earshot. They had a brief conversation.

When he returned to me, Chaffee demanded again, "What's the story?"

"I'm working on the Hoffa case," I explained. "I'm a crime reporter and an author who published a book about Jimmy Hoffa. Pat and I expected to meet with a source who said he had some information. There are a number of people in Detroit who know that I'm here, conducting this investigation, including the FBI and the local news media."

"Who's your source?" Chaffee asked.

"I'm not naming him—even though I now think he's the one who just set me up."

Then, not even waiting for a confrontation, I said, "There is one thing in the car that's not mine. The source I was to meet here gave me a sealed package of what I believed contained tape recordings and demanded that I not open the package until I received his permission."

I added that I had executed a chain-of-custody form when I received the package, as well as taken photographs of the tapes, sealed in plastic, before they were placed in the black-vinyl pouch.

Chaffee asked me where the pouch was. I told him that it was in my briefcase in the backseat of my car.

When I started to move towards the back door of my Jeep, Chaffee stepped in front of me and told me to get back. He then opened the door, and I pointed to my black Zero Halliburton briefcase on the floor behind the passenger's seat.

Chaffee grabbed the briefcase and opened it.

He pulled out the pouch and placed it on the hood of Hairston's squad car. He then opened the pouch and slid out the six tapes sealed in plastic.

Meantime, the dog sniffed around the exterior of my car, as well as my briefcase and the black-vinyl pouch. The dog had no reaction.

While that was going on, Trooper Aguzzi returned to the scene, along with Pat Clawson who had also been detained as he sat in his car by the farm. Clawson was driving his own car and pulled in after Aguzzi.

All I could say to the deputy was, "Pat's wife if going to kill me for getting him involved. He has nothing to do with this. He was just here, helping me."

As I started to walk towards Pat, Aguzzi instructed me to stay put and not speak with him. She asked me who the source was that I was supposed to meet.

I replied that I would not name him, repeating that I now believed that he was the one who had set us up.

She responded that Clawson had already named the source.

When I still refused to name him, she gave me his correct name.

I replied, "Let my silence be my answer."

"I have a case against [AH] in Genesee County next month," she said, now smiling. "He's one of the biggest con men in the state. . . . Mr. Clawson said that you were waiting to meet with him for information about the Hoffa case."

"Are you Robin?" I asked her.

"Robin who?" She replied.

"Are you Robin from the Michigan State Police?"

"I know Robin. How do you know her?"

"The source dropped her name. She was supposed to be the law-enforcement official who was going to receive the information we learned here about the Hoffa case."

With that exchange, the tense situation was completely diffused. Trooper Aguzzi walked to the other officers and spoke with them.

After that, all four of the officers came over and shook my hand, saying that they had received information that something illegal was happening, and that they had to check it out.

"I understand completely," I replied with considerable relief. "But I would really like to get to the bottom of how this happened."

None of them seem to know anything more than a call was received, giving the dispatcher descriptions of my car and me.

While I was talking to Clawson—who said he saw my situation unfold through binoculars before Trooper Aguzzi detained him—a fifth police car entered the parking lot.

The driver was Detective Sergeant Scott Wright of the Genesee County Sheriff's Office. He walked over to me and shook my hand, apologizing for any inconvenience this had caused me.

"Well, I should probably thank you for making this story a little more interesting. . . . Clearly, I'm not going to be getting Jimmy Hoffa's dead body today."

Sergeant Wright laughed as Trooper Aguzzi asked him what had initiated this situation.

Wright replied, "We received a call from a confidential source. I can't tell you who it was."

Aguzzi then motioned to Wright, and the two of them stepped away to talk privately.

When Aguzzi returned—without actually naming AH as the confidential informant—she speculated that he might have pulled this stunt in a cynical effort to curry favor with the Genesee County prosecutor in his upcoming criminal case. In other words, AH wanted to show that he was cooperating with the law-enforcement community by helping to entrap someone he had falsely portrayed as a corrupt journalist.

Before we left the scene, I took pictures of all the officers next to a Michigan State Police squad car. Also, Pat took photographs of me with them. In the money shot, Aguzzi had my hands behind my back and was pretending to handcuff me.

All of us exchanged business cards. Also, I had two copies of *The Hoffa Wars* in my car, and I gave them to Deputy Hairston and Trooper Aguzzi, signing each, "Thank you for scaring the hell out of me. Best wishes, Dan."

All in all, I had been detained and questioned for about an hour.

I drove onto the freeway and headed back east—with Clawson following me to Interstate-75, making sure that I wasn't followed.

Five days later, the story of my recent adventure by reporter Paul Egan made the front page of the *Detroit News*—above the masthead. Mercifully, the article did not include the final scene behind the Mobil station.

In part, the story stated:

> Moldea, who began looking into [AH's] claims earlier this month, said he was aware [AH] had credibility issues but was hoping he was telling the truth when he told Moldea he would lead him to Hoffa's body. That never happened, he said.
>
> Another ex-con, Donovan Wells, got an early release from a federal hospital prison after he came forward with the information that FBI agents used to get a warrant to tear down a barn and dig at a Milford Township horse farm in 2006.
>
> Moldea said he believes Wells was telling the truth and said [AH's] story was compelling because he described what he witnessed as a "reburial," presumably after Hoffa was buried in Milford Township and subsequently dug up. Moldea said [AH] and his attorney were cooperating with federal investigators and said officials appeared to be taking him seriously.
>
> [AH] gave Moldea permission to approach the FBI with [AH's] claims that he witnessed Hoffa's burial. . . .
>
> Later, Moldea said he completely lost faith in [AH].

PROLOGUE: CHASING A GHOST

Shortly thereafter, AH was convicted on state criminal charges and returned to prison in December 2009. He has since been released. Meantime, the search for Jimmy Hoffa continues.

PART ONE:
Entering the fray

1. Kent State

On **Friday night, May 1, 1970,** a group of us from the University of Akron did the bar scene on North Water Street near Kent State University, about twelve miles northeast of Akron. While at The Cove, a popular nightclub with a dance floor, I saw an attractive co-ed from Kent whom I had met once before. Like me, Susan was a totally naïve and completely self-absorbed sophomore. We talked with friends, drank 3.2-draft beer, and danced until she asked me for a ride back to her dormitory.

As we were leaving the bar, we saw *Wild in the Streets* come to life. Students and townies were clashing; fights were seemingly breaking out everywhere. Windows were broken; parked and moving cars were vandalized.

Craziness on the first nice night of spring, we thought.

Susan and I picked our way through the mayhem to my 1964 Thunderbird and drove to Kent State's campus, just a few minutes away. I walked her to the front door of her dorm and asked to see her again the following afternoon.

To be sure, I wasn't a very sophisticated guy, but I did come from a good family. Middle class in Middle America, we ate dinner together every night while my sister, Marsha, and I were growing up in our three-bedroom home in Akron. Also, we went to church every Sunday, and I attended Sunday school until I was fifteen. And, before that, I was even an altar boy, as well as a Boy Scout. My favorite television character was The Lone Ranger, a classic do-gooder.

My parents taught us about sportsmanship, living by The Golden Rule, and always staying loyal to our family and friends. As far back as I can remember, they never punished me for something I didn't do. And I don't remember ever getting punished too harshly for something I did do. In fact, I cannot think of a single time that my parents were unfair either to Marsha or me.

I went to elementary school, junior high school, and high school in South Akron—which we also called Lower Akron or just plain "L.A."

Throughout my childhood and teen years, I was always a skinny kid with chronic dark circles under my eyes. I wasn't really a sickly boy—in fact, I had perfect attendance during my three years of high school. But I did lack confidence.

Earlier, while playing Class-G baseball, I was beaned with a high and inside fastball that I stepped into, thinking it was going to break over the plate. Suddenly gun-shy, I never completely recovered from that incident.

Injury prone because of playing scared, I wound up riding the bench in nearly every organized prep sport I played in the years that followed. I had simply stopped believing in myself but always hoped that I would suddenly snap out of it and find the ability to compete—which I never did by the end of my junior year in high school.

Also, in the midst of all of this, adding insult to injury, I lost my best gal to my best pal, a star football player.

Student politics would up as my salvation. I became one of those student-leader types who was elected to student council and as president of my senior class, Akron Garfield's Class of 1968.

Senator Robert Kennedy was shot and fatally wounded during the early-morning hours on the day of my high-school graduation, June 5, 1968. I announced the tragedy to my class during our morning commencement rehearsal. He died the following day.

Yet, despite how dramatically the world was changing at the time, I remained relatively insulated by my environment and mostly unaffected by the events of the outside world. Even though I had been deeply moved, like everyone else, by the murder of President John Kennedy in 1963 when I was thirteen and had even known a few guys who had been killed in Vietnam since then, I still viewed politics as a game of make-believe.

Consequently, I was a mass of political contradictions. For instance, while I was in high school, my congressman had nominated me to the Air Force Academy. While working hard for the actual appointment, I simultaneously campaigned for Democratic anti-war Presidential candidate Senator Eugene McCarthy. And, on top of that, I was a member of Young Republicans.

All I knew was that out of respect for my dad—a former football and track star at Ohio State and a lieutenant colonel in the Air Force Reserves whose oil portrait as "The Typical Officer Candidate" still hung in the Pentagon—I wanted to serve either in the military or in politics. Also, like any other kid, I wanted to make my mom proud.

But after I failed to receive the appointment to the academy, my only back-up plan was to stay in town and attend the University of Akron, which, actually, is a wonderful school.

Meantime, after a friend and I were injured and hospitalized after nearly getting killed in a head-on car collision after a church basketball

PART ONE: ENTERING THE FRAY

tournament in Youngstown, I became the epitome of the self-serving male, getting a little crazy in the process.

By the middle of my sophomore year, I had become a complete wild man, living in a group house with a pack of wild men. A close friend, nicknamed "Mad Dog," even taught me how to eat glass as a means of intimidation.

One night at a local bar, I stood up to two bigger guys who wanted to kick my skinny ass. Knowing that I was at risk as the crowd formed around us—no fewer than fifty eyewitnesses—I picked up my glass, took a bite out of it, and started chewing it. Shocked, both guys apologized to me and immediately left the bar, probably thinking that I was nuts.

By May 1970, the ideal Friday night for many of us was going drinking with the guys, getting into a fight, somehow surviving the fight, then picking up a girl, and bringing her home.

But, as I drove back to Akron, alone, after leaving Susan at her dorm at Kent State, I had no idea how dramatically life would change during the next few days.

On Saturday, May 2, 1970—two days after President Richard Nixon announced the U.S. invasion of Cambodia—the random madness from the night before had already evolved into something quite political. Stop the War activists spoke to a crowd of students on Kent State's Commons. Some of the speakers sincerely tried to educate the uninformed, like Susan and me, about the war in Vietnam. Others were just angry, taunting anyone who disagreed with them.

After spending the evening with some friends in Akron, Susan and I returned to Kent on Sunday afternoon and saw the burned-out remnants of the ROTC building that had been torched the previous night, as well as the presence of the Ohio National Guard, which had just come from a wildcat strike of truckers in another part of the state.

What first appeared as a friendly, carnival-like, late-afternoon scene of students and Guardsmen became more confrontational and even frightening during the early evening hours in the midst of a large sit-in of students on the street in front of Kent State's campus.

Frankly, I was terrified. Neither Susan nor I wanted to deal with any of this, so I drove her to her parents' home in nearby Cuyahoga Falls and went back to my fraternity house in Akron. I told Susan that I would pick her up the following morning and drive her back to Kent for her first class.

When we arrived on Monday, May 4, just before 9:00 A.M., the atmosphere on campus was tense. Even though we smelled no tear gas and saw no Guardsmen point their guns at anyone, both of us were afraid. And, because nearly everyone else seemed either equally scared or just plain pissed off, we decided to leave Kent, especially since Susan's morning classes had been canceled because of bomb threats. She didn't even want to go to her room in the dorm to pick up anything.

Susan was lucky that her parents lived nearby, and I was lucky to have a car. Most of the kids on campus were trapped there. I took Susan to a diner just outside Kent for breakfast and then back to her parents' home. Returning to the University of Akron, I then attended my own classes.

When I walked into the student center at a little after 2:00 P.M., the entire place was buzzing. Seeing some friends playing bridge at a corner table, I asked what was going on.

They told me that the National Guard had opened fire into a crowd of anti-war demonstrators at Kent State. Few details were available. But rumors were flying that scores of students had been shot and killed, and that several Guardsmen had been hit by sniper fire.

Shocked and shaken, I simply couldn't believe what I was hearing, telling them that I had been on Kent's campus earlier in the morning but hadn't seen any violence, just fear and anger.

That same afternoon, while listening to a bitter debate about the war in the lobby of the student center, a friend and I were surprised to find ourselves in agreement with the anti-war activists. Then, along with several others in the crowd, both of us grabbed our wallets, pulled out our draft cards, and burned them.

For me, this overt act of defiance was a point of no return.

By nightfall, news reports clarified some of what had happened at Kent State. Four students had been shot to death and nine were wounded. There had never been any student snipers. The thirteen-second barrage of gunfire had occurred at 12:24 P.M., a little over three hours after Susan and I had left Kent.

That night in Akron, I was at my part-time job as an ID checker at an off-campus bar. The guy who owned the joint was a friend and saw how overwrought I was over the shootings. Midway through my shift, he instructed me to clock out for the evening and go to the rally on Akron's campus, protesting the shootings and the war.

I went and was just another face in the crowd. Jim Heinisch, one of my fraternity brothers, was the editor of the student newspaper and a leader of the demonstration. He picked me out of the mass of people

PART ONE: ENTERING THE FRAY

and invited me to be among the dozens of students who were delivering brief statements.

When I told him I didn't know what to do, he instructed me to say whatever was in my heart. It was the first time I had ever spoken to an angry crowd. I'm sure that whatever I said was completely unintelligible—but I did get up there and speak.

During the days that followed, like tens of thousands of other students across the nation, I wore a black arm band and participated in the national moratorium for the four dead white students at Kent State—Allison Krause, Jeff Miller, Sandy Scheuer, and Bill Schroeder—and later two black students at Jackson State—Phillip Gibbs and James Earl Green—who were shot and killed in a hail of police gunfire on May 14. None of us knew any of these kids when they were alive, but nearly all of us now felt a genuine connection to them and their families in the wake of their deaths.

After that, I heard Dick Gregory, the civil-rights activist, speak about "students as niggers," and he just blew me away. I had never heard anyone talk like that before.[1] And then, another girlfriend and I went to see the movie, Z, Costa-Gavras's Oscar-winning French-language film about the brutal murder of an anti-war political leader by right-wing military officers in Greece.

The sheer concentration of all these life-altering experiences was absolutely breathtaking. With everything happening so fast, I no longer viewed myself as the center of the universe. And, like so many others during this remarkable period of time, I changed as a person and never looked back.

In lieu of remaining a "self-serving" creep, I wanted to become a "society-serving" man. Suddenly, I sought to become an independent person and to lead what Martin Luther King often called, "a committed life."

While remaining in my fraternity—to which I was always very loyal regardless of my personal politics—I broadened my college friendships with others on campus, especially among those in the civil-rights, anti-war, and student-power communities. Also, on the downside, I started doing speed—like a long-haul trucker. I began staying up nights and earned the nickname "The Bat," a handle that still remains with me.

Much of my time at night, I spent writing. I found that the mere act of putting my confused thoughts down on paper gave me distance and perspective, permitting me to think about what I planned to do before I actually did it—or to better understand something I had already done. This simple therapy probably saved me from prison or death.

But not completely reformed, I launched what became one of the most popular term-paper businesses on campus, advertising it as a "research service." For an agreed upon fee, my staff of four and I wrote papers on any subject and of any length. We promised a "B" with a money-back guarantee for a lesser grade. I hardly got rich, but I did make enough money to pay my bills—until the university's faculty senate banned these operations and put me out of business.

Once again, I was forced to write for fun but not for profit.

One of my instructors at the university—who in earlier years had been an editor for a New York publishing house—took a particular interest in what I was writing. Her name was Nancy Nolte, an intelligent and caring middle-aged woman, happily married to an executive with a local engineering firm and the mother of three sons. She encouraged me to write and offered to read anything I wrote.

After reviewing my first batch of work, "Mrs. Nolte," as I would always call her (even after she earned her doctorate), wrote me a note on August 10, 1970, saying: "As the old song says: 'You've come a long way from St. Louis (South Akron), but you still have a long way to go.'" Because of her attention, concern, and encouragement, I started to fight off the demons that were still haunting me and continued writing.

In the wake of an unpleasant experience with some bad speed and then meeting Lynn, a wonderful woman who was the daughter of a respected local businessman, I straightened up.

Meantime, I had dropped my 2-S student deferment for the military draft and went 1-A, knowing that if my lottery number was not selected by the end of the year, I would receive an ironclad exemption. The numbers drawn nearly came to mine—but, mercifully, did not, making me exempt from military service and Vietnam.

My dad, who had left the Air Force Reserves and now opposed the war in the wake of the shootings at Kent State, could not have been more supportive.

2. Surviving the revolution

The following year, I wrote and published a one-man campus newsletter and served as president of my fraternity. Also, during the summer of 1971, I received a job driving a truck after working the previous two

PART ONE: ENTERING THE FRAY

summers loading trucks. I loved my new job as a driver, hauling ass down the highway and feeling free.

In early July, while carrying a load of automotive parts and two large oil drums to Columbus on Interstate-71, my cargo exploded. After jumping from my large pickup truck, escaping a second blast, I brushed myself off on the wide median at the bottom of a grassy hill next to a highway patrolman who had actually witnessed the incident while driving in the opposite direction.

Fearing that I would be fired for losing my truck, I then returned to my flaming vehicle, grabbed a pair of gloves, and dropped the tailgate. Back in my cab, I maneuvered the truck to the top of the grassy hill near the edge of the highway. By shifting gears from low to reverse, I rocked the truck back and forth several times up and down the hill, causing the burning load to slide off the back of the truck.

Real truckers stopped to help extinguished the fire on my truck and its gas tank. Suffering nothing more than a minor shoulder injury, along with some cuts and bruises and a hell of a sunburn from the fire, I was credited by the Ohio State Highway Patrol with saving my truck.

The Akron Beacon Journal, my hometown newspaper, published a story, saying:

> A quick-thinking Akron truck driver en route to Columbus "rocked" a flaming load of merchandise out of his pickup truck Thursday morning, preventing a serious explosion which could have cost him his life. . . .
>
> "All I could think was that if the truck blew up, I would lose my job," said the Akron University student.[2]

The truckers who stopped to help me were credited with saving my life, and I obtained most of their names and addresses before I left the scene.

My boss yelled at me for going back into the burning truck—but he gave me a small raise in pay. He and I also wrote letters to those truckers who had saved my life. I promised each of them that I would try to repay them somehow, someday.

In May 1972, without any experience in university politics outside of the Greek system and the moratorium after Kent State, I ran for student body president against two well-known student activists, veterans in the battle for student rights. Breaking with Greek tradition, I selected a popular dorm student who was a non-Greek as my running mate in an attempt to form an unprecedented Greek-dorm campus alliance.

The Buchtelite, the student newspaper, endorsed one of my opponents and then took a swipe at me, saying I would be "too disposed to represent only the Greek point of view as student body president."[3]

But, by turning out the vote, our ticket nearly captured the three-way race on the first ballot. We easily won the election after the two-man runoff.

By the end of the first quarter—with the help of numerous student leaders, especially my new political mentor, Tim Davis, a Vietnam veteran who had nearly been killed after stepping on a land mine and now ran the local Stop the War movement—we had created a strong coalition of student groups, including Greeks, dorm students, commuters, anti-war activists, jocks, the arts and theater crowd, the gay community, the freaks, the Black United Students, and our international students, among others. We even brought ROTC students into the fold—because we openly supported citizen-soldiers, as well as the ROTC program for those students who needed the scholarship money to get through school.

We developed further skills and organizing tactics after attending the 1972 Congress of the National Student Association at Catholic University—my first trip to Washington, D.C. The featured speakers at the conference included such famous icons as Ralph Nader, Gloria Steinem, Julian Bond, and members of the Chicago 7.

Although the NSA had been previously compromised because of its covert association with the Central Intelligence Agency, revealed by *Ramparts* magazine in 1967, its 1972 incarnation was nothing less than a hotbed of student commitment to causes and issues. For me, it was another moving, even radicalizing experience.

Meantime, as a reward for our work with the student groups on Akron's campus, as well as with student governments at other universities around the state, a surprising op-ed article appeared in the *Buchtelite*, in which the newspaper's former editor, who had earlier trashed me, now wrote: "Moldea has proven in the last four months to be more committed to opening up student government than has any other student politician on this campus during the last four years."[4]

Also, Tim Davis and I worked hard to gain the trust of school administration officials—with whom we were already in the midst of numerous battles. We hoped to gain their respect—and concessions—with their grudging recognition of our sincerity, commitment, and hard work.

PART ONE: ENTERING THE FRAY

In January 1973, a group of black students and white radicals occupied the administration building, protesting an alleged act of racism in off-campus housing. The leaders of the protest asked me to be their liaison to Dr. Dominic Guzzetta, the university's president, who was in his office while uniformed and plain-clothes police officers crowded in front of his door.

After a lengthy discussion, Dr. Guzzetta told me that he was willing to meet with four representatives of the protest to discuss their concerns. I thanked the president for being so reasonable and returned to the mob of students who immediately rejected the offer, insisting that the university president negotiate with all of the students, *en masse*.

The *Buchtelite* accurately described what followed:

> Moldea told everyone to wait there, then he went by himself to talk to Guzzetta.
>
> While Moldea and the president argued about the situation, students began talking of storming the president's office.
>
> Moldea returned to the students and said, "If we wanted to scare the administration, if that's what we're after, we have successfully intimidated the administration. Guzzetta will not come out here and subject himself to verbal abuse." [Moldea] also said that this would best be settled by sending in representatives....
>
> Students started walking toward the president's office. [Leaders of the protest] continued to argue with Moldea. Police stood in front of Guzzetta's door blocking the entrance.
>
> As students approached the president's office, Moldea moved between the police and the students. Moldea suggested [that they] take some other course of action.
>
> At that point [one of the leaders of the protest] asked all students to sit in front of Guzzetta's office.[5]

With this potentially dangerous situation now defused, the students finally agreed to send in representatives to talk to the president.

There were no arrests, and no one was hurt. And I received the best press of my young life for physically stepping between the police and the students in the midst of such a volatile situation.

But, three months later, as the student government's relationship with the administration and the board of trustees deteriorated, university police officers "arrested" me during a protest in the student center. Threatened with violations of the Ohio Campus Riot Act and faced with possible suspension from the university and, worse yet, eighteen months in prison, I retained Bill Whitaker, a leader of the anti-war movement at Kent State, who had recently graduated from the University of Akron's School of Law. Whitaker refused to accept any fee from me or my family.

In the midst of Whitaker's legal maneuvering on my behalf, Tim Davis sent me a Ziggy-cartoon greeting card. Ziggy was depicted on the front, trying to hold back a large globe, which was starting to roll over him.

"Looks like it's you and me against the world..." the front of the card read—with the inside adding, "and I think we're gonna get creamed."

Fortunately, the attorney representing the university was an older fraternity brother of mine and a reasonable man. Because of him and my own attorney's stellar work, all of the charges against me were dropped.

3. Into the real world

Washington, D.C. is a mecca for former student body presidents at America's colleges and universities. So after receiving my B.A. in June 1973, I packed up my 1966 Thunderbird, which I had bought used in 1972, and drove to Washington, trying to get a job as a staffer for, among others, Senator William Saxbe, a maverick Republican from Ohio with whom I once had lunch when he visited the university.

Even though President Nixon was taking extreme heat for the Watergate cover-up, I had decided to remain a Republican despite my enthusiastic support for Senator George McGovern during the 1972 campaign. I believed that the chances of Nixon being forced from office were high, and that progressive Republicans would seize the responsibility—and the opportunity—to clean up his mess.

Meantime, nearly all of my friends—few of whom were Republicans—continued to be perplexed about my party selection. Misguided or not,

PART ONE: ENTERING THE FRAY

I always explained that I believed in decentralization, bringing power from the federal government down to state and local levels.

But after examining my record as an anti-Nixon, anti-war, pro-student rights Republican who supported Eugene McCarthy and George McGovern, no Republican in official Washington, including Saxbe, wanted anything to do with me. And when I applied for a job at a Washington poverty program run by liberal Democrats, they initially expressed delight with my student-activist credentials but then looked at me with total incredulity when they learned that I was a Republican.

A simple party change could have solved all of my political problems, but I was determined to be on the ground floor of the new GOP after Nixon was forced from office.

So, while in Washington in my delusional state, I stayed with a friend from Akron who worked as an intern for our congressman, Representative John Seiberling, a liberal Democrat. I attended the Watergate hearings at the Russell Senate Office Building during the day and found a part-time job at night, working on the loading docks at a trucking company in Kensington, Maryland.

Every day, I wrote to Lynn, still an undergraduate, who had remained in Akron but decided to stay with me while I tried to find myself.

In a letter to Mrs. Nolte, who was still encouraging me to write, I wrote:

> I have quickly discovered that anyone who comes to this place seeking fame and fortune immediately had better prepare for the big letdown. I was one of those wild-eyed idealists shot down during the first week after believing that I'd have Washington by the horns within a matter of hours.

In her reply, she insisted:

> Unless you tell me otherwise, I [have] the impression that contacts are most important in getting a job—especially in Washington. There must be three million well-qualified ex-student presidents looking for jobs there. How does someone choose among them? By giving the nod to acquaintances or protégés of old friends or professional contacts.

Mrs. Nolte gave me good advice. But—because I had decided to go it alone, without asking for favors from political figures back home—I was more dependent on good luck than anything else. Finding none,

I surrendered and left Washington on August 21, just two months after I had arrived.

Five days later, back in Ohio, Tracy Lewis, an old friend who was the first president of the Black United Students at the University of Akron, offered me a job as a planner for the Community Action Council in Ravenna, Ohio, a federal poverty program under the U.S. Office of Economic Opportunity, just a few miles from Kent State University. However, Lewis, the executive director of the agency, was already in the midst of a battle with the CAC board of directors. Frustrated with the internal politics, Lewis resigned on October 31, 1973, taking all eight of us on his staff with him.

I didn't expect to be gone so soon and had just traded in my 1966 Thunderbird and bought a 1970 Thunderbird, which I couldn't afford without another job. Frustrated, while seeing all of the action happening in the world, I wanted to do something important but found myself powerless to do anything.

Once again, Mrs. Nolte grabbed me by the scruff of the neck and pulled me back to reality, saying:

> You had better face the fact that you are going to have little of either power or independence for the next few years. I would hope that you would view such a situation not as intolerable subjection, but as a learning experience, a garnering of experience....
>
> [I]t's time to look outward on the world—as an observer on its edge, and not at its center—and learn something about it, so you can master it; so you won't be thrown for continual losses by ignorance. Running your head into a brick wall isn't always the best way of triumphing—sometimes all you get is a broken neck. You better find out what is on the other side of the wall first—and there might be an easy path around it....
>
> You've got a jock and an artist struggling within you. The problem is how to get them working in tandem.

In November, I was accepted to the graduate program in American history at Kent State and received an assistantship for the rest of the academic year with a new federally-funded center based at the university to assist Ohio school districts with problems relating to desegregation.

PART ONE: ENTERING THE FRAY

Among other assignments, I helped edit and write the program's monthly newsletter.

Also, along with my assistantship, I taught a course for undergraduates, "Racism and Poverty," in Kent State's Honors and Experimental College—where I held weekly seminars on racism in government, business, education, housing, law enforcement, and sports.

The window in my office at Wright Hall at Kent State's Tri-Towers complex gave me a panoramic view of the site where the National Guard had opened fire on the students in May 1970, which still remained the biggest turning point in my life.

Starting to find my legs and confidence, I asked Lynn to marry me on Christmas Day 1973, and we began to plan for what we hoped would be a long future together.

4. Running for office

On January 21, 1974, a month before my twenty-fourth birthday, I attended a hearing of the Akron City Council, which was considering a resolution to support the impeachment of President Richard Nixon. Rising from the audience, I went to the public microphone to speak in favor of the motion.

Announcing that I was a card-carrying Republican, I went on to say:

> The President has not only destroyed the integrity of the executive branch, which also includes the Justice Department and the Department of Defense, but he has nearly destroyed the credibility of the Congress, the courts, state and local governments, the press, and the Republican Party. . . . The American people must regain their perspective as to what a free society is, and whom a responsive, representative government represents.

I received loud applause from the crowd, mostly composed of Democrats, as well as the attention of a handful of dissident Republicans who had attended the hearing and agreed with the resolution but had decided not to speak. After the meeting, I had dinner with several of them, and they encouraged me to run for office.

Ten days later, without any money or organization, I formally announced my candidacy for a seat in the Ohio State Legislature. Democrat Dr. Vernon Cook, a professor of political science at the University of Akron—whom I knew, liked and respected—was the first-term incumbent whom I sought to unseat.

Campaigning on the need for Republicans to reform their own party, I quickly found that the local party's high command didn't share my enthusiasm for change. More importantly, Raymond C. Bliss—the revered former chairman of the Republican National Committee from 1965 to 1969 who had engineered Nixon's 1968 election—ran the party in Akron with an iron fist, and he didn't care for me or my ideas at all.[6]

In response to my candidacy, Bliss and the local GOP served up a good family man and computer programmer at the Firestone Tire & Rubber Company from the most conservative section of our district to run against me. It would be the only contested Republican primary in the county.

Now, I had to wage an open fight against my own local party.

On February 14, at the county's annual Lincoln Day Dinner, party leaders introduced the latest crop of Republican candidates. My opponent stood when his name was called and received a sustained ovation from the audience. When I heard my name, I stood but only received a smattering of polite applause.

After the dinner, my fiancé and I ran into Ray Bliss who was putting on his overcoat. When I said hello to him, he replied, "Dan, I'm going to destroy you in this town."

"Give it your best shot, Ray!" I replied insolently, knowing that it was the wrong thing to say, even as the words tumbled out of my mouth.

On April 8, Mark Figetakis, the Republican candidate for Congress in my home district attacked his Democratic opponent, the incumbent John Seiberling, for promoting the grand-jury investigation of the shootings at Kent State, which had led to the recent indictment of eight Ohio National Guardsmen. At the time, I was still a graduate student at Kent State.

Specifically, Figetakis had said, "There is something drastically wrong today when we have rioters and buildings burners remaining unindicted and the enforcers of the law are indicted and face possibly being thrown in jail as criminals."[7]

In fact, twenty-five people, mostly students, had been earlier indicted in connection with the incident at Kent State. However, the charges against them were dropped.[8]

Two days later, during a speech at Kent, I criticized Figetakis for getting his facts wrong, saying, "Party loyalty ceases when such absurd statements are made. Mr. Figetakis's view of the Kent State killings epitomizes the insensitivity of many Republican leaders toward students, minorities, old people, and Middle America, as well as the justice afforded to these groups in our society. Such statements should indicate to all thinking Republicans the need for change within our party."

During the question-and-answer period, I committed the ultimate Republican act of heresy by publicly endorsing Figetakis's Democratic opponent, John Seiberling—a member of the U.S. House Judiciary Committee, which would soon vote for Nixon's impeachment. I also endorsed the Democratic ticket for Ohio governor and lieutenant governor, John Gilligan and Richard Celeste, respectively. Gilligan was running for reelection against Republican James A. Rhodes, the governor at the time of the Kent State tragedy who had received widespread criticism for his poor handling of the situation before and after the shootings.

Perhaps the most accurate portrait of my campaign appeared in a story by Mickey Porter, a popular columnist for the *Akron Beacon Journal*, which had won a Pulitzer Prize for its coverage of the Kent State shootings four years earlier.

Writing about my recent address to the rank-and-file of Goodyear Tire & Rubber Company Local 2, Porter wrote:

> Dan Moldea is not your average Republican. He campaigned for Eugene McCarthy. He campaigned for George McGovern. He favors the President's impeachment. And last year he was the activist president of Akron University's student body. . . .
>
> Being asked to speak at the union hall, Moldea worked up a 10-minute speech and then was told there was a misunderstanding, that he couldn't speak at all. . . . Dejected, he left the hall and headed for his car. But wait . . . what's that lying there in an adjacent vacant lot? Nothing other than a discarded soap box.
>
> Moldea grabbed the box . . . waited for the meeting to end and then climbed atop his soap box and began orating.
>
> The members stopped in their tracks, wondering who that long-haired nutball was. But they stayed, and they listened, and now they know who Dan Moldea is.[9]

A few days after that experience, the *Beacon Journal's* editors invited all May primary candidates to meet with them before they published their endorsements in the newspaper. Considering my off-beat politics, I dreaded the thought of my scheduled interview with these respected editors.

The endorsement from the *Beacon Journal* was the key to my low-budget campaign. Without it, there was no way that I could win. With the endorsement, I had a chance.

When I walked into the editorial meeting on April 19, I remember trembling a little bit. As I sat down at the table, one of the editors said to me, "You've been a very busy young man, Mr. Moldea. I see you still haven't gotten over the need to raise hell."

For the next thirty minutes, the editors peppered me with questions about state and local issues, all of which I had studied and knew well—funding for public education, no-fault divorce, gun control, property taxes, metropolitan regionalism, and even probate-court reform, among other issues of the day.

Just before the end of the half-hour session, they asked me why I had advocated Nixon's impeachment—and why I had remained a Republican, considering all the grief I was taking from my friends, nearly all of whom were Democrats.

Once again, I explained that I believed in decentralization, bringing power from the federal government down to state and local levels. To me, that was the pristine core of the Republican philosophy—regardless of how perverted that ideal had become by the spring of 1974. Furthermore, I boldly predicted that after Watergate and Nixon, the Republican Party would become the party of reform.

In other words, I was betting heavily that anti-Nixon, anti-war Republicans who had supported Gene McCarthy and George McGovern would soon be viewed as visionaries within the new-and-improved Republican Party.

Obviously, I had to respect the skepticism of all in the room, including those who laughed out loud.

When the meeting with the *Beacon Journal's* editors concluded, I felt that I had just completed one of my final exams in graduate school. I shook hands with all of them before I left, but none of them really looked at me. I thought that my political career was over right then and there.

Two weeks later, after canvassing a few neighborhoods, I stopped off to see my parents at their new home in Fairlawn, a western suburb of Akron. When I walked through the front door, my mother gave me a hug and asked if I had seen the afternoon newspaper. "No, Mom," I replied. "What's happened now?" Dad, who had a big grin on his face, came into the room, holding the *Beacon Journal*. "Here," he said, "read it for yourself."

Under the endorsement for the Ohio House 39th District, the editors had written an editorial, saying:

> [Moldea] is running a hard campaign. . . . [His opponent] shows little desire to pursue the issues this time.
>
> From what we've seen, [the other GOP candidate] was put on the ballot by party officials to counter Moldea, who is a maverick. But he couples his criticism of the ethics and morality of the Nixon administration with support of Republican philosophy. He favors, for example, a move away from highly centralized government.
>
> Mr. Moldea has studied state issues, is eager to prove his political worth, and places a high premium on integrity. Orthodox or maverick, we favor Dan E. Moldea.[10]

Actually, my parents had obtained one of the few available copies of the newspaper. Unfortunately for me, on May 1, the day before this remarkable endorsement for my candidacy, the *Akron Beacon Journal* was struck for the first time in its 136-year history and did not publish at all. As a result of the work stoppage by Teamsters Local 473, only a limited number of copies were actually published and distributed on May 2 and for duration of the six-day strike. Most of the voters in my district never even saw what the newspaper had written about me.

On the night of primary election on May 7, my opponent—the good and decent family man who had "little desire to pursue the issues" but enjoyed the monumental backing of the GOP's entire county organization—wiped the floor with me, defeating me by nearly a three-to-one margin.

Indeed, Ray Bliss had his way with me after all.

Later that evening, I received a telephone call from a friend who was out of town on business, a successful elderly gentleman and one of my biggest supporters. He knew the bottom line about most things in life.

"How'd you do?" He asked when I answered the phone.

Trying to be upbeat, I replied, "Hey, we ran a clean race. We stuck to the issues. We stood on principle. We . . . "

"Cut the bullshit, Dan," my old friend interrupted. "Did you win, or did you lose?"

5. On selling out

After losing the May 1974 primary by such a wide margin, I felt devastated and humiliated. Dealing with a new crisis of confidence and spirit, I couldn't seem to get back on track. Earlier, on the eve of the election and sensing defeat, I had started to move away from Lynn who had been supportive through it all. Recognizing that I was getting ready to go through a dark period in my life, we broke off the engagement and ended our three-year relationship.

Shortly after the break up and when classes at Kent State ended for the summer, five college buddies asked me to go with them for a weekend in the mountains of Pennsylvania to fish, shoot guns at paper targets, drink beer, smoke cigars, play cards, and talk about women.

When we arrived, I wandered off alone to look around. Our large wooden cabin sat on a hilltop overlooking a clear lake while the green forest of the mountains surrounding this scene appeared to go on forever. The sun shone brightly in the beautiful blue sky and reflected off the water like a mirror, but the shade from the trees made the scene idyllic.

Beautiful surroundings, warm weather, and low humidity, it was paradise. I just wanted to lie back in the tall grass and not think about anything in particular, maybe not think about anything at all—just dig my back in that grass and get comfortable. Man, it felt good. I felt happy.

Later, when I returned to the cabin, one of the guys on the trip began hustling me to come to work with him at his boss's insurance company. I simply told him, "Hey, I don't think I have what it takes to be an insurance salesman. . . ."

"Estate planner," he corrected me.

"Sorry, estate planner. I just don't have what it takes."

But the more he talked and the more beer we drank, the better the idea sounded. He told me that I could have a guaranteed monthly salary, plus a 55-percent commission on the specific policies I sold, in addition to a twenty-percent monthly bonus and a twenty-two percent quarterly bonus, as well as an annual bonus that would also be determined by total sales. He told me about the Million Dollar Roundtable, his fabulous Tudor home, his Corvette, and his knockout trophy wife.

PART ONE: ENTERING THE FRAY

"You have the American Dream, my friend," I said to him with admiration.

"And you can have it, too," he replied.

After thinking for a few moments, I said, "What the hell, let's give it a try. I don't have to go back to school until fall."

The following week—to the shock of nearly everyone who cared about me in Akron and Kent—I went into a six-week training program to become an estate planner/financial consultant: an insurance agent. I didn't have to sell anything yet, just attend classes.

I cut my hair. I put on a conservative suit, tie, starched shirts, and Florsheims—and started carrying a briefcase to classes every day. Abandoning the public courses I had grown up on, I started playing golf on the weekends at an exclusive country club with wealthy older friends who were members. And I started seeing a girl who did nothing but volunteer work for the Junior League.

Suddenly, I wanted personal happiness, and I was willing to do whatever it took to get it.

At the same time, with my hat in my hand, I made an appointment to see my principal tormentor, Ray Bliss. During our meeting, I pledged my support to the guy who had defeated me in the primary. When I said I wanted something else to do, he threw me a bone, asking me to help reorganize the county's dormant Young Republicans' organization. I happily agreed to consider it and suggested some ideas about attracting young disenchanted people into the GOP.

As I sat there completely debasing myself, I could hardly believe what I was saying. Then, really rubbing my face in it, Bliss asked me, "So, Dan, Jim Rhodes is going to need some help before the gubernatorial election. Have you changed your mind about him yet?"

At that exact moment, I started to feel like Paul Newman on the prison road crew in *Cool Hand Luke* after his second escape and capture—when prison bosses beat him over and over again until he "got his mind right." Soon after, he started fetching water for them.

"Let me get back to you on the Rhodes campaign, sir," I cringed.

I had written to Mrs. Nolte and asked whether she considered my sudden change of life a complete and total sellout.

Although she encouraged me to find happiness, she warned:

> There are dangers. As my definition has it, selling out comes when you narrow your interests; let your intellect, aesthetic tendencies, and sense of humor atrophy; make your primary interest the acquisition of things....

> You do well to worry. Money is addictive (if you've never had any, you don't miss it; once you have established a certain standard of living, however, it is very difficult to retreat from it). And power corrupts.
>
> Sell lots of insurance, but guard your soul and psyche. And keep your dreams, baby.[11]

Tim Davis had continued as a trusted friend after I graduated. Trying to get through his final year at the university, he had remained involved with student government and served as one of its representatives to the faculty senate.

I had also become a close friend of Davis's older brother, Bob, an Akron rubber worker and working-class hero at General Tire. Bob, one of the smartest people I have ever known, was a former honors student at Purdue University who had left school to join the Army and to fight in Vietnam.

On November 4, 1969, Davis's base in Tay Ninh Province came "under intense ground attack," according to an official report by the Department of the Army, which continued:

> Staff Sergeant Davis was personally responsible for halting the initial thrust of seven sappers who had penetrated the last row of barbed wire and were at the outside wall. By throwing grenades and placing down effective fire, he killed several enemy [soldiers] and prevented them from entering his area. He then rallied his men and set up a defensive position that was so effective that there were no further enemy penetrations in his area.[12]

For this remarkable act of heroism, Bob Davis earned the Silver Star.

The only person who had more respect for Bob Davis than me was his brother, Tim. But after three years of living together, they had started driving each other crazy.

Tim was a gourmet cook who drank fine wine and always insisted on having his home in immaculate condition. Divorced after his return from the war, Bob still lived like a soldier in the field. His bedroom had long been known as "The Bunker," because it reminded combat veterans of their sleeping quarters in the jungle. To him, a typical meal was peanut butter and honey on a hunk of white bread.

PART ONE: ENTERING THE FRAY

Before they killed each other, Tim moved into a house around the corner on Elmore Avenue, which was owned by a college friend of ours, Jim Switzer, "The Bishop of Elmore" as we called him.[13] He and his family owned four houses on the block. Jim's home was always a warm and pleasant gathering place for his legions of friends. He and his long-time girlfriend and future wife, Gretchen, did a considerable amount of volunteer work in the community, focusing on public libraries and the arts.

Knowing that I was cash poor and as much of a noble savage as he was, Bob Davis—who spent most of his time with his future wife, Kaye, a dance coach for the Ohio Ballet—allowed me to stay at his home until I got on my feet.

Hearing about my new job, as well as my recent political cataclysm, Bob took the news in stride. His brother, Tim, did not.

On July 16, Tim Davis and I had dinner at a local greasy spoon. When he asked me what I had been doing, I told him that I was in training to be an insurance salesman. Also, I gave him the mortifying details of my meeting with Ray Bliss.

Davis nearly choked on his cheeseburger. "What the fuck are you doing?" He scowled at me, drawing the attention of everyone in the joint. "What the fuck are you doing?"

I laughed, at first, but seeing that he was serious, I became serious, too. "Tim, I'm tired of trouble. I'm tired of not knowing who I am or where I'm going. I'm tired of not having enough money to do the things I want to do. I'm tired of being an outsider. . . . Plus, I like this Junior Leaguer."

Without saying another word, Davis dropped five dollars on the table for his unfinished dinner and stormed out of the restaurant alone.

Upset over Davis's reaction, I went home. Checking my messages, I received one from Curtis Davis, the new executive director of the Portage County Community Action Council—no relation to Tim and Bob Davis—and I returned his call. To my surprise, Curtis said that he wanted to bring me back to the CAC in Ravenna. When I told him that I would be willing to talk about it, he instructed me to be in his office on July 19 at 4:00 P.M.

Hanging up the phone, I sat down and started to do the homework for my insurance class the following morning. Although I had become a firm believer in the need for insurance—all kinds of insurance—I started to wonder whether selling insurance was the future I really wanted.

At some point that night, I threw down my pen and simply said, "This just isn't me." I immediately went to my typewriter and wrote my letter of resignation to the insurance company.

Tim Davis called me on the morning of July 19 and said he wanted to talk. I went to his house and immediately apologized for pissing him off three days earlier. When he started to give me a lecture, I interrupted him, telling him that I had done a lot of thinking and decided to grow my hair back, to put the blue jeans and cowboy boots back on, to quit the insurance business before I had to sell anything to anyone, to start playing golf at the old public courses again, and, finally, to register as a Democrat.

I added that I might be going back to work for the CAC federal poverty agency—while keeping my graduate assistantship at Kent State.

Looking relieved, Davis balked momentarily when I said there was one proviso.

"What's that?" He asked sternly.

"I get to keep the Junior Leaguer. . . ."

That afternoon, I met with Curtis Davis at CAC headquarters in Ravenna. He told me that his agency had an opportunity to receive some federal-grant money and asked me to write the proposal required for the grant. I immediately accepted the job.

That same night, in an event I took as a reward for my decision to change my own life, a friend and I went to Cleveland Stadium where we witnessed Cleveland Indians pitcher Dick Bosman throw a no-hitter against the Oakland A's. If not for Bosman's own throwing error in the fourth inning, he would've pitched a perfect game. We were among the 24,000-plus fans who leaned with every pitch after the seventh and gave Bosman a standing ovation when he reemerged from the dugout after completing this rare feat.

It was an absolutely thrilling experience.

Back to my own world: After completing the grant assignment—which I presented to the CAC board of directors on August 8, the same night as President Nixon announced his resignation in the midst of the Watergate scandal—Curtis Davis named me as his deputy director.

To be sure, I now had a good but low-paying job, doing important work at a federal poverty agency while I continued my studies in graduate school and taught a class about the causes and effects of racism to undergraduates.

Even though the Junior Leaguer dumped me in the aftermath of my latest transition, I felt back on track.

But, that, too, would be short lived.

PART ONE: ENTERING THE FRAY

On Wednesday, October 9, the CAC's bookkeeper asked me to come to his office. When I arrived, he alleged that two CAC checks—one of which had been payable to a local accounting firm—had been used by Curtis Davis as collateral for a personal loan. Davis had endorsed at least one of the checks, even though it had not been made out to him. The second check had not yet cleared. Continuing through the agency's financial records, we documented other financial discrepancies involving the executive director.

After I confronted Davis with the evidence the following day, he immediately fired me. And, to the surprise of nearly everyone, the CAC board of directors, which later forced Davis's resignation, allowed my firing to stand, even though my actions were supported by members of the board, as well as the county prosecutor and the local media. The board members claimed that I was in the midst of a 120-day probationary period as a federal employee, and that there was nothing they could do.

I hated the idea of filing a lawsuit, especially for money damages against a federal poverty agency. But I needed some act of good faith from the CAC board—which had refused to correct the situation—so that I could walk away from this matter without it haunting me for the rest of my life.

But when the CAC board refused to budge, I went to Nick Roetzel, a local attorney in Akron, who had served as chapter advisor for my fraternity at the university. Roetzel—who had also been a member of a team of four attorneys representing the National Association for the Advancement of Colored People (NAACP) in *Hunter v. Erickson*, a 1969 landmark open-housing case, before the United States Supreme Court—reviewed my situation and said we had a sure winner.

In the end, we reached an out-of-court settlement in which the CAC board gave me my old job back . . . so that I could simply resign. Knowing how financially strapped the agency had been, I, of course, waived any claims to back pay.

For his own payment, attorney Roetzel accepted one of my prized possessions: a baseball signed by the 1954 pennant-winning Cleveland Indians.

In the wake of the final settlement, an editorial in the *Akron Beacon Journal*, "Fighting the good fight," summed up the episode:

> Many talk about carrying on a fight against some wrong as a matter of principle. Few do so. Dan Moldea is one of the few.
> . . .

Moldea gained nothing from this in a tangible sense. He doesn't have the job back and he doesn't have the money. But he gained something far more important—the satisfaction of vindication, of a clean record, of a reputation of integrity. That made it a fight worth waging.[14]

6. Becoming a writer

After I left my job as deputy director of the Portage County Community Action Council in October 1974, I attended a party for an old friend from the Black United Students at the University of Akron and met William Ellis, Sr., the owner and publisher of *The Reporter*, an Akron-based newspaper, serving the black community in northeastern Ohio. Years earlier, Ellis had worked as a young attorney with the NAACP on its historic 1954 landmark case, *Brown v. Board of Education*.

When I told him that I was in graduate school at Kent State, taught a course about racism, and had always wanted to be a writer, he invited me to be his "token white guy" at the newspaper and offered me my own weekly column. To the delight of my writing coach, Mrs. Nolte, I accepted his offer, even though I would only receive fifteen dollars per article. My first column appeared on November 30, 1974.

Most of my early work was fairly lightweight, dealing with sports and the arts, covering the U.S. Olympic Boxing team and the Harlem Globetrotters during their local appearances, writing about a professional hockey game that went into double overtime, and pushing for greater funding for the Ohio Ballet.

Meantime, an acquaintance from the American Friends Service asked me to speak to the local Kiwanis Club about world hunger. I collected some research and put together a twenty-minute talk after which I also wrote a column.

My world-hunger article attracted the attention of Dick Nixon, a United Farm Workers' organizer in Akron. (Nixon was no relation to President Richard Nixon who had just resigned from office.) Nixon called and asked me if I'd be interested in writing about the UFW's ongoing battle with the International Brotherhood of Teamsters.

When I replied that I was, Nixon gave me a box of documents and introduced me to a couple of sources. Reading the material and talking

PART ONE: ENTERING THE FRAY

to his contacts, I also went out and did some new reporting. It was the first hard news story I had ever written. And I later received a letter from UFW President Cesar Chavez, thanking me for publishing it.

Dick Nixon liked the column, too, and he asked me if I was willing to do more reporting about the Teamsters. When I replied that I was looking for a topic for my master's thesis at Kent State, he gave me the telephone number for Gordon "Mac" McKinley, a leader in the rank-and-file's national battle for Teamster reform who lived in the Akron area.

On December 14, I called McKinley who belonged to the Professional Drivers Council on Safety and Health (PROD), a Washington, D.C.-based, spin-off group of Ralph Nader's Public Citizen. McKinley and other union rebels in PROD had been battling the Teamsters' power structure for years, insisting that it was abusing its members and their pension funds.

Three days later, McKinley and I met at 3:15 A.M. on a cold and dark, snow-covered street corner in downtown Akron. From the outset, he made it clear that he had a gun in his pocket and was prepared to use it if there was any trouble. Terrified, I replied that I was simply there to learn something new to write about in my little column and possibly for my thesis in graduate school.

McKinley and I talked for a few moments, and, after things settled down, he handed me a black ledger, containing the complete list of loans from the Teamsters' Central States, Southeast and Southwest Areas Pension Fund, many of which had gone to the underworld.

When I returned home, I leafed through the ledger, spotting everything from Las Vegas casinos and real-estate ventures to country clubs and trucking companies, some of which had received loans of astronomical amounts from the union. One large loan had even gone to the popular Akron televangelist, Rex Humbard, and his Cuyahoga Falls-based Cathedral of Tomorrow.

Although completely uninformed about the subject of the Teamsters and the Mafia, I was obviously intrigued by the contents of this document—even though I didn't have any idea what all this stuff meant. Determined to find out, I stayed in touch with McKinley.

For several days over the Christmas break, like a student in class, I went to his home, sat at his kitchen table, drank coffee, smoked Kools, and listened as he taught me about the Teamsters Union.

After I earned his trust, McKinley told me to contact PROD's executive director, Arthur Fox, a well-known and respected Nader attorney. I called Fox in Washington, D.C. and told him that I had been referred by McKinley who had already told him about me. During our friendly exchange, Fox offered to send materials to me about a breaking story, involving a major lobbying campaign by the American Trucking Association for what he viewed as a bad piece of legislation in Congress.

I wrote the story, which received some attention, and Fox was pleased.

The following week, on January 24, 1975, I began the first of my eight-part series, "The Teamsters, Their Pension Fund and the Mafia," which was based, in part, on the black ledger McKinley had given me during our first meeting. Much of this information had never been published.

Although extremely busy with her own work in academia, Mrs. Nolte reviewed each of my columns. In a letter written on March 15, she advised me to collect all of my data and published works about the Teamsters and "Go for it!" In other words, she wanted me to write a book in concert with my master's thesis.

For encouragement and inspiration, she gave me a gift: *The Autobiography of Lincoln Steffens*, the fascinating memoir of one of the great early investigative journalists. I added it to my growing library, which also included another book I had recently received from a rank-and-file Teamster, *The Fall and Rise of Jimmy Hoffa* by Walter Sheridan, the chief investigator for former Attorney General Robert Kennedy, who was principally responsible for sending the ex-Teamsters leader to prison in 1967.

Just before publication of the eighth and final installment of my series about the Teamsters and the Mafia on March 21, 1975, I took my boss, Bill Ellis, to lunch. I told him that I had to leave his newspaper and thanked him for allowing me to be his "token white guy." He laughed and slapped me on the shoulder, understanding that I could no longer work for fifteen dollars a week. Then, suddenly looking at me with concern, he asked, "Are you still going after the Teamsters?"

I laughed, "Bill, I'm still going after the Teamsters. And I expect you and Mrs. Nolte to come and pick up the pieces when they come after me."

7. Set up in Chicago

During Easter break, I drove my 1970 Thunderbird to Washington, the first stop of a planned five-city tour, and spent the day with Arthur Fox and his administrator, Michael deBlois, a great organizer with a terrific head for politics. For several hours, Fox, deBlois, and I swapped stories and information. I really admired these dedicated guys and what they represented.

I also gave Fox and deBlois a proposal for the thesis/book I wanted to write about the Teamsters. Fox arranged for me to speak with Ralph Nader. While student body president at the University of Akron, I was among several students who had met with Nader after his speech at the 1972 National Student Association Congress in Washington.

Now, during our conversation in March 1974, Nader encouraged me to write a book about the Teamsters and gave me the name of his New York literary agent, Philip Spitzer, who also represented several authors in Public Citizen.

Spitzer, a terrific guy who spoke fluent French and drove a new Peugeot, received his Masters degree in publishing from New York University—in addition to a degree in French literature from the University of Paris. After seeing some of my raw materials, he agreed to represent me.

In the wake of spending the following day at the Department of Labor, combing through union records, I drove to Dayton where I spoke at a rank-and-file rally, arranged by union reformers associated with Mac McKinley in Akron. Following my speech, an irate Teamster loyalist who had been drinking heavily pulled a handgun out of his jacket pocket. He waved it around and threatened to shoot me. Several of his friends talked him into putting away the gun and then helped him out of the building.

But, unlike my first meeting with McKinley the previous December, when he scared me by simply claiming to have a gun in his pocket, this incident startled me but wasn't nearly as traumatic. Shocked by my own lack of terror, I couldn't believe that I was already getting used to this.

My trips to Louisville and Nashville were much calmer. I did my interviews, collected documents, and then headed north.

During my final stop in Chicago on April 1, I attended the Gaylur Products/Central States Pension Fund trial at the federal courthouse—which featured, among others, defendants Allen Dorfman, the notorious one-time fiduciary manager of the Teamsters pension fund, and Teamsters bail bondsman, Irwin Weiner. Both had been accused of defrauding the Central States Fund.

Prior to the trial, two ski-masked, shotgun-wielding assailants had murdered a key prosecution witness, slated to testify against the defendants—who were later acquitted.

In the midst of a recess, I saw Dorfman and Weiner sitting on a bench outside the courtroom. Intruding on their conversation, I walked up and introduced myself as a graduate student at Kent State who was writing a master's thesis about the Teamsters. Both men were courteous.

During our brief conversation, I asked Dorfman, the primary target in my eight-part series for *The Reporter*, whether he was as bad as everyone was claiming. He laughed, insisting that he was "no different and no worse than anyone else in a position to manipulate money and power."

While in Chicago, I stayed at the home of reform leader Robert Grant of the local independent Teamsters union. For three days, I ate with his family, used his telephone, and slept on his couch.

Totally committed to his cause, Bob Grant embodied the quintessential union rank-and-file reformer—smart, tough, brave, and selfless. Through Grant, I was introduced to other Chicago dissident leaders, including Dan La Botz, a scholar and writer as well as a Teamster. As with Grant, I really looked up to La Botz.

Because I had been equally impressed with Arthur Fox and Mike deBlois, I encouraged the Chicago rebels to join forces with PROD. However, Grant, La Botz, and their colleagues were unenthusiastic about the Nader group—because it wasn't operated by rank-and-file Teamsters. I told them that I thought that they were making a big mistake.

During my final day in Chicago, I received a telephone call at Grant's home from an anonymous person, promising to provide me with damaging information about Allen Dorfman. A contact, the caller said, would be waiting for me at a bar just north of the city at 4:00 P.M.

Because the meeting had been set at a public place and in broad daylight, I did not even hesitate to go. Ever since my initial contact in the middle of the night with Mac McKinley, this whole experience had been a series of adventures. I assumed that this meeting would yield another. Then, I planned to drive back to Ohio.

Also—at 25-years-old, six-feet-four, and a hard 175 pounds—I knew how to take care of myself. And, even if I couldn't handle a particular situation, I still had good speed on a dead run. And, if all else failed, my Thunderbird had a powerful V-8 engine, and I had never been shy about driving fast. My collection of speeding tickets in no fewer than four states was evidence of that.

But, most of all, I viewed myself as being invulnerable.

Arriving at the bar at about 3:45 P.M., I parked in the corner of an empty adjacent lot. I took my tape recorder and notepad out of my backpack and placed them in the pockets of my leather jacket. Then, I walked up a cement walkway towards the entrance of the bar—a thick oak door with a black wrought-iron handle. I thought nothing of it when

PART ONE: ENTERING THE FRAY

I heard two car doors slam and people walking up behind me. I don't remember much of anything immediately after that.

When I finally regained consciousness during the early evening, I was lying on my left side across the front seat of my car in my own blood and urine. Someone—or, presumably, the people I heard walking up behind me—had torn me apart.

I felt as though the right side of my face had been bashed in. My chest, neck, upper and lower back, lower abdomen, and right leg ached badly. My right hand was so swollen that I thought it was broken. Propping myself up so that I could look in the rear-view mirror, I switched on the interior light of my car and saw that my badly bruised right eye was nearly closed. Blood from my nose, mouth, and a cut over my right eye had trickled across my face. And, adding insult to injury, I had wet my pants. I was a complete mess.

With no health insurance since I left the CAC, and nothing but a gasoline credit card and only about fifty bucks in my pocket, I drove slowly from the bar and stopped at a gas station a few blocks away. Using the bathroom, I tried to clean up. I took a change of clothes out of my backpack, but it must have taken me five minutes simply to pull a turtleneck over my head, because I was in so much pain. Then, I wrapped my right hand in a mound of paper towels doused with cold water, which I also held up against my right eye.

I drove to a nearby hospital but never went in for treatment, deciding instead to save the expense and simply go home to reevaluate my injuries from there.

When I returned to Akron, I rested quietly and missed the next week of classes at Kent. Fortunately, I had no broken bones. More than anything else, I felt humiliated by the thrashing I had taken.

Although I quickly healed physically, I felt a mixture of "lucky to be alive" and overall despair. Regardless of their proportions, it was far from the invulnerability I had felt before Chicago.

In short, other than the Kent State shootings, I could not think of a single event at that point in my young life that had so dramatically changed me and the way I viewed the world. Among other upheavals that followed, my childhood religious upbringing kicked in as I developed a healthy belief in a benevolent God, as well as a sense of an ultimate impartial justice in the universe—a faith system that has sustained me ever since. However, for reasons I never fully understood, I felt embarrassed by these views and kept them to myself.

Losing much of my innocence in the wake of that horrible incident in Chicago, I left the master's program at Kent State and moved forward with my full-time investigation of the Teamsters. And, as I entered this dangerous world of probing labor racketeers and Mafia figures, delusional or not, I was now willing to sacrifice myself for what I believed was a righteous cause.

8. Jimmy Hoffa disappears

In the midst of my recovery from the ass-kicking I had received in Chicago, Jonathan Kwitny, a staff reporter for the *Wall Street Journal*, contacted me after hearing from Arthur Fox of PROD that I had been doing work on the Teamsters' Central States Pension Fund.

I had read Kwitny's 1973 book, *The Fountain Pen Conspiracy*, a few months earlier, and viewed him as among the best investigative journalists in the country, along with my other favorites: columnist Jack Anderson, Seymour Hersh and David Burnham of the *New York Times*, Donald Bartlett and James Steele of the *Philadelphia Inquirer*, and, of course, Bob Woodward and Carl Bernstein of the *Washington Post*. To me, all of these guys—along with Senate investigator Walter Sheridan, the author of *The Fall and Rise of Jimmy Hoffa*, and Clark Mollenhoff, the author of *Tentacles of Power*—were gods.

During the spring of 1975, only a handful of journalists, like Kwitny and me, were specializing on the Teamsters and the Mafia. They included Jim Drinkhall of *Overdrive* who published truly amazing stories about Teamster corruption for his California-based trucking magazine, Pulitzer Prize-winner Denny Walsh of the *Sacramento Bee*, and Lester Velie of *Reader's Digest*, an old pro whose earlier work had helped to spark many of the investigations of the union during the 1950s and 1960s. And then there were "The Giants," the published authors of a long list of great mobology books: Ovid Demaris, Hank Messick, and Ed Reid.

During my conversations with Kwitny, he asked me for the documentation contained in my eight-part series—"The Teamsters Union, Their Pension Fund, and the Mafia"—which I had recently published in *The Reporter*. I sent him everything he wanted—*except* the black ledger of loans from the pension fund that union reformer Mac McKinley had given me the previous December. I jealously guarded that document, knowing few people had it, and that I would remain in demand as long as I did not give it away.

PART ONE: ENTERING THE FRAY

When Kwitny's three-part series about the Teamsters and the Central States Pension Fund ran in the *Wall Street Journal* on July 22-24, he generously spread the word that I had made an important contribution to his work. The problem was that in late-July 1975 few people cared about the Teamsters and the Mafia.

Then, on July 30, Jimmy Hoffa disappeared. . . . Now, suddenly, everybody cared.

—⚍—

Eyewitnesses had last seen Hoffa outside the Machus Red Fox restaurant in Bloomfield Hills, Michigan, northwest of downtown Detroit, at about 2:30 P.M. He was reportedly waiting for a scheduled meeting with two Mafia figures, Anthony Giacalone of Detroit and Anthony Provenzano of Union City, New Jersey.

On August 1, after the public announcement of Hoffa's disappearance, Kwitny telephoned me from New York to discuss the matter. During our conversation, he good naturedly demanded a theory from me. Aiming to please, I concocted an outrageous one, speculating that Hoffa might be alive and hiding in northern Wisconsin, near the Canadian border, at the Jack O'Lantern Lodge in Eagle River. I added that the resort was owned by the family of Allen Dorfman, the former fiduciary manager of the pension fund. At one time, Hoffa, who fished and hunted, had been a frequent visitor.

Kwitny told me that he wanted to discuss my idea with his editor, even though I reminded him that it was nothing more than a wild theory.

In a piece Kwitny later wrote about our misadventure, he picks up the story:

> Tepidly, I approached the *Journal's* managing editor, Fred Taylor, describing Dan, and his idea. I said it had the scent of logic and the genius of novelty, but was still a very long shot, just a roll of the dice. Taylor wanted to go for it. Money was looser in those days, and finding Hoffa would be one hell of a scoop. But while Taylor wasn't worried about the financial risk, he did express concern over the physical risk. I shrugged it off. Nevertheless, he instructed me to make sure that either Dan or I wait in town at a phone while the other visited the lodge. If the scout wasn't heard from by an appointed hour, the person at the phone would call Taylor at home. Lord knows what

Taylor would have done in such an event, but I agreed and headed for LaGuardia.

Airplane schedules being what they were and are, I first cast eyes on Dan at O'Hare Airport in Chicago, where he had arrived from Cleveland to meet me for the connecting flight to [Rhinelander]. I hadn't really known what to expect, but it certainly wasn't what I saw. Dan was a height and physique that might make one of Hoffa's professional legbreakers drop his tire iron and flee. A stranger seeing Dan board a plane to Wisconsin would have to assume he was reporting for duty to the Green Bay Packers.

Furthermore, he was dressed head to foot in black, body-clinging clothing and was carrying a rope, underwater flashlight and snorkel gear. It might be necessary, he explained, to approach the Jack-O' Lantern Lodge stealthily, underwater from across the lake. I immediately decided that I would be the one who waited in town by the telephone.

We rented a car and drove slowly by the entrance of the lodge, trying to look as innocent as possible. The fences were decorated with jack-o' lanterns. Buildings were visible in the distance, but the only signs of life were some German [S]hepherd dogs. The dogs convinced me I had made the right decision about who would go and who would wait.

At about dusk, we pulled into Eagle River, a sleepy little place . . . I forget the name of the cafe with the public phone where I decided to hole up. . . .

Dan was to have called the cafe to assure me of his safety no later than ten o'clock, which was eleven New York time; I didn't know when Taylor went to bed. Dan drove off looking confident. I sipped my coffee and watched eight o'clock pass. Nine. It grew to be five minutes of ten, and I started wondering what I would say if I had to make the phone call to Taylor.

At two minutes of ten, Dan strode into the cafe looking serious and plopped down across from me, holding his arm. A dog had bitten him. But two guards had pulled the dog off. He was all right. He . . . talked his way past the guards and gained an audience with Allen Dorfman's mother, an elderly lady who asserted that neither her son nor Mr. Hoffa was there. On the grounds, Dan met up with some other people and talked to them. There were a group of kids. . . . That cinched it for Dan. We were barking up the wrong tree. . .[15]

After this crazy attempt to find Hoffa, Kwitny and I laughed until we left Wisconsin on Sunday, August 3, and went our separate ways. Our running joke revolved around the newsroom scene at the *Wall Street Journal* when Kwitny would have to explain our wild-goose chase to his boss, Fred Taylor—and to all of the others who were sure to find out about it. And, while Kwitny was taking all this grief in New York, I was going to wind up with rabies, because I had refused to seek any medical attention after my brawl with one of the German Shepherds.

When I arrived back in Ohio, I decided to drive to Detroit and get into the mainstream action swirling around the Hoffa case. However, my Thunderbird had been vandalized and wouldn't start. I tried to fix it but only made it worse.

9. At the Red Fox

The following day, August 4, with a credit card and only two dollars cash in my wallet, I flew to hot and humid Detroit and hitchhiked about thirty miles north of the Detroit Metro Airport to the Red Fox restaurant where Hoffa was last seen on July 30. I really had no specific plan after that. I simply assumed that the Red Fox would be filled with news people who might be interested in my work.

When I arrived at the restaurant in a golf shirt, blue jeans, and cowboy boots, I saw a sign near the front door, noting a dress code. That was bad news. I was still bandaged after my dog-bite experience in Eagle River, and I didn't have a tie. I did have a rumpled sports jacket jammed in my backpack. But, when I put it on and walked into the Red Fox, the maitre d' told me to go home and put on the proper attire.

As I stepped back outside, I saw a priest wearing a small Eastern Orthodox crucifix on his jacket, standing near the door and appearing to be waiting for someone—just like Hoffa a few days earlier. I struck up a conversation with him, noting the summer heat and the fact that I, too, was a member of the Eastern Orthodox Church.

Then I said to him, "Father, I need to get into the restaurant, but I'm not dressed right. May I accompany you in there? I don't think that the management will say anything if I'm with a priest."

The reverend smiled and walked into the restaurant, holding me by the arm. When the maitre d' looked up at me, I simply said, "I'm with him," pointing to the priest. He smiled and let me pass.

Needing something to happen very quickly, I spotted the bow-tied NBC News correspondent, Irving R. Levine, a respected economics and labor reporter, walking down the stairs. I thanked the priest for helping me, shook hands with him, and then took off after Levine.

Downstairs, I saw the famous correspondent on a pay phone, getting ready to make a call. When he glanced at me, I nodded, pointing at him and then at me.

"May I help you?" Levine asked before finishing the number he was dialing.

"Mr. Levine, you need me," I blurted right out.

"I need you?"

"You need me for the Hoffa case."

Giving me a once over, Levine inquired, "Do you know something about the case?"

"I've done a lot of reporting about the Teamsters, and I helped with the research for the *Wall Street Journal* series last week."

Placing the phone back on the hook, Levine asked, "Are you that graduate student from Kent State?"

Assuming that he had heard about me from Jon Kwitny or someone who had talked to him, I grinned and spread my arms apart, saying, "That's me!"

As we shook hands, Levine asked, "Do you have plans for lunch?"

"No, sir, I don't."

Without making his call, Levine put his arm around my shoulder as we walked back up the stairs. "Then join us," he said.

When I saw the maitre d', I pointed at Levine and said, "Now, I'm with him." This time, the maitre d' laughed out loud.

Levine and I walked to his table where we joined several members of his NBC crew, including Bob Toombs, an NBC field producer assigned to the Hoffa case. Levine introduced me, adding that I was the graduate student who had helped Jon Kwitny with his series in the *Wall Street Journal*.

PART ONE: ENTERING THE FRAY

As Toombs and I shook hands, he asked me if I was working with any news organization. I replied that I was an independent writer, "unaffiliated at present."

"Are you looking for work?"

Surprised that he wanted to get right down to it, I responded, "Yes, sir. I've come to Detroit to work on the Hoffa case."

Toombs, who was on my right, looked over at Levine, on my left. Levine just smiled and said, "Go ahead." Toombs then started peppering me with questions, a trivia quiz about the Teamsters.

When they were satisfied that I knew something about the union, we started talking seriously about Hoffa and his background.

Born in Brazil, Indiana, on February 14, 1913, Hoffa, a former dock worker for a grocery store chain, became an organizer for Detroit's Teamsters Local 299 in 1937, rising quickly to lead his local, as well as Detroit's Joint Council 43, the Michigan Conference of Teamsters, and the Central Conference of Teamsters.

During a battle with a rival union which threatened the Teamsters' turf in Detroit in 1941, Hoffa enlisted the support of several local Mafia figures who successfully ran the CIO raiders out of town. However, the subsequent pact that Hoffa created with the underworld reduced him from a potentially great union leader—as was Walter Reuther of the United Auto Workers Union, also of Detroit—to nothing more than a labor racketeer. As a further contrast, Santo Perrone, one of the gangsters who aided Hoffa's rise to power, was later implicated in a murder plot against Reuther.

Creating a fiefdom for himself in the Midwest, Hoffa founded the union's health & welfare and pension funds with the cooperation of Chicago labor racketeer Paul Dorfman and his stepson, Allen Dorfman—the same guy I had met four months earlier at the Gaylur Products trial in Chicago. With the approval of Hoffa and the Dorfmans, these funds were bilked by the underworld.

The Kefauver Committee had targeted Hoffa during its U.S. Senate investigation in 1950-1951 but failed to discover a smoking gun that could lead to his prosecution. The year after the hearings ended, Teamsters general president Dave Beck appointed Hoffa as an international vice president. Then, after feeding Beck to the newly created Senate Rackets Committee in 1957, Hoffa, who routinely supplied information about his enemies to the committee, succeeded him as the union's general president.

Soon after Hoffa's election, the AFL-CIO expelled the Teamsters, and the federal government placed the union under the supervision of a court-ordered Board of Monitors. Later, Hoffa ravaged the monitors and won the union's independence in 1961. He immediately rewrote the union's constitution, centralizing power in his own hands and giving himself the ability to throw dissident locals into trusteeship.

Meantime, Hoffa had been indicted and acquitted in separate bribery and wiretapping cases. Also, federal prosecutors indicted him in a third case for his role in a land-fraud scheme in Florida. That case was later dropped.

Senator John Kennedy, a member of the Senate Rackets Committee, was elected President in November 1960, defeating Vice President Richard Nixon, whom Hoffa had supported. For his selection as the new U.S. Attorney General, the new President appointed his brother, Robert Kennedy, the chief counsel of the Senate Rackets Committee—who had several explosive confrontations with Hoffa during the Teamster boss's appearances before the committee. After winning the White House, the Kennedy brothers immediately declared war on organized crime and its associates, especially Jimmy Hoffa.

After a lengthy investigation, the Department of Justice indicted Hoffa for extortion, stemming from the earlier aborted prosecution for the land-fraud scheme. However, the trial ended in a hung jury. The Justice Department then indicted him again—this time for his role in a successful jury-tampering effort during the extortion trial.

Hoffa was finally convicted in Chattanooga for jury tampering in March 1964—just fifteen weeks after a sniper shot and killed President Kennedy in Dallas. Later that summer, Hoffa was convicted in Chicago for pension fraud. He was sentenced to a total of thirteen years in prison.

While appealing his convictions in 1966, he was reelected to his third five-year term as union president.

Hoffa entered Lewisburg Penitentiary on March 7, 1967. He selected his long-time friend, Frank Fitzsimmons, as his day-to-day caretaker of the union. But, soon after, Hoffa and Fitzsimmons had a falling out.

While Hoffa was in prison, Fitzsimmons became his own man and quickly began to decentralize power in the union to members of his general executive board who created their own fiefdoms around the country. In return, they, along with their allies in the Mafia, became fiercely loyal to Fitzsimmons who gave them just about anything and everything they wanted.

PART ONE: ENTERING THE FRAY

At the July 1971 Teamsters convention, Fitzsimmons was elected general president, officially replacing Hoffa.

During the Christmas holiday in 1971 with Hoffa out of power, President Nixon, who was elected president in 1968 and had become a close friend of Fitzsimmons, commuted Hoffa's prison sentence—with the proviso that he not engage in union politics until 1980. If Hoffa violated this restriction, he would be sent back to jail to finish his term. Hoffa accepted this at first but later blamed Fitzsimmons and others for making a secret deal with Nixon to push him out of the union.

At the time of Hoffa's disappearance, he and Fitzsimmons, along with their supporters in and out of the Mafia, were locked in a bitter dispute—as Hoffa and his attorneys attempted to overturn the commutation restrictions in court.

After he vanished, nearly everyone assumed that Fitzsimmons's allies in the underworld had murdered Hoffa in an effort to end his bid to regain the presidency of the union.

After lunch at the Red Fox and our lengthy discussion about Hoffa, Bob Toombs said to me, "We have a few interviews to do this afternoon. Why don't you join us? Maybe we can work something out."

Driving around the Detroit metropolitan area with the NBC people, I tried to get a feel for the politics between Levine and Toombs. Clearly, Levine, the big-name correspondent, was the star, but field-producer Toombs made things happen before, during, and after the interviews. Even though Levine had brought me into this situation, I decided, at least until I officially received a job, not to speak to him unless he spoke to me. Instead, I stayed close to Toombs. If Levine missed a line of questioning with someone he was interviewing, I didn't tell him directly. Instead, I quietly told Toombs and let him pass it on to Levine.

By the end of the day, I knew that I had made a real contribution to their reporting. I also knew that Toombs appreciated the deferential treatment I had given to him, and that he and Levine recognized me as a team player.

When we arrived at their hotel, the Southfield Sheraton, they asked me to come in with them. Standing in the lobby and having no idea where I was going to stay that night, I saw Levine and Toombs talking. After a few moments, Levine gave Toombs a pat on the back as they both turned and smiled at me.

Toombs went to the registration desk and talked to a clerk who handed him a key. Then, Toombs walked over and put the key in my hand, saying, "You're staying here with us. We'll give you a hundred dollars a day, plus all of your expenses. Tomorrow, we'll rent you a car and get you an office downtown with us. . . . Agreed?"

"Agreed!" I replied with considerable appreciation and relief.

"Welcome aboard, kid," Toombs declared, shaking my hand. "Don't fuck up."

10. The goon squad

On Tuesday, August 5, the day after I was hired by NBC News, I was given a desk in the newsroom of WWJ-TV, an NBC affiliate in downtown Detroit. For my first assignment, Bob Toombs gave me a long list of questions he needed answered and people he wanted contacted.

At 10:45 A.M., with my work nearly completed, I received a call from a very nervous man who refused to identify himself. He said that he had received my name from someone in the Teamsters rank-and-file reform movement, adding that he had important information about the Hoffa case.

"Do you know where he is?" I laughed, opening my notepad and picking up a pen.

"No," he answered. "I don't know for sure what happened to Jimmy. But I do know who was behind some of the bombings and shootings."

"What bombings and shootings?"

"The bombings and shootings against some of those people in Local 299, Jimmy's home local."

I thought for a moment and said, "I know that Frank Fitzsimmons's son's car was bombed about a month ago near Tiger Stadium."

"I know who was behind that," he responded. "It was a ruse."

"You know who bombed Dick Fitzsimmons's Lincoln?"

"Yeah, I know. I can't prove they did it, but I know they did."

Every few minutes, I heard him dropping coins into a pay phone.

Believing that this guy might be for real, I grabbed my tape recorder. Then, I attached a common wiretapping device with a suction cup to the telephone. Because I did not want to inhibit what he had called to tell me, I didn't tell him when I switched on the recorder.

"Okay, let me understand this," I said, trying to get him to repeat what he had just said off tape. "You're saying that you know who bombed Dick Fitzsimmons's car last month."

"Yeah, but, like I said, I can't prove it," he said. "I just know they did it."

"And you say it was a ruse?"

"Yeah . . . most of the bombings and shootings in Local 299 were against pro-Hoffa people. Then, just before Jimmy disappeared, Dick Fitzsimmons's car was bombed. . . . It had been too one way. They wanted something to happen to a Fitzsimmons person to make it look like both sides were involved in the violence."

"You're telling me that some pro-Fitzsimmons people blew up Dick Fitzsimmons' car?"

"Yeah, that's it."

"Does Dick Fitzsimmons know about this?"

"I don't think so. He didn't need to. He was someplace else when it happened. . . . Nobody got hurt, and it wasn't even Fitzsimmons's own car. The union gave him that car to use."

"Okay, who are the guys who did the bombing?"

With no equivocation, the source gave me the names of two men I had never heard of before: Larry McHenry and Jim Shaw, alleging that they had actually bombed the car.

"I'm sorry, sir, I don't know those names. Who are these guys?"

"They used to work for Rolland McMaster, and they might be still working for him."

"Okay, I'm sorry again," I said with some frustration. "I'm not familiar with him either. What's his name?"

Remaining patient with me, the source repeated McMaster's name and spelled it for me, adding that he was a "general organizer" for the Teamsters who worked directly for Fitzsimmons.

A few minutes later, I asked, "Okay, so what kind of work did these two guys do for McMaster?"

"They were part of an 'organizing unit' McMaster ran for Fitzsimmons and the Teamsters. . . ."

"You mean, like a goon squad?"

"Yeah," he laughed, "it was a goon squad."

"And do you know these guys personally: McMaster and Larry McHenry and Jim Shaw?"

"Yes, I do. I know all three of them pretty good."

"And how do you know them?"

"Because I was in the unit, too."

We spoke for a few more minutes until he ran out of change. Before he hung up, I asked him to stay in touch.

After my conversation with the source, I looked for Bob Toombs who was at a meeting outside the office. Then, I called John Sikorski, PROD's new research director in Washington, and asked him what he could find out about Rolland McMaster.

A few minutes later, Sikorski called back, telling me that McMaster had worked as a long-time aide to Jimmy Hoffa and had held several elected and appointed offices in Local 299. A large man with a huge reputation for toughness, McMaster, born in 1914, was known as a leg-breaker for Hoffa and, later, for Fitzsimmons. He also had a glass eye.

During the Senate Rackets Committee hearings, chief counsel Robert Kennedy had accused McMaster of shaking down trucking companies. In one extortion case, McMaster had been charged for allegedly extorting a woman who owned a trucking company to make payoffs for labor peace.

After the Department of Justice indicted McMaster, he married the woman who refused to testify against her new husband. Federal prosecutors later dropped their charges against him.

After Kennedy became attorney general, the Justice Department indicted McMaster again—this time for extorting an Ohio trucking company, Youngstown Cartage. Upon his conviction, a federal judge sentenced him to eighteen months at the federal prison in Terre Haute, Indiana. Since his release, McMaster had become the Teamsters' principal expert on trucking matters involving special commodities and steel hauling.

Topping off all of this, Sikorski warned me that McMaster was widely known as a very, very dangerous man.

When Toombs returned to the office, I briefed him, telling him what I had learned about Rolland McMaster, his Teamster organizing unit, and the violence in Local 299 prior to Hoffa's disappearance, particularly the bombing of young Fitzsimmons's car.

When Toombs expressed some skepticism, I grabbed my recorder and played the tape. After hearing the source's own words, Toombs started to believe. He asked me whether the source would agree to go on camera. I told him I didn't know.

"Why did he let you tape him?" Toombs asked.

"I didn't tell him, Bob. I didn't want to spook the guy."

Toombs became angry with me for taping the telephone conversation without the source's permission. I tried to give him the "people lie, tapes don't" argument, but he didn't want to hear about it.

PART ONE: ENTERING THE FRAY

"We don't do that around here!" He shouted.

Seeing me slump in my seat, Toombs stood up and then patted me on the back. "Unofficially, though," he said quietly, "good job."

Toombs reached into his pocket and placed five one-hundred dollar bills in front of me, telling me that this was an advance against my salary and expenses. Then, he instructed me to spend the rest of the day checking out my new source's story.

11. The Local 299 violence

I called a rank-and-file member of PROD who lived in Detroit and had some friends in high places at Local 299. I asked him to put me in touch with someone who could explain the violence in Local 299 prior to Jimmy Hoffa's disappearance.

A few minutes later, Hoffa's uncle, Steve Riddle, a local business agent, called me at the television station. During our brief conversation, I asked him if he would talk to me in person. He told me to meet him at the Local 299 union hall in a half hour.

After grabbing a quick lunch at a fast-food joint, I drove to Local 299 on Trumbull Avenue. The two-story building, made of alternating patterns of light and dark brown brick, looked like a fortress, with right angles and heavy, three-paned windows.

Steve Riddle, a short and thin man with glasses, met me in the lobby. He had brought along Mike Raggish, a tough looking former police officer who served as an occasional bodyguard for another Hoffa supporter, Dave Johnson, the president of Local 299. I shook hands with Riddle and Raggish as we walked into a conference room.

"Who is Rolland McMaster?" I asked Riddle as we sat down.

Riddle's head jerked when he heard that first question.

Seeing his reaction, I asked, "I'm sorry Steve, is he a friend of yours?"

"No!" Riddle shot back. "He's no friend of mine, and he is no friend of Jimmy Hoffa!"

"Do you think your nephew is still alive?"

"I don't know what to think. Probably not. But if he was murdered, I'd start my investigation with McMaster."

Riddle explained that the Local 299 drama featured four principal characters: Jimmy Hoffa and Frank Fitzsimmons, along with Rolland McMaster and Dave Johnson. All others were simply members of their supporting cast. Prior to 1967, these four men had worked as a team within Local 299. Hoffa was president; Fitzsimmons, vice president; McMaster, secretary-treasurer; and Johnson, the recording secretary.

Riddle explained that the split between Hoffa and Fitzsimmons began in March 1967 after Hoffa went to prison and Fitzsimmons appointed McMaster to run the Detroit local—contrary to Hoffa's instructions to give the job to Dave Johnson. From there, the situation became worse, as Fitzsimmons defiantly protected McMaster.

In 1970, during the escalating turmoil between the Hoffa and Fitzsimmons forces, Johnson accused McMaster of ordering one of his organizers, Don Davis, to attack and beat him. Immediately after the alleged assault, Johnson used this politically supercharged incident to purge McMaster from Local 299.

Soon after the Don Davis incident, the membership elected Johnson as president of the local. Simultaneously, Fitzsimmons quietly named McMaster as a general organizer for the international union. Although spotted occasionally in Detroit, McMaster appeared to have vanished from the local scene after the Johnson beating.

Meantime, in the wake of Fitzsimmons's election as union president in July 1971 and Hoffa's release from prison five months later, the ex-Teamsters boss began to fight the restrictions Nixon had placed on his commutation. Always remaining loyal to Hoffa, Johnson publicly announced that if the restrictions were overturned, he would yield the Local 299 presidency to Hoffa—who could then use it as his springboard to unseat Fitzsimmons at the 1976 Teamsters Convention.

While the legal drama of Hoffa's desperate fight made national headlines, a rash of violent acts against Hoffa's supporters in Local 299 received virtually no attention, including:

> * A barn, owned by Local's 299's new secretary-treasurer Otto Wendell, was torched.
>
> * Four sticks of dynamite were placed under the car of Local 299 business agent Jimmy Clift.
>
> * And the home of another business agent, Gene Page, was bombed.

Following these first three incidents in which no one was injured:

PART ONE: ENTERING THE FRAY

* A pro-Hoffa Local 299 trustee, George Roxburgh, was wounded during a shotgun attack as he sat in his car. Hit in his head, arms, and chest, Roxburgh survived—although the blast cost him his right eye.

* A few months later, someone fired another shotgun blast into Dave Johnson's empty office at the union hall. When Johnson arrived at the local the following morning, the entire room was covered with buckshot and glass.

* Johnson's cabin cruiser was bombed at its mooring behind his home on Grosse Ile, near Detroit.

* Following that, during the 1974 independent truckers' national shutdown, the home of William "Red" Anderson, one of Hoffa's liaisons to the independents, was bombed.

In August 1974, Richard Fitzsimmons, Frank's oldest son, announced his candidacy for president of Local 299. Everyone predicted that. But no one expected him to select McMaster as his running mate.

In retaliation, Johnson fired three pro-Fitzsimmons business agents. Consequently, McMaster and young Fitzsimmons organized a massive protest against Johnson in front of Local 299 which threatened to become extremely violent.

International vice president and Detroit Local 337 president Robert Holmes—a long-time friend of both Hoffa and Fitzsimmons who had managed to remain neutral in their dispute—negotiated a settlement whereby the union would be operated by a coalition of Hoffa and Fitzsimmons supporters with Johnson remaining as president and Dick Fitzsimmons serving as vice president.

Remarkably, Riddle and Raggish told me, the person who nearly scuttled the arrangement was Jimmy Hoffa who feared that he might be running out of time to gain a union office before the 1976 Teamsters Convention where the union's top officers would be elected. Hoffa knew that, in order to run for general president, a candidate must be a delegate to the convention. And a delegate was usually an appointed or elected union official from one of the 800-plus Teamster locals.

Obsessed with his personal comeback, Hoffa had announced that he might allow his name to be put up for the Local 299 presidency in the upcoming December 1974 election. By not participating in the campaign and permitting others to rally support for him, Hoffa believed that he could win without technically violating his commutation restrictions. Then, after his victory, he would allow Dave Johnson to serve in his place until his legal challenge to the restrictions worked its way through the courts. If the restrictions were overturned, Johnson would step aside for Hoffa.

Also, Hoffa believed that in a Presidential election year, his old friend, President Gerald Ford of Michigan, would not risk losing Teamster votes by attempting to block his candidacy. Interestingly, during the spring of 1975, President Ford granted disgraced former Teamsters general president Dave Beck a full pardon. Many wondered if Ford was considering another for Hoffa prior to the 1976 presidential election.

As Hoffa's strategy unfolded, union member Larry McHenry, loyal to McMaster, filed suit against the local, trying to block Hoffa's attempt to run for Local 299 office. Viewing the suit as a blessing in disguise, Hoffa told Johnson and secretary-treasurer Otto Wendell to use McHenry's litigation as justification for postponing the Local 299 election, thus, buying Hoffa more time.

When Riddle mentioned McHenry's name, I sat in my chair like a statute, saying nothing about the information my secret source had earlier given me about McHenry's alleged role in the bombing of Dick Fitzsimmons's car, along with that of another McMaster operative, Jim Shaw.

Riddle continued, saying that after the postponement of the election, Frank Fitzsimmons weighed in with his considerable power, threatening to throw Local 299 into trusteeship if Hoffa's name actually appeared on the ballot. And, if Fitzsimmons needed additional justification for his action, he could use the ongoing violence in Local 299 as another reason to step in and take over.

However, a U.S. Justice Department spokesman mooted the need for any of this when he warned that the federal government would take legal action against Hoffa if he ran for Local 299 president. Threatened with a return to prison to finish his sentence, Hoffa relented and hoped for better luck in court.

McMaster, still working as a general organizer directly under Frank Fitzsimmons, decided to defy the local's coalition slate, announcing that he would challenge Johnson for president. McMaster also put up a slate of candidates for other offices—one of whom was Larry McHenry.

Furious, Johnson threatened to torpedo the earlier compromise if McMaster actually ran. Consequently, in another peace negotiated by Bobby Holmes, Fitzsimmons asked McMaster to bow out. Reluctantly, McMaster complied. But, even with McMaster gone, McHenry still didn't want to leave—until Fitzsimmons stepped in again and simply ruled him ineligible for office.

Between then and Hoffa's disappearance, McMaster started packing local union meetings with his supporters and out-of-state thugs—who sounded suspiciously like members of the goon squad my new secret source had described. Several of these meetings, led by Dave Johnson, were disrupted by McMaster's men.

At the end of June 1975, the Local 299 violence resumed when Ralph Proctor, a local business agent, was mildly roughed up by persons unknown as he left a tavern in Melvindale. The Proctor ambush, which some viewed as a staged event with Proctor's full cooperation, was the first alleged act of violence against a Fitzsimmons-McMaster supporter.

Proctor, who wasn't really hurt, publicly accused the Hoffa-Johnson forces of ordering the attack.

Then, on Thursday, July 10, while Dick Fitzsimmons was getting ready to leave Nemo's Bar near Tiger Stadium, his union car, a 1975 Lincoln Continental, exploded.

Twenty days later, Hoffa disappeared.

I thanked Riddle and Raggish for the briefing and returned to my desk at WWJ-TV, spending the rest of the day typing up my notes.

In my mind, there was a very possible, even likely connection between Rolland McMaster and Jimmy Hoffa's murder.

12. Manitoulin Island

That evening, Bob Toombs took me to dinner, and I told him what I had learned earlier in the day.

"With the exception of Hoffa's bid for the union's presidency," I reported, "the national media is completely ignoring what's happened right here in Detroit. I just can't believe that the people behind all of this local violence against Hoffa's supporters didn't play some role in the events leading up to his disappearance."

Toombs nodded without really agreeing or disagreeing and said he would call New York to discuss it. Meantime, he told me to work exclusively on this new local angle.

The following morning, August 6, Irving R. Levine left Detroit and was replaced by two other respected NBC reporters, Robert Hager and Mike Jackson. Also, another outstanding NBC field producer, Bert

Medley, joined the mix. Toombs, who still ran the show, briefed all three of them about my secret source and what I had learned.

During the late morning, the anonymous source called me again. When I asked him to tell me more about McMaster's 32-member organizing unit—which he started calling the "McMaster Task Force"—he recalled incidents of bombings and shootings conducted between 1972-1974 against a variety of trucking companies. He added that, more often than not, McMaster had used the facade of organizing simply as a means to shake down trucking executives by getting them to pay for labor peace.

Seeing Toombs walk into the newsroom, I motioned to him to come to my desk. When he did, I asked the source if he would speak to my boss. The source agreed, and Toombs picked up an extension. During the three-way conversation, the source repeated the information about the McMaster Task Force, adding that he had heard that McMaster was on Manitoulin Island in Ontario, along with several of his men, including Larry McHenry and Jim Shaw. He claimed that McMaster owned a farm on the eastern portion of the island, which was located in Lake Huron. Then, my source speculated that McMaster and his goon squad might be holding Hoffa, dead or alive, on that island.

When I saw Toombs jump out of his chair after hearing that, I winced. I knew what Toombs was thinking. And I had intentionally kept quiet about my wild-goose chase in Eagle River with Jon Kwitny of the *Wall Street Journal* a few days earlier, knowing that the story made me look like an idiot.

At the conclusion of the ten-minute conversation, Toombs slammed down the phone and shouted at me, "Did you get that on tape?"

I stammered, "Um, ah, ah, I—I thought you told me not to do any more secret taping, Bob. . . . No, I didn't."

Toombs walked away from my desk—this time, disappointed that I hadn't memorialized the call. Now, he was on the spot and had to make a decision.

A few minutes later, Toombs called a joint meeting of the NBC and WWJ staffers who were working on the Hoffa case. Bob Hager was out of the office and didn't attend the meeting. Mike Jackson and Bert Medley were present, along with WWJ news manager Robert Giles, WWJ news anchorman Lowell James, and WWJ investigative reporter Robert Vito.

Toombs announced that he had just talked to my source, adding that he appeared to be extremely credible. Then, he recounted that portion of the conversation about the possibility of McMaster's men holding Hoffa, dead or alive, on McMaster's Manitoulin Island farm.

PART ONE: ENTERING THE FRAY

"I think we ought to check this out right away," declared Toombs. "What do you think, Dan?"

Still cringing inside, knowing that the source was only speculating, I mocked enthusiasm, replying, "Hey, I'm ready, Bob! When do I go?"

"No," Toombs responded to me, "we need you and Mike [Jackson] here for other things."

Toombs conferred with Medley and concluded, "We're going to call New York and talk it over." Then, pointing at Vito, who had interviewed Hoffa shortly before his disappearance, Toombs asked, "If we do it, how about you, Bob?"

Vito laughed, "Let's do it! But let me call my wife first!"

Later that afternoon, Vito formally received the assignment to look for Jimmy Hoffa on Manitoulin Island. I didn't know whether to laugh or to cry, especially after I heard Toombs on the telephone, arranging for a helicopter to fly to Manitoulin Island in the event that Vito hit paydirt.

While Vito trekked up north, Steve Riddle called me and asked if I wanted to talk to Dave Johnson, the president of Local 299. When I said I did, he told me to meet them at the union hall later that afternoon.

At my meeting with Johnson, we discussed the politics and the violence in Local 299, especially the 1974 bombing of his cabin cruiser. Johnson refused to speculate who had been behind that particular incident or any of the other beatings, bombings, or shootings. However, he seethed with anger whenever I brought up McMaster. Johnson couldn't even refer to him by name, calling him instead "that union organizer."

Clearly believing that Hoffa had been murdered but refusing to say so out loud, Johnson kept his political edge, saying, "Frank Fitzsimmons is a good friend of mine, and I want everyone to know that, just as everyone knew that Hoffa was my friend. I have no ax to grind with Frank."

—⚏—

A few days later, Bob Vito returned from his misadventure on Manitoulin Island where he had posed as a camper. He reported that during a check of local property records he discovered a parcel of land on the eastern portion of the island registered in the name of "Harold R. McMaster"—but he had no idea whether this McMaster had any connection to our McMaster whom I later learned did have a cousin named "Harold R. McMaster."

Although Vito did not attempt to enter the property, he did confirm that a number of people were occupying the area. However, Vito did not learn their identities or what they were doing there. Concluding that Hoffa was not on the island, dead or alive, he simply returned to Detroit.

With Vito's safe return and the white heat of the Hoffa case subsiding in Michigan, Bob Toombs called me to his office. When I walked in, believing that he was going to rip my head off for the Manitoulin Island debacle, he smiled and shook my hand, telling me that I had been reassigned to NBC News in New York, adding that my $100-a-day salary had been doubled.

13. A guerrilla writer in New York

As I wrapped up my work in Detroit and prepared to fly to Manhattan, I typed up a long memorandum for Bob Toombs, giving him the current state of evidence in the Hoffa case. Briefly, this is what I wrote:

> On Wednesday, July 30, Hoffa left his cottage in Lake Orion, twenty-five miles north of Detroit, for his scheduled 2:00 P.M. meeting with Detroit Mafia figure Anthony Giacalone and New Jersey labor racketeer Anthony Provenzano. The sitdown had been arranged three days earlier after Giacalone had a series of meetings with Hoffa, imploring him to meet with Provenzano, a former Hoffa-friend-turned-enemy. Vito Giacalone, Tony's brother, and Louis Linteau—a trusted Hoffa confidant who owned an airport limousine service in Pontiac, Michigan—had been present for these earlier meetings.
>
> Wearing a dark-blue shirt, trousers, and sunglasses, Hoffa drove his dark-green 1974 Grand Ville Pontiac to the Red Fox, the site for the meeting. His wife later reported that Hoffa appeared uncommonly nervous prior to leaving their home.
>
> En route to the meeting, Hoffa stopped to visit with Linteau who was out of his office. Hoffa chatted with several employees. He told one of them that he was on his way to see Giacalone and Provenzano and wanted Linteau to accompany him.

After arriving at the restaurant alone, he parked his car at a shopping center next to the Red Fox. Waiting nearly a half hour—during which time several pedestrians spotted him—Hoffa probably realized that he had been stood up. He called his wife at 2:30 and asked if Giacalone had called. When she said he hadn't, he told her—if he did call—to tell him that he was still waiting.

Hoffa then called Linteau who had returned from his lunch. "Giacalone didn't show up," Hoffa barked. "I'm coming out there."

Other than Hoffa's abductors, nobody knows for sure what happened next.

Both Giacalone and Provenzano had iron-clad alibis for their whereabouts: Giacalone was in plain sight at the Southfield Athletic Club; Provenzano was at Teamsters Local 560 in Union City, New Jersey, playing cards with several business agents.

Suspicion immediately fell on Hoffa's "foster son," Charles "Chuckie" O'Brien, a once-trusted top Hoffa aide whose relationship with his "father" had fallen on hard times. He had been driving a car owned by Giacalone's son, Joseph, running errands for Local 337 president Bobby Holmes, including transporting a fresh salmon packed in ice from the local to Holmes's home.

Later, when federal investigators found blood on the back seat of the car, O'Brien claimed that the package had ripped, causing fish blood to leak. O'Brien said that he then took the car to be washed, but traces of the blood stains remained. Even though the subsequent blood analysis indicated that it was not human blood, tracking dogs reportedly picked up Hoffa's scent in the car.

After going through the car wash, O'Brien stopped at the Southfield Athletic Club where he had prearranged to meet Tony Giacalone in the lobby at 2:15 P.M. During their three-minute meeting, Giacalone gave him gifts for the upcoming birthdays of O'Brien's children.

Speculation was rampant that after meeting with Giacalone, O'Brien went to the Red Fox—either alone or with others—to pick up Hoffa.

Although O'Brien vehemently denied any role in the abduction, his story was so filled with contradictions that suspicions intensified.

—⁂—

Detailing my upcoming responsibilities in New York, NBC news manager Bob Reid wrote a memorandum to Lonnie Guida, a top NBC executive, saying:

> Moldea, who is a recognized expert on the Central States Teamster Pension Fund, will be helping us to prepare background materials for use in any special programs we do in connection with Hoffa's disappearance. . .
>
> In addition, we have agreed to pay Moldea for an in-depth report on the history of organized crime within the [pension fund]. Moldea will provide access to certain research materials which are otherwise not available to us, help us gain access to his confidential sources within the Pension Fund management and otherwise provide any information, assistance and other materials as we may request.

When I saw Reid's memorandum, I was disappointed that NBC was no longer interested in my task-force source—the mysterious Teamster official who had been anonymously calling and feeding me information about Rolland McMaster and his goon squad. I still believed that the key to understanding the politics behind Hoffa's disappearance lay in the preceding violence in Detroit's Local 299—just as my task-force source had suggested. But I decided to wait until I arrived in New York to make the case to my new bosses.

On Thursday, August 14, I flew to New York where I went to work in the Special Projects Division of NBC News under executive producer Gordon Manning, who had just joined the network after a long and distinguished career at CBS News where he served as executive producer of its evening news program with anchorman Walter Cronkite.

I went to the office of the 58-year old Manning to introduce myself and to plead with him to allow me to continue my work with the Master Task Force source.

"Dan, is this the guy who gave us Manitoulin Island?" Asked Manning with justifiable sarcasm.

PART ONE: ENTERING THE FRAY

"Sir," I said, smiling but reeling on the defensive, "I know what you're thinking, but everything he said he knew for sure was confirmed. Regarding Manitoulin Island, he said a guy named McMaster had a farm on the eastern portion of the island, and that people were meeting there. Bob Vito confirmed all of that."

"What about Hoffa's body?" Manning continued, refusing to let me off the hook. "Didn't he say something about Hoffa being up there, too?"

"That was nothing but speculation on his part, sir. He labeled it that way. Bob Toombs just played his hunch."

Relenting, Manning allowed me to continue working on the McMaster Task Force, as long as it didn't interfere with what I had been brought to New York to do.

"Thank you, sir," I replied respectfully, "because my source wants to meet with me this Sunday."

Manning laughed and instructed me to work it out with Bob Reid.

That same day, I met another legendary news producer who had just come to NBC, Stanhope Gould, also a veteran of CBS News. Gould had heard about my work from Manning and tagged me as "a guerrilla writer"—an advocacy journalist, an investigative reporter who embraces a particular cause and openly takes sides.

Inasmuch as Gould was the new head of NBC's investigative unit and had come from the school of *objective* journalism, I didn't really accept his depiction of me as a compliment. But—considering the nature of my work and my alliances with, among others, the rank-and-file reform movement within the Teamsters—I did consider it a fair description.

In fact, I had become an advocate, and I had taken sides.

On Saturday, August 16, Reid and I flew to Harrisburg, Pennsylvania, where *Overdrive* magazine was holding its annual Roadmasters convention for independent truckers in nearby Gettysburg. After meeting and interviewing the publication's editor, Mike Parkhurst, we learned that the magazine's chief investigative writer, Jim Drinkhall, was flying in to attend the conference that afternoon.

I had great respect for Drinkhall's work for *Overdrive*. Because of what he had published about the Teamsters—and the publicity the magazine had scored in the aftermath of Hoffa's disappearance because of his blockbuster stories—the convention had already become a total media circus.

Knowing that Drinkhall would be the center of attention and wanting to spend as much time with him as possible, I asked Parkhurst, "Do you mind if Bob and I pick up Jim at the airport?" Parkhurst had no objection.

A tall, good-looking man, Drinkhall—quiet, modest, and in his early thirties—seemed pleased to see me when Bob Reid and I met him at his gate in the airport. During the past few months, Drinkhall and I had talked several times on the telephone, especially about Allen Dorfman, and he never seemed to get tired of talking about his work. As a result, Drinkhall and I chattered for the entire trip back to the convention center while Reid drove our rented car and listened with fascination to endless stories about Teamsters corruption.

When we arrived at the hotel, I even grabbed Drinkhall's luggage and carried it inside with the hope that we could spend a few extra minutes with him while walking to his room.

After Drinkhall stepped into the lobby, he was swarmed by independent truckers and members of the press. Just seeing the top of his head in the crowd and clinging to his luggage, I turned to Reid and laughed, "We're not going to see this guy again for the rest of the day."

Just as I said that, Drinkhall called over to us, shouting, "Hey, Dan, do you guys want to have dinner with us tonight?"

"Absolutely!" I replied.

The dinner began with only six of us. During the five hours we sat in the restaurant, nearly fifty people came over and stood around the table, just listening to Drinkhall's stories. I couldn't believe how fabulous this guy was.

14. The man in the black Cadillac

Early the next morning, Sunday, August 17, Bob Reid and I flew to a Midwestern airport where I was scheduled to meet my source from the McMaster Task Force. As instructed, I stood by the front entrance of the airport, holding my copy of Walter Sheridan's book, *The Fall and Rise of Jimmy Hoffa*.

As I nervously waited for him to drive up, all I could think about was the beating I had taken in Chicago four months earlier under, basically, the same circumstances—a scheduled meeting in broad daylight with an anonymous source who supposedly wanted to give me some information. But in this case, I was completely vulnerable. My source was going to pick me up and then drive to an unknown destination.

Sitting on a bench and hiding behind a newspaper, Reid watched the scene from a distance, ready to take down the source's license-plate number.

When a big black Cadillac pulled up in front of me, I showed the driver Sheridan's book.

"Get in," he said gruffly as he leaned over and opened the passenger door. I quickly glanced back at Bob Reid, now on his feet and looking really concerned, and smiled at him, somehow sensing that my life was about to change forever.

Seeing how jumpy I was in the car, the source told me to light up if I wanted to smoke. I pulled a pack of Kools from my pocket and slid out a cigarette. He immediately noticed my hands trembling as I lit it with a match.

"Relax," he said, "I'll have you back in a couple of hours. Between now and then, I'll make it worth your while."

Taking a long hit off my cigarette, I turned to him and said, "Listen, I have to ask you: Why are you putting yourself on the line like this? Is this business or personal with you?"

"It's a lot of both," he replied.

"Are you looking for money?"

"Naw, I do all right. I don't want anything."

"You know that I'm making money off what you're telling me. I mean, this has become part of my work."

"No, you go ahead. I'm just going to be able to tell you things. I don't have any proof. You're going to have to come up with that yourself. Believe me, if you get into this, you're going to earn whatever money you make."

"So why are you doing this?"

"Let's just say I want to do something good now."

I pulled out the recorder from my backpack and asked him if I could tape our interview. He gave me permission to turn it on. Also, he handed me his own ninety-minute, tape-recorded statement, which he made while working for McMaster.

The task-force source explained that nearly six months before Hoffa's release from prison, the Teamsters general executive board presented what appeared to be a benign resolution to the delegates of the 1971 Teamsters Convention which, upon acceptance, would give the board *carte blanche* in the union's efforts to organize America's independent truckers. The delegates passed the resolution by voice vote.

Soon after the convention adjourned, the board created the IBT's Freight, Steel and Special Commodities Division. Fitzsimmons appointed Rolland McMaster to head this national organizing effort. McMaster's immediate supervisor was Roy Williams of Kansas City, a mobbed-up IBT general vice president.

The Teamsters had created this task force to counter the threat posed by the Pittsburgh-based Fraternal Association of Steel Haulers (FASH).

Earlier, on October 28, 1969—in one of the most violent moments in recent American labor history—a squad of 120 Teamster goons clashed with sixty FASH partisans during a wildcat strike at the Stop Five security gate of the Republic Steel Company in Youngstown, Ohio. The Teamsters had tried to crash the FASH picket line.

When they failed, the Teamsters retreated, grabbed their guns, and fired into the crowd of dissidents. One Teamster had actually set up a machine-gun on a tripod and opened up. In retaliation, a FASH striker firebombed a car owned by the president of the local Teamsters.

Remarkably, after a half hour of armed warfare, only one man had been killed: the Teamster goon who had manned the machine-gun. Eight others were hospitalized. Dozens had a variety of lesser injuries.

Significantly, FASH held them off. The Teamsters never crossed the picket line. The incident, known to many as "The FASH Shootout," made national headlines.

FASH chairman William J. Hill later told me that McMaster had engineered the confrontation.

After the bloody battle, an angry Bill Hill led the movement for his members to decertify from the Teamsters and to create a new union with an expanded membership, the Fraternal Association of *Special* Haulers. Achieving immediate success, FASH organized its first trucking company—Tajon, Inc. of Mercer, Pennsylvania—in October 1970. Then, FASH filed an additional forty petitions to represent nonunion carriers, as well as several companies under contract with the Teamsters.

FASH's successes, especially those against the Teamsters, forced the National Labor Relations Board to rule that the new union could not raid companies with existing Teamster contracts until their agreements had expired. And, in two subsequent head-to-head NLRB-sanctioned elections, FASH demolished the Teamsters, setting the stage for the creation of the McMaster Task Force to strike back against the rival union.

McMaster began recruiting the thirty-two members of his organizing team, many of whom had long criminal records. One particular

PART ONE: ENTERING THE FRAY

member, a reputed explosives expert, was Jack O. Robison who had been twice convicted for grand larceny, twice for breaking and entering, three times for disorderly conduct, and drunk driving. Also, he had been arrested for punching out a trucking executive who refused to sign a union contract. Further, he had been indicted for murder but was acquitted, because he had acted in self-defense. Sentenced to a total of thirteen years in prison, Robison had served just over half that time.

All of McMaster's organizers had business cards, identifying each as an "IBT organizer" with the "Central, Eastern, Southern and Western Conferences of Teamsters." Organizers received $18,000 in annual salary and "unlimited" expense accounts, as well as full pension, health and welfare benefits while on the job. All funding for the task force was channeled from the IBT to the Central Conference of Teamsters in the guise of "special organizing grants."

McMaster selected a former top FASH official, Mike Boano of Local 377 in Youngstown, Ohio, as his second-in-command. Earlier, Boano had a bitter falling out with Bill Hill.

During its two-year history—between January 1972 and February 1974—the McMaster Task Force organized only a handful of truckers, but it left a pattern of beatings, shootings, arson, and bombings in its wake.

"Here's something I learned," my task force source told me. "I'll tell you how to start a fire. It's very slick. There's no way you can tell. They'll take oxygen, and they'll find out where the boiler room is, say, in a warehouse. And they'll fill that son of a bitch up with about eight to ten bottles of oxygen. Eventually, that oxygen is gonna find its way to that flame, and when it does, there's a flash. Oxygen doesn't burn, it just helps fire burn. And there's no smell, no trace. Nobody knows what happened. There's nothing. Because after they load the place up with oxygen, they walk away from it.... The arson squad comes in and everybody.... They can't figure out how these fires start."

Regarding the violence in Local 299, the source told me that he had received a telephone call from McMaster after Dave Johnson announced his candidacy for reelection as Local 299 president in 1974. McMaster had asked him to come to Detroit for "a special project."

Remembering this project well, the source explained, "The main thing was: Don't let Jimmy [Hoffa] into 299. If he gets into 299, that makes him eligible [to run for Teamsters president]. So the main thing was to stop him. The international tried all the legal things in the courts and everything.... The main fight, though, came out of Detroit.

"The idea was [to] keep Dave Johnson out. If Hoffa would have come in, [Johnson] was going to resign, turn the power over to Hoffa, which would have made him the [local's] principal officer, a delegate to the convention in '76. And when it came to nomination, he would stand up and say, 'I'm challenging you, Frank, for my old job!' . . .

"This is why Fitzsimmons gave McMaster a 'blank check.' When I say a 'blank check,' I don't physically mean a check. I mean, 'Whatever it costs to do it, you do it.'"

My source refused to participate, as did several other former members of the task force who were asked. However, three former task-force alumni did agree, including Jack Robison and the two men allegedly responsible for bombing Dick Fitzsimmons's car: Larry McHenry and Jim Shaw.

Unfortunately, my source possessed no documentation of any of the alleged payoffs for labor peace during the life of the organizing task force and no evidence of specific crimes by task-force members during the Local 299 violence.

In short, when he returned me to the airport where I rejoined Bob Reid, I had a great story but absolutely nothing to back it up—with the exception of a couple of fascinating tape recordings.

The following day, Monday, August 18, I tried to convince NBC to stay with the McMaster Task Force story, but Gordon Manning denied my request, citing the obvious time and expense involved.

Relenting for the moment, I returned to my room at the Warwick Hotel in midtown Manhattan and spent the rest of the day and night completing my promised report about the Teamsters' pension fund.

After I turned in my work the following morning, Manning—who was famous for his memoranda, called "Gordograms"—wrote one to NBC News executive Lee Hanna on August 19, saying:

> What would you think of lifting the whole Hoffa project out of the realm of a stand-by 11:30 P.M. Special Report pegged to some uncertain future climax in the disappearance, and definitely schedule it as a full-hour, prime-time Special Report this autumn under this approach and title:
>
> HOFFA, THE TEAMSTERS & THE MOB
> Narrated by Francis Ford Coppola
> Producer of The Godfather and The Godfather II

PART ONE: ENTERING THE FRAY

> It may sound too theatrical—or indeed totally inadvisable or impractical—to you, but practically everyone who reads our research on Hoffa points out its fascinating parallels and overtones with The Godfather. I enclose a copy of a report by Dan Moldea, a young graduate student at Kent State who was hired via Irving R. Levine to provide background and information in Detroit while NBC was hot on Hoffa right after he vanished, and who is now contributing his knowledge and contacts to two of our prepared pieces for a possible special. Moldea's report itself reads like a scenario from *The Godfather.*
>
> It was my thought that a thoroughly factual script on Hoffa's career—and the facts known to date on his disappearance, plus authoritative speculation on his fate—in the hands of Coppola would take on added drama.

Unfortunately, Hanna and the NBC brass decided against Manning's idea.

After completing my assigned tasks for NBC on the Hoffa case on August 29, I tried, once again, to interest Manning in an investigation of the McMaster Task Force. But, yet again, he denied my request. However, he did offer me a possible job with the impressive NBC News organization, doing general assignment research.

Grateful for the consideration, I refused, telling Manning that I wanted to stay on the Hoffa case and adding that I really believed that I was onto something with the McMaster angle.

He laughed while shaking his head in disbelief.

We shook hands, and then I returned to Ohio and to freelanceland.

PART TWO:

The Teamsters & the Mafia

15. Dealing with the FBI

On September 11, 1975, soon after returning to Ohio, I received a letter from my agent, Philip Spitzer, notifying me that Star Lawrence, a top editor at W.W. Norton & Company, had rejected my proposed book about Allen Dorfman and the Teamsters' pension fund.

Spitzer, whom I had seen while I was with NBC in New York, wrote:

> Here is what I gather is the situation: The editors see an interesting subject; they see the groundwork for a book; and they see the chapter-by-chapter outline. When I first spoke to you about the book, I reacted in the way that Star Lawrence did: How can you get all of this information in a book, a book that has a logical beginning, middle, end, and logical development? I guess it still isn't clear, since the proposal covers enough to boggle the mind. Apparently it's not enough simply to tell an editor you can handle it. It's not enough either to show samples of your other writing, which can't be indicative of how you'd handle the problem the editors are concerned with.
>
> So it may be that you'll have to provide some sort of sample chapter, or part of a chapter, just enough to show the tone, style, and organization of the book—to show how the pieces of the story will fit together without the book's reading like a news report, encyclopedia, or whatever. In the end, the editor does have to be able to visualize the book, and nothing really can be left to his imagination.

Reading Spitzer's letter, I knew he was giving me sound advice, but, at the same time, I felt my early edge with exclusive information about the Teamsters already slipping away—especially now after leaving NBC.

I really respected my competition in the field. Jim Drinkhall, Jon Kwitny, Lester Velie, and all of the others who were continuing to report on Teamster matters had institutional support and financial resources that far outdistanced mine. With the backing of their newspapers, magazines, and television networks, they could now learn in a few days what it had taken me months to uncover.

In other words, because of my stubborn self-imposed isolation and limitations as an independent writer, I feared that any book I submitted would be old news by the time of its publication a year later.

I realized that in order to remain effective I had to go into areas of investigation where establishment reporters—not as hungry as I—might hesitate to go. And my source in the McMaster Task Force had given me that opportunity, which would take me into the world of Teamster terrorism, extortion plots, and goon squads.

Through it all, I hoped to solve the violence in Local 299 and, perhaps, even the murder of Jimmy Hoffa.

Because I had not yet developed a single source in the FBI, the lead law-enforcement agency in the case, I went to the bureau's Akron field office and submitted a fifteen-page theory about the Hoffa disappearance—which combined what everyone already knew with some of what I had recently learned. Also, I submitted a list of written questions about the Local 299 violence and the Hoffa case to a specific special agent in Detroit and requested his response. Almost immediately, the FBI agent called and asked if he could come for a visit. Of course, I agreed.

For two days, October 16-17, the FBI agent from Detroit, accompanied by the special agent in charge of the Akron field office, came to my home and questioned me.[16]

The Detroit agent said that he was interested in what I knew about Rolland McMaster and three of his trusted men, Larry McHenry, Jack Robison, and Jim Shaw. Before responding, I replied that I was interested in what he knew about these same people, as well as the violence in Local 299 and Hoffa's murder.

The agent said, "Obviously, we're interested in some of the same things." However, he went on to give me the standard "one-way street" lecture—that the FBI receives but does not give information.

"Then neither one of us is going to find out very much," I smiled, trying to set the stage for some negotiation.

"I'll tell you what," he replied. "You tell me what you know. And, for the time being, I will confirm or deny your information based on what we know. Either way, I'll make sure that you don't go off the track with what you're investigating. If I believe you're right about something, I'll encourage you to stay on that track. If I know you're wrong, I'll warn you to get off."

Agreement made, I gave him an oral recitation of my chronology of events while protecting the identity of my source in the McMaster Task Force. However, I did play portions of my tape-recorded interview with the source—after I received my source's permission to do so.

PART TWO: THE TEAMSTERS & THE MAFIA

When I asked the Detroit FBI man whether I was on or off the track with my belief that the McMaster Task Force had been behind the violence in Local 299, he replied, "I wouldn't be here if I thought you were wrong about that."

When I specifically asked him whether Larry McHenry and Jim Shaw had bombed Dick Fitzsimmons's car on July 10, he responded, "Stay on track with that one. That might be one of the biggest stories you have."

"Do you guys think they did it?" I asked.

"What we believe and what we can prove are two different things."

"Do you guys think that McMaster was involved in Hoffa's murder?"

"I can't respond to that one way or the other, because we honestly don't know what happened. We have information from a variety of sources about a number of different scenarios. But I can tell you that McMaster is not above suspicion here. We are actively investigating him."

The agent did tell me that McMaster had been arrested in Bay City, Michigan, on September 26, after he and a friend, Jack Ferris, allegedly pistol-whipped a motorist who had tailgated them on Interstate-75 in Michigan. The incident appeared in the Detroit newspapers.

At the end of our two-day marathon meeting, the FBI agent encouraged me to return to Detroit and continue my research on McMaster.

16. Back to Detroit

On Tuesday morning, October 28, I came off the bench and drove to Detroit. Back in the hunt, I wanted to freelance a story about the McMaster Task Force to a major newspaper. From the outset, the *Detroit Free Press* had been far ahead of the pack in its coverage of Hoffa's disappearance. When I worked for NBC in Detroit, the *Free Press* was required daily reading.

Soon after arriving in town, I arranged to have breakfast with Jo Thomas, the top investigative reporter for the *Free Press*, at the coffee shop in the *Free Press* building. Although Thomas said that she had heard about my work on the McMaster Task Force from her friend, Jim Drinkhall, she also indicated that her newspaper did not publish freelance work. However, she did offer to swap information.

Sensing that she was blowing me off, I told her that I would get back to her.

I went to Local 299 where I met again with Hoffa's uncle, Steve Riddle, asking him to arrange an interview for me with James P. Hoffa, Jimmy Hoffa's attorney-son. Riddle picked up the telephone, called young Hoffa, and set up a meeting for the following day.

On October 29, I met the 34-year-old Hoffa in his law office on the 33rd floor of Detroit's Guardian Building, overlooking the Detroit River. An all-state linebacker at Detroit's Cooley High School, Hoffa had gone to Michigan State where a knee injury ended his football career. Later, he attended law school at the University of Michigan. In 1967, while a practicing labor attorney, Hoffa ran unsuccessfully for a seat in the Michigan state legislature. After the election, he concentrated on his law practice at the firm of Hoffa Chodak & Robiner. He became a trusted legal advisor to Local 299, as well as to his father.

With Hoffa's law partner, Murray Chodak in the room, Hoffa vehemently defended his dad, saying, "There was a mutual love between my father and the Teamsters' rank and file. They knew that he sincerely cared about them and their welfare. He was a real leader."

Making it respectfully clear that I didn't agree at all with his appraisal of his dad, I quickly changed the subject and explained my theory about the Local 299 violence and his father's murder, along with Rolland McMaster's possible role.

Excited by this news, Hoffa asked, "Does the FBI know what you know?"

Not knowing how to handle that question, I simply replied, "I don't know what the FBI knows."

Immediately, Hoffa picked up his telephone and dialed a number. "I've got a man here I want you to meet," Hoffa said. "Can you come over now? He's here."

When he hung up the receiver, he said, "The FBI is coming over here. Is that okay? I know these guys. You can trust them."

I shrugged, saying nothing but fearing that I had just been bullied into an awkward situation.

Hoffa, Chodak, and I continued to talk for the next half hour until his secretary buzzed and told him that the FBI agents had arrived.

Within seconds, three special agents walked into Hoffa's office while I was looking out the window on the other side of the room. I immediately recognized one of them as the FBI agent who had visited me in Ohio two weeks earlier. I didn't say a word, waiting to see how he wanted to handle the situation.

Shaking hands with Hoffa first, the FBI agent I knew turned and saw me by the window. He paused momentarily. But other than "hello," he

PART TWO: THE TEAMSTERS & THE MAFIA

didn't say a word as Hoffa introduced us. "Nice to meet you," I simply replied.

For the next forty-five minutes, Hoffa and the three FBI agents listened as I did my song-and-dance routine. When I completed the performance, Hoffa and the FBI agents asked me several questions. Then, still in my presence, Hoffa asked the FBI agents what they thought.

"We can't confirm everything he's saying," one of the other FBI agents responded. "But you can trust what he's saying—if that makes any sense."

When Hoffa asked what that meant, the agent added, "You can trust Dan and his information."

A few minutes later, the three FBI agents left, leaving Hoffa, Chodak, and me behind.

Hoffa asked me if I needed any money. I replied that I did, and that I was looking for a newspaper to finance my research. When Hoffa asked me if I had talked to the *Detroit Free Press*, I recounted that I had spoken with Jo Thomas the previous day, adding that she said her newspaper didn't hire freelancers.

Once again, Hoffa picked up the telephone. This time, he called the *Free Press*'s labor editor, Ralph Orr. Hoffa arranged a meeting for the following day.

After my interview with young Hoffa, I went to another, also arranged by Steve Riddle, at the Southfield Sheraton, the same hotel where I had stayed while working for NBC.

My contact was a Local 299 officer and a long-time confidant of Jimmy Hoffa and Dave Johnson.

As soon as I walked into the room, I noticed that the official, there alone, was extremely nervous. I brushed it off because I wasn't. I viewed him as a friendly source—like Riddle and Johnson—even though he wouldn't permit me to tape the interview. I figured that he would allow me to turn on the recorder after I gained his trust.

As I jumped right into a series of questions about Rolland McMaster, the official became almost overwrought.

Suddenly, after I innocently asked him if he had a problem, he pulled a revolver from his pants and pointed it between my eyes.

"Jesus Christ!" I exclaimed.

Lowering the gun to my mouth, he shouted, "Open!"

"Why are you doing this to me?" I asked desperately.

"Open!" He yelled again.

As I opened wide, he placed the gun in my mouth, exclaiming, "Don't even think about fucking with me! . . . Do we understand each other?"

With my eyes as wide open as my mouth, I nodded my head slowly. Then he jerked his gun out of my mouth.

I was so badly shaken that I had tears in my eyes. He had cut the back of my throat and chipped a couple of back teeth with the muzzle of his gun. For the next few minutes—while he watched with seemingly mixed emotions over what he had just done to me—I walked quietly around the room, keeping my distance from him as I spit out blood and particles of teeth.

I don't remember exactly what he and I said after that, but I was afraid that he would actually shoot me if I tried to leave.

After a few terrifying minutes, the Local 299 official finally apologized, saying that he had been under enormous pressure and thought I was there to betray him.

Clearly obsessed with McMaster, he appeared more afraid of him than anyone I had met to date. And he could not understand why I would leave my safe place in the world and voluntarily put myself at risk to go after someone like McMaster.

At that moment, I didn't feel like explaining anything. I just wanted to get the hell out of that room as quickly as possible.

After the 299 official said some additional conciliatory words, he stuck out his hand as I grabbed my things and made my way for the door. Seeing he was sincere, I shook his hand, half-heartedly. He added that he wanted to reschedule the interview. Still trembling, I told him I would call him.

The following day, October 30, Ralph Orr met with Hoffa and me. Orr brought along Jo Thomas and *Free Press* city editor John Oppedahl.

I gave all three *Free Press* staffers copies of my resume and played the tape of my entire ninety-minute interview with the task-force source, again with the source's permission.

Afterwards, the people from the newspaper invited me to lunch where we continued to discuss McMaster and his organizing unit. In the midst of our conversation, Oppedahl asked me for references. I told him to contact Arthur Fox, Jon Kwitny, Jim Drinkhall, Bob Toombs, and Gordon Manning. Jotting down their names and numbers, Oppedahl told me to call him the following week.

After my morning interviews on Friday, October 31, I met my FBI contact for what I thought would be a quick lunch. As we were leaving the restaurant, he asked me if I wanted to take a ride with him. Agreeing, I got into his car, and he gave me a tour of some of the local sights.

Our first stop was the Leland House, an old hotel and apartment building just a few minutes from the federal building. When I asked why he wanted to show it to me, he replied that Larry McHenry had been living there for several months.

He added that the owners of record were Mayer Morganroth, the attorney who had accompanied McMaster when he was questioned by the FBI about Hoffa's disappearance, and Jack Ferris, a suspected McMaster front man. The FBI agent reminded me that Ferris had been with McMaster the previous month during the alleged pistol-whipping incident on the highway.

The FBI agent continued that, while living at the Leland House, McHenry had been frequently visited by Jack Robison and Jim Shaw. Knowing that McHenry and Shaw were suspects in the bombing of Dick Fitzsimmons car, I asked if Robison had been involved in the Local 299 violence. The FBI man said that Robison was a suspect in the bombing of Dave Johnson's cabin cruiser and had been seen at several Local 299 meetings with McHenry and Shaw—who had attempted to disrupt them.

At the time Hoffa disappeared in late July, Shaw had a room at the Leland on a day-to-day basis while Robison occasionally stayed there on weekends.

The federal agent also wanted me to know that prior to Hoffa's disappearance, McHenry's nineteen-year-old son, Patrick, had been living and working as a doorman at the Leland House. The kid often boasted about his father's activities in the Teamsters.

On August 1, 1975—just two days after Hoffa disappeared—Patrick McHenry's girlfriend found him dead in his room after an apparent drug overdose. "There was enough heroin injected into Patrick to kill an elephant," the FBI agent told me. "If Patrick was murdered because of something he knew, we'd like to know what it was."

The agent added that young McHenry's death came less than a week after the FBI had questioned McHenry and Shaw about the bombing of Dick Fitzsimmons's car.

Stunned, I asked my FBI contact, "Then, you guys suspected McHenry and Shaw of doing the bombing even before I came along?"

"Yeah," he laughed. "That's why we absolutely had to talk to you. So if you're asking me if you should stay on this McMaster track, I'm telling you to stay on it. You're on to something important there."

For our final stop on the tour, the FBI agent showed me McMaster's Southfield home on Wildbrook Drive in a wooded area a few miles northwest of Detroit. Trying to get my bearings, I looked around and suddenly realized where we were . . . just off Telegraph and Twelve-Mile Roads, only five minutes from the Red Fox restaurant.

17. The Hoffa Reward Fund

On Wednesday, November 5, city editor John Oppedahl of the *Free Press* and I signed a "letter of understanding" for which I received a whopping $250 advance for my help "in connection with a story relating to the Teamsters Union." Also, I agreed that, during the "two to three weeks" of our investigation, I would not "aid any other news gathering organizations." Further, I would be "credited in the paper" for my work "if it is published." At that time, the newspaper would pay me an additional $250. Although I received no expense money, I did get a desk and telephone in the newsroom.

During my assignment, I worked at the direction of Ralph Orr and Jo Thomas, with whom I was expected to share all of my information—including the tape of my interview with the task-force source.

I knew that I had signed a lousy deal because the project would easily take longer than three weeks to complete. But, upon signing the contract, I gave the *Free Press* all of my material about McMaster's organizing drive between 1972 and 1974, which meant that I had lost control of my documentation from the outset.

I knew nothing about the daily newspaper business, but I did believe in the people with whom I'd be working. Thomas and Orr were real pros, and Oppedahl was a great editor, as well as a very nice guy. As a total rank amateur, I knew I could learn a lot from all three of them. I viewed it as an internship.

During lunch after the deal was struck, Orr told me that Jo Thomas, a former Nieman Fellow at Harvard, had "dated" the controversial Chuck O'Brien, who had allegedly appeared on her doorstep soon after Hoffa's disappearance while federal agents were looking for him. When I asked whether the newspaper considered that a conflict of interest, Orr nodded but added, "She's the best we got. We need her."[17]

After lunch, I went to Jimmy Hoffa's office to thank him for his help and to tell him of my arrangement with the newspaper. When he heard the deal, Hoffa said that I couldn't live on what the *Free Press* was paying me. He also agreed that the investigation would take much longer than three weeks, so Hoffa suggested that I bargain for more money.

I told him that it was the best the newspaper would do.

Hoffa then said that he was prepared to give me an additional $200 a week from the Hoffa Reward Fund—a growing reservoir of money, specifically designated to help solve his father's murder—as a reward for my previous work on the Local 299 violence. I asked him if there were any strings attached. Hoffa, who was the sole administrator of the fund, replied, "No strings. It's just reward money for what you've already done."

I told him that I would get back to him.

Later that day during a meeting with Oppedahl, I asked him whether there was any way that I could pry any more money out of the *Free Press*. Oppedahl politely said no.

Then, I told Oppedahl that Hoffa was willing to pay me an extra $200 a week from the Hoffa Reward Fund for my previous work on the Local 299 violence, which would support me during our investigation. I added that no strings were attached.

Oppedahl replied, "Look, Dan, as long as you come to work and do your job, and I come to work and do mine, I don't see any problem in your dealings with Hoffa."

Hearing Oppedahl say that, I decided to go ahead and accept Hoffa's reward money. And, just to make sure that there would never be any question about the permission I had received from the newspaper, I put the arrangement in writing.

—⁂—

When I arrived at my desk at the *Free Press* on Monday, November 10, I received a telephone call.

"I understand you're trying to get me before a grand jury," the voice said.

Even though he didn't identify himself, I knew exactly who it was.

"Mr. McMaster!" I exclaimed, taken completely by surprise. "I'm so glad to hear from you! How did you know where to find me?"

"I've been shocked to hear from some of the people I've heard from. They've been telling me that you and the *Free Press* are trying to get me before a grand jury."

"Not true, not true. We're just looking at that special commodities division that you headed in 1972, 1973."

"Well, hell," McMaster shouted in mock anger, "before you murder me, why don't you meet me?"

"That's our ultimate intention," I assured him, adding that as soon as we concluded our investigation we would ask him for a formal interview. "You'll see nothing in print before then."

"You know, sometimes I go to church," McMaster continued, "and I don't like people looking at me."

Also, on Monday afternoon, I went to see Hoffa and told him that I would accept his offer to receive money from the Hoffa Reward Fund for my previous work on McMaster. For the first and each subsequent $200 cash payment, Hoffa asked me to sign a receipt.

To be clear, I was not at all uncomfortable with this situation because, in my view, I had already earned this money in my role as a freelance writer—and I had received the permission of my boss at the newspaper to accept it. Also, I had notified Orr and Thomas, as well as my FBI contact about my deal with Hoffa. No one expressed any problem with the arrangement.

Already, Hoffa and I had spent hours in his office and on the telephone talking about new leads and theories. From the beginning, he and I had developed a strange relationship, even a potential friendship. We knew that on other issues involving his father and the Teamsters, our positions were greatly at odds.

Knowing of my loyalty to Arthur Fox and PROD, as well as to Ken Paff of Cleveland, the leader of the newly formed Teamsters for a Decent Contract, Hoffa predicted that we would be adversaries at some point in the future.

I predicted that he would one day become president of the Teamsters Union.

During the next three weeks, I located and contacted over half of the former members of the 32-man McMaster Task Force. But, other than my original source, I received quality cooperation from only six of them. The rest were either totally defiant in their defense of McMaster or completely terrified of him and refused to say anything.

Also, during those first few weeks, Thomas and I called numerous trucking executives whose companies had been targeted by the McMaster Task Force. Some admitted to receiving sweetheart contracts, but no one would admit that they had actually made a payoff for labor peace.

In the midst of these interviews, while I was staying at the Michigan Inn in Southfield, someone tampered with my Thunderbird as it was parked in the hotel lot, cutting all of the belts in my engine.

PART TWO: THE TEAMSTERS & THE MAFIA

On November 13, I cold called Paul Jeffries, the former owner of Eck Miller Trucking in Owensboro, Kentucky, who had sold his company earlier in the year. When I asked him about the task force's attempts to unionize his company, Jeffries talked openly, saying that Mike Boano, McMaster's number-two man in the unit, had taken the point position during the organizing drive that led to an employee strike.

"It was a very violent strike in which the FBI was called in after one of our trucks was firebombed," Jeffries told me. "There were so many shootings that we lost count. Bullets were flying everywhere. It was a miracle that nobody got killed."

Jeffries named several of McMaster's organizers who were involved in the effort, including Jack Robison and especially Jim Shaw who was a former driver for Eck Miller and had joined the McMaster unit during the campaign.

At the peak of the violence, according to Jeffries, McMaster came in and offered him a sweetheart contract—with, among other concessions, no employer pension or health and welfare payments.

Jeffries also stated that he had been approached to pay for total labor peace. In other words, for x-amount of dollars, the Teamsters would agree to go away with no contract at all.

"No specific amount of money was ever mentioned," Jeffries recounted, "but what was said was, 'Look, you probably think that this is going to cost you more than it is.'"

Jeffries added that he refused to accept the sweetheart contract and never made the payoff. His story mirrored those of numerous other trucking executives Jo Thomas and I had interviewed.

However, Jeffries made another very disturbing allegation. He charged that while the McMaster Task Force was trying to organize his company, a "stranger" came into town and received a $6,000 payment from the Teamsters to aid their effort against Eck Miller. When I pushed for a name, Jeffries alleged that the "stranger" was Jim Drinkhall of *Overdrive*.

After Jeffries named Drinkhall, one of my favorite people in the world, my entire body quaked. In fact, when I expressed skepticism and even anger towards Jeffries, he refused to back down from his story, adding that Drinkhall had written two *Overdrive* articles critical of Eck Miller and supportive of McMaster's Task Force during the organizing campaign.

I quickly typed up my notes and gave them to Jo Thomas. Also a friend of Drinkhall, she, too, expressed anger and disbelief about what Jeffries had said about him.

Consequently, Thomas insisted on seeing Jeffries in person. A week later, on November 20, Thomas and I flew to Kentucky to meet with Jeffries who repeated his story—including the part about Drinkhall and the alleged $6,000 payment, which Drinkhall had actually written about and vehemently denied in one of the two stories for *Overdrive*.[18]

After the formal interview with Jeffries, I called Drinkhall at his office in California and told him what Jeffries had said. Although I did not believe the crazy story about the alleged payoff, I did become concerned when Drinkhall did not give me the reaction I wanted to hear when I asked him about his relationships with McMaster and Boano. I came away from the conversation with the clear impression that both men considered him a friend.

18. A surprise witness at the grand jury

By the beginning of December 1975, progress on our task-force story had stalled because of other important articles that Orr and Thomas had to complete. Nevertheless, I still had to clear everything with my senior partners, so I often found myself waiting for decisions while they went about their lives and other work. Getting frustrated, I started going off on my own, getting back into the Hoffa murder case—and McMaster's possible role in it—to see if I could develop anything new.

Both Orr and Thomas, who were still the lead reporters on the Hoffa caper for the *Free Press*, appeared willing to believe my theory about McMaster's alleged involvement in the Local 299 violence, but they had always cautioned me against trying to link him to Hoffa's disappearance. "The murder was strictly a mob thing," Thomas told me repeatedly. "McMaster wasn't involved."

On December 3, one of Thomas's sources telephoned, telling her that the U.S. Strike Force Against Organized Crime in Detroit had called several key witnesses in the Hoffa case to appear before a federal grand jury the following day. As all of us jumped on telephones to call our sources, word quickly spread that the witnesses were the suspects actually thought to have murdered Hoffa. This appeared to be the big break in the case everyone had been waiting for.

PART TWO: THE TEAMSTERS & THE MAFIA

Filtering out the bad rumors from the good, we learned that the witnesses were several union officials from New Jersey. All of them were associated with Tony Provenzano, whom Hoffa was scheduled to meet on the day he disappeared.

Also, the FBI had conducted searches of at least three locations in New Jersey: a file cabinet used by Salvatore Briguglio, a business agent in Local 560; a safety deposit box leased by his brother, Gabriel Briguglio, the vice president of Local 84 in Fort Lee, at a bank in Union City; and Brother Moscato's garbage dump in Hackensack.

After hearing Salvatore Briguglio's name, I called Don Vestal, a one-time Hoffa aide who later became an enemy of the union's power structure and then a leader of the Teamsters United Rank and File (TURF), a rank-and-file reform organization. I asked him whether he had ever heard of Briguglio—without telling him why I was interested or even mentioning McMaster's name.

Vestal's response was contained in my December 3 memorandum to Orr and Thomas:

> Don Vestal said that Briguglio is known by Dave Johnson, a former business agent in 299, and McMaster. Vestal said that Briguglio . . . was generally considered to be McMaster's bodyguard. He said Briguglio was close to both Tony and Sal Provenzano [who was Tony's brother]. . . . McMaster and Briguglio traveled together; their association goes back to the late '50s or early '60s.

Neither Orr nor Thomas had anything to say about my memorandum. Instead, they continued their own work, digging out the names of those who were going to appear at the grand jury: the Briguglio brothers and another set of brothers, Stephen and Thomas Andretta, who were also associated with Provenzano.

A fifth witness could not be identified.

All five of these men were represented by William Bufalino, who was related to Russell Bufalino, the Mafia boss of northeastern Pennsylvania.

On Thursday, December 4, while Ralph Orr and I worked in the newsroom, Jo Thomas covered the chaotic scene outside the grand-jury room at the federal courthouse, across the street from the *Free Press* building. Periodically, she phoned in reports to our boss, John Oppedahl, who relayed the messages to Orr and me.

After a few hours of this, Oppedahl, laughing almost uncontrollably, walked up to my desk and asked, "Guess who the unidentified fifth man at the grand jury is?"

Without saying anything, I jumped out of my seat and left the newsroom. Passing by the elevators, I ran down the steps, out the building, across the street, and into the federal courthouse.

When I arrived, I saw Rolland McMaster, standing alone by the elevator, waiting for his turn to testify.

Wearing a trench coat, sports shirt, and a hat with a wide brim, the 62-year-old union organizer epitomized the classic stereotype of the term "Teamster." Although he and I were both the same height—six-feet-four-inches—he weighed 245, seventy pounds more than me. His hands were as big as shovels. His face was highlighted by a thick, protruding upper lip.

He wore a pair of designer eyeglasses. Behind them, his right eye was penetrating. His left eye, which was made of glass, simply stared straight ahead and into the distance.

I walked up to McMaster and introduced myself. McMaster simply said, "I thought that was you."

Tastelessly jubilant and even a little sarcastic, I asked him, "Gee, Mister McMaster, why have *you* been called before the grand jury investigating Hoffa's disappearance?"

Allowing me to get away with my bad attitude, he simply replied, "I don't know. You're welcome to call me after it's over, and I'll tell you what happened."

Another reporter walked up to us and began to question McMaster. I excused myself and walked away.

As I looked for Jo Thomas, I heard someone behind me say, "Hey, Moldea!" McMaster had left the other reporter and followed me. "Do you think you got me?" McMaster asked in a good-natured tone.

Surprised by his reaction, I timidly replied, "Probably not, sir."

Later, I did make a courtesy call to McMaster at his farm in Wixom for a brief interview. He told me that, like the Briguglios and the Andrettas, he had taken the Fifth Amendment before the grand jury, because, "It was just one of those things." He added that he had volunteered during the hearing "to serve on a search committee" for Hoffa.

McMaster said that Salvatore Briguglio was merely an old acquaintance, adding that he had met his brother, Gabriel Briguglio, and Steve and Tom Andretta for the first time at the courthouse that day.

He stated that he could not understand why Tony Provenzano was being implicated in Hoffa's disappearance. "They were the best of friends," he said. "Anyway, the Teamsters have professional ethics like reporters do. We don't shoot people and kill people."

McMaster recalled that he had not seen Provenzano since the previous fall and described Tony Giacalone—the Detroit mobster who was scheduled to meet with Hoffa on the day of his disappearance—as nothing more than "an acquaintance."

I did not ask McMaster about an earlier report I had received that he had picked up Provenzano and another man at the Pontiac Airport a day or two before Hoffa vanished.

Regarding Chuck O'Brien's possible involvement in Hoffa's murder, McMaster insisted, "He couldn't be involved. Jimmy was like a father to him."

I asked McMaster what he did on the day Hoffa disappeared, and he replied, "I don't remember, to tell you the truth. You might want to ask the FBI because they seem know more about that than I do." He said that the FBI first questioned him "three or four days" after Hoffa vanished.

On Friday, December 5, the day after the grand-jury hearing, the *Free Press* reported that Hoffa might have been killed, stuffed into a 55-gallon drum, loaded onto a Gateway Transportation Company truck, and shipped to some unknown destination. Many people speculated that Hoffa's body might have been buried at Brother Moscato's—the site of a recent FBI search.

The FBI agent did tell me that officials of Gateway's steel division in Detroit had been subpoenaed to testify before the federal grand jury, along with their records of dispatch from July 30 to August 10.

"When I talked to McMaster," I said to the FBI agent, "he told me that he didn't remember where he was. He told me to ask the FBI."

The agent replied, "McMaster was with Teamsters Local 142 secretary-treasurer Donald Sawochka in Gary, Indiana, for two or three hours on the day Hoffa disappeared. That's what Sawochka told us."

"What was the purpose of the meeting?"

"They were meeting with representatives of Gateway's steel division."

Laughing at that response because of Gateway's alleged link to Hoffa's murder, I asked, "Did McMaster go to the meeting alone or with another union official?"

"No, he went with Stanton Barr."

"Who is Stanton Barr?"

"He's McMaster's brother-in-law. He married the sister of McMaster's wife."

"Why would he go with McMaster to a union meeting with Gateway executives?"

Then the FBI agent started laughing, too. "Because," he replied, "Stanton Barr is the head of Gateway's steel division in Detroit. He was among the Gateway people who testified at the grand-jury hearing on December 4. . . . All of you guys in the press completely missed that."

In the wake of the grand-jury hearing, I managed to anger Jo Thomas and Ralph Orr who thought that my personal obsession with McMaster had compromised me, especially since I was still accepting reward money from Hoffa.

In the midst of all this, I called Jon Kwitny at the *Wall Street Journal*, still a close friend, and explained the situation to him. He shouted at me over the telephone, "Stop your financial relationship with Hoffa! I don't care whether it's reward money or what! I don't care whether the *Free Press* approved it! End it! Now!"

On January 9, 1976, I told Jimmy Hoffa, Jr. that I didn't want any more money from the Hoffa Reward Fund. By then, I had received a total of $2,100, all of which I later declared on my 1975 federal income tax return. Hoffa had no reaction to this, except to request that I stay in touch.

No longer receiving money from Hoffa, I had a conversation with Ted Joy, an independent writer from Kent, Ohio, who told me that I might be eligible to receive a grant from the Fund for Investigative Journalism in Washington, D.C.

The next day, I telephoned Howard Bray, the executive director of the fund. Immediately, Bray sent me the paperwork, describing the process for obtaining grants. I quickly applied, asking for $2,000 and attaching a letter of recommendation from John Oppedahl.

On February 27—my 26th birthday—the Fund for Investigation Journalism approved my grant proposal.

19. The payoff man

Since the beginning of our investigation of the McMaster Task Force, several trucking-company executives had told us that at the peak of the violence in McMaster's organizing campaigns against them, "a man from Indianapolis" would call and offer to make the union go away—for a price. However, the executives either could not remember or refused to tell us the name of the man we came to refer to as "The Indianapolis Connection."

On January 16, 1976, during an interview I was conducting with the owner of an Ohio steel-hauling firm, the executive remembered the name and gave it to me.

I immediately called Jo Thomas, to whom I had not spoken in several weeks. Because she was busy, and I was on the road calling from a pay phone, I asked to speak with Ralph Orr who wrote her a memorandum, saying: "Dan Moldea called while you were on the phone. He has the Indianapolis contact—a retired labor consultant named Richard Dininger. Moldea got a guy with a trucking company . . . to admit that Dininger and he had negotiated a sweetheart contract."

The trucking executive gave me a copy of his union contract, as well as letters written by Dininger that outlined their negotiations. In one particular letter, Dininger wrote of meeting with McMaster to discuss the contract.

When I returned to Detroit, I gave Oppedahl, Orr, and Thomas copies of all of this material. Also, I had learned that Dininger, a former Local 135 business agent in Indianapolis, served with McMaster on the 1971 Central States Iron and Steel Negotiating Committee. In retirement after twenty years with the union, Dininger had founded a labor/management consulting firm, Labor Associates.

—⁂—

On March 3, 1976, I drove to Pittsburgh and spent the day interviewing Bill Hill, the chairman of the Fraternal Association of Steel Haulers (FASH), the organization that had forced the Teamsters to create the McMaster Task Force in 1971 after "The FASH Shootout." Tough and uncompromising in business matters but almost gentle and even funny in repose, Hill—another big steel hauler with combed-back, jet-black hair—opened his files, allowing me to see and to copy anything I wanted.

During my talks with Hill, I asked him whether he had ever heard of Jim Drinkhall of *Overdrive* magazine being friends with any members of the McMaster Task Force. Hill immediately went to his file and pulled Mike Boano's sworn deposition of April 30, 1971, in the case *U.S. Steel Corporation v. Fraternal Association of Steel Haulers*, two years before the Eck Miller situation occurred.

While reading the deposition, I noticed that Boano—who had served as McMaster's chief lieutenant during the life of the goon squad—testified that he had met Drinkhall and Mike Parkhurst, the owner of *Overdrive*, during the early 1960s. At the time, Drinkhall worked as a young writer; Parkhurst was a freelance photographer, trying to start a magazine for truckers. For years, Boano had driven a steel-hauling rig for Youngstown Cartage—while the company was being shaken down by Rolland McMaster. The Justice Department indicted and convicted McMaster for the Youngstown Cartage extortion scheme in 1961. Ironically, Boano had been a government witness against McMaster.

According to his own deposition, Boano was a friend of both Drinkhall and Parkhurst. In the February 1968 issue of *Overdrive*, they had published a letter from then-FASH official Boano, thanking the magazine for helping FASH during a protest. Among other things, *Overdrive* had paid for the lawyer Boano used during his protest.

When an attorney asked him during his testimony if he had remained in touch with Drinkhall and Parkhurst, Boano replied, "Yes, we were personal friends, and they liked me a lot."[19]

However, after Boano's falling out with Bill Hill, he resigned from his job with FASH. Drinkhall and Parkhurst pledged to support Boano in the dispute. Soon after, Parkhurst became Hill's avowed enemy.

The following day, I drove to Johnstown, Pennsylvania, and interviewed a top official with McQuaide Freight Lines. During our discussion, he told me that in the midst of McMaster's organizing campaign, he had been offered labor peace for $3,000 a month for an indefinite period by Richard Dininger, my newly discovered Indianapolis Connection.

When the company refused to make the payoff, the Teamsters allegedly bombed its warehouse and airplane hangar. Damages totaled nearly five-million dollars. In the end, McQuaide dropped its charges against the Teamsters in return for the Teamsters ending its organizing campaign against the company.

The McQuaide interview was a major score, and I immediately reported it to the *Free Press*.

On a roll, I left Johnstown and drove to Kentucky, where I spent two days developing several sources who were directly and indirectly involved with the new Teamsters task force, which my original source had discussed with me.

This new unit, the Tri-State Energy Haulers Division, was headed by IBT general organizer Jackie Presser of Cleveland. The energy division's efforts were concentrated on non-union coal carriers in the Ohio Valley which encompassed portions of Ohio, Pennsylvania, and West Virginia.

In addition, I had learned that the United Mine Workers had pledged full cooperation with the Teamsters and had signed a mutual "no-raiding pact."

During an interview I conducted on March 5, I obtained a copy of a detailed August 29, 1975, three-page letter from Ohio Conference of Teamsters boss Presser to Teamsters general president Frank Fitzsimmons, which outlined the new energy division.

With Presser's letter—and proof of the new goon squad—in my possession, I returned to Ohio. There, I talked to the head of a company organized by the new unit who gave me a copy of its sweetheart contract—with substandard wages, hours, and benefits.

It appeared to be the McMaster Task Force all over again. In fact, two of its organizers were Larry McHenry and Jim Shaw who were still the government's top suspects for the bombing of Dick Fitzsimmons's car.

20. Brother in The Bond

I returned to Detroit on Thursday, March 25, 1976, and attended a staff meeting with my colleagues at the *Free Press*. Going through all of the material we had collected, we planned our final assault on the McMaster Task Force story.

During the discussion, I told them that I planned to go to Indianapolis that night. Jo Thomas asked if I had scheduled an interview with Richard Dininger. I told her that I had not, but that I might ambush him at either his home or office.

"Could you hold off talking to him until we finish talking to all the companies?" She snapped. With no resistance, I agreed not to contact Dininger.

Appearing puzzled as to why I had acquiesced so easily, Thomas continued, "What are you going to Indianapolis to do?"

"I talked to Don Davis last week," I replied. "He wants to see me, so I'm going to meet with him tomorrow afternoon."

Knowing that the reputedly violent Davis, an alleged explosives expert, continued to be vilified in Local 299 after allegedly beating up Dave Johnson in 1970 upon the orders of Rolland McMaster, Thomas advised me to cancel the interview with Davis, saying, "This guy's a thug! He probably still works for McMaster! I just don't want to see you go down there, and walk into something you can't get out of!"

The usually laid-back Ralph Orr spoke up, agreeing with Thomas. Even Oppedahl appeared concerned.

"Guys, I'm fine. I have a contact down there in case I have any problems."

Thomas told me to call her, too, if any problems arose.

Then, without me even asking him, Oppedahl gave me a couple of hundred dollars for my trip. This was the first time in nearly five months—when I received my original advance of $250, now long gone—that the *Free Press* had given me any additional money.

I left for Indianapolis during the early evening but only drove as far as Jackson, Michigan, where my Thunderbird's water pump broke. The AAA towed me to a nearby service station where I was told that my car could not be repaired until the following morning. With no hotels nearby, I spent the night reading and catnapping in a chair at the gas station, which was open around the clock.

On Friday, March 26, at 1:00 P.M, I checked into a motel in Greenwood, just outside of Indianapolis. I called Don Davis who asked me where I was staying. I politely refused to tell him, so he instructed me to meet him at his place of business—a gun store—in an hour. He added that his attorney, Loren Comstock, would join us.

I parked my Thunderbird in front of his shop in the midst of a small strip of stores and walked in. Behind the counter, I saw Davis—a massive 350-pound former Teamster organizer. I stepped up and introduced myself.

Very warm and friendly, Davis, with a broad smile on his face, pumped my hand and offered me a soft drink. "I like this guy," I immediately thought to myself. "I can't believe this is the same Don Davis whom I have heard so many terrible things about."

As Davis telephoned his wife to tell her that I had arrived—concluding the call with "I love you, dear"—I was busy looking at all the guns in his shop.

"You really like guns," I said, stating the obvious.

"It's a living," he replied.

"The book on you is that you're a bomber, not a shooter," I said, smiling.

"I'll bet that I can tell you a few stories about me that even you haven't heard," he responded. "Of course, all of them are bullshit."

After a lengthy conversation between Davis and me, Loren Comstock walked into the shop. A tall, distinguished-looking attorney, Comstock and I shook hands. He asked me to join them for an early dinner.

I went with Comstock in his car, leaving my Thunderbird behind, parked in front of the gun shop. Davis followed us in his own car. On the drive to the restaurant, Comstock was cool towards me.

During the dinner, Davis excused himself to go to the bathroom. While Davis was away, Comstock, who specialized in criminal-defense work, noticed the college ring on my right hand, which had the Greek letters for Phi Delta Theta on the stone.

He asked me the traditional Phi Delt greeting.

Surprised that he was a brother, too, I gave him the secret required response. Somehow, that simple connection warmed everything up between us.

After dinner, we went to Comstock's office for the formal, taped interview with Davis. Although Davis admitted that he had been involved in some questionable acts during certain labor disputes, he vehemently denied that he had beaten up Dave Johnson in 1970. And, after hearing his side of the story, I believed that Davis was telling the truth, especially after I saw the results of a polygraph test he had taken shortly after the Johnson incident.

In fact, I even believed Davis when he added that he had merely been used by the pro-Hoffa forces to purge Rolland McMaster as the head of Local 299. Returning to Indianapolis after the alleged beating, Davis eventually lost nearly everything, including his job.

Until I had arrived in Indianapolis that day, not one reporter had ever asked Davis his side of the story.

Several hours into the interview, Davis became noticeably ill. Apologizing, he excused himself and drove home alone.

While Comstock and I were driving back to my car, he asked me if I wanted to grab a bite to eat. It was about 1:30 A.M.—the middle of the day for me—and so I agreed to stop. We walked into a small diner and ordered breakfast. The food came quickly.

As I talked with my fraternity brother, he became extremely serious and told me that McMaster knew I was in the area, alone. Apparently, Davis had innocently given him a heads up about my visit.

I laughed, accusing him of trying to frighten me.

Comstock then told me that McMaster's loyalists were receiving pressure from the FBI because of my investigation, and that the Strike Force office in Pittsburgh would soon present evidence before a federal grand jury. He suggested that there had been "a lot of talk" among McMaster's people to have me killed—along with my mysterious task-force source who had been feeding me information.

"Loren, I have a lot of friends, too," I replied, feigning confidence. "If anything happens to me, McMaster and his men are going to have more problems than they ever dreamed of."

Concerned for my safety, Comstock exclaimed in clipped syllables, "You just don't get it, Dan! You have to understand that you aren't going to live unless McMaster allows you to! You could be killed tonight when you go back to your motel!"

Now overwhelmed with fear, I excused myself from the table—with no objection from Comstock who probably knew that I was going to make a telephone call.

Even though it was just after 2:00 A.M., I called my FBI contact in Indianapolis. There was no answer at the number I was given.

Then, I called Jo Thomas at her home. She screamed at me, "I told you! You've been set up! Get out of there!"

As I hung up the phone, all I could think was that I was about to get my ass kicked again, just like in Chicago—or worse. I felt absolutely horrified at the prospect of what was about to happen to me.

When I returned to the table, I had tears in my eyes. There was no way Comstock didn't see them.

He asked me if I was okay and whether I wanted to leave. Without saying a word, I nodded my head. I dropped a twenty-dollar bill on the table, and we went to his car.

We drove a short distance and pulled into the unlit parking lot in front of Davis's gun shop. Still visibly upset, I thanked Loren for everything, shook his hand, and got out of the car. He wished me the best of luck before he sped away. I prayed that this guy—my fraternity brother—had just done me a huge favor.

Now standing in the dark, I walked to the front of my Thunderbird, the only car in the parking lot, and felt the piece of scotch tape that I had placed where the hood opened. Seeing that the tape was still there and attached, I assumed that no one had opened the hood.

Opening my car door, I put my hand under the driver's seat, feeling for any containers or loose wires. There were none.

I damned myself for parking right in front of Davis's gun store instead of several blocks away. Sitting behind the wheel of my car, I placed the key in the ignition, straddled my legs across the front seat, covered my head and face with my left arm, and turned the key—fully expecting the car to explode.

The car started right away.

Screeching my B.F. Goodrich tires out of the parking lot, I decided not to go back to my motel. I left behind a sport coat, a pair of slacks, and some unimportant miscellaneous materials. But even if I had a suitcase filled with hundred-dollar bills there, I still would not have returned to my room that night.

When I finally turned east onto Interstate-70, I knew that I had not been followed. I honestly believed that Loren Comstock, my Phi Delta Theta fraternity brother, had just saved my life. I had survived whatever was supposed to happen to me—or whatever I imagined was supposed to happen to me.

Driving fast and hard on that dark and empty highway, I opened all of the windows on my Thunderbird—my Batmobile—and stuck my head and left arm out of the driver's side, allowing the cold spring night air to go right through me.

I never felt more alive in my entire life.

21. Confronting McMaster

On April 12, 1976—just as Comstock had predicted—a federal grand jury in Pittsburgh began investigating members of the McMaster Task Force for their alleged roles in the bombing raids on three companies: Interstate Motor Freight System, McQuaide Freight Lines, and Don Martin Trucking. Outside the grand jury's secret sessions, the FBI, the Alcohol Tobacco and Firearms Division of the Treasury Department, and the U.S. Strike Force Against Organized Crime continued their probes of McMaster's operations.

When I received word about the investigation from a new FBI source in Pennsylvania, I told him that I had not heard of the bombing at Don Martin Trucking. He gave me the number of the company's president, and I called him.

The executive candidly provided details of the incident, which actually were minor in comparison to what had happened at Interstate and McQuaide. At Don Martin, a stick of dynamite had exploded near a trailer parked on the company's lot, causing minimal damage. The McMaster organizer spearheading the Don Martin campaign was Jack Robison who was clearly a target of the grand-jury probe.

Also, the president of the company told me that he, too, had been approached by Dick Dininger who offered him a sweetheart contract—for a price.

I reported all of this information to the *Free Press*.

On April 16—during an interview with an executive at Noble Graham Transport, a small family-run steel and lumber hauler in Michigan's Upper Peninsula—Jo Thomas uncovered actual transcripts of taped conversations where a payoff had been suggested by Dininger.

When a company official called Mike Boano, who headed the campaign, and asked if Dininger could deliver labor peace, Boano replied on tape, "He's a pretty understanding gentleman. . . . I do know he's reliable, and he can usually substantiate his claims. I have had quite a few dealings with him."

Dininger had proposed that the company pay him between $20,000 and $25,000 over a five-year period. In return, he would guarantee labor peace. Noble Graham refused to make the payoff, and its employees voted down the Teamsters at the NLRB-sanctioned election.

Over the next month—during which Thomas had gone on a two-week vacation, and Orr had been hospitalized for a kidney infection—I contacted dozens of trucking companies, many of whom had been hit with the full force of the McMaster Task Force before Dininger stepped in, trying to make a deal.

On Friday, May 14, Thomas authorized me to interview Dininger. After a lengthy search, I finally found him in Sarasota, Florida, and fenced with him for an hour during a taped conversation.

Dininger portrayed himself as an honest businessman. "I would hear reports," he told me, "and when I did, I'd make a telephone call." He added, "If I heard [a company] was on strike, I would call management up and ask if I could help them. That would be my business."

He denied ever working in concert with McMaster, Boano, or anyone else from the task force to shake down a trucking company.

With Dininger's statement memorialized, Thomas further authorized me to set up the long-awaited formal interview with McMaster for Thursday, May 20 at 2:30 P.M. in the office of the general counsel of the *Detroit Free Press*.

I located McMaster at his farm in Wixom and extended the invitation. He agreed to be there.

On the morning of the McMaster interview, Orr, Thomas, and I met to plan our strategy. We agreed to obtain as much background information as we could on McMaster's personal life and union career, and then Thomas would take the lead with the questioning about the task force.

They instructed me *not* to ask McMaster any questions about the Local 299 violence or the Hoffa disappearance. Fearing that this would be the last time McMaster would allow me to talk to him, I protested that decision. Getting tough with me, Orr and Thomas insisted, so, once again, I backed off.

At 2:15 P.M., I met McMaster and two of his associates in the lobby of the *Free Press* building and escorted them to the general counsel's office. No one else had arrived, so I offered them some coffee or soft drinks as we talked briefly about matters unrelated to the Teamsters. McMaster looked relaxed and confident. Both of us had tape recorders to memorialize the interview.

After *Free Press* counsel Kenneth Murray, assistant city editor Ladd Neuman, Jo Thomas, and Ralph Orr arrived, the interview began.

Thomas skillfully led McMaster through his early career in Local 299, discussing his significant role in Jimmy Hoffa's rise to power. Speaking freely, McMaster moved into the government investigations of the Teamsters, especially his bout with Robert Kennedy and the Senate Rackets Committee.

During her questioning, Thomas yielded occasionally to Neuman, Orr, and me. As I ran down my list of questions, I asked McMaster about a secret agreement he had with Hoffa, regarding his own role in the local after he went to prison.

McMaster replied that after his indictment and conviction for extortion at Youngstown Cartage, Hoffa had ordered him to resign as secretary-treasurer of Local 299. McMaster agreed to do so, but only if he received Hoffa's assurance that he would regain his position in the union after McMaster's release from prison. Hoffa authorized Dave Johnson and Frank Fitzsimmons to make the deal with McMaster, which was signed on a paper napkin during a meeting at the Pontchartrain Hotel in downtown Detroit. McMaster went to prison after resigning from his post. Johnson succeeded him as secretary-treasurer.

McMaster added that in April 1968, after Hoffa had been in prison for just over a year and McMaster was out of jail and now on probation, Fitzsimmons decided to honor his contract with McMaster, selecting him to run Local 299. Hoffa protested from behind bars, but Fitzsimmons defied him, allowing Johnson to remain secretary-treasurer but appointing McMaster as the local's "administrative assistant" and chief executive officer.

According to McMaster, his appointment by a defiant Fitzsimmons caused the initial rift between Hoffa and Fitzsimmons. Specifically, McMaster said, "Jimmy was in the [prison] down there and heard about that. And he didn't like that. And he put that machinery to work to chop me up. Not so much me, but he knew that I couldn't do any of this without Fitzsimmons's blessing. So [Hoffa] chopped up the organization, and it has never run smoothly since."

After Don Davis allegedly beat up Johnson at McMaster's behest—an act for which I now believed that Davis and McMaster were completely innocent—Hoffa, through his people in Detroit, engineered McMaster's ouster from Local 299. McMaster bitterly charged, "It was all caused by Jimmy's behind the scenes chopping me up."

In retaliation, Fitzsimmons appointed McMaster as a general organizer with the Central Conference and as the director of the union's special commodities and steel operations. "FASH was making a lot of noise," McMaster explained. "They were criticizing us extensively for not doing some things."

So, as we had already learned, the Teamsters created the special unit—the McMaster Task Force—to deal with the situation.

As the questioning turned to matters directly related to our story, the rest of us sat back as Thomas, once again, took control of the interview. Responding to Thomas's sharp questioning, McMaster depicted his organizing drive as a legitimate operation. Confronted with evidence of sweetheart contracts, McMaster danced around the issue, saying, "If there's any contract I can't explain, there's something wrong.... Practically everything that was done in this field, they got the approval from me."

Thomas then asked him, "There was a lot of rough stuff in the organizing. Were you aware of this?

"This was one of the things that puzzled me very much," McMaster replied, "and I reprimanded people for allowing this to happen."

Speaking specifically about the Eck Miller campaign in Owensboro, Kentucky, McMaster said, "I had a strange thing happen. I went to Kentucky. We had so many problems. I went to this company, and the workers are a fine bunch of workers. One of the [pro-Teamster employees for the company who was on] the picket line, pulled out a pistol and shot at the trucks."

Blaming the company and its employees for the violence, McMaster continued, "[Eck Miller] started a campaign which, I don't know—but that burning the truck up in the center of the street and leaving it there as a monument—I blame them for that. And so did *Overdrive* magazine which investigated it very carefully. It's the first time they ever wrote anything nice about us. I think they were kind of sympathetic to our problems."

During another pre-interview decision, we chose not to broach the subject of Jim Drinkhall's alleged friendships with McMaster and Boano.

PART TWO: THE TEAMSTERS & THE MAFIA

When pushed hard on the violence, McMaster insisted, "I can't control people who drink beer and get tanked."

Thomas continued, "One of the characters that turned up at a lot of the trucking companies was a guy named Dick Dininger.... Did you have any knowledge that he contacted companies and offered to make the Teamsters go away?"

McMaster responded, "If he did, I don't know about it. Make them go away? We never went away.... He never negotiated with me."

Thomas confronted McMaster with a document we had uncovered, indicating that he had been personally dealing directly with Dininger.

Seeing the evidence before him, McMaster simply replied, "He could have said something to me. I remember the company.... [Dininger] had to talk with the guy who was down there directly on the scene. I stayed out of those kinds of things."

Thomas continued, "We have ten companies... that show that, at just about the time your people show up, Dininger calls [each company]. He's a friend of yours. Did you know about this?"

"I don't know how he would even find out, unless he saw our publicity.... Did you talk to Dininger?" McMaster asked.

"Yes," Thomas replied sternly.

McMaster said, "I don't know how he would find out."

Orr asked, "Did the International feel they got enough bang for their buck?"

"Oh, yeah. They were satisfied. It produced even more than you can imagine, because it created activity.... We did hard work. There was no skullduggery going on."

To everyone's surprise, as the interview wound down, McMaster pulled out a confidential report, which he permitted us to keep. It listed fifty-four companies which had been supposedly unionized by the McMaster Task Force—which appeared to yield 1,587 new union members. Most of them were trucking firms we had never heard of.

Although we were pleased with most of the results of the three-hour interview, McMaster's list of alleged organizing successes completely threw us for a loop. As a result of this new information, McMaster successfully forced us to postpone our anticipated Sunday, May 23, publication date.

I told Thomas that I would call every company McMaster had listed when I came to work the following day.

Assistant city editor Ladd Neuman came to my desk and told me to have a good dinner. Also, he had reserved a room for me at the Howard Johnson Motor Inn near the *Free Press* building. He said that the newspaper, which gave me an additional $300, would pick up the bill for everything.

I returned to my desk the following morning at 7:00 A.M. and began calling the companies on McMaster's list.

By the end of the day, representatives from most of the companies told me that they had never heard of McMaster and were either nonunion or had been organized long before the task force was created. And those executives whose companies had been organized by McMaster admitted to accepting sweetheart contracts. Also, an official from a Minnesota trucking company conceded that he had paid for labor peace after being approached by Dick Dininger.

Later that month, on May 27, PROD released its investigation of the Teamsters' top leadership, *Teamster Democracy and Financial Responsibility: A Factual and Structural Analysis*. The report completed nearly a year of work by the PROD staff—Arthur Fox, Mike deBlois, and John Sikorski, PROD's research director and the report's principal author. Included in the bound 177-page document were references to McMaster and his task force in anticipation of the publication of our story.

Finally, on June 20, 1976, the *Free Press* published our article about the McMaster Task Force, which was nationally syndicated. We reported that the 32-man unit had been part of a 48-state extortion scheme to get trucking companies to pay for labor peace. During its two-year history, the unit had used extreme violence, including bombings and shootings, to shake down its targets.

However, to my disappointment, I did not receive a byline line with Orr and Thomas. Instead a box appeared on the jump page of the story, which read:

> The story of the Teamsters Union task force was developed after the *Free Press* was approached last fall by free-lance journalist Dan E. Moldea, who had gained knowledge of the task force operations from union sources. Moldea was then hired by the paper on a part-time basis to obtain more information and to aid the staff of the paper.
>
> On the strength of his work and recommendations of *Free Press* editors, Moldea obtained a fellowship with the Fund for Investigative Journalism in Washington, D.C. early this year.

PART TWO: THE TEAMSTERS & THE MAFIA

> Moldea had a close working relationship with elements both inside and outside the union opposed to the present Teamster leadership and received some pay from them.
>
> Any information received by the paper, both from Moldea and from other sources, was verified independently by the *Free Press* before publication.

On the morning of June 22, two days after publication, I came to the *Free Press* building for the final time to clean out my desk. I decided not to make an issue about the byline matter. Unlike NBC News, the newspaper did not ask me to stay. By this time, Jo Thomas and I were barely speaking to each other, even though our story was receiving widespread praise.

I walked around the newsroom, shaking hands with staff members who did not work on the story but whom I had enjoyed seeing and having lunch with over the past eight months.

Ralph Orr wasn't around, so I left a short note on his desk, thanking him for seeing the project through to publication. John Oppedahl came to my desk while I placed all my paperwork in a box and jammed other materials into my backpack. He handed me the rest of my money, put his hand on my shoulder, and simply said, "Good job." Saying it the way he did meant more to me than anything else he could have said or done.

Gesturing towards Jo Thomas, Oppedahl suggested, "Go over there, and say good-bye to her. You'll regret it later if you don't."

I shook hands with John, picked up my things, and went over to Thomas's desk where she was typing away on another big story.

I stood there, smiling at her until she finally looked up at me and smiled, too. "Thanks, Jo," I said quietly. "I just wanted to say good-bye."

Thomas, who later moved to the *New York Times* and became an even bigger star, stood and shook my hand, reminding me to read the newspaper's lead editorial that day.

Picking up the morning edition on my way out of the newsroom, I saw that the *Free Press's* editorial board had commended our investigation, adding: "Still it is just one more example of the terrible state of the Teamsters union—and the crying need for massive, top-to-bottom reform within it."

Just a few days earlier, the Teamsters for a Decent Contract (TDC) had changed its name to the Teamsters for a Democratic Union (TDU). And, soon after, union delegates to the 1976 Teamsters' convention in Las Vegas reelected Frank Fitzsimmons to his second term as their general president.

22. "Jimmy ran off to Brazil with a black go-go dancer"

On Wednesday, June 29, 1976, I returned to Washington, D.C. and visited my friends at PROD. When I arrived, John Sikorski introduced me to Marc Smolonsky, an associate of Jack Anderson, who had contacted PROD for some information. Smolonsky and I hit it off immediately, and we agreed to stay in touch.

The following day, Smolonsky told me that Anderson was planning to do a column for the first anniversary of the Hoffa disappearance. "Jack wants you to work with us on the story. Interested?" Smolonsky asked.

Working with Jack Anderson would be a dream come true, so, of course, I agreed. Smolonsky took me to Anderson's office on Sixteenth Street in northwest Washington and introduced me to him.

Friendly but tough, Anderson talked to me for about a half hour. He asked how I wanted to approach the story. I proposed that we concentrate on the Local 299 violence because the story had gone untold while the Hoffa case remained unsolved. We had not even mentioned it in our *Free Press* story.

Anderson agreed with my suggestion and welcomed me aboard, saying that he would have his secretary draw up a contract between us.

On July 1, I received a letter from Anderson, authorizing me to use his name during my continuing investigation of the Teamsters. He also gave me a couple of hundred dollars to get started and used his influence at the Fund for Investigative Journalism to get me another grant.

I used part of the money to take my new friend, Marc Smolonsky, out to lunch.

That same day, I called McMaster's former organizer, Larry McHenry, a member of the new energy-division task force. The FBI still believed that he, along with Jim Shaw, had been involved in, among other things, the bombing of Dick Fitzsimmons's car twenty days before Hoffa disappeared.

Although we had not mentioned McHenry's name in the *Free Press* article, I asked him what he thought of it.

"One word," he said. "Bullshit!"

PART TWO: THE TEAMSTERS & THE MAFIA

McHenry added that he had been subpoenaed to appear before the federal grand jury in Pittsburgh. He admitted being with McMaster's men at the Local 299 meetings that were disrupted, but he denied having any role in the violence against local officials.

McHenry, without any prompting from me, turned the conversation to his son. "The so-called investigations of me . . . are based mostly on phone taps of my son's conversations before he died."

"I don't know whether you want to talk about that," I replied, not pushing him to answer questions about his son, Patrick, who had been found dead in his room at the Leland House after a drug overdose two days after Hoffa disappeared.

"I don't mind. . . . The kid was sick. There's no doubt about that. And anything to do with the Teamsters, he talked to a lot of people. And he tried to play the big wheel, like his old man was into everything. . . . What you have is based upon [the FBI's] phone taps of conversations overheard as far as Patrick is concerned."

I then asked, "Were you questioned with regard to the bombing of [Dick] Fitzsimmons's car?"

He responded, "That was brought up. In fact, [the FBI] even asked me if I was surprised that they had brought it up. I said I sure was. They asked me if I knew who was responsible, and I said no."

In short, McHenry denied that he and Jim Shaw were involved in the bombing—with or without McMaster's authorization. He also denied any involvement in Hoffa's murder or with the disposal of his body.

For my next interview, I then turned to McHenry's partner, Jim Shaw.

At six-foot-five and 245 pounds, Shaw, in his mid-thirties, appeared as a youthful image of McMaster. A former mechanical-engineering student at the University of Maryland and a U.S. Army veteran, Shaw confirmed to me that he had joined the McMaster Task Force in the midst of the organized campaign against Eck Miller, where he, as an owner-operator trucker, had worked for Paul Jeffries.

To my surprise, Shaw admitted that he had come to Detroit to attend Local 299 meetings with McHenry. During the political turmoil preceding Hoffa's disappearance, Shaw confirmed that he had moved into the Leland House—just as the FBI had told me. Shaw added that he worked as a "part-time bouncer" for the hotel.

Shaw continued that on April 17, 1975, his new Kenworth truck, valued at $50,000, was firebombed at a trucking terminal in suburban Detroit. The truck was insured, and the bombing remained unsolved.

Soon after, Shaw explained, McMaster helped him get a job in Detroit's steel division of the Gateway Transportation Company.

My mind began racing after I heard that, particularly since Gateway officials—including McMaster's brother-in-law, Stanton Barr—had been questioned by the grand jury investigating Hoffa's murder.

When I asked him if he and McHenry had bombed young Fitzsimmons's car, Shaw replied, "Me and Larry were bumming around together for some time. Then, a couple of weeks after Dick Fitzsimmons's car was bombed, a couple of FBI agents came out to see me at work. I wasn't there any of the times they were, so I called their offices in Detroit and even went down to see them. When I got there, they told me that they had enough evidence on me and Larry to bring us before a grand jury for bombing Fitzsimmons's car. I couldn't believe it."

After Shaw denied any role in the bombing, I asked him whether he knew anything about Hoffa's disappearance. He replied, "The only reason why I was suspected of anything was because of my friendship with Larry McHenry."

On July 23, I scheduled my final interview with Rolland McMaster, my last opportunity to confront him with the questions the *Free Press* would not allow me to ask. I wanted to go back to Detroit to see him, but Jack Anderson, fearing for my safety, insisted that I not meet McMaster in person. Instead, Anderson told me to conduct the interview over the telephone and to tape the conversation—with McMaster's permission.

While making the arrangements for the formal interview that night, McMaster told me, "I got some advice. I was told to stop talking to you. . . . The counsel [for the Teamsters] said that it was very dangerous for me to talk to you."

I replied, "I can understand why you would feel that way. . . . I will tell you this, this next article [by Jack Anderson] is really going to be tough on you, really tough."

To his great credit, McMaster still decided to do the interview that night.

When I called him back, I was a little nervous and asked him questions in rapid succession.

First, I told him that FASH leader Bill Hill had told me of a conversation he had with Ohio Teamsters leader William Presser. During their talk, Presser had accused McMaster of being behind "The FASH Shootout" in 1969.

"I heard that same damn thing," McMaster responded. "Of course, it was cleared up in my crowd."

PART TWO: THE TEAMSTERS & THE MAFIA

Then, I asked him if he knew Jim Drinkhall of *Overdrive*.

"I consider him a friend of mine," McMaster replied.

I then turned the conversation to the violence in Local 299, asking, "What is your theory about who was behind it?"

McMaster explained, "I think Jimmy was in very heavily and giving money to various screwed-up groups. . . . Some of them have made tentative confessions that Hoffa was paying all the bills and stuff like that." McMaster viewed these groups as being independent-trucker organizations, as well as the reform groups that led to the newly-created Teamsters for a Democratic Union.

McMaster completely rejected the suggestion that his men were behind any of the violence, including the bombing of Dick Fitzsimmons's car.

Slowing down, I continued, "It's the awesome power that you appear to wield that absolutely fascinates me. . . . I am as fascinated with you as I was with Allen Dorfman. And I think you're more powerful than Allen Dorfman. . . . "

McMaster replied, "He's a different type of person than me."

"Yeah, that's the whole thing. You've been through the rough-and-tumble part of it. That's what I respect. You've clawed your way up there to become as powerful and wealthy as you are. And Dorfman, it was handed to him by Hoffa."

"That's right."

"He didn't start out on a truck like you. That's why I decided, 'I think I'm going to stay with McMaster rather than go back to Dorfman.'"

After this melodramatic confessional which appeared to amuse McMaster, I returned to the Hoffa case, asking him about his relationship with Salvatore Briguglio—who, according to the FBI, was the likely triggerman in the murder. And, according to Teamster leader Don Vestal of Nashville, Briguglio was one of McMaster's former bodyguards and an occasional traveling companion.

"Did you know Salvatore Briguglio?" I asked.

"No," McMaster insisted.

"Previously, you told me that you did."

"If I did, it was at one of those meetings, and we shook hands. I can't remember those guys."

"Okay, but you were never in business with him?"

"Never."

"Did you ever travel with him?"

"Never."

When I asked McMaster about Chuck O'Brien's suspected role in the Hoffa murder, McMaster said, "He's got the biggest mouth in the whole goddamn world. And he runs off at the mouth all of the goddamn time and doesn't know what he's talking about," adding that he "can't believe" that O'Brien could have been involved. McMaster said that Hoffa had given him the responsibility to watch over O'Brien in the union.

When I asked McMaster what theory he had developed about the murder, he said, "I think that Jimmy ran off to Brazil with a black go-go dancer to avoid more persecution from the government. I hired a soothsayer and asked her where Jimmy was. That's what she told me."

I laughed, telling him, "The FBI and federal investigators can't rule you out . . . but no one can bring you into it."

He shot back, "If I was involved in that thing in any way, shape, or form, I'd be heading for the hills. They told me that they were still fishing."

After completing my interview with McMaster, I collected all of my materials and submitted a fifteen-page report to Jack Anderson. His column appeared on July 30, 1976 and was nationally syndicated. Anderson wrote:

> It was a year ago today that Jimmy Hoffa, the tempestuous Teamster, disappeared. Federal investigators have told us Hoffa was murdered. They claim to know who did it and why. All they lack is the evidence.
>
> But part of the story can now be told. It's a story of violence that began after Hoffa's release from prison in 1971. . . .

Pleased with the story—even though it was greatly reduced to only a few hundred words—Anderson wrote a "To Whom It May Concern Letter" for me, saying, "Dan Moldea is one of the few investigative reporters dedicated to exposing the corrupt and illicit activities of the Teamsters. He seems to have an unsurpassed knowledge of the union."

PART TWO: THE TEAMSTERS & THE MAFIA

23. Calling Sally Bugs at Local 560

In early September 1976, John Sikorski replaced Arthur Fox as executive director of PROD while Fox, remaining faithful to the cause of Teamsters reform, became PROD's general counsel.

On September 15, while I was still in Washington, Sikorski invited Lowell Bergman, an associate editor at *Rolling Stone*, and me to join him for dinner. I had known of Bergman because of a March 1975 article he had co-authored with reporter Jeff Gerth in *Penthouse* about the Teamsters-financed La Costa Country Club.

While talking about the Teamsters and Hoffa's murder, Bergman suggested that I do an article about the Hoffa case for possible publication on the first anniversary of the Hoffa grand-jury hearing in early December. We exchanged business cards and agreed to talk in the near future.

For the most part, Bergman and I got along well. I really liked and respected him from the outset. However, Sikorski nearly had to pull us apart after Bergman brought up Jim Drinkhall's name. Bergman boasted that Drinkhall was a long-time friend of his. Shooting off my mouth, I told Bergman that Drinkhall had been a hero of mine—but that we had become estranged because of his friendships with Rolland McMaster and Mike Boano.

Bergman and I got into a heated argument. Although we both cooled off, I knew that I had not heard the last of this matter.

—⚍—

Federal investigators had a protected witness, Ralph Picardo, a former driver for Tony Provenzano, who had given them the alleged details of Jimmy Hoffa's murder. Somehow, Picardo had implicated Provenzano, the Briguglios, and the Andrettas in the plot. On the basis of Picardo's information, the federal grand jury in Detroit had called them, along with McMaster and Gateway executives, the previous year.

With Picardo—a former union business agent and convicted murderer—now the star witness in the case, the focus of the Hoffa investigation had shifted from Detroit to Union City, the home of Tony Provenzano's Teamsters Local 560.

I told Sikorski that I knew the Detroit angle of the case as well as anyone, but I was not as familiar with the probe in New Jersey. Sikorski suggested that I partner up with Bob Windrem, an investigative reporter from the *Home News* in New Brunswick, New Jersey.

Actually, I had already met Windrem, by telephone, through Sikorski. Windrem had recently done an excellent series of articles about the New Jersey Teamsters, and we had exchanged information about the Hoffa case during my work for Jack Anderson.

Taking Sikorski's advice, I called Windrem and pitched the idea to him. Windrem was excited about the proposed partnership, regardless of where we published our story.

On October 17, I drove from Washington to New Brunswick to begin the collaboration. Windrem and I immediately became friends. He gave me a car tour of northern New Jersey, which included everything from the Local 560 building in Union City to Brother Moscato's garbage dump in Hackensack. When we went to his home, he had his files laid out in an orderly fashion and plenty of office supplies at our disposal.

Two days later, after drinking a few beers, Windrem and I started laughing about crazy things we could do to break open the Hoffa case, like bringing in our own heavy equipment to dig up Brother Moscato's.

But, when Windrem suggested calling up Local 560 and trying to interview Salvatore Briguglio, the alleged triggerman in the Hoffa murder, I stopped laughing.

"That's a great idea!" I exclaimed.

The next morning, I called Local 560's headquarters and asked to speak with the 48-year old Briguglio. To my surprise, "Sally Bugs," who had never been interviewed and had only given the feds the Fifth, took my call.

"What do you need?" Briguglio barked.

"I want to interview you, sir," I replied.

"What about?"

"The Hoffa murder."

"What makes you think I have anything to say about that?"

"Because, Mr. Briguglio, you have neither been arrested nor indicted, and yet you are still being accused of murdering Jimmy Hoffa. . . . And I think that the government might be violating your civil rights."

In fact, I had never met a mobster or mob associate who wasn't against wiretapping or in favor of strong personal privacy laws. Already during my career as a crime reporter, I had been repeatedly bored by bad guys who were whining about the alleged impingements upon their rights and freedoms by the FBI and IRS.

PART TWO: THE TEAMSTERS & THE MAFIA

True to form, Briguglio, who put me on hold for a minute or so, came back and said firmly, "Be here on Monday, October 25th, twelve o'clock noon. Ask for me at the receptionist's window."

Windrem and I celebrated—even though Windrem refused to come along with me. "I gotta live here," he said.

24. My lunch with Hoffa's alleged killers

On Monday, October 25 at 11:45 A.M., I arrived alone at Local 560. Asking for Sal Briguglio and being directed into a waiting room filled with bowling and softball trophies, I nervously skimmed magazines months out of date. After about a twenty-minute wait, Briguglio came through the door. Following close behind was his attorney, William Bufalino.

I had known the boisterous, glad-handing, and heavy-set Bufalino from my earlier work in Detroit, so he was particularly cordial when we shook hands. Briguglio, a short but wiry man, was more laid back, just staring and sizing me up.

"Join us for lunch across the street," Bufalino said cheerfully.

Still a little nervous, I smiled and nodded.

We then climbed aboard a small elevator in which I had to crouch my six-foot-four-inch frame. I remembered that the elderly elevator operator had been one of Tony Provenzano's alibi witnesses for the day Hoffa disappeared. When the elevator door opened, we were in the midst of a basement-parking garage.

"I thought we were just going across the street," I whispered to Bufalino.

"Yeah, but I thought we'd drive over," Bufalino replied.

With some trepidation but total surrender, I stepped into the back seat of Briguglio's late-model Buick. As I squirmed momentarily, Briguglio pressed a button that opened the garage door. Within seconds, we were across the street in front of the restaurant.

Inside, as the maitre d' led us down an aisle to a back room, I saw two other men seated at our table. No introductions necessary, I already knew who they were.

The first was Briguglio's brother, 31-year old Gabriel, the vice president of the Provenzano-controlled Local 84 in Fort Lee and one of Sally Bug's alleged coconspirators in the Hoffa murder. The second man was

40-year old Steve Andretta, a former Local 560 business agent and the brother of Tom Andretta, another alleged witness to the killing.

Thrilled by what I was in the midst of and simultaneously wolfing down my portion of the antipasto and a plate of linguini in clam sauce, I kept asking for permission to turn on the tape recorder in my pocket. Bufalino refused each time, saying, "Later, Danny, later."

After a 90-minute lunch, Bufalino and I left the restaurant and returned to Local 560. This time we walked while Briguglio and Andretta drove over in Briguglio's car.

Because of another appointment, Gabe Briguglio had to leave. During the lunch, he insisted that he had nothing to do with the Hoffa murder. Tom Andretta, whom I talked to on the telephone that afternoon, also denied any role in the killing.

Led into the local union president's office by Bufalino, I finally pulled out my tape recorder and laid it on the table in full view of the others who soon walked in. Salvatore Provenzano—Tony's brother and the president of the local who had not been present for the lunch—joined us, as did Sal Briguglio and Steve Andretta.

For the next three-and-a-half hours, I recorded the first and only taped interview with the man suspected to have murdered Jimmy Hoffa.

Briguglio was loud and defiant, refusing to admit that he had been involved in the Hoffa murder while I kept trying to prod him into a confession. Ever protective of his client, Bufalino, never known to be shy, kept trying to deflect the interview away from Briguglio's alleged complicity and toward the government's allegedly illegal tactics to gather information—the subject I had supposedly come there to discuss.

In response to my question about who was paying Bufalino's legal bills for his representation of Hoffa's alleged killers, the attorney replied, "If someday they have some money, they can pay me. If Hoffa were here right now, he'd say, 'Continue to defend these people. They weren't the ones who did it.'"

Also, I asked Bufalino whether his family relationship with mob boss Russell Bufalino of eastern Pennsylvania was the reason he had been selected as counsel for them. Bufalino shot back, "If you want to charge me with something regarding Russell Bufalino, charge me with the fact that I selected him as my number-one friend! I would rather be accused of being his friend and brother by choice, not by an accident of birth!"

Throughout the interview, William Bufalino appeared to suggest that the government suspected Russell Bufalino as the man responsible for ordering the hit on Hoffa. And that was news to me.

PART TWO: THE TEAMSTERS & THE MAFIA

At the time, Russell Bufalino was reportedly the interim head of the Vito Genovese crime family. Tony Provenzano was a Genovese caporegime.

When I inquired of Salvatore Provenzano why his brother, Tony Pro, was being accused of engineering the Hoffa murder, he shot back, "Jimmy and my brother were friends to the very end. . . . I have seen letters that Jimmy sent to Tony, but I can't show them to you. They burnt up when Tony's house went up in flames."

Turning to Briguglio, I said, "You are the main man in this whole thing. You're the person everyone alleges blew [Hoffa's] head off. How do you react to these allegations?"

Briguglio responded coolly, "They're very, very serious allegations. And I'm very, very concerned about them, of course. But I know since I had nothing to do with it, I'm not too concerned about it. But I'm still being hurt by the publicity that's being generated by it. . . . That's [the government's] game plan: subpoena after subpoena. They haven't stopped; they aren't ever going to stop."

Distressed about being recently indicted for the sixteen-year-old murder of Anthony Castellito, a union rival, Briguglio continued, "[The government] will say, 'Although we didn't solve the Hoffa mystery, in order to justify the grand jury, we got this guy indicted on that, and the other guys on the other thing.' In the meantime, the Hoffa grand jury is going to fizzle out. . . . So, if you're asking me if I'm worried, the answer is, 'Yes.' I'm very, very worried and very, very concerned."

He explained that in early-December 1975, federal agents had roused Tony and Salvatore's brother, Nunzio Provenzano, the secretary-treasurer of Local 560, out of bed. Armed with subpoenas, the agents demanded access to a file cabinet in the union hall often used by Briguglio.

"They were looking for two .38s with silencers," Briguglio explained. "They came in; they didn't find any."

While government investigators searched through the union hall, other federal agents converged on the Garden State Bank across the street, holding subpoenas and demanding access to safety-deposit boxes that had been rented by Steve Andretta and Gabe Briguglio.

"This box I had only opened up two days prior," Andretta told me. "This was the first time in my life I had opened a safety-deposit box." He added that he used it to store his jewelry: two watches and two rings.

"You know what they found [in Gabe's safety-deposit box]?" Briguglio asked. "A sock, an old sock with some old coins in there. That's all they found. So that's another blank. God knows what they were looking for, the bastards, what they expected to find in there!"

However, he knew as well as I did: the FBI was looking for the weapon used to kill Jimmy Hoffa.

Pressing Briguglio and Andretta as to how federal agents knew to target the union file cabinet and the safety-deposit boxes, Andretta, somewhat sheepishly, replied, "They asked me about my visit to prison."

In August 1975, Andretta had visited Ralph Picardo, an old friend, in the readjustment unit of the prison hospital at Trenton State Penitentiary. Andretta and Picardo talked on telephones and could see each other through a thick glass barrier.

Federal agents alleged that during this visit, Andretta gave up some of the details of the Hoffa murder to Picardo. After receiving this information, Picardo made a beeline to the closest federal prosecutor and tried to make a deal to get out of prison.

During his subsequent appearance before the federal grand jury, Andretta testified under a forced grant of immunity. "I was highly insulted," he told me. "[I] never discussed anything about Hoffa with Picardo. . . . Picardo is trying to use us to bargain his way out of jail."

Consequently, cited with contempt for refusing to answer questions, Andretta spent sixty-three days in Michigan's Milan Prison.

I asked Andretta what he was asked during the grand-jury hearing. Andretta replied, "What did Sal [Briguglio] do with [Hoffa's] body? What did my brother do with the body? What did Tony Provenzano do with the body? What did Gabe Briguglio do with the body?"

After Andretta's release, Tony Provenzano threw a party for him and gave him a new Cadillac.

"They spent ten million dollars trying to throw Hoffa in jail," Andretta said bitterly. "And now they've spent a figure close to it, trying to find out what happened to him. And they're trying to get anybody involved in it for whatever reasons they want. They're very embarrassed."

When I asked Briguglio—who revealed that he had been identified as a "target" of the Hoffa probe during an earlier September 8, 1975, solo appearance before the federal grand jury in Detroit—where he was at the time of Hoffa's disappearance, he replied that he was playing Greek rummy in the Local 560 union hall with his two alleged coconspirators, Gabe Briguglio and Tom Andretta, as well as Tony Provenzano and other union officials.

However, during the interview, Briguglio, who said he had personally known Hoffa "very well," contradicted that version, saying that he had left Local 560 earlier in the day because of a flaring pain in his mouth after oral surgery the previous day.

In a final denial to me about committing the murder, Briguglio said, "I wish they would find out who did it, so they would take the heat off me and Tony [Provenzano]. Other than that, I don't even know if the guy is dead. . . . The government is on a fishing expedition. I don't know anyone in the world who would want to hurt Jimmy. He wasn't a threat to anyone to my knowledge. . . .

"There has to be law enforcement—but not like this when they go out and solicit phony witnesses to make a target out of certain individuals. What [the FBI] wants is a Briguglio or a Provenzano, any name they can build up. They build you up to knock you down, so they can make a name for themselves."

Over the next four days, Windrem and I cranked out a 36-page, double-spaced story, highlighted with portions of my interview at Local 560. However, predictably, when I called Lowell Bergman at *Rolling Stone*, he was no longer interested in my work, especially in the wake of our earlier argument over Jim Drinkhall.

After *Rolling Stone* and, later, *New Times*, another publication that featured investigative work, rejected our article—supposedly because of potential libel problems—I freelanced a story about my interview with Hoffa's alleged killers through the North American Newspaper Alliance/United Feature Syndicate.

I later gave a copy of my typed transcript with Hoffa's alleged killers to Windrem, telling him that we might trade it to the FBI in return for an exclusive interview with Ralph Picardo.

On October 30, my last day in New Jersey, Mike Hoyt, a reporter from the *Home News* prodded by Windrem, published a feature story that gave a fairly accurate picture of me at that time.[20] He wrote:

> In his beat-up blue Thunderbird, Moldea travels to Detroit, Washington, Chicago and points in between looking for information. Last week, it was New Jersey. . . . He's a free-lance investigative writer, a rare commodity in a profession that takes a lot of time and money. Moldea, 26 and single, has survived on borrowed cash, an occasional grant, and the articles and television research work he writes or collaborates on from time to time. . . . . When he travels, he works constantly. Reporters often look harried at the typewriter, but Moldea looks manic.

He writes late, smoking constantly, and the circles under his eyes get nearly black. . . .

"Hoffa was probably as crooked as the rest of them," he said. "I'm not interested in avenging Jimmy Hoffa.

"But you just don't go out and kill a guy like Jimmy Hoffa. Somebody very powerful had to make that decision, and I want to know who."

25. Death threat

After returning home to Ohio on November 2—Election Day 1976—my father called and asked me to have lunch with him. Dad sounded a little shaky. In the years since I had left home, he never called to ask me to a private lunch. Because he was in the midst of a bout with throat cancer, diagnosed the previous January, I came to the restaurant extremely concerned.

I had known a lot of tough guys in my life, but I had never met anyone as tough as Emil Moldea.

In 1940, Dad, an All-City lineman at Garfield High School in Akron—where I would later go to school—received a scholarship to play freshman football at Ohio State for Coach Francis Schmidt. While at OSU, he became a close friend of, among others, his Delta Tau Delta fraternity brother, future Pro Football Hall of Famer Dante Lavelli of the Cleveland Browns.

Dad played spring ball under the legendary coach, Paul Brown, who tried but failed to get him a draft deferment in 1941.[21] As a sophomore, Dad was slated to be one of the starting tackles on Brown's celebrated 1942 Ohio State football team, which shared the national championship with the University of Georgia.

Instead, after his basic training, Dad was assigned to the 41st Training Squadron at Denver's Lowry Field where he was in charge of troop conditioning. Simultaneously, he worked without pay as an assistant line coach at the University of Denver where he also continued his undergraduate work. In 1943, after he attended Officer Training School and received his commission, the Army shipped him to England.

PART TWO: THE TEAMSTERS & THE MAFIA

Dad's portrait as the Army-Air Force's "Typical Officer Candidate" during World War II, painted by the military artist Charles Baskerville, still hangs in the E-Ring of the Pentagon. A captain, although not a pilot, he had served in the 357th Fighter Group in England with one of my childhood heroes, famed fighter pilot Chuck Yeager, the first person to break the sound barrier.

After his military service, Dad returned to Ohio State and played football for Coach Wes Fesler in 1947. Then twenty-nine and the oldest player on the varsity by three years, Dad, still playing defensive tackle, was trapped twice by two offensive linemen during an inter-squad scrimmage. The coach instructed Dad "to leave the game to the kids." However, he kept him on the roster as the team's place-kicking specialist.

Dad would always be remembered for his last-second heroics during a game against Northwestern on November 8, 1947. According to the *ESPN College Football Encyclopedia*, which described the game as having the "wildest finish" in Ohio State football history:

> Buckeyes QB Pandel Savic had a pass from the Northwestern 12-yard line intercepted on the apparent final play of a 1947 game. The Ohio State band, figuring the home team had lost, took the field. Northwestern, however, was penalized for having 12 men on the field. The Buckeyes then tried a reverse, but Rodney Swinehart was tackled at the 2-yard line. Northwestern was penalized for being offside. Savic then threw a TD pass to Jimmy Clark to tie the score. The Wildcats blocked Emil Moldea's point-after kick, but they were again called for offsides. Head linesman E.C. Curtis called all three penalties with time expired. Moldea's second PAT was good for a 7-6 Ohio State win.[22]

The following month, Dan Reeves, the owner of the Los Angeles Rams, invited Dad to try out for his professional football team.[23] But now considered an old man after several years in the military and married, Dad passed on the offer.

However, the following spring, he went on to star on the Buckeyes' track and field team—with which he had lettered in 1941, 1946, 1947 and 1948. He had also set the Ohio State record for the shot put, which stood for seven years.

A real football lover, Dad had always wanted to coach and, after graduation with a degree in education, had been offered several low-paying jobs at small colleges, which could have led to bigger assignments. In fact, one of Dad's college buddies, Don McCafferty, went that route, starting as an assistant coach at Kent State University. He eventually became head coach of the Baltimore Colts, which won Super Bowl V in 1971, his first season on the job.

But I came along in 1950 as did my sister, Marsha, three years later, causing him to scuttle his plans. He had to raise a family and never really had the chance to go for his dream. Meantime, though, he had assembled a wonderful group of close friends—war veterans, former college and professional athletes, truckers, business executives, tavern owners, and even a pizzeria proprietor—so much so that I always enjoyed spending time with his crowd as much as I did with friends my own age.

To be sure, he was a hard act to follow, and I always looked up to him, especially because of his toughness.

Once, during a visit to my uncle's farm when I was just ten years old, Dad picked up an old German rifle with a tight, spring-action bolt. Holding back the bolt with his left hand, he tried to clean the chamber with his right index finger. Suddenly, the bolt slipped and slammed shut.

Spattered with some of his blood, I was looking at Dad's face when the accident occurred. I don't remember him flinching, even though the top part of his finger had been shredded. The rest of us in the family had to coax him to go to the hospital to get stitched up.

This was one very tough man.

At our lunch on Election Day, Dad apologized for the drama, saying he wanted to tell me something—but not in front of Mom. Saying nothing, I waited to hear the bad news about the cancer.

Instead, Dad told me that while I had been in New Jersey the previous week he had been threatened at his office. For years, he had worked as a salesman at Consolidated Freightways, which was one of the largest trucking companies in the United States.

When I asked him to describe the threat, he replied that he had received a telephone call from an anonymous man who, very coolly, told him that he was going to be killed and stuffed in the trunk of his car if he didn't get me under control.

When I heard that, I shouted, "God damn these guys!"

Dad told me that he didn't really feel in danger, but that he thought I should know what had happened. He encouraged me to keep exposing corruption in the trucking industry and working with the rank-and-file reformers.

PART TWO: THE TEAMSTERS & THE MAFIA

Immediately after I left Dad, I went back to my apartment and called the FBI to report the threat. And then, without any hesitation, I picked up the telephone and called a friend of mine in the U.S. Strike Force Against Organized Crime in Pittsburgh. After months of balking, I finally agreed to cooperate openly with the federal grand-jury investigation of McMaster's goon squad, which was the target of the probe.

"What do you need?" I asked my friend when he came to the phone.

This was no longer just business. This was personal. And I was no longer just a journalist, I was, indeed, an advocate who was further prepared to take sides—just as Stanhope Gould had alleged when he derisively described me as a "guerrilla writer" while I was at NBC.

For threatening my dad, I wanted these people indicted.

Within twenty-four hours, I had provided prosecutors with my evidence of wrongdoing by the McMaster unit. Also, I had convinced several of my own confidential sources to cooperate with the government, as well. However, I continued to keep confidential the names of those sources who, for reasons of their own, had refused to work with the prosecution, especially my original task-force source.

26. The contract

On November 6, 1976, a Teamster official with whom I had become friendly called me at home. He said that he had just attended a meeting of Teamster leaders in Pittsburgh during which there had been a discussion about having me eliminated. Immediately upon hearing that, I switched on my tape recorder.

"What's the talk?" I asked.

"I'm telling you," he replied, "you'd better watch it!"

"What do you mean?"

"I'm just telling you! You better watch your goddamn step, or you're going to get yourself killed!"

"Why's that?"

"I'm telling you."

Laughing, I continued, "Why? Who said something now?"

Getting angry with me for not taking him seriously, the Teamster said, "You think it's a joke!"

Getting serious, I responded, "No, I don't think it's a joke at all! Why? What's going on?"

"Hell, Dan, some time ago, I just happened to be in an office, and I pick this thing up. And, man, they have the history on you, your family, and everybody else!"

"What's going on? Tell me what the story is! How bad is it?"

"You'd better cool it up in that area!"

"Up in what area?"

"Up in the Michigan area! You've stepped on some pretty big toes!"

"Like who?" I asked. "McMaster?"

"Like Rolland McMaster!"

"Level with me! What's the story?"

"The only thing I can tell you is: you better cool it, you know? I can't tell you to cool it. Just watch your step, because you've been pretty fair with me."

"Yeah, that's right. And that's why I'm asking. Tell me what's going on. . . ."

"You better watch them up in the Detroit area! You better watch the Teamsters! I'm telling you. . . . Oh, man, they got a biography on you that's ten miles long! They know every step you make!"

Now, really concerned, I pleaded, "Give me the whole story. . . . Come on, level with me! Tell me what's happening. . . . "

"I'm telling you one guy you should watch out for is ol' Mac!"

"McMaster? He and I get along!"

"You and him get along? Don't you better believe that!"

"I talked to him about three or four months ago. We got along just fine. . . . Were you up in Michigan when you heard this stuff?"

"Oh, no. I heard it through Pittsburgh. . . . "

"Well, I know that people were pretty upset with me, because of the grand jury that my work started."

"On McQuaide?"

"McQuaide [and] Interstate. . . . Well, tell me about this thing with me."

"I saw a biography on you, complete, you know?"

"A biography?" I asked.

"I mean, complete: Your life, your family, where they work, so forth, everything!"

"Why? Do they do this for all reporters?"

"Do they do it? You're the only guy I've ever heard! Your name was mentioned in a few conversations!"

"And there's no way that anyone could know about you and me! There is no way!" I assured him.

"No! They don't know!"

PART TWO: THE TEAMSTERS & THE MAFIA

"There is no way, because I've never mentioned your name. I don't even keep your telephone number listed anyplace where anybody can find it. . . . [How has] it been discussed?"

"I didn't want to get involved in the conversation when I overheard it, you know? . . . The only thing I'm saying is stay clear of some of them, especially guys that are really loyal to Mac."

The source assured me that I was the target, not my father. Whatever threat had been leveled against Dad was clearly a means to get to me.

Later, I had a second telephone conversation with my source and then a face-to-face meeting with him—where he said that he had heard that a mere $1,500 had passed hands to kill me.

To be sure, I was more humiliated by the embarrassingly low price on my head than fearful about the actual threat to end my life.

After receiving this information, I went to my key sources at the FBI and played the tape for them. When the recording ended, I turned and said to them, "There, what do you think of that?"

One of the FBI agents said. "What are you going to do, Dan?"

"What do you mean: what am I going to do? What are you going to do?" I asked.

"Dan, no crime's been committed yet."

"Guys, in order for a crime to be committed, I've got to be dead! And that's why I've come to you!"

One of them replied, "All we can do is advise you to move to a neutral city."

"A neutral city?" I asked. "What's a neutral city?"

"A neutral city is a city that's not controlled by any particular organized-crime group."

"Like where?"

"Like Miami. Like Las Vegas. Like Washington, D.C. All of the crime families are in those cities. No one group controls any of them."

After this conversation with these federal agents, I telephoned both the person who had allegedly put up the $1,500, as well as the person who had allegedly accepted the money. I knew both of them from my previous work.

Although both adamantly denied any plans to have me killed, I angrily told each of them: "If any member of my family is harmed—if I'm harmed in any way, if I get struck by lightning—you are going to be held responsible for it! I have a tape, which shows that you guys discussed killing me. And the feds now have this tape."

I didn't know whether these calls would do any good, but I did feel better after making them. Regardless of their impact, I decided that it might finally be time to move out of the Midwest.

Next stop: Washington, D.C., a neutral city.

27. To Washington

During a trip to Washington, D.C., in July 1976, I had met Walter Sheridan who had earlier headed Kennedy's "Get Hoffa Squad" while Robert Kennedy served as U.S. Attorney General. I had helped a truck driver with a pension matter, and, in appreciation, he had given me a copy of Sheridan's book, *The Fall and Rise of Jimmy Hoffa*, as a gift. When I gave Sheridan the book for his signature, he added: "Welcome to the fray!"

After the latest conversation with my friends in law enforcement, Sheridan was the first person I called. Telling him about my precarious situation, he also advised me to move to Washington—but to arrive with my eyes open. Underscoring his point, he gave me an article, "Organized Crime in Washington," that appeared in the April 1976 issue of *Washingtonian* magazine. Detailing the history of the mob in Washington, journalist Frank Browning had written:

> No large business can long survive without knowing its territory and its market. This is as true in the underworld as it is in the overworld of legitimate business. To survive is to specialize, for underworld boss and corporate executive alike. That is why the DC police are so misleading when they say there is no "Godfather" for Washington, no single boss or organization of family like Lansky or Gambino or Marcello or Bonanno. For in Washington today there are underworld operators who work with organizations directed by each of these men.

However, if I did move back to Washington, I didn't want to return flying by the seat of my pants as I had in 1973 after graduating from college.

By coincidence, Thaddeus Garrett of Akron, a long-time aide to U.S. Representative Shirley Chisholm (D-New York) and a college friend, had just received a Presidential appointment from Gerald Ford who had lost the November 2 election to President-elect Jimmy Carter. Soon after his defeat and during the transition period, Ford selected Garrett, a black Republican, as a member of the U.S. Consumer Product Safety Commission in Washington.

Garrett called me on November 12 and offered me a job as one of his two special assistants, a position with a GS-13 grade level and a $24,300 annual salary. The other special-assistant post went to attorney Barry Boyd, a former VISTA volunteer and an acquaintance from the University of Akron.

From the outset, I understood the job to be temporary—perhaps six months at the most. Garrett didn't believe that Carter would reappoint him. Still, I was ecstatic about receiving even a temporary federal job in neutral Washington with a good salary, as well as health and life insurance benefits.

It couldn't have come at a better time.

Two weeks later, in early December, I moved to Washington. John Sikorski of PROD and I, along with one of John's friends from their days at Harvard and a woman they both knew, rented a four-bedroom group house on Sixteenth Street—just across the street from the Woodner Hotel, where Jimmy Hoffa had lived in suite B-1250 while he was president of the Teamsters.

I began working for Garrett and CPSC on Monday, December 6, studying such timely issues as the fire risks of TRIS-treated clothing for children and the horrible effects of asbestos in the workplace. Also, Garrett permitted me to continue writing about the Teamsters in my spare time.

Soon after my arrival in Washington, I went to Walter Sheridan's home in Bethesda to pay my respects. After dinner and a long conversation in his living room, Sheridan left momentarily and returned with a large box, which he handed to me.

"What's this, Walt?" I asked.

"It's a present, welcoming you to Washington."

Sheridan had given me his extra set of the Senate Rackets Committee hearing transcripts and reports from 1957-1960. He also handed me a list of other Kennedy aides and their telephone numbers, telling me to contact them and to use his name.

These were very serious gifts.

Meanwhile, Richard Thornburgh, then the head of the Criminal Division in Edward Levi's Justice Department under President Ford, had engineered the elimination of the U.S. Strike Forces Against Organized Crime in several cities, including the unit in Pittsburgh. Consequently, the entire grand-jury investigation of McMaster and his coconspirators had collapsed—even though I knew, as a fact, that federal prosecutors were about to hand up no fewer than five indictments.

Although U.S. Attorney Blair Griffith tried to pick up the case where the Strike Force had been forced to leave it, he was unsuccessful in his efforts to revive it. Later, the new Carter Administration replaced the Republican prosecutor as U.S. attorney, ending the federal investigation of the McMaster Task Force once and for all.

If my calls to the two people who allegedly planned to kill me had not dissuaded them from carrying out their measly $1,500 murder contract because of my cooperation with federal prosecutors, then Thornburgh's decision to wipe out the Pittsburgh Strike Force made killing me completely unnecessary.

In effect, a political maneuver which I openly opposed probably wound up saving my life.

PART THREE:
Hoffa, Marcello & Trafficante

28. "Who is Frank Sheeran?"

On February 22, 1977, a law-enforcement official called and began reading verbatim portions of my exclusive interview with Hoffa's alleged killers at Local 560. Stunned, I asked him where he had received a copy of my transcript, which I had only given to five trusted friends.

He replied that one of his supervisors had laid it on his desk earlier in the day. I asked him to cross-check it and identify the source of the material.

He called back later that day, only saying that the transcript had been passed to his source by an FBI agent in New Jersey.

Immediately, I called Bob Windrem in New Brunswick and confronted him, asking if he had given the transcript of my interview with Sal Briguglio and his colleagues to the FBI.

An honest guy, Windrem immediately admitted it, saying that he needed some information from the FBI for a story he was writing, unrelated to the article that we had worked on together. Apparently, with nothing else to trade, he gave his FBI contact my transcript with Hoffa's alleged killers.

It was a really rotten thing to do, especially to a friend and colleague. And, needless to say, Windrem's out-of-character betrayal put an immediate damper on our friendship.

Two months later, on April 25, Steven Brill, a talented writer and legal columnist at *Esquire*, called me. Brill explained that he had recently received a contract with a large advance from Simon & Schuster to write a major book about the Teamsters Union, adding that he was planning to hire Jim Drinkhall and Bob Windrem as his consultants.

Nearly dropping the receiver after hearing those two names, I politely asked Brill why he was calling me. Equally polite, he replied that he wanted me to send him copies of my articles from the *Free Press* and Jack Anderson. He also asked whether I would authorize Windrem to give him a copy of my interview with Hoffa's alleged killers.

Trying to get along with this guy and assuming that Windrem had probably already given him the transcript, I authorized the release and agreed to send him the two articles he requested.

Knowing that I was now competing with Brill—who probably had access to much of what I knew through Windrem—I began working even harder on my own book.

I sent a new proposal to Philip Spitzer, asking him to resubmit it to Doubleday, which had rejected my earlier idea but still remained interested. However, this time, I had a strong letter of support for the project from Clark Mollenhoff, a Pulitzer Prize-winning reporter from the *Des Moines Register and Tribune* whose investigations into Hoffa and the Teamsters had led to the formation of the Senate Rackets Committee in February 1957.

Then, four days after his first call, Brill telephoned again to discuss my interview with Hoffa's alleged killers.

My new girlfriend, Tina—a smart and politically-savvy women's-rights activist with whom I was now living in Georgetown—predicted that Brill was going to try to cut my throat after he got everything he needed out of me.

The following week, Brill and I met for the first time over breakfast at the Capitol Hilton in Washington. I had respected him from the first time I talked to him on the phone, even though—thanks to Tina—I now saw through the competitive-edge game he was playing with me.

Brill—who, like me, was born in 1950—said that he had heard that I was in the midst of writing my own book about the Teamsters. Confirming that, I added that I saw no problem trading information. However, I was embarrassed when he asked whether I had a publisher, and I had to reply that I did not.

Trying to make it clear that he had already left me in the dust, Brill boasted that he "owned" Ohio Teamster boss Jackie Presser, who was introducing him to the top people in the Teamsters high command, including Frank Fitzsimmons.

Also, Brill informed me that he had obtained a secret FBI report, the *Hoffex Memo*, as he called it. According to Brill, this document detailed what the FBI knew about the events surrounding July 30, 1975, the day Hoffa vanished, including a likely scenario of his murder.

Now truly impressed, I asked Brill to tell me more. He alleged that a Teamster official named Frank Sheeran had been involved in the murder, and that everyone had missed him at the December 4, 1975, federal grand-jury hearing in Detroit. Like McMaster, the Briguglios, and the Andrettas, Sheeran had also taken the Fifth.

Completely deflated by all of this, I returned to my office and called one of my FBI sources.

"What the hell is the *Hoffex Memo*? I asked.

"I don't know," he replied. "What is it?"

"I just had breakfast with a guy named Steve Brill who's writing a book about the Teamsters, and he says he has a copy of the *Hoffex Memo*, which tells everything about what happened to Hoffa on the day of the murder!"

"Dan, *Hoffex* is the code name for our entire Hoffa investigation. We've had a lot of reports...."

I interrupted, clearly not knowing what I was talking about, "What about the one that spells everything out?"

"We don't know what really happened, so we couldn't write a definitive document about what did happen."

"Well, who, then, is Frank Sheeran?"

My FBI source fell speechless.

Hearing his screaming silence, I asked with dread, "Oh, shit! What have I missed?"

"I can't talk about him, Dan."

"Wait a minute! What about confirm and deny? What about keeping me on track?"

Pausing for a moment, he replied, "Okay, yes, we're interested in Sheeran. This is the first time you've asked me about him. So, I'm telling you now, stay on that track. We can't prove anything, but he could be important."

29. "To do two things at once is to do neither"

On May 23, my agent, Philip Spitzer, called to tell me that Doubleday had rejected my book proposal for a second time, so I still had no publisher. When I asked Spitzer what the problem was, he honestly told me that my work read like a report from a police blotter. I replied with considerable frustration that I would prepare another proposal—*after* I learned how to write. I asked him to give me a couple of days.

I called Mrs. Nolte and explained my dilemma. She instructed me to get my copy of the book, *The New Journalism* by Tom Wolfe and E. W. Johnson, which she had sent me for Christmas 1976, and to re-read it. Telling me that I had to learn how to make my nonfiction prose read like fiction, she added that the most important element in successful writing was good storytelling—and that the secret to good storytelling was the use of immediacy to grab the reader's attention.

That night, after reading portions of the Wolfe and Johnson book, I composed a section of my chapter about the 1967 steel-haulers strike, writing:

> The rust-colored carbon vapors from towering smokestacks of steel mills billowed into the skies over Gary, Indiana, while their grimy residue covered the city below. Impoverished steel haulers could only look to the filthy heavens for relief from their low wages and poor working conditions. . . .

"Okay, so it was my first shot," I told Mrs. Nolte after I read it to her, and she stopped laughing.

But, later, I wrote:

> Owner-operators had to keep moving to make ends meet. They broke speed limits, hauled longer than the ten hours a day the government permitted, and sometimes popped pills to stay awake. Pushing themselves to the brink, some drivers broke under the strain, destroying their family lives or themselves.
>
> "Trade that damn white elephant in, and come to work in the factory," their friends say.
>
> Bill Kusley didn't like the conditions of the industry but would give anybody who told him to leave it a "fuck you" scowl as he climbed into his rig to deliver another load of steel. A part-time farmer and son of a United Steel Workers organizer, Kusley was a barely literate "deez" and "doze" person who talked constantly, insufferably about the truckers' revolution.
>
> "If deez sonobitches runnin' ya 'round, we'll strike da mothafuckas. Take his fuckin' tires; shut 'em down."

Mrs. Nolte liked this new approach and instructed me to keep going. Also, she told me that since Brill already had a contract to do a book about the Teamsters, I should write my book about Jimmy Hoffa, incorporating my materials about Allen Dorfman and the Central States Pension Fund, the rank-and-file reformers, the steel haulers, the McMaster Task Force, Local 299, and Hoffa's murder into an investigative biography of Hoffa. She reminded me that Walter Sheridan had given me his contacts from the Justice Department, as well as an entire set of hearings from the Senate Rackets Committee, which focused on Hoffa's early career.

PART THREE: HOFFA, MARCELLO & TRAFFICANTE

After calling Sheridan to seek out his advice, I went back and rewrote the proposal, now pitching the book as a chronicle of Hoffa's rise and fall: *Legacy of Violence: Inside Hoffa's Detroit.*

Philip Spitzer hated the title, but he liked what I had done with the proposal and my sample chapter on the steel haulers. He told me that he believed that he could now sell the book.

On Wednesday, June 15, Joan Tapper, the editor of the New Republic Book Company in Washington, D.C., and I had a luncheon meeting arranged by Spitzer. She said that she was interested in my book but wanted to see additional sample chapters. Two days later, I gave her two more.

While waiting for the New Republic to make its decision, I flew to Detroit on June 24 for a meeting with another member of the McMaster Task Force who said he wanted to talk. Steve Riddle and one of his assistants accompanied me to the meeting.

During the discussion, the task-force organizer and I got into an argument after he was suddenly stricken with a bad case of amnesia. Furious with him for making me come to Detroit for nothing, I taunted him, trying to get him to open up.

Instead of talking, we wound up in a fistfight. Both of us landed punches, but neither of us was hurt. Riddle and his aide, who was bigger than both of us, broke up the fight after which the organizer stormed out of the room.

Back in Washington, my work on the Hoffa book had already begun to clash with my work at the CPSC. With my parents coming to Washington for the weekend to meet Tina, I decided to stall a decision until I had a chance to talk to them and get their advice.

On Saturday night, July 9, Mom and Dad took us to Trader Vic's. During dinner, I explained the situation to my folks. Of course, they advised me to keep my job until I had the book contract in hand. But, concerned with Brill's head start with his own book, I feared that if I didn't start working on my book full-time, he would come out long before me.

Then, after dinner, I broke open my fortune cookie, which simply read: *"To do two things at once is to do neither."*

On Monday, I went to my boss, Thadd Garrett, thanked him for giving me the job that allowed me to come to neutral Washington, and then gave him my two-week notice.

A month later, on Wednesday, August 10, Philip Spitzer called. Joan Tapper and the New Republic Book Company had offered an ego-shattering $5,500 advance for my proposed book.

But, because I wanted to take on Brill, I decided to swallow my pride and accept this lowball deal.

30. The *Hoffex Memo*

While I continued my research on Hoffa and the Teamsters, Bob Windrem had left New Brunswick and the *Home News* to take a job as PROD's new research director. Now spending time in Washington, Windrem continued working as a consultant for Brill.

Knowing that Windrem and I would be constantly running into each other, John Sikorski tried to make peace by getting the three of us together for dinner on July 26. I agreed to the sitdown, but I had only one item on my agenda: To find out what Brill knew.

When I first saw Windrem, I couldn't have been colder. I wanted him on the defensive from the outset. Sikorski, always the peacemaker, tried to warm things up by recounting our individual adventures in our wars against the Teamsters' high command.

I remained quiet for several moments. Then, acting as if we were three mob guys trying to prevent the big war, I finally said with a straight face, "Bob, you betrayed me. And, now, you must atone. I gotta know about this *Hoffex Memo*."

Sikorski, who had heard me talk about this mysterious document, became very quiet and sat back, waiting for Windrem's response.

Windrem thought for a moment and then laid it out for us.

In January 1976, FBI Director Clarence Kelley had convened a conference about the Hoffa case. In the wake of this meeting of FBI agents and federal prosecutors, a fifty-to-sixty page document resulted—the *Hoffex Memo*.

"Have you seen this report?" I asked. "What's in it?"

Windrem said that Brill had flashed it at him but didn't allow him to study the document. However, Brill did highlight the report for him, verbally. Windrem then recounted his conversation with Brill for Sikorski and me.

To my great relief, the *Hoffex Memo* contained very little that I didn't already know. However, Windrem said that the report did implicate

Frank Sheeran, the president of Teamsters Local 326 in Wilmington, Delaware, in the murder. When I asked Windrem what role Sheeran played, he replied that Brill was keeping the Sheeran material close to his chest.

Then, Windrem volunteered that Brill would allege in his book that Frank Fitzsimmons had personally arranged for the disposal of Hoffa's body via Detroit Mafia figures Peter Vitale and Jimmy Quasarano. The two mobsters had allegedly placed Hoffa "in a waste compactor at Central Sanitation Services."

Hearing this news, Sikorski was stunned, and I pretended to be shocked, too. However, without saying anything to Sikorski and Windrem, I immediately realized that Brill's theory about Central Sanitation was wrong. That scenario had been among the first to surface after the disappearance. And I already knew as a fact from my own sources that the FBI had rejected it.

The following day, I called one of my sources at the FBI and told him what I had heard about the *Hoffex Memo*.

"Don't worry about it," he said. "It's nothing. Just keep working with what you already know."

But, before we ended our conversation, I said to the FBI man, "Let me ask you about Central Sanitation. Do you guys believe that Vitale and Quasarano disposed of Hoffa's body at Central Sanitation?"

"Central Sanitation? Are you kidding? We told you nearly two years ago that we had dismissed that theory. There was a proposed draft search warrant that was drawn up for Central Sanitation, but it was never executed. That story is bullshit."

31. The killing of the President

On Tuesday, September 27, during a meeting about my book with Howard Bray, the executive director of the Fund for Investigative Journalism, and its board president Milton Viorst, they suggested that I contact a researcher named Michael Ewing, who had worked with Viorst and received grants from the fund for a story about the murder of President John Kennedy.

Viorst and Ewing had written an interesting article in the November 1975 issue of *Washingtonian*, "The Mafia, the CIA, and the Kennedy Assassination," in which they presented evidence that the CIA and the

Mafia might have worked together in a plot to kill the President. Viorst added that Ewing had also co-authored the paperback book, *Coincidence or Conspiracy?*, a compendium of all the major conspiracy theories about the Kennedy assassination.

When I went home and told Tina about my conversation with Bray and Viorst, she rolled her eyes, saying skeptically, "The Kennedy assassination?"

But, despite my trusted girlfriend's reaction, I was intrigued by Hoffa's possible connection to this murder case.

By mid-1977, most critics of the Warren Commission were either directly or indirectly agreeing with the discredited, mobbed-up New Orleans District Attorney Jim Garrison that the CIA was involved in the President's murder. Some were trying to prove that three hobos arrested in Dealey Plaza on the day of the murder later became the Watergate burglars—a theory that was soon annihilated when evidence surfaced that the hobos were, in fact, hobos. No one had even suggested, at least in writing and in any detail, that the President's murder was a straight mob hit with Hoffa's participation.[24]

That same day, I called Mike Ewing and had a long conversation with him. He said that he had been looking for an opportunity to investigate a possible Hoffa connection to the JFK murder, adding that there was also some evidence that Hoffa could have been involved in the CIA-Mafia murder plots against Fidel Castro, which had recently been revealed by a U.S. Senate panel called the Church Committee, named after its chairman, Senator Frank Church (D-Idaho).

In addition, Ewing had obtained Jack Ruby's telephone toll records. They showed that during the days and weeks before Kennedy's murder, Ruby had called and received calls from several people close to Hoffa and Carlos Marcello, the Mafia boss of New Orleans.

Ewing asked me if I had ever talked to Edward "Grady" Partin, the key government witness against Hoffa at his 1964 jury-tampering trial in Chattanooga. I told Ewing that I had spoken with Partin in 1975 in the aftermath of Hoffa's disappearance while I was working with NBC News in Detroit. Walter Sheridan had introduced me to him.

Ewing told me to call Partin and ask him about Hoffa, the Castro plots, and the Kennedy murder. That night, I interviewed Partin again. He told me about Hoffa's 1959 gun-running activities in Cuba, his illegal $500,000 contribution to Richard Nixon during the 1960 Presidential election, and a proposed plot by Hoffa to kill Robert Kennedy in 1962.

Partin also explained that—during Hoffa's appeal process in the aftermath of his conviction in Chattanooga—New Orleans District

PART THREE: HOFFA, MARCELLO & TRAFFICANTE

Attorney Jim Garrison, as a favor to either Hoffa or Marcello or both, had actually tried to implicate Partin as a suspect in his already off-the-wall New Orleans investigation of the murder of President Kennedy. An attorney for Hoffa, Frank Ragano, had approached Partin and told him that he could make Garrison go away—if Partin agreed to sign an affidavit recanting his earlier testimony in Chattanooga against Hoffa.

Partin refused, and Hoffa went to prison.

Earlier, Walter Sheridan had given me a March 13, 1967, FBI 302-interview report with I. Irving Davidson, a Washington public-relations man who did work for both Hoffa and Marcello. In this document, captioned, "Assassination of President John F. Kennedy," the FBI wrote:

> Edward G. Partin . . . will be subpoenaed by [Garrison's] grand jury in New Orleans, Louisiana, in the near future in connection with his possible involvement in captioned matter. Davidson stated that he has heard there is a photograph available of Partin in the presence of Jack Ruby (deceased), convicted of killing Lee Harvey Oswald.

Partin also went into a long recitation about Davidson, to whom Jack Anderson associate Marc Smolonsky had introduced me in July 1976. According to Partin, Davidson, who had shared an office with Anderson, was Marcello's man in Washington.[25]

The following day, before I talked to Ewing again, I called Davidson, and we had an argument over the questions I was asking. But he admitted his business relationships with Hoffa and Marcello, as well as his role in shipping arms and ammunition to both sides in the Cuban Revolution. Davidson explained that the people he represented, who had financed the arms deals, wanted to make sure that they supported the winning side.

The Mafia had made millions of dollars from its gambling and narcotics networks in Cuba, protected by President Fulgencio Batista who was on the Mafia's pad. When Castro threatened the status quo, the underworld tried to buy his goodwill, as well.

When Castro seized control of Cuba on January 1, 1959, the Mafia believed that its operations would remain intact. In fact, Jimmy Hoffa had attempted to arrange a Central States Pension Fund loan for a company that would deliver a fleet of Army surplus cargo planes to the new Cuban government.

However, the deal collapsed after Castro double-crossed the mob, closing the gambling casinos and imprisoning Marcello's partner, Mafia boss Santo Trafficante of Tampa. In addition, Castro shut down the narcotics-supply network operating in Cuba and exiled Marcello back to New Orleans.

Consequently, Meyer Lansky, the legendary "financial wizard of organized crime," put out a million-dollar murder contract on Castro. At first, no known takers stepped forward. But, by December 1959, Castro was widely viewed as a communist. Now, he not only angered the Mafia but the United States Government.

That same month, the CIA began what became known as the CIA-Mafia plots against Castro.

Eight months later, in August 1960, James O'Connell, a CIA support chief—working under Richard Bissell, the head of covert operations—contacted a close friend, Howard Hughes aide Robert Maheu. O'Connell wanted to bring Trafficante, recently released from a Cuban prison, into the caper and asked Maheu to help. Maheu received the support of an old friend, Chicago mobster Johnny Rosselli, who solicited the cooperation of Sam Giancana, who then brought in Trafficante—with the likely advice and consent of Trafficante's long-time partner, Carlos Marcello.

On October 5, Ewing and I met for the first time at the Library of Congress. During our meeting, I asked him to help me with my book. In return, Ewing said that he wanted $1,200, which was over twenty percent of my $5,500 advance from the New Republic. I agreed.

To offset the money I wanted to give Ewing, I applied for another grant to the Fund for Investigative Journalism. "As you know," I wrote to Howard Bray, "I have had financial difficulties in my freelance career, and I want to make sure that Mr. Ewing is treated fairly."

With a strong letter of recommendation from my editor, Joan Tapper at the New Republic, the fund approved my request for $1,200 on October 21. I gave all of the money to Ewing.

Three days before receiving the grant, I had lunch with Walter Sheridan. I told Sheridan about my deal with Ewing, whom he knew, and the nature of our probe. Sheridan replied that he had a healthy respect for Ewing but advised me to watch myself in any investigation of the Kennedy assassination. He warned that writing a book that included a JFK conspiracy theory could jeopardize the credibility of everything else contained in the manuscript, including my new revelations about the violence in Local 299 and Hoffa's murder.

32. "I think my dad knew Jack Ruby"

While Ewing and I moved fast and hard with our Kennedy murder investigation, I continued my interviews with the Teamsters' crowd. Remaining in touch with Bill Bufalino, I had a second exclusive interview with Salvatore Briguglio and, separately, another with Steve Andretta.

Chuck O'Brien refused to sit down for a face-to-face interview, but I did catch him at a weak moment. We had a long telephone conversation during which he, of course, continued to deny any role in Hoffa's murder, but he did discuss some of the key players in the case.[26]

During a quick trip to Detroit, I spent several hours with Louis Linteau, the last known person to speak by phone with Hoffa—after which he introduced me to his employees who had talked to Hoffa in person while he was en route to the Red Fox. In addition, I finished my interviews with some of the victims of the violence in Local 299—Jimmy Clift, Gene Page, George Roxburgh, Red Anderson, and even Ralph Proctor and Dick Fitzsimmons. And I wrapped up my discussions with several leaders of the Teamsters for Democratic Union and its previous incarnations in the heroic rank-and-file reform movements.

Also, in mid-November, I again interviewed Otto Wendell, the local's secretary-treasurer. The following month, on December 12, Wendell was found shot twice in his car. He never regained consciousness and died on Christmas Eve. He had been killed with his own gun. The police, who ruled out suicide, didn't know whether Wendell had shot himself accidentally or whether he had been murdered.

Tina and I were in Detroit when Wendell died, spending the Christmas holidays with her parents at their home in Southfield.

Two days after Christmas, I visited Jimmy Hoffa, Jr., whom I had not seen since I left the *Detroit Free Press*, at his law office. Murray Chodak, Hoffa's law partner, was also present.

"How's your book going, Dan?" Hoffa asked.

"Pretty good, pretty good," I replied. "I've been busting my ass on it. . . . I should probably tell you something, though."

"What's that?"

"I've collected a lot of evidence, and I'm going to claim that your father, Carlos Marcello, and Santo Trafficante arranged and executed President Kennedy's murder in 1963."

Clearly agitated, Hoffa shot back, "That's such bullshit, Dan. I think my dad knew Jack Ruby, but from what I understand, he [Ruby] was the kind of guy everybody knew. So what?"

Seeing me react to his statement, Hoffa started to backpedal, saying he couldn't recall any specific information upon which he based his opinion. However, he did add, "It doesn't make any sense." Pausing for a moment, he continued, "If my dad had decided to kill Kennedy, he would have gotten a gun, walked right up to him, and blew his brains out."

Actually, I was still stunned over Hoffa's statement that he believed his father "knew Jack Ruby." No one, not even among the hard-core conspiracy theorists, had ever made that allegation.

Seeing me pull out my notepad to write down the quote, Hoffa exclaimed, "That's off the record!"

"Bullshit, Jimmy!" I replied. "You know the rules. When you want something off the record, you say so. And then you make your statement. You don't wait to see my reaction, and then try to take it off the record. That statement is on the record."

Turning quickly to Chodak, Hoffa said, "What did I just say, Murray?"

"I didn't hear you say anything, Jim," Chodak insisted.

Turning towards me, Hoffa concluded, "See, Dan? It's our word against yours! What do you have? You have nothing!"

As the conversation quickly deteriorated, I left the office but finished writing down Hoffa's quotes on my notepad as I walked to the elevator.

—⚏—

Although I had collected a great deal of information about the Teamsters, I needed as much information as I could get about the inside workings of the Mafia, particularly as they related to Hoffa's rise and fall.

On February 2, I conducted my first of three five-hour interviews over dinner at the Monocle Restaurant on Capitol Hill with Ralph Salerno, the former supervisor of detectives for the New York City Police Department. Actually, more than being interviewed, Salerno, one of the top organized-crime experts in the country, talked while I took notes and asked questions. He was the knowledgeable teacher, and I was the eager student.

During my last session with Salerno—who had recently been appointed as the chief consultant on organized crime for the U.S. House

PART THREE: HOFFA, MARCELLO & TRAFFICANTE

Select Committee on Assassinations—we discussed the murder of President Kennedy. Telling him what Ewing and I believed, he would later say to me, "There is no solid evidence yet that Carlos Marcello, Santo Trafficante, Jimmy Hoffa, or any other criminal or criminal associate had been involved in a conspiracy to kill President Kennedy. Regardless of whether they knew or not, they should have built the largest statue in the world to Lee Harvey Oswald. No one man has ever done as much damage to this country's war on the underworld as he did."

33. Findings

In early March, my associate, Mike Ewing, like Ralph Salerno before him, received an appointment to join the staff of the U.S. House Select Committee on Assassinations from its new chief counsel, G. Robert Blakey, who had replaced former federal prosecutor Richard Sprague of Philadelphia. Like Salerno, Blakey was widely known as one of the world's top experts on the subject of organized crime.

Completing his excellent work for me, Ewing gave me an eighty-page summary of our findings. Combining that with what I had learned since my investigations of the Teamsters began in late 1974, I drew up a list of my conclusions, which included:

> * Hoffa, who was directly involved in gunrunning activities in pre-revolution Cuba, might have been involved during the early CIA-Mafia plots against Fidel Castro. Ewing and I had learned that mobsters Russell Bufalino, Salvatore Granello and James Plumeri of New York's Lucchese family, as well as John LaRocca and Gabriel Mannarino of the Pittsburgh Mafia—all business associates of Hoffa—had been directly involved in the plots. Mafia figure-turned-protected witness Charles Crimaldi specifically told me that Hoffa was the "original liaison" between the CIA and the Mafia.
>
> * During the 1960 Democratic convention, Sam Giancana, via Frank Sinatra, introduced Presidential nominee John Kennedy to a woman, Judith Campbell, with whom Kennedy had an affair. Ewing and I believed that this was a blatant but unsuccessful attempt by the Mafia to blackmail the Kennedys to relent

in their war against organized crime, which they had initiated during the Senate Rackets Committee.

* Even after the Mafia's blackmail scheme over the Campbell affair became known to the Kennedys in 1962, the Kennedy Administration's war against the mob intensified.

* Upon being elected President and appointing his brother as attorney general, John Kennedy authorized an official, full-scale war on the Mafia, targeting Hoffa, Marcello, and Trafficante, among others.

* John and Robert Kennedy knew nothing about the CIA-Mafia plots until the spring of 1962 when FBI Director J. Edgar Hoover, who had earlier denied the existence of the Mafia, told the President about them.[27]

* After learning about the CIA-Mafia plots against Castro in May 1962, an angry Robert Kennedy went to the CIA and ordered them stopped.[28]

* During September 1962, three important discussions took place. 1) Hoffa had a conversation with Ed Partin about having Robert Kennedy killed. 2) Marcello had a conversation with government informant Ed Becker, nixing the idea of killing the Attorney General and targeting the President instead.[29] 3) Trafficante had a conversation with government informer Jose Aleman, saying that the President was "going to be hit" and that Hoffa was making the arrangements.

* Further, I believed that the assassination of President Kennedy had been arranged and executed by Marcello, Trafficante, and Hoffa. Our investigation included details about those who were in contact with Jack Ruby prior to the assassination: Hoffa aides Barney Baker, Irwin Weiner, and Murray Miller, as well as Marcello confidant Nofio Pecora. (Ewing had interviewed Baker, and I interviewed Weiner, whom I had previously met in Chicago with Allen Dorfman, whose stepfather, Paul Dorfman, was the head of the Chicago Wastehandlers Union where Ruby had worked as a union organizer.)

PART THREE: HOFFA, MARCELLO & TRAFFICANTE

* The FBI and CIA, which were *not* involved in the President's murder, had engaged in institutional coverups in the wake of the killing. The FBI wanted to conceal its failure to recognize the existence of the Mafia. The CIA wanted to conceal its murder plots against Castro with the Mafia.

* It is reasonable to assume that if CIA Director Allen Dulles, who sat on the Warren Commission, had revealed the existence of the CIA-Mafia plots against Castro that a whole new avenue of investigation would have resulted.

* The investigation of President Kennedy's murder by corrupt New Orleans District Attorney Jim Garrison was nothing more than a deliberate effort to deflect attention away from Marcello who had Garrison on his pad. Garrison had also used his fraudulent probe to help Hoffa—by claiming that Ed Partin, the key witness against the Teamster leader in his 1964 jury-tampering trial, had been seen with Lee Harvey Oswald and Jack Ruby. Hoffa's attorney, Frank Ragano, assured Partin that Garrison would clear him—if he recanted his testimony against Hoffa.

* Murdered in the midst of the Church Committee hearings during the summer of 1975—which was investigating the CIA-Mafia plots against Castro—Hoffa had been leaking information to the committee about the activities of his former mobster-partners who had since become his enemies.[30] Also, he was cooperating with federal and state law-enforcement officials who were investigating corruption in the Teamsters Union.

* The same mobsters who authorized the Hoffa killing had ordered the murder of Sam Giancana on June 19, 1975, fewer than six weeks before Hoffa disappeared and a year before the murder of Johnny Rosselli in August 1976. (Rosselli was last seen on a boat owned by Santo Trafficante.)

* Russell Bufalino, who was involved in the earliest stages of the CIA-Mafia plots against Castro, authorized Hoffa's murder which was handled by Salvatore Briguglio, upon the orders of Anthony Provenzano. Others allegedly complicit in the Hoffa

murder included Gabriel Briguglio, Thomas and Stephen Andretta, and Frank Sheeran.

* The Hoffa murder had more to do with silencing him in the midst of the investigations of his participation in the Castro plots and John Kennedy's murder than with his attempts to return to power in the union—and that Marcello and Trafficante had both checked off on the Hoffa hit. Chicago mobster Charles Crimaldi specifically told me that Hoffa had been killed on orders from the same mobsters who had been involved in the CIA-Mafia plots.

* Also, Crimaldi told me that Hoffa's body had been crushed and smelted in a car compactor—which was consistent with my belief that Hoffa's body had been picked up by someone driving a truck from Gateway's steel division in suburban Detroit, which hauled tons of steel each day for crushing and smelting. In addition, Partin informed me that Chuck O'Brien had allegedly told him that Hoffa was now either a hub cup or a fender.

* Rolland McMaster—along with his two associates, Larry McHenry and Jim Shaw, who were both involved in the Local 299 violence before Hoffa's disappeared—might have been involved in the disposal of Hoffa's body. On the afternoon of Hoffa's murder, McMaster's alibi was that he was out of town with his brother-in-law, Stanton Barr, the head of Gateway's steel division. When McMaster returned that night, he went to his home in Southfield, which was just a five-minute drive from the restaurant where Hoffa was last seen.

34. Brill and S & S get tough

When I signed my book deal with the New Republic, I did not realize that my publisher had an exclusive distribution contract with Simon & Schuster, the publisher of Brill's book. After I discovered this arrangement, my heart nearly stopped—even though the New Republic assured me that the situation posed no threat to my work.

Then, on Tuesday, February 7, 1978, Joan Tapper, my editor at the New Republic, told me that she had received a call from Alice Mayhew, Brill's editor at S & S. The powerful editor of Bob Woodward and Carl Bernstein's *All the President's Men*, among many other best-selling books, Mayhew expressed a growing concern about my book, adding that she wanted Brill to come out alone and in an open field.

Surprised by the call, Tapper politely defended her right to publish my book, suggesting that she would put up a fight if Simon & Schuster gave the New Republic any distribution problems. After the conversation between Mayhew and Tapper, Raphael Sagalyn, the publicity director of the New Republic, sent a conciliatory follow-up letter to Mayhew, insisting that the two books would actually complement each other.

Eight days later, on February 15, Brill called me, asking for Rolland McMaster's date of birth. Not very threatened by that question, I gave it to him.

During our continuing conversation, Brill said that he was upset because he could not get his book out until the end of January 1979 at the earliest. Then, Brill started pumping me for my publication date. I replied that my book would come out at Christmas.

Actually, both of us were being cagey, and both of us knew it. In fact, both of our books were scheduled for late-summer releases, even though they were on the fall list.

That same night, Bob Windrem, still one of Brill's two consultants, called and made a formal offer on Brill's behalf: Brill would give me some of his "exclusive" material, like the *Hoffex Memo*, if I would simply credit him for those items I used. Certainly, I had no problem with that arrangement, assuming that Brill had anything I really needed or wanted.

The following day, as Windrem had directed, I called Brill, who confirmed that he had authorized the offer made by Windrem. However, Brill added, "There's a problem if your book is going to come out before mine."

Then, Brill said that he would give me anything I wanted in his book—if I delayed publication until after his book was released. I laughed, saying that, under those conditions, I didn't really need his help, adding that my book was strong enough to compete with his, head-to-head.

At that moment, even though I was simply protecting my work, I knew that a spirited competitor had now become an unwanted adversary.

On Wednesday, March 8, I called Rafe Sagalyn at the New Republic to ask him a question about the anticipated promotion of my book.

Suddenly, he interrupted me and became deadly serious, predicting that Simon & Schuster might "move slowly on our book" because of the competition with the Brill book.

I asked what the chances were that Simon & Schuster would flatly refuse to distribute my book. Sagalyn replied that it was unlikely, because that decision would invite legal action. He told me that it would be easier for S & S to remain in control of my book by telling their salesmen to downplay it. Sagalyn added that Simon & Schuster was already promising booksellers around the country that Brill's book would be "the book of the year."

That same day, I called my agent, Philip Spitzer, who had stuck with me during my four years of research on Hoffa and the Teamsters and finally sold my book to the New Republic. He advised me to find a good lawyer.

The next day, I telephoned Tina's personal attorney and explained the situation. He predicted that there was going to be trouble, and that Simon & Schuster was going to suppress my book, giving Brill no competition at all.

Immediately after that, I slaved day and night for nearly three weeks to finish my book. I'd type on my manual typewriter for twelve straight hours, crash for twenty minutes, and then get back to my desk.

Wearing headphones, I'd listen to anything that kept me up and moving, ranging from Dvorak's *New World Symphony* to the theme song from *Rocky* to just about anything on the Motown label.

I started living again on my version of the four basic food groups: Chinese food, pizza, fried chicken, and cheeseburgers. Smoking between three and four packs of Kools a day, I literally beat myself into the ground.

When Tina saw me slowing down, she would walk up behind me, slide off my headphones, and simply whisper in my ear, "Steven Brill."

35. Briguglio and I get whacked

On March 14, my new attorney's law partner, Steve Martindale—a popular Washington man-about-town who also represented Perrier Water and the Beach Boys' record company—called Martin Peretz, the publisher of the *New Republic* magazine and the owner of its book company. Martindale asked if Simon & Schuster was going to pose a problem for us.

Peretz responded that the worst that could possibly happen would be for Simon & Schuster to sit on my Hoffa book and not try very hard to sell it. However, he added that he was prepared to defend his interest in my work.

The next day, after I received Mrs. Nolte's critique of my book and made several necessary changes, I gave my nearly completed manuscript to the New Republic. The only chapter missing was about Hoffa's disappearance.

In a letter to my publisher—drafted by my attorneys—I promised to deliver this chapter after the crisis with Simon & Schuster played out. Meantime, I gave the book to three trusted friends for their comments: Arthur Fox, Ralph Salerno, and Walter Sheridan.

Also, to the delight of Philip Spitzer and the New Republic, I had changed the name of the book from *Inside Hoffa's Detroit* to a title Tina had suggested, *The Hoffa Wars*.

On Monday, March 20 at 4:00 P.M., Joan Tapper and Rafe Sagalyn were informed that Simon & Schuster had flatly refused to distribute my book. The decision was made by Richard Snyder, the president of the publishing house since 1975, shortly after the conglomerate Gulf & Western bought S & S.

Snyder had the audacity to instruct the New Republic to hold my book until the spring of 1979. Snyder claimed that, under the contract I had signed with the New Republic, he could legally take this action.

I knew nothing of this decision, even after I telephoned Sagalyn that same night at 8:00 P.M. For whatever reason, Sagalyn chose not to tell me about Simon & Schuster's action, probably assuming that it was not yet a *fait accompli*.

The next day, March 21, at 10:00 A.M., I called Tapper to discuss the chapter about Hoffa's murder. By the tone of her voice, I knew something was wrong. But like Sagalyn the night before, she refused to discuss it. Stalling me, she said that she was in a meeting and would call me back later. Finally, at 2:30 that afternoon, Tapper called and asked me to come to the New Republic in two hours. She said it was not a matter that could be discussed on the telephone.

At 4:30 P.M., Tapper and Sagalyn dropped the bomb, explaining what had transpired over the past two days.

Storming out of Tapper's office, I immediately called my attorneys from a pay phone on the street and asked them to move against Simon & Schuster and, if necessary, the New Republic.

When I returned home later that evening, Tina had more bad news for me. Sal Briguglio, whom I had interviewed for a fourth time the previous month, had just been murdered in New York.

Many believed that Briguglio, who was under indictment for the 1961 murder of a union rival, was on the verge of flipping and turning state's evidence about the Hoffa murder.

During my final taped interview with him, Briguglio—worn and tired, showing the strain of the enormous federal pressure he was under—told me, "I've got no regrets, except for getting involved in this mess with the government. If they want you, you're theirs.... I have no aspirations any more. I've gone as far as I can go in this union. There's nothing left."[31]

Devastated from everything that had happened that day, I called one of my sources in the FBI's Washington Field Office who was actively involved in the Hoffa case. He gave me the known details about Briguglio's murder. In short, two unidentified men had walked up to him in New York's Little Italy and knocked him to the sidewalk. Then, they pulled out guns and shot him four times in the head and once in the chest.

Trying to finish my chapter on the Hoffa case, I again asked one of my FBI guys in Detroit what he believed had happened to Hoffa *after* his murder. Once again, the FBI agent told me not to worry about Brill's Central Sanitation theory about the disposal of Hoffa's body... because he was dead wrong.

On March 28, one week after Briguglio's murder, I called Frank Sheeran and tape-recorded the conversation, trying to get him to discuss anything—just as long as I got him talking. As it turned out, I caught him on the run. But he said that he was going to be in Washington the following Monday.

During our brief conversation, I brought up the testimonial dinner that his Teamsters local in Wilmington, Delaware, had thrown for him in 1974—at which Hoffa was the keynote speaker. Sheeran told me, "The only thing I can say about [Hoffa] is all good.... Now, the thing is that you just want to talk about Jimmy and his personality, *per se?* You're not talking about any other bullshit?"

"Not unless you want to get into it," I replied.

"No," he laughed, "I don't want to get into that shit, my friend. I don't know anything to get into. As far as he goes, I could tell you my feelings towards the guy, and my relationship, and the kind of man I thought he was. That I can tell you. Anything else, I don't know."

Sheeran said that he was going to check me out and call at the end of the following week.

We never spoke again.

As I had already learned, Hoffa and Sheeran were, indeed, very close friends. In fact, I believed that Sheeran could have been in the car that picked up Hoffa on the day of his disappearance. To be sure, Hoffa would have gotten in a car with him.

But that was nothing but pure speculation. I had absolutely no evidence to justify placing Sheeran in that car for publication in my upcoming book—even though I now had enough evidence to implicate him in the overall murder conspiracy.

36. Paddington to the rescue

After we learned of Simon & Schuster's blatant attempt to suppress *The Hoffa Wars*, my lawyer, Steve Martindale, contacted Paddington Press, a small but aggressive London-based publisher. Martindale was in the midst of negotiating a deal with the company to publish a book by another client, Margaret Trudeau, the estranged wife of Canadian Prime Minister Pierre Trudeau.

On March 29, I flew to New York and met Paddington's publisher, John Marqusee. I asked my agent, Philip Spitzer, to accompany me to the meeting. Within ten minutes of shaking hands with us, Marqusee offered to buy my book.

Spitzer asked me what I wanted him to do since he had not been responsible for the Paddington deal. I told him that he had been loyal to me from the outset. Without him, there would be no book. I instructed him to negotiate the contract with Paddington and accept his well-deserved, ten-percent commission. Since Martindale had arranged the Paddington deal, I also agreed to give him and his partner another ten percent.

The Hoffa Wars had now transcended contracts, books, and publishing. It had become a crusade. I was prepared to do anything—and pay anything—to get this book out at the same time as Brill's.

With the tentative publishing deal made, I gave Marqusee my final chapter about Hoffa's murder—which included my exclusive interviews with Hoffa's alleged killer, the late Salvatore Briguglio. The New Republic Book Company remained our only stumbling block to our deal with Paddington.

Finally, on Tuesday, April 4, because of Martindale's friendship with Marty Peretz, Joan Tapper and the New Republic graciously allowed us to void our agreement without a legal battle.

Soon after, Paddington and I signed a new contract.

On Thursday, June 8, my new editor, Mary Heathcote, and I wrapped up the editing work on my book. We had saved the sections about the CIA-Mafia plots and John Kennedy's murder for last. To celebrate, I invited her to the Georgetown Inn for dinner. While waiting in the dining room for Heathcote to join me, I saw a man I recognized seated alone on the other side of the room.

I quickly called the maitre d', asking him if that man was Robert Maheu, the former top aide to billionaire Howard Hughes, who became the liaison between the CIA and the Mafia during the plots against Castro.

When the maitre d' confirmed it, I offered him twenty bucks if he would bring Maheu to my table. The maitre d' did as I asked, and, to my surprise, Maheu came over and sat down with me.

I introduced myself and told him, "I have just spent part of the day writing about you."

Explaining that I was interested in his role in the plots against Castro, Maheu proclaimed proudly, "I was willing to kill ten Castros to save a single American life."

When Mary arrived, she audibly gasped when I introduced her to Maheu.

As his dinner guest had arrived and he stood to join him, I asked Maheu if I could see him the following day. He told me to meet him there at the Georgetown Inn for breakfast.

At our meeting the following morning, I did for Maheu what I had done for many of my sources. I allowed him to read what I had written about him and gave him an opportunity to amend or amplify this material.

Maheu read and approved the section about him with some minor changes. During our on-the-record interview, he explained how he had become acquainted with Johnny Rosselli, as well as how he became entangled with the Castro plots—which began eight months before he was brought into the conspiracy. Regarding Hoffa's possible role in the plots, Maheu did not know for sure but conceded, "Things were happening before I became involved." For instance, Maheu knew nothing about Russell Bufalino's early role in the plots, along with those of his supporting cast: mobsters Jimmy Plumeri, Salvatore Granello, John LaRocca, and Gabriel Mannarino.

Then, while discussing the Castro plots, Maheu appeared to slip and identified the then-unknown Cuban exile leader who was passed the poison pills by the CIA, via Rosselli, for the purpose of killing Castro: Antonio de Varona, the former president of the Cuban Senate.

Maheu and I both knew that was big news.[32]

37. *The New York Times* creates me

After Mary Heathcote finished her massive editing job on my 900-plus-page manuscript, a prominent New York libel attorney, David Lubell, and one of his associates vetted *The Hoffa Wars*, driving me crazy for two full days as they made me jump for every piece of documentation.

In the wake of Lubell's legal review, he wrote to Paddington Press, saying: "We must note that rarely have we encountered an investigative reporter, or any non-fiction writer, who had as great a command of his source material, both primary and secondary, as did Mr. Moldea."

Simultaneously, trying to smoke out whatever I was missing about the Hoffa murder case and aiding my vetting process, my attorneys and I decided to leak what we knew about the investigation, including the possible role of Frank Sheeran, to my friend, Jon Kwitny at the *Wall Street Journal*. I even introduced him to some of my key sources at the FBI and in the Strike Force Against Organized Crime.

At first, Kwitny couldn't believe that I was giving him this gift. But I knew that, if anyone could get to the bottom of this case and steal Brill's thunder, Kwitny was the one to do it.

Kwitny's story—"Suspects in Hoffa Case Are Constantly Feeling Long Arm of the Law"—appeared on the *Journal's* front page on June 12. Acknowledging that "the case is no closer to official resolution now than it was back in 1975," Kwitny featured mini-sketches of the key suspects in the case—Russell Bufalino, Tony Provenzano, Tony Giacalone, Sal and Gabe Briguglio, Tom and Steve Andretta, Chuck O'Brien, and Frank Sheeran.

He did not mention Rolland McMaster, who, next to Hoffa, was the major character in my book—and, I believed, had been behind the Local 299 violence and might have played a role in the disposal of Hoffa's body. I kept McMaster exclusively for my book.

Regarding Sheeran, Kwitny wrote:

> Sheeran hasn't been charged with anything criminal since the Hoffa disappearance, but he is in Tax Court contesting the $2,532 that the Internal Revenue Service wants to charge him for allegedly using a union car for personal business. The car came to the attention of federal agents during the investigations that followed Hoffa's disappearance. Sheeran also has been kept hopping for months by federal grand juries investigating sweetheart contracts and pension-fund fraud. Last week it was learned that the Justice Department has authorized attorneys in the field to seek a grand-jury indictment against Sheeran for criminal contempt of court in failing to cooperate with a federal grand jury in Syracuse, N.Y., after he had been given immunity from prosecution. Mr. Sheeran's lawyer says his client answered all questions the grand jury had a right to ask.

Along with mentioning my upcoming book in his story, Kwitny confirmed privately that I hadn't missed anything.

On June 22, I received a telephone call from Herbert Mitgang, literary columnist at the *New York Times*, who wanted to discuss the publishing controversy between Brill and me, concentrating on Simon & Schuster's actions against the New Republic Book Company, which forced me to break my original book contract and to sign with Paddington. I agreed to cooperate with Mitgang and told him what I knew.

One week later, on Thursday, June 29, Mitgang's article appeared in the *Times*. And it was just fabulous, saying:

PART THREE: HOFFA, MARCELLO & TRAFFICANTE

> Two forthcoming books on the same controversial subjects—James R. Hoffa and the International Brotherhood of Teamsters' covert role in American political and criminal life—have pitted their authors and publishers in a behind-the-scenes contest, with possible broad implications for publishing independence or suppression. . . .
>
> At issue is not censorship, but a growing trend to contractual arrangements in which smaller publishers use larger ones to sell their books. The Hoffa books, according to the publishing community, point up the difficulties involved for independent houses in today's marketplace.
>
> The first book is *The Hoffa Wars: Teamsters, Rebels, Politicians and the Mob* by Dan E. Moldea, to be published by Paddington, a small but vigorous independent house with offices in New York and
>
> London. . . . The second is *The Teamsters* by Steven Brill, to be published by Simon & Schuster, which is owned by the Gulf and Western Industries conglomerate.[33]

The story included praise for *The Hoffa Wars* by Marty Peretz, the publisher of the New Republic Book Company, which was forced to give up the project. Peretz told Mitgang: "I very much regret it because it's a powerful book."

Mitgang was extremely critical of Richard Snyder, the president of Simon & Schuster, who actually confessed to the *Times* reporter: "I was surprised when I heard that New Republic was selling its book to Paddington. We requested them to postpone it, not to sell it."

Also, after discussing my interview with Hoffa's alleged killers and reporting details from the tape of the November 1976 threat to my life, Mitgang quoted Brill about an alleged taped confession he had supposedly received from Frank Sheeran, writing:

> Mr. Brill also says he has been threatened—by an official of the Federal Bureau of Investigation—for supposedly not sharing a taped "confession" about the Hoffa murder. "Please stress that I have no such tape—it's just not true," Mr. Brill said.

Mitgang concluded in his *Times* article:

> Publishing lawyers ... said that the attempted delay of the Moldea book was one of the first examples of [a] possible loss of independence—with implicit censorship—where there is a conflict on a controversial nonfiction book.

That same day, inspired by the article in the *New York Times*, *Playboy* magazine purchased the first-serial rights to *The Hoffa Wars* for nearly twice as much as my original advance for the book. Also, the Book-of-the-Month Club purchased the book-club rights to *The Hoffa Wars*. Soon after, *The Observer* of London bought the worldwide syndication rights for another huge chunk of change, and, to everyone's delight, the *New York Times* syndication service bought the U.S. rights.

At the same time, Paddington announced a $50,000 advertising budget for the book and a 50,000-copy first printing.

Tina and I went out to celebrate that night—after she finished scraping me off the ceiling. I had just experienced the greatest day of my life—the day the *New York Times* recognized and, thus, created me as a new American author.

Motivated by the market power of the *New York Times*, publications all over the country suddenly began writing about the pending release of *The Hoffa Wars*—written by a completely unknown 28-year-old author and published by a little British company no one had ever heard of before.

Riding the wave, I went to New York on Monday, July 24 to work on the excerpt for *Playboy*. The story concentrated on the violence in Local 299 and the politics behind the Hoffa murder, as well as the possible Marcello-Trafficante-Hoffa scenario in the murder of President Kennedy.

During an early morning breakfast with Barry Golson, *Playboy's* executive editor, on Saturday, July 29, I felt exhausted after the week's work. It was 2:30 A.M., and we had just put the story to bed.

Golson—who had edited the article along with his top lieutenant, Tom Passavant—offhandedly remarked, "It's too bad that we don't have anyone saying that Hoffa personally knew Jack Ruby."

"Yeah," I replied. "The only thing I ever heard was ..." and I told Golson about my meeting with Jimmy Hoffa, Jr. the previous December—during which he said he believed his father knew Ruby.

Astonished, Golson exclaimed, "Why isn't that in the story?"

"Barry, it's my word against both Hoffa and Murray Chodak."

"Did he say it?"

"Yeah, of course, he said it."

PART THREE: HOFFA, MARCELLO & TRAFFICANTE

"Did you write it down?"

"Yeah, as I left Hoffa's office."

Golson paid the check and said we were going back to the office to add Hoffa's quote to the *Playboy* article. He assured me, "Our attorneys will back you up if Hoffa comes after us."

Emboldened by Golson's confidence, I also added the Hoffa quote as a last-minute endnote to my book's galleys.

In addition, I had told Golson—and gave him a written statement—about the circumstances revolving around my acceptance of the money from the Hoffa Reward Fund, administered by Jimmy Hoffa, Jr. Golson suggested that I defuse any potential criticism by writing a brief preface to my article about receiving the reward money, which I did.[34]

On Tuesday, August 15, I played golf in Washington with Rafe Sagalyn of the New Republic—who, like his boss, Joan Tapper, had been very fair to me. He told me that—during a meeting he attended in New York at Simon & Schuster—Dick Snyder had exploded over Mitgang's article in the *New York Times*. Sagalyn warned me that the S & S chief would "pull out all the stops" in his promotion of Brill's book.

Soon after, the *Village Voice* published what appeared to be an S & S flack's story, saying: "There's little doubt that *The Teamsters* will be the next 'big' book. Brill is scheduled for, not one, but three consecutive interviews on the *Today Show*, beginning September 11."[35]

While promoting Brill's work, Snyder clearly wanted to bury Paddington, my book, and me. And, frankly, Paddington and I were up for this fight.

38. Yes, we have no Central Sanitation

On Wednesday, August 23, Tina and I drove to a huge printing plant near Gettysburg, Pennsylvania, where *The Hoffa Wars* had just been completed. Paddington's sales manager had asked me to sign 800 copies purchased by Hudson's, a Michigan-based, department-store chain, in the wake of Mitgang's article in the *New York Times*.

When we arrived, a plant executive gave us a tour of his impressive facility, showing us hundreds of newly-bound books.

Then, he placed us in a small room. Tina had walked out momentarily to get something from the car when another executive of the company came in and handed me the first copy of my book.

Knowing that this was a big moment for me, he smiled and left the room, shutting the door behind him as if I was going to do something weird with it.

I did stare at it, though, cupping it in both hands and treating it as an icon. Then, I gently ran my fingers along the smooth and shiny dust cover as I looked at it front and back. I opened the book and slowly removed its jacket, feeling its hard cover and the raised print on its spine.

And then I did what nearly every nonfiction author does when he or she first sees his or her finished book: I went to the index. Other than the text itself, there is nothing more important than a good index. And, "This," I said out loud to myself, "is a great index!"

By the time Tina returned, she found me sitting alone in the room, just reading my own book.

On or about the same day in early September, both books, *The Hoffa Wars* and *The Teamsters*, were released. I bought a copy of Brill's book when I saw it on display next to mine in a Cleveland bookstore.

I had real problems with the manner in which he had depicted Hoffa as a working-class hero and Robert Kennedy as a malicious wiretapper who had violated Hoffa's civil rights. However, Brill organized his book masterfully and written it extremely well.

As predicted, Brill's material about the Hoffa murder contained no surprises, and I was absolutely joyful when I saw that he had actually featured the Central Sanitation theory about the disposal of Hoffa's body—just as Bob Windrem had told John Sikorski and me.

Although his most interesting chapter was a profile of Ron Carey, the maverick president of Teamsters Local 804 in New York, my biggest complaint about his book was his portrayal of the corrupt Ohio Teamsters boss Jackie Presser as a quasi-reformer. Meantime, he gave backhanded treatment to the contemporary rank-and-file reform movements, like the Teamsters for a Democratic Union (TDU) and PROD.

Bill Wallace of the *Berkeley Barb* later wrote, "Moldea gives a much fairer view of the Teamster rebel movement."

Convoy, the voice of TDU, which actively promoted my book, said in its review by Mike Friedman, "Moldea explains the rank and file tradition for today's reform movements. He understands that tradition, because he's no outsider to it."[36]

But public interest in the rank-and-file reform movement paled by comparison with their fascination with Hoffa's disappearance. Right off the bat, it was Brill who took the early advantage, and, to my chagrin, my former employers, NBC News and the *Detroit Free Press*, helped him get it.

On Saturday night, September 9, correspondent Brian Ross of *NBC Nightly News* opened the program with an exclusive report about Brill's book, claiming that, according to Brill, the FBI believed that Hoffa's body was disposed of at Central Sanitation in Detroit. Ross added that the FBI had no comment.

As Ross's accurate report about Brill's erroneous theory went off the wire services that night, Ralph Orr at the *Detroit Free Press* published a huge banner headline story, "Hoffa slain by 2 N.J. men, author says," on Sunday, September 10.

In his article, Orr wrote: "Brill pinpoints Central Sanitation at 8215 Moran in Hamtramck as the place when Hoffa's body was taken. . . 'Hoffa's body was destroyed at the premises.'"[37]

Once again, the FBI had no comment on Brill's theory.

I knew that Brill's Central Sanitation theory was wrong—based on what the FBI had repeatedly told me—and was upset that the FBI had not said so to either Brian Ross or Ralph Orr.

I called one of my FBI sources, saying, "What's wrong with you guys? You've been telling me for years that the Central Sanitation theory is wrong. And now you're saying, 'no comment?' Is this what you believe or not? If not, you have a responsibility to correct what's being said."

The FBI agent replied, "I told you, we don't believe it."

"Then, damn it, say so! Please issue a statement!"

Later that same day, the FBI finally issued a joint statement from its Washington headquarters and Detroit field office, saying:

> The theory that Mr. Hoffa's remains were disposed of at a private suburban sanitation facility [Central Sanitation] was explored at the outset of the case. It was subsequently determined that the source of the information was not reliable. No search warrant was ever requested, issued or executed by the FBI, concerning the sanitation company.

Nevertheless, despite the FBI's denial, Brian Ross returned to the *NBC Nightly News* and stood by Brill's inaccurate conclusion. And, even though the *Free Press* had trumpeted Brill's allegations on Sunday's front page, the newspaper only played the FBI's denial of Brill's claim and Ralph Orr's story in a short piece on page three the following day, September 11.

In its no-byline story, the *Free Press* reported:

> The FBI Sunday said author Steven Brill's claim that the bureau searched a Hamtramck incinerating company [Central Sanitation] for James R. Hoffa's body was wrong and that his theory on how Hoffa disappeared and was killed is not the agency's 'subscribed solution to the case.[38]

The FBI repeated that the source for Brill's scenario was deemed "not reliable."

The following day, Tuesday, September 12, Helen Fogel, another reporter at the *Free Press* wrote a second, front-page story, "TV story on Hoffa called lie," in the wake of the FBI's denials.

The newspaper quoted Brill, saying: "I was told by the highest possible sources in the Hoffa investigation that the theory advanced in the book was the investigators' leading explanation of Hoffa's disappearance. . . . If they are now denying it, well, I can't speak for the FBI."

Any other book by any other author would have been crippled by this news—yet, Brill continued to survive. And I felt the unrelenting power of Dick Snyder and Simon & Schuster hovering over this entire fiasco. In fact, Rafe Sagalyn at the New Republic, who attended meetings with Simon & Schuster executives, including Snyder, wrote me letter on September 12, saying, "Remember one thing: whatever perfidious efforts are/will be made against you—and S & S machinations notwithstanding—*The Hoffa Wars* will be read. The word about *The Teamsters* will get out. Your accomplishments have been significant, against formidable odds."

Still, I had some explaining to do with my own people—specifically why did NBC and the *Free Press*, two places where I had worked, take the lead on Brill's book and ignore mine?

In short, both NBC and the *Free Press* believed that I was flying off walls with my claim that Carlos Marcello, Santo Trafficante, and Jimmy Hoffa had arranged and executed the murder of President Kennedy.

Even Brill chimed in on this matter, describing it as "total garbage," and telling the *Dallas Morning News*, "I would be embarrassed to put that in the book."[39]

PART THREE: HOFFA, MARCELLO & TRAFFICANTE

39. The U.S. House Assassinations Committee

On Sunday, September 24, the first tandem review of the two books appeared in the *Detroit News*. Reviewer Michael Wendland, who had covered the Teamsters for years, wrote:

"Moldea rips away at the Hoffa mystique, shattering that image Hoffa so carefully cultivated. . . . Moldea's [book] is the most readable and presents the most new information."

In a second joint review in *New York* magazine, critic Michael Novak stated:

> "Jimmy Hoffa's most valuable contribution to the American labor movement came at the moment he stopped breathing on July 30, 1975," writes Dan E. Moldea in the more passionate, detailed, and coherent of these two books. Moldea has a working class view of the struggle; before becoming a journalist, he drove trucks. . . . Steve Brill comes to the Teamsters after legal training at Yale. He tries to be sympathetic to his material, like a courteous visitor to a foreign country. He organizes his book around nine key unionists. . . . These portraits have a point, but the superiority of the Moldea book lies in the inherent drama of the unfolding history.⁴⁰

Regarding my theory about the President's assassination, Novak concluded: "It all seems crazy. But suppose the mob helped organize the killing of John F. Kennedy?"

On Monday, September 25, the U.S. House Select Committee on Assassinations opened its public hearings on the possible role of the Mafia in the President's murder. National Public Radio covered most of the gavel-to-gavel action.

Listening to NPR while waiting to go on a television show in Boston, I nearly fell off my chair when Nina Totenberg, who anchored the NPR broadcast, began reading long excerpts from *The Hoffa Wars*, which already contained much of what the committee was now presenting.

On Wednesday, September 27—as Totenberg continued reading from *The Hoffa Wars* and later featured my work on four consecutive nights for NPR's *All Things Considered*—committee chief counsel, Robert Blakey, masterminded a dramatic lead-in to his most explosive evidence.

Having set the stage the previous two days by interviewing peripheral witnesses to the organized-crime investigation, he now brought in his two key witnesses: mobster Santo Trafficante and Cuban businessman Jose Aleman, who had supposedly heard Trafficante threaten the President because of Robert Kennedy's war against the underworld, adding that Hoffa was making the arrangements for the President's murder.

However, Aleman—who was supposed to reveal details about Trafficante's threat—panicked in the witness chair, claiming that his life had been placed in jeopardy when committee staffers allowed him to fly to Washington National Airport unescorted.

Consequently, Aleman's failure to perform immediately hurt the committee's plan to show a possible organized-crime conspiracy. Neither Ralph Salerno's testimony, nor that of the Warren Commission's chief organized-crime investigator—who admitted under oath that the Mafia had been virtually ignored by that panel—could help the committee rebound in the eyes of those in the press gallery, most of whom were hearing about the controversies in the Kennedy case for the first time.

Soon after, even though the committee had not finished presenting its evidence, the negative articles and editorials began. The headline for the story about the September 27 hearing in the *Washington Post* was: "JFK death probers can't link syndicate."

Suddenly, the honest and responsible work of Blakey and his staff was no longer taken as seriously as it deserved. And, thus, as Walter Sheridan had feared, there was a perception that *The Hoffa Wars* simply contained just another conspiracy theory.

In his own assault on me for my Marcello-Trafficante-Hoffa theory, Ralph Orr of the *Detroit Free Press* quoted Jimmy Hoffa Jr., denying that he had ever told me that his father had known Jack Ruby. Hoffa told Orr, "That is a complete fabrication. I categorically deny that any such conversation ever took place."

Orr continued: "Said [Hoffa's] law partner, Murray Chodak, whom Moldea said was present for the interview: 'Jimmy never, never said that. I was stunned when I read it. We would sue, but we don't want to help hustle the damned book.'"[41]

Soon after, a staff investigator for the U.S. House Select Committee on Assassinations called and told me that Hoffa had called me "a liar" and denied making the statement during an interview with the committee. Specifically, the investigator's report stated:

PART THREE: HOFFA, MARCELLO & TRAFFICANTE

> Speaking of the recent book, *The Hoffa Wars*, Hoffa stated that "It is completely inaccurate. It is a scandalous and malicious book. An outrage. It's the worst fabrication and worst book since *The Enemy Within*, [Robert Kennedy's 1960 book about Hoffa and the Mafia]." In response to the question of whether the book accurately quotes him as having stated that he believes his father knew Jack Ruby, Hoffa stated, "That's a total lie. I never said my father knew Jack Ruby or anything like that. He made that up for the book."[42]

The staff investigator asked me if I had any corroboration for my claim that Hoffa had made this statement.

"Come over to my place," I told him.

When he arrived, I gave him a copy of a tape.

"What's on this?" He asked.

"Hoffa called me on the phone on September 14," I replied. "During our discussion, he confirmed the quote. To protect myself, I taped the call. This is the tape of my conversation with Hoffa."

In short, Hoffa, Jr.—after seeing either my book or the article in *Playboy*—had called my home and verbally attacked me for alleging that his father had been involved in President Kennedy's murder. After reminding Hoffa what he had told me on December 27, 1977, in his office, Hoffa confirmed his statement to me—that his father had personally known Jack Ruby.

On September 18, after my appearance on a WCVB-TV morning radio show in Boston, I called my attorney, Steve Martindale, who told me that he had been contacted by attorney Frank Ragano of Tampa, the former legal counsel to Santo Trafficante, as well as Carlos Marcello and Jimmy Hoffa, during the time of the Castro plots. According to Martindale, Ragano made an offer of $250,000 to buy the rights to my book—supposedly to make a movie. He said that his project was backed by television talk-show host David Susskind. Martindale asked me what I wanted to do. I telephoned Walter Sheridan who told me to stay clear of Ragano because he was "bad news."

I called Martindale back and told him to tell Ragano to forget it. However, I instructed him first to ask Ragano his opinion with regard to my chapters on the Castro and Kennedy murder plots and, specifically, the possibility of Hoffa's involvement.

Later that day, Martindale reported that Ragano had said that I was "essentially correct." but that I had "oversimplified" the scenario. Ragano would say no more.

On October 1, the *News Journal* of Wilmington, Delaware, published a story about the allegations that both Brill and I had leveled against Frank Sheeran whom we had implicated in Hoffa's murder. Reporter Mary Jo Meisner quoted Sheeran's attorney who said, "Mr. Sheeran has been advised by counsel not to make any comments in regard to the allegations contained in the two books. However, at the appropriate time and after our own investigation, I expect that we will have a full statement to make."

On Thursday night, October 5, Steve Martindale threw a book party for Tina and me at his home in Georgetown. Numerous celebrities were in attendance, ranging from Mayor Walter Washington of Washington, D.C. to model Margaux Hemingway, the granddaughter of Ernest Hemingway—along with executives from Paddington Press, the New Republic, and *Playboy*, as well as my parents, Mrs. Nolte (who had moved to Boulder, Colorado), Philip Spitzer, other close friends, numerous reporters and authors, and a number of steel haulers and rank-and-file reformers. Also, actress Elizabeth Taylor, a close friend of Martindale, was confirmed to attend, but other matters complicated her evening so she could not make it.

The *Washington Post* prominently featured a story about the party the following day in its Style section.

Earlier on the day of the party, still five days before our official publication date, *The Hoffa Wars* went into its second printing. On our pub date, Paddington ordered its third printing.

During my book tour, along with my initial appearance on ABC's *Good Morning America*, my publisher arranged for me to travel coast-to-coast and to appear in twenty-two cities in the U.S. and Canada, beginning in New York and ending in Los Angeles.

In the "Public Eye," the *Chicago Sun-Times's* gossip column, Bob Herguth wrote a small piece, saying: "Dan E. Moldea visited Chicago to promote his best-selling book, *The Hoffa Wars*. He popped into Walden Books and bought another book, *The Only Investment Guide You'll Ever Need*, by Andrew Tobias."

Although I constantly felt that all fame and fortune was fleeting, I enjoyed every minute of this experience.

40. Helping TDU and PROD make peace

On October 21, in one of the biggest honors I had ever received, the executive board of the Teamsters for a Democratic Union asked me to be the keynote speaker at its third annual convention in Windsor, Ontario.

"As I look around this room," I said to my old friends, "all I see are a great number of reasonable men and women who are looking for reasonable solutions to the seemingly insurmountable problems they face as members of the Teamsters Union.

"Four years ago, I started my investigation of the union, and I feel that I have aged at least forty years. Many of you sitting in this room tonight were responsible for educating me and protecting me. I can never repay you for your patience and kindness. . . . "

Also, in my attempt to help settle the differences between TDU and PROD, I called Arthur Fox just before my speech and asked him to give me an olive branch that I could carry to the TDU membership. As always, Arthur responded with real class.

What he gave me was best told in the newspaper, *In These Times*. Teamster reform leader and author Dan La Botz, whom I met in Chicago in 1975, wrote about my speech, reporting:

> Dan Moldea . . . said, "From the moment I saw what was going on in the fight of the rank and file against Teamster official— I aligned myself with your cause. . . . TDU and PROD now stand alone as the great reform organizations. As the National Master Freight Agreement approaches, I appeal to you to work together."
>
> Moldea added that PROD had taken a big step towards unity when their attorney, Arthur Fox, repudiated and apologized for a letter he had written three years ago [criticizing] members . . . active in building TDU.⁴³

Soon after, TDU and PROD made their official peace and then merged, solidifying the Teamsters' rank-and-file reform movement.

The reviews for both Brill's book and mine, for the most part, were quite favorable, recognizing the dedication to our work—and the fact that the two books in many ways actually did complement each other, just as Rafe Sagalyn had predicted.

For instance, respected labor expert Jack Barbash, a professor of economics and industrial relations at the University of Wisconsin, wrote in the *Christian Science Monitor*: "I have nothing but admiration for the passion, investigative skill, scrupulous regard for the facts, and commitment to trade union principles which Brill and Moldea have shown."[44]

Others were not quite so kind. On November 5, the 88-day strike by newspaper workers against the *New York Times* ended. During the interim, the *Times* had not been published. There had been no Sunday *Book Review* and no *Times* Best Sellers list since the release of the two books about Hoffa and the Teamsters.

A week later, Fred J. Cook, a writer to whom I had referred and attacked in my book for his delusional pro-Hoffa apologia in *The Nation* on the opening day of Hoffa's pension-fraud trial in Chicago in 1964, published a tandem review of *The Hoffa Wars* and *The Teamsters* on the front page of the first edition of the *New York Times Book Review* after the strike.

I could not believe that the *Times* had selected someone my publisher and I, among many others, considered such an obviously biased reviewer, especially after the contentious history of these two books. Of course, Cook used the opportunity to wax my tail while giving Brill his best review of all.

From the outset, I suspected that the selection of Cook was nothing less than a huge favor to Dick Snyder and Simon & Schuster, one of the *New York Times Book Review's* biggest advertisers, in the wake of Herb Mitgang's clearly fair and balanced story five months earlier which was much more favorable to my book.[45]

I was so upset by Cook's assault on me that I actually spoke to a libel attorney, asking if I had a case. Agreeing that Cook's false statements were egregious and even provable lies, he replied that winning would be difficult and expensive—since opinion writers enjoyed wide protections under the First Amendment. He advised me to grow up and accept the consequences of the profession. Unfair reviews—even lying reviews, like Fred Cook's—came with the territory.

So, in the end, I backed down.

All the while, I continued to get ripped apart over the Marcello-Trafficante-Hoffa theory of the Kennedy murder in my book. Here is a sampling:

PART THREE: HOFFA, MARCELLO & TRAFFICANTE

* Labor reporter Sidney Lens of the *Chicago Tribune* wrote:

> Among the claims made by Moldea is that Hoffa and gangsters Carlos Marcello and Santos Trafficante 'had discussions with their subordinates about murdering President Kennedy.' They also seem to have been in contact with Jack Ruby, the man who killed Kennedy's presumed assassin, Lee Harvey Oswald. Too much of what appears in this book dangles, without proof of reference to a good source.[46]

* Robert Merry of the *Wall Street Journal* added:

> Shunning widespread speculation that Mr. Hoffa was murdered by Teamster-connected mobsters bent on preserving their cozy arrangements with the union, Mr. Moldea seems to believe Mr. Hoffa's killing stemmed from some ominous inside knowledge he harbored about the Mafia's—and perhaps his own—connection to the Kennedy assassination . . . And so in the end Mr. Moldea's theme, while stunning as a consolidated answer to all kinds of arcane questions about Teamsters behavior, simply lacks credibility.[47]

* Kenneth Crowe of *Newsday*, another labor reporter, continued:

> Moldea also puts forth the questionable and admittedly speculative theory that Hoffa and the mob were linked to the assassination of President John F. Kennedy, because of Kennedy's war on both Hoffa and the hoods . . . [S]eeing the mob everywhere may be a special form of paranoia endemic to "guerrilla writers."[48]

Meantime, the fabled Murray Kempton published his version of Hoffa's history in the February 1979 edition of the *New York Review of Books*, in which he wrote:

> Brill and Moldea are both investigative reporters. Investigative reporting is the best, probably the only, excuse for journalism; but, welcome as its renaissance is, we ought to recognize that it is an extractive and not a redefining process.

> Moldea's book is the more striking instance of the method's virtue as an inspiration to energy and of its vice as a discouragement to reflection. His shovel throws up the ore and slag in one indiscriminate mass. On the one hand we have page after page of conscientious, if recondite, detail about the grievances of steelhaulers, the tribulations and treasons of innumerable uprisings against the union's bravos, and the beatings and the bombings in the quarrel over Detroit Local 299. . . .
>
> On the other hand we have any number of fantasies about the malignant authority exercised by Hoffa over our national history, an authority in a coalition of the Teamsters Union and organized crime. This is the coalition that may or may not have murdered President Kennedy. . . . The great defect of the method may be that it will dare the wildest degree of speculation about events and none at all about first causes.[49]

I immediately wrote a letter to the *NYRB* after reading the Kempton review, my only such public response to anything written about *The Hoffa Wars*. In that letter, which was published, I stated:

> Although I feel that I was completely responsible in my handling of this obviously sensational material which is now being taken seriously by the government as well as the press, I am at a loss when reviewers, like Mr. Kempton, indicate that this is one of the 'fantasies' in my book. I simply hope that Mr. Kempton and those other reviewers who have written that I have "ruined an excellent book with the Kennedy assassination theory" remember where they heard it first when the House Assassinations Committee releases its final report.[50]

On March 22, Paddington Press received a letter addressed to me from Frank Sheeran's attorney, F. Emmett Fitzpatrick, Philadelphia's former district attorney, who wrote:

> Mr. Sheeran has recently become familiar with the book authored by you entitled *The Hoffa Wars*.

Mr. Sheeran wishes me to inform you that he emphatically denies the allegations about his involvement in Mr. Hoffa's alleged death and to state specifically that your allegation that he was present in Detroit on the last day that Mr. Hoffa was seen is false, unfounded and has been specifically contradicted by evidence supplied by Mr. Sheeran to the Federal Government.

On Mr. Sheeran's behalf, I demand a retraction and a public apology for all of your many allegations of his activities surrounding and contributing to the alleged disappearance or death of Mr. Hoffa.

My attorney replied to Sheeran, simply saying: "Mr. Moldea stands by his reporting."

I never heard from Sheeran or his attorney again.

Sheeran later held a press conference at which he told reporters: "The government feels I have information on the Hoffa case, which I don't."[51]

41. "The mob did it. It's a historical fact."

Jeff Goldberg and Carl Oglesby, two leaders of the Assassination Information Bureau, wrote the first in-depth analysis of the anticipated report of the U.S. House Select Committee on Assassinations, which they published in the Outlook section of the *Washington Post*.[52] They predicted that the committee would conclude that Marcello, Trafficante, and Hoffa might have been involved in the President's murder—just as I had claimed months earlier in *The Hoffa Wars*.

Goldberg became a close friend, especially after he and I started hosting a Thursday-night poker game, the first of which was on December 28, 1978.[53] Others at the table included Oglesby, a former national president of the Students for a Democratic Society (SDS), and Carl Shoffler, a detective with the Intelligence Division of the Metropolitan Police Department. Shoffler was best known as the arresting officer of the Watergate burglars on June 17, 1972. Almost immediately, Shoffler became a trusted friend.

As renewed interest in the select committee's upcoming report became more widespread—after the panel stumbled the previous fall in the aftermath of Jose Aleman's testimony—a remarkable story appeared on the front page of the *New York Times*, saying:

> The report, to be released later this summer, says the two-year House investigation could not determine who the conspirators were, but it specifies evidence and allegations it gathered on organized crime figures and the Cubans. The report also discusses speculation that James R. Hoffa, former president of the International Brotherhood of Teamsters, may have had a role, but it draws no conclusion. . . . The report identifies the organized crime figures most likely to have taken part in a conspiracy as Carlos Marcello of Louisiana and Santos Trafficante of Florida. . . .
>
> Aides to Mr. Marcello, Mr. Trafficante and Mr. Hoffa were all linked in the committee's public hearings to Jack Ruby, who killed Lee Harvey Oswald two days after Oswald was arrested and accused of assassinating the President. The link was made through telephone calls that Ruby made.[54]

The article made no reference to my work, even though the reporter who wrote the story had interviewed me.[55] He later said that he had credited me—but that the *Times's* high command had edited out the references to my book.

By this time, I was really hungry for some real recognition as the first reporter to lay out the scenario that could eventually lead to the final solution to the assassination of President Kennedy.

Adding to my growing list of complaints against the *New York Times*—especially in the wake of Fred Cook's attack on me in the *Book Review* for my Marcello-Trafficante-Hoffa theory in *The Hoffa Wars*—Aljean Harmetz, the newspaper's controversial Hollywood correspondent, published a story on June 11, featuring a newly-released "documentary novel" called, *Blood Feud*.

This book, published nearly nine months after *The Hoffa Wars*, was written by screenwriters Edward Hannibal and Bob Boris and contained a completely fictionalized account of the rivalry between Jimmy Hoffa and Robert Kennedy. The authors had also changed the names of Marcello and Trafficante and linked them with Hoffa in a plot to murder John Kennedy.

PART THREE: HOFFA, MARCELLO & TRAFFICANTE

Playing off the recent story on the *Times's* front page, Harmetz's article—headlined, "History Catches Up to Hoffa-Kennedy Book"—stated:

> Last February [1979], a manuscript was delivered to Ballantine Books linking James R. Hoffa, former president of the International Brotherhood of Teamsters, and two organized-crime figures, Carlos Marcello and Santos Trafficante, to the assassination of President Kennedy.
>
> Greatly interested in the book but fearful of lawsuits, Ballantine persuaded the authors to use fictional names in place of Mr. Marcello and Mr. Trafficante. The "documentary novel" that resulted was published 10 days ago as *Blood Feud*, just days before the leak of the House Assassinations Committee's final report. . . .
>
> And Robert Boris, *Blood Feud's* co-author, says wryly, "I spent a year and a library card finding out what it took the committee two and a half years and $5 million to discover."[56]

I simply couldn't believe that the *New York Times* had decided to credit this work of fiction instead of my earlier published nonfiction book.[57]

Upon the release of its final report on July 17, the U.S. House Select Committee on Assassinations concluded that, indeed, Jimmy Hoffa, Carlos Marcello, and Santo Trafficante each had the "motive, means, and opportunity" to have President Kennedy killed. Then, placing an exclamation point on all of this at the end of the committee's investigation, Chief Counsel Robert Blakey insisted, "The mob did it. It's a historical fact."

42. The Paddington bankruptcy

On Wednesday, September 26, 1979, a reporter/friend telephoned me at my home. He said that Investigative Reporters and Editors (IRE)—a journalists' organization created in the wake of the 1976 murder of

Arizona Republic reporter Don Bolles—was in the midst of an informal probe of Jim Drinkhall, Brill's consultant for his book who had left *Overdrive* and joined the staff of the *Wall Street Journal*. He asked me if I knew anything about him.

After a brief conversation, my reporter/friend asked me if I would talk to a prosecutor with the U.S. Strike Force Against Organized Crime in San Francisco. I agreed to do so.

The following day, September 27, I received a call from Strike Force prosecutor Michael Kramer who—along with another federal prosecutor, John Dowd—was in the midst of a legal battle with Drinkhall and the *Journal*.

I told Kramer about my earlier hero worship of Drinkhall, as well as his friendships with Rolland McMaster and Mike Boano, which had deeply concerned me.

Interestingly, Bob Windrem, Brill's other consultant for *The Teamsters*, wrote a defense of Drinkhall and an attack on Mike Kramer, published in the January 1980 edition of Brill's new magazine, *American Lawyer*, where Windrem worked as a staff reporter.[58]

Meantime, after receiving an early partial payment for royalties owed from Paddington Press and awaiting publication of our mass-market paperback edition, I paid off all my outstanding debts, voluntarily returned the grant money I had received from the Fund for Investigative Journalism, and bought a condominium in Washington's Dupont Circle area where Tina and I moved on November 1, 1979.

And I anticipated another big check from Paddington for royalties owed.

However, the excitement over my anticipated financial windfall was premature. In the midst of my spending spree, Paddington Press suddenly filed for bankruptcy, taking with it much of the money I had earned from *The Hoffa Wars*. Paddington had been crushed under heavy costs from its distributor, Grosset & Dunlap, and numerous other problems endemic to small independent publishing houses.

After the initial devastation, I just felt horrible—not only for me but for Paddington, which had fought so bravely to survive. I retained an attorney to deal with the situation. But when he wanted to go for Paddington's throat to collect whatever he could, I asked him to back off. I just didn't have the heart for it.

Going to war with Simon & Schuster was one thing, but going to war with Paddington was something else. That little publishing house still meant too much to me.

43. Fear causes indecision

During the fall of 1979, while I was dealing with my troubles, my girlfriend, Tina, who had become a nationally known and respected women's rights leader, introduced me to Mary King, the deputy director of ACTION/Peace Corps, the federal volunteer agency.

A brilliant and dedicated woman who had worked as a photographer with the Student Nonviolent Coordinating Committee (SNCC) in her youth, King was married to Peter Bourne, President Carter's former drug advisor, who had lost his job after writing a prescription to a White House aide in the name of a fictitious patient. The scandal took its toll on King and Bourne, two of the most decent people I had ever met. After leaving the Carter Administration, Bourne accepted a prestigious job with the United Nations and spent much of his time out of the country.

Sensing that Washington knives were out for her, too, King just wanted to do her quality work quietly and in a safe place. She wanted protection—someone loyal who would run interference and fight for her. Hearing about my trials and tribulations, she told Tina that she believed I was that guy.

Knowing that I was burned out from all of my recent battles, Tina encouraged King to offer me the job in which I would be primarily working on issues related to Vietnamese resettlement in the United States while investigating the violence waged against these refugees.

Appointed as King's executive assistant, I had a Schedule-C political appointment and a GS-16 grade with an annual salary of nearly $50,000. I also received a "Top Secret" security clearance.

Frankly, aside from the fact that I now needed the money in the wake of Paddington's collapse, I loved my job, doing work that reminded me of my days with the Community Action Council and associating with several people whom I had first met during the student-rights movement and at the 1972 National Student Association convention.[59]

Intuitively, Tina, whose own career was taking off, recognized that events were starting to pull me in opposite directions. But, with regard to my chosen profession as an author and investigative journalist, she saw me balking, seemingly settling for the life of a well-paid, behind the scenes, nine-to-five bureaucrat—which she viewed as a bridge, not as a career.

In the aftermath of a referendum in New Jersey to legalize gambling in Atlantic City, I considered writing a book about Resorts International, the casino corporation, but backed away without ever submitting the proposal I had completed. Then, I flirted with doing an investigative biography about Carlos Marcello but retreated from that, too—just as I had with another proposed project about the Mafia's influence on Wall Street and yet another I considered writing about the mob's role in the garment industry in New York, which I wanted to call *Seventh Avenue*.

However, my reticence was not without cause. After surviving a sudden and quite unexpected encounter with one of McMaster's men while I was jogging on the Towpath in Georgetown—an ambush more intended to frighten than to harm—I had begun to play scared once again, just as I had during my youth after I was hit in the head by a high-and-inside fastball.

In the midst of all of this, Tina, who had always tolerated and even enjoyed my high-wire act, decided to leave me. After the incident on the Towpath—even with my new friend and poker buddy, MPD Detective Carl Shoffler, handling this situation personally—I simply couldn't figure out how to regain my courage.

PART FOUR:
Ronald Reagan & MCA

44. Reagan courting Teamsters

On February 16, 1980, Republican presidential candidate Ronald Reagan told an odd joke to Senator Gordon Humphrey (R-New Hampshire) and several other people within earshot.

> How do you tell the Polish one at a cockfight?
>
> He's the one with a duck.
>
> How do you tell the Italian one?
>
> He's the one who bets on the duck.
>
> How do you know the Mafia is there?
>
> The duck wins.

Still burned out in the summer of 1980—two years after the release of *The Hoffa Wars*—I was still doing anything and everything, trying to stay away from investigations of the Teamsters and the Mafia. For the first time in a long time, I finally felt safe and secure.

Then, on Wednesday afternoon, August 27, 1980, I received a telephone call from one of my Teamster sources in Ohio. He told me that Ronald Reagan had just kicked off his fall campaign in Columbus with an appearance before the Ohio Conference of Teamsters, chaired by the union's new vice president, Jackie Presser of Cleveland. Surprised by Reagan's odd selection for such an important event, I asked my source to stay in touch with me.

Later that day, he called back, saying that Reagan had just spent the past forty-five minutes behind closed doors with Presser and Roy Williams of Kansas City, another Teamsters vice president—in concert with the decision by the Teamsters' general executive board to endorse Reagan's candidacy.

Williams, who had supervised the McMaster Task Force, was not just another union man. Earlier that same morning, the wire services, newspapers, radio, and television networks had carried stories about Williams's sworn testimony the previous day before the U.S. Senate's Permanent Subcommittee on Investigations. Williams had taken the

Fifth Amendment twenty-three times when asked about his personal and financial dealings with several top organized-crime figures.

Among the mobsters with whom Williams had been associated was Carlos Marcello, who recently had been memorialized on tape during the FBI's BRILAB sting operation, boasting, "We own the Teamsters."

I called a reporter and spoon fed the information to her, adding that there was no way that Reagan had not received a briefing about Williams's appearance before the subcommittee. Reagan knew exactly what he was dealing with. She broke the story on National Public Radio's *All Things Considered.*

The story later appeared in newspapers across the country. However, the political impact was minimal, and Reagan's campaign did not even break stride.

On Tuesday, November 4, Reagan defeated Jimmy Carter for President of the United States as the Republicans also took control of the U.S. Senate. Consequently, my days as a political appointee in ACTION were numbered.

Following his victory, Reagan made his first trip as President-elect to Washington on November 18. Accompanied by Vice President-elect George H. W. Bush, Reagan went to Teamster headquarters, the union's marble palace on Louisiana Avenue near Capitol Hill. Attending another general executive board meeting, Reagan and Bush joyfully invited the Teamster leaders, especially Jackie Presser and Roy Williams, to help them select their secretary of labor and other administration officials.

To many of us who had investigated the Teamsters and the Mafia, President-elect Reagan's sweetheart relationship with the union, which he was not even trying to conceal, was our worst nightmare come to life. And, in the wake of Reagan's shocking invitation to the Teamsters, we knew that his cavalier attitude about organized crime would be reflected in the upcoming appointments to his administration.

Sure enough, in mid December, Reagan and Edwin Meese, the chief of his transition team, selected the mob-connected Jackie Presser, an eighth-grade dropout, as a "senior economic advisor." Presser boasted to the media that he had been appointed to screen potential appointees to "the Labor Department, Treasury, and a few other independent agencies," presumably any government entity that would have jurisdiction in any future investigations of the Teamsters.

Remarkably, at the same time, Presser and other former trustees of the Central States Pension Fund were targets of several civil suits brought by the Department of Labor, seeking reimbursement to the fund of $120 million in illegal loans made to Las Vegas casinos, as well as to organized-crime figures and their associates. All of the trustees had been forced to resign in 1976 because of their approval of such questionable loans.

On bended knees, White House beat reporters gently prodded Reagan at a press conference to discuss the Presser appointment, asking if he had been informed about the charges against the Teamster leader. Reagan coolly replied, "If that's true, that will be investigated and brought out."

Later, Meese contradicted Reagan, saying that Presser had been investigated prior to his appointment. The charges against Presser, according to Meese, were "mostly innuendo."

While the controversy over Presser stewed, Reagan nominated Ray Donovan as U.S. Secretary of Labor. Donovan, the executive vice president of the Schiavone Construction Company of Secaucus, New Jersey, had raised money for the Reagan-Bush campaign and even hosted a fundraiser, featuring Frank Sinatra, which yielded over $200,000 in contributions.

Given Donovan's past dealings with the Teamsters, their support for him was no surprise. During his confirmation hearings, Donovan was accused of making past payoffs to a New York Teamsters official on behalf of his New Jersey construction company. In addition, he was charged with associating with top Teamster racketeers, including Salvatore Briguglio of New Jersey's Local 560, the alleged killer of Jimmy Hoffa, who, himself, had been murdered in March 1978. Also, Donovan had allegedly done business with William Masselli, a top Mafia figure in New York.

Remarkably enough, one of the key government witnesses against Donovan was Ralph Picardo, who had also served as the government's chief informant in the Hoffa murder probe. Picardo was the FBI witness who had suggested that Sal Briguglio was Hoffa's killer and that Gateway Transportation was the vehicle that hauled the former Teamsters boss to his final resting place.

45. The Institute for Policy Studies

Because of my increasing concern about Reagan and his intentions, I reluctantly decided to get off the bench again and return to the game. But, because I was still gun shy, literally, I wanted to play on a team.

My good friend, Washington writer Barbara Raskin, introduced me to her ex-husband, Marcus Raskin, who, along with Richard Barnet, had founded the Institute for Policy Studies, a Washington-based New Left think tank, in 1963.

Located at the corner of 19th and Q Streets in Dupont Circle, IPS had been the victim of one of the first acts of contemporary political terrorism in the United States. On September 21, 1976, Orlando Letelier, an IPS fellow and Chile's former ambassador to Cuba, and another IPS staffer, twenty-five-year-old Ronni Karpen Moffitt, were killed in a car bombing while they were near Sheridan Circle in Washington, just a few blocks from IPS. Anti-Castro Cubans and officials of the right-wing dictatorship of General Augusto Pinochet in Chile were indicted and convicted for their roles in the murders.

Both Raskin and Barnet appeared receptive to the idea of bringing me aboard—even though most of those at IPS dealt with issues revolving around war and peace. Regardless of the fact that I had numerous friends in the law-enforcement community, that I supported court-authorized wiretapping, and that I was, generally, a hardliner on crime issues—as well as a journalist who had made his reputation by investigating a corrupt labor union—Raskin and Barnet believed that I would fit in with their community of progressives.

All I knew was that I was second to none in my concern over the incoming Reagan Administration's puzzling view of organized crime, as well as the New Right's determination to crush the Old and New Left. And I wanted to be in that fight against the Reaganistas, recognizing that IPS would be an early target.

I sent a proposal to Raskin and Barnet, outlining an IPS program to deal with the issues of organized crime in American society, stating:

> Organized crime has an uncanny ability to thrive under either conservative or liberal governments.
>
> The real problem in waging a war against organized crime—whether as a reporter, a public official, or a private citizen—is political: the left balks at any suggestion of electronic surveillance, which is the only effective means of gathering intelligence against organized crime. You must bug these guys; you must wiretap them. The right has a tendency to decentralize power in America from the federal government down to the state and local levels. Because of decentralization, organized crime figures have, in many cases, come to a first name

relationship with state and local political figures—with all of this newfound power—within their own jurisdictions.

Consequently, mob guys have an uncanny ability to be civil libertarians and support right-wing causes simultaneously. . . .

During the next four years, the Institute for Policy Studies and other liberal think tanks will be targeted by the Reagan Administration and Congress. Its motives, sources of funding, and activities will be placed under close scrutiny, undermined and perhaps even subverted. IPS, in particular, should begin to prepare a solid offensive attack against the assault from the New Right.

On February 12, three weeks after Reagan's inauguration, the IPS board of directors appointed me as a Visiting Fellow. Also selected were Indochina expert and former *Washington Post* reporter Elizabeth Becker, Chilean novelist and poet Ariel Dorfman, economist Michael Parenti, housing expert Chester Hartman, and labor writer Curtis Seltzer. I was proud to be associated with all of these writers and scholars, as well as the entire IPS community.[60]

Although I did not receive a salary with IPS, I did have an office and a telephone, which I quickly gave up because I preferred to work at my condo, just a drive and a three-iron away from the Institute.

On Thursday, May 28, 1981, I held my first formal seminar at IPS, "The Reagan Administration, Organized Crime and the Left." A few days earlier, Teamsters general president Frank Fitzsimmons had died of cancer and was replaced by Roy Williams, with whom Ronald Reagan had met privately, along with Presser, the previous August.

The day after Williams's appointment, I was quoted in *Newsday*, saying: "If I could pick somebody I wanted to see as president of the Teamsters, it would be Roy Williams, because he will continue to symbolize the corruption in the Teamsters union. My fear was a Mr. Clean type . . . would be picked," resulting in an easing of the government's scrutiny of the union.[61]

Immediately after becoming president of the Teamsters, Williams was indicted for conspiring to bribe Senator Howard Cannon of Nevada. Williams's co-conspirators included Allen Dorfman, the former fiduciary manager of the Teamsters' Central States Pension Fund, and several organized-crime figures. Also, the Senate's Permanent Subcommittee on Investigations released an interim report on the Teamsters, describing

Williams as "an organized-crime mole operating at senior levels of the Teamsters Union."

In spite of all of the damning evidence, both incoming Attorney General William French Smith and Labor Secretary Ray Donovan refused to take any action to remove Williams from office.

During my seminar at IPS, I railed against Reagan's ties to mobbed-up Teamsters, like Roy Williams and Jackie Presser, as well as Reagan's appointments of Smith and Donovan. Further, I attacked Senator Paul Laxalt of Nevada, the head of the National Republican Committee and Reagan's closest political friend, for his three recent meetings with Smith, specifically to discuss minimizing the role of the Justice Department's Strike Force Against Organized Crime in Las Vegas.

Predictably, the right-wing media responded harshly to my seminar. In the radical-right newspaper, *Human Events*, reporter Cliff Kincaid, who was present at IPS for my talk, published an article, "Left Launches New Line of Attack Against Reagan." In his article, Kincaid wrote:

> The charge is now being made—and chances are that it will surface in the major media—that the Reagan Administration is soft on the Mafia.
>
> Incredibly, the source of the charge is the Institute for Policy Studies (IPS), a pro-Marxist 'research organization' that may face a congressional investigation into its links with Communist regimes and terrorist movements....
>
> Moldea, despite IPS' efforts to portray him as just an intrepid prober of organized crime, also revealed himself as a man of the radical left.... Despite Moldea's admission that the Mafia has operated under liberal and conservative and Democratic and Republican administrations, there was agreement on one point: The Reagan Administration must be portrayed as Mob-connected. And the main target is clearly President Reagan himself.[62]

PART FOUR: RONALD REAGAN & MCA

46. The CIA and the Mafia again?

Following my seminar at IPS, the situation became even worse for the anti-organized-crime advocates. In President Reagan's September 1981 budget revisions, he imposed a one-third cutback on the FBI's investigations of gambling, prostitution, arson-for-hire, gangland murders, and pornography. In addition, according to the November 20 edition of the *Washington Post,* Reagan indicated that "no new undercover operations would be authorized in fiscal 1982 against either organized crime or white-collar crime." And all of this came in the wake of a hiring freeze and dramatic staff reductions within the FBI.

Also in his budget, Reagan severely curtailed the investigative and enforcement abilities of the Securities and Exchange Commission, the Internal Revenue Service, and, of course, the Strike Forces Against Organized Crime.

Further, I viewed Reagan's appointment of a Cabinet-level task force to coordinate federal efforts to combat drug smuggling as nothing more than a public-relations gimmick. Reagan had selected Vice President George Bush, a former director of the CIA, to head the anti-drug task force in South Florida. It wound up as a classic case in which the Reagan Administration pulled its punch, rounding up some little ponies while leaving the stallions locked up in the barn.

Regarding U.S. Secretary of Labor Ray Donovan, a panel of appellate judges had appointed an independent counsel, Leon Silverman, to investigate him in the wake of further allegations of underworld associations. As Silverman began his grand-jury probe, which would lead to Donovan's eventual indictment, the Senate continued its own investigation into allegations that mob money had been laundered through Donovan's construction firm.

In the end, two potential trial witnesses—Fred Furino, a long-time associate of Sal Briguglio, and Nat Masselli, the son of Mafia figure William Masselli—were both found murdered, the targets of gangland executions.

Subsequently, Donovan was acquitted, bitterly lamenting to reporters in the aftermath of his trial, "Which office do I go to get my reputation back?"

Reagan's new CIA director was William Casey who had been the overall chairman of the Reagan-Bush campaign committee. An intelligence officer during World War II, Casey had been the founder, general counsel, and a member of the board of directors of Multiponics, an agribusiness firm. One of Casey's partners in the company had been identified by law-enforcement agencies as an associate of Carlos Marcello's crime family in New Orleans. Wiretaps showed that Casey's partner had worked with the underworld since the 1950s.

In another business concern, Casey, the former head of the Securities and Exchange Commission under President Nixon, represented SCA Services, a New Jersey-based waste-disposal company, during the company's efforts to hold off an SEC investigation in 1977. The SEC had accused SCA executives of diverting $4 million of company funds for illegal purposes. Casey negotiated a settlement with the SEC in which SCA neither had to confirm nor deny the charges.

Later, a government witness told congressional investigators that SCA had been "involved with organized crime in the garbage business and now they're moving into hazardous waste." Officials of the Intelligence Division of the New Jersey State Police had identified no fewer than three recent SCA executives as having "strong, deep-rooted connections to organized crime." In fact, the SEC forced the president of SCA to leave the company because of his own underworld connections.[63]

At a subsequent IPS seminar, I warned of a rebirth of a "degree of common cause and a covert working relationship" between the Casey-controlled CIA and organized crime, as had been seen during the CIA-Mafia plots to kill Castro that began in 1960 during the final year of the Eisenhower Administration, adding:

> Even though the CIA-Mafia plots to kill Castro failed, crime bosses used information from this alliance to bargain for immunity from prosecutions, as well as to blackmail the United States Government....
>
> To sum all of this up, in my first seminar on this subject last May, I charged that the Reagan Administration had "shown a frightening tolerance of organized crime," as evidenced by its cavalier attitude toward this institutional problem. I believe that everything that has happened since May clearly shows this to be true, except that now this attitude has become a disturbing and even dangerous pattern.
>
> I am not alleging guilt by association; I am simply questioning this pattern of associations, particularly when the Administration claims to be taking the hard-line on the organized-crime problem. It is quickly becoming apparent

that this, indeed, is nothing more than a charade, and that the Reagan Administration simply prefers "organized" crime to "disorganized" crime—because a degree of internal discipline and control is implicit with the former.

My investigation of the Reagan Administration had put a hook in me as deeply as the McMaster Task Force had. But working for free at IPS while still not prepared to pitch a new book proposal about Reagan and the Mafia, I found myself in financial trouble again.

My only real asset was the condominium I had just purchased in 1979. And, although I loved my home and its location, I loved my causes even more. As I grappled over what appeared to be a difficult decision, it seemed much simpler after Mrs. Nolte wrote a timely letter to me, saying:

> To misquote Thoreau: "Most men go down the road of life bent under the weight of too many material goods." You are now entering that category. As much as you treasure the ownership of that apartment, it makes you a hostage to the world of material rewards....
>
> If you don't find another source of income soon, you will be condemned to the 8-5 life of a bureaucrat. No doubt work at ACTION was more interesting and rewarding than selling insurance, but it is not being your own man, which is what you seem to want. If you want to be independent and also own worldly goods, you'd better start pounding that typewriter.

After receiving Mrs. Nolte's letter, I decided to sell my condo.

The first prospective buyer the real-estate agent brought to my home was Richard Queen, one of the hostages taken by the Iranian militants during the November 1979 siege in Tehran. Queen, who had been diagnosed with multiple sclerosis, had received his freedom prior to the general release of the other hostages on the day of Reagan's inauguration.

Returning to the United States and given a considerable amount of back pay, Queen wanted to spend his money. As the real-estate agent gave him a tour of my place, he asked for the price. When she told him, Queen replied, "That's very reasonable. I think I might take it."

Watching and hearing this scene from the other side of the room, I couldn't take it any longer. Angering my real-estate agent, I walked over to Queen, put my arm around his shoulder, and said, "Listen, kid, you've had enough problems. This place is not worth what we're asking. I'm not going to sell it to you."

A few weeks later, my real-estate agent, who had settled down after I blew the Queen deal, sold my home to an executive for a local chemical company—for our asking price. The agent insisted that I not be present during her client's walkthrough.

With the money made, I paid my bills and moved into a smaller, less expensive rental. The sale of the condominium bought me some time while I tried to figure out what I was going to do next.

47. Writers' rights

On March 10, 1980, I received a letter from Senator Howard M. Metzenbaum (D-Ohio), the chairman of the U.S. Senate Subcommittee on Antitrust, Monopoly and Business Rights, asking me to testify before his panel, along with a handful of other authors and publishing executives, at a one-day hearing about corporate concentrations in the publishing industry. What had sparked Metzenbaum's interest in my statement was the June 29, 1978, article by Herbert Mitgang in the *New York Times* about Simon & Schuster's brazen attempt to sabotage and suppress *The Hoffa Wars*.

After receiving the senator's letter, I spoke with my "big sister," Barbara Raskin, who then worked for Sam Brown, the director of ACTION. Raskin, the author of three books at that time, was a founder and a former president of Washington Independent Writers, an organization I had joined the previous July. A strong advocate of writers' rights issues, Raskin encouraged me to accept Senator Metzenbaum's invitation and to provide testimony to the subcommittee—even though I risked alienating potential publishers of books I hoped to write in the future.

On Thursday, March 13, accompanied by Barbara, I appeared before the senate panel.[64] During my testimony, I ran the committee through my battles prior to switching publishers from the New Republic to Paddington Press after Simon & Schuster had refused to distribute my book. Before answering questions, I concluded my prepared remarks, saying:

> As a member of Washington Independent Writers, I am concerned for others who have been, are now, or will in the future [be] confronted with a similar dilemma—without agents and attorneys, like mine, who are willing to gamble on the future of equally unknown freelance writers. . . .
>
> As Herbert Mitgang wrote in his June 29 article, each such case is an example "of [a] possible loss of independence—with implicit censorship—where there is conflict on a controversial nonfiction book."

Naively or not, I walked away from this experience absolutely convinced that only by remaining free and independent could I become the crime reporter and author I always wanted to be, unencumbered by the politics and conflicts of interest inherent with the Big Media. However, I also realized that by following this course, I would open myself up to professional isolation and a complete lack of institutional protection, as well as a harrowing feast-and-famine existence—just as Mrs. Nolte had warned in her last letter.

From the outset of this realization, I knew that I had to learn how to parlay moments of success into a strategy for long-term survival—while attempting to discover sources of strength and even joy during those moments of inevitable failure that were sure to arise during my writing career.

Also, I sought to discover how other independent writers handled similar situations in their own lives, wondering if there was any common ground upon which we could help each other.

The week after my appearance before the Senate subcommittee, Barbara Raskin asked me to accompany her and author Kitty Kelley, who had recently published a best-selling book about Jackie Kennedy Onassis, to a meeting of the board of directors of the Washington Independent Writers (WIW). The previous Christmas Eve, Kitty and I had been featured together in a story written by reporter Rudy Maxa and published in the *Washington Post Magazine*, entitled, "Be An Author, Make Enemies." Soon after, I became involved in the writers' rights movement, accepting a vacant seat on the WIW board, which Kitty gave up for me.

Just as independent truckers viewed their own profession, many authors believed that the term, "independent writer," was more of a hope than a reality. That belief was supported in the spring of 1981 by the results of an Authors Guild poll, which revealed that the median writing income of its members was less than $5,000 a year. In other words, a writer who didn't make enough money probably couldn't remain independent for very long, especially if he or she had family responsibilities.

No one needed a crystal ball to understand that corporate concentrations in the publishing industry, among other institutional problems, would continue to hurt those who wrote and published for a living. Also, problems with uncooperative publishers and editors, as well as uncommitted memberships and officers, were monumental obstacles for most writers' groups. Confronting all these problems without large sums of independent money had caused many of these organizations to fade or disband between crises. Sometimes the old faces returned, but personal, professional, and financial problems usually took their toll. The latest crop of writers' leaders were usually those who had been most recently abused by the publishing industry and would, sometimes, organize for motives other than a real commitment to writers' rights issues.

A major problem for each wave of writers' organizations was a lack of continuity from one to the next. There didn't seem to be any way to learn from the mistakes of earlier groups or parallel organizations. Group after group—with different names and acronyms—searched for their own unique identities, throwing away yesterday's rulebook and writing their own.

By May 1981, after nearly a year on the WIW board of directors, I had become extremely pessimistic about the direction of the publishing industry, as well as the writers' rights movement. Still, even though I had delivered a gloomy keynote speech about the state of the writing profession at the second annual WIW Spring Writers Conference in May, I was elected president of WIW the following month.

In a written statement to the membership during my campaign, I explained that I wanted to fight for writers' rights while building coalitions with other national and local writers' organizations.

Also, I proposed a "feasibility study" for a Washington writers' union, similar to the Writers Guilds in Los Angeles and New York. That idea was extremely controversial—especially among some independent writers who did not want a union or anyone else speaking for them, as well as among those who did not write for a living and wanted organizations, like WIW, to remain small cliques of hobby writers who only wrote occasionally for profit.

Although I stood firmly against "politicizing" WIW outside the arena of writers' rights, I knew that the interests of politicians and writers would occasionally clash, forcing us to become more political—as in the anticipated fight with the Reagan Administration, which had already announced its intention to water down the Freedom of Information Act.

To me, politicizing the association meant taking stands on issues like abortion or the then-current war in El Salvador. Regardless of my personal positions on these matters, I did not think that WIW, which had a remarkably conservative membership, had any business getting involved in them. Many of us wanted to help to unite writers, not look for issues to divide them.

Soon after my election, the Nation Institute, the public-interest arm of *The Nation* magazine, announced that it would sponsor the American Writers Congress, the first such conclave of writers in forty years, scheduled for October 9-12 at the Roosevelt Hotel in New York.

During a local organizing meeting in Washington, author E. Ethelbert Miller, the head of the Ascension Poetry Reading Series at Howard University, and I were selected to co-chair the Washington delegation to the Congress—where many hoped that the first national writers' union would be created.

48. The American Writers Congress

On September 11, 1981, Ethelbert and I took the train to New York for a meeting about the American Writers Congress, scheduled for the following day at the New School for Social Research, across the street from *The Nation*. Hosting the meeting were members of the Congress's steering committee, mostly staffers at the Nation Institute. The editor of *The Nation*, Victor Navasky, also attended, along with a couple of dozen writers from around the country, representing a variety of writers' organizations.

In a written statement, the New York Media Alliance, promoting the immediate establishment of a writers' union, stated:

> A national writers union would bargain collectively with publishers, editors, and other employers for the rights of writers. It would establish and enforce standards and practices pertaining to such issues as: wages and fees, payment schedules, kill fees, advances, editorial accountability to writers, indemnity and warranty clauses, copyrights, royalties, and subsidiary

rights. It would represent writers in grievances against employers. It would supply standard contracts for book and magazine writers.

As a large organization, the union would be able to gain medical, legal and other benefits for members. It would act as a lobbying organization to advance the rights of writers and to oppose laws that discriminate against us. It would fight censorship.

Even though I fully supported a feasibility study for the eventual creation of a writers' union—which, while running for WIW president, was a major plank on the platform I had won on—I wanted to know more about this particular effort by the Media Alliance.

In my own written statement—fully aware that I was responsible to WIW's conservative board and membership—I posed several questions to the organizers of the proposed union, based upon my knowledge of the problems that the independent truckers had experienced with their own collective-bargaining efforts: How would the issue of unionizing independent contractors be addressed? Would there be local affiliations? If so, how much power would the national union have over its locals? How would the national board be elected? What would be the dues structure? Would dues be paid to both the national union and to its locals? And, generally speaking, would there be bottom-up union democracy or a top-down autocracy?

None of these questions were even addressed in the union organizers' written statement.

Pushing my own agenda, I concluded in my prepared statement:

I believe that a strong and militant—but loosely organized—national alliance of writers' organizations is presently needed. ... [A]n activist national board, broadly-based in its national representation, could help defend individual writers and publicize their problems. Money which would be used fighting the National Labor Relations Board under the union scenario would be better spent if poured into legal and education funds with non-profit, non-partisan tax status. Each dollar spent would be a contribution toward the critical issues writers are facing in these very conservative, very dangerous times.

In other words, short-sighted or not, I wanted a radicalized version of a WIW-like trade association operating on the national level. And I was not alone in this belief. During the meeting, Doug Ireland of the *Village Voice*, a key member of the Congress's steering committee and a union supporter, also advocated "a fighting writers' organization," a National Rifle Association for writers.

The pro-union people did not disagree with our ideas. In fact, most of them supported a national trade association of writers' organizations. However, they also strongly believed that the time had come for the creation of a national writers' union, concentrating on organizing individual writers, which would be launched at the American Writers Congress in October.

By the end of the meeting, Ethelbert and I couldn't have been more impressed with *The Nation* crowd, who were also heavily promoting the idea of the National Writers Union. Even though they represented "management," we were convinced that they were essentially telling the Congress's participants, "Okay, the American Writers Congress is yours. Take it wherever you want. And we'll help you in any way we can."

Because of this remarkable gift from *The Nation*, the 1981 American Writers Congress was a smash hit. Nearly 3,500 writers—an anthology of novelists, poets, investigative journalists, short story writers, technical writers, and small press operators, among many others—attended four days of meetings, hearings, panels, workshops, and roundtable discussions while learning about each other and finding some common ground.

"We don't need any more writers as solitary heroes," author Toni Morrison declared during her keynote address to the Congress. "We need a heroic writers' movement—assertive, militant, [and] pugnacious."

The Congress's action-packed, five-hour plenary session—along with supporting the writers' union and my proposed association of writers' organizations—considered and passed resolutions on numerous issues facing writers, as well as a variety of programs dealing with writers/consumers' services, alternative channels for publishing, review and distribution of books, publishing contracts, paperback rights, book burnings, and censorship, among others.

In my subsequent report to the WIW membership, I wrote:

> If those of us who attended the Congress learned nothing else from our conversations with writers from San Francisco to New York and Minneapolis to Houston, we learned that all of us are essentially facing the same problems. Thus, the defense

of a writer or a writers' rights issue in St. Louis will eventually translate into a defense of all writers nationwide.

In the midst of the weekend Congress, I had also developed a healthy appreciation and respect for the organizers of the new national writers' union, whom I had the opportunity to meet and speak with. All of my questions about the union's structure and organization still weren't answered, but I recognized that the people behind the evolving union movement were making sincere attempts to make the union as broadly based as possible.

Yet, although I was listed in a promotional pamphlet among dozens of supporters of the new National Writers Union, I still felt that I had no choice but to temper my new enthusiasm as I tried to walk the tightrope between the union's local organizers in Washington, who were trusted friends of mine—especially writers Barbara Raskin, Ethelbert Miller, Jeff Stein, and John Dinges—and the anti-union members of WIW's board and membership to whom I was accountable as WIW president.

Consequently, in the wake of the Congress, I felt that I had been placed in a political vise. But I sensed that, in the end, the inevitable conflict between the new writers' union and the established WIW trade association would be good for everyone who wrote for a living—even though I was probably going to get crushed in the process.

Almost on cue, after the American Writers Congress and the creation of the National Writers Union, WIW board meetings at the National Press Club became incredibly contentious and notorious. Writers from New York and as far away as San Francisco came to witness the verbal slugfests between and among those members of the board who wanted WIW to become a national leader in the fight for writers' rights and those who wanted WIW to remain a benign local writers' club. With few exceptions, everyone on the board, including me, showed up for every meeting loaded for bear. The carnage was absolutely breathtaking for onlookers who had the stomach to stay and watch. They had ringside seats to a bare-knuckled brawl for the heart and soul of the organization.

In the midst of all this combat, conservative board members made an issue of my association with the left-wing Institute for Policy Studies and claimed that I was attempting to turn our trade association into a union. That was nonsense, but, unfortunately for me, a lot of people believed it.

Towards the end of my term, after losing my slight majority on the board, I sensed that I was finished as WIW president, announcing that I would not seek reelection. I then threw my support behind the association's former executive director, WIW vice president Judith Saks, a gentle but committed woman who would have made a wonderful president. However, soon after, Saks, who had just given birth to her first child, declined to run, deciding instead to concentrate on her family and career.

Later, after the positive public reaction to my May 4 testimony in support of the Freedom of Information Act—along with those of Coretta Scott King, authors Seymour Hersh and Kurt Vonnegut, and citizen-activists Joan Claybrook and Lois Gibbs—before a joint hearing of senators and congressmen on Capitol Hill, I changed my mind and decided to run again, touting a long list of accomplishments. No previous WIW president had ever sought—or wanted—a second term for this volunteer job.

In my prepared statement, announcing my bid for reelection, I wrote:

> WIW is now the largest and most respected local organization of free-lance writers in the United States. Because of our size and our strength—as well as our location—we have a responsibility to provide our membership with more than just workshops, newsletters, and health insurance. We should be something more than just a clearinghouse for information. No doubt, these services are important—in fact, they're the backbone of our organization. But we now have the responsibility to stand with other writers' groups at the forefront of this battle, and to defend and protect writers from the abuses which we are starting to read and hear about daily.
>
> Also, I made a pledge to keep WIW, the trade association, and the WIW Legal and Education Fund, our 501(c)(3) group, autonomous. However, I added that I wanted to explore the possibility of inviting the local writers' union to become a third, independent branch of WIW.

The reaction to my announced reelection bid and plans for the future was swift and severe. A popular founding member of WIW and the soon-to-be owner of a small, Washington-based publishing house, whom I always liked and respected, was recruited to run against me. A strategy of mass mailings and phone calls to WIW members became the centerpiece of his campaign, which was managed by the conservative members of the sitting board of directors.

After hearing from other WIW members what was going on, Doug Ireland of the American Writers Congress wrote a fund-raising letter on my behalf to his personal friends in New York and Washington, declaring:

> Dan is the target of a smear campaign of red-baiting based primarily on Dan's association with the Institute for Policy Studies and his steadfast support of the work of the Congress. A coalition of conservatives, Cold War liberals, and anti-political types are attempting to paint Dan as a tool of the IPS 'disinformation' apparat. The opposition to Dan is well-heeled and plans a number of mailings and other outreach activities prior to the voting.

To my complete surprise, these tactics had an immediate impact. Suddenly on defense after this final assault on my tenure as WIW president, I failed to put together an effective counteroffensive. After a year of nimble tap dancing and careful tightrope walking, I was caught completely flatfooted.

On June 16, two days before the sealed mail ballots were even counted, I had already accepted defeat, stating in my final written report to the WIW board of directors: "Writers' rights activists don't die. They just start writing again."

49. The Milo murder

On June 30, 1981—in the midst of my volunteer work with IPS and WIW—I received a telephone call from Akron attorney Barry Boyd, a friend who had worked with me in Thadd Garrett's office during our brief assignment at the U.S. Consumer Product Safety Commission in 1976-1977. I had last seen Boyd the previous Christmas at a party thrown by a mutual friend.

Boyd called to tell me that he had been arrested for his involvement in the highly publicized murder of Dean Milo, the wealthy CEO of the largest barber and beauty supply wholesaler in the country, which was based in Akron. Privately owned by Milo's family, the Milo Corporation grossed nearly $50 million a year, doing business with companies like Faberge, L'Oreal, and Clairol, among others.

PART FOUR: RONALD REAGAN & MCA

Automatically assuming that Boyd was innocent, I started suggesting some ideas for his legal defense. In the midst of this, Boyd stopped me in mid-sentence and confessed that he had been involved in arranging this murder, adding that he was now cooperating with the prosecutor's office.

Hearing this, I was completely stunned, especially when he suggested that I might want to write a book about the case. Actually, I had been looking for a professional reason to stay close to Ohio because of my dad's looming health problems, including his long bout with throat cancer.

41-year-old Dean Milo was slain on August 10, 1980, at 2:30 A.M. at his home in Bath, Ohio, a fashionable suburb of Akron, while his wife and three children were visiting her parents in Clearwater, Florida. When the police arrived at the scene the following day—after his best friend's wife had found his body and called 911—they saw Milo lying face down in the blood-covered foyer near his front door. He was wearing only a pair of urine-stained, blood-splotched boxer shorts—which were on backward, the fly over the buttocks.

A yellow, foam-filled cushion with white trim, apparently taken from a chair ten feet from his body, covered his head and shoulders. In the middle of the cushion, police officers could see the clear impression of a single bullet hole. Criminalists removed the cushion and found a second bullet wound in his back. Above Milo's head were two spent cartridge shells, fired from a .32-caliber revolver.

Also, investigators noticed cotton particles on Milo's neck and back, in and around one of the entrance wounds. Another wad of cotton protruded from Milo's mouth, prompting early speculation that the murderer or some unknown person in the house had tried to administer first aid after the shooting.

Just inside the front door, the police discovered a crumpled Western Union telegram still in its yellow envelope. When the police opened it after lifting a single fingerprint, they saw that the telegram form was blank.

Because Milo had a business relationship with at least one reputed Mafia figure, James Farina, who had expressed an interest in buying Milo's company, law-enforcement officials initially suspected that Milo had been the victim of a contract killing.

Immediately, the scope of the murder investigation rocked the state of Ohio. The Summit County Sheriff's Office, in cooperation with the Bath Township Police, concentrated their probe on the Milo Corporation. They quickly learned that, although Milo had full control over the firm, the stock had been divided in thirds among Dean; his younger brother, Fred; and their sister, Sophie Milo Curtis. But in recent months, family troubles had developed, and Dean Milo had fired his brother and sister from their jobs, specifically accusing his brother of embezzling $300,000 from the family business.

In the aftermath of Dean Milo's murder, Fred Milo took over as the president of the company. Investigating Fred and his sister—as well as her husband, another company executive who had lost his job—the police learned that all three had been out of town at the time of the murder.

Nevertheless, shortly after his arrest, my friend, attorney Barry Boyd, immediately confessed to being part of the murder conspiracy, which he claimed was engineered by Fred Milo, who had promised him the moon and the stars in return for his cooperation.

Boyd stated that he had brought a topless dancer, Terry Lea King, into the plot. Then, she contacted a personal friend, Tom Mitchell, a Vietnam veteran who said he was willing to kill for money.

With Boyd's confession, the police arrested King and Mitchell. However, even though the Boyd-King-Mitchell group had plotted Milo's murder, they never carried out their plan.

Instead, after realizing that King and Mitchell were not up for the job, Boyd looked inside the company and approached Ray Sesic, an employee of the Milo Corporation who was loyal to Fred Milo. Sesic brought in Tony Ridle, another Milo employee. Ridle hooked up with Harry Knott, an old friend of his who was a vending-machine operator in Arizona. Knott brought in his brother-in-law, Frank Piccirilli, who allegedly had mob connections.

By the time I came into the case in July 1981, Knott and Piccirilli were still at large. However, King, Mitchell, Sesic and Ridle, like Boyd, had pleaded guilty and were working with the prosecution. In addition, the police had captured Milo's actual killer, David Harden, a troubled young speed freak, and flipped him.

Yet, even with the cooperation of these six co-conspirators, Fred Milo's first trial had already ended in a hung jury on May 25. In fact, the prosecution, fearing a mistrial, had decided not to place Harden, who had been arrested in the midst of trial, on the stand.

Fred Zuch, who prosecuted the Milo case, did use Harden during the retrial. And, on July 29, 1981—with the sworn testimonies of Boyd, Sesic, Ridle, and Harden—Fred Milo was convicted of aggravated murder.

PART FOUR: RONALD REAGAN & MCA

After his initial call to me, Barry Boyd introduced me to William C. Dear, a flamboyant but capable and very successful private investigator from Dallas, Texas, who had played an important role in the investigation.

I also met Lieutenant Larry Momchilov of the Summit County Sheriff's Office, an intelligent and tough detective, as well as the lead investigator in the Milo case. Then, through Momchilov, I met two other talented detectives in the case, Bill Lewis of Summit County and Richard Munsey of the Bath Township Police. After gaining the trust of these outstanding officers, Momchilov took me to the county jail in late September and arranged for me to meet, separately, with four of the co-conspirators: Barry Boyd, Tom Mitchell, Tony Ridle and David Harden. With their permission, I taped all of these interviews and photographed each man.

Completely remorseful, Boyd, Mitchell, and Ridle gave me detailed accounts of their roles in the murder conspiracy, repeating what they had previously told the detectives.

Milo's killer, Dave Harden, then a very rough and scary young man, agreed to talk to me but refused to say very much about the killing. Although he had given a confession to the sheriff's detectives and retold his story at Fred Milo's trial, he had never given up all of the specific details about the actual murder.

Seeing that I was having difficulties with Harden, one of the detectives asked me if he could do anything. I took him outside the interrogation room and asked him to place the black-and-white and color photographs of Milo's body at the crime scene and at the autopsy in a manila folder. The detective cooperated, quickly realizing what I planned to do.

With these graphic pictures inside the folder on the table between us, I began asking Harden hard questions about the personal life of the man he had killed. Clearly, he did not know very much. Then, I started to wax sentimental about Milo, telling Harden about Milo's devoted wife and his three wonderful children who were now fatherless.

Seeing Harden respond and getting him to admit that he did not bother to look at Milo after he had shot him twice, I pulled all of the graphic photographs from the folder and fanned them out on the table in front of him.

Harden looked away at first, but then his head slowly turned toward the pictures. For whatever reason, he just had to see them. As he spread these gory photos with his fingers and actually studied a few, Harden started to choke up and then instinctively pushed the pictures back towards me. Giving him a minute to compose himself, I asked, "Dave, can you tell me what happened now?"

Then, Harden gave me his whole story.

In addition, police detectives introduced me to John Harris, a 350-pound loan shark who had been arrested two weeks after Fred Milo's conviction. Harris, whom Harden indicated had solicited him to commit the murder, was scheduled for trial in January 1982. During my interviews with Harris, he was amicable but remained defiant, insisting on his innocence.

My agent, Philip Spitzer, had tried to pitch the Milo-book project to several publishers, but there were no takers. The problem, the editors explained to Spitzer, was that this murder conspiracy had happened in a suburb of Akron, Ohio. If a sensational conspiracy case like this had occurred in New York City or Los Angeles, it would have been worldwide news—and the story behind the murder would have been huge.

Spitzer then introduced me to Neil Nyren, a senior editor at Atheneum. After my meeting with Nyren, the man who had recently turned *Sixty Minutes's* Andy Rooney into a best-selling author, Atheneum offered me a deal—but only for a $10,000 advance, $5,000 on signing of the contract and $5,000 on acceptance of the completed manuscript.

Why did I accept such a low advance? My dad, who had been battling throat cancer for several years, had now been diagnosed with pancreatic cancer, as well. And he didn't have much time left.

I had already left my home in Washington and moved into a rented house on Elmore Avenue in Akron, owned by my college buddy, Jim Switzer, "The Bishop of Elmore." And I lived next door to my old friend, Tim Davis, now the popular Summit County Auditor, and his wife, Dawn, a professor at the university.

In short, there was no choice. I needed the deal and had to accept whatever was offered.

PART FOUR: RONALD REAGAN & MCA

50. Paying respects

On January 17, 1983, libel attorney Robert G. Sugarman of the New York law firm, Weil Gotshal & Manges, responded to a vetting request by Neil Nyren and Atheneum for *The Hunting of Cain*, my book about the Milo murder. And Nyren nearly had heart failure when Sugarman returned a very serious forty-page memorandum, jam-packed with potential legal problems in my book. Frankly, I wasn't concerned at all, knowing that I had the goods.

Ten days later, I met with Nyren and the attorneys in New York and listened as the lawyers called out specific legal challenges to the manuscript. Responding to each, I pulled out a document from a police file or a tape-recorded interview I had conducted with one of the principals in the book.

In the end, to the relief of Nyren and the attorneys, their only real concern was with James Farina, the reputed Mafia associate, whom the sheriff's detectives had initially believed might have been behind the Milo murder. Although I had made it clear in my book that he was innocent of any involvement in the killing—and that I had even changed Farina's name to "James Licata"—the libel attorneys felt uncomfortable about him, fearing that he might sue. So they instructed me to obtain more documentation from another credible authority about his connections to the underworld.

Nearly six weeks later—after I had failed to get any law-enforcement agency, other than the Summit County Sheriff's Office, to identify Farina as an associate of the Mafia—I was out of time. Consequently, Nyren and the Atheneum's attorneys wanted to cut Farina out of my book.

In a last ditch effort to keep him in the text, I decided to go directly to Farina and just ask him, straight out, whether he was connected to the Mafia. Everyone, including Nyren, thought I was crazy to handle it that way, but I had no other acceptable options.

On March 3, after making an appointment, I drove to Farina's office in Canton, Ohio, gave him a fruit basket as a gift, and generally paid my respects to him. Early during our two-hour meeting, I explained that I was the guy doing the book on the Milo murder, that I specialized in organized-crime investigations, and that I had linked him to organized-crime figures in northeastern Ohio.

"Now," I said, "I need your approval for what I have written about you."

Farina, along with his two associates who witnessed this bizarre scene, appeared amused by my direct approach and asked to see the specific references to him. I then handed him every page of the book's galleys in which he was mentioned or even referred to—and waited anxiously as he and his associates read the text.

After completing the chapters and walking out of the room for a private discussion with his aides—leaving me a nervous wreck in his office—Farina returned and said, "There is nothing in this book that will damage me."

Relieved, I pushed his cooperation a little further, asking if he would be willing to repeat what he had just said to my editor. He laughed and, remarkably, agreed to do so.

I picked up the telephone on his desk and called Neil Nyren in New York, charging the call to my home phone, so that I would have a record of it.

When Nyren answered and heard it was me, he immediately asked, "So how did we do with Farina?"

"He's right here and wants to talk to you." I replied.

"What?"

"Neil, he's right here!"

Farina took the phone and confirmed to a very surprised Nyren that he had no objections to what I had written.

―⁂―

On Friday, March 25, reporter Steve Love of the *Akron Beacon Journal* wrote a profile about the hometown author who had just finished a manuscript about the Milo murder. Realizing that the book wouldn't be released until June, Love stated:

> Fred Zuch, the assistant Summit County prosecutor in charge of the case, says he was skeptical of Moldea.
>
> "It wasn't Dan," Zuch said. "I would have been skeptical of anybody who wanted to write a book about the case."
>
> With his obsession for accuracy and documentation, Moldea erased Zuch's skepticism. "I was impressed with the way he was able to absorb the Milo case and understand it."

"Dan," agreed editor Nyren, "is one of the most scrupulous and painstaking researchers I've ever come into contact with.

"When we met with our lawyers to go over the book, he brought along a [collection] of documents. They'd ask a question about something and he'd pull out a file. . . . I've never seen anyone like him."

Love also added a personal note from me, writing:

Moldea said, "I never thought this would be a big book, but I'd always had a fantasy of being a writer and writing about my hometown.

"To me, the book is a success right now. I did what I wanted to do."[65]

However, my bigger reason for returning to my hometown had been to help my family as Dad continued to battle pancreatic cancer, which had been diagnosed the previous August. To everyone's delight, he had gone into remission just before Thanksgiving. The tumor had not grown since.

Then, in late April, after a routine examination by his oncologist at the Cleveland Clinic, I received the report that the tumor had not only grown but had spread to other parts of his body. Because Dad didn't want to hear any bad news, I kept the final prognosis to myself.

At most, he had only six weeks left.

Determined to spend as much time as I could with my family, my plans were nearly sidetracked by a sudden and unexpected twist in the Milo murder case.

51. Subpoenaed

On January 22, 1982, John Harris was convicted of aggravated murder for his role in the Milo killing. Unlike some of the others in the conspiracy—Barry Boyd, Terry Lea King, Tom Mitchell, Ray Sesic, Tony Ridle, and Dave Harden—Harris had never confessed to the prosecution.

The following day, Saturday, January 23, Harris, whom I had interviewed on three previous occasions in the jailhouse, telephoned me at my home in Washington. During our conversation, he began to give me a full confession about his involvement in the murder conspiracy. In doing so, he implicated co-conspirator Frank Piccirilli who had not yet stood trial.

When I realized what Harris was saying, I switched on my tape recorder and memorialized the conversation. By the end of the interview, Harris, who did not know that I had taped him, understood that his confession would be added to the book I was writing, which was set to be released in June 1983.

Then, on April 5, 1983—well over a year after his telephone confession and nearly a month after my book had been shipped to the printer—Harris sent me a letter from prison, saying:

> The word is out here that you have agreed to turn over to the Summit County prosecutor tapes of the interviews that you had with me; that these tapes supposedly contain damaging information against Frank Piccirilli . . .
>
> I am not sure at this point whether or not I will take the stand in Frank's defense. But I can assure you if I do, it will be the real truth. . . .

When I read the letter, I wasn't too concerned. At that point, I had neither given the tape of our January 1982 conversation to the prosecution, nor had I discussed Harris's confession with the police and the prosecutor.

However, on April 20, a deputy in the sheriff's department informed me that Harris was going to testify on Piccirilli's behalf and was prepared to say that Piccirilli had nothing to do with Milo's murder at his upcoming trial. Upon hearing that, I told the deputy that I had Harris on tape, revealing that Piccirilli was the key man behind the Milo murder plot.

According to my agreement with Harris in January 1982, I had pledged not to use his confession until his attempts to plea bargain with the prosecutor had been exhausted. By this time, Harris's efforts had failed—according to both the prosecutor's office and even Harris. Thus, I had fulfilled my agreement with him and considered his confession to be non-privileged and non-confidential. Also, as I had told Harris during our taped conversation, his confession had become the centerpiece of the book's Epilogue, which I still had not shown to either the police or the prosecutor's office.

The following day, April 21, the deputy called and asked if I would be willing to play the Harris tape for Fred Zuch, the prosecuting attorney in the upcoming Piccirilli trial. I replied that I was willing to do so, particularly if Harris was serious about testifying as a defense witness.

Specifically—during our taped conversation in January 1982—I had asked Harris for details about the murder. On tape, Harris told me:

> One day, Frank Piccirilli called me up and said he wanted to get together. He owed me $100 or something, I forget. So we met at this restaurant. . . .
>
> Frank told me he had this guy in Ohio he wanted killed. And he was offering $5,000. So I said, "Why don't you let me make the money?" He says, "Can you handle it?" I told him I could get it handled. . . . After that, at some bar, I met this guy, Dave Harden.

Capitalizing on this chance meeting with Harden, Harris offered him $2,000 to commit the actual murder. Because Harden was desperate for money, he accepted.

Driving a borrowed car, Harris and Harden arrived in Cleveland in early August and spent several nights hotel hopping and partying. "Harden was driving me crazy," Harris added during our taped conversation. "He was so goddamn nervous. And all he wanted to do was get drunk, get high, and get pussy."

Throughout this period of time, Harris told me that he stayed in constant touch with Piccirilli.

Then, early Sunday morning, August 10, 1980, they heard that Milo had returned from a business trip and was at his home in Bath, Ohio. They cased the executive's house and left but then returned shortly thereafter. This time, Harden, with a .32 revolver in his hand, went to Milo's door, posing as a Western Union delivery man.

"Who gave you the gun?" I asked Harris.

"The gun? Frank Piccirilli. Frank gave it to me—a .32 automatic, with a homemade silencer, stuffed with cotton."

At the crime scene, police detectives could not figure out the source of the cotton particles on Milo's neck and back, in and around one of the entrance wounds, as well as another wad of cotton in his mouth.

As it turned out, a homemade silencer—a steel pipe, stuffed with cotton—had initially thrown off the investigation.

With the first shot, all the cotton blew out, according to Harden's subsequent statement to the prosecution team. To muffle the second shot, he grabbed a cushion from a chair in the living room, pressed his gun against it, and fired.

On May 2, 1983, realizing that I was going to catch hell, I played the Harris tape for Fred Zuch. Immediately, the prosecutor told me that he had to tell Piccirilli's attorneys about the recording.

Two weeks later, on May 16, the jury for the aggravated murder trial, *State of Ohio v. Piccirilli*, was selected. Just prior to opening arguments, Piccirilli's defense attorney, Paul Collins, recognized me sitting in the back of the courtroom. He walked up and asked, "Are you Dan Moldea?"

"Yes, I am," I replied as I stood up, thinking he wanted to shake hands.

As I extended my hand, he slapped a piece of paper in it, saying angrily, "This is for you!"

When I unfolded the paper, I saw that it was a subpoena. Specifically, it demanded that I supply the defense with a "copy of [the] book involving Milo case you are writing, records and tapes of interviews, records of any statements given you by any police officer or prosecutor."

A few minutes after I was served, Collins asked Frank Bayer, the trial judge, to order me out of the courtroom because I was a potential witness. The judge agreed, instructing me to appear at a hearing the following morning.

That same afternoon, I called attorney George Farris, one of my closest and most trusted friends since our days in college, and asked him to represent me at the hearing.

The next morning, during the hearing to consider the merits of the subpoena, Farris charged that the defense was on nothing more than a fishing expedition. After a lengthy debate, Judge Bayer asked defense-attorney Collins to be more specific with his request for information and scheduled another hearing for the following day.

At the second hearing on Wednesday, Piccirilli's defense team demanded that I reveal my confidential sources and the contents of the Harris tape. In addition, they asked that I be placed under oath to answer specific questions.

Farris objected, but Judge Bayer insisted that I take the oath. When I balked, he threatened to find me in contempt and to order me imprisoned immediately. Farris then asked for a recess, so that he and I could speak in private.

To me, there was really nothing to discuss. Knowing that my book would be out in a few weeks, I was prepared to surrender and give the defense attorneys anything they wanted, except my confidential sources—since everything else was already in the book.

Another trusted friend who had joined our conversation pleaded with me to hang tough and go to prison. "Think of the publicity for your book!" He exclaimed.

"Listen," I told Farris and my other friend, "you guys know that my dad is dying. There is just no way that I have any time to go to jail. Under normal circumstances, no problem—but not with Dad in trouble! Tell the judge that I'll give them the tape and even take the oath to answer questions about Harris's confession. Give them anything but my sources."

Overruling me, Farris, a fine attorney whom I trusted totally, wanted to take the hard line, insisting, "If the defense gets you on the stand, they're going to ask you about your confidential sources. And when you refuse to answer, you're going to be right back where you started, and you could still wind up in jail.... Trust me, I can work this out."

Relenting, I went along with Farris, and he proved to be right.

When we returned to the hearing, Farris offered Piccirilli's attorneys the opportunity to listen to Harris's soon-to-be-published taped confession in which he had implicated Piccirilli in the Milo murder. However, Farris politely insisted that I not be forced to reveal any sources or to answer any questions, tactfully predicting a monumental First Amendment battle if his offer was rejected.

Persuaded by Judge Bayer, the defense agreed to our offer. We allowed Piccirilli's defense team to hear the tape at 4:00 that afternoon. Of course, after listening to the tape, the defense immediately dropped Harris from its witness list.

On May 25, the jury convicted Piccirilli of aggravated murder. Judge Bayer sentenced him to life in prison.

On June 8, I received two finished hardbound copies of my second book, *The Hunting of Cain: A True Story of Money, Greed, and Fratricide*, which I had dedicated to my family. My editor, Neil Nyren, had moved heaven and earth to get them to me as quickly as he did.

Dad, who had never cared much for my life as a scuffling independent writer, spent the next two days reading this book, and then finally started in on *The Hoffa Wars*, which he could never quite get through. Also, we received a copy of *The Nation*, which featured one of my stories about President Ronald Reagan and the Teamsters, which he did manage to finish.[66]

At 6:50 A.M., on June 12, at home with his wife and two children at his bedside, Dad took his last breath and died very peacefully.

52. Going back East

As predicted, *The Hunting of Cain* didn't sell anywhere near as well as my first book, *The Hoffa Wars*. Even though it had been mentioned in Herbert Mitgang's preview of spring 1983 books in the *New York Times Book Review*, the *Times*, for reasons unknown, decided not to review it. For many people, without a *Times* review, *The Hunting of Cain* simply did not exist. However, I did receive three particularly favorable reviews in other newspapers.

Dennis McEaneney of the *Akron Beacon Journal*, an excellent reporter who had written over 200 stories about the Milo murder case during a sixteen-month period and was easily capable of writing his own book, could not have been more gracious, saying in his review:

> The best of the book, and it is truly fine, rests in the word-for-word tape recorded conversations between the detectives—or Moldea—and the murder conspirators. The interviews are amazing. They'll set the hair on the back of your neck on end....
>
> *The Hunting of Cain* should not be ignored by any truthseeker.[67]

Jim Quinlan, writing his review for the *Chicago Sun-Times*, stated:

> If you savor non-fiction crime accounts, with detectives grinding it out in a painstaking yearlong investigation to solve a murder, then you won't be disappointed with Dan E. Moldea's *The Hunting of Cain*.
>
> A master of investigative research, Moldea won high marks for documentation and detail in his previous book, *The Hoffa Wars*. In *The Hunting of Cain*, he repeats his zealous devotion to fact-finding.[68]

And, in my favorite review for this book, Pulitzer Prize-winning book critic Jonathan Yardley of the *Washington Post* wrote:

> Dan Moldea doesn't get cute in this tough, resourceful, intelligent book. . . . In *The Hunting of Cain*, Moldea is after bigger game that the mere question of whodunit. This meticulously researched book is about the unfolding of a criminal investigation, and about the freaky consequences of coincidence and accident in the lives of human beings. It is not an especially reflective book, and Moldea doesn't hammer the reader over the head with the conclusions that can be drawn from it; but this reticence is one of the book's greatest strengths, and it stands in revealing contrast to the breathless tone in which many nonfiction crime stories are told these days. . . *The Hunting of Cain* is an impeccable job of research and storytelling.[69]

By the beginning of the fall of 1983, the daily visits to my parents' home in Ohio from friends and relatives had subsided, and my sister, Marsha, had returned to her life in Florida. Consequently, Mom found herself alone, even after I started spending three nights a week at her house, just to keep her company.

Fortunately, Dad had provided well for her, financially. Also, Mom had taken care of herself by keeping her job at B.F. Goodrich and remaining closely connected to our church.

Born in Cleveland in 1922, my mom, Mary Craciun—"Mary Christmas" in English—was the youngest of five children. Her mother, Ana Farcasiu, had come to the United States from Romania in 1906 at eighteen. In 1910, she married John Craciun, another Romanian immigrant, who owned a local tavern.

Extremely religious, my grandparents brought up their children in a strict and disciplined environment. As a student at the Cleveland Institute of Music after high school, Mom studied voice. She also attended Fenn College where she developed secretarial skills—just in case she needed a day job. Although she didn't wind up in the opera, Mom regularly sang in the church choir and was active in local civic organizations.

Mom adored her mother who went blind in her later years, but she dedicated her life to my dad after they were married on August 11, 1946, just before his senior year at Ohio State. After graduation, they moved to Akron, Dad's hometown, where they later raised Marsha and me.

Now, like most widows in the wake of their husband's death, the new void in her life could not be filled. Seeing me growing restless in Akron in wake of the publication of the Milo book, Mom, always generous and loyal, encouraged me to return to the East Coast.

Although I had initially intended to return to Washington, my new girlfriend, Leslie, an accomplished novelist whom I had met while we were conducting separate seminars at the Georgetown Writers Conference in July 1981, invited me to stay with her in Manhattan. We had been seeing each other since I called her during my trip to vet *The Hunting of Cain* the previous January.

In short, I was still a basket case after Dad's death. But I was keeping the hurt well hidden from my family and friends. Leslie was the only person in my life who truly understood the pain I was in. As a consequence—more for me than for her—she took me in and helped me through the most difficult time in my life.

Because her apartment in Chelsea was so small, I decided to keep my rented house in Ohio where almost everything I owned remained. I had hoped that I could secure a book deal and get us a bigger place before we drove each other crazy.

When I moved to New York on October 30, I remained as low key as possible. I did not contact any of my friends in town. I made no public-speaking appearances. And I really did not want to make the scene in The Big Apple. I came to town with just over $2,000 in my pocket and had to hit very quickly or else everything I wanted would collapse. I had a job to do, and I just wanted to get it done.

What little I did have in New York had to be stashed under tables or scattered about in this very cramped apartment. My designated workspace consisted of the corner of Leslie's dining room table.

In the past, when I faced an absolute deadline or a difficult situation, I did what I had conditioned myself to do: live like a savage, work at all hours of the day and night, catnap when necessary, and, generally, throw myself into my work. Now in a similar situation, I encouraged Leslie to continue her life, see her friends, and keep her routine.

But, in the end, it was all for naught. I failed to sell the proposal for what I had hoped would be my next book. And I left New York on January 20, 1984. Understanding my situation, Leslie put up no fight.

Returning to Washington, I moved into a group house with several independent journalists—including Jeff Stein of *The Progressive* and Peter Ross Range of *Playboy*—in the Mount Pleasant section of town. With some of the freelance-writing money I quickly earned in D.C., I bought a CPM-driven Kaypro II computer, with no hard drive and only 64K of RAM.

After years of using a manual typewriter, I was thrilled to be in the computer age.

53. *The Wall Street Journal* settles

Shortly after arriving in Washington, I received a subpoena from Washington attorney Tom Green, who represented former U.S. Strike Force attorneys John Dowd and Mike Kramer in their libel case against Jim Drinkhall and the *Wall Street Journal*. I made no attempt to resist.

The Drinkhall controversy had already become an open wound within the community of investigative reporters, particularly among those of us who covered the Teamsters and the mob. And, because I was one of the few reporters who had actually agreed to testify against Drinkhall—who continued to be well liked and respected—I found myself with a serious public-relations problem. Some of my colleagues viewed me as a cop who had agreed to testify against another cop. One *Wall Street Journal* reporter, Edward Pound, refused to speak to me. Even, my old friend, Jon Kwitny, another *Journal* reporter who had helped Drinkhall get his job at the newspaper, was upset with what I had done but reserved any final judgment until the case concluded.

But, then, just days before the beginning of the trial, the *Wall Street Journal* suddenly settled, agreeing to pay $800,000 to the former prosecutors.

Washington Post reporter Al Kamen wrote on June 8:

> U.S. District Court Judge Harold H. Greene yesterday dismissed the cases against the *Journal* and reporter James A. Drinkhall after both sides reached an agreement that included an acknowledgment by the *Journal* that it could not prove some of the allegations in the articles.
>
> Veteran libel lawyers said yesterday that the settlement was unusually large and that it was surprising given the *Journal's* reputation for aggressively defending its articles.

Journal associate publisher Peter R. Kann said the settlement is "an exception to, not a change in," the paper's policy of not settling libel suits.

The New York Times added:

> The payment is the largest reported settlement in a libel suit that did not go to trial, and it is the first known departure from the *Journal's* announced policy of contesting all such actions at least through the trial process.
>
> As part of the agreement, the company acknowledged for the first time that it could not prove a major allegation reported in the articles: that the prosecutors had improperly harassed a prisoner to force him to cooperate with an investigation they were conducting as members of a Federal Organized Crime Strike Force."
>
> The *Journal* also conceded that it could not prove that Dowd and Kramer had engineered a conspiracy of harassment against Drinkhall, as Drinkhall had alleged in his second article.

Shortly after the settlement, Drinkhall left the *Wall Street Journal*.

54. Reagan and the Hollywood Mafia

In early-June 1984—soon after I had left the group house and moved to my own apartment in Washington's Glover Park section—I received a call from Marc Raskin at the Institute for Policy Studies where I was now an Associate Fellow.

Welcoming me back to D. C., Raskin asked if I was interested in conducting another investigation of Ronald Reagan. When I replied that I was certainly ready to start rolling again, he offered me a $5,000 grant, allowing me to proceed in any direction I chose.

Sensing that this was an opportunity to find my next book project, I also sought and received a $3,000 grant from the Fund for Constitutional Government. I split that money with my close friend and Thursday-night poker buddy, Jeff Goldberg, who was writing a book about Richard Nixon and had offered to help me compile whatever I found during my upcoming research trip to Los Angeles. If all went well, I planned to use this information as a pitch for my third book.

Meantime, on June 15, Neil Nyren of Atheneum, the editor of my recently published second book, *The Hunting of Cain*, wrote a letter to me, saying:

> As of the end of the month, I'm leaving Atheneum. Yes, things do change, don't they? I've been made the proverbial offer I cannot refuse from G. P. Putnam's Sons, and the opportunities are splendid, career and otherwise. . . . We'll get another book together going someday.

Happy for Nyren, who became the company's new publisher, I remembered that Putnam's parent company was MCA, Inc., the Hollywood-based entertainment conglomerate—which also owned Grosset & Dunlap, the publisher that had bought the paperback rights to my first book, *The Hoffa Wars*. With my relationship with Nyren, whom I really liked and respected, fairly solid, I believed that Putnam might be the publisher for my possible new book on Ronald Reagan.

But, before I left for Los Angeles to do my research, the prospect of Nyren and Putnam publishing a book critical of Reagan suddenly appeared extremely unlikely.

While packing, I stumbled across an extraordinary article buried in the Calendar section of the *Los Angeles Times*, dated August 17, 1980, and titled, "Ronald Reagan in Hollywood." Two independent journalists, Ellen Farley and William K. Knoedelseder, had written the story, which included information about Reagan's term as president of the Screen Actors Guild and his simultaneous sweetheart relationship with MCA, whose president, Lew Wasserman, just happened to be Reagan's talent agent.

After reading this article, which completely blew me away, I decided to find out more about MCA before leaving Washington.

No single corporation in Hollywood—or, for that matter, in the entire entertainment industry—could rival the power of MCA. Formed by Jules Stein, a Chicago ophthalmologist, in 1924, MCA, which began as a talent agency, later became a multi-billion-dollar business, owning and controlling Universal Pictures. It produced such recent films as *The Sting, The Deer Hunter, Airport, American Graffiti, Jaws, E.T. the Extraterrestrial, On Golden Pond,* and *Back to the Future*; while Universal Television created such programs as *Marcus Welby, M.D., Columbo, McMillan and Wife, Kojak, The Six-Million-Dollar Man, The Rockford Files, The Incredible Hulk, Simon & Simon, Magnum, P.I.,* and *Miami Vice.* And MCA Records featured Elton John, The Who, Neil Diamond, and Olivia Newton-John.

Like the Teamsters, MCA was a very powerful American institution.

With the grant money in my pocket and my preliminary work completed, I flew to Los Angeles on Monday, August 20, determined to find out everything I could about MCA and its relationship with Ronald Reagan.

Upon my arrival at LAX, I rented a Thunderbird and drove to Pacific Palisades for an appointment with Mae Churchill, a long-time friend of several people in the IPS community. Churchill lived in a fabulous home, tucked in the woods on a mountain overlooking Malibu and the Pacific Ocean. A wonderful *grande dame* of the left, she had been a local leader in the battle *for* civil rights and *against* organized crime for decades. A former assistant to studio executive William Fox in Hollywood, Churchill had left management to become an activist in nearly every pro-democracy union movement in the film industry.

In her youth, she had an affair with another leftist, Jeff Kibre, an honest labor leader in Hollywood. During the late 1930s, the now-deceased Kibre had led a reform movement among dissident members of the film industry's corrupt unions. In addition, Kibre revealed evidence that proved a partnership between Hollywood studio heads and powerful Mafia figures. In return for cash payoffs, mobsters guaranteed labor peace to film moguls, specifically from the International Alliance of Theatrical Stage Employees (IATSE), which was controlled by the Chicago Outfit.

In the biggest scandal ever to hit Hollywood, Kibre's information led to the indictments of the president of the Motion Picture Producers Association, Joe Schenck of Twentieth Century-Fox, two corrupt IATSE union leaders, George Browne and Willie Bioff, and seven dangerous mobsters, most of whom were from Chicago.

Of course, Hollywood blacklisted Kibre for his landmark anti-corruption work—but did so under the guise of his participation in left-wing political activities. Redbaited and labeled a communist, Kibre was forced to leave the film business.

Churchill explained to me that Ronald Reagan—as a member of the board of directors of the Screen Actors Guild, and, later, as

SAG's president—had aligned himself closely with the IATSE and the Teamsters, both of which were mob-controlled.

The day after my meeting with Churchill, I drove down the coast to Playa del Rey where I met with the legendary Jack Tobin, "The Godfather of Mafia Reporters" and a close friend of Walter Sheridan. A former ace with the *Los Angeles Times*, Tobin and his then partner, Gene Blake, had written a series of nearly sixty articles about the Teamsters' pension fund between May 1962 and August 1964. Since leaving the *Times*, Tobin had worked for the *Los Angeles Herald-Examiner* and, for the past decade, consulted for Time, Inc., including its subsidiary, *Sports Illustrated*.

The tall and thin 70-year-old Tobin and his lovely wife, Virginia, lived in a beautiful beach house on the ocean. Downstairs in his office, Tobin maintained an incredible file room, filled with government documents, newspaper clippings, and assorted correspondences. Tobin collected everything and knew about everything he collected.

When I told Tobin I was looking into Reagan's ties to MCA, he replied, "You'll have to go after Sidney Korshak. . . . He's where Reagan's connections to MCA, as well as to the underworld, will begin and end."[70]

55. Finding gold in Los Angeles

After spending two-and-a-half days with Jack Tobin and his files, I went to Santa Monica on Thursday, August 23, 1984, to visit author Larry Leamer and his wonderful wife, Vesna, two close friends from Washington who had recently moved to California.

Looking at the books in Leamer's library, I grabbed a copy of *Washington Post* reporter Lou Cannon's reputedly definitive biography, *Reagan*, which had been published in 1982. However, in Cannon's index, there were no cites to MCA or its founder Jules Stein and only a brief, anecdotal reference to Lew Wasserman, Reagan's personal agent who wound up succeeding Stein as MCA's chairman of the board.

Then, looking at Cannon's title page, I was shocked to see that his hardback book had been published by Putnam, MCA's publishing subsidiary—prior to Neil Nyren taking over as its publisher.

"How could a reporter like Lou Cannon miss the Reagan-MCA connection?" I asked Leamer who simply shrugged.

Later, after hearing me mention the 1980 Knoedelseder-Farley article in the *Los Angeles Times*, Leamer shuffled through some papers on his desk and pulled out a large clipping from *Daily Variety*, "New Info on Reagan, MCA Waiver Probe," dated April 18, 1984. Written by staff reporter David Robb, the article explained previously untold details of Reagan's relationship with MCA, culminating with his testimony before a federal grand jury in February 1962 in which he was questioned about his relationship with the corporation.

The story was so remarkable that I had to sit down to read it. And, when I finished, I read it again.

"Does this Robb guy live in L.A.?" I asked Leamer.

"Just call *Daily Variety* and ask for him."

I looked up the telephone number in the phone book and called the paper. When the receptionist answered, I asked for Robb.

"Dave Robb," a stern voice answered.

"Is this *the* David Robb?" I asked.

"Yeah."

"My name is Dan Moldea. I'm an independent journalist and author from Washington, and I'm interested in your fabulous story about Reagan and MCA last April. Do you have plans for dinner tonight?"

Reluctant, at first, to help someone he didn't know, Robb finally relented, telling me to meet him at Patys, a popular diner with an unusual name in Toluca Lake.

Tall and thin with a round Eastern European face, the 35-year-old Robb and I could have passed as brothers. However, Robb was extremely gruff and suspicious. When I first saw him and introduced myself, I gave him a copy of *The Hoffa Wars*, which had my name on the cover and picture on the back flap. Not good enough for Robb, he wanted to see some real identification and demanded my driver's license. Obliging him, I pulled out my wallet and showed him everything I had, including my driver's license and even my student-identification card from Kent State.

After a very pleasant dinner and a quick stop at a poker club in Commerce, we went to Robb's apartment in Hollywood where he showed me a huge box, containing 6,000 pages of unsorted Department of Justice documents about Reagan, MCA, and the Screen Actors Guild that he had received through the Freedom of Information Act.

It was an absolute gold mine.

Even though Robb invited me to sleep on his couch, I wound up spending the entire night skimming through this astonishing material, which included the complete transcript of Reagan's 1962 testimony before a federal grand jury.

The following day, Robb—who, despite his tough-guy exterior, turned out to be one of the finest people I had ever known—allowed me to photocopy anything I wanted. In fact, I copied everything, most of which had not been published in Robb's only article about this subject. And, even though I had been extremely critical of Lou Cannon for missing—or ignoring—the Reagan-MCA connection, the fact was that none of the dozens of other books about Reagan had addressed this matter either.

I offered to pay Robb, who became a long-term friend, a consulting fee or even give him a percentage of my book's royalties. Incredibly, he refused to accept any money from me.

Ronald Reagan had come to Los Angeles in 1937 to make motion pictures. In 1940, MCA bought out the talent agency that represented Reagan. Lew Wasserman, a rising star at MCA, became Reagan's personal agent, later negotiating his first million-dollar contract with Warner Brothers on Reagan's behalf, based on the success of the actor's 1942 film, *King's Row*.

In 1946, Wasserman became the president of MCA, and the following year, Reagan, with his film career already in decline at the end of his seven-year contract, became the president of the Screen Actors Guild (SAG).

A sweetheart relationship developed between MCA and SAG, which culminated in July 1952 during Reagan's fifth consecutive term as SAG's president. Reagan and Laurence Beilenson—an attorney for MCA who had previously served as SAG's general counsel and represented Reagan in his 1949 divorce from actress Jane Wyman—negotiated an exclusive blanket waiver from SAG that permitted MCA to engage in unlimited film production.

In fact, the agreement violated SAG's bylaws, which prohibited talent agents from employing their own clients. At the time, no other talent agency could receive a similar arrangement.

A Justice Department memorandum in Dave Robb's FOIA cache indicated that the waiver became "the central fact of MCA's whole rise to power."

At the end of Reagan's fifth term as SAG president, he began to have serious financial problems, particularly with the IRS. MCA negotiated a deal with a Las Vegas hotel-casino, which was owned and operated by associates of the Chicago Outfit, for Reagan to host a song-and-dance show and to receive enough money to cover his back-tax debt.

When Reagan returned to Hollywood, MCA, through its newly-formed film company, Revue Productions, selected him to host its flagship television program, the *General Electric Theater* for $125,000 a year. He was paid additional fees when he actually produced episodes for the series.

Despite his status as a television producer, Reagan remained on SAG's board of directors in another violation of the guild's bylaws, which prohibited producers from holding office in the actors' guild. In 1959, when Reagan ran for an unprecedented sixth term as SAG's president, his opponents raised the bylaws issue. However, Reagan denied, on the record, that he had ever produced any episodes for the *General Electric Theater*, which was an outright lie.

Wasserman had encouraged Reagan to seek his sixth term. MCA was facing sensitive negotiations with SAG over residual television and motion-picture rights for actors. The issue eventually forced SAG to strike in 1960, and Reagan, as SAG president, became the actors' chief negotiator.

The contract that Reagan arranged with the studios is still known in Hollywood as "The Great Giveaway." It did provide residuals for actors—but only for films made *after* 1960. The studios kept everything *before* 1960, which was worth billions of dollars. This greatly benefited MCA, which had recently purchased Paramount Pictures's huge film library in 1959.

(Later, Richard Walsh, the president of IATSE during the 1960 SAG strike, told me that labor lawyer and Mafia mouthpiece Sidney Korshak, a close friend of Lew Wasserman, was directly involved in the negotiations with Reagan—just as Jack Tobin had predicted.)

In 1962, the Justice Department filed a federal antitrust suit against MCA, alleging that it was both a talent agency and a production company. SAG was charged as a coconspirator.

Reagan became the subject of both criminal and civil investigations by the FBI and a federal grand jury in Los Angeles. A Justice Department memorandum quoted a Hollywood source as saying, "Ronald Reagan is a complete slave of MCA who would do their bidding on anything."

Reagan was subpoenaed to testify before the grand jury, but he experienced amnesia during his testimony on February 5, 1962, failing to recall significant details of his role in the SAG-MCA blanket-waiver decision in 1952.

Federal prosecutors were so convinced that Reagan had perjured himself repeatedly during his testimony that they subpoenaed his and his wife's federal income-tax returns for the years 1952 to 1955. His second wife, actress Nancy Reagan, had been a member of the SAG board of directors since 1951.

However, in July 1962—in the aftermath of MCA's purchase of Decca Records, the parent company of Universal Pictures—MCA agreed to abolish its talent agency as part of a consent decree with the Kennedy Justice Department. As a result, all charges against and investigations of the company and its alleged coconspirators, including Reagan and SAG, were dropped, and the record of the case was sealed.

Universal quickly became the biggest film producer in the entertainment industry.

Claiming that he was deeply affected by the breakup of MCA—which, in fact, had turned the company into an even more powerful multibillion dollar international corporation—Reagan, supposedly a lifelong Democrat, suddenly became an anti-big government Republican, just like his political mentors at MCA, board chair Jules Stein and vice president Taft Schreiber, both of whom were active in Republican Party politics.

In return for Reagan's long-time loyalty to his benefactors, MCA, through its cooperation in the selling of Reagan's Malibu properties, helped Reagan to become a multi-millionaire—and, then, the governor of California.[71]

On September 1, 1984, I left Los Angeles, feeling triumphant as I returned to Washington. Jeff Goldberg and I began working on our 20,000-word article about Reagan and MCA, trying to get it published before the November 6 Presidential election, in which former Vice President Walter Mondale was challenging Reagan's bid for reelection.

Barred from approaching monthly magazines because of their tight deadlines and knowing that the daily newspapers would try to steal our story, Goldberg and I went to the new editor of *City Paper*, Mark Perry, an old friend from Washington Independent Writers who had joined our Thursday-night poker group. Perry agreed to publish our story, "That's Entertainment: Ronald Reagan's Four Decades of Friendship with World Showbiz Colossus MCA," which appeared on the front page of the October 5-11 issue.

But, despite our best efforts in this little publication, we had absolutely no impact on the election. The President slaughtered Mondale, whose running mate, Geraldine Ferraro, had a husband who had been linked to New York mobsters in a devastating article co-written by Jon Kwitny of the *Wall Street Journal*.

On the subject of Reagan and his own connections, the President continued to receive a pass.

56. William Morris Agency, Viking Press

On November 7, 1984, immediately upon returning to Washington after lecturing at a conference of Caribbean journalists in Jamaica, I drew up a book proposal, stating:

> President Ronald Reagan has won his second term by an overwhelming margin. Incredibly, despite all that has been written about him, little is really known or understood about how he acquired both his wealth and power. Previous books on Reagan—even those by Lou Cannon of the *Washington Post* and respected Reagan biographer Bill Boyarsky of the *Los Angeles Times*—have not even addressed the impact of MCA, Inc., the entertainment conglomerate, on Reagan's professional and political careers. I propose to do such a book, concentrating on the rise of MCA.

I added that my principal characters were Ronald Reagan, Lew Wasserman, and Sidney Korshak—three of the most powerful people in the worlds of politics, show business, and the underworld, respectively.

On January 24, Marie Arana-Ward, the Washington editor for Harcourt Brace Jovanovich, greeted me at the headquarters of her publishing house on Fifth Avenue in New York where I met Peter Jovanovich, the heir to his family's publishing empire, to discuss my Reagan-MCA book proposal.

The meeting had been scheduled by an associate of Sterling Lord, my new, big-name, hot-shot literary agent.[72] Earlier, he had convinced me to leave Philip Spitzer, my loyal agent for the past ten years who had held my hand while I was trying to find a publisher for my first book about Jimmy Hoffa and then stuck by me when I decided to write my second book about a murder in an Akron suburb, which he totally opposed.

I quickly realized that leaving Spitzer was one of the worst mistakes I had ever made, because, by doing so, I had lost my guardian angel through the fiery hell that is the publishing world. And that message came through loud and clear during my meeting with Harcourt Brace.

When Jovanovich arrived nearly forty-five minutes late for our meeting at his office, Arana-Ward, who was as agitated as I, managed to introduce me to her boss, but that was about all either of us said for the rest of the meeting. Without specifically addressing my proposal, Jovanovich said that any book about Reagan had to make the President "come alive."

Nodding in agreement, I then simply sat there with Arana-Ward and listened while this neo-conservative pontificated about what a wonderful guy Reagan was—without any further discussion about my project in which Jovanovich clearly had no interest.

Finally, about a half-hour into his monologue, I turned to the Arana-Ward—with Jovanovich in mid-sentence—and laughed, "What the hell am I doing here?"

Mercifully, the meeting collapsed immediately after that.

Arana-Ward—who, soon after, left Harcourt Brace and went to Simon & Schuster—couldn't stop apologizing as I walked out of Jovanovich's office, still laughing. Actually, I wasn't angry with her or even her boss. However, I was absolutely furious with my new agent, whom I fired later that day for not screening this situation beforehand. Philip Spitzer would have never allowed me to walk into something like that.

A few hours later, I returned to Washington, agentless.

The following day, I called an old acquaintance, Washington author Robert Pack, who had just published the biography, *Edward Bennett Williams for the Defense*, about the famous Washington attorney who had represented notorious people, like Jimmy Hoffa, and respected institutions, like the *Washington Post*.

Upon hearing my predicament, Pack offered to introduce me to his agent, Mel Berger of the William Morris Agency.

Berger and I spoke to each other, and he asked to see my proposal, which I shipped to him overnight. Upon receipt, he accepted me as a client.

On March 1—just two days after my 35th birthday—my agent of less than ten days called, telling me that Viking Press had just bid $75,000 for my Reagan book, which, at that time, was the largest advance I had ever been offered for anything.

57. Korshak gets a pass

After paying off all of my debts and buying my first *new* Thunderbird after three used T-Birds, I completely threw myself into my work. I now had the William Morris Agency representing me and Viking Press publishing my third book. I felt that I was finally hitting my stride as an independent journalist and author.

On Sunday, May 19—after throwing a huge party at IPS two days earlier for everybody I knew—I packed up my 1985 Thunderbird and drove across country to Los Angeles. Holing up in my summer digs in Westwood, near UCLA, I went into my Bat-mode, working day and night, crashing for twenty minutes at a time, getting up and going back to work again. Other than an occasional poker game with Dave Robb or dinner with the Leamers, the Tobins, Mae Churchill, or any of a handful of other friends, I had no life other than researching and writing. But, as a result of this rigid self-discipline, I was cranking out the manuscript.[73]

One big problem I did have with this book was that my three major characters—Ronald Reagan, Lew Wasserman, and Sidney Korshak—were all alive, at the height of their power, and still kicking ass. Although I scored a coup by finding and interviewing Richard Walsh—the former president of the IATSE, who made the Reagan-Korshak connection for me while recalling the events of the 1960 strike by the Screen Actors Guild—I couldn't get many others to go on the record with their criticisms of these powerhouses, especially Wasserman and Korshak, who still wielded incredible power in the Hollywood film industry.[74]

I did experience an off-the-record interview of a lifetime with a big, box-office superstar actor, who actually started to cry when I pushed him about his professional relationship with Wasserman, whom he knew could destroy his career by simply snapping his fingers. Another big-name talent gave me several stories about Wasserman but insisted that I couldn't use any of them until after Wasserman died—and, even then, without attribution as if Wasserman could reach him from the grave.

In the end, although I interviewed 127 people, I couldn't get more than twenty on the record. Fortunately—thanks to Jack Tobin, Mae Churchill, Dave Robb, Bill Knoedelseder, and several others—I had primary-source documents coming out of my ears. I felt uncomfortable basing my work mostly on these written records, but there was simply no other way to source this book—because so many people were afraid to talk.

On January 6, 1986, I finished the draft manuscript and sent it to my editor, Dan Frank at Viking Press—nearly three months before my April 1 deadline. As usual, Mrs. Nolte had already gone through it, giving me her solid advice about what should stay in or come out—and how to smooth the rough edges of what remained.

Neither Mrs. Nolte nor I could come up with a legitimate title for the book, so Frank named it, *Dark Victory: Ronald Reagan, MCA, and the Mob*—based on the 1939 Bette Davis film, *Dark Victory*, in which Reagan had a supporting role. Frank was struck by the obvious double meaning in the title.

While Frank and his staff edited and vetted my book, I still had time to add new details to the manuscript, based on unfolding events.

On Sunday, January 12, an article appeared under President Reagan's byline in the *New York Times Magazine*, entitled "Declaring War on Organized Crime." The story celebrated the "success" of the Reagan Administration's war on the underworld. Without ever mentioning the corrupt Teamsters Union or its new president, Jackie Presser, Reagan added, "There will be no détente with the mob. It's war to the end. We mean to cripple their organization."

Remarkably, two days after this almost laughable article was published, Reagan's own President's Commission on Organized Crime issued an interim report, criticizing the Reagan Administration for its close ties to the mobbed-up Teamsters Union, adding that "the appearance of impropriety" had been created. The commission report shook up the White House and Justice Department so badly that Attorney General Ed Meese called a press conference to defend the White House-Teamsters relationship, defiantly saying that he did not see anything improper about it.

Then, Meese added:

> At no time have I, nor, to my knowledge, any member of the administration, done anything which was designed to assist or aid anyone involved with organized crime. The fact that people did meet with labor leaders was certainly not designated or intended to in any way interfere with the proper investigation of organized crime.

In response, a column appeared in the January 23 issue of *L.A. Weekly*, which stated:

Last week, the *New York Times Sunday Magazine* stooped to printing—and the *Herald Examiner* to reprinting—a shameless piece of self-promotion in the form of an article "by" the president in which Reagan . . . celebrates [his] "long-standing" anti-mob position, with exhibit A his purported heroic expulsion of the underworld from the IATSE studio union. It would read better if investigative reporters Dan Moldea and Jeff Goldberg hadn't turned up a very different set of facts 18 months ago in [*City Paper*].

Their story documented the efforts made in the 1940s by the Conference of Studio Unions (CSU) to "replace IATSE, which had been dominated by the Chicago mob." A CSU strike broke out and the union asked the Reagan-led Screen Actors Guild for support. But Reagan bought the IATSE line the CSU was pro-communist. So "Reagan forged the SAG/IATSE alliance that crushed the progressive CSU." Moldea and Goldberg continue: "During the violent IATSE-CSU battles, the SAG leadership was protected by IATSE guards. Reagan . . . carried a .32 caliber Smith and Wesson as he crossed the CSU picket line. [Reagan] has also told and retold the story about how a handful of Teamsters protected him from 'communists.'"

The President's Commission on Organized Crime's 222-page final report, *The Impact: Organized Crime Today*, was a major disappointment upon its April 1986 release. Over half of the eighteen commissioners filed supplemental views or dissenting opinions to the report. Dissenters charged, "Poor management of time, money, and staff has resulted in the commission's leaving important issues unexamined . . . . The true history of the commission . . . is a saga of missed opportunity."

I asked one commissioner, Philip Manuel, why Sidney Korshak's name had not appeared in the final report. He replied, "That's a sensitive area. Korshak did come up in a couple of interviews and in one of the staff reports. But there was dissension about him throughout the life of the commission. . . . Several of us wanted to highlight him. . . . But it was just not meant to be. There were forces that didn't want Korshak touched. So the commission just rounded up the usual suspects."

Notably, Manuel questioned commission witness Jimmy "The Weasel" Fratianno, a top Mafia figure who had flipped and turned state's evidence, about Korshak.

PART FOUR: RONALD REAGAN & MCA

Manuel: Mr. Fratianno, when you were active with the La Cosa Nostra, did you have occasion to meet the man by the name of Sidney Korshak?

Fratianno: Yes, sir.

Manuel: Would you tell the Commission what you know about him and what function, if any, he provides for organized crime?

Fratianno: He is a Chicago man for thirty years that I know of. He practically runs the Mafia industry. . . .

Manuel: Would Sidney Korshak be the type of person you had in mind when you were telling the Commission about front men that operate for organized crime?

Fratianno: He is one of them. Yes, sir.

Speaking of Korshak, another commissioner went even further, citing a nine-hour meeting prior to the release of the final report. "Leaving Korshak out of the final report was no accident," the commissioner said. "A conscious decision was made to leave out any reference to him, and we were told about it at that meeting. It was too late to do anything about it. We [the commissioners] really never had a chance to see the final version of the report before it was released. . . . I felt that there was pressure to keep Korshak out. And where that pressure came from, well, your guess is as good as mine."

58. Political Isolation

In my third book, *Dark Victory*, I made—and documented—five basic charges:

1. That Ronald Reagan—the actor, the union leader, and the national political figure—was the creation of an entertainment conglomerate known as MCA, the Music Corporation of America.

2. That Reagan was the subject of and subpoenaed to testify before a 1962 federal grand jury. Specifically, federal prosecutors investigated kickbacks and payoffs that Reagan had allegedly received in return for concessions he had made to MCA, then his talent agency, while serving as the six-term president of the Screen Actors Guild. These concessions helped to make MCA a multi-billion-dollar corporation; and, as a quid pro quo, MCA helped Reagan become a multi-millionaire.

3. That MCA had worked with organized-crime figures throughout its history. Most recently, a federal investigation of MCA and the mob—which revolved around MCA's appointment of an identified Mafia figure to a top post in MCA's Record Division—was quashed by the Reagan Justice Department.

4. That Reagan had been influenced throughout his career by people associated with organized crime (a) beginning with his days in the Screen Actors Guild during which he had aligned himself with mob-controlled unions, (b) through his job at a mob-operated Las Vegas casino while he was having tax problems with the IRS, (c) through his negotiations during the 1960 SAG strike, and (d) during the bizarre sale of his California properties at a hugely inflated prices while he was running for governor of California.

5. That Reagan's appointments and policies as President of the United States had been influenced, in part, by these underworld associations.

These were the charges I had to defend over the coming months—during Reagan's growing popularity in the midst of his second term. Thus, I was grateful for the support I expected to receive from my colleagues at the Institute for Policy Studies where I continued to serve as an Associate Fellow, as well as from the liberal community, which had been demonized by Reagan's right-wing allies during the past six years.

On May 23, 1986, Bob Borosage, the executive director of IPS, called and asked me to have lunch with him. He did not want to talk about why over the telephone. When I arrived at Cafe Rondo, across from the Institute on Q Street, Borosage was waiting for me at a table, sitting with

IPS co-founder Marc Raskin and the respected journalist, attorney, and civil-rights activist, Roger Wilkins.

"To what do I owe this honor?" I asked.

None of them blinked or even smiled. Seeing how serious and uncomfortable they were, I simply asked, "No kidding, guys. What's up?"

"Tell us about your book about MCA," Borosage said, speaking for the others.

I gave them a ten-minute verbal tour of the book, emphasizing its major characters: Ronald Reagan, Lew Wasserman, and Sidney Korshak.

"And how do you deal with the Institute in your book?" Asked Raskin, who had really started this Reagan-MCA project in June 1984 when he provided me with a $5,000 grant to investigate the President.

Now very serious, I replied, "I acknowledge you guys, individually, on the Acknowledgments page. I also have a separate paragraph, thanking the Institute for its support, and I identify myself as an Associate Fellow on the back flap of the book's dust jacket. . . . Guys, what's up here?"

Wilkins then launched into a long explanation about his friendship with Jean Stein, the daughter of MCA founder Jules Stein and the heiress to his fortune. Unlike her widely respected conservative father, Jean Stein was a widely respected liberal.

"I'm sorry, Roger" I said when he concluded. "What does any of this have to do with me and my book? Honestly, there's no mention of your relationship with Jean Stein. It's none of my business."

"It's not that," Raskin then declared. "Jean Stein runs a big foundation up in New York, and she gives grants to worthy causes."

"Like IPS?" I asked.

"Like IPS," Raskin replied. "The other thing that complicates matters is that Lew Wasserman wants to throw a big Hollywood fundraiser for IPS."

Wasserman, MCA's chairman of the board, was still a liberal Democrat who had supported Jimmy Carter—until Carter ran against Ronald Reagan in 1980.

Knowing exactly what I was being told but forcing them to tell me out loud, I asked, "So what are we saying here?"

Speaking for the others, Borosage dropped the bomb, saying, "You have to take all references to the Institute out of your book. We just can't jeopardize our fund-raising efforts because of what you've written."[75]

"Done!" I replied without a fight. "Do you want my resignation from the Institute, too?"

When, to my disappointment, none of them said anything, I quietly surrendered, "Okay, you'll have it by the end of the day." Then, I shook hands with all three men and left the restaurant without ordering lunch.

After six years as a loyal team player at IPS, I now found myself alone and, worse yet, politically isolated and professionally vulnerable—just when I needed every friend I could get.

59. Bad timing

During the first week of August, the early reviews for *Dark Victory*—which featured the full text of Ronald Reagan's 1962 grand-jury testimony—began running in the trade publications. *Kirkus* gave me a bad review, describing my book as "a mountain of jellybeans." *Publishers Weekly* printed a neutral review, neither particularly good nor bad. However, *Library Journal* gave me a favorable review, calling *Dark Victory* an "extraordinary book."

More good reviews followed in *Booklist*, ("Moldea mounts a strong case"), *Best Sellers* ("a fast-paced gem"), and the *West Coast Review of Books*, which gave the book four stars ("a real page turner").

In the midst of all of this, my agent, Mel Berger, called to tell me that Norman Brokaw—the CEO of the William Morris Agency and talent agent for celebrities ranging from Marilyn Monroe and Elizabeth Taylor to Bill Cosby and Clint Eastwood—had said that *Dark Victory* was "the greatest book he's ever read, anywhere, anyplace, anytime." Berger added that Brokaw had ordered copies for all of the members of his company's board of directors.

Also, my publisher, Viking Press, purchased a full-page ad for *Dark Victory* in the *New York Times Book Review* and smaller ads in the *Washington Post* and the *Los Angeles Times*. In addition, Viking sent me on a first-class book tour to several cities, including Boston, Chicago, Los Angeles, New York, Philadelphia, San Francisco, and Washington, among others.

Although we scored well with local television and radio, I was unable to get a single invitation on any of the network-television programs—all of which routinely did business with MCA and its subsidiary, Universal Television.

We found the print media less conflicted. Pete Yost, a reporter for the Associated Press, called and asked me to do an interview about *Dark*

Victory. I came to the meeting well prepared, deciding to spoon-feed him my documentation for the critical portions of the book.

On Sunday, September 21, Yost's AP wire story appeared all over the country. In the *New York Times*, Yost's article was headlined, "Reagan Was a Subject of 60's Screen Inquiry," and also credited Dave Robb's earlier reporting at *Daily Variety*.

Concentrating on the Justice Department's 1962 investigation of MCA—during which Reagan had been called before the federal grand jury in Los Angeles—the AP story, published in the *Times*, stated:

> In Mr. Reagan's grand jury testimony, reprinted in the book, he repeatedly said he could not recall details of the 1952 [MCA blanket] waiver.... Mr. Moldea's book says that any criminal proceedings were dropped as a condition of a consent decree. In addition, MCA executives, Mr. Reagan and others "avoided having to appear in open court to answer messy questions about their financial relationships," the book said.

Spokesmen for President Reagan, MCA, and the Screen Actors Guild refused to comment about the charges in my book.

Regardless of the print attention *Dark Victory* was receiving, my publisher and I had a major problem: Nearly six weeks after its release, few potential readers could find any copies in bookstores outside of southern California—where the book appeared to be flying off the shelves. Consequently, all of this great print media was going to waste while Viking searched for the bottleneck in its distribution network.

I even found unexpected support from the *Hollywood Reporter*—although the other trade publications for the entertainment industry, like *Variety* and *Electronic Media*, slapped me down. Thomas Pryor, the executive editor of *Variety*, accused me of naiveté while simultaneously making my case of MCA's ties to the underworld, writing:

> Naturally, MCA did business with gangsters; it wasn't possible to book talent into a nightclub without becoming involved, for, with very few exceptions the rumrunners controlled the niteries.[76]

The Los Angeles Times disagreed with Pryor's evaluation of my work, as reviewer David Pecchia insisted:

> *Dark Victory* is indeed a victory for author Moldea. He has through sheer tenacity amassed an avalanche of ominous and unnerving facts. . . .
>
> There is much information that is fresh in this book, and through numerous interviews and previously unattainable federal documents, Moldea has woven a myriad of previously separated facts into a startling political pattern.[77]

Reporter Kim Masters of the *Los Angeles Daily News* wrote a news story, allowing MCA executives to slough off my allegations, as well as an ongoing federal grand-jury investigation of MCA's ties with reputed Mafia figure Salvatore Pisello, whom I had also discussed in *Dark Victory*.[78] (In the end, the investigation of MCA was quashed by the Reagan Justice Department.) Masters stated:

> Until now, MCA has ignored the book, refusing to be interviewed by its author. In an interview last week, [MCA president Sid] Sheinberg said he has not read it, [but still remarked,] "I was sent a copy by someone . . . [but] I have no idea what it really says."[79]

Then, completely ignoring the Pisello probe, Sheinberg added, "I don't think there's a sane individual anywhere that believes MCA is involved with the Mafia. Anyone who does believe that should . . . get some professional psychiatric help. Our worst detractors don't believe we have Mafia ties."[80]

Masters continued:

> The book has received some favorable reviews and has become a best seller in Los Angeles, but it is turning in only a fair performance in other cities, and it is not achieving national recognition.

Trying to explain this, Ron Curran of the *L.A. Weekly* insisted:

> Moldea's findings certainly deserve national attention. But whether most Americans will even hear of Moldea's work has come into serious question in recent weeks, as his publisher has been repeatedly rebuffed in trying to arrange promotional

appearances to support the book. Major media outlets apparently feel the topic is just too controversial.[81]

In Palo Alto, California, John McClintock wrote in the *Times-Tribune*, wrote:

> All three television networks have refused to have investigative reporter Dan Moldea on their morning talk shows to discuss his book.
>
> It seems unusual, given TV's seemingly insatiable appetite for interview subjects. The networks say it's because they don't want to offend President Reagan. Moldea says it's really because they don't want to offend MCA, the largest show business conglomerate in the world.
>
> Whatever the explanation, this interesting blackout of television promotion for *Dark Victory* gives you a fair idea of just how hot it is.[82]

This television "blackout" over *Dark Victory*, which was also discussed in an article in the *Los Angeles Times*, had become very troublesome. Without national television for such a controversial nonfiction work, I had a zero chance to make the national best-sellers lists.

Addressing this problem in perhaps my favorite review of all for *Dark Victory*—which was neither particularly favorable nor unfavorable—author Nicholas von Hoffman, writing for the winter issue of *Grand Street*, wrote a lengthy and reflective essay, stating, in part:

> Civic morality may indeed ebb and flow with the passage of the decades, but there is more involved in the flaccid public response to a book like Moldea's than that. Implicitly, the author is inviting us to do something we don't want to do—he's asking us to live with the proposition that a sitting President is some kind of crook. In short, civic morale is to be sacrificed to civic morality. Only a few of us want to do that. It's too dispiriting to know that our President, given the symbolic place the office has, is a grievous and egregious violator of the higher standard we set for ourselves. We're delighted to learn that John Kennedy was a philandering adulterer, but only after he's dead and gone. While he was alive and in the White House,

we needed to believe that when the lights went out at night he
was bedded down with his wife.... There may come a time...
when *Dark Victory* will have a greater impact than it is having in
the autumn of 1986. Until then it may help to remember that
only occasionally does the truth make us free; the rest of the
time it merely ruffles our feathers.[83]

Of course, no one anticipated the Iran-Contra scandal would break in November.[84] But, by then, renowned historian Garry Wills had published his own book, *Reagan's America*, in which he offered an abbreviated version of the Reagan-MCA connection. To his credit—Wills, whose book, with the help of the scandal, shot to the top of the national best-sellers lists—acknowledged the work Jeff Goldberg and I had done in our earlier article about Reagan and MCA for *City Paper*.

In his review of Wills's book, Pulitzer Prize-winning reporter Al Delugach wrote in the *Los Angeles Times*: "The new Wills book appears better positioned to achieve wider public interest than another fine one published ... a few months ago, *Dark Victory: Ronald Reagan, MCA, and the Mob*."[85]

In other words, my book suffered from bad timing.

However, among the bright spots, Tina, my ex-girlfriend who had become very successful in her new career in Manhattan, threw a fabulous book party for me on the Upper East Side where—in the midst of seeing many long-time friends and colleagues—I also had the pleasure to meet her equally successful husband-to-be.

Tina, who could not have been kinder to me, was happy at last.

60. Trouble with the *New York Times*

Even though I had criticized journalist Fred J. Cook in my first book, *The Hoffa Wars*, the *New York Times Book Review* selected him to write the review of that book. When I complained, the *Times* editor who fielded my call replied that I had not specifically named Cook in my book. Indeed, I had referred to a famous story Cook had written but did not name him as the author. Acknowledging that Cook had a responsibility to tell the *Times* about any conflict of interest, the *Times* editor added that the *Book Review* had a strict policy not to make assignments to people who were criticized *by name* in the book under review.

Then, after Cook and the *Book Review* criticized me for my Marcello-Trafficante-Hoffa theory about the murder of President Kennedy in *The Hoffa Wars*, *New York Times* Hollywood reporter Aljean Harmetz chose to credit a "documentary novel," published nine months *after* my nonfiction book, for breaking the story—just before the final report of the U.S. House Select Committee on Assassinations was released.[86]

In addition, even though the *New York Times's* literary columnist, Herbert Mitgang, had listed my second book, *The Hunting of Cain*, in his spring 1983 forecast of upcoming books, the *Times* opted, for reasons I never fully understood, not to review that book.

Then came my third book, *Dark Victory*, which the *New York Times Book Review* assigned to Jeff Gerth. In that book, I had quoted a named source who was critical of an article co-written by Gerth, whom I had identified by name, which should have eliminated him as a reviewer. In addition, I had been openly critical of Gerth's role as a co-defendant in a libel suit against *Penthouse* for an article he had co-authored. I simply could not believe that the *Times* had chosen Gerth to critique my work.

Predictably, Gerth published a negative review of *Dark Victory*, saying that it was "an ambitious book that sheds some light on past events but falls short in showing that old ties make for current scandal."[87]

But, the *New York Times*, which usually has the final word on these matters, demonstrated schizophrenia about the importance of the Reagan-MCA matter—based on who reviewed what book by which author.

Two months after Gerth shrugged off my revelations, the *New York Times* published its review of *Reagan's America* by Garry Wills, who had footnoted his material about Reagan and MCA to my work. *Times* reviewer Michiko Kakutani lauded Wills, saying that his reporting of Reagan's "possibly conflicting involvements with MCA and the Screen Actors Guild . . . help shed light on some of the messy convulsions of the current Iran-Contra affair, as well as other problems of this Administration. And, in that sense, Reagan's America is both a timely—and necessary—book."[88]

Even though my book was in the midst of a ten-week run on the *Los Angeles Times's* best-sellers list, my frustration with the *New York Times*, which began with its false and misleading review of *The Hoffa Wars*, continued. I did complain to the editor of the *Times* about the *Book Review's* selection of Jeff Gerth as the reviewer of my work, but I backed down and did nothing when the *Times* refused to correct the situation.

However, right on the heels of this controversy, another problem with the *New York Times* developed. And I was determined not to allow this one to pass so easily.

—⚏—

On March 16, 1987, Jon Kwitny, still a top reporter for the *Wall Street Journal* and now the host of public television's *Kwitny Report*, taped a program about the charges made in *Dark Victory*. Kwitny was enthusiastic about the book and asked me to appear on the program, along with journalist Nicholas Lemann, who had written a critical review of my book in the *New York Review of Books*.

During the taping, at the beginning of an exchange between Kwitny and me, Kwitny said that he personally felt that I had done a "disservice" by "trying to put a smoking gun in Mr. Reagan's hands." However, Kwitny quickly followed this criticism up by saying that my book had "amassed a powerful case that Mr. Reagan spent the middle decades of his life running blindly and jovially through a bustling anthill of corruption, at times presiding over it as if he didn't know it existed but always relying on it to make his own world function smoothly."

A review of the *Kwitny Report* appeared in the *New York Times* on April 15, 1987, written by media critic, John Corry—whose wife, Sonia Landau, had headed the "Women for Reagan-Bush" campaign and had been appointed by Reagan as a member of the board of directors for the Corporation for Public Broadcasting.

In his review, Corry wrote:

> The dud *Kwitny Report*—the one that seemed to last hours—was a discussion of Ronald Reagan's alleged connections to the mob. The configuration wasn't sufficiently mixed. The program was dreary Reagan bashing. Mr. Kwitny, though, seemed to know it. When he introduced his principal guest, Dan E. Moldea, author of *Dark Victory*, he said forthrightly that Mr. Moldea was a personal friend. *He also said his book was a "disservice."* Without firm evidence, Mr. Kwitny said, the book linked Mr. Reagan, the Music Corporation of America and gangsters. [Emphasis added.]

However, Kwitny, who had been completely supportive of *Dark Victory*, had never described my book as a "disservice."

PART FOUR: RONALD REAGAN & MCA

I was absolutely incensed by this latest attack on me by the *Times*, written by another reviewer with a clear conflict of interest. And, this time, I wanted to do something about it. When I called the *Times* and requested a correction, the newspaper, of course, refused yet again to correct its mistakes.

I then called John Sikorski, the former executive director of PROD who was now a private attorney in Springfield, Massachusetts. Sikorski wrote a letter to Max Frankel, the executive editor of the *Times*, on April 22 and asked for a correction.

Sikorski wrote:

> Overall, Mr. Corry's article recklessly presents a false impression that Mr. Kwitny did not think highly of *Dark Victory*. Indeed, Mr. Kwitny spent the first third of the show summarizing the book with great enthusiasm.
>
> These observations can be confirmed by the *Times* which received a videotape of the broadcast in questions from WNYC prior to April 15.
>
> Accordingly, we demand that the *New York Times* run a notice clarifying Mr. Corry's review.... Any proposed clarification should be reviewed with this office if it is to have the effect of settling this matter without the need for further proceedings.

Even Jon Kwitny wrote a letter to the *Times*, insisting that Corry was wrong and that a correction was necessary.

On Saturday, April 25, while I was out of town—covering the National Rifle Association Convention in Reno, Nevada, for National Public Radio—I called my home in Washington to collect the messages on my answering machine. Joel Swerdlow, another close friend, had called to congratulate me for getting the *New York Times* to publish a correction, which he had read in the *Times* that day.

I immediately went to a newspaper stand in my hotel and picked up a copy of the *Times*. When I turned to the corrections box on page three, I saw several corrections but not mine.

I then called Swerdlow in Washington who read the correction to me. Same newspaper, different edition—the *Times* had only published the correction in a limited number of editions, even though Corry's review had appeared in all editions. And my correction was the only one that hadn't run in all editions.

In the limited number of editions in which it appeared, the correction read:

> A television review of the *Kwitny Report* on Wednesday [sic] incompletely characterized Jonathan Kwitny's remarks about the book *Dark Victory*, whose author, Dan E. Moldea, was a guest on the show. Mr. Kwitny said the book was in some ways a "disservice" because without firm evidence it linked President Reagan, the Music Corporation of America and gangsters. But Mr. Kwitnys praised other aspects of the book.

Making the situation worse, the *Times* had now even screwed up the correction.

Furious, I called Sikorski who had already seen the correction and was nearly as upset as I was.

"What do you want to do, Dan?" Sikorski asked.

"I want to sue these motherfuckers!" I shouted, completely losing it. "That's what I want to do! I am so fucking tired of these fucking arrogant assholes with their fucking conflicts of interest at the fucking *New York Times* misrepresenting my goddamn work and fucking with my goddamn life! Let's sue 'em!"

Still functioning in the real world, Sikorski suggested instead that he write another letter to the *Times*.

Simultaneously, Geoffrey Stokes, the media critic at the *Village Voice*, had followed this controversy over the Corry review. In the May 5 issue of the *Voice*, Stokes wrote:

> Just this week . . . the *Times* was forced to run a correction (itself inaccurate, but that's another story) of Corry's biased version of a *Kwitny Report* that focused on Dan E. Moldea's book *Dark Victory*. . . .
>
> A transcript of the program, however, reveals . . . almost precisely the opposite of what Corry claimed.

Sikorski's second letter went out on May 11 to both Frankel and Jack Rosenthal, the *Times's* editorial page editor. This time, Sikorski wrote:

> We have reviewed the correction in the *New York Times* ran on April 25, of Mr. Corry's review of April 15, 1987. The

PART FOUR: RONALD REAGAN & MCA

> correction the *Times* ran is unacceptable and in violation of good journalistic ethics and basic notions of fairness.
>
> Your correction again misstated what Mr. Kwitny said on the show. . . .
>
> Recognizing that litigation is often not the best way to resolve disputes, we hereby demand that the *Times* issue another clarification on its reviewing pages.

Sikorski also suggested that, as an alternative to another correction, the *Times* publish my letter to the editor, allowing me to defend myself.

I had concurred with Sikorski's wording, especially the threat to sue—even though we both knew that I didn't have the money to go through with it. In other words, we had decided to play a straight-out bluff with the most powerful newspaper in the world.

But the *Times* called that bluff on Thursday, May 14, in a letter from *Times* attorney David Thurm, who wrote:

> I have carefully reviewed the underlying story, the correction and your letter and find that the Times's correction is fully responsive. The reader is sure to understand what was intended by the correction, and your suggested changes are purely quibbles over semantics. . . .
>
> [W]e cannot accede to your request for a further correction or a letter to the editor.

Because I could not afford to sue, I had no choice but to back down from the *New York Times*—just as I had done twice before.

But I swore to myself that I would never do it again.

PART FIVE:
The NFL & the Mafia

61. The *Frontline* broadcast

On Monday, January 17, 1983, *Frontline*, a weekly news-documentary series, premiered on the Public Broadcasting System, featuring a program entitled, "An Unauthorized History of the NFL." Jessica Savitch, an NBC News correspondent on loan to PBS, narrated the one-hour show, which criticized the close association between the worlds of professional football and syndicate gambling.

Two extremely controversial stories were highlighted on the program. One involved a bookmaker who claimed that he had fixed an unnamed head coach, an unnamed quarterback, and an unnamed team captain who played for an unnamed NFL team. The second detailed allegations that the late owner of the Los Angeles Rams, Carroll Rosenbloom—the one-time owner of the Baltimore Colts who had died in what was ruled as an accidental drowning in April 1979—might have been murdered.

Frontline also spotlighted the Teamsters' Central States Pension Fund and its millions in loans to Las Vegas casinos, which had accepted billions in legal bets over the years. In this portion of the program, the primary target was Allen Dorfman of Chicago, the former fiduciary manager of the pension fund, who had ties to numerous NFL team owners, coaches, and players.

Two friends of mine were involved in the production of the program: Scott Malone, its chief investigator, and Tom Mechling, the former executive director of the National Center for Gambling Information, who served as the program's consultant, a role he had earlier played for the NFL Players Association.

On the night of the *Frontline* broadcast, I called both Malone and Mechling to congratulate each of them for their work. Both told me that they were already besieged with calls, warning them about the political dangers of going up against the NFL.

The following day, as expected, NFL commissioner Pete Rozelle—via the league's public-relations man, Joe Browne—issued a statement, condemning the *Frontline* broadcast. In part, Rozelle/Browne said:

> The program presented by PBS Monday night was chiefly a rehash of press clippings, gossip and rumor, some almost 25 years old. The innuendoes and unsupported allegations, including the circumstances of Carroll Rosenbloom's death and the so-called fixed games, were, in my view, disgraceful examples of cheap sensationalism and checkbook journalism.

On January 20—just three days after the *Frontline* broadcast—three ski-masked gunmen ambushed and murdered Dorfman. They approached him while he and Teamsters bail bondsman Irwin Weiner, whom I had met with Dorfman in April 1975 at the Gaylur Products trial, walked across a parking lot in Lincolnwood, a Chicago suburb.

Just the previous week, Dorfman had been convicted of conspiring to bribe U.S. Senator Howard Cannon of Nevada, culminating the FBI's *Pendorf*—Penetrate Dorfman—investigation that had been initiated in 1979. Four other men were convicted with Dorfman, including Teamsters general president Roy Williams.

A federal judge had sentenced the sixty-year-old Dorfman to a fifty-five-year prison sentence. No doubt, the Chicago mobsters who ordered his murder feared that he was about to flip and turn state's evidence for the government.

Because of my familiarity with many of the key characters in the *Frontline* story—like Dorfman, Weiner, and Williams—Scott Malone asked me to co-author a book with him about the NFL and the Mafia, based on the research he had accumulated for his program.

Six months later, my Dad, who was then losing his battle with pancreatic cancer, and I were talking alone in his bedroom. "You know where I'm going with my career as a crime reporter," I whispered to my father who lay helpless and dying in his bed. "Do you have any advice for me?"

Wracked with pain, Dad suddenly became very still. After a few thoughtful moments, just three hours before he died, he quietly replied, "Yeah. . . . Don't write that damn book about the NFL."

Ignoring his last piece of advice four months later, I moved to New York while already in the midst of writing a proposal for this book. Finally, on November 21, Malone and I completed the NFL proposal and delivered it to our agent who immediately submitted it to several publishers.

But, soon after, the rejections and low bids for the book started to pour in. The best offer we received came from Villard Books, which put up a mere $40,000 for what we considered a two-year project. Malone and I, who would have to split the money, decided to pass.

Every single publisher, including Villard, had expressed fears of potential libel problems with the book. One top editor, Donald Hutter, wrote to my agent, saying: "I'm truly sorry this one didn't work out—I was very impressed by Dan and his carefully considered approach to getting the goods—but at the same time I can understand the qualms of others."

PART FIVE: THE NFL & THE MAFIA

The final blow came on January 15, 1984. *The New York Times Sunday Magazine* published a cover story, "Pete Rozelle: The Man Who Made Football An American Obsession," a remarkably detailed story about the NFL commissioner by David Harris, the former antiwar activist and an editor at the magazine, whom I had always respected. Within days, I learned that Harris, who had also been shopping a book on the NFL, had sold it for a big number to Bantam Books.

I made a courtesy call to Harris whom I had met once before and asked him several specific questions about his project, trying to get a feel for how far along he was. Friendly and even quite candid, Harris told me that he had secured the cooperation of Rozelle, several NFL team owners, and the league's front office. Recognizing that he was an honest reporter with a great project and a huge head start, I suggested to Malone that he get behind Harris's effort.

Harris's book about the NFL, *The League*, was released during the fall 1986—at the same time as my third book, *Dark Victory*. Although I found Harris's book very well written and extremely fascinating, it primarily concentrated on the business of professional football and not its corruption.

As a result, Malone insisted that there was still a book to be written about the NFL and the mob. But, he added, he was inundated with work at *Frontline* and proposed that I be the sole author of the book and simply hire him as a consultant.

62. Investigating professional football

On Friday, July 17, 1987, I had lunch with Bill Regardie, the owner of *Regardie's*, a stylish Washington-based, monthly business magazine. During the past few months, I had published two major cover stories for *Regardie's*—one on the National Rifle Association and a second about the murder of Senator Robert Kennedy. Also present for my lunch with Regardie were his executive editor, Brian Kelly, and managing editor Bob Vasilak. During the meeting, I gave them a written proposal for an article about the NFL and the mob.

On July 27, I signed two contracts, one with *Regardie's*, which gave me $10,000 for the story, and the second with Scott Malone for his work as a consultant. Then, a few days later, I left for the West Coast and spent a month doing research and interviews for my NFL story in Los Angeles, San Diego, and Las Vegas.

For the next several months, I ate, drank, and slept professional football. As part of this process, I conducted two interviews with Warren Welsh, the director of NFL Security, the private police force of the National Football League, on November 16 and November 29.

Clearing the story, the editors at *Regardie's* encouraged me to attempt to interview NFL Commissioner Pete Rozelle, whom I had saved for last. However, after contacting Joe Browne, the NFL's director of public relations, I was informed in a letter from Browne that Rozelle would not consent to the interview.

After Rozelle refused my request, I called Welsh again and read my finished manuscript to him for the purpose of soliciting his comments and criticism. In short, I wanted to make sure that my story was right. After hearing the article and making several suggestions as to how it could be improved, Welsh described it as a "fair and accurate" report.

After this conversation, Welsh wrote a memorandum about me on January 5, 1988, which accurately stated:

> During the week of December 28, 1987, I spoke with Dan Moldea regarding an article he is writing for the February issue of *Regardie's* magazine. The article will discuss in detail the League's history with gambling matters including the backgrounds of owners and their relatives, e.g. Bert Bell, Charles Bidwill Sr., Hugh Culverhouse, Al Davis, Edward J. DeBartolo, Jr. Barron Hilton, Lamar Hunt, Eugene Klein, Tim Mara, Arthur "Mickey" McBride, John Mecom Jr., Art Modell, Clint Murchison Jr., George Richards, Art Rooney, Sr., Carroll Rosenbloom, and David "Sonny" Werblin.
>
> Additionally, the author will note taped conversations between Sammy Baugh and a known gambler. Also, he will note government investigations that surfaced the names of Len Dawson, Bob Griese, Paul Hornung, Sonny Jurgensen, Alex Karras, Lou Michaels, Joe Namath, Vince Promuto, Johnny Robinson, Art Schlichter, Jake Scott and Ken Stabler.
>
> The author acknowledged that he was assisted in the preparation of the article by Scott Malone, a writer who was an associate producer and investigator on the *Frontline* program

entitled, "An Unauthorized History of the NFL" that aired in January, 1983.

Moldea said that he would send me a copy of the article during the week of January 18. The magazine will appear on the stands during the week of January 25.

The week before the Super Bowl, *Regardie's* released its February 1988 issue, featuring as its cover story, "The NFL and the Mob: Pro Football's Dirty Secret."

In its review of my work, the *Washington Post* wrote:

> Washington's Dan E. Moldea is one of a kind, and the kind in question is the tireless hunter-gatherer of evidence that some people would just as soon see left alone. There is evidence of legwork here, and of reality.[89]

In its own review of my article, *Extra!*, the house organ of the media watchdog group, Fairness and Accuracy in Reporting (FAIR), complained about the press coverage of my article:

> [T]he major media, with few exceptions, are still ignoring a very embarrassing subject. Moldea appeared on *CBS Night Watch* (1-29-88) and CNN *Crossfire* (1-30-88), but his story wasn't picked up by the nightly news or the national print media. As an NBC employee told Moldea, "We spend [$2] billion to broadcast NFL games. We can't have you on saying it's crooked."[90]

Meantime, I submitted a revised proposal for the NFL book to attorney Ronald Goldfarb, who was also a Washington literary agent and WIW's long-time general counsel.[91]

Surprisingly, Friday, January 29, 1988—the day of the auction for my book and just two days before the Super Bowl—came and went with little enthusiasm for my project. However, I did receive one bid from Lisa Drew, a senior editor at William Morrow, who offered $40,000, which was $35,000 less than I had received as an advance for my last book. Also, it was the same price that Villard had offered to both Malone and me four years earlier.

Still, I wanted to do this book and decided that, if I did it well, I could make more money from the back-end royalties. Thus, I asked my agent to make a counteroffer of $50,000, which I would accept. On February 9, Drew convinced company executives to up the bid to $50,000. I signed the contract on March 9.

I couldn't afford to buy a new Thunderbird with this kind of money. So, to celebrate the new NFL book contract, I replaced my Kaypro II computer with an IBM PS/2 with a twenty-megabyte hard disk. I also bought a Hewlett Packard LaserJet printer.

All the while, I never even gave a second thought to Dad's admonition on his deathbed: "Don't write that damn book about the NFL."

During the fall of 1987, a friend invited me to a party at the home of a wealthy insurance executive who owned a magnificent penthouse apartment in the Washington Harbor, overlooking the Potomac River in Georgetown.

Among the people at the dinner party was Mimi, a blonde knockout who took my breath away when I saw her. Because she had a date, I minded my manners and kept my distance. However, a friend of hers told me that she and her boyfriend were in the final stages of their relationship.

On Saturday, January 16, 1988, Mimi called and asked me to have dinner with her and her girlfriend that night. Kind, thoughtful, and independent, she turned out to be a combination of the best women I had ever known. A studio art teacher at a private school in Washington and an artist from a family of artists, Mimi, one of the world's experts on contemporary African art, had lived all over the world and spoke several languages.

After our first evening together, even with a chaperon, I knew that this was the woman I had always wanted.

63. Game fixing in the NFL

In my January 1988 article about the NFL and the mob for *Regardie's*, I had primarily concentrated on the suppressed and killed investigations of NFL corruption by the law-enforcement community. But I had no hard evidence of actual game fixing and received a considerable amount of criticism from the media—especially on the CNN program,

PART FIVE: THE NFL & THE MAFIA

Crossfire—for making such a fuss about corruption in the NFL without finding it. So, for my book, I concentrated most of my resources on proving that NFL games had, indeed, been fixed.

The NFL and its commissioner, Pete Rozelle, had claimed that no game in its history—since the formation of the league in 1920—had ever been fixed. However, the NFL did acknowledge two unsuccessful attempts to fix NFL games. The first was the 1946 NFL Championship Game between the New York Giants and the Chicago Bears. The second was a 1971 regular-season game between the Houston Oilers and the Pittsburgh Steelers.

Nevertheless, several people had made allegations about NFL game fixing, and I began working to confirm or reject those charges based on my own investigations.

For instance, Bubba Smith, a defensive lineman for the Baltimore Colts, had told *Playboy* that the 1969 Super Bowl, featuring the heroics of New York Jets quarterback Joe Namath, had been fixed, and that Carroll Rosenbloom, then the owner of the Colts, had bet against his own team.

This was not true, according to my own investigation, which included my interview with the bookmaker who had actually handled Rosenbloom's bet that was placed on his own team.

In 1983, when I began my preliminary work for the NFL book in the wake of the *Frontline* program, I had contacted Vincent Piersante, the head of the organized-crime division of the Michigan state attorney general's office. Piersante, who had been helpful to me during my research for *The Hoffa Wars*, said that if I wanted to write about game fixing in the NFL, I would have to investigate Donald Dawson, a top bookmaker from Detroit.

Piersante explained that Dawson had been involved with members of the Detroit Lions and other NFL teams during the 1950s, 1960s, and 1970s. "Professional football, we had cold," Piersante said. "It was clear to us that games had been fixed by players [who were] shaving points in cooperation with several organized-crime connected bookmakers."

Piersante added that Dawson was among those bookmakers who were financing the players' game-fixing schemes.

After speaking with Piersante, I then went to other law-enforcement officials, including Herbert Hinchman, a former top official with the Criminal Intelligence Division of the Internal Revenue Service. Hinchman had coordinated the agency's 1969-1970 investigation of Dawson.

During the IRS probe, several NFL players were proven to have been in regular contact with and provided inside information to Dawson, who was later convicted and sentenced to prison for his bookmaking activities.

Also, numerous other law-enforcement officials with the FBI and the U.S. Strike Force, whom I also interviewed, agreed with Piersante and Hinchman in their assessments of Dawson's activities.

At this point in my investigation, I had enough evidence to print that that Don Dawson had allegedly engaged in game fixing.

But, wanting more, I went after Dawson and found him living in Las Vegas. He had never been interviewed by any reporter and, at first, tried to dismiss me. But I kept prodding him, playing to his enormous ego. When that didn't work, I started to recount what my law-enforcement sources had told me about him. That placed Dawson on the defensive, forcing him to reply to each charge in detail.

After finally getting Dawson to admit for the first time that he had been involved in NFL game fixing, I asked him to explain the mechanics. Dawson replied, "A player, usually a quarterback, would come to me and say, 'I need some bread.' Then he'd ask me to make a bet for him and myself. If the Lions were ten-point favorites, he'd say, 'Well, we'll probably win by six or seven. We won't cover the spread.'"

Naming names and teams, Dawson continued:

> Naturally, I wanted to do business with the quarterback, because he handles the ball on every play. And a lot of quarterbacks were shaving points. Sure, it happened. The players didn't make any money [from playing football], and so they bet. In those days, they were barely getting by. They were getting their brains beaten out for almost nothing.
>
> ***I was involved with players in at least thirty-two NFL games that were dumped or where points were shaved.*** I knew a lot of players and then through them I got acquainted with other players and then did business with them. [Emphasis added.]

Indeed, Dawson had just confessed to fixing "at least thirty-two NFL games." Of course, I tape recorded this conversation.

In another game-fixing conspiracy, Leo Halper, the head of Project Layoff, an IRS gambling investigation in Nevada, provided me with evidence, indicating that two referees had allegedly participated in the fixing of no fewer than eight additional NFL games.[92]

PART FIVE: THE NFL & THE MAFIA

64. Rosenbloom was *not* murdered

Another major target of my book was the cadre of NFL team owners who had turned the league into what I had started to view as a money-laundering operation. I made a particular issue out of the gambling and underworld associations of Edward J. DeBartolo, Sr. of the San Francisco 49ers, who, to me, had the most nefarious connections.

In 1970, DeBartolo's name had appeared on the U.S. Justice Department's Organized Crime Principal Subjects List, a catalog of people who were suspected of having links to organized crime.

DeBartolo was an admitted gambler who had a $100,000 line of credit at Caesars Palace in Las Vegas. Also the owner the Pittsburgh Penguins of the National Hockey League and the Pittsburgh Civic Arena, DeBartolo had made several unsuccessful attempts to purchase Major League Baseball teams during the late 1970s. Among those teams were: the Chicago White Sox (twice), the Boston Red Sox, the Cleveland Indians, and the Seattle Mariners. He also tried to bring a major league baseball franchise to New Orleans.

In the end, DeBartolo withdrew his bid when it became clear that he would be facing stiff opposition because of his ties to racetracks and gamblers. "My father has too much class for baseball," DeBartolo's son, Edward J. DeBartolo, Jr., told the *New York Times*.[93]

In March 1977, the elder DeBartolo purchased ninety percent of the stock of the San Francisco 49ers for $17.6 million and made it a subsidiary of his corporation. Then, he gave the team to his thirty-year old son. "Eddie Jr. bought it from me," DeBartolo told the *Pittsburgh Press*. "Everyone thinks I gave it to him, but Eddie financed it and paid for it."

However, the senior DeBartolo personally secured his son's purchase.

Meantime, during another long research trip on the West Coast during the summer of 1988, I found the four missing photographs taken during Carroll Rosenbloom's autopsy after his 1979 drowning in Golden Beach, Florida. For years, rumors had been flying that these four very graphic pictures would prove, once and for all, that Rosenbloom had been murdered.

Along with interviewing just about everyone involved in the official investigation, I gave the photographs and accompanying official reports to several friends in the law-enforcement community for their analyses.

In direct conflict with the conclusion of the 1983 *Frontline* documentary that Rosenbloom had been murdered, the pictures showed *no* evidence of foul play and confirmed the reports filed by the Dade County Department of Public Safety, as well as the original autopsy report.

"In short," I wrote in my manuscript, "the evidence appears to be clear that Rosenbloom died in a tragic accident and was not murdered."

In early November, I finished a very rough draft of my NFL book and sent it to Mrs. Nolte for her initial comments. In her November 29 letter, she wrote:

> You've heard the old saying: "Inside every fat person is a thin person crying to get out?" Well, inside this overstuffed, cumbersome manuscript is a lean, hard-hitting book waiting to be cut free. I have tried to give you suggestions for that major task, as well as for some less important grooming of the book. So steel yourself, Dan. Crank up your will-power to jettison your much-loved mob detail, and do what everyone is telling you your "baby" needs: slimming down.

65. Predicting the media's reaction

On December 1, 1988, I sent letters to each of the NFL team owners, requesting interviews. As it turned out, Gene Klein, the former owner of the San Diego Chargers, was the only past or present NFL team owner who agreed to sit for an interview with me. Also, I had sent yet another letter to NFL Commissioner Rozelle, requesting an interview.

Seven days later, I received a note from Joe Browne, again turning down my request for a meeting with Rozelle.

Fearing yet another public-relations problem, the NFL, early on, had started to react strongly to my work. On January 9, 1989—eight months before the book's official release—the NFL placed its own spin on the facts. Without any provocation from me or my publisher, the *New York Post* ran an article by staff writer Eileen Daspin in its Page Six column, reporting that I had a book coming out about the National Football League and organized crime, adding:

PART FIVE: THE NFL & THE MAFIA

An NFL spokesman said a magazine article Moldea wrote on the same subject "was a cut-and-paste job and not very factual. It was filled with inaccuracies, gossip and innuendo." He said league commissioner Pete Rozelle didn't intend to talk to Moldea.

Warren Welsh later identified the unnamed "NFL spokesman" as Joe Browne, who appeared to protect the NFL with the same ferocity that he would protect his own family.

Reacting to Browne's preemptive attack on my book, I added a section to the Prologue of my manuscript—in my own effort to preempt the NFL's future challenges to my work. This section stated:

> What this book does is outline the patterns of association that have been tolerated by the NFL while the league and the federal government were claiming to take a hard line against organized crime and its influence on professional sports. In fact, the NFL has too often been lax in the enforcement of its own rules, and law-enforcement agencies have permitted the NFL to get away with it. This sweetheart relationship has greatly contributed to the myth about the integrity of the NFL.
>
> Consequently, the NFL is sure to discredit this book, which strikes at the heart of the business of professional football, in any way it can—just as it did with an article I wrote about this subject after the 1987 regular season. An unnamed league spokesman [Joe Browne] said that the story "was a cut-and-paste job and not very factual. It was filled with inaccuracies, gossip and innuendo." But that response was a complete turnabout.
>
> In fact, I read my article to the current NFL Security director, Warren Welsh, prior to publication to solicit whatever changes he felt were required. And, because of Welsh's expertise and inside information, I trusted him and made several necessary modifications upon his advice. In the end, he told me that it was a "fair and accurate" report. However, the NFL, for reasons only its unnamed spokesman can explain, changed its tune after the story was made public. But no one from the league would meet me face-to-face in a public forum to explain what its specific objections were, even after having been

invited to do so on two national television programs on which I appeared.

> *Predictably, with the publication of this book, the league's now-familiar tactic will be to remain aloof from the charges, deny them from afar, and then send its front line of defense, the loyal sportswriters, to attack the messenger.* But, once again, in good faith and asking only for confidentiality, I offered this manuscript to Welsh for his review. But neither he nor anyone else from the NFL responded. [Emphasis added.]

My criticism of sportswriters was well founded. For years, Neil Amdur had worked as a top sportswriter for the *New York Times*. In 1971, he published a book entitled, *The Fifth Down: Democracy and the Football Revolution*, featuring a section called, "The Captive Press," which began:

> Football writers and members of the media are among the most intense rooters for the teams they are assigned to follow as a "beat.". . .
>
> Broadcasters face similar problems. It is much easier to chronicle the exploits of a team that is ahead 42-14 than one behind 35-7. If a broadcaster is attached to a specific college or pro team, or even a league like the National Football League, he is not about to shimmy his surroundings with dialogue that will endanger his financially secure position.
>
> This is the reason why broadcasters telecasting the 1970 Super Bowl game conveniently disregarded any mention of the word "gambling" in their lengthy discussions about the "problems" that Len Dawson, the Kansas City quarterback, had endured during the week.[94]

Bernie Parrish, a former All-Pro defensive back for the Cleveland Browns, wrote his groundbreaking book, *They Call It A Game*, also in 1971. His chapter on the sports press, "The Emperors Footmen," was particularly penetrating, stating:

> The special-assignment sportswriters who regularly cover pro football are a major key to the suffocating control Pete Rozelle and the owners exercise over their monopoly. There

is at least one special writer assigned to cover pro football in every National Football League franchise city. This gives the league a free multimillion-dollar propaganda machine with an influential voice in twenty-four [now twenty-six] major cities and population centers in the country. Almost on cue they promote a merger, push legislation, attack an opponent of the league, justify ticket-price increases, trades, and rule changes, or generally create a cover for whatever dealings the owners may be plotting.

These sportswriters find life easier and more profitable if they remain in management's favor. Without cooperation from the team's management, a sportswriter would be unable to fill his daily column. It doesn't pay to oppose management's interests too often, and back scratching can be very rewarding.[95]

And, in the January 24, 1988, issue of the *Washington Post Magazine*, sportswriter Christine Brennan chronicled her experiences covering the Washington Redskins. Included in this article was Brennan's reported conflict with owner Jack Kent Cooke and other members of the Redskins' management team. In part, Brennan wrote:

You see, I thought I was just doing my job when I asked the owner of the Redskins if the team was considering trading a key player. I didn't expect such a simple question would cause me to be declared *persona non grata* by one of the world's richest men for three months.

I thought I was well within my rights to write about the contract that the team's general manager was about to sign. I didn't expect him to get angry and refuse to give me a private interview for nearly two years.

And I figured if a former star player on the management staff said something on television, I could report it in the sports pages of my newspaper, right? Wrong. I did that and it ended a fine working relationship I had with that good man—just like that.

This was typical of what happened when honest sports reporters attempted to demonstrate their independence from their sources in the NFL.

Facing the inevitable wrath of the sportswriters who covered the NFL, I also added to my Prologue:

> I am a crime reporter, not a sportswriter. My job is not contingent on maintaining access to and the goodwill of the personnel of any particular team or sports institution. Friends of mine who do write about sports have expressed the need "to behave" and admit that they have willingly become part of the NFL's sophisticated public-relations machine on occasion in order to maintain their sources of information. I believe that the need for this professional access and goodwill has prevented a fair and responsible analysis of the relationship between professional sports and organized crime by all forms of the sports media.

66. Pre-publication

In January 1989, I submitted my completed manuscript to my publisher on deadline, along with drafts of the final chapter and Epilogue—both of which were still chronicling ongoing matters.

I made five principal charges in this book, based upon an enormous accumulation of never-before-published information. Specifically, I challenged the integrity of the National Football League, citing that:

> 1. No fewer than 26 past and present NFL team owners have had documented personal and/or business ties with members of the gambling community and/or the organized crime syndicate.
>
> 2. There is evidence that no fewer than 70 NFL games may have been fixed.
>
> 3. No fewer than 50 legitimate investigations of corruption within the NFL have been either suppressed or killed as a

PART FIVE: THE NFL & THE MAFIA

result of the sweetheart relationship between NFL Security, the internal police force within the league, and a variety of federal, state, and local law-enforcement agencies.

4. The illegal gambling economy has become an adjunct to the First Amendment because of the insistence by the sports media to print and broadcast the betting line and to hire oddsmakers and handicappers for the purpose of predicting the outcomes of NFL games.

5. The movement toward legalizing sports gambling by the states will cause a proliferation of illegal bookmaking and organized-crime activities.

Also, I gave my manuscript to four experts to ensure the accuracy of its contents:

* Mike Duberstein: The research director for the NFL's Players Association.

* Phil Manuel: The former chief investigator of the U.S. Senate's Permanent Subcommittee on Investigations who was recognized as one of the top organized-crime investigators in the United States.

* Mort Olshan: The publisher of the *Gold Sheet*, a "bible" for America's sports gambling community, and perhaps the country's most respected legal handicapper on professional football.

* Jack Tobin: The highly respected former *Los Angeles Times* reporter and "Godfather of Mafia Reporters," who was also a consultant for *Sports Illustrated*. Tobin had become like a second father to me after our first meeting in 1984 during the research for my first story about Ronald Reagan and MCA.

Further, there were numerous sources whom I had interviewed who also aided in the fact-checking process. During many of these conversations, I read them the entire sections in which they were mentioned to ensure that the facts were right and that they had been quoted accurately.

On January 23, my editor, Lisa Drew, after reading my manuscript, wrote a private memorandum to William Morrow's editor-in-chief, Jim Landis, stating:

> I must say, the author has done an incredible job of research, synthesis, writing and documentation, which is a requirement, because the Mob is all over the NFL. This is going to create enormous comment and controversy when we publish next fall. ... In addition, Moldea is very responsible, and has never been sued for any book ... he has written.

The following month, Al Marchioni, the president of William Morrow, changed the title of my book—which I had been calling, *The Integrity of the Game*—to *Interference: How Organized Crime Influences Professional Football*.

Upon completing her excellent editing work, Drew sent my manuscript to William Morrow's attorneys for vetting. At the end of this process, there were no substantial changes in the text, except for a decision not to name the two referees who had allegedly fixed the eight NFL games, which were investigated by the IRS during Project Layoff.

On March 21, an "editor's presentation" was made to in-house personnel at William Morrow about my book. In her memorandum to the staff, Drew wrote:

> *Interference* is one of the most anticipated, feared and talked about football books ever—it is a hard-hitting look at the billion-dollar influence the mob has over professional football by one of the top Mafia experts in this country.

By coincidence, the following day, March 22, Pete Rozelle, after twenty-nine years on the job, suddenly resigned as NFL commissioner—the same day as the Pete Rose gambling scandal exploded, stemming from his long association with bookmakers.

As with the publication of *The Hoffa Wars*—but unlike the releases of *The Hunting of Cain* and *Dark Victory*—the timing for the publication of *Interference* appeared absolutely perfect.

Nevertheless, I tried not to lose sight of the fact that the NFL's high command, along with their legion of loyal sportswriters, would do anything and everything they could to protect the institution of professional football.

PART FIVE: THE NFL & THE MAFIA

67. "A troublesome book"

In early June, Peter King, a sportswriter for *Newsday*, wrote a column in anticipation of the publication of *Interference*. King had interviewed Joe Browne, and, not unexpectedly, Browne repeated what he had told the *New York Post* the previous January: "The book is an outgrowth of a magazine piece and a tabloid TV show, both of which contained a series of long-repudiated rumors, distortions, half-truths and outright factual errors."

On July 3, the *Sporting News* published its own story about *Interference*, "NFL Worried." In part, the story stated: "As if it already hasn't been a topsy-turvy off-season for the NFL, now comes word about a troublesome book scheduled to be published in August."

Joe Browne's quote from the *Newsday* article was republished in the *Sporting News* article.

Clearly, the NFL's strategy in its pre-publication assault on my work consisted of labeling my work as sloppy, dishonest, and old news.

On July 5, William Morrow, already jazzed about the early controversy over the book, purchased four ads for *Interference* in the *New York Times* for its August 7, August 14, August 21, and August 28 editions.

Two days later, my publisher began distributing *Interference* to bookstores around the United States—nearly six weeks before the official pub date.

Greg Mowery, my publicist at William Morrow, called me early on the morning of July 21. During the conversation, Mowery said that he had booked me on twenty-nine major radio and television shows in twelve cities. In other words, my publisher was giving me a first-class book tour.

Three days later, New York public-relations executive Wayne Rosso, a friend of mine, called and said that he had some free time and wanted to help me. During the course of the day, I received a call arranged by Rosso from Billy Heller of the *New York Post's* Page Six. I spoke with Heller and recited the basic charges in my book.

I also predicted that when he contacted the NFL for comment, Joe Browne would attack the book—because it was based on the *Frontline* program and my article in *Regardie's*, just as he had said repeatedly in the past. I also gave Heller my reply to Browne's now-predictable response.

On July 25, the Page Six story ran. My charges were accurately reported, and Joe Browne of the NFL gave the same quote I had predicted. But the *Post* did not bother to run my reply to his mantra, thus, giving Browne the last word. Specifically, the *Post* stated:

Gridiron powers that be aren't overly concerned with the book's blitz. League spokesman Joe Brown [sic] called the book "a padded magazine piece." Although he wouldn't respond to specific allegations, Brown [sic] contended "the book is based on a TV show . . . and a 1988 magazine story, both of which contained a listing of long repudiated rumors, distortions, half-truths and frankly, outright factual errors."

On July 26, I appeared on my first program for the *Interference* tour, *Morning Edition* on National Public Radio. The show was taped and scheduled to be broadcast the following day. In his introduction, interviewer Scott Simon said:

> According to author Dan Moldea, the NFL threw away its integrity regarding gambling long ago. Moldea's new book is, *Interference: How Organized Crime Influences Professional Football.* It's Moldea's fourth book on mob influence in various aspects of American society. The author alleges that instead of discouraging gambling, many NFL owners gamble themselves and encourage it in others. He says there are links to organized crime. And he says that NFL owners hire security officers, with ties to the Justice Department to ensure that drug and gambling investigations go nowhere.

The following day, my publicist sent a memorandum to "All Concerned" within the publishing house, indicating that I was going to appear on *Good Morning America* on August 9, the *Larry King Show* later that same day, *Entertainment Tonight* on August 10, and CBS's *Pat Sajack Show* on August 23. He also said that Las Vegas had been added to the list of cities I would be touring, adding in his memo: "[W]e've got an excellent media launch for Dan and *Interference!*"

On July 30, my mom called and read an article about my new book on the front page of the *Akron Beacon Journal*, which had gone off the Knight-Ridder news wire. Cleveland Browns owner Art Modell, a target in my book, was quoted as saying about me:

> The man is a muckraker, the man is sick. He has no credibility, he has no credence. . . . We're a popular game and he's trying to take advantage of that by looking for a fast buck. I wouldn't even look at the book, let alone buy it. Outrageous. It's all outrageous.

PART FIVE: THE NFL & THE MAFIA

Also, that same day, Jim Baker, a reporter for the *Boston Herald*, published a lengthy story: "Moldea's claims big headache for NFL." In part, Baker wrote:

> [I]t will be most interesting to see how the networks, local stations, and yes, those NFL writers and broadcasters who've been riding the NFL gravy train for years, will treat this one. Those media members with strong connections to the owners will make especially compelling observation.

On August 1, Lisa Drew called and said that *Interference* had just gone into a second printing. The book appeared to be moving fast, and Drew was already predicting that it had an excellent chance to wind up on the *New York Times* Best Sellers List.

Meantime, in the midst of nothing but good news, I went out to my parked 1985 Thunderbird on Wisconsin Avenue and found it totaled. The police told me that a speeding cab had run a red light, caromed off a another car entering the intersection, spun out of control, and crashed into eight parked cars. My T-Bird was the only one completely destroyed. Incredibly, no one was injured.

However, this bizarre accident seemed to foreshadow the chain of events that would soon follow. Unknown to me, I had already run the red light and was spinning out of control.

68. Looking for fights

My interviews on the big, national programs, like ABC's *Good Morning America*, and Larry King's evening radio show were contentious but fair. But, more than anything else, I looked forward to those interviews with the sports broadcasters, those who actually knew what I was complaining about and had to make a decision how to handle me.

On Friday, August 11, at about 1:00 P.M., in a pouring New York rain, I was picked up by my publicist and taken to Mickey Mantle's Restaurant on Central Park South for the popular sports show with Bill Mazur of WFAN radio.

Mazur and I sparred good-naturedly for a few minutes before the show. He wanted to get a fix on who I was, what I knew, and how well I could deliver my message. I really liked Mazur and, knowing how many people listened to him on the radio, I wanted to give him a good show.

In the midst of the on-air interview, Mazur said, "Now, when you talk about National Football League owners, Dan—I know a few of the owners. And I would be very, very surprised if any of them had ever had direct dealings with the Mafia."

In response to Mazur's challenge, I replied, "Edward J. DeBartolo, Sr., San Francisco Forty-Niners. . . . The Forty-Niners are a ninety-percent subsidiary of his Edward J. DeBartolo Corporation. DeBartolo has been investigated by numerous federal and state law enforcement agencies. I published federal reports with corroborative reports by state agencies, saying that DeBartolo has been doing business with Carlo Marcello, the Mafia boss down in New Orleans; Santo Trafficante, the former Mafia boss in Tampa, Florida; and Meyer Lansky, when he was alive.

"[These agencies] have linked DeBartolo to gun-running operations, drug-trafficking operations, and money-laundering operations. Five times, DeBartolo tried to buy into Major League Baseball—turned down for the fifth time just the other day—tried to buy the Cleveland Indians. Five times, because of his associations with racetracks, his associations with gamblers and organized crime.

"He comes into the NFL in 1977. Jack Danahy, the former chief of NFL Security, whom I interviewed at length for this book—that is the only question he refused to answer: 'Why [did] DeBartolo get into the NFL?'

"When you look at DeBartolo's connections to the underworld, when you look at the other NFL team owners' connections to the underworld, DeBartolo was let into a sport—where he could not get into baseball—but he was allowed into football because in the NFL, DeBartolo was right at home. He was with people like him."

Stunned, Mazur came back, "You know that really is a devastating comment to make because . . ."

"And I'm legally responsible for everything I've written in the book."

After the show with Mazur—who jokingly predicted before I left the restaurant that I was "a dead man"—my publicist took me to WOR for Gil Gross's radio show for more of the same.

On August 15—three days before the book's official pub date—I appeared as a talking head from Boston on Scott Ross's *Straight Talk* program on the Christian Broadcasting Network, which aired live from Virginia Beach. In the CBN studio were college basketball coach Lefty Driesell and Steve Howe, a former pitcher for the Los Angeles Dodgers, among other teams.

PART FIVE: THE NFL & THE MAFIA

During this interview, I decided to go after Howe, who was suspended from Major League Baseball for drug use seven times by the end of his career.

Howe gave me an early opening when he said, "If you want to talk about ethics, our society is a mess. You know? It doesn't matter whether I'm out there throwing ninety-mile-an-hour fastballs. Yes, there is pressure. But we have coping skills, and we have areas where we can deal with that."

Scott Ross then turned to field a question from a member of his audience as I asked, "May I jump into this someplace?"

"Yes," Ross said, "go ahead. Jump in."

"One of the things everyone is talking about—and I disagree with Coach Driesell in the comments he made early on about drugs being the number-one problem in this country. I mean, drugs are chemicals. The number-one problem in this country are the people who are manufacturing and distributing and selling the drugs. The number-one problem is organized crime. And there is a severe failure on the part of our political leaders and by the media to educate people as to what organized crime is and what the impacts of organized crime are. To all intents and purposes, when a player has a relationship with a drug dealer, he, in effect, has a relationship with organized crime."

Then, going after the ball player, I continued, "Steve Howe—I'd like to ask him—he had a relationship with a dealer or a series of dealers. Now, I'm under the impression that dealers are not in this business for philanthropic purposes. They are in this to get inside information on games or on teams or on this particular individual. They want some sort of an advantage or some on-field edge. And I'm wondering if anyone whom Steve Howe received drugs from ever tried to get this inside information or tried to affect his performance on-field? There is an extortionate quality to that relationship."

"No, absolutely not," Howe replied angrily. "No one has ever approached me about inside information on any game. When I went and saw a dealer—Some people that I used were basically my friends. . . . Now, if they took some information elsewhere, I didn't know about it. Hey, when I was going out to get high, I sure didn't want to talk about how I pitched the night before."

Ross tried to get beyond this, but I interrupted, "Once you have that chemical dependency, you are, therefore, dependent on that dealer in order to provide those drugs to you. At what point does he extort you for information or for an advantage on field?"

Howe fired back, "Certainly, anything is a possibility. There are possibilities and ifs and ands and shoulds and should nots all over the place."

Cutting off this exchange just as it was getting good, Ross took a question from a wide-eyed twelve-year-old in the audience who changed the subject.

However, I just couldn't believe that Howe and any other player could associate with drug dealers—or just sit around getting high with their friends—without talking about their on-field performances, as well as those of their teammates. After all, I knew gamblers who, on principle, would refuse to sell drugs. But I was not aware of many drug dealers who, on principle, refused to gamble.

Warren Welsh had once told me during the research for my book, "Our worst case would be the athlete who is strung out on drugs and has a line of credit with his drug dealer and can't pay the bill. Then he gets that knock on the door. And [the player] says, 'Hey, I told you. I can't pay the bill.' And then [the dealer] says, 'Hey, I don't want your money, but now you're going to work for us.'"

69. Debating an empty chair

When I arrived home in Washington after the first leg of my book tour, my publicist had left a message, saying that I was scheduled for a debate the following day on *CBS Nightwatch* with Jim Feist, a Las Vegas sports-gambling tout. Immediately, I called sports arbitrageur Lem Banker in Las Vegas to check out Feist. By coincidence, Banker was on his other line with Feist who had also called to check me out.

Predictably, *Nightwatch*, hosted by Charlie Rose, was a dogfight between Feist and me that lasted for three segments. Although our battle remained in good humor—especially after we recounted our simultaneous calls to Lem Banker to vet each other the night before—Rose and I went at it with considerably more zeal.

This sideshow started during the second segment when Rose interrupted the debate between Feist and me to allow Joe Browne, who had been invited on the program but declined, to take a free shot at me by repeating his mantra.

Rose said, "Here is what the director of communications of the NFL says about this book: 'The book is an outgrowth of a magazine piece and a tabloid television show, both of which contained a series of long-repudiated rumors, distortions, half-truths, and outright factual errors.'"

"Then the NFL," I laughed, "should be sitting here in the chair across from me, answering these allegations. The NFL has not denied anything that's in the book. As far as anything that happened in the article that I wrote in *Regardie's* magazine in 1988, I gave that article to Warren Welsh, the chief of NFL Security, not after it was in galleys, not after it was out. I gave it to Warren Welsh, the chief of security, before the article was even turned in to the publisher."

"To give them an opportunity to respond?" Rose asked.

"To give them an opportunity to respond—and to make sure that the story was right. And Warren Welsh's response after hearing the story was that it was a 'fair and accurate' report. I offered the NFL Security people a copy of this manuscript before it came out, because I wanted to make sure that, again, my work was fair and accurate—which, of course, it is. I take my legal responsibilities very seriously. This is my fourth book. I've never not only lost a suit, I have never been sued [for any of my books]. And I don't expect to be sued for this book. The NFL is coming at me with nothing. They have nothing. They are not denying anything. All they are hoping is that I just go away."

On August 23, I flew to Los Angeles where I was to appear on CBS's *Pat Sajack Show*. Prior to the program, I called Jack Tobin, who told me that he had lunch the previous day with Warren Welsh, who said that he wanted to see me. Tobin told me where Welsh was staying in the Los Angeles area. I told Tobin that I would call him after the television program.

On camera, Sajack opened the interview by asking, "What do you hear from the powers-that-be? Anything?"

"They just want me to go away, right now," I smiled.

"We've spoken to them, and they don't want to talk about it either. They have nothing to say."

"But they're not denying anything," I continued, "and they are not refuting any of the facts in the book."

After a recapitulation of everything I had been alleging during my tour—the fixed games, the corrupt owners, and the killed investigations—Sajack asked me what should happen next.

I replied, "Well, I'm hoping that there will be a federal investigation—hopefully a Senate select committee—to investigate organized-crime's influence in all professional sports, not just football but in baseball and basketball, as well.

"I'm hoping that there will be registration and licensing of anyone with a financial interest in a professional sports team; that there will be public disclosure of financial transactions involving professional sports teams. And that there will be a further examination of public ownership of teams, so that the citizens of the cities in which these teams play—the public—can have, literally, a piece of stock in those companies."

After the Sajack show, instead of calling Welsh, I asked my escort to take me to the hotel where Welsh was staying. When I arrived, I learned that he had already checked out. However, Welsh had left a forwarding number for me at the front desk.

I called Welsh in West Covina and told him that I had interpreted his comments to Jack Tobin as a sign of good faith, and that I wanted to respond in kind. We agreed that he would call me in Las Vegas at the Stardust Hotel on Sunday afternoon.

As a further act of good faith, I gave Welsh the names of the two referees who had allegedly participated in fixing several NFL games in 1979—an allegation in my book that had become the subject of considerable debate. And I added that I would give him any other documentation he wanted.

70. A secret meeting in Las Vegas

I flew to Las Vegas and arrived at about 10:30 A.M. on Sunday, August 27. I rented a Thunderbird and visited some local friends and acquaintances, including the always controversial but fascinating Bob Maheu, with whom I had lunch at his home, and Howard Schwartz, the colorful manager of the Gamblers Book Club.

While I was with Schwartz, I called the Stardust and asked for my messages. The clerk told me that Warren Welsh had called. After I returned Welsh's call, we agreed to meet in my room at the hotel at 4:30 P.M.

I checked into the Stardust where I had been comped by Scotty Schettler, the popular manager of the casino's sports book, whom I had interviewed for *Interference*. I then waited for Welsh who arrived at exactly 4:30.

Welsh and I were very friendly. He knew that I had not been attacking him personally. In fact, he mentioned that he had heard a tape of the *Roy Leonard Show* in Chicago in which I had been complimentary of him.

PART FIVE: THE NFL & THE MAFIA

Before Welsh asked me anything, I listed my complaints against the NFL, especially against Joe Browne for what I considered his neverending false and misleading comments about my book to the media.

Welsh then asked about the game-fixing case involving the two NFL game officials. I gave him the details of the IRS's Project Layoff investigation and showed him, among other documents, an FBI report in which the alleged fixes were chronicled.

I also provided him with a flow chart about the organized-crime ties of Edward J. DeBartolo, Sr., the owner of the San Francisco 49ers, which was prepared by the Florida Department of Law Enforcement, as well as a U.S. Customs report that provided even more details of his relationships with numerous major Mafia figures.

Welsh then started questioning me about Don Dawson, the Detroit bookmaker. I took Welsh step-by-step through the Dawson process. Welsh listened intensely and took notes.

When he started questioning me about whether Dawson was really admitting to fixing games or whether his words had another meaning, I pulled out a copy of Dawson's taped confession and played portions of it for him. After hearing the recording, Welsh agreed that Dawson had flat out claimed to have fixed 32 NFL games.

In our continuing conversation, which was really quite friendly throughout, I tried to convince Welsh that I was not the enemy of honest football and Pete Rozelle, who had remained as NFL commissioner until his still-to-be-named replacement was selected. I insisted that I was an ally—and that I could not believe that he and Rozelle were disagreeing with my thesis: that the NFL team owners were a bunch of greedy plutocrats, some of whom were deeply involved with the gambling community and even the Mafia.

Welsh was non-committal about all of this, but I genuinely believed that I was getting through to him.[96]

I had a television taping to do at KVBC-TV, an NBC affiliate located in North Las Vegas, so I left Welsh in my hotel room, alone with my loose-leaf notebook of key documents about the charges contained in my book. I also gave him my tape recorder, so that he could listen to the entire Dawson tape.

When I returned to my room at the Stardust, Welsh was still there, listening to the recording.

He laughed when I told him that I had been asked during the KVBC interview whether I had any contact with the NFL—and that I had refused to answer the question. The reporter conducting the interview did not understand why—but I couldn't explain that, while in the midst of this particular interview, the director of NFL Security was sitting in my hotel room.

I only stayed with Welsh for a few minutes, because I had to meet sports handicapper Arnie Lang, who was interviewing me that night on the Stardust Sports Book's weekly radio show. I told Welsh that I would return after dinner and before the show.

After dinner with Lang, I returned to my room. Welsh was still there, reading my book of documents. He was very upset that there was not a radio in the room, and he could not listen to the program. After spending some more time with Welsh, I went to the sports book for the live radio show.

71. "We have to destroy you now"

To me, my appearance on the *Stardust Line* was the ultimate test of whether my work and I could stand up under deep and penetrating questioning, which probed the extent of my knowledge about gambling, bookmaking, oddsmaking, organized crime, and their connections to the NFL.

For reasons never explained, Arnie Lang had made no prior public announcement that I was going to be on his program that night. In a series of promotions on the radio station, I had only been described as "a mystery guest."

When I was called up to the stage, the crowd in the sports book immediately started to grow. Lang was complimentary of me and my work in his introduction. The soon-overflow crowd appeared to be friendly and even supportive.

Initially, I had been scheduled to be on the program for only ten to fifteen minutes. However, the program went so well that Lang asked me to stay on for the entire first hour of the program. The hour then stretched into ninety minutes.

The telephone call-ins were mostly supportive. Two callers were semi-hostile. One complained that Lang was not being tough enough with me.

When the interview was over, Lang asked me to join him and his crew for a drink at midnight at the bar next to the sports book. He said it had been the best show the *Stardust Line* had ever broadcast.

PART FIVE: THE NFL & THE MAFIA

Before meeting Lang after the program, I went back to my room. As I walked up the hallway, Welsh came out of my room. He had decided to take a late plane and return to Los Angeles.

I walked Welsh outside to the brightly lit entrance of the Stardust in the midst of Las Vegas's brightly lit Strip. While we were shaking hands, I asked Welsh to call off Joe Browne—for whom I had established a grudging respect for his loyalty to duty and his fighting spirit. Also, I asked Welsh to whisper in the ears of a couple of influential sports reporters, and tell them that I had the goods to support my charges.

Again, Welsh was noncommittal and simply joked, "Dan, we have to destroy you now."

I laughed and shook hands with Welsh again. To this day, I still don't believe that Welsh had any idea of what was about to happen to me.

When I returned to my room, all of my materials—the book of documents, the recorder, and the tapes were all neatly stacked on a table. Welsh had only taken the papers I had given him permission to take.

The following day, after a couple of morning shows in Las Vegas, lunch with oddsmaker Michael Roxborough, and three more interviews that night, I took the red-eye to Cleveland, arriving at about 6:00 A.M. on August 29.

I rented another Thunderbird and drove to my mother's home in Fairlawn. Having nothing scheduled early, I slept late and then took my mom to lunch. That afternoon, from Mom's house, I fielded my 4:00 P.M. phone interview from a Montreal radio station. Then, I drove to downtown Cleveland and checked into the Stouffer Hotel.

The next day, I felt absolutely triumphant as I made the rounds to all the local radio and television talk shows whose hosts were as kind as they could be to a local author.

That night at my hotel, I checked my answering machine in Washington. Among other calls, two friends of mine in Los Angeles—documentary filmmaker Rhys Thomas and author Bob Ward, who was the co-executive producer of NBC's *Miami Vice*—had left messages, telling me that Keith Olbermann, the sports anchor at KCBS-TV, had reported on his evening sports program that he had just returned from New York with former football star Dick Butkus.

Olbermann wrote an article about the incident, saying:

> Dick Butkus was grunting. I mean Butkus, Hall of Fame linebacker of the Chicago Bears, was grunting as he snapped the pages of an innocent-looking book.

— 249 —

We were facing each other for the five-hour cross-country flight, yet we must have already passed Topeka when he looked up and glared at me. "You're that sportscaster in L.A., aren't you?" I nodded my reply. "You read this yet?" He tapped the book, *Interference* by Dan E. Moldea, fiercely. "Everybody I know is in this book. And it's all true."[97]

Later, Olbermann specifically said of *Interference*, "Moldea has written perhaps the most important sports book in the history of the language."

72. A sudden problem

Rushing between shows in Cleveland, I called Greg Mowery, my publicist at William Morrow, who had just received an early copy of the September 3 edition of the *New York Times Book Review*. Mowery said that a *Times* sportswriter, Gerald Eskenazi, had given me a bad review.

After Mowery quickly read brief portions of the review over the phone, I really wasn't too upset, telling him that there were a lot of mistakes in it, and that it could not be defended. Undaunted, I went on with my busy day.

The following morning, Thursday, August 31, after my last radio show, I arrived at Cleveland Hopkins Airport. While waiting to return to Washington, I had some time, so I called my editor, Lisa Drew, and asked her what she thought about the *New York Times* review. She said that she wasn't too concerned, because she never expected the sports media to be anything but hostile toward us—just as I had predicted in my book.

That same day, sportswriter Desiree Ward of the *Milwaukee Journal* wrote her own review of *Interference*, stating in her first paragraph:

> Don't buy this book. Don't borrow this book. Don't swap anything for this book. If it's too late and one of the above has already taken place, put the book down and don't read it. It's not that Dan Moldea hasn't done his homework on gambling within the National Football League. He has. In fact, he has done so much homework that it takes 52 chapters, plus a prolog and epilog, to present it. And that's part of the problem with this book: There is simply too much information....[98]

PART FIVE: THE NFL & THE MAFIA

Back in Washington, on Friday, September 1, I took a cab to ABC News where I was interviewed by correspondent Dave Marash for the filmed portion of an upcoming *Nightline* program.

During the pre-interview, Marash told me that my friend, sports arbitrageur Lem Banker of Las Vegas, had said that gamblers had tampered with two Minnesota Vikings' games in 1988—against Green Bay Packers and Tampa Bay Buccaneers. Banker hinted at this during our August 12 appearance together on Bill Moran's radio show on KFI in Los Angeles and mentioned it again while we were having dinner together at Binion's Horseshoe Club while I was in Las Vegas.

According to Banker, eight to ten players with the Vikings had been poisoned during a locker-room meal by syndicate-connected gamblers in an attempt to influence the outcomes of the games. Minnesota did not cover the spread in either contest.

Marash was in the process of tracking down the story. He also told me that the NFL was not giving *Nightline* anyone to refute my charges—although Joe Browne said that he might agree to a taped interview.

I begged Marash to convince Browne to go on the air because I verbally wanted to take him apart on national television.

I also notified Marash about the Gerald Eskenazi's review in the *New York Times Book Review*. I told him that I would send him my written response after I actually saw the review.

That afternoon, I did the *Mark Scott Show* on WRC Talk Radio in Washington. He had notes about the *New York Times* review in front of him, but he didn't have an actual copy of the review. He did not quote any of the negative parts, only Eskenazi's statement that there was "hot stuff" in the book.

Although everyone was talking about it, I still could not get a copy of this review that was already bedeviling me.

All I knew about Eskenazi was that he was a respected sportswriter who had been on staff at the *New York Times* for many years. In fact, I had an endnote in my book which cited his work.

That night, I did *The Winner's Circle*, a sports show run by Brad Segall in Princeton, New Jersey. Once again, the *New York Times* review was brought up. This time, I attacked Eskenazi during the program for the mistakes I remembered that he had made. I also accused him of trying to protect his friends and sources at the NFL by attempting to knock me out with one punch.

On September 1, Howard Schwartz, the manager of the Gambler Book Club in Las Vegas, sent a letter to a sales person at William Morrow, which stated:

— 251 —

> [*Interference*] is selling well here—200 copies in less than 2 weeks. I don't care what the reviews said in the *NY Times Book Review* section by Eskenazi or *Football News's* Yarbro. I like the book. . . . We can hardly keep the book in stock.

This was the first time I had even heard about the Yarbro review.

73. The review in the *New York Times*

On Sunday, September 3, Mimi and I were having breakfast at the Zebra Room in Washington, which was near her apartment building. I had bought a copy of the *Times* at a nearby drug store and brought it to the restaurant. Because she wanted to read it first, I gave her the *New York Times Book Review* while I scanned the front section of the newspaper.

When I saw tears welling up in her eyes, I took the *Book Review* from her. "How bad can it be?" I asked.

I was completely shocked after I saw the review in black and white and finished reading it for the first time. The impact of seeing it in print far exceeded the mere sting of hearing it read quickly over the telephone.

Incredulous, I told Mimi, "First, Fred Cook, then Aljean Harmetz, then Jeff Gerth, and then John Corry. This is the fifth goddamn time the *New York Times* has done this to me!"

By then, both Mimi and I had lost our appetites, so I walked her home and returned to my apartment. I immediately wrote an eight-page response to the review.

Eskenazi—in his attempt to make *Interference* appear to be a book filled with major errors—had based his written opinion on a series of provably false statements. Incredibly, he had claimed that I stated facts I never did, or that I omitted other facts that were clearly contained in my book. Using these gross misrepresentations, he concluded that my book contained "sloppy journalism," a charge that, if true, could end a nonfiction author's career.

Immediately, I knew that I had no choice but to challenge the review, which I considered both reckless and malicious—the thresholds for libel against a public figure or even a limited public figure, assuming I was one.

In short, Eskenazi's review sounded like another Joe Browne press release, and I immediately suspected a connection.

PART FIVE: THE NFL & THE MAFIA

Specifically, the five principal charges upon which Eskenazi based his conclusions about me and my book and my responses to these charges were as follows:

1. Charge: Eskenazi claimed that I did not properly identify Joe Hirsch as a writer on horse racing for the *Morning Telegraph*, which later became the *Daily Racing Forum*.

Response: This was untrue. In the second paragraph of page 139 of my book, I quoted former New York Jets quarterback Joe Namath as saying: "I met Joe [Hirsch] at his place of business, the race track. No, he doesn't book bets; at least, he's never booked any of my bets. Joe writes for the *Morning Telegraph*, which is read by known gamblers."

2. Charge: Eskenazi wrote that I claimed that there was something premeditated and "sinister" about a meeting in a Miami bar between Namath and Baltimore Colts placekicker Lou Michaels during the week before Super Bowl III in 1969.

Response: This was a clear misrepresentation. I never made this charge and wrote in the second paragraph on page 197: "[Lou] Michaels told me that the meeting at a Miami bar/restaurant was quite accidental and even confrontational."

3. Charge: Eskenazi wrote that I "revived the discredited notion" that former Los Angeles Rams owner Carroll Rosenbloom, who drowned in 1979, was murdered.

Response: This was untrue. In the fourth paragraph of page 360 of the book, I wrote: "The evidence appears to be clear that Rosenbloom died in a tragic accident and was not murdered."

4. Charge: Eskenazi claimed that my version of the alleged betting on the 1958 NFL championship game between the Colts and the New York Giants was based on nothing more than my own speculation.

Response: This was untrue. In paragraphs five through seven on page 91 of my book, I quoted three knowledgeable

— 253 —

sources—oddsmaker Bobby Martin, as well as bookmakers Ed Curd and Gene Nolan—who described the betting and how it was accomplished.

5. Charge: Eskenazi wrote that I did not "state in the text that Steve Myhra was among the worst placekickers in the league."

Response: This was untrue. In the third paragraph of page 90 of the book, I quoted Colts' head coach Weeb Ewbank, who told me, in part: "We did not have a great field goal kicker." Also, in footnote #1 on page 444 of my book, which refers to the Ewbank quote, I wrote: "Baltimore, in 1958, had the second worst field goal percentage in the NFL, 35.7 percent, making five of fourteen attempts."

Also, the review noted that I had misspelled the names of three minor characters in my 512-page book—who had a combined total of four cites in my index. However, I had spelled these names just as they appeared in both the *Washington Post* and the *Los Angeles Times*.[99]

Remarkably, in the credit line to Eskenazi's review of my book, he was simply identified as "a sportswriter for the *New York Times*, [who] is currently working with Carl Yastrzemski on his autobiography."

In other words, the *Times* had tried to represent Eskenazi as an impartial baseball writer, failing to mention that he had covered the NFL for nearly thirty years and, specifically, as his personal beat, the New York Jets, upon whom he depended for professional access and goodwill.

74. Pigs and sausages

On Labor Day, everything appeared closed, and no one seemed to be at work. However, my old friend, attorney John Sikorski—who had handled my complaint against the *Times* in the wake of the John Corry review of the *Kwitny Report*—was at his office, so I faxed him a copy of my eight-page response to the *Times*.

Sikorski called after reading the material and said that we had a good case to ask for a retraction from the *Times*.

PART FIVE: THE NFL & THE MAFIA

On Tuesday, September 5, I Federal Expressed copies of my response and summary to my publisher and to Warren Welsh. After I returned home, I wrote a private message to myself, saying:

> Eskenazi and the *New York Times* have severely crippled me... The fact that my own people at Morrow were surprised to learn that I had a response to the review is very disconcerting. If they didn't understand the details of my book in contrast to Eskenazi's review, how will the general public and, more importantly, the media and the booksellers? ...
>
> I am up for this battle, but I feel myself quickly losing my enthusiasm for writing these kinds of books, which force me to spend 95% of my time fighting not the bad guys but the media.

I then called the former executive director of the Fund for Investigative Journalism, Howard Bray, at the Department of Journalism at the University of Maryland where he worked. Bray told me that he thought my only recourse against the *Times* was to write a letter to the editor. He added that my agent, Ron Goldfarb, was a personal friend of *Times Book Review* editor, Michael Levitas.

Before calling Goldfarb, I called Sikorski. He had faxed my eight-page statement to Lisa Drew—who had already responded in a letter to me. Drew wrote that she had discussed the matter with Al Marchioni, the president of William Morrow, adding:

> While we are sympathetic with your distress about both the tone and the many statements and implications of inaccuracy in the review, ... our show of support is to publish, publicize and advertise the book in the first place. Beyond that, we cannot go.

After Sikorski read Drew's disappointing letter to me—publishers defend their authors all the time—I told him about Goldfarb's relationship with Levitas. Agreeing with Bray's assessment, Sikorski told me to call Goldfarb to get his perspective. He added that Goldfarb might be able to negotiate our way into a favorable settlement. Sikorski said that our best goal was to get a retraction and then try to interest a *New York Times* sports columnist into writing a fairer assessment of the book.

I called Goldfarb at his office. He had not seen the review yet. I immediately sent it over by messenger.

Goldfarb told me that Levitas was no longer the editor of the *Book Review*. The new editor was Rebecca Sinkler, whom he didn't know very well. Instinctively, we recognized that I had a big problem—inasmuch as the publication of the review came in the midst of a leadership change at the *Book Review*.

After I told Goldfarb that I would sue for libel if this matter was not handled properly, he warned, "People who sue for libel go in looking like pigs; and, even when they win, they come out like sausages."

After Goldfarb saw the review and my response, he called, expressing disbelief over what the *Times* had done to me. I then put Goldfarb and Sikorski on a conference call. But, regardless of the false and misleading statements in the review, they agreed that I had little chance of winning a libel suit against the *New York Times*.

In the September 5 edition of *Football News* that Howard Schwartz had referred to in his earlier letter to William Morrow, columnist Gar Yarbro—prior to seeing Eskenazi's review in the *Times*—had written a review of *Interference*, entitled "Moldea's book based on rumors, half-truths."

Reading again like a Joe Browne press release, Yarbro wrote:

> The book reviewers will list Dan E. Moldea's news sports book
> ... as non-fiction. But there are so many rumors, half-truths
> and unsubstantiated stories that, in my mind, it would be best
> classified as fiction. Why anyone would pay $19.95 for this
> rehash of old material is beyond me.... The author has a great
> imagination.... Moldea should be writing television scripts.

It came as no surprise that *Football News* was owned and operated by the National Football League, which further piqued my suspicion of Browne's involvement with Eskenazi.

The following morning, I telephoned Washington attorney Tom Green at his office. Green had handled the John Dowd-Mike Kramer libel suit against Jim Drinkhall and the *Wall Street Journal*, winning an $800,000 settlement for the two ex-prosecutors.[100]

Green had not yet seen the review and asked me to pull everything together for him to read. He then sent a messenger to my home to pick up the package.

On the evening of September 6, I wrote another private note to myself, saying:

PART FIVE: THE NFL & THE MAFIA

> My whole nature has changed to a totally defensive posture. Anyone I talk to gets my explanation about the review—whether they want to hear it or not. That makes me cringe when I think about what I'm putting the people around me through.
> . . .
>
> I believe that I have no choice but to sue for libel. If I haven't been libeled, then I really don't know what it is. But if truth is a defense for libel, then the *Times* has no defense.
>
> I await Tom Green's decision . . . . I want this fight, even though I dread the thought of what I'm up against.

On September 7 at 11:00 A.M., Tom Green called. He said that he still did not know exactly how he felt about the case, stating, "Clearly, the review is horseshit, a trivialization, and inane." He added, the entire review, despite all of its mistakes and misrepresentations could be viewed by the court as "fair opinion."

Green proposed that I write a letter directly to Eskenazi and send copies to the managing editor of the *Times*, as well as to Becky Sinkler, the new editor at the *Book Review*. He instructed me to make the letter very strong, advising me to give them "a short fuse." He suggested the following Monday at noon as the deadline.

In the first sentence of my letter to Eskenazi, I charged that his review was "deceptive, misleading, reckless, and malicious and has placed my book and me in a false light. Thus, you have libeled me." I then listed his specific charges and my responses, asking for a full retraction and giving Eskenazi and the *Times* until Monday, September 11, at noon, to respond.

Tom Green called at about 6:30 P.M. and asked what was happening.

I told him that I had followed his advice and was sending the letter to Eskenazi with copies to *Times* managing editor Arthur Gelb and Becky Sinkler. I asked him if he was willing to sue if this did not work. He told me that we would talk about it after the *Times* made its decision.

When I returned from the Federal Express office, I received a message from Richard Harris, *Nightline*'s chief booker, who asked me to be on its NFL and gambling program, scheduled for Monday night, September 11—after ABC's *Monday Night Football* game between the Washington Redskins and the New York Giants.

75. Combat on *Nightline*

On September 11—the day after the 1989 NFL regular season began—Richard Harris of *Nightline* called just before 11:00 A.M. and informed me that our program had been bumped because anchor Ted Koppel had arranged to interview Russian leader Boris Yeltsin.

Then, at 7:05 that night, Tracy Day, a *Nightline* producer, called and said that our program was on again, adding that the Yeltsin interview had been canceled. "Yeltsin's drunk, and they can't sober him up," she told me, adding that the other two guests were Warren Welsh and Michael Roxborough.

A chauffeur in a black, stretch limo picked me up at my home and drove downtown to ABC's Washington bureau. After the make-up process, I was then taken into a small studio adjacent to the control room. It was the set for David Brinkley's Sunday morning talk show.

There were five people in the room, including a cameraman and an assistant director who was responsible for counting down the seconds before we went on the air. The camera was about eight to ten feet in front of me at eye level. I was instructed to look straight into it and not move my eyes. I saw myself briefly on a monitor, but the image was only in black and white. Because it was a distraction, I asked that it be turned off. My thinning hair seemed a little awry, and so I combed it without a mirror—wishing I had not done so after I did.

Everything I heard came through an earpiece. I spoke into a small microphone clasped to the lapel of my suit jacket. During a quick sound check, I joked briefly with Welsh in New York and Roxborough in Las Vegas, wondering out loud whether the Giants-Redskins game had been fixed. All three of us, who knew each other, laughed, but we were clearly nervous.

Then, the game was turned off, and *Nightline's* taped background report on gambling and the NFL began. On the filmed portion of the program, correspondent Dave Marash was seen walking through the Stardust Sports Book. After that, he showed his taped interviews with Roxborough, former NFL Security chief Bill Hundley, Warren Welsh, and then me.

Marash also interviewed Lem Banker, who spelled out the details of the two Minnesota Vikings' games against the Green Bay Packers and the Tampa Bay Buccaneers after eight to ten players were stricken with food poisoning. Agreeing that the incident should have been, but was not, placed on the NFL's weekly injury and illness reports released to the wire services, Welsh spoke for the league, saying that he did not believe anything nefarious had happened.

After the taped segment, it was our turn. Jeff Greenfield, who was filling in for Ted Koppel, introduced us in alphabetical order. I was first followed by Roxborough, and Welsh.

Then, there was a cut to a commercial.

When we returned, I went on auto-pilot. After a quick exchange between Greenfield and Welsh, Greenfield asked me a question. Completely ignoring what he had asked, I ran down the key points I had really come there to say about the NFL and the Mafia. When Greenfield repeated the question, I answered it directly.

After that, I just reacted and tried to keep Welsh on the defensive by attacking the NFL team owners. Throughout the program, I kept thinking that being on with two men I liked and respected—Roxborough and Welsh—was to my disadvantage, because I didn't want to go for their throats.

According to the official *Nightline* transcript, a brief exchange was precipitated after I claimed that there was evidence that no fewer than 70 NFL games had been fixed:

> **Greenfield:** I can't forbear from picking up on the point you [Moldea] said earlier. Are you talking about games that have been fixed within recent history, recent NFL history, last 10 years or so?
>
> **Moldea:** I'm saying that the last games I have where there's allegations of fixed games were 10 years ago. There were eight games that were allegedly fixed by two referees who were paid $100,000 each for each game by a New York Mafia guy, and their job was to basically make sure that that Mafia guy covered the spread.
>
> **Greenfield:** Mr. Welsh, quickly, what do you have to say about those allegations? Have you looked at Mr. Moldea's book? Can you respond to them?
>
> **Welsh:** I have, and I would like to say that in contact with law enforcement sources, that the informant that Mr. Moldea refers to is termed a "pathological liar" by the FBI.

Moldea: Well, the IRS has a different feeling about him, Warren, and basically they viewed him as being credible, and that—the IRS believed that the investigation itself concluded that the games were indeed fixed. They had the information in advance of the games on those eight fixed games.

During a discussion about the state of Oregon's recent legalization of an NFL sports lottery, the debate became even more contentious.

Roxborough: Sports betting is growing tremendously, and not just in Nevada, all over, and it's good, low-cost entertainment, and that's the main reason it's growing.

Moldea: Low-cost entertainment? I look at the situation in Oregon right now, Roxy, and the only thing I respect about the Oregon betting lottery is the fact that you're setting the line—a man I trust, a man I admire, a man who I know is honest is going to be setting the line. But, basically, what's going to—

Greenfield: Could I interrupt, Dan? [I want to] explain that Oregon has begun a system where a bettor can go to his local grocery store and bet the spread, pick a number of teams and whether they'll beat the spread, put down a buck or ten or 20, I guess. . . . I just wanted to clear that up. Some of our audience may not be into this pastime, but go ahead.

Roxborough: It started this weekend. It was very successful. And it's one-dollar to twenty-dollar bets. And I call that entertainment. In fact, I call that better entertainment than going to movies these days.

Greenfield: Dan?

Moldea: Well, that may be true. What I'm afraid of is that Oregon is going to end up educating the public as to how to gamble, how to use the point spread, and everyone's going to realize that Oregon is taking a huge skim of the handle—the total pool of bets. And what the public is going to realize within a few weeks is they can get a bigger bang for their buck from Charlie the Bookie, the friendly local bookmaker at the

PART FIVE: THE NFL & THE MAFIA

corner bar who's going to be making them put up $11 to win $10—and is only going to be taking a ten percent commission on the losing bets he books.

Roxborough: But see, Dan, that's not always true, Dan. First of all, the Oregon odds are pretty good, and, in fact, as parley cards go, some of the odds are much higher than illegal bookmakers. And, also, where should the money go? Should it go to an illegal bookmaker to buy a new Cadillac, or should it go to fund the intercollegiate and athletic sports in Oregon, like it does with the lottery up there?

Greenfield: If I may . . .

Moldea: Well, what . . .

Greenfield: I'd like to . . .

Moldea: Excuse me. What I'm saying is that, Roxy, the Oregon lottery is going to cause a proliferation of illegal bookmaking and organized crime activity. And I think in recent cases, the evidence is clear on that.

Greenfield: Can I bring, please . . . I'd like to bring Warren Welsh, who represents the league, into this. Mr. Welsh, your league was very down on this idea of Oregon's, right?

Welsh: We certainly were. And our premise is: why use the National Football League to promote betting? We just don't like it. We certainly encourage new fans to come our way, but we certainly don't need new bettors.

Moldea: Warren, why didn't you file a lawsuit against Oregon before they started taking your product and selling it? I mean, why didn't the NFL file suit, as they did in Delaware back in 1976 when Delaware had their own disastrous lottery? Why isn't the NFL taking some legal action? And I don't think you've taken any legal action against Kentucky, which is going to have its own NFL lottery next month.

Welsh: Our lawyers are continuing to review this case, and we have many options open to us.

76. A game of chicken

At 2:00 P.M. on September 12—after Eskenazi and the *New York Times* had apparently refused to respond to my earlier letter—I met with Tom Green who had tried to reach Becky Sinkler at the *New York Times Book Review*. However, she was on vacation. Her number two was out to lunch, so Green called the *Times's* general counsel's office.

As I sat in a chair in front of his desk, Green talked to a *Times* attorney and told him that he expected an official response to my letter from the *Times*—any kind of response. He said that if we didn't get an answer or if the reply was unsatisfactory, then we would sue.

Apparently, the *Times* attorney had not heard about the issue and promised to investigate. Green and the *Times* lawyer agreed to talk again the following day.

At 6:00 P.M., Green telephoned me, saying that the counsel for the *Times* had just called and asked that we give the newspaper until Monday for a decision. Green agreed.

On Monday, September 18, Green called me at noon and said that the *New York Times* counsel had told him that Eskenazi had been ordered to attend a meeting at 3:00 P.M. on Tuesday, September 19. He promised to telephone Green with a decision.

The next day, I flew to Hattiesburg, Mississippi, to present a campus-wide lecture at the University of Southern Mississippi about sports gambling. Before the lecture, I received a message to call Green at his home. Doing so immediately, I asked him what the *Times* attorney had said.

Green told me that he had talked to him for an hour. As Green had predicted, the conclusion was that Eskenazi's review was "protected opinion." Therefore, the *Times* would issue no retraction and no corrections.

I was just getting ready to do my lecture and could not talk for very long. Green told me to call him when I returned to Washington.

Back in D.C. on September 20, I called Green, who gave me additional details of his conversation with the *Times*.

Green added that everything he had done for me to that point was free. Now, I was on the clock. For him to proceed further would require a detailed analysis of my book—after which he would make a final determination as to whether we really had a good, winnable case.

I told Green to do whatever was necessary. I wanted to know what my legal options were.

Soon after, I received a call from Marnie Inskip, a producer for a Fox-TV program called *The Reporters*. She explained that while preparing her story about my book, her boss walked up to her, tossed the *New York Times* review of *Interference* on her desk, and said that the segment had been canceled.

On Sunday, September 24, in the midst of a mix of generally favorable reviews from journalists and customary unfavorable reviews from sportswriters, I received a positive review in the *Los Angeles Times*. The review was written by reporter Michael Harris. Too little, too late, Harris wrote: "*Interference* is like a hard-nosed fullback . . . packed with names, dates and places, hitting the holes until the defense—one's incredulity—gives way. The weight of evidence is overwhelming."

On Monday, September 25, I flew to Des Moines, Iowa, for a Tuesday campus-wide lecture at Des Moines Area Community College. While changing planes in Chicago, I checked my messages and had received one from Tom Green. When I called him back, he told me that he had completed his analysis of the review and my book. He explained that he no longer had any doubts: I had been clearly libeled by the *New York Times*. He suggested that we sit down and discuss the situation.

On Friday afternoon, September 29, Green and I had lunch at The Palm in Washington. Early in the meeting, Green handed me the *New York Times's* written response from its counsel.

When I looked at the letter, I nearly choked on my Gigi Salad. I immediately noticed that it had been written by *Times's* attorney David Thurm, the same attorney who had handled my 1987 complaint against John Corry.

Green saw my reaction and asked me if I had a problem. I recounted the story about how the *Times* had published an unsatisfactory correction to Corry's review. I explained that when the *Times* refused to make amends in that case, my attorney and I had bluffed litigation—a bluff David Thurm had called and won.

Now, in his letter to Green, Thurm had attempted to defend Eskenazi's review, taking my complaints and addressing each. In doing so, Thurm specifically misquoted the actual wording of my book, twisting what I wrote and didn't write. Thurm added:

> The main thrust of your client's concern seems to be the characterization of the book as "sloppy journalism." From a legal viewpoint, this is clearly protected as opinion. The words are those of opinion and as such are not capable of being objectively characterized as true or false.

However, Green and I believed that Eskenazi's opinion had been based on a series of provably false facts cited in the review—such as Eskenazi's claim that I had written that Carroll Rosenbloom was murdered, when, in fact, I had clearly written that he "had died in a tragic accident and was not murdered."

Later, I came to believe that David Thurm's letter was the turning point in this entire dispute. Thurm and the *Times* had copped their position and became immovable. Thurm likely assumed that my attorney and I were bluffing again and would never file suit—while I really never believed that Thurm and the *Times* would ultimately stand by Eskenazi's error-ridden review.

Thus, this entire situation was reduced to nothing more than a game of chicken. In effect, we were like two teenagers in fast cars, drag racing towards the edge of a First Amendment cliff.

Who, if anyone, would jump out first?

On Saturday, October 14, I called Alexander Greenfeld, whom I had met at the 1988 WIW Spring Writers Conference. Greenfeld, with whom I had become friendly, was a former legal counsel for the *New York Times*. Now, he was a professor at the University of Maryland's School of Journalism. I told him that I wanted his advice as to how to handle the *Times*.

He asked me to drop off a package of information for him to review before our scheduled luncheon meeting the following week.

Greenfeld, who personally knew Eskenazi from his days at the *Times*, called me later that afternoon. From the outset, he described Eskenazi as "a good sports reporter, an excellent writer, and a wonderful family man."

PART FIVE: THE NFL & THE MAFIA

But, after his examination of the facts of my case, Greenfeld—just like Sikorski and Green—expressed his legal opinion that I had been clearly libeled, based on the errors of fact and blatant misrepresentations in the review.

"Great damage has been done to you," the former *New York Times* attorney insisted. "There's no defense for opinion when it's based on a misstatement of facts or misleading facts. The general rule is that an opinion has to be supported by the facts and it cannot misrepresent facts. ... I believe that the *Times* wants to be fair. [*New York Times* executive editor] Abe Rosenthal used to say that—and Max Frankel is the same way."

Also, he brushed off David Thurm's response as simply "boilerplate," predicting that I would prevail in court. The problem, he said, was that the lawsuit would take five years to litigate, and the *Times* would fight it all the way. However, he did reveal, "They have quietly settled a few cases from time to time."

Greenfeld advised against litigation and advocated a "journalistic solution." He knew all of the top executives at the *Times* and told me that he might be able to negotiate some sort of settlement. I gave him the green light to do so.

But, soon after, Greenfeld called and told me that he had tried but failed to negotiate a peace for me with the newspaper.

In the wake of this final act of diplomacy, both Tom Green and John Sikorski gave me realistic but prohibitive prices for them to litigate against the *Times*. In other words, I was back to square one.

On the night of November 14, in a last-ditch effort for a peaceful solution, I wrote another response to Becky Sinkler at the *New York Times Book Review*—along with a cover letter, asking her to print my defense against Eskenazi's review. I Federal Expressed the package to her the following day. However, the *Times* refused to publish my letter to the editor, never allowing me to defend myself.

As my eagerly anticipated war with the NFL degenerated into a dreaded conflict with the *New York Times*, the NFL team owners selected Paul Tagliabue, a prominent attorney with Covington & Burling in Washington and an outside NFL counsel, as their new commissioner, replacing Pete Rozelle. By coincidence, Tagliabue's younger brother, John Tagliabue, was the *New York Times's* bureau chief in Warsaw, Poland.

On December 10—as Paul Tagliabue settled into his new job and I fought for my personal and professional survival—Gerald Eskenazi wrote a major article for the sports page of the *New York Times*: "Game Day on the Sidelines: Frenetic World Come to Life."

The NFL had given Eskenazi an early Christmas gift, allowing the sportswriter to take an exclusive "behind-the-scenes" look at the exciting world of professional football.

77. "I'll give you a good fight!"

On the morning of June 22, 1990, while I was reading the *Washington Post*, I came across a story, "Statements of Opinion Can Be Libelous, Court Rules." It reported a U.S. Supreme Court decision in the landmark case, *Milkovich v. Lorain Journal Company*. The story's lead read: "The Supreme Court ruled yesterday that expressions of opinion can be the subject of libel suits if they contain 'false and defamatory' facts."

A sports columnist for the *Lorain Journal*, a newspaper in northeastern Ohio, had written a column, calling a local wrestling coach, Michael Milkovich, a "liar." In response, Milkovich sued.

The lower courts decided that the columnist had expressed a privileged opinion about Milkovich. However, the U.S. Supreme Court ruled, 7-2, against the lower courts' decision.

I clipped the story and placed it on top of my desk.

The following day, during a private conversation with Washington radio talk-show host Sheldon Tromberg, I told him about my situation with the *New York Times*, as well as what I knew about the *Milkovich* decision. Tromberg suggested that I call a friend of his, attorney Stephen M. Trattner of Lewis & Trattner in Washington, D.C.

Immediately after my talk with Tromberg, I called Trattner at his office. He listened to my problems but was noncommittal. However, he agreed—as a favor to Tromberg—to do an analysis of the *Times* review and my book. I put together a package for Trattner and messengered it to his office.

On July 5, like attorneys John Sikorski, Tom Green, and Alex Greenfeld before him, Steve Trattner rendered his professional legal opinion that, in fact, I had been libeled, "recklessly and maliciously."

Realizing that we were coming up on the one-year statute of limitations, Trattner introduced me to a friend of his, Roger C. Simmons, a partner in the law firm Gordon & Simmons in Frederick, Maryland. He was my last hope before the statute ran out.

PART FIVE: THE NFL & THE MAFIA

Finally, after a couple hours of frank discussions during our first meeting, Simmons, a big man with a tough but friendly demeanor, agreed to take my case against the *New York Times*.

Just before our meeting ended, I said to Simmons, "Roger, I am forty years old. After publishing four books I'm really proud of, I should be enjoying the prime of my career. Instead, I am now battling for my basic survival. . . . I wouldn't even think of asking you for a guarantee that we're going to win, because I have some idea of what we're up against. All I'm asking for is a good fight."

Simmons smiled, "You want a good fight? . . . I'll give you a good fight!"

That night, I had my first full, uninterrupted sleep since the publication of the *New York Times's* review of *Interference*. After everything I had been through—and everything I had put Mimi, as well as my family and friends through—I was finally going to be able to say loudly and clearly that I was challenging the *New York Times* in court.

This time, there would be no backing down.

PART SIX:
Moldea v. New York Times

78. At war with the *New York Times*

On August 23, 1990, Roger Simmons filed a $10 million libel suit—*Moldea v. New York Times*—in the U.S. District Court for the District of Columbia. In our complaint, Simmons charged that the September 3, 1989, review, written by *Times* sportswriter Gerald Eskenazi, was "intended to protect the NFL by personally attacking Moldea, discrediting his reputation and smearing his good name as an investigative reporter."

Specifically, the suit cited seven errors and misrepresentations in the review, which were the basis for Eskenazi's claim that I had engaged in "sloppy journalism." Among our examples was the reviewer's allegation that my book "revives the discredited notion that Carroll Rosenbloom . . . met foul play when he drowned in Florida 10 years ago," when, in fact, I had written, "The evidence appears to be clear that Carroll Rosenbloom died in a tragic accident was not murdered."

The following day, after an AP wire story, *Washington Post* book-chat columnist David Streitfeld published a lengthy article on the front page of the Style section. He quoted a senior attorney for the *New York Times* and three prominent First Amendment lawyers, all of whom attacked the merits of our case. However, in his depiction of me as a crazy person, he failed to quote—or even identify—my attorney, Roger Simmons, anywhere in the article.

Then, having some fun with the idea of a disgruntled author filing a libel suit over a review, Streitfeld concluded: "And if, in the end, he loses the case? [Moldea said,] 'I guess that means I'm a sloppy journalist and I'm dishonest and everything else.'"

On August 26, 1990, two days after the Streitfeld story, the *Washington Post* published an editorial: "Suing the Reviewer," attacking me and my suit against the *Times*. In this editorial—which was mostly based on Streitfeld's own sloppy reporting—the *Post*, articulating its fear of the linkage of my case to the earlier *Milkovich* decision by the Supreme Court, wrote:

> That fear now takes a faintly absurd but still troublesome twist with the lawsuit of writer Dan Moldea against the *New York Times*, which Mr. Moldea accuses of having libeled him by publishing a negative review of his book. . . . [Moldea's] claim of factual falsity [against the *Times*] seems something of a stretch. The review does, as he charges, accuse him of 'sloppy

journalism'; it goes on to give a string of examples, including spelling errors. . . .

However, the *Washington Post* conveniently omitted from the Streitfeld story and its editorial that the *Post* had misspelled the same names in its own newspaper.

Hearing me complain about the unfairness of the biased reactions in the press to our litigation, Simmons laughed and simply advised me to grow some very thick skin as quickly as possible, because this was just the beginning. He added that—despite my long career as a good guy, investigating some of the most dangerous bad guys in the country, alone, as an independent writer—I would now be cast in the media as a villain. And I would have to learn how to live with that.

"I thought you understood this," Simmons chided me. "The press has a vested interest in the outcome of this case. Do you really expect them to report it fairly?"

Although I had no second thoughts about filing the case, I did find myself in a *Catch-22* dilemma: If I had ignored the review and did nothing, I would be dead, branded by the *New York Times* as a sloppy journalist. If I sued but lost, I would really be dead with a stake rammed through my heart. But even if we proved the merits of our case and won, I'd still be dead—because I would be viewed as wreaking havoc on the First Amendment.

I began to lose sleep again, just trying to figure out how I could come out of this situation alive and still in one piece.

On the public-relations front, I put together a press kit, which contained a copy of *Interference*, a statement about the case, my letter to the editor that the *Times* refused to publish, and some biographical material.

Even though the nature of this fight emboldened me to work even harder, Mimi seemed to absorb most of the impact of all the bad news. I repeatedly gave her opportunities to leave me, so that she could find some degree of peace and serenity in life, knowing that she couldn't find much of either with me. But, incredibly, Mimi continued to stand by me.

Meantime, coming to my short-term financial rescue, my old friend, the former chief investigator for the U.S. Senate Permanent Subcommittee on Investigations, Phil Manuel—now president of the Philip Manuel Resource Group, a successful Washington private investigations firm—asked me to come to work as a consultant for him on one of his cases. And my booking agents, Bob Katz and Jodi Solomon, had nailed down three new lectures for me at Michigan Technological

University, Valparaiso University, and the University of Central Florida—for which I cleared an additional $7,000.

Focusing my attention on my libel suit, I organized my files for easier access and began logging in everything relevant to the *Times* case. If I had been a chronology freak before, I had now evolved into a timeline monster. Everything I had ever done, was in the midst of doing, or would do in the future had a place in some topical chronology.

And, then, trying to give Roger Simmons and his associates everything they could possibly use during the case, I started a series of memoranda for their consideration. During the first few weeks, I wrote memos on such subjects as: "Prior Conflicts with the *New York Times*," "Reviving the Carroll Rosenbloom Murder Theory," "The NFL's On-the-Record Reactions to *Interference*," "Preliminary Background Report on Gerald Eskenazi," "Corrections Published by the *New York Times*," "Killed NFL Investigations," "Alleged Fixed Professional Football Games," and even my "1975-1989 Federal Income Tax Returns," among others, which would total over 700 memoranda by the end of the case.

On September 5, the WIW board of directors, led by WIW president Tim Wells, passed a resolution, saying, in part:

> Overt misstatements of fact, when published in a book review, should be viewed in the same light as misstatements of fact that appear in any other section of the newspaper, or any other forum. If such errors appear in a review and are brought to the attention of the publisher and conclusively demonstrated beyond a reasonable doubt, the publisher has a moral and ethical obligation to either retract any libelous portions of the review or to provide the author in question with the opportunity for a rebuttal.
>
> Further, we believe such misstatements of facts are apparent in a review... published by the *New York Times* on September 3, 1989, that dealt with Dan Moldea's book, *Interference: How Organized Crime Influences Professional Football*.

Later, the WIW board generously voted to give me $5,000 from its Writers Defense Fund to pay my required retainer to my attorney, allowing me to use the money I still had for my war chest.

Meantime, Roger Simmons sprayed the terrain with subpoenas for discovery, going after files held by William Morrow, the National Football League, and, of course, the *New York Times* and Gerald Eskenazi. My publisher, William Morrow, was the only party that cooperated fully. Attorneys for the others vigorously resisted our attempts to secure their files.

Actually, I prayed that we would find something in the NFL files that could make it culpable in our complaint. We wanted to find some way to bring the NFL in as a defendant—even if it meant dropping our complaint against the *Times*.

We believed that what the *Times* had done to *Interference* was tantamount to an act of censorship, and that the National Football League was the beneficiary of that act.

But, for now, in order to get to the NFL, we had to get past the *Times*.

79. Joe Browne and Gerald Eskenazi

On November 5, after the *Times's* lead outside counsel, Bruce Sanford—a talented and respected First Amendment attorney with the influential law firm, Baker & Hostetler—filed a motion with the court to stay discovery, Simmons and Sanford faced off for the first time in open court to provide their first status reports to U.S. District Judge John Garrett Penn.

At the end of the hearing, Judge Penn allowed 180 days for discovery—with the understanding that he would reconsider after seeing the *Times's* anticipated motion for summary judgment.

Two days later, on November 7, Simmons dropped a subpoena on Eskenazi for his sworn deposition. We were confident that Simmons, a skilled and aggressive interrogator, would annihilate Eskenazi under oath. We honestly believed that in the wake of Eskenazi's deposition, this case would be over. We thought that the *Times* would beg us to settle.

As I had repeatedly told anyone who would listen, the similarities in tone and substance between the Joe Browne's public statements on behalf of the NFL and Gerald Eskenazi's subsequent review were incredibly striking. From the outset, I had predicted a relationship between Browne and Eskenazi in this matter—especially after I discovered Eskenazi's acknowledgment to Browne in the sportswriter's 1976 book about the New York Giants, *There Were Giants in Those Days*, a celebration of professional football for which Eskenazi received the full cooperation of both the NFL and the Giants' top management.

In addition, according to documents released by the *Times* under the required discovery, Eskenazi's personal calendar indicated that he had been scheduled to talk to Browne on the first day of my book tour, July 26, 1989. Soon after, Eskenazi received the assignment from the *New York Times* to review my book.

Also, Eskenazi had handwritten Browne's name in a margin of his personal notes about *Interference*, suggesting that Eskenazi had consulted with Browne prior to writing the review. In addition, Eskenazi appeared to have listed and numbered Browne's criticisms of my book in another margin, apart from the rest of his notes. And most of these points wound up in Eskenazi's error-filled review, suggesting that Eskenazi and Browne had actually worked together on this piece.

As all of the legal maneuvering on both sides continued after the *Times* submitted its motion for summary judgment on November 30, we prepared for Eskenazi's deposition on Thursday and Friday, December 20 and 21. Well in advance, we had our train and hotel reservations for the anticipated two-day bloodbath—if it even went that long before the *Times* unconditionally surrendered.

Throughout December 19, the day before Eskenazi's anticipated day of reckoning, telephone calls and faxed documents burned up the phone lines among the attorneys and me. Roger Simmons seemed so pumped up that I thought he was ready to climb into the ring with Mike Tyson.

Then, just before 5:00 P.M.—while I was in the midst of packing my luggage—Simmons called. Badly shaken, he simply told me, "Judge Penn has just stayed all discovery. Eskenazi's deposition tomorrow has been postponed indefinitely."

I just sat at my desk in total disbelief. Then, I called Mimi, asking if I could take her to a movie and dinner that night—because I would not be going to New York the following day.

On May 29, 1991, I participated on a panel of journalists and attorneys to discuss the topic, "The First Amendment: What's Its Worth Today?"[101] Warren Burger, the former Chief Justice of the U.S. Supreme Court, served as moderator of this event, which was held at the National Press Club.

During my opening statement, I decided to express my reconstituted view of the media, saying:

> Other than the government, I can think of no institution in which the temptations for abuses and the potential for sheer corruption are greater than within the media itself. Yet no other business in American society enjoys the same constitutional privilege that the media enjoys. And no institution in America, not even the government, can wipe out a person's reputation as fast and as thoroughly as the media can.
>
> Now, all of us can speak in broad terms about the principles of the First Amendment being more important than the problems of one individual. Thus, the individual, in view of the overall principle, is viewed as being dispensable and should be willing to be sacrificed. However, speaking from experience, when you—yourself—become the individual expected to be sacrificed, you then develop a little different perspective on such matters. You find yourself in a position where you are literally fighting for your own personal and professional survival. And, at the moment, I am fighting for my life. And I simply refuse to be sacrificed.
>
> Another consequence is that this entire matter has pitted me against former colleagues, like the established pro-First Amendment groups, whose supporters have never met a libel suit they either like or respect—regardless of its merits, regardless of the unjustified personal damage the offending publication has done. As a consequence, these respected groups desperately search for any means available to defend occasionally indefensible abuses of the First Amendment while hanging people, like me, out to dry in the process. Again, the individual is expected to be sacrificed in order to protect the perceived overall principles of the First Amendment.
>
> And, in my particular case—in which I am challenging a review to which I was not permitted to respond—I believe that the First Amendment issues cut both ways. My First Amendment rights have been violated. By the *Times* refusal to publish my letter, I was not permitted to participate in the full and robust exchange of ideas that the *New York Times*

attorneys now claim that my suit threatens. Where are the First Amendment organizations, which should be questioning the violations of my rights? Again, I am the individual up against a powerful institution; and thus I am the one who has to be sacrificed.

At the same time, I cannot say enough about the pro-First Amendment groups. The Reporters Committee came to my rescue three years ago after I was subpoenaed by several Mafia figures in a federal RICO case in New Jersey and ordered to give up some FBI sources.[102] . . .

But the Reporters Committee and the big media are going to have to stop viewing the First Amendment in absolute terms—because they have developed distorted views of what the First Amendment should and should not protect. Every word, written or broadcast by a journalist, is not necessarily sacrosanct, endowed by a divine spirit and protected from legitimate legal challenge. The media, on occasion, screws up. . . .

When Chief Justice Burger asked me for my recommendations for reform, I replied that I had four:

1. Public disclosure should not be limited to public officials; it should also apply to those who write about them. This disclosure of individual journalists should include details about stock and investment portfolios, incomes, speaking engagements, and other matters which could demonstrate the appearance of or actual conflicts of interests.

2. The Congress should investigate the impact that the increasing corporate concentrations within the media have had on the reporting of the news.

3. The Justice Department's Antitrust Division, asleep now for over ten years, should reexamine recent media mergers and where necessary begin busting these violations to the public trust; and

4. Ultimately, the only checks on the growing and abusive power of the media conglomerates are the courts. The courts are

the only places where private individuals can finally demand accountability from First Amendment abuses. Consequently, the courts should provide for a faster track in the hearing of libel suits, thereby creating a balance between media conglomerates and the individual who has been defamed.

After I completed my entire statement, Chief Justice Burger paused for a moment and said, only half-jokingly in front of the large audience which was taken aback by my words, "I would be surprised if you weren't excommunicated from the press club for what you've just said."

80. *Cooke v. Washingtonian*

Harry Turner had worked as a chauffeur for Jack Kent Cooke, the owner of the Washington Redskins. In the December 1989 issue of *Washingtonian* magazine, Turner, after being fired by Cooke, published a story about his experiences with his former boss.

Immediately after publication, Cooke filed a $30-million libel suit against Turner and the magazine, challenging three stated facts in the article. First, Cooke denied Turner's allegation that he had expressed support for Jimmy "The Greek" Snyder after the colorful oddsmaker had aired his racist views about black athletes during a television interview. Second, Cooke denied Turner's charge that he had used his political influence to fix a traffic ticket.

Finally—and, obviously, most significantly—Cooke denied Turner's allegation that the owner of the Redskins had once warned him not to bet on NFL games, because they "can be fixed."

Although Turner never alleged that Cooke personally participated in game fixing, Cooke clearly felt it necessary to challenge this statement. Of course, the NFL agreed with his position and supported this litigation while vigorously resisting subpoenas from the magazine's defense attorneys.

In spite of all evidence to the contrary, NFL officials had continued to claim that no professional football game had ever been successfully fixed since the creation of the league in 1920.

After Cooke filed his complaint, an attorney for *Washingtonian* contacted me. Since the release of my book, not one reporter, covering either news or sports, had ever asked to examine my evidence of game fixing in the NFL. Thus, I had been searching for a forum—other than the media—to release this documentation, especially after the filing of *Moldea v. New York Times.*

I told the *Washingtonian* lawyer to have Jack Limpert, the magazine's long-time executive editor, personally invite me onto their defense team. At that time, my relationship with Limpert was lukewarm at best. He had been stalling an answer to a proposed article I wanted to write for the magazine about the Black Mafia in Washington. So, before we discussed anything else, I wanted an answer to that.

After not hearing from him for several months, Limpert finally called me in mid-August 1990 with his hat in his hand, asking for my help with his magazine's defense. During our conversation, he addressed me as "Mr. Moldea" and "Sir," a manner in which he had never before referred to me.

Perplexed by Limpert's unfamiliar tone, I then called a close friend and source, asking him to find out how much trouble *Washingtonian* was really in over the *Cooke* case. Twenty minutes later, my friend called back, laughing. When I asked him what was so funny, he told me that Harry Turner—the sole source for the story and the key witness in this $30 million libel suit—had once claimed to have been kidnapped by space aliens and taken to another planet.

Essentially, Turner had self-destructed. The magazine's only hope was to use outsiders and their evidence to prove that the three contested allegations in his article were actually true.

Because I am not a negotiator, I immediately called my attorney, Roger Simmons, and asked him to work out my deal with *Washingtonian*, providing him with our newfound bargaining power.

According to the spectacular arrangement he worked out for me, I agreed to serve as an expert witness for the defense during which time I would be required to turn over my documentation of the game fixing in the NFL. In addition, I pledged to provide *Washingtonian's* legal team with at least two other experts who could testify that NFL games "can be fixed."

Clearly, *Washingtonian's* attorneys felt that if they could get past the NFL game-fixing count then they could win the entire case.

I provided the attorneys with the promised list of law-enforcement experts who agreed to testify about NFL game fixing. However, instead of only providing two witnesses, as my contract with *Washingtonian* required, I gave them six. From this list, the magazine's attorneys selected three to sit for depositions—in addition to my own testimony.

The other witnesses were: Herbert Hinchman, a former top federal agent with the Criminal Investigative Division of the Internal Revenue Service; Carl Shoffler, a former detective with the intelligence division of the Washington, D.C. police department; and Leo Halper, another former IRS/CID agent, who headed *Project Layoff*, a federal sports-gambling probe in Nevada.

All four of us testified under oath that not only can NFL games be fixed, but that, in fact, they have been fixed.

During my sworn deposition on February 11, 1991, I was asked about my documentation in *Interference*. Also, Cooke's attorney peppered me with questions about my evidence of game fixing, especially the role of Don Dawson in the thirty-two fixed NFL games:

> **Question:** Did you bring Dawson's allegations to the attention of any law-enforcement officials, apart from publishing it in the book?
>
> **Moldea:** It was more like the law-enforcement officials brought it to my attention.
>
> **Question:** In what way?
>
> **Moldea:** Well, when I first got into this whole investigation, I went to a top organized-crime investigator with the Michigan State Attorney General's office, and he told me, "If you're going to do something on the NFL, you're going to have to investigate Don Dawson, because he was fixing games. We knew it." So then I went to my friends and sources at the IRS, the criminal intelligence division, and they told me the same thing: Don Dawson was fixing games. They knew it. Their investigations were quashed.
>
> **Question:** Is fixing games a federal crime?
>
> **Moldea:** It would be a violation of the *Sports Bribery Act*.
>
> **Question:** I take it, it might involve other crimes like income tax evasion?
>
> **Moldea:** Absolutely. . . .

PART SIX: MOLDEA V. NEW YORK TIMES

Question: It was [also an IRS official] who indicated to you that you should pursue Dawson. Is that correct?

Moldea: Right. At that point, I had enough evidence to say, "Allegedly, according to law enforcement sources, Don Dawson had been fixing NFL games." But I went that extra step and jumped through the hoops and interviewed Dawson. And he confessed. So law enforcement agents made charges; he confessed. That was evidence in a court of law as far as I was concerned.

Question: Did Dawson understand when he confessed that he was exposing himself to criminal prosecution?

Moldea: I made it very, very clear to him that I was publishing this material. Again, I went out to him. I showed him the manuscripts. I showed him the galleys. I sent his son, who is an attorney, the galleys so his son would know.

Question: I'm not suggesting you did anything wrong to him. I was just trying to figure what your understanding of his state of mind was.

Moldea: I made it very clear to him that he was going to be published and was going to get famous.

Question: Now, do you have any idea why no federal authority—I mean, in our parlance, this is a lay-down case—

Moldea: Statute of limitations.

Question: Oh, the statute of limitations. He believed that he was okay because of the statute of limitations?

Moldea: I don't know if that's what he was thinking. He was not, *per se*, a target of my investigation. Not really. What I was simply trying to show is that despite the NFL's claims that they're investigating organized crime, the fact is that these things are going on.

In the wake of our depositions, *Washingtonian* filed a motion for summary judgment, asking the presiding judge to dismiss the *Cooke* case. The judge took the matter under consideration.

On July 25, the judge ruled on the motion. After weighing "the various pleadings and the record," he dismissed the NFL game-fixing count.

Clearly, the judge had given *Washingtonian* a major victory with this ruling.

Further, during a conference call with all of the attorneys in the case, the judge told Cooke's lawyers that he would permit them to present their case on the other two minor counts at trial. However, the judge warned that before *Washingtonian* had to present its defense, he would consider a directed verdict on *Washingtonian's* behalf.

In other words, Cooke's case was in very serious trouble. *Washingtonian's* talented attorneys had taken an extremely difficult case and turned it into a likely winner.

The judge scheduled the trial—which would concentrate on the lesser issues of Cooke's alleged support for Jimmy the Greek and the circumstances revolving around the traffic ticket—for September 10. *Washingtonian's* attorneys—as well as those of us who served as their expert witnesses—were ecstatic. All of us who had been deposed on the magazine's behalf about game fixing in the NFL were now out of the case. We had no further responsibilities.

Then, suddenly, on Thursday, August 8, *Washingtonian* settled out of court with Cooke.

Washingtonian, with its victory at hand, inexplicably admitted "a lapse in editorial judgment" and accepted defeat.

Even those of us who were now out of the case were in complete shock.

As part of the settlement, *Washingtonian* actually agreed to apologize publicly to Cooke for all three of the challenged passages in the article and to make a "substantial" contribution to Cooke's favorite charity. The apology would include the NFL game-fixing count, which had already been dismissed by the judge!

Also, the principals agreed not to comment about the case.

To make matters worse, the depositions of our expert witnesses—all of whom documented evidence of NFL game fixing—were sealed as part of the final settlement.

Shortly after the case ended, the magazine's executive editor, Jack Limpert, appeared in Jack Kent Cooke's owner's box at RFK stadium for the Washington Redskins's 1991 home opener.

PART SIX: MOLDEA V. NEW YORK TIMES

81. A slow judge makes a fast decision

As our battle with the *New York Times* continued, I decided to upgrade some of my equipment. I bought an IBM PS/2 386-55SX with greater speed, more RAM, and a larger hard drive. Also, since I had not owned a car since the runaway cab totaled my Thunderbird during the summer of 1989, I went to an auto auction in Washington, looking for another Thunderbird. Instead, I wound up buying a very large 1979 Jeep Wagoneer with four-wheel drive.

Meantime, with U.S. District Judge John Garrett Penn under fire from the *Washington Post* for his newly discovered backlog of cases, my attorneys—Roger Simmons, Steve Trattner, and Ed Law—and I had a conference call about Penn's endless delay in ruling on the *Times's* motion for summary judgment. At that point, we almost didn't care which way Penn ruled. We just wanted our case moving again. Regardless of how he decided, the losing side would appeal, and we assumed that, sooner or later, the case would wind up with the U.S. Supreme Court.

In order to jump-start Judge Penn, Simmons filed a motion to lift his order to stay discovery, concentrating, in part, on a direct personal connection I had discovered and documented between Arthur Sulzberger, the publisher and chairman of the *New York Times*, and the mobbed-up NFL team owner, Edward J. DeBartolo.

Times attorney Bruce Sanford responded with fury in his January 27, 1992, opposition to our motion, stating:

> Moldea makes the wholly preposterous suggestion that former *New York Times* publisher Arthur Ochs Sulzberger would be an important witness. His statements in support of this theory are not merely speculative, but patently false. Sulzberger has not been to a professional football game since the Giants left New York some 18 years ago, does not have any "relationships with NFL owners." .... There neither is, nor could be, any legitimate reason for seeking discovery from Sulzberger, and the *Times* would vehemently resist such a transparent attempt to harass the head of the family that controls the *Times*.

Obviously, we disagreed with Sanford's claim and pushed the issue—because we had the hard evidence of the association between Sulzberger and DeBartolo, which, indeed, had nothing to do with football. And we believed that the *Times* actually knew what we had.

Immediately after receiving our motion and the *Times's* reply, Judge Penn suddenly shut everything down on January 31 by granting the *Times's* motion for summary judgment.

Officially, our case was now dismissed.

But we experienced no trauma over this action. Three days later, Roger Simmons filed our notice of appeal, already realizing that nothing about our case against the powerful *New York Times* would be routine.

As Simmons went through the process of preparing for our appeal, the press—still not taking our case very seriously—continued firing shots at me.

In one of the funniest instances, Judith Colp, a feature writer for the *Washington Times*, called and asked if I would sit down for an interview about the case. I was acquainted with her husband, so I agreed to meet with her after receiving permission from Simmons.

Because my apartment looked like it had been hit by a thermonuclear device—with papers and books everywhere—I balked when she wanted to come to my home. Instead, I told her that I would be willing to come to her newspaper's headquarters on New York Avenue.

"What about your documentation?" She asked. "I'll need it for my editors.... Why don't you just throw it in a suitcase and bring it with you?"

Agreeing with her suggestion to haul a suitcase to our meeting, I met with Colp who seemed very nice and professional.

In her April 23 article in the *Washington Times*, trying to portray me as a nutcase, she wrote: "Mr. Moldea has become, well, obsessed with his case. He meets a reporter toting a large briefcase filled with files and videotapes."

After the WIW board of directors passed its resolution supporting me in the litigation, I decided to approach other writers' groups, hoping for official consideration and professional legitimacy.

Earlier, on September 4, 1991, I had gone to the most unlikely writers' group of all for support: the National Book Critics Circle, the trade association of America's book reviewers.

I contacted Jack Miles, the president of NBCC and the editor of the *Los Angeles Times Book Review*, and explained the case to him. He was obviously aware of the dispute and expressed an interest in examining our materials, so I sent him a package of information. He also suggested that I become a member of NBCC, which I agreed to do.

On January 16, 1992, Miles called to tell me the results of the NBCC's board of directors' meetings on January 9-10, saying that the board had decided to form a three-person committee—composed of Miles; Patricia Holt, the book editor for the *San Francisco Chronicle*; and Carlin Romano, the book editor of the *Philadelphia Inquirer*.

Later, after a seven-month examination of the facts of *Moldea v. New York Times*, the committee proposed three options to the full NBCC board—all of which were critical of the manner in which the *Times* had handled my situation.

However, when the board met to decide which of the options to accept, its members balked. Miles later wrote an article in the *Los Angeles Times*, saying:

> After much consideration, the board decided to take no position on the matter. Thinking as reviewers faced with the prospect of future litigation if their work struck an author as defamatory, some on the board tacitly sided with the *New York Times*... Others on the board, perhaps thinking of their vulnerability as authors to essentially unaccountable reviewers, tacitly sided with Moldea, who claims: "If I win this case, the worst that can happen is that reviewers and other opinion-writers will suddenly have a responsibility to be accountable for what they write. Any writer who cannot live with that should not be in this profession."[103]

After the interesting result from the NBCC experience, I sent similar requests to two other organizations, in which I had long-time memberships: the Authors Guild and Investigative Reporters & Editors (IRE).

However, like NBCC, both the Authors Guild and IRE refused to take sides.[104]

As a result, I simply declared victory, telling journalist Debra Gersh of *Editor & Publisher* during an interview, "Officials from all three of these organizations reviewed the key documents in this case. If the facts didn't support what I've been saying all along, these organizations, especially the NBCC, wouldn't have hesitated to kick my ass and defend the *New York Times*."

The 1963 murder of President Kennedy suddenly became news again soon after the release of Oliver Stone's controversial film, *JFK*. I viewed this movie as a great cinema but terrible history in which Stone had attempted to rehabilitate New Orleans District Attorney Jim Garrison who was played by Kevin Costner. Stone made Garrison appear as a dogged investigator, as well as another misunderstood visionary instead of what he really was: a mobbed-up stooge for New Orleans mob boss Carlos Marcello—just as I had alleged in *The Hoffa Wars*.

Simultaneously, reporter Jack Newfield of the *New York Post* published a story about attorney Frank Ragano, who had represented Santo Trafficante, as well as Marcello and Jimmy Hoffa—the same lawyer who had offered me a $250,000 bribe through my attorney in 1978 for the rights to *The Hoffa Wars*. In the opening paragraph of his story, Newfield wrote:

> A lawyer who represented Jimmy Hoffa says the slain Teamsters boss recruited two Mafia chieftains to carry out the assassination of President John F. Kennedy.
>
> The lawyer, Frank Ragano of Tampa, told *The Post* yesterday he now believes he carried a deadly message from Hoffa in early 1963 to Florida mob boss [Santo] Trafficante and New Orleans mob boss Carlos Marcello that led to the Nov. 22, 1963, assassination in Dallas.[105]

The article noted that Hoffa had disappeared in 1975; Trafficante had died at 72 after heart surgery on March 17, 1987; and Marcello was alive and in prison but supposedly suffering from Alzheimer's disease.[106]

To my delight, *Newsweek* credited the first reporting on this matter to "Dan E. Moldea, who made the Teamsters-JFK-Ragano link in his 1978 book, *The Hoffa Wars*."[107]

Shortly thereafter, I called Ragano in Tampa. He could not have been happier to hear from me—even after I reminded him about the attempted bribe. Ragano, who was appealing a three-year prison sentence for income-tax evasion, invited me to participate on a team of experts he was assembling to help him get out his story. Along with Newfield and me, he had selected Bob Blakey, the former chief counsel of the U.S. House Select Committee on Assassinations, and author/screenwriter Nick Pileggi, among others.

Later, Charles Stuart, a respected documentary filmmaker, produced an excellent episode on PBS's *Frontline* about Ragano in which all of us appeared.[108]

During my own interviews with Ragano, I asked him about Ed Partin's earlier statement to me that Ragano had offered to make Jim Garrison back off from his absurd investigation of Partin's alleged involvement with Lee Harvey Oswald and Jack Ruby—in return for a sworn affidavit from Partin, recanting his testimony against Hoffa during the Teamster leader's jury-tampering trial.

Ragano confirmed Partin's story, admitting that he did make that offer to Partin who had died in March 1990. Ragano added that he had the clout with Garrison to guarantee it.

Also, in an article I later did for the *Washington Post*, I wrote:

> Earlier this year, Frank Ragano offered to turn state's evidence regarding his knowledge of the roles of Hoffa and Marcello in Kennedy's murder. According to Ragano, Marcello and Santo Trafficante, the former Mafia boss of Tampa, accepted a murder contract on Kennedy from Hoffa in 1963. Ragano has told me that Garrison did nothing more during his 1967-1969 investigation than divert public attention away from Marcello. "Garrison was shielding Marcello from being implicated in the Kennedy murder case," Ragano says.[109]

Throwing me a bouquet, Ragano gave my publisher a quote for the 1993 re-release of *The Hoffa Wars*, in which he said:

> In 1978, a Washington journalist released a controversial book that began to unlock the secrets of the brutal murder of President Kennedy. He did it by piecing together the Hoffa-Marcello-Trafficante puzzle for the first time. That journalist was Dan E. Moldea, and his book was *The Hoffa Wars*.[110]

82. The U.S. Court of Appeals

With all of my activities swirling around work and litigation, Mimi had been busy promoting her late mother's recently-published book, *New*

Currents, Ancient Rivers, about contemporary African art, which had been published and distributed by the Smithsonian Institution in Washington. However, Mimi's tireless work on behalf of her mother, Jean Kennedy, was one of few bright spots in her life. I certainly wasn't providing many, and, even though I loved her dearly, I again offered her the opportunity to escape.

This time, after five years together and three years of rejecting that suggestion, she took it. I wasn't particularly surprised and almost relieved. I had felt nothing but guilt over how my chaotic life had affected hers since the publication of the *New York Times's* review of *Interference* in September 1989.

I had absolutely no interest in any other women—not that many women would have been interested in me. Along with all my other problems and dilemmas, I had lost almost all of my hair and, after quitting smoking Kools for the umpteenth time, was as big as I had ever been—six-feet-four, 245 pounds, the same size as Rolland McMaster, whom I had once viewed as enormous. Also the usual dark circles around my eyes were now nearly black.

When a woman said she wanted me in my younger hard-body, full-head-of-hair days, I expected it. Now, if a woman came on to me, I automatically assumed that I was getting set up. Because of the way I looked, I simply refused to believe it. It just made no sense.

Meantime, because I felt so estranged from the writing community in the midst of my case against the *Times*, I started organizing dinners for writers at Musso & Frank's restaurant on Hollywood Boulevard in Los Angeles whenever I came to town.

Seeing how well the Los Angeles dinners worked, I organized another group of authors—writers who had written at least one book—in Washington. However, unlike the Los Angeles dinner party, the Authors Dinner Group, which later grew to a stable of nearly 100 published authors, remained stag—men only. A few years earlier, we had tried a co-ed group, but members started dating each other, which caused some hard feelings and eventually destroyed the group. In the end, the women authors, led by Barbara Raskin, went in one direction; the men went in another, specifically to the Ratskeller of The Old Europe restaurant in the Glover Park section of town for our twice-a-year conclaves.[111]

These author dinners—as well as my Thursday night poker group and other friendships—helped me to keep my sanity in the midst of another horrible period of my life.

In a profession where people generally do not wish each other well, I wanted to surround myself with people who do.

PART SIX: MOLDEA V. NEW YORK TIMES

Prior to the oral arguments before the U.S. Court of Appeals in *Moldea v. New York Times*, I had my first and only argument with our lead counsel, Roger Simmons. Nearly every article written about the case had highlighted and even tried to limit our dispute to the use of the term "sloppy journalism," in lieu of the actual provably false facts contained in the review—for example, what I did and did not say about Los Angeles Rams' owner Carroll Rosenbloom's death.

I had come to believe that as long as the "sloppy journalism" count remained in our complaint, the media would continue to portray me unjustly as a thin-skinned author with "a wounded ego," and that the entire foundation of our case would still be misunderstood, as well as misrepresented by the media and the courts.

I asked Simmons—as well as my other lawyers, Steve Trattner and Ed Law—to consider conceding the *Times's* point that the term "sloppy journalism" was, in fact, a statement of non-defamatory opinion, which would force the *Times*, the media, and the courts to start dealing with the specific errors in the review, the provably false facts.

Although very concerned with the severe thrashing I was taking in the press, Simmons refused, arguing that Eskenazi's use of the term "sloppy journalism" had been based on the specific provably false facts contained in the review. Thus, Simmons reasoned, if Eskenazi's errors were defamatory, then the broad conclusions which summed them up—like the term "sloppy journalism"—were defamatory, as well.

In the end, Simmons won our argument, persuading me that we had to continue to fight the battle over the term "sloppy journalism," regardless of how much grief I was taking for it.

On September 14, 1993, Simmons was nothing short of spectacular, stressing our now-united point of view during the hard-fought oral arguments against the *Times's* attorneys before the three-judge panel of the U.S. Court of Appeals for the D.C. Circuit in Washington.

When Simmons, Trattner, Law, and I walked out of the courtroom, we were absolutely jubilant. But, then, seeing Bruce Sanford and the *Times* legal team conferring in the hallway, we quickly straightened up and tried to be humble. As we shook hands with Sanford and company, we saw the looks in their eyes.

They looked scared and rightfully so. Simmons had just smacked them down in open court, and we were now expecting a big win.

83. "Reversed and remanded"

On Friday, February 18, Debbie Wise, Roger Simmons's executive assistant, called to tell me that the U.S. Court of Appeals had rendered a decision in our case against the *New York Times*. Simmons and Ed Law were not in their offices—and she couldn't reach Steve Trattner—so she was not completely sure how "reversed and remanded" applied to our case.

It sounded like good news to me, as if the court had reversed the lower-court decision and remanded the case to trial. I called Tom von Stein, my close friend and another Thursday night poker buddy, at the Securities and Exchange Commission where he worked as a top attorney in its enforcement division. Von Stein believed that it was good news, too, but we both wanted confirmation. Von Stein ran off to the federal courthouse to get the paperwork.

After von Stein left his office, reporter David Streitfeld of the *Washington Post* called and officially gave me the news. Reading the AP and Reuters stories as they were coming off the wire, he said that the federal appellate court had ruled, 2-1, in our favor, restoring all three counts of our case.

I knew without asking that Judge Abner Mikva—a former U.S. congressman from Chicago who was close to the Korshak family—had been the dissenter, based on his statements during the oral arguments. No doubt, Mikva had completely ignored my harsh criticism of Sidney Korshak in *Interference*, not to mention what I had earlier written about Korshak in *Dark Victory*.[112]

Although I was extremely happy with the court's decision, I trembled a bit, knowing that the media would hardly be celebrating our big victory. In fact, when Streitfeld asked me for comment, I simply told him, "We are about to see a demonstration of raw power coming at us like a rifle shot."[113]

After my conversation with Streitfeld, von Stein called and started faxing the opinion to me. However, because my telephone and fax machine were the on the same phone line—which also had Call Waiting—any fax transmission was disrupted by the incoming calls. For the next few hours, von Stein tried and retried to fax the opinion—but to no avail. The flood of calls from the media and friends who heard the good news precluded my ability to receive the 39-page opinion and dissent.

During the late morning, after they messengered the opinion to me, Simmons, Steve Trattner, Ed Law, and I had a conference call—in which I heaped praise on them. This was their victory, which had been led by Roger Simmons.

But, again, even though all of us were thrilled by the panel's opinion, we remained relatively subdued, not knowing exactly what lay ahead. No one even suggested breaking out the champagne.

One reason for our reticence was that we had read and understood the opinion. Judge Harry Edwards, who had written it, stated that four of the five statements of fact contained in the review—including Eskenazi's false claim that my book "revives the discredited notion that Carroll Rosenbloom . . . . met foul play"—could be meaningfully determined by a jury to be true or false.

That, we appreciated.

However, Judge Edwards also insisted: "[I]f the *Times* review had said nothing more than 'Moldea's work is sloppy journalism,' this statement would be actionable because it is capable of defamatory meaning, and it reasonably can be understood to rest on provable, albeit unstated, defamatory facts."

Although grateful for the overall decision, I shuddered when I first read it, because it appeared that Judge Edwards had taken the controversy over the term "sloppy journalism" to an extreme—much further than even Roger Simmons sought.

All we had ever wanted was our day in court to present our evidence. But now, suddenly, we found ourselves at the hub of a potentially dangerous First Amendment issue.

The following day, the *New York Times* and the *Washington Post* published articles, featuring their predictable negative spin about our case.

However, David G. Savage, a reporter for the *Los Angeles Times* appeared to understand that something more was happening, writing:

> [The Moldea appellate] ruling illustrates a new trend in libel law. Since 1990, courts have increasingly held critics and opinion writers to the same strict standards for accuracy as news reporters.
>
> Before then, critics, columnists and editorial writers generally were seen as immune from libel suits because their words were labeled opinion, not fact. . . . [Roger C. Simmons,] who represented Moldea praised the ruling as a "victory for the small guy" against the most powerful force in book publishing.[114]

Predicting the general media's reaction to the decision, Paul Barrett of the *Wall Street Journal*—in a long feature article, aptly headlined, "Author Who Sued Over Scornful Review Is Now Scorned by the Publishing World"—added:

> The media are up in arms over the panel's decision, pointing to a dissenting judge's assertion that it could "open up the entire arena of artistic criticism to mass defamation suits." Until recently, courts made a sharp distinction between assertions of fact and opinion, and opinion was completely shielded from libel suits. . . . Some journalists and First Amendment buffs see Mr. Moldea as a traitor. "For Dan Moldea, an investigative journalist who has been the beneficiary of libel-defense law, to turn around and file a libel suit is unconscionable," says Jane Kirtley, executive director of the Reporters Committee for Freedom of the Press.[115]

Media critic Edwin Diamond of *New York* continued:

> Kirtley . . . criticizes Moldea "for bringing in the lawyers." Instead, she says, he should have raised hell, gone public, written letters to the editor. But that's exactly what Moldea says he did do. First he wrote Eskenazi "questioning his use of misleading facts." According to Moldea, Eskenazi never replied. Next, Moldea asked the *Times* to run a corrections box and was turned down. Next, he wrote a letter to the editor of the *Book Review*. It never appeared.[116]

George Freeman, the *Times's* senior attorney, commented to Debra Gersh of *Editor & Publisher*: "The issue is not if we're right or wrong. Certainly the book is subject to multiple interpretations. It's wrong that it goes to a jury."[117]

Indeed, the reinstatement of the case by the court of appeals had brought a new phenomenon in our case. Suddenly, real journalists—like Savage, Barrett, Diamond, and Gersh, among many others—were now asking for our side of the controversy, as well as our documentation, which we had always made available to the media.

During the late morning of Friday, February 25, author Tim Wells, the former president of WIW, called and asked me if I would be willing to meet that afternoon with a Mafia figure about whom he wanted to write a book. Of course, I agreed to attend the meeting, which had been set for 5:00 P.M. at Quigley's, a restaurant near American University, just up the street from my home. Wells said he would pick me up at 4:30.

Getting ready for the meeting with this mob guy, I put on a pair of blue jeans, black cowboy boots, a black-linen shirt, buttoned to the top, and a black leather jacket. I looked like the Prince of Darkness.

When Wells arrived at my apartment, he said that there had been a change of plans, and that the meeting had been moved to the Sign of the Whale, another popular Washington watering hole on M Street. I threw on a long dark gray overcoat and got into his car and went downtown. We parked in a lot on 19th Street, strolled across M, and into the restaurant. Wells walked ahead of me, and I followed him.

In the back room, instead of meeting a Mafia guy, I stepped into a surprise party with scores of cheering authors, journalists, attorneys, and trusted friends, toasting and celebrating our David and Goliath victory.

84. "Beyond a Bad Review"

On February 28, Roger Simmons picked me up, and we drove downtown for two scheduled afternoon meetings. Before the first, we went for corned beef and cabbage at Duke Zeibert's with Washington's power-lunch crowd where Simmons immediately became the center of attention among his friends and colleagues in the legal community.

At 2:00 P.M., after this really fun lunch, Simmons and I met with op-ed page editor Steve Rosenfeld and editorial writer Patricia Shakow at the *Washington Post*, which still refused to cut us any slack.

We had asked for the meeting in an attempt to have Simmons's reply published in response to yet another cataclysmic *Post* editorial, along with a poorly-researched column by ombudsman Joann Byrd and a heart-breaking piece of trash written by *Book World* columnist Jonathan Yardley who had earlier written my favorite review for *The Hunting of Cain*.

Simmons and I complained that the *Post* had been uniquely misleading about the issues of our case in its transparent effort to carry water for its traditional rival, the *New York Times*.

Rosenfeld, whom I had known for years, and Shakow, whom I had never met, could not have been colder toward us. While we attempted to remain measured and respectful to them in spite of their one-sided articles and editorials, the two *Post* staffers dripped with sarcasm every time they opened their mouths.

Simmons and I specified numerous errors made in the *Post's* editorials and op-ed pieces, providing them with our written documentation—including the evidence that the *Post* had misspelled the same names I had in my book. Seeing that we were speaking to a couple of brick walls, we reluctantly accepted Rosenfeld at his word that they would publish Simmons's reply.

On March 2, after hearing nothing, Simmons called Rosenfeld who replied, "We'll get back to you next week. The story is in the pipeline."

On March 12—after still hearing nothing from the newspaper, which continued to attack us—I wrote a polite letter to the *Post's* executive editor, Leonard Downie, whom I had a met a few times and always respected.

Finally, on March 23, the *Post* published Simmons's article, "Beyond a 'Bad Review,'" on the op-ed page.

Once again, regardless of how long it took, the *Washington Post* had diffused a volatile situation by merely publishing an aggrieved party's defense.

In his firmly-worded article, Simmons insisted:

> [Moldea's] complaint argues for honesty and accuracy in opinion writing—something that has long been mandatory in news reporting. It was filed only after the *Times* explicitly refused both to print a correction and to publish any rebuttal letter regarding its review of Moldea's book.
>
> Contrary to the image the [media have] projected, *Moldea* is not an assault on the foundations of the 'marketplace of ideas.' It is, however, a demand for opinion writers and reviewers to take a few basic steps to get their facts straight.
>
> Two judges on the U.S. Court of Appeals for the District of Columbia Circuit, who are longstanding protectors of the First Amendment and who are among the finest minds in the legal profession, joined in the opinion at issue. They made it clear that *Moldea v. The New York Times* is most distinctly not a suit over a 'bad review,' or about the use of the term 'sloppy'

standing alone. It is a suit challenging verifiably false factual assertions...."

Speaking for the court of appeals, Judge Edwards said: "We certainly do not mean to suggest that all bad reviews are actionable. We do hold, however, that assertions that would otherwise be actionable in defamation are not transmogrified into nonactionable statements when they appear in the context of a book review."

Moldea also contends that the *Times* should be required to accurately identify the biases and credentials of its 'neutral' reviewers, ensure that its reviewers actually read the books they review, and insist that its editors fact-check reviews against the books under review. Where errors of verifiable fact are made, Moldea's suit argues that the *Times* should give an author the opportunity for a rebuttal. [118]

Finally, Simmons's outstanding op-ed piece had correctly laid out our case.

85. Kenneth Starr and *The World Amicus*

In late March, attorneys for the *New York Times* petitioned the entire eleven-judge Court of Appeals for the D.C. Circuit for a rehearing of my case, *en banc*, arguing that its 2-1 decision "undermines two centuries of jurisprudence protecting literary criticism, ... [placing] at risk virtually every unflattering review."

In concert with the *Times's* sky-is-falling brief, prominent Washington attorney Kenneth Starr of Kirkland & Ellis, a former judge with that same appellate court and the former Solicitor General of the United States under President George H. W. Bush, filed an *amicus curiae* that reeked with the power and prestige of its author.

In his well-argued brief—which, we believed, completely distorted the facts of our case—Starr represented the Newspaper Association of America, Dow Jones & Company, the Associated Press, Scripps Howard, the Copley Press, the *Christian Science Monitor*, Time Inc., *U.S. News &*

World Report, the *New Yorker,* Magazine Publishers of America, the Society of Professional Journalists, among many other media organizations.

From the moment of its filing on March 21, my attorneys and I referred to Starr's work with awe, simply calling it, *The World Amicus.*[119]

The following day, trying to alleviate some of the sting after the filing of *The World Amicus,* I made a copy of the *Ziggy* greeting card that my old friend Tim Davis had given me twenty-one years earlier after my April 1973 arrest at the University of Akron while I was student body president. I sent the Ziggy card to Simmons, thanking him for the great fight he was giving me.

Seemingly applicable to our situation, the card still read: "Looks like it's you and me against the World. . . . and I think we're gonna get creamed."

However, after years of receiving passes from the fray, the *New York Times* and Gerald Eskenazi were finally starting to receive serious criticism for misrepresenting what I had written and not written in my book. For instance:

> * Ed Diamond in *New York,* who had earlier written: "More germane is this sentence from the book review: '[Moldea] revives the discredited notion that Carroll Rosenbloom, the ornery owner of the Rams, who had a penchant for gambling, met foul play when he drowned in Florida 10 years ago.' In fact, Moldea interviewed witnesses who were at the scene, obtained the autopsy photos, and concluded on page 360 of *Interference*: 'Rosenbloom died in a tragic accident and was not murdered.'"
>
> * Christopher Hanson in the *Columbia Journal Review* continued: "In fact, Moldea ended up discrediting the notion that Rosenbloom was murdered. He unearthed new evidence, interviewed experts, and concluded that the man died by accident."[120]
>
> * D. T. Max of the *New York Observer* late wrote: "[T]he judge found that Mr. Eskenazi, as a reviewer, had the obligation to be as factually accurate as a writer 'of a hard news story' in statements affecting Mr. Moldea's reputation. Without judging the facts as such, the court . . . found that since it was probable that Mr. Eskenazi might have erred, and perhaps erred in a way that defamed Mr. Moldea as a journalist, Mr. Moldea had the right to his day in court. . . . 'I may be crazy, but I'm not stupid,' said

the author, . . . 'I wasn't looking for a way to commit suicide by suing the *New York Times.*'"[121]

* Sports journalist Allen Barra, also of the *New York Observer,* decided: "I think Mr. Moldea is right when he charges Mr. Eskenazi with writing a review that, at the very least, was misleading in regard to several facts presented in the book and wrote that opinion for another publication. . . . I'm not suggesting that Mr. Eskenazi had that kind of natural bias against Mr. Moldea's book, but I think the *Times* could have fended off some charges by not giving the assignment to a beat writer—one who could risk losing precious 'access' to important National Football League information if he gave aid and comfort to a scathing critic of the league like Mr. Moldea."[122]

* John Leonard, the former editor of the *New York Times Book Review,* insisted in *The Nation*: "How nice, though, if, between opinions, we got the facts straight. Strong feelings are no guarantee of intelligent thinking. . . . I've read *Interference,* and Gerald Eskenazi's *Times* review of it, and if we are to deplore sloppy journalism we must admit that sloppy reviewing is one of its drearier subdivisions."[123]

And Steve Love, a reporter from the *Akron Beacon Journal,* wrote:

> In the dozen years I have known Moldea, I've always expected that one day someone would get him. I just never figured it would be the *New York Times.* . . .
>
> I can testify that Eskenazi misrepresented some of what Moldea wrote in *Interference,* in particular a meeting between New York Jets quarterback Joe Namath and Baltimore Colts placekicker Lou Michaels. He also charged that Moldea didn't "state in his text" another point he clearly made in the 63 pages of notes at the end of the book. . . .
>
> Eskenazi did what the mob could not: He killed Moldea.[124]

Actually, while we were turning the corner in this fight and now winning, I was still alive and well. And, for the first time since their review of *Interference* in September 1989, the mighty *New York Times* finally found itself on defense.

86. An unprecedented reversal: *Moldea II*

On Tuesday, May 3, at 9:00 A.M., Roger Simmons called and told me that the U.S. Court of Appeals had issued a second opinion regarding our case. Unclear about what had happened, he instructed me to go to the courthouse and get a copy.

I ran out the door, grabbed a cab, and went downtown. When I arrived at the clerk's office, I saw a sheet of paper taped to the wall, stating, "Opinions filed May 3, 1994 in the following . . . ." Only naming *Moldea v. New York Times*, the announcement noted that the new opinion had been written by Judge Edwards who also wrote the first opinion.

Under the category "Action," the word "Affirmed" appeared.

"Affirmed," I said out loud to myself. "That sounds like good news."

I walked into the clerk's office, smiling, gave the person behind the counter my name, and asked for a copy of the opinion.

When the clerk handed me the document, I opened it to the first page. Edwards began by recalling Justice Potter Stewart's statement in the wake of a U.S. Supreme Court's decision to reconsider and overrule an earlier decision. Edwards wrote:

> This remark has special poignancy for me now, because it underscores the distress felt by a judge who, in grappling with a very difficult legal issue, concludes that he has made a mistake of judgment. . . . Like Justice Stewart, I will take refuge in an aphorism of Justice Frankfurter:
>
> "Wisdom too often never comes, and so one ought not to reject it merely because it comes late."

I stopped reading momentarily and murmured to myself, "Where the hell is he going with this?"

Continuing, Edwards stated:

> In a 2-1 decision, the panel reversed on the ground that some of the review's characterizations of Moldea's book were

> potentially actionable because they were verifiable, and could not be held to be true as a matter of law. . . .
>
> The original majority opinion was generally correct in its statement of the law of defamation. Unfortunately, that opinion failed to take sufficient account of the fact that the statements at issue appeared in the context of a book review, a genre in which readers expect to find spirited critiques of literary works that they understand to be the reviewer's description and assessment of texts that are capable of a number of possible rational interpretations. . . .

Reading that, I clearly remembered Edwards writing in his first opinion that the "analysis of this case is not altered by the fact that the challenged statements appeared in a book review rather than in a hard news story."

Then, Edwards dropped the bomb:

> In light of our reconsideration of this case, we hold that the challenged statements in the *Times* review are supportable interpretations of *Interference*, and that as a matter of law the review is substantially true. Accordingly, we affirm the District Court's grant of summary judgment in favor of the *Times*.

I glanced up towards the counter and saw several people looking at me and then quickly look away.

Then, as the clerk offered me a few extra copies of the opinion, he said quietly, "I'm sorry, Mr. Moldea."

I smiled and replied, "Hey, I fought the law, and the law won."

The smile on my face disappeared within seconds after I walked out of the clerk's office. I then went to a nearby pay phone, called Simmons, and gave him the bad news—which he had already heard from a barrage of reporters who had called since we last talked. I was so numb that I don't even remember the specifics of what either of us had said during this conversation.

By the time I reached the elevator, I had a pretty good idea of what was going to happen to me after Edwards's latest opinion—which he called *Moldea II*—became public. But, even though I expected the opinion writers to tear me apart once again, I also anticipated the continued involvement of news reporters who would certainly investigate and ask questions about this incredible reversal.

Returning home, I heard my telephone ringing as I walked up the stairs. I didn't rush to get it, allowing my answering machine to record the message instead.

When I entered my apartment, I sat down on the couch as Noodles, my golden retriever, came over to me. She always seemed to know intuitively when I was in distress. For the next few minutes, as more calls came in, I stroked the fur on Noodles's back while looking around my living room, fully expecting to lose what little I had left.

After I finally decided to get up and face the music, the first call I returned was to Tamar Lewin, a reporter for the *New York Times*, who had called for comment. I gave Lewin what would become my mantra for the rest of the day:

> These judges spent over six months reviewing the case history as well as my book. On that basis, they ruled in our favor. Since then, the only new contribution has been the avalanche of misleading articles and editorials overreacting to this decision. I think it's legitimate to question what impact all of that had on this very bizarre reversal.[125]

The following day, the media coverage told the story. Paul Barrett in the *Wall Street Journal* wrote:

> In an extraordinary action, a federal appeals court retracted a controversial ruling that would have made it easier to file libel suits against publishers of negative book reviews and other critical works.
>
> A three-judge panel of the U.S. Court of Appeals said its 2-1 decision in February had simply been wrong—a stunning admission for an influential court to make, especially in a celebrated case....
>
> *Even if a reviewer is trying to damage an author's reputation, there may be nothing the courts can do about it,* "at least not without unacceptably interfering with free speech," Judge Edwards asserted.[126] [Emphasis added.]

In a turnabout of his own, David Streitfeld of the *Washington Post* wrote a surprisingly fair article about the judges' reversal, quoting Carlin Romano, the president of the National Book Critics Circle, saying: "None of the big media outfits seem to take seriously that it may be Moldea who's on the right side of freedom of expression here. His argument—that he and authors like him have little chance to respond to book reviews in major publications—is well taken."

Streitfeld also received comments from the attorneys on both sides:

> Lawyers for the *Times*, which had been hoping at best for a rehearing by the full 11-member appeals court, were happily stunned yesterday. Bruce Sanford [the *Times's* lead outside counsel] saluted Edwards's "enormously rare" action as "a testament to the quality of the man and the judge." . . .
>
> Simmons [said] that "we have certainly not given up. Dan Moldea is a fighter, and we intend to win. We will pursue at the next level. . . . "[127]

Did anyone agree with me that the judges caved in to outside pressures?

Streitfeld quoted respected First Amendment expert Rodney Smolla of the College of William & Mary's School of Law: "This is impossible to understand. . . . They argued this out, thought this out, thrashed it out . . . It's inexplicable."

Also, reporter Joan Biskupic, who covered the courts for the *Post*, wrote on May 5:

> [T]he sheer rarity of a reversal by the D.C. Circuit Court of Appeals, dismissing [the] controversial lawsuit . . . continued to reverberate yesterday.
>
> "It was and is the talk" of the law firms, said Kenneth W. Starr, a former appeals court judge and former solicitor general, now in private practice . . . . Judge Abner J. Mikva, who dissented in the original case, was vindicated this week. But he took no credit yesterday.
>
> "I certainly did not lobby them on the issue," he said. "I didn't send them copies of the editorials or anything. They could read those on their own."
>
> So did the original majority give in to outside pressure, as Moldea and others suggested Tuesday?

"These are very strong-minded judges," Mikva said. 'They don't cave to pressure. Even good pressure." . . .

Others were not as generous. A libel lawyer who spoke on the condition of anonymity attributed the reversal to the "firestorm of public criticism that the earlier decision received."

Separately, Columbia Law Prof. Kent Greenwalt said, "We could talk about conscious and unconscious levels of response to public reaction. I think well enough of Edwards and [Patricia] Wald to rule out the possibility they said to themselves, 'I think my decision was right the first time, but now that I'm going to be embarrassed and attacked I'm going to change my mind.' But it's possible to be influenced unconsciously."[128]

Five years later, Mikva, then retired from the bench, was extremely candid about the impact of media pressure on Judges Harry Edwards and Patricia Wald, his two colleagues during *Moldea v. New York Times*. In a June 14, 1999, article for the *Legal Times*, Mikva, confirming what I had alleged, wrote:

I wish I could claim that my eloquence, either in my dissent or otherwise, persuaded my colleagues to change their minds. It was more likely the drumbeat of criticism begun in the editorials of the *Washington Post* and the *New York Times* about the "serious threat" to the First Amendment posed by the original decision. While my dissent was quoted widely in those editorials, the panel ignored it when the second *Moldea* opinion held that book reviews are entitled to special protection.[129]

Indeed, if the beneficiary of this "bizarre reversal" had been an oil company or pharmaceutical concern, the media would have demanded a federal investigation into the circumstances of this ruling.

But, because media organizations were the beneficiary, they sat back and did nothing.

PART SIX: MOLDEA V. NEW YORK TIMES

87. The Simmons-Starr debate

On Thursday, May 5—just before *Time* magazine and its subsidiary, *Entertainment Weekly,* named me in their separate editions as "Loser of the Week"—I decided to take off for the weekend and get away from the telephone. I flew home to Ohio to take my mom out to dinner for Mother's Day and to play golf with my college buddies. Among my family and friends in Akron, no one could have cared less about *Moldea v. New York Times.*

The following night, Roger Simmons, still defending me as passionately as ever, appeared on Court-TV to debate Kenneth Starr, the author of *The World Amicus.* Host Fred Graham moderated.

After the issues were laid out, Graham spoke of my criticism of the judges for allowing the media criticism in the wake of *Moldea I* to influence their decision.

> **Graham:** Well, let's ask Ken Starr. What else did change other than all this criticism?
>
> **Starr:** I think in all honesty, Fred, the court had a fuller understanding of the implications of its opinion. Its first opinion was very far reaching. It was a monumental opinion. It was a dynamite opinion. And I don't think that the court apprehended what it had done. And that may seem odd, but it happens. Judges are very busy—
>
> **Graham:** Morning after? [laughing]
>
> **Starr:** Morning after. And then the *Times* comes in and says, "Here is what the court has done." It was supported by media interests, indicating, "This is very far reaching." And the court has, perhaps, over read—I think it did, and Roger is a wonderful lawyer but I disagree with him on the state of the law. I think the panel opinion, the divided panel opinion, had just misapprehended what the law was. They got it wrong the first time. And, then, to their great credit they said, "We goofed. We made a mistake, and we're going to get it right." And they did.

Graham: Now, those two judges who switched, Judge Harry Edwards and Pat Wald, they are both strong-minded judges. They had to know when they issued the first "monumental decision" that people were going to look at it and analyze it. And then, suddenly, they changed their mind. Is there any precedent? I don't know a precedent for this.

Starr: Judges change their minds. You will see—to Judge Edwards's credit—when he begins the second opinion, he talks about quoting . . . that "wisdom sometimes comes late," and that it's better that it comes late than never at all. And judges need to be open minded about this. So I think this—by the way, Fred—is a great tribute to the court. And I feel very, very strongly that the court institutionally should be viewed as not having catered and not been courageous to stick up for what it thought was right—but being open minded enough to take a second look.

Simmons: No one, I think, to my knowledge, would ever begin to criticize the intellectual integrity and the capability of Judge Edwards and Judge Wald. They are two of the finest judges in the country. There is no doubt about it. I think the question here that got created was what exactly the Supreme Court case in 1990—the *Milkovich* case, which preceded the filing of our complaint by about four months—what it really means. That's the critical issue. We see *Milkovich* as cleanly and clearly and specifically wiping away the difference between opinions and normal news reporting. And the *Milkovich* case—

Graham: Well, pardon me for interrupting. You're going to the issue here, and we'll go there in a minute. But it does seem—Do you know of any precedent like this?

Simmons: This is, I think, *sui generis*. It stands on its own.

Graham: Yeah.

Simmons: It's unique. There are certainly instances—as Mr. Starr well points out—where judges will change their mind, where they've seen—missed a case, missed a precedent or something very different about a case that is brought to their attention. This is a case where the judges looked at it for six months before they ruled on the opinion. There was a vigorous oral argument. There was a 2-1 split on it. There was vigorous debate within the court over how it would come out. And they came out passionately for Dan Moldea.

Graham: Uh-huh.

Simmons: Ten weeks later, they came out rather ambiguously for the *New York Times*. And, I think, what it points to is a need for clarification of this area of the law.

Meantime, continuing to misrepresent what my case was all about—the provably false facts contained in Eskenazi's review—the *New York Times* published a self-congratulatory editorial, celebrating its big win against little me on May 7, "Critical Freedom," in which the newspaper embraced God and country, as well as the First Amendment, saying:

> The Court of Appeals judges have rebounded with sensitivity, and with courage, given the difficulty of changing judicial minds. The whole society, freer to speak and argue about matters of public concern, is the winner.

Of course, to the *New York Times*, that "critical freedom . . . to speak and argue about matters of public concern" applied to everyone but me. Just as it had done after its false review about my book, the *Times* again refused to publish my response. In my unpublished reply to the *Times* editorial, I stated:

> Contrary to what the *New York Times* has bullied its readers to believe—that this litigation is merely over the use of the term 'sloppy journalism' in a vacuum—my suit really questions whether reviewers with conflicts of interest can voice their hidden agendas with the publication of probably false facts that are merely disguised as opinions. In short, my attorneys and I believe that opinion writers should be held to the same standard of accuracy and honesty as news reporters. . . .
>
> The *New York Times* asserts in its May 7 editorial that the appellate court's second opinion safeguards "spirited argument,"

adding: "The whole society, freer to speak and argue about matters of public concern, is the winner."

Ironically, your newspaper's original failure to publish my letter to the editor in response to a false and misleading review of my book denied me the opportunity to participate in this "spirited argument." Had I been given the opportunity to respond, I never would have filed this lawsuit.

Writing on my behalf, Roger Simmons stated in his own letter to the *Times*:

I must say I am not particularly surprised that the *New York Times* would not want to publish Dan Moldea's reply to its false editorial about him and his case inasmuch as the *Times* has never desired to publish his view of the controversy. The *Times* obviously does not want to permit Dan Moldea to participate in the free exchange of ideas in the marketplace.

Soon after realizing that, once again, the *Times* would not publish either of our responses, I wrote an article about the case for the *Los Angeles Times*.[130] This op-ed piece served as the basis for my speech at a symposium at the 1994 American Booksellers Association in Los Angeles, which had been arranged and sponsored by the National Book Critics Circle. The event pitted Roger Simmons and me against *Times* attorney Bruce Sanford and three other supporters of the *New York Times*.

In both the speech and my article, which was published on the same day of the symposium, I explained:

In effect, the appellate court, in its virtually unprecedented act, created an exemption from libel for opinion writers when they engage in "mischievous intent," as the court now calls it. News reporters and nonfiction authors have no such exemption and continue to be held to a "malice" standard.

In other words, a person expressing an opinion may deliberately set out to make misstatements of fact without the critic's victim having any recourse.

In the midst of the debate at the ABA, Carlin Romano, the president of NBCC and the moderator of this slugfest, stunned everyone in the large meeting room when he suddenly came out publicly for our side. It was a show-stopping moment.

Later, Romano wrote in his lengthy two-part series about my case in *The Nation*:

> Learning to love *Moldea v. New York Times* as a watershed libel ruling requires bringing together the facts of the case, the legal analysis they generate and the realities of power politics in book reviewing. It isn't a pretty picture....
>
> As with most complex litigation, it would take a lifetime to disentangle every contested element of *Moldea v. New York Times*. But despite the reflex posturing of big media organizations praising *Moldea II* as a victory for freedom of speech, it's actually the opposite. It's a victory not for working journalists, authors and critics who thrive on debating issues and interpretations but for corporate media managers who want to squelch criticism of what they publish, escape tightening their standards to eliminate shoddy reviewing, evade questioning of the judgment of their critics, avoid paying for their mistakes as other corporate managers must and, above all, prevent ordinary Americans—the members of a jury—from getting a look at their practices.[131]

Even according to Bruce Sanford's own account of the ABA event in his 1999 book, *Don't Kill the Messenger*, Simmons and I had won over the audience:

> What interested me most about the afternoon was not the reprise of the legal arguments, which sounded the same familiar melodies as the courts were hearing, but instead the responsive chords which Moldea was finding with the audience of authors, publishers, bookstore owners and affiliated denizens of the book world. Whenever Moldea would rant against the power of the *Times Book Review* to make or break a book with a positive or negative review, the audience would nod in agreement as if a flashing "Nod Now" sign had been turned on from the podium.[132]

Once again, Sanford had created a fantasy about what really happened. In fact, Simmons and I—along with NBCC president Carlin

Romano—swung this sophisticated, book-savvy crowd to our point of view because, for the first time, they had heard our side of the story. Regardless of Sanford's subsequent rationalizations, the audience simply did not buy his defense of the *Times's* actions, especially its decision not to publish my letter to the editor, which would have averted all of this.

88. The Supreme Court says "no"

On October 3, in another unprecedented moment in judicial history that brought *Moldea v. New York Times* to an anticlimactic conclusion, the U.S. Supreme Court refused to review any of the nearly 1,700-newly-petitioned cases pending before it, including our case. Thus, once and for all, I was denied my day in court. In addition, we were never allowed to take a single deposition, including that of the reviewer, Gerald Eskenazi.

On its front page the next day, the *New York Times* described it as "the day the Supreme Court of the United States said 'no.'"[133]

Amidst all of the comment and analyses that followed, a thoughtful and responsible editorial in the *Los Angeles Times* stated:

> Moldea's claim was that errors made by the reviewer amounted to libel against the author. In fact, the review did contain some errors; Moldea did have some valid points. The Court of Appeals first ruled that the errors in the review could constitute libel. But then, months later, the court, to general amazement, reversed its decision, stating that it had "failed to take sufficient account of the fact that the statements at issue appeared in the context of a book review...."
>
> Was this distinction raised by the *New York Times* the one that persuaded the high court, or was it something else? At this point, we do not know. The *Moldea* case was settled without that point having been nailed down.... Claiming our First Amendment freedom to criticize legal briefs and court decisions, we suggest that the complex matter of responsibility to fact even within the expression of opinion deserves further attention.[134]

As the winners of this war, the *Times's* partisans took the opportunity to dance on my head—just as I would have danced on theirs had I won. David Streitfeld of the *Washington Post* talked to an associate of Bruce Sanford, reporting: "Reacting to yesterday's high court action, Henry Hoberman, outside counsel for the *Times*, said that 'opinion writers and commentators are now safe from would-be censors and opinion police like Dan Moldea.'"[135]

However, Streitfeld added: "While many commentators were of the opinion that the review in this case shouldn't be used to rewrite the First Amendment, some still felt that Eskenazi was—well, sloppy."[136]

Streitfeld went on to quote Christopher Hanson, who had written about the case in the *Columbia Journalism Review*, saying: "Moldea has reason to be upset. After comparing what the book says with what the review says it says, one might conclude that Eskenazi was some distance from Pulitzer territory."

The *Post* reporter concluded his story with a quote from me:

> "Now I have to get a life," [Moldea] said yesterday. His career has rebounded; he is publishing a book in the spring on the police investigation into the murder of Robert Kennedy. Presumably, the *Times* will review it.
>
> "I'm sure they'll be very fair," Moldea said.

Immediately after hearing the news, former NBCC president Jack Miles of *the Los Angeles Times*, who would win a Pulitzer Prize in 1996 for his book, *God: A Biography*, faxed me a very kind personal letter that meant a great deal to me.

I wrote him back, saying, in part:

> Personally, I feel like a guy who has been slugging down a fifth of gin every day for the past five years, and now I have to stop, cold turkey. This case has already lasted longer than World War II, and now I am preparing to put it behind me...
>
> Anyway, the bad news is: It's over. The good news is: It's over.

Borrowing a scene from David Mamet's film, *Things Change*, I taped quarters to each of the letters I sent to my attorneys—Roger Simmons, Steve Trattner, and Ed Law—and wrote:

There is an old Sicilian proverb: "It takes a big man to appreciate the value of a small coin."

Enclosed is a small coin. If you are ever in any trouble or in need of something I can help you get, please drop this small coin in a telephone and call me. You guys are the best fighters I have ever seen in my life, and you have successfully brought my career back to life.

I will always be grateful.

Also, on the day of the decision, I wrote a note to both Bruce Sanford and George Freeman, simply saying to the victorious attorneys for the *Times*: "Congratulations. And thank you for a great fight."

89. *Alien Ink*

In the wake of my loss in *Moldea v. New York Times*, I received documents that likely would have impacted the manner in which we had conducted the case. This new information provided important insights into the relationship between the FBI and the National Football League, as well as the *Washington Post* and its selection of a journalist who was also a well-known stalking horse and informant for the FBI, to review *Interference*.

In early 1992, I received a call from a colleague, journalist Dick Brenneman, who told me that a newly-released book—*Alien Ink: The FBI's War on Freedom of Expression*, written by author Natalie Robins—revealed that the FBI had maintained a covert "Book Review Section," which had been used to sabotage authors and their published works.

Brenneman added that my embattled 1989 book, *Interference*, was named in Robins's book and, according to the author, had been one of the FBI's targets—in fact, one of its last two targets before the section went out of business. Brenneman knew that I had been extremely critical of the FBI in my book for its suppression of numerous investigations involving National Football League personnel and a variety of underworld figures.

I had never heard of Robins—who was the wife of Christopher Lehmann-Haupt, the *New York Times's* widely respected daily book critic.

PART SIX: MOLDEA V. NEW YORK TIMES

For whatever reason, she never attempted to interview me. But I certainly appreciated her fine work.

I began making my own inquiries, going first to the *New York Times Book Review.* Explaining the contents of Robins's new book, reviewer David Traxel had written:

> Since antiquity, governments have feared writers because of their willingness to subvert official truths while seductively arguing for visions of their own. . . .
>
> The Federal Bureau of Investigation had begun gathering information on American writers at least a decade before J. Edgar Hoover assumed command in 1924, but he brought an energetic efficiency and sense of mission to the task that resulted in hundreds of journalists, novelists, short-story writers and poets receiving unwanted reviews. . . .
>
> What they [independent researchers] found ranged from the banal (newspaper clippings, extracts from Current Biography, bone-headed interpretations of the writings that would make a freshman blush with embarrassment) all the way up to serious trouble (malicious and anonymous letters, wiretap transcripts, agent reports)—all perhaps evidence that they had been victims of the sabotage programs the agency ran against those it considered a threat.[137]

Did the FBI's "book-reviewing" operation end with J. Edgar Hoover's death? In Robins's book, she wrote:

> In the eighties, the Book Review Section of the FBI, which had begun life in 1920 as the Publications Section, was placed under the Public Affairs Section. During the 1950s, book reviews had been handled by the Central Research Section, and in the 1960s, by the Research Satellite Section. In the 1970s, they were back under the Central Research Section.
>
> Today, FBI deputy assistant Milt Ahlerich says that certain books are of interest to the FBI "not from an investigative standpoint necessarily," and that "in a very limited fashion we will review five or six books a year." The FBI is no longer looking for subversive writing, but "technique or new research

that's being done—maybe a current work on terrorism, a current work on foreign counterintelligence."

In addition, according to FBI special agent Susan Schnitzer, "The authors of books reviewed are not indexed, because it is not done for investigative reasons."

What interested the FBI in the eighties? Thirteen books. . . .

Robins then noted these thirteen books, including:

> In 1989, the Bureau reviewed *Interference,* by Dan E. Moldea, and *Donnie Brasco: An FBI Agent Undercover in the Mafia,* by Joseph D. Pistone and Richard Woodley. As of May 1990, no further books were reviewed. [138]

In the wake of calling several sources at the FBI—who, unfortunately, did not have access to records in the bureau's Book Review Section—I filed a Freedom of Information Act request, asking for the FBI's "review" of *Interference* referred to in *Alien Ink.*

Then, after a four-year wait, I finally received the FBI's files regarding my book about professional football. These documents indicated that—unknown to me—the FBI had essentially placed me under investigation in August 1989, within days after the release of *Interference.*

The collection of records in the FOIA package ranged from my probe of the Teamsters Union—which led to my first book, *The Hoffa Wars* in 1978—to my work at the left-wing Institute for Policy Studies to my 1986 book, *Dark Victory, Ronald Reagan, MCA and the Mob,* to my probe of the NFL in *Interference.*

In a portion of a background report to Milt Ahlerich, the FBI deputy assistant who coordinated the investigation of me and my work, an unnamed FBI special agent wrote:

> I am responding to your request for information concerning the author, Dan Moldea. Mr. Moldea is the subject of Bufile 190-3181, containing five sections. These files contain FOIPA requests dating from 1977 and continuing to the present. The primary subjects of his requests appear to relate to alleged organized crime figures and the Teamsters Union.

PART SIX: MOLDEA V. NEW YORK TIMES

> Mr. Moldea is also identified in Bufile 9-60052, Serial 855, dated October 1975. This file identifies Moldea as a self- identified, free-lance writer.... [Moldea] previously lived in the Detroit, Michigan, area, and did extensive research on the Teamsters Union. He developed valuable sources close to the Teamsters Union, and planned to put this information into book form.... It appeared from Moldea's [theories about the disappearance of Jimmy Hoffa] that he was quite knowledgeable of local Teamster politics and individuals associated with the disappearance of Hoffa.

Dealing specifically with *Interference*, FBI Special Agent Scott Nelson wrote in another report:

> Ostensibly providing a public service, the author has turned out a glaring commentary on law enforcement's efforts, or the lack thereof, to rid professional sports of organized-crime influence. At the Federal level, he charges that only the Kennedy and Carter administrations made a serious attempt at curbing organized crime.
>
> Mr. Moldea is highly critical of Attorney General Richard Thornburgh and provides a mixed review of the FBI. While he acknowledges the positive results of some Bureau investigations, he also points out an instance in which the FBI was allegedly uncooperative with the IRS [the Donald Dawson case], that a new Agent working a major gambling case [the Computer Group investigation] was naive to the practices of bookmakers and that the FBI conducted electronic surveillance without court authorization.[139]

The FBI, which widely disseminated these and numerous other reports about me, also featured and highlighted the horrific reviews of *Interference* by Gerald Eskenazi for the *New York Times* and Sandy Smith for the *Washington Post*.

Did the FBI attempt to sabotage *Interference* as a favor to the NFL? I believed that there was clear evidence that it did.

And, if there was any doubt, in January 1996—with hundreds of qualified candidates to choose from—the NFL's high command selected Milt Ahlerich, the special agent who had supervised the FBI's investigation of *Interference* and me, to succeed Warren Welsh as the new chief of NFL Security.

90. *The Washington Post* and the FBI informant

My war with the *New York Times* over the Eskenazi review was well known. However, very little was known about my battle with the *Washington Post* over the review by Sandy Smith, then an investigative reporter for *Time* whom I had openly accused of being a shill and informant for the FBI.

Here was part of what I wrote about Smith in a memorandum to my attorney, Roger Simmons, who was handling the *New York Times* case.

> On October 29, 1989, Sandy Smith published a review of my book, *Interference*, in the *Washington Post Book World*. The major point of contention between Smith and me was which federal agency had conducted the investigation of Detroit bookmaker Donald Dawson. I had claimed in my book that it was the IRS and that, according to federal sources quoted in my book, the FBI had refused to cooperate. Smith claimed that it was the FBI.
>
> Along with my letter to the editor, I gave *Book World* an IRS surveillance report on Dawson, challenging Smith to support his claims about the FBI. I even asked *Book World's* editors to publish an "Editor's Note" to determine, once and for all, who was telling the truth: the author or the reviewer.
>
> On November 26, 1989, *Book World* published my response to Smith's review. However, *Book World* refused to intervene as a third party to resolve the dispute, even though its editors were in possession of my evidence that Smith was wrong about the question of which federal agency had conducted the investigation.
>
> Consequently, to the readers of *Book World*, it was my word against his. And he had the first word with his review and last word in his response, which immediately followed my published letter.

PART SIX: MOLDEA V. NEW YORK TIMES

Completely frustrated by the *Post's* refusal to correct the record, I wondered: (a) where did Smith receive his false information about the FBI's investigation of Dawson; and (b) what his association with the FBI really was.

While trying to find the answers to these questions, I found two interesting sources about Smith's relationship with the FBI:

* In Sanford J. Ungar's 1976 book, *FBI*, a critical examination of the bureau, the author wrote:

As chief spokesman for the Bureau, [Cartha] DeLoach kept a stable of trusted journalists well supplied with information—people such as Hoover's close friend Walter Trohan of the *Chicago Tribune*, labor columnist Victor Riesel, Jeremiah O'Leary of the *Washington Evening Star*, **Sandy Smith** of *Time* and *Life* magazines. . . . Like many other government agencies in Washington, the Bureau profited from selectively leaking material to its friends that it wanted to see in print or on the air.[140] [Emphasis added.]

* In former FBI Special Agent William F. Roemer's 1990 book, *Roemer: Man Against The Mob*, the author added:

[T]here was one guy in Chicago who was in a position to help us a lot. His name was **Sandy Smith**, the ace of the investigative reporters in Chicago. Sandy had been with the *Chicago Tribune* for a decade or so. . . . In general, Sandy's help was invaluable. *Whenever we possessed information that we could not use to make a case or to assist in gathering further intelligence, we fed info to Sandy for publication in the Tribune and later, when he left the Trib, in the Sun-Times.* (Sandy later left the *Sun-Times* for *Life* magazine and eventually *Time*, where he cemented his reputation as the top crime reporter in the country.)[141] [Emphasis added.]

Furthermore, at the time of his review of *Interference*, Sandy Smith was in the midst of a litigation against Little, Brown, the publisher of his recently canceled book about organized crime. Smith and his co-author were represented by Washington attorney William Hundley, the former chief of the U.S. Justice Department's Organized Crime and

Racketeering Section, who had been retained by the two authors in June 1989.

What was the significance of Hundley's representation of Smith at the time of his review of my book about the NFL? After Hundley left the government in 1966, NFL Commissioner Pete Rozelle selected him as the director of NFL Security.

In Chapter 18 of *Interference*, entitled "Bill Hundley and NFL Security," I was extremely critical of Hundley's role as NFL Security chief, providing specific details of his alleged participation in the suppression and/or killing of official probes, including several investigations of game fixing.[142]

However, when I reported Smith's brazen and well-documented conflicts of interest, the *Washington Post* still decided to do nothing—thus, allowing Smith's biased and unfair review of my book to stand without an official challenge from the newspaper.

I knew then that I was now in a perpetual penalty phase for my case against the *New York Times*, and that I had received a life sentence without the possibility of parole.

PART SEVEN:
From RFK to OJ

91. An appearance of conspiracy

During the summer of 1985—while living in Los Angeles and working on my third book, *Dark Victory*—I met Gregory Stone, an ex-aide to former U.S. Representative Allard Lowenstein (D-New York), and Dr. Philip Melanson, a political science professor at Southeastern Massachusetts University. Both men were in the midst of a public crusade to reopen the murder investigation of Senator Robert Kennedy of New York.

At 12:15 A.M. on June 5, 1968, an assassin shot and mortally wounded Senator Kennedy in a narrow kitchen pantry of the Ambassador Hotel in Los Angeles. Just moments earlier, the 42-year-old Kennedy had left a ballroom celebration in the wake of winning the California Democratic presidential primary. No fewer than seventy-seven people were crowded in the pantry when twenty-four-year-old Palestinian immigrant Sirhan Bishara Sirhan, using an eight-shot .22-caliber revolver, opened fire on the senator.

With hotel security guards only in a crowd-control capacity, no official police presence, and only a single unarmed bodyguard nearby, Kennedy was shot three times and died early the following day. Five other people were each shot once but all survived.

During our 1985 meeting, Stone summed up his research on the continuing controversies involving muzzle distance and alleged extra bullets: "Consider this," he told me, "the existing crime-scene evidence supports the probability that more than eight shots were fired from more than one gun, and that the three shots that struck Kennedy were fired from point-blank range—no more than three inches from the senator's body. A fourth shot passed through Kennedy's jacket but did not hit him.

"No one but the police, who were not present at the time of the shooting, claimed that the barrel of Sirhan's gun was any closer than a foot-and-a-half from Kennedy, who was shot from the right rear at a leftward and steeply upward angle. Eyewitnesses stated that the senator was moving towards Sirhan, shaking hands, when the assassin opened fire. They also claimed that Sirhan, whose arm was grabbed after the first or second shot, never had an opportunity to shoot Kennedy in the back once—let alone four times—at point-blank range."

Overwhelmingly, Stone insisted, the eyewitnesses' versions of events directly contradicted the official police reconstruction of the murder. When confronted about this, Los Angeles Police Department officials referred instead to the panic and confusion that had broken loose inside the pantry while Sirhan was emptying his .22 revolver into the crowd.

In essence, the police said, the eyewitnesses lacked the training and experience necessary to make their stories credible.

Stone and Melanson told me that the only hope for learning the full truth was to expand responsible efforts of independent investigation. And they wanted me to try to break new ground in the case, hoping that I could help force the city of Los Angeles to release all of its files in the RFK case, which had been locked up for nearly twenty years.

Considering the flak I had earlier taken for getting involved in a probe of President John Kennedy's assassination while writing my 1978 book, *The Hoffa Wars*, I needed to be convinced that the Robert Kennedy murder merited further study. In the Hoffa book, I was the first journalist to allege that Mafia bosses Carlos Marcello of New Orleans and Santo Trafficante of Tampa, along with Teamsters president Jimmy Hoffa, had arranged and executed the murder of the president—a position I still defend.

In 1979, a year after the release of my book, the U.S. House Select Committee on Assassinations stated in its final report that Marcello, Trafficante, and Hoffa had the "motive, means, and opportunity" to kill the president. The committee's chief counsel, the legendary Robert Blakey, publicly declared, "The mob did it. It's a historical fact."

Because the committee had essentially corroborated what I had published a year earlier, I came out of that episode in one piece.

Finally, in late 1986, after the release of *Dark Victory*, I started to read the limited amount of available documents about the RFK murder and was shocked by what I saw. Without question, the case I assumed was open-and-shut had been badly mishandled by the LAPD. It was clear that law-enforcement officials had misrepresented key facts in the case, destroyed material evidence, and obstructed independent attempts to resolve the critical issues of the case. Evidence that had not been tampered with made it seem unlikely that Sirhan was the only person to fire a gun that night.

So I began to wonder: Did Mafia figures and their associates—specifically Marcello, Trafficante, and Hoffa—have Robert Kennedy killed, just as I believed they had earlier murdered his brother, the President?

When I asked Stone and Melanson to name their best suspect as the second gunman in the RFK case, they replied, almost in unison, "Thane Eugene Cesar," a security guard with extreme right-wing views who hated Kennedy and supported George Wallace, the racist independent candidate for president in 1968.

Seen by eyewitnesses with his gun drawn, Cesar, who told the police that he was carrying a .38-caliber revolver that night, had been standing directly behind Kennedy at the moment of the shooting. Also, Cesar had owned a .22, with class characteristics similar to Sirhan's weapon. However, soon after the murder, Cesar sold his .22, which then mysteriously disappeared—and then he gave the police false information about this matter, saying that he had sold the gun *prior* to the murder.

In mid-March 1987, I pitched the RFK project to *Regardie's*, where I had just published a cover story about the National Rifle Association for the recently released April issue. *Regardie's* offered me a contract for the Kennedy article, which included a large bonus if I found security guard Gene Cesar and got him on the record.

No one connected with the Kennedy case had seen or heard from Cesar since November 1975 when he was interviewed for the final time by the Los Angeles District Attorney's Office. In fact, an assistant district attorney had put out the word that Cesar was dead. Los Angeles journalist Theodore Charach, who was the first to reveal the evidence against Cesar, had been the last reporter to interview him in October 1969.

However, through a network of sources and public-records searches in southern California, I found Cesar living in Simi Valley. Immediately, I Federal Expressed a letter to him, requesting an interview and asking him to call me by 6:00 P.M. on the day of receipt. When he did not reply, I decided to confront Garland Weber, identified in divorce and real-estate records as Cesar's attorney.

Without calling ahead, I went to Weber's office in Van Nuys and waited in his reception room until he had time to see me. Not knowing what I wanted to discuss, Weber brought me into his office after I had been waiting for only about twenty minutes.

"What can I do for you?" Weber asked.

"Sir, I'd like you to help me get an interview with Gene Cesar," I replied.

"He won't talk. Gene had a bad experience a long time ago with a reporter, and he said he would never speak to another one."

Refusing to accept that, I smiled, "Well, he's going to talk to me."

"Why's that?"

"Because if he doesn't, I am going to talk to his family, his friends, his neighbors, his employer, and every goddamn person in his life. And when they ask me why I'm asking questions about him, I'm going to tell them why."

Taken aback, Weber responded, "How do I know you're not going to fuck my client, like the last reporter did?"

Getting up from my chair and leaning over his desk, I paraphrased a line from the Al Pacino movie, *Scarface*, saying, "Hey, Garland, let's get this straight right now. I've never fucked anybody over in my life who didn't have it coming. You got that? All I have in this world are my balls and my word. And I don't break 'em for anybody."

I couldn't keep a straight face after saying that, so I started laughing. And Weber, who also had seen the movie, did, too.

"Let me see what I can do," Weber said, still laughing. "You call me here tomorrow."

With Weber present, my first interview with Gene Cesar took place on Friday, March 27. I had three tape recorders memorializing the discussion—two tapes for me and one for them.

Because of the evidence Stone and Melanson had shown me, I believed that it was possible, even likely, that Cesar had been the second gunman in the murder of Senator Kennedy. Thus, I had never been more prepared for an interview in my life. I was in a high confidence mode and genuinely believed that I was going to make history that day.

During the three-hour interview, Cesar and I had several sharp, even heated exchanges when I confronted him with the evidence of more than one gun being fired in the pantry and his position in relation to Kennedy's gunshot wounds—as well as the fact that he had drawn his gun, was possibly carrying a second gun (specifically the missing .22), and his false and conflicting statements to the police and the FBI about his movements that night.

In the midst of one of these confrontations, I looked Cesar right in the eyes and asked, "Did you shoot Bobby Kennedy, intentionally or accidentally?"

Cesar glared right back at me and simply replied, "No."

This was how Cesar saw his dilemma: "I got caught in a situation I can't get out of. But no matter what anybody says or any report they come up with, I know I didn't do it. The police department knows I didn't do it. There're just a few people out there who want to make something out of something that isn't there—even though I know that some of the evidence makes me look bad."

PART SEVEN: FROM RFK TO OJ

92. Releasing the LAPD's files

My article, "Who Really Killed Bobby Kennedy?," appeared on the cover of the June 1987 issue of *Regardie's*, which hit the newsstands on May 20, featuring the inconsistencies with the LAPD's case. In addition to examining the problems with the official version of the killing, the story also contained my exclusive interview with Cesar.

I concluded the article with the following observation:

> Gene Cesar may be the classic example of a man caught at the wrong time in the wrong place with a gun in his hand and powder burns on his face—an innocent bystander caught in the crossfire of history. However, considering the current state of evidence, a more sinister scenario cannot be dismissed. Until the City of Los Angeles complies with its repeated promises of full disclosure of the murder investigation, monumental questions about the most basic issues surrounding the case remain. And after nineteen years these issues deserve to be resolved.

What had become clear at the time of the publication of the *Regardie's* article was that there could not be a truly legitimate appraisal of the crime-scene issues until the release of the LAPD's investigative files in the case. Thus, I neither publicly advocated nor advanced any theory about what had happened on the night of the shooting. Instead, I simply concentrated on the crime-scene issues—although, privately, I did believe that two guns had been fired with Cesar still my top suspect as the second gunman.

Bolstering the impact of the *Regardie's* article, an Associated Press wire story and two surprisingly strong reviews supporting my work appeared in two unlikely publications, both of which had long defended the official version of the case: the *Washington Post* and the *Los Angeles Times*.

On May 26, Charles Trueheart of the *Washington Post* stated:

> Moldea, whose appetite for byzantine intrigue is no secret, has exercised considerable restraint in not taking his speculation beyond the evidence. He portrays no conspiracy as such, but illuminates those elements of the case and investigation that make it implausible that Sirhan was the only assassin at the scene.[143]

Then, on June 12, Bill Steigerwald of the *Los Angeles Times* said of the *Regardie's* article:

> Moldea makes a convincing case that the official story is rife with crucial inconsistencies and unanswered questions and remains an unsolved mystery. Moldea marshals a great deal of evidence to support his claims that the LAPD botched its original investigation.[144]

Steigerwald had called the LAPD for comment, adding:

> [Commander] William Booth of the LAPD, who had not seen Moldea's piece, said that all the material that can be released has been released and that "everyone has access to the same evidence and they can come up with their own theories." The LAPD's position, he said, is summed up by the fact that Sirhan Sirhan was tried and convicted and is still in prison.

Booth's statement infuriated Greg Stone because the LAPD appeared to have altered its position once again, now insisting that no more files would be released. But while the LAPD seemed to be backsliding, Stone and other advocates of full disclosure were buoyed by the sudden public clamor for the release of the files in the wake of my story's publication.

Stone—with the active support of Paul Schrade, one of the five other people shot on the night Kennedy was fatally wounded—immediately launched a public-relations attack on the LAPD for its continued efforts to conceal the files.

Then, suddenly—while the *Regardie's* article was still on the newsstands—the city of Los Angeles reversed the LAPD's position, ordering the release of the entire Robert Kennedy murder case file. Almost immediately, boxloads of documents were transported to the California State Archives in Sacramento where nearly a year-long declassification process began.

On Friday, June 26, reporter Chuck Conconi of the *Washington Post* wrote in his column:

> Nineteen years after the assassination of Robert F. Kennedy, the Los Angeles Police Department's investigative files on the case are about to be released. Ever since Washington investigative reporter Dan Moldea's article "Who Killed Bobby

Kennedy?" was published in this month's issue of *Regardie's* magazine, interest in the murder case has had resurgence.[145]

And Kevin McManus of *Insight* magazine acknowledged:

> The [Cesar] interview and subsequent [*Regardie's*] article appear to have had the result of forcing the Los Angeles government to do something others have been urging it to do for many years: open the police records on the assassination.[146]

Also, as a result of the sudden release of the RFK files, several producers asked me to appear on radio and television programs to discuss the matter.

On June 30, in the midst of all this activity, I received an invitation to be a guest on NBC's *Today Show*. Although I was excited about the offer, I soon learned that the National Association of Broadcast Employees and Technicians (NABET) had struck NBC and its owned-and-operated stations nationwide.

With no settlement by the time of my scheduled appearance—and inasmuch as I was still a member of the National Writers Union—I refused to cross the picket line and did not appear on the program.

93. Interviewing the cops

By the time the California State Archives released the Robert Kennedy murder case files in April 1988, I was steeped in work on my fourth book, *Interference: How Organized Crime Influences Professional Football*, for which I had a tight deadline. Consequently, I did not play much of a role in the debate over the fact that the LAPD's files were incomplete and that valuable evidence and records had supposedly been destroyed. Once again, the indefatigable Greg Stone led the charge against the police, alleging that a cover up was still in progress.

Even though I had no intention of returning to the Kennedy case after the publication of *Interference* in July 1989, Stone dragged me back into the battle, kicking and screaming. Providing me with a grant from his Inquiry and Accountability Foundation to sweeten the arrangement, he convinced me that new information in the state archives was worthy of exploration.

Returning to Los Angeles, one of my first stops was Parker Center, the downtown headquarters of the LAPD. I had earlier given my *Regardie's* article to three homicide detectives, whom I had used as sources for my previous work on organized crime, and asked for their opinions of my story. One of them had played a minor role in the Kennedy murder investigation.

The four of us met in a small interrogation room at the LAPD's Robbery-Homicide Division.

"Dan, I read your article," one of the detectives said, "and you don't have it."

"What do you mean I don't have it?" I asked defensively.

"You don't have it! You based nearly all of your research on eyewitness testimony. Eyewitness testimony? You talk about seventy-seven people in a room and twelve actual eyewitnesses to the shooting. These are people who were in the wrong place at the wrong time. You're expecting accuracy in their statements? Twelve different eyewitnesses will generally give you twelve different versions of a story."

"But in this case," I insisted, "especially with regard to muzzle distance, they're all saying the same thing: Sirhan never got off a single point-blank shot at Kennedy. There's no dispute here. There are not twelve different versions."

"Yeah, but eyewitnesses are not trained or experienced or qualified to make judgments about what they see in such situations. Don't get me wrong, eyewitness testimony occasionally makes convictions. But nothing beats physical evidence or a police official's expert testimony."

"So you're saying that only cops have the training, experience, and qualifications to know truly what they saw."

"Essentially, yes, that's what I'm saying."

I started laughing while all three of the detectives looked puzzled at my reaction. One of them asked, "What's so funny, Dan?"

"I think I've just figured out how I'm going to approach the next phase of my research."

This time I would not rely on the supposedly shaky statements of eyewitnesses who found themselves thrust into a violent moment of American history. Instead, I decided to conduct a series of interviews over the next several months with the people whose training and experience would be above reproach: the officials, detectives, and patrolmen in the Los Angeles Police Department, the Los Angeles Sheriff's Department, the Los Angeles Fire Department, and the FBI, who performed their routine duties at the crime scene after the shooting. And the lists of these law-enforcement personnel involved in the RFK murder

PART SEVEN: FROM RFK TO OJ

investigation were located at the California State Archives in Sacramento. They were now public record.

Although I also had access to both the active and retired LAPD rosters to help locate sources, I soon found that my most difficult problem was identifying those officers and officials pictured in the captionless official and non-official LAPD photographs taken during the crime-scene investigation.

I began carrying these pictures to the various divisions at Parker Center and to the LAPD's individual stations in and around Los Angeles. Through my police contacts, I was permitted to visit the various detective and patrolmen's offices. Upon my arrival at each location—where I was usually accompanied by one of my LAPD sources—I walked to the middle of their large group offices and held the photographs high in the air, shouting out, "Who wants to see some pictures of cops?"

Usually a party atmosphere quickly developed as LAPD officers and officials crowded around and identified their colleagues in the photographs. Because of this enthusiastic cooperation, I was able to identify most of the LAPD personnel in the pictures.

Of the 187 principal law-enforcement officials, detectives, and officers identified in LAPD records as having been involved in the 1968 Kennedy crime-scene investigation, I was able to locate or learn the fate of 158 of them. A total of 114 agreed to be interviewed and speak on the record with me. Another twenty-six refused comment for various reasons. Of that number, eight refused to respond to my written requests for interviews, and four did not return my calls. No fewer than eighteen had died since the 1968 murder. And I was simply unable to locate twenty-nine, many of whom were also thought to be deceased.

Few of these law-enforcement professionals had ever been interviewed about the Kennedy case. During our conversations, most of them were honest and unguarded in their responses to my two basic questions about their work on the night of the RFK shooting: "What did you do?" and "What did you see?" Many officers had kept their field officer's notebooks, and some even referred to their notes in the midst my interviews with them.

During these discussions, several recalled seeing, what they described as, bullet holes in the walls and door frames in Sirhan's line of fire—consistent with matter-of-fact notations buried in a little-known FBI report, which included photographs of four identified "bullet holes," all of which had been circled by a police officer at the crime scene.

The problem? Sirhan only had an eight-shot revolver. Since Kennedy had been shot three times and one bullet was removed from each of the other five victims, there shouldn't have been any bullet holes at these locations—although the LAPD did identify one shot that passed through Kennedy's chest and was lost in the ceiling space.

To me, this information was absolutely devastating, because it almost surely proved that a second gun had been fired in the kitchen pantry at the Ambassador Hotel on that terrible night in June 1968.

And this evidence wasn't coming from shaky civilian eyewitnesses. It was coming from experienced police officers and FBI agents.

94. The suicide of Greg Stone

On May 13, 1990, I published the results of my latest investigation in the *Washington Post*. In this article, I concluded:

> Theoretically, the firing of another gun besides Sirhan's at the Ambassador might have been accidental, defensive, or sinister; it would be a mistake to rush to quick or simplistic judgments concerning the origin of additional assassination gunshots. The importance and complexity of this matter demand that it be examined impartially by a reconstituted official investigation.[147]

But, during an appearance on NBC's *Unsolved Mysteries* three days after the publication of my article, I did not take my own advice, declaring on national television, that two guns had been fired at the crime scene. Because the evidence appeared so overwhelming, I never thought that I would eat those words.

After approaching two publishers but unable to sell a proposed book about the RFK case, I left the investigation in July 1990, which caused a falling out between Greg Stone and me. Stone, a brilliant man who had abandoned his doctorate work to investigate the RFK murder, had wanted me to remain on the case, full-time. To him, this crime had become an obsession, and he spent his career trying to solve it, casting aside any semblance of a personal life while rejecting positions in academia, which would have allowed him to escape from this world of evidence minutia and conspiracy theories.

Me? I had my own problems. As a result of the false and misleading review of *Interference*, I was in the midst of fighting for my personal and professional life in a very bitter public dispute that would lead to my libel case, *Moldea v. New York Times*, which my attorney filed in August 1990. Consequently, in order to pay my bills, I was only accepting projects with guaranteed money. I really had no choice.

On November 8, Stone and I—along with former FBI agent William Bailey, who was at the crime scene on the night of the Senator's murder, and Phil Melanson—participated in a symposium at Southeastern Massachusetts University where Melanson taught political science.

After the well-attended event, Stone, Melanson, and I went out to dinner—even though there was still some tension between Stone and me. But, after we shook hands and made peace, the atmosphere lightened up considerably as the three of us had a great time, telling and retelling our old war stories.

Soon after, Stone again began sending me his memoranda about the RFK case and drafts of his proposal to the district attorney's office in which he was requesting a grand-jury hearing to investigate police procedures during the RFK case. Also, he asked me to execute my third sworn affidavit in his Freedom of Information Act lawsuit against the FBI, which I agreed to do. As usual, we exchanged Christmas cards and talked occasionally on the telephone.

Late on the evening of January 28, 1991, Stone called me at my home in Washington for the second time that week. He had no specific agenda, no particular subject he wanted to discuss. He seemed perfectly normal but a little tired.

I remember advising him to take a vacation. "Go sit on a beach, get a tan, chase women," I said.

The following night at 10:45 P.M., I received a telephone call from Phil Melanson who told me that he had just spoken to a man who identified himself as an investigator from the Los Angeles County Coroner's Office. The investigator told Melanson that Greg Stone had committed suicide.

Melanson seemed to think that the call was a cruel joke. Taking it more seriously, I asked Melanson if he had tried to call Stone. He said that he had not.

Immediately, I telephoned Stone at his home in the East Hollywood section of Los Angeles. When he didn't answer, I left a message on his answering machine, demanding that he call me as soon as he received it. After failing to reach Stone, I called his next-door neighbor, Floyd Nelson, who worked nights and also was not home. I left a desperate message on Nelson's answering machine, as well.

Then, I called the coroner's office in Los Angeles. The same investigator who had spoken to Melanson confirmed that Stone was dead. He had committed suicide in the Fern Dell section of Griffith Park about a mile from Stone's home.

Specifically, the investigator said that between 3:00 and 4:00 that afternoon the 41-year-old Stone had sat down under a tree in the park, placed a .38 Smith & Wesson revolver in his mouth, and pulled the trigger. A park employee had found him just after the shooting—while the blood was still gushing from his head. Two LAPD officers responded to the call.

According to the coroner's investigator, the officers had found a note in Stone's clothing, directing them to his red Volkswagen, parked in a nearby lot. When the police found his car, they discovered another note. This one provided the names of several people who were to be contacted, including his sister and uncle, his personal attorneys and a mortician, as well as Melanson and Nelson. The police also found a psychiatrist's business card in his possession.

The coroner's investigator told me that he had talked to Stone's psychiatrist, who said that Stone was as depressed as anyone he had ever seen. He added that his suicide came as no surprise—that he had threatened to kill himself on several occasions during the past couple of weeks.

Stunned, I told the investigator that I didn't have any idea that Stone was in trouble or had sought professional help, even though I had spoken to him twice in the past week.

At 3:00 A.M., I called Floyd Nelson again. This time, he was in. Overwhelmed with grief, he explained that he had heard about Stone's death from a friend at work and immediately left his job. When he arrived home, he grabbed the key Stone had given him and went into his apartment. On Stone's desk was a file folder marked "Post Mortem," which contained numerous documents.

Stone had handwritten and signed a suicide note, stating:

> This is my own decision and came out of my own problems and shortcomings. It is not the fault at all of my family, friends or the people I've worked with.
>
> I'm sorry to have let my family and so many others down.

Several days later, when I returned to Washington after visiting a funeral home in southern Ohio to pay my respects to Stone and his family, I was looking through my mail and noticed a letter from him. My hands were shaking as I opened it.

Inside, the handwritten note simply said: "Sorry about this, Dan. Stay a survivor."

95. Back in the game

Two years after Stone's suicide—in the midst of a hiatus in my case against the *New York Times*, while the U.S. Court of Appeals for the D.C. Circuit weighed its merits—I decided to re-enter the RFK battleground and tried, once again, to sell a book about this case.

Through investigative journalist Bill Knoedelseder, I met a fabulous literary agent, attorney Alice Martell, the no-nonsense but smart and congenial president of the successful Martell Agency on Fifth Avenue in New York. Although very critical of my libel case against the *Times*, Martell still expressed an interest in my story about the murder of Senator Kennedy and asked me to submit a proposal for her consideration.

On May 27, 1993, I completed the proposal and sent it to her. In my cover letter, I wrote, in part:

> Here is what my proposed book will prove:
>
> 1. That at least two guns were fired at Senator Kennedy on the night of his murder.
>
> 2. That Sirhan Sirhan, although shooting to kill, did not fire any of the bullets that hit Kennedy.
>
> 3. That the investigations conducted by both the Los Angeles Police Department and the FBI were sidetracked by an incompetent crime-scene investigation during the hours after the shooting. Consequently, in order to cover-up official incompetence, these agencies misrepresented key facts, destroyed material evidence, and obstructed independent attempts to review the critical issues in the case.
>
> 4. That members of organized crime had the motive, means, and opportunity to have Senator Kennedy murdered.

5. That a security guard with a gun in his hand and powder burns on his face—who was standing directly behind Kennedy—individually possessed the motive, means, and opportunity to have killed Kennedy.

In short, I am guaranteeing documentation for the above five items. [Emphasis added.]

On June 6, Martell sent my proposal—with all of these extraordinary claims and promises—to her contacts in the publishing industry.

Twenty-two days later, I took the train to New York to meet with Star Lawrence of W.W. Norton, who had a reputation as one of the best but toughest editors in New York. After taking Martell and me to lunch at the Princeton Club, Lawrence asked us to return to his office and attend a meeting with Norton's editorial board.

During the discussion about the RFK murder with company executives, they repeatedly asked me if I could deliver on what I had "guaranteed" in my proposal, especially the claims that two guns had been fired at the crime scene and that the three bullets striking Senator Kennedy had not come from Sirhan's gun.

Confidently, I replied that I could and that I would.

They also inquired about my libel suit against the *New York Times*, which I was actually anxious to answer, considering how badly the press was misrepresenting the facts of this case. Because of all the irresponsible reporting about this litigation, I was facing a potential career-ending public-relations problem.

Since that nightmare began in 1989, my meeting with Norton was the closest I had come to getting another book deal. One of my former editors candidly assured me that I had not been officially blacklisted. However, he did say that I had been widely tagged in the publishing industry as "a real troublemaker," mostly because of my case against the *Times*, as well as my take-no-prisoners approach to defending my work.

On Wednesday afternoon at 5:00 P.M., Martell called and gave me the good news: Star Lawrence and W.W. Norton had bought the Kennedy book. Norton only offered a $75,000 advance—the same price I had received for *Dark Victory* eight years earlier. But so what?

I felt that I was back in the game again and honestly believed that I could deliver on the guarantees made in my book proposal. Plus, I was really happy and even honored to work with Lawrence.

Based on what the FBI reports had stated and LAPD officers and officials had told me, I was as convinced as I could be that two guns had been fired in the kitchen pantry at the Ambassador Hotel on the night Robert Kennedy was fatally wounded. Thus, I continued to target Gene Cesar as my principal suspect as the second gunman—just as many other investigators had before I came into this case.

The difference was that I had exclusive and unlimited access to him—in spite of the fact that Cesar was well aware of my suspicions.

However, after my numerous interviews with Cesar over the telephone and in person, I finally realized that I had asked him every question I could think of.

At the conclusion of one of our lengthy face-to-face interviews, Garland Weber, Cesar's attorney, saw the puzzled look on my face and asked me what I thought.

I replied that I still didn't know what to think. However, I did express my belief that Cesar was not a sinister force at the crime scene. He did not intentionally shoot Robert Kennedy. Yet, questions remained for me as to whether he had fired his gun accidentally or in retaliation to Sirhan's barrage of gunfire.

I still suspected that, somehow, Cesar might have shot Senator Kennedy during all the confusion at the crime scene.

Without any foolproof way to extract the truth, I simply decided to start treating Cesar just like any other witness to the murder. I called him on occasion from my home in Washington to see how he was. I visited him during my frequent trips to Los Angeles. I found the time I spent with him and his wife to be pleasant. He had an offbeat sense of humor. He was a funny guy.

During one of those trips to the West Coast, Cesar and I had lunch at a restaurant near Anheuser-Busch in Van Nuys, his place of employment. I brought no tape recorder, and I took no notes during our conversation.

In the midst of this meeting, Cesar casually told me about some unusual diamond purchases he had made. He added that he had bought the diamonds from a local businessman who was an associate of the Chicago Outfit.

Needless to say, the story shocked me, and I questioned him about it at subsequent meetings, which were tape-recorded. There were several discrepancies in the date of the initial purchase—which Cesar had ranged from 1968 to 1974.

Because of such discrepancies—and because of the enormous amount of time and money I was spending trying to prove or disprove Cesar's innocence—I asked Cesar if he would be willing to be either hypnotized or polygraphed. Surprisingly, he immediately agreed to such a test—with no particular preference.

I contacted a federal prosecutor whom I had known and trusted for several years and asked for his advice about which test to arrange. He warned against hypnosis, because it could be tantamount to tampering with a potential witness. Thus, he suggested that I have Cesar polygraphed.

He also proposed that I hire Edward Gelb, a Los Angeles polygraph expert, to administer the test. Gelb, arguably the best polygraph operator in the country, was the former president and executive director of the American Polygraph Association.

I decided that if Cesar clearly passed the test, I would back off and accept his innocence. However, if he failed the test or it proved inconclusive, I would spend every waking hour and every dollar I had trying to bring him down. And I told him that.

As anyone in such a situation, Cesar was understandably nervous on the day of the test. He and his attorney arrived at Gelb's office a few minutes early while I was completing my briefing to Gelb about Cesar and the Kennedy murder case.

"How do you feel?" I asked Cesar.

"Let's do it," he replied with some irritation. "Let's get it over with."

Gelb invited us into his private office and had Cesar sign several standard documents and releases. After a quick explanation of what would be happening over the next few hours, Gelb politely ordered Weber and me to leave. As Weber and I went off to a breakfast on Sunset Boulevard, Gelb and Cesar got down to business.

A few hours later, after Weber and I returned and were sitting in Gelb's waiting room, Gelb came out and invited us into his private office.

"Are you okay?" I asked Cesar who appeared very relaxed.

Laughing, Cesar replied, "I didn't shoot Bobby, but I've been thinking about shooting you for making me go through all of this."

"You're going to be happy," I said. "You passed, right?"

"That's what he told me."

"Okay, now you're set. You don't have to do this anymore."

Gelb, who gave me graphs and the tape recordings of the entire session, began to explain the results. In short, Cesar had passed with flying colors.[148]

After hearing all of this, I suddenly wondered out loud: "Then, who really did kill Senator Kennedy?"

PART SEVEN: FROM RFK TO OJ

96. Getting to Sirhan

After Gene Cesar passed the polygraph, I called Paul Schrade—one of the five other victims who had been shot on the night Senator Kennedy was fatally wounded—and told him that I wanted to interview Sirhan Sirhan. He suggested that I call Lynn Mangan of Carson City, Nevada, a close friend of the Sirhan family, who was the key to seeing the convicted assassin.

I telephoned Mangan, and she was quite friendly. She knew about my work on the RFK case and asked me to send a written request that she could forward to Sirhan.

By 6:00 P.M., my letter was at the Federal Express office.

On August 21, 1993, Mangan called me in Washington and said that Sirhan wanted to see me. That night, Mangan wrote a letter to Sirhan, which she later shared with me, saying:

> I just [spoke with] Dan Moldea. Lots to talk about when I see you. Among the things we discussed were his articles, interviews and his upcoming book. I relayed to him how genuinely pleased you were with his writings and that you wanted to meet with him when he is in California. . . . I'm just sorry we didn't get together sooner.

On Sunday, September 19, the day after I flew to Los Angeles, I had dinner in Pasadena with Schrade, along with Adel Sirhan, Sirhan Sirhan's older brother, and Larry Teeter, who was being considered as Sirhan's new attorney. For the most part, I spent the evening angling for a specific date that I could interview the convicted assassin. But, while Adel Sirhan wanted it to happen as quickly as possible, Teeter seemed to be blocking me.

"Why are you fucking with me, Larry?" I finally asked him in front of Schrade and Adel.

"I'm the new lawyer," he replied, standing his ground. "You're the reporter. I haven't talked to my client yet. And I think the new lawyer should talk to the client before the reporter does."

Knowing that Teeter was absolutely right but refusing to say so aloud, I glanced over at Adel Sirhan who rolled his eyes. I knew right then that I was going to see his brother very soon. There was no way that Adel and especially Lynn Mangan were going to yield control of Sirhan to an attorney who had not yet been retained.

From the time of his conviction in 1969 to 1975, Sirhan Sirhan had lived at San Quentin. The first two of those years, he spent on death row. From 1975 to 1992, after the death penalty was repealed in California, he was held at Soledad Penitentiary. Finally, on June 1, 1992, he moved to Corcoran State Prison, a maximum-security facility, tucked between Bakersfield and Fresno. He lived with thirty-four other "high-profile" inmates, including convicted murderer Charles Manson, in the prison's protective unit.[149]

On Saturday afternoon, September 25, Adel Sirhan called, saying that he was going to go to Corcoran the following morning at 6:00 A.M. He asked me if I wanted to accompany him. Of course, I jumped at the invitation and even offered to drive. Early Sunday morning, Adel and I—along with Bill Klaber, who had produced a controversial pro-conspiracy program about the RFK case on National Public Radio—made the three-hour-plus drive from Los Angeles to Corcoran in my rented Thunderbird.

I had already taken an immediate liking to Adel. A decent man, he seemed to bear the weight of his brother's conviction and imprisonment, a classic example of a big brother who felt responsible for his little brother's actions. A talented musician, Adel had become a tragic figure over the years. Even if happiness could have been handed to him on a silver platter, he would not have accepted it unless it included the release of his brother and the reunification of his family. Getting his family back together now appeared to be his only ambition, especially since his mother, another very decent person and an innocent victim, was in failing health.

Arriving in the parking lot at Corcoran, I finally met Mangan, a friendly but very tough woman. From the outset, I knew that she was in charge simply by her firm tone and strong demeanor. Other than Adel and his mother, no one had worked harder to free Sirhan than Mangan.

After everyone greeted each other, we boarded a shuttle bus with the visitors to other inmates. Getting off at Sirhan's cell-block, we signed in, produced ID, walked through a metal detector and then a bolted door into a steel cage with razor wire along the top. A guard came, unlocked another door, and took us through a courtyard to the visitation room.

As I faced a Coke machine and fumbled for change in my pocket, I waited for the prison guards to bring Sirhan to us. After I placed two quarters in the slot and heard a can of soda drop, Adel, in a quiet voice behind me, began to introduce us.

"Dan Moldea," he said, "Sirhan Sirhan. Sirhan, this is Dan Moldea."

I turned around, and we both smiled at each other. Sirhan bowed modestly, gently clasping both of his hands together as if in prayer. He took my extended hand and pumped it heartily like a politician on Election Day, placing his left hand over my right hand for emphasis. I couldn't help but be struck by how kind and polite he appeared to be.

Dressed in blue-denim prison fatigues and a pair of simple black-canvas shoes, the five-feet-two-inch Sirhan appeared much shorter than I had imagined, slightly built but in good shape and well groomed. He had a full head of black but slightly graying hair, cut conservatively. His deep brown eyes were bright and clear. His natural bronze coloring made him appear like a man who had spent the summer on the beach.

In short, he looked pretty good for a guy who had spent the past twenty-five years in prison.

After the initial small talk, I pulled a religious item from my pocket: two small brown rectangular pieces of cloth, joined together by a band of brown cloth. I told him, "Even though you and I are both Eastern Orthodox Christians, I want to give you a Scapular, a Roman Catholic sacramental that you wear around your neck. . . . On one side it reads, 'Whosoever dies wearing this Scapular shall not suffer eternal fire.'"

Sirhan was clearly moved by my gift, but he had to get permission to accept it. He motioned to a prison guard who walked over to us. Sirhan handed the Scapular to him, and he examined it. A few seconds later, the guard whispered something to Sirhan, who then returned the Scapular to me.

Disappointed, Sirhan said, "I'm sorry, Mr. Moldea, but, for whatever reason, I'm not going to be allowed to accept this. . . . But, once again, I really appreciate it."

During the first several minutes of our interview, Sirhan remained clearly agitated, giving the hard eyes to the guard who refused to allow him to keep the Scapular.

At Sirhan's insistence, I had to visit him on the weekend when family and friends met with prisoners. Although I had been cleared by Corcoran officials to visit Sirhan as a journalist during the week when I would be permitted to bring along recording equipment, Sirhan refused to allow me to do so. I sensed that he, literally, didn't want to go "on the record." He never explained why.

So I met him when no recording equipment, pens, or notepads were permitted through prison security. Instead, I scrounged up some paper and a small pencil from the prison guards who were standing watch nearby. When the pencil went dull, I sharpened it on the edge of my

Diet Coke can. And then, throughout my interview with Sirhan, I frequently read his quotes back to him, allowing him to amend or expand on what he had just said.

During that first six-hour interview, I sat at a round table next to Sirhan, believing that I was probably speaking with an innocent man who, somehow, had been used by forces unknown to take the fall for this murder.

According to Sirhan, on the day of the shooting, he had fired his .22 revolver at a pistol range for several hours and, after having dinner with a friend, eventually wound up at the Ambassador Hotel. There, he attended a victory party for Max Rafferty who had won the Republican primary for the U.S. Senate. While at that celebration, Sirhan said that he began drinking and became intoxicated.

Sirhan told me that, after leaving Rafferty's party, he was so drunk that he did not remember grabbing his gun when he walked to his parked car. But, instead of driving home in his condition, he returned to the Ambassador with his gun in his pocket, searching for coffee, and eventually wandered into the celebration for Senator Kennedy's victory in the California Democratic primary for President.

Although he remembered speaking with a woman in a plain-white dress—not a polka-dot dress—who was standing near a coffee urn outside the kitchen pantry, Sirhan insisted that he had no memory of entering the pantry or firing his weapon, claiming that he had been disoriented by the booze and the bright lights in the hotel. "I don't remember shooting him," he told me. "All I remember is being choked and getting my ass kicked."

Further, Sirhan claimed to have absolutely no recollection of writing, among other things, "RFK must die!" over and over again in his now-infamous notebooks before the murder.

Even though Sirhan's entire story was nothing less than bizarre, the one thing that kept me clinging to the two-gun scenario—which could possibly prove Sirhan's innocence—was the identification of extra bullets by the police and the FBI. Still, I decided to push Sirhan harder the next time I spoke to him.

During my second interview with Sirhan the following month on October 10, I became much more confrontational in my questioning, especially with regard to his 1969 confession, which he had since recanted. Essentially, Sirhan told me that, even though he never had any

PART SEVEN: FROM RFK TO OJ

recollection of firing his gun, he did admit to killing Senator Kennedy during his trial, because his attorney told him to—in an effort to prevent Sirhan from going to the gas chamber.

By the end of my second interview with Sirhan, which lasted four hours, I was even more uncomfortable with his story. But, because I was drafting my manuscript in a straight chronology—with my interviews with Sirhan near the end of my planned thirty-chapter book—I didn't panic, deciding that I needed another interview with him in order to clear up my lingering problems.

97. Doubts

During the next eight months, I completed twenty-seven chapters and sent them to Star Lawrence, my editor at W. W. Norton, on May 4, 1994. These chapters appeared consistent with my book proposal, in which I had "guaranteed" to deliver proof that two guns had been fired at the crime scene, and that Sirhan had not fired any of the shots that hit Senator Kennedy. Then, I awaited Lawrence's reaction to my work, as well as approval on the West Coast for my third interview with Sirhan.

Meantime, I came up with an offbeat idea. I wanted suspected second gunman Gene Cesar—who had conclusively passed a lie-detector test I had arranged with a prominent polygraph operator—to accompany me to my next interview with Sirhan, scheduled for May 18. I was curious to see how both of these men would react to each other.

Adel Sirhan and Lynn Mangan approved, as did Cesar. However, after the interview with Sirhan was postponed, along with another one on May 25, the meeting between Sirhan and Cesar never materialized.

My next scheduled meeting with Sirhan was June 5.

While preparing for this interview, I spoke with Los Angeles attorney Francis Pizzulli, who had filed a defamation suit against the author of a little-known book, which alleged that Pizzulli's client, an Iranian student, had murdered Senator Kennedy with a gun concealed in a camera. While collecting his evidence for the case, which he later won, Pizzulli received a letter about journalist Robert Blair Kaiser, a former investigator for Sirhan's defense team who had written an important 1970 book about the case, *"R.F.K. Must Die!"*

The letter, handwritten by Sirhan, was sent to his trial attorney, Grant Cooper, whom he simply referred to as "Punk." Over the telephone,

Pizzulli read me the undated letter, which was probably written during Kaiser's book-promotion tour:

> Hey Punk,
>
> Tell your friend Robert Kaiser to keep mouthing off about me like he has been doing on radio and television. If he gets his brains splattered he will have asked for it like Bobby Kennedy did. Kennedy didn't scare me; don't think that you or Kaiser will; neither of you is beyond my reach. [A]nd if you don't believe me—just tell your ex-monk to show up on the news media again—I dare him.
>
> R.B.K. must shut his trap, or die.

Pizzulli offered to give me a copy of the letter but only if Kaiser—who had earlier studied for the priesthood, thus, the reference to "your ex-monk"—approved.

While speaking with Bob Kaiser, who did give me his approval, he also informed me about a conversation that Michael McCowan, another investigator on the Sirhan defense team, allegedly had with Sirhan. During this meeting, the convicted assassin had supposedly admitted that he remembered when his eyes met Kennedy's just before he shot him. Kaiser wasn't sure of all the details, except that Sirhan's alleged statement had contradicted his long-standing claim that he had no recollection of seeing Kennedy or firing his gun.

Before my third interview with Sirhan, I tried but failed to locate McCowan. Nevertheless, I obviously found the "Hey Punk" letter extremely troubling. It gave credence to the alleged McCowan episode and caused me to question not only Sirhan's entire story but my long-held position about this case.

On Monday, May 30, 1994, the day after Roger Simmons and I appeared at a symposium during the American Booksellers Association in Los Angeles to discuss *Moldea v. New York Times*, my editor, Star Lawrence, and I had lunch at the convention center. Bringing up our book about the RFK murder, he said, "I've just read the first twenty-seven chapters. Fantastic! I'm a believer, man! There were two guns in that room!"

I stuttered and stammered, "Um . . . well . . . listen . . ."

"Oh, no!" Lawrence exclaimed.

"Yeah," I replied, giving it to Lawrence as straight as I could, "as you know, I've been talking to Sirhan and reviewing some new evidence. I'm very concerned that I've been wrong. He might have done it and done it alone."

Astonished and a little agitated, Lawrence asked, "So what are you going to do about it?"

"I'm supposed to see Sirhan on Sunday. I'm already planning to get in his face, big time, and see how he reacts. By the end of that interview, I'll know."

Looking at me sternly while reminding me about the "guarantees" in my book proposal, Lawrence replied, "Dan, all I can say is: You better make this work."

I nodded respectfully and later left the lunch with my tail between my legs.

98. Confronting Sirhan

On Sunday, June 5, 1994—the 26th anniversary of the shooting of Senator Kennedy—Adel Sirhan and I drove to Corcoran for what would be my third and final interview with Sirhan Sirhan. During the trip, I told Adel that I planned to get rough with his brother during this session. Adel simply shrugged and told me, "Go for it."

Go for it, I did—even though Sirhan insisted that he had no memory of writing the "Hey Punk" letter to Grant Cooper and flatly denied ever saying to anyone that he recalled when his eyes met Kennedy's just before he shot him. However, the climax of the interview began as I asked Sirhan, yet again, whether he had confederates.

"Were you a participant in a conspiracy?" I asked.

Sirhan replied, "Do you think I would conceal anything about someone else's involvement and face the gas chamber in the most literal sense? I have no knowledge of a conspiracy."

"But, yes or no, were you part of a conspiracy, Sirhan?"

"I wish there had been a conspiracy. It would have unraveled before now."

"Then, why do you even talk about the possibility of being mind controlled?"

"My defense attorneys developed the idea of *The Manchurian Candidate* theory."

"Then, once again, why don't you just accept responsibility for this crime?"

"If I was to accept responsibility for this crime, it would be a hell of a burden to live with—having taken a human life without knowing it."

"Then you are saying that you are willing to take responsibility, but you have no memory of committing the crime?"

"It's not in my mind, but I'm not denying it. I must have been there, but I can't reconstruct it mentally. I mean no disrespect here, but I empathize with Senator Ted Kennedy in the Chappaquiddick incident. He was supposedly under the influence of alcohol and couldn't remember what he had done. When he finally did realize what had happened, someone was dead."

"Why did you take credit for the murder at your trial?"

"Grant Cooper [Sirhan's attorney] conned me to say that I killed Robert Kennedy. I went along with him because he had my life in his hands. I was duped into believing that he had my best interests in mind. It was a futile defense. Cooper sold me out. Charles Manson once told me that defense attorneys treat their clients like kings before their trials. After the trials begin, they treat their clients like shit. This was true of the manner in which Grant Cooper treated me. I remember Cooper once told me, 'You're getting the best, and you're not paying anything. Just shut up. I'm the lawyer, and you're just the client.'"

I continued, "You were willing to go to the gas chamber for a crime you didn't remember committing?"

"I did a lot of self exploration while I was on death row. It changed my whole vision of the world. I was trying to justify that I was going to the gas chamber. I wanted to search myself to find the truth, but I could never figure it out. I had nothing to lose."

"Did you ever examine whether you had acted with premeditation?"

"When I got to death row, I started reading the law about diminished capacity and the requirements for premeditation. There was no way that I could have summoned the prerequisite for first-degree murder. That was not part of me. They said that I didn't understand the magnitude of what I had done. They're right. I don't truly appreciate it, because I have no awareness of having aimed the gun at Bobby Kennedy."

"Why did you admit to the murder before the parole board?"

"They want the prisoner to admit his guilt and take responsibility for the crime. They want us to confess and to express remorse, which is what I have done. In fact, I have been told that I won't be paroled because of the Kennedys."

"So, once again, you were willing to take credit for the crime without remembering that you had committed it?"

Suddenly, Sirhan became overwrought, exclaiming, "It's so damn painful! I want to expunge all of this from my mind!"

At that exact moment, as these words tumbled out of Sirhan's mouth, I suddenly realized that Sirhan had been lying to me and everyone else all along.

In response, I stated firmly, "I am not a court of law. I am not a parole board. I'm a reporter who doesn't want to be wrong. I want to know, Sirhan: Did you commit this crime?"

Sirhan fired right back, "I would not want to take the blame for this crime as long as there is exculpatory evidence that I didn't do the crime. The jury was never given the opportunity to pass judgment on the evidence discovered since the trial, as well as the inconsistencies of the firearms evidence [the bullet evidence] at the trial. In view of this, no, I didn't get a fair trial."

With that reply, I finally began to understand Sirhan's entire strategy. As long as people, like me, continued to put forth supposed new evidence, he still had a chance to experience freedom. And, more than any other person in recent years, I had been keeping this case alive with all of my supposed new revelations about alleged extra bullets and the possibility that at least two guns had been fired at the crime scene.

As I sat there, I became furious with myself for nearly being hoodwinked by Sirhan and the circumstances of this entire case. I didn't even attempt to conceal my feelings.

With Adel still present, I barked angrily at Sirhan, "You don't remember writing in your notebooks in which you articulated your determination to kill Robert Kennedy and why—That's motive! You don't remember getting your gun when you returned to your car from the Rafferty party—That's means! You don't remember having been in the pantry, getting close to Kennedy, and firing your gun—That's opportunity!

"Every time you have a memory lapse, it goes to motive, means, or opportunity!"

In response, Sirhan sat quietly, saying nothing but looking puzzled, probably wondering where I was going with all of this. But I could tell that he wasn't very concerned. He knew, probably more than anyone else, that I had nearly bet my professional reputation on the second-gun theory. "What's Moldea going to do now that he's in so deep," Sirhan must have thought, "turn around now and say that I acted alone?"

Knowing how close Sirhan was to his ailing mother, whom he deeply loved and respected—and understanding how much pain Sirhan knew he had inflicted on her—I asked him, "Sirhan, when your mother dies, God forbid, are you going to remember everything and come clean?"[150]

Now furious with me for bringing his mother into this, Sirhan exclaimed, raising his voice with each syllable, "Change my story? Mr. Moldea, you're a motherfucker! Mr. Moldea, you're a fucking asshole!"

I smiled at Sirhan and started jabbing my finger in his face. "Sirhan, it's 'Dan, you're a motherfucker. Dan, you're a fucking asshole.'" As I started to laugh out loud, Sirhan paused for a moment and started laughing, too, breaking a very tense moment.

As I would later write in my manuscript: "But he wasn't laughing for the same reason I was: I had just wanted Sirhan to remember the first name of his last hope."

After this bitter third and final interview, fully aware that I did not have Sirhan on tape and fearing that he might deny what I had written in my notes, I sent Sirhan a letter on July 2, saying:

> Thank you for meeting with me again. As always, I appreciated your candid remarks—even when I got rough with you, especially on June 5th. As you know, that's my job; I did the same thing with the LAPD and particularly with Gene Cesar.
>
> Here is the composite made from my notes of our three interviews—on September 26 and October 10, 1993; and June 5, 1994. . . . I wanted you to have the opportunity to amend or to expand upon anything else you read. I still would like to memorialize an interview with you either on video or audio tape. I have received permission from the prison to do this, if you are willing.
>
> Also, as I told you on the 5th, I would like to arrange a polygraph for you, concentrating on what you do and do not remember. You rejected that idea then, but I am asking you to reconsider.
>
> I don't know what the situation is with prison correspondence, so if I don't hear from you by July 31, I will assume that

everything is fine, as written. Of course, you may always call me collect to give me your comments.

Please keep this correspondence as your written record of our interviews.

Predictably, Sirhan, who was extremely angry with me after our final interview, did not responded by the July 31 deadline—which technically indicated his approval of the "transcript." But I still could foresee a problem in which my book came out, and Sirhan—who was, up to that point, still unaware of my final conclusions—would retaliate by denying the quotes I had attributed to him.

To neutralize this scenario, I returned to Los Angeles and met with Adel Sirhan, the only witness to all three of my interviews with his brother—totaling fourteen hours. I provided him with a copy of the "transcript" and asked for his approval, which he gave me with only minor corrections.

Then, as I came down the wire to deliver my finished manuscript to my publisher, I finally located Michael McCowan, the one-time investigator for Sirhan's defense team. During our conversation, McCowan confirmed—and, at my request, signed a statement, attesting to—the story I had earlier heard from Bob Kaiser.[151]

Specifically, McCowan revealed that during one of his interviews with Sirhan, the assassin described the exact moment when his eyes met Kennedy's just before he shot him. Shocked by what Sirhan had just confessed—in view of his previous insistence that he had no recollection of firing his gun at the crime scene—McCowan asked, "Then why, Sirhan, didn't you shoot him between the eyes?"

With no hesitation and no apparent remorse, Sirhan simply replied, "Because that son of a bitch turned his head at the last second."

Completing my manuscript, I concluded:

> Gene Cesar [is] an innocent man who since 1969 has been wrongly accused of being involved in the murder of Senator Kennedy.... Sirhan Bishara Sirhan consciously and knowingly murdered Senator Robert Kennedy, and he acted alone.

99. When wisdom comes late

When the U.S. Court of Appeals reversed itself and took away my momentary victory in *Moldea v. New York Times* on May 3, 1994, the appellate judge who wrote this opinion quoted former U.S. Supreme Court Associate Justice Felix Frankfurter, saying: "Wisdom too often never comes, and so one ought not to reject it merely because it comes late."

Sensing the irony of my own situation, I used that same quote as the lead-in to the final chapter of my new book, *The Killing of Robert F. Kennedy: An Investigation of Motive, Means, and Opportunity*, in an effort to foreshadow my own reversal about the events surrounding the murder of Senator Kennedy.

I submitted my completed manuscript to my publisher, W.W. Norton, on October 3, 1994, the same day that the U.S. Supreme Court refused to hear my case against the *New York Times* and nearly six months before the deadline in my contract.

My writing coach, Mrs. Nolte, who had earlier reviewed the manuscript, thought that the RFK book was my best work ever. However, she feared that my surprising 180-degree turnaround would dampen Norton's enthusiasm while providing the critics—whose knives would be out for me in the wake of losing my libel suit—with ample cause to tear me apart.

But, because this was my first published book in six long years, I had no choice but to remain positive. To me, this was the ball game. A bad outing would probably end my career as both an author and an investigative journalist.

Even though I had guaranteed in my book proposal to deliver evidence that extra bullets proved that two guns had been fired at the crime scene and that Sirhan never hit Senator Kennedy at point-blank range, Star Lawrence, my editor at Norton, did not complain about my reversal after reading the completed manuscript. In fact, he told me that I had handled the situation well and vindicated my integrity as a journalist by admitting that I had been wrong while setting the record straight. As a result, Lawrence and I believed that our book would be viewed as the definitive account of what had really happened on the night Senator Kennedy was shot and mortally wounded—even though my friends in the conspiracy crowd were sure to disagree.[152]

Still, two questions remained: How would America's book reviewers react—especially in the wake of my five-year litigation against the *New*

PART SEVEN: FROM RFK TO OJ

York Times? Would these reviewers seek retribution and finish me off, once and for all?

Before we had to face any of that, Lawrence invited me to speak to the entire W.W. Norton publishing operation at its semi-annual sales conference in Manhattan on December 5. Viewing this as a huge break, as well as an opportunity to explain what had happened between my book proposal and completed manuscript, I rode the train to New York, picked up my agent, Alice Martell, at her midtown office, and took a cab to the big meeting.

Nervous at first, I told the large crowd, "I am honored to be speaking today before the real power in the publishing industry: the sales people. Authors like me would be nothing without people like you, and I am proud to be on the Norton team for my new book."

Then, after paying my respects to the sales force, as well as to Star Lawrence and Norton's editorial board, I gave them an overview of the book, explaining:

> As I write in the Preface: "This book is the story of a murder investigation. It is neither a political melodrama nor a paranoid's paradise."
>
> Chapter One, which is entitled "Intersection," traces the lives of the four major characters of the book on the day of the primary election—Kennedy, Sirhan, shooting victim Paul Schrade, and security guard Thane Eugene Cesar, who has long been accused of being the second gunman at the crime scene and Kennedy's actual killer. This chapter ends when the lives of these four people converge in the kitchen pantry.
>
> The rest of Part One is the story of the police investigation of this murder, which is told almost entirely by the officers and investigators themselves—most of whom had never before been interviewed. At the end of Part One, the reader should be convinced that Sirhan committed the crime and acted alone.
>
> Part Two chronicles the controversies in the case—questions about extra bullets at the scene, firearms evidence, discrepancies between eyewitness accounts and the official version the case, and the evidence that Gene Cesar might have fired the fatal shots at Senator Kennedy. At the end of Part Two, the

reader should have serious concerns that two guns were fired at the crime scene.

In Part Three, I enter the case, skeptical of the official version, believing that two guns had been fired and that Cesar might have fired the second gun. I receive an FBI report, stating that four bullets—not accounted for by the LAPD's crime lab—had been photographed and logged. These were four more bullets than Sirhan's eight-shot revolver could hold. When I interview the individual LAPD officers and officials involved in the case, nearly twenty of them confirm the existence of these bullet holes identified in the FBI photos. These are not conspiracy nuts saying this; these are experienced, trained, and qualified law-enforcement officials.

Also in Part Three, I chronicle my collection of all this evidence, including my exclusive interviews with Cesar, who admits that he was working for George Wallace at the time, that he hated Robert Kennedy, and that he had a business connection to a Mafia associate in 1968.

By the end of Chapter Twenty-Seven of this thirty-chapter book, even the most skeptical reader will believe that it is more than likely that two guns were fired, and that Cesar may, indeed, have fired the shots that killed Senator Kennedy—whether intentionally or accidentally in the midst of clumsiness or retaliation against Sirhan.

But, then, in Chapters Twenty-Eight and Twenty-Nine, there is The Twist—the essential element of nearly every great story. In Chapter Twenty-Eight, Cesar takes and conclusively passes a polygraph test. Then, in the final conflict in Chapter Twenty-Nine, Sirhan and I face off in a very dramatic confrontation in a prison-visitation room at Corcoran State Penitentiary in central California over what Sirhan does and does not remember about the night of the murder.

In the final chapter, Chapter Thirty, I authoritatively answer the six principal questions that have lingered for years in this case:

PART SEVEN: FROM RFK TO OJ

* Who was hit with the first shot?

* What was the order of shots hitting Kennedy?

* How was Kennedy hit at point-blank range when not a single eyewitness saw the barrel of Sirhan's revolver get closer than a foot-and-a-half away from Kennedy's body?[153]

* Were there really extra bullets in the walls and the door frames of the kitchen pantry—as the FBI report and key LAPD officials have alleged?[154]

* Why did the court-authorized firearms panel in 1975 fail to match Sirhan's gun with the three intact victim bullets?

* What was Sirhan's motive?

In the end, while Sirhan's guilt is reaffirmed, two men wrongly accused for twenty-seven years—one a police criminalist and security guard Cesar—are finally vindicated.[155]

Indeed, the LAPD did solve this murder in 1968. But, nearly twenty-seven years later, I have solved this case by finally explaining why the evidence of a possible second gunman appears as it does.

Lessons learned? Placing into a new context what I had known all along about this case, I now realize that even law-enforcement officials—who possess the training, qualifications, and experience to determine the significance of crime-scene evidence—do make mistakes if their abilities are not put to the test under the proper circumstances and conditions.

In other words, if one does not account for occasional official mistakes and incompetence, then nearly every such murder could appear to be a conspiracy, particularly if a civilian investigator—like me, with limited access and resources—is looking for one.

I am very excited about this true crime book, which I hope you will find is both honest and intelligent.

Norton threw a luncheon for me where Star Lawrence gave me a note that the head of Norton's sales division had handed him after my speech. It simply read: "Knockout presentation!"

100. Bad photograph, great review

In early-April 1995, I received four finished copies of my Kennedy book, sending the first, as always, to my mom. I had dedicated the book to two people, one of whom was Mrs. Nolte who received the second book. The other person on my dedication page was Walter Sheridan, Robert Kennedy's long-time friend and aide, who had died just three months earlier. I sent the third copy to his widow.

Shortly before his death, Sheridan had called and asked for my conclusions. He was relieved when I told him that I had reversed course and concluded that Sirhan had acted alone. If there really had been a conspiracy against Senator Kennedy, Sheridan would have discovered it.

I kept the fourth copy for my own collection.

Soon after, the *Washington Post* accepted a lengthy article about my 180 on the RFK case. Because the *Post's* editors had published my article about the case in May 1990—in which I made the case that extra bullets, identified by the FBI and LAPD officers, might have been fired at the crime scene—I felt that I owed them this consideration, even though many of the *Post's* people had been so difficult during *Moldea v. New York Times*.[156]

In mid-April, *Kirkus* published the first review for the Kennedy book. The anonymous *Kirkus* reviewer stated:

> Moldea has reexamined every piece of available evidence and, in an example of indefatigable journalism, tracked down virtually every policeman and FBI agent who worked on the case, is still alive, and would agree to talk to him. He also interviewed Sirhan and Thane Eugene Cesar, a security guard the night of the shooting often named as the second assassin. . . . Moldea has left no stones unturned in his examination of the Robert Kennedy assassination, uncovering many worms and perhaps, finally, the true smoking gun.[157]

However, *Kirkus* took a shot at me in the midst of the review but quickly turned it into a compliment, saying:

> Moldea can be criticized for the deceptive way he presents evidence as credible and then, Sherlock Holmes-like, explains only at the end why it is tainted. But this infuriating device works, holding the reader riveted as he reconstructs the crime scene and reviews the investigation.

Publishers Weekly printed the second early trade-publication review of the Kennedy book, following suit with *Kirkus* with an almost identical analysis.

Gilbert Taylor of *Booklist*, the third of the early trade reviews, wrote in the May 15 edition:

> Moldea revisits [the murder case] comprehensively but unprejudicedly, so readers swayed by his forensic skill at examining ambiguous evidence will be surprised by his ultimate conclusion. . . . Moldea adopts no theory until he has analyzed all the evidence, culminating in interviews with [Sirhan] and the guard, Thane Cesar. Detailed and definitive, Moldea's persistent investigation might close the book on the tragedy.[158]

So far so good, I held my breath while awaiting the reviews from mainstream publications.

British journalist Godfrey Hodgson, in his review for the *Washington Post Book World*, completely ripped my head off, calling me, among other things, a liar.

Apparently, Hodgson could speak with authority about the Kennedy murder case, in which the assassin sprang out of a large crowd and opened fire. Hodgson even boasted:

> As it happens, I was in that crowd, a few feet away from the senator, on my way to a promised interview with Kennedy for the *London Sunday Times*. I have an indelible memory of the grief and confusion of that moment.[159]

The day after Hodgson's review of my book, while I was drafting my response to the *Post*, a former FBI agent, who is a still close friend, called and said that he had seen Hodgson's review. As I started to recite my complaints with Hodgson, the FBI man ordered me to hang up the phone and go to my fax machine.

A few minutes later, I received a fax of the report that detailed the FBI's interview with Hodgson.

The following is the text of my response to the very embarrassed *Washington Post*:

> Dear Editor:
>
> It is particularly disturbing to me that Godfrey Hodgson, in his June 25 review, implies that my book, *The Killing of Robert F. Kennedy*, is premised on 300 pages of "lying." Then, he quickly retracts that charge, because he knows he cannot support it. Still, planting the idea, Hodgson writes: "We might even be tempted to say, in Moldea-speak, 'This [expletive] guy [Moldea] has been lying to us all along.' That wouldn't be quite fair: teasing us, maybe, to make the most of a losing hand, but not lying."
>
> Very cute.
>
> Earlier in the review, Hodgson makes a statement about himself that brings this issue of "lying" into sharper focus.
>
> Following Kennedy's emotional speech after winning the June 1968 California Democratic primary, his aides pushed to get the senator out of the hotel's jam-packed Embassy Room and over to a press conference in the adjacent Colonial Room. To get there quickly, they decided to take a short-cut.
>
> Describing his proximity to Kennedy, Hodgson states in his review:
>
> "Instead, as he was hustled through a kitchen pantry in the Ambassador Hotel in Los Angeles after a victory rally with his campaign workers, Robert Kennedy encountered a young Palestinian Christian called Sirhan Bishara Sirhan and was shot to death.
>
> "<u>As it happens, I was in that crowd, a few feet away from the senator, on my way to a promised interview with Kennedy for</u>

PART SEVEN: FROM RFK TO OJ

the <u>*London Sunday Times.* I have an indelible memory of the grief and confusion of that moment.</u>" [Emphasis added.]

Clearly, Hodgson includes this personal account in his review to establish his authority when writing about the Kennedy murder and to give greater weight to his opinion of my work. After all, he appears to have been an eyewitness.

But was he really?

According to the LAPD's official list of the 77 known persons in the kitchen pantry at the moment of the shooting, Hodgson is not mentioned either as an eyewitness or as even being present in the room!

In fact, according to his own 1969 book, *An American Melodrama: The Presidential Campaign of 1968*, Hodgson detailed on pages 353-354 that he was on the floor below the kitchen pantry, perhaps even outside the hotel, while Kennedy was upstairs being gunned down!

Remarkably, a third version of these events comes from Hodgson's own statement to the FBI. According to the FBI's official report of the Hodgson interview—dated July 8, 1968, just over a month after the murder—Hodgson "furnished the following information":

"As soon as KENNEDY finished his speech and before he began to move through the crowd, HODGSON [and two colleagues] left the Embassy Room by going down an iron staircase to the parking lot. They did this to avoid getting trapped in the crowd. They did not know which way the Senator would go after making his speech or what his exact plans were.

"While outside HODGSON heard about the shooting and he went back inside the hotel. He went towards the kitchen area but was unable to enter the area because of the crowds. He did not see the Senator or SIRHAN at that time."

Hodgson's now-embellished claim that he was just "a few feet away from the senator" deceitfully gives the impression that he was an actual eyewitness to this terrible event. This gross exaggeration—debunked by LAPD and FBI records, as well as his own 1969 book—is as dishonest as his review of my work.[160]

Dan E. Moldea
Washington, D.C.

In mid-May, a photographer from the *New York Times* called and asked for an appointment to take my picture. I reluctantly scheduled the meeting, assuming this assignment was part of some follow-up report about my defeat to the *Times*.

Then, on late Wednesday afternoon, May 24, I received a call from a reporter-friend of mine at the *New York Times*.

"Hey, Dan!" He said, excitedly. "Did you hear the news here?"

"About what?" I asked.

"We're reviewing your new book in the *Times* tomorrow."

"You've got to be kidding me. Who's doing it?"

"Christopher Lehmann-Haupt."

"Jesus! What's he going to say? Do you know?"

"No one knows yet, but people around here are buzzing about it."

For the next twelve hours, I couldn't work. I couldn't eat. I couldn't sleep. I couldn't sit still. I felt like a condemned man the night before execution, waiting for a call from the governor.

Finally, at 6:00 in the morning, I couldn't take it anymore. Instead of waiting for the *Times* to arrive on my doorstep, I went to a 24-hour convenience store to get a copy.

When I walked into the 7-11, a large stack of the *New York Times* rested on the wire stand. I picked one up and opened it to the book-review page which, indeed, ran only one featured review: *The Killing of Robert F. Kennedy*.

The first thing I saw was my photograph, which I nearly didn't recognize. My face appeared so large and contorted that I looked like a wrestling promoter. But, within seconds, it didn't matter how I looked in the picture because Lehmann-Haupt had made my book look great in the review, writing:

> Carefully reasoned . . . ultimately persuasive . . . dramatic. . . . The author meticulously dissects how the various disputes arose and how critics were drawn into the orbit of the case.

> ... The cleverness of [Moldea's] strategy in the book lies in his playing so effectively the part of devil's advocate. ... His book should be read, not so much for the irrefutability of its conclusions as for the way the author has brought order out of a chaotic tale and turned an appalling tatter of history into an emblem of our misshapen times.[161]

Absolutely joyful, I bought three copies of the *Times*. While driving, I had to pull over momentarily: I couldn't see the road because my eyes had welled up.

When I arrived back at my apartment during mid-morning after a breakfast-business meeting, I already had 47 messages on my answering machine from friends and colleagues who were thrilled about the review—even though nearly everyone poked fun at me about the picture.

That afternoon, I wrote a letter to Lehmann-Haupt—the husband of Natalie Robbins, the author of *Alien Ink*—simply saying: "Thank you for your consideration and thoughtful review. You and the *Times* have demonstrated nothing less than pure class, and everyone is saying so."

Soon after, Alex Kuczynski of the *New York Observer* published an article, saying:

> A rave review by the *New York Times'* venerated book reviewer Christopher Lehmann-Haupt is every author's dream. But are your chances even better if you've brought a lawsuit against the *Times* for their last review of one of your books? On Thursday, May 25, the *New York Times* published a highly favorable review, by Mr. Lehmann-Haupt, of Dan E. Moldea's *The Killing of Robert F. Kennedy*. ...
>
> Mr. Moldea told the *Observer*, "Sometimes when you're reviewed, you get a real pro and other times you get a shill for the institution you're writing about. The last time I got a shill, this time I got a pro."
>
> Said Mr. Lehmann-Haupt: "I just sort of put my head in the sand and tried to judge the book on its own merits. That to me is the job of a good reviewer."[162]

Reporter John Diamond of the Associated Press followed with a wire story, saying:

"Sirhan Bishara Sirhan consciously and knowingly murdered Senator Robert Kennedy, and he acted alone," Moldea concludes. . . . What makes the book notable is that Moldea, an investigative reporter who has been working on the RFK case since the mid-1980s, rejects his own earlier suspicion that the assassination was a conspiracy by more than one gunman.[163]

On my June 5 publication date, *Newsweek* released its June 12 issue, featuring a full-page article about the Kennedy book. Reporter Steve Waldman wrote:

> If there had been a conspiracy to assassinate Robert F. Kennedy, as many people believe, Dan Moldea probably would have found it. . . . [I]n 1987 Moldea had written an influential article in *Regardie's* magazine demanding that the RFK case be reopened because of mounting evidence that a second gunman was involved. But after doing extra research for a book, Moldea concluded that he was wrong the first time—and that the sole killer of Robert Kennedy on June 5, 1968, was a deranged Sirhan Sirhan. . . .
>
> If this reporting doesn't seal the case, Moldea's chilling prison interviews with Sirhan do.[164]

On June 8, three close friends—Barbara Raskin, Herb White, and well-known Washington publicist Janet Donovan, all of whom had hosted a party for my third book, *Dark Victory*, in 1986—threw another one for my Kennedy book at White's restaurant, Herb's, in downtown Washington. The crowd consisted of a couple of hundred long-time friends from Akron to Detroit and New York to Los Angeles, as well as numerous authors and journalists, attorneys, cops, spooks, and even a couple of ex-mob guys from the Federal Witness Protection Program.

Ethelbert Miller, still a leader in Washington's community of writers, introduced me, saying: "The last few years have been difficult ones for Dan Moldea. He has fought to uphold his good name and continued writing. . . . Moldea loves the writers' battlefield."

After Miller's generous introduction, I pretended to get very serious and said to the large crowd, "Today, my attorneys and I announce that we have filed another defamation suit against the *New York Times*—this time for the publication of that goddamn picture two weeks ago that made me look like Luca Brasi in *The Godfather*. We are seeking millions in damages."

The day after the book party, another rumor circulated that a second review of my book would soon be published in the Sunday *New York Times Book Review*. But, frankly, I didn't want it. I was still overjoyed with the Lehmann-Haupt review, and I didn't want another to cancel it out.

On Wednesday, June 14, Star Lawrence faxed me the review that would appear in the *New York Times Book Review* on Sunday, June 18. To my complete surprise, it was even better than the first, declaring:

> In *The Killing of Robert F. Kennedy*, a persuasive reexamination of the assassination, Mr. Moldea does what many journalists would lack the courage for—admit that his earlier work was wrong.... But because of the honesty and logic with which he approaches his study, Mr. Moldea's journalistic instincts have never looked sharper.

Written by Gerald Posner—the author of *Case Closed*, the best-selling anti-conspiracy book about John Kennedy's murder—the review also finally gave credit where credit had long been due: "Mr. Moldea dedicates the book to his writing coach, Nancy Nolte, and properly so, because this is the best written of his books, finished in a clear and easy style."

On August 31, John Aloysius Farrell—an investigative journalist for the *Boston Globe*, which was now owned by the *New York Times*—wrote a feature story about me on the front page of the newspaper's Living Arts section. Entitled, "Dan Moldea's Lonely Beat," Farrell stated:

> Dan Moldea may qualify as a Last Angry Man. A tough guy. A rough and rugged knight-errant in a world of corporations and computers....
>
> The literary world is filled with gripes and braggadocio, but it was Moldea who sued the *New York Times Book Review* and, shrugging off the reprobations of newspaper editorialists and other protectors of the First Amendment, carried his case to the U.S. Supreme Court.
>
> Not a great career move: taking on the bible of book reviews. Pretty nervy for a free-lance writer.

Speaking specifically of the Kennedy book, Farrell continued:

> Moldea performs a public service. His book is, above all else, an anatomy of conspiracy theory: a dissection of how blundering public officials, in trying to cover up their own quite human mistakes, can fuel wider suspicions and doubts. . . .
>
> That Moldea could carry off such a trick is a testament to his skill as a writer and investigator. . . . Of all the writers who have challenged the official verdict on the Kennedy assassinations, his careful work won the quiet respect . . . of the Kennedy family's aides and advisors.
>
> In the end, Moldea chose journalistic integrity over the commercial possibilities of a fresh conspiracy theory.

Concluding his story, Farrell quoted me, saying, "The jury is out on me. I love the work. I love the investigations, the reporting, [and] the colleagues. I love everything I do except the business. The business is something I've never been good at.'"

101. Old problems become a new reality

Telling people what they already knew—like that Sirhan Sirhan had killed Senator Kennedy and acted alone—did not make bookstore owners bang down W.W. Norton's door for my work. Every author knows the cycle: If the bookstores do not order a book, then people can't purchase it. If readers cannot buy the book, there are no royalties.

And, even when there were royalties, sometimes I couldn't collect them. Just recently, the publisher that had released the fifth edition of *The Hoffa Wars* had suddenly gone out of business, taking down whatever money I had made in the process—just like the original hardback publisher of that work. Then, another publisher, which had purchased the mass-market paperback rights to my embattled book, *Interference*, suddenly went out of business, just five weeks before its scheduled release.

To complicate matters even more, the then ongoing trial of O. J. Simpson in Los Angeles had effectively obliterated the true-crime book market in New York. To most people who read this genre, the O. J. case was the only legitimate true-crime game in town.

Consequently, I was having difficulty selling another project, regardless of all the fabulous reviews I had received for the RFK book. And, because of my deteriorating financial situation, I was unable to move as freely as I usually did.

I tried to get work again as a consultant, but—with the stunning growth of the Internet, computer databases, and search engines for every conceivable subject—potential clients and law firms could have their assistants and clerks pull up information in seconds that I had previously charged $200 an hour to deliver.

Meantime, I watched as my existing tax bill to the IRS grew with interest and penalties while my credit cards hit their limits. Most painful of all was when I voluntarily surrendered my beloved American Express Platinum Card after paying off my debt. For years, regardless of my financial situation, that Platinum Card had symbolized the fact that I paid my bills. Now, with more important priorities, I could not even afford to pay its $300 annual fee.

On top of all of that, back when my hopes were still high for the financial success of the RFK book, I had agreed to buy a 1990 Jeep Cherokee Laredo from William Jahoda of Chicago, one of the Mafia's most successful bookmakers who had flipped, turned state's evidence, and was entering the Federal Witness Protection Program.

Even though I had tried but failed to sell a proposal about Jahoda's fascinating story to a New York publisher, Jahoda and I remained on good terms, and he had made an offer I couldn't refuse for the car—"no money down, pay me whenever you can." But, despite our friendship, he still expected to get paid.

Now, I had to face an age-old existential dilemma: If one owes the IRS and a Mafia guy, who gets paid first?

Actually, Jahoda's Cherokee had some sentimental value. The previous year, word came out of Chicago that a Mafia hitman had received a contract to find and kill Jahoda who was then living in Washington, D.C. Federal prosecutors, who needed Jahoda's testimony in an upcoming murder trial, ordered him to leave his rented house and to move into a local hotel where federal marshals could better protect him. They also advised him to get rid of his car, so Jahoda gave me his Jeep to use until the feds gave him the all-clear sign.

The problem was that Jahoda, in violation of Wit-Sec rules, had been using my address as an occasional mail drop, including on Federal Express airbills—which were discovered by the people who had supposedly sent the contract killer. And, oblivious to all of this, I was now driving Jahoda's car.

Soon after, federal agents called and advised me to leave town, concerned that I could be whacked by someone who believed me to be Jahoda with whom I shared similar physical characteristics. Although I refused to leave my home, I did experience some comic relief each time I went out to start his car.

Within a couple of weeks, the feds managed to get the situation under control and allowed Jahoda to return to his home. I gladly returned his Jeep to him—until I later agreed to buy it.

Meantime, Mimi, who earlier left me during the spring of 1993, had now returned in the midst of the worst financial crisis I had ever experienced. With bankruptcy a very real possibility—a trigger I mercifully never had to pull—Mimi insisted on standing by me through this horrible time.

I was very grateful that after our long separation, we had "found" each other again.

Watching me continue to sink into the mire of money problems, Mrs. Nolte sent me a very tough letter in late September, saying:

> Don't be afraid or ashamed to start over. I think most successful people who have dared to be different go through a really bad period like this—and have to start near the "bottom" again. It's hard on the ego, but I have seen it happen. The new career [might be] more satisfying than the old.
>
> You had the daring, the guts and the imagination when you first started out to get into something you knew nothing about (except a bit about the Teamsters). Yes, it would be harder at this point in your life. But now you have a lot of skills you didn't have then. . . .
>
> All I know is I have more confidence in you and your abilities now than I did years ago when I saw something special in you and first encouraged you to write.

In the midst of everything else that was happening in my life, I had yet another problem, something that started as a minor hassle but now threatened to overshadow everything else.

During the spring of 1992, I had signed a collaboration contract with Howard Safir, the former head of the U.S. Federal Witness Protection Program, who selected me to write a book about his career. I reluctantly agreed to share the risk with Safir, working for several months—gratis

PART SEVEN: FROM RFK TO OJ

and under a cloak of confidentiality but with a promise of future royalties. Actually, I enjoyed working with Safir, a very accomplished man with a fascinating story.

Before we made our deal, I had asked Safir what he had previously done with his project. He simply replied that he had sold an option to a film producer, which had since expired.

But, after completing our 96-page proposal, I discovered that Safir had attempted but failed to sell his autobiography in each of the previous two years, rendering our new project damaged goods.

After learning that Safir, for whom I had always showed great respect, had been less than candid with me, I angrily confronted him. In response, Safir unilaterally ended our arrangement—despite my months of free work on his behalf.

I was fully prepared to walk away from this entire matter and say nothing more about it. But my attorney, Roger Simmons, who had become my most fiercely loyal friend, refused to tolerate this situation and filed suit against Safir in June 1993 in the midst of our hiatus between the lower and appellate courts' actions in *Moldea v. New York Times*.

After a long and bitter period of discovery and depositions, *Moldea v. Safir* was finally heard in Maryland's Circuit Court for Anne Arundel County.

On December 11, 1995, after a two-week trial, the six-member jury ruled in my favor, finding that Safir had engaged in negligent misrepresentation and breach of contract, awarding us $17,500 in compensatory damages. After winning the case, I told the *New York Daily News*, which had called for comment, "When you're asked to share the risks, you have to know what the risks are."[165]

Shortly after the case ended, Mayor Rudolph Giuliani appointed Safir as the police commissioner of New York City.

Because all but $2,000 of the damage award in *Moldea v. Safir* went to pay my attorney's expenses, my financial situation still appeared hopeless.

Then, as all seemed lost, a consulting firm in the Washington, D.C. area needed an investigator to go to Europe to find a very specific piece of information. This caper was tantamount to looking for a needle in a haystack of needles—but offered a huge reward if solved.

Former D.C. detective and organized-crime expert, Carl Shoffler, who had been like a big brother to me since he came to our first poker game in December 1978, convinced the firm that I was the right man for the job.

Meantime, the trip gave me the opportunity to do research on a book I wanted to write about Roberto Calvi, the chairman of Europe's second-largest bank, Banco Ambrosiano. In June 1982, Calvi had been found hanging from the scaffolding beneath the Blackfriars Bridge in London after the collapse of the bank, which had done business with The Vatican, as well as the Mafia. An initial ruling of suicide later evolved into proof of a murder—which still officially remains unsolved.[166]

With my client allowing Mimi, who spoke a variety of languages, to help me on this assignment, we went to Europe and found the required information in just three days. Pleased with our success—which yielded me enough money to pay off both the IRS and the ex-Mafia guy, along with most of my other debts—the firm asked us to remain in Europe to find some additional materials. Meantime, the information I had hoped to obtain about Calvi and Banco Ambrosiano never materialized, later causing me to abandon that book project.

However, our trip was cut short when we received word that Shoffler, who had arranged for this assignment that became my financial salvation, had slipped into a lingering coma—without ever realizing that he had liver cancer.

Immediately after our return to the United States, I drove to Johns Hopkins Hospital in Baltimore to visit the still comatose Shoffler in the intensive-care ward.

Just ten minutes after I arrived—and with his family, another former D.C. detective, and me, standing at his bedside—the 51-year-old Shoffler took his last breath and died without ever regaining consciousness.

102. The O. J. Simpson case

On January 22, 1996, Washington attorney Ron Goldfarb—the literary agent who had represented my book about the NFL and the Mafia—called and asked me if I wanted to compete for a proposed book by Tom Lange and Philip Vannatter, the two detectives who led the LAPD's investigation of O. J. Simpson and his alleged role in the June 12, 1994, murders of his ex-wife, Nicole Brown, and her young friend, Ron Goldman.

On October 3, 1995, a Los Angeles County jury had acquitted Simpson in the wake of his attorneys' charges that the former NFL star had been the victim of a police conspiracy. Only recently had a gag order on the detectives been lifted. They were now free to defend themselves and to tell their story.

Immediately, as Goldfarb directed, I sent a package of personal information to the detectives. Eight days later, Lange called from Los Angeles and interviewed me. Knowing that my recent book about the murder of Robert Kennedy had been extremely critical of the LAPD, Lange told me that he and Vannatter were looking for someone with the independence to challenge their work, believing that even the most skeptical but fair analysis would conclude that they had performed well—contrary to the manner in which they had been portrayed by Simpson's defense team and in the media. Also, as it turned out, Lange and I had several mutual friends within the LAPD's legendary Robbery-Homicide Division, and I encouraged him to call them and check me out.

The following day, Goldfarb notified me that Lange and Vannatter had selected me to write their book.

One immediate problem I had was Alice Martell, the agent who had helped to save my career by selling my book about the murder of Senator Kennedy to Star Lawrence and W.W. Norton. When I told Goldfarb that I was loyal to Martell, he made it clear to me that he was in no mood for splitting commissions, adding that he would find someone else for the Lange-and-Vannatter assignment if I insisted on keeping Martell.

Consequently, just as I shamelessly abandoned Philip Spitzer—the wonderful agent who had sold my first two books—in favor of a higher-profile agent who wound up a monumental disappointment, I deserted Martell in order to get this deal. Martell, who always exhibited pure class, made it easy for me, and she let me go.

Goldfarb said that I did not even have to write a book proposal because one already existed. In fact, I was not the first choice for this project. The two detectives had earlier worked with Jim Newton, a top reporter for the *Los Angeles Times* who had covered the Simpson case for his newspaper. After writing an excellent proposal, Newton faced a conflict-of-interest situation with the *Times* and decided to withdraw from the book project. Nevertheless, he told the detectives to use his proposal, which Goldfarb sent to me.

While reading Newton's proposal and giving myself a crash course on the Simpson case, Lange called and invited me to meet with him and Vannatter in New York during their one-day stay on February 6. That morning, I took the Amtrak Metroliner to New York and met them at the Radisson Hotel in midtown Manhattan.

Lange and I hit it off immediately, but I felt a little tension with Vannatter who was a very tough guy. But, as the meeting progressed,

Vannatter and I warmed up to each other. I quickly learned to respect his demeanor, and he seemed to appreciate my candor.

When the detectives asked me to detail my specific problems with their handling of the Simpson case, I replied somewhat high-handedly, "For starters, I have problems with the decision to go over the gate at Simpson's house, the circumstances of the search warrant, the early handling of the blood evidence at the crime scene, the decision to throw a blanket taken from the house over Nicole Brown's body, the interrogation of Simpson, and the transport of the blood vial from the police station to Simpson's residence."

After hearing this recitation, both detectives addressed each of my concerns in considerable, almost overwhelming detail, citing portions of the case history with which I was completely unfamiliar. Immediately after hearing their responses, I knew that they had a terrific untold story, filled with inside information and evidence not used at the Simpson trial.

Further, Lange had kept a personal journal from the first day of the murder which continued through to Simpson's acquittal. Although he refused to give it to me until we secured a book deal, I suspected that it would become the backbone of our manuscript.

Of course, I had big problems with the role of Mark Fuhrman—who was still facing charges for perjury, stemming from his sworn testimony during Simpson's criminal trial. However, early on, Lange and Vannatter, two supercops from the Robbery-Homicide Division, made it clear that they had not known Fuhrman, who was a junior detective in the West Los Angeles Division, prior to the Brown-Goldman murders.

As we concluded our first meeting, Lange, Vannatter, and I were in sync, agreeing to keep Newton's excellent proposal intact but deciding to add a brief, five-page introduction to highlight the revelations in the book. After receiving their ideas, I drafted these pages on the train back to Washington, typing them up that night and faxing them to Goldfarb and the detectives the following day.

In the first two paragraphs of the proposal, I wrote:

> Tom Lange and Phil Vannatter know more about the case against O. J. Simpson than anyone on earth. And above everything else, the history of the most celebrated murder investigation in modern times, perhaps all time, begins and ends with these two cops. Attorneys, jurors, witnesses, and reporters may write what they will, but this is and always has been a police story.

PART SEVEN: FROM RFK TO OJ

Lange and Vannatter took over the investigation when it was just hours old and ran it from that moment on. For more than a year, their names and faces became almost as well known as Starsky and Hutch. Suddenly, before a national television audience, they represented not just the controversial Los Angeles Police Department but the 175,000 police officers in America, who were simultaneously cheering them on.

Soon after, the detectives worked out an arrangement with the producers of *Larry King Live* on CNN, in which they agreed to sit for their first media interview ever about the Simpson case on February 22. They asked me to appear with them, but I refused, saying that my presence would come across as a hard sell of the book. These were two good cops who had a wonderful chemistry. I thought that the country—and, hopefully, the publishing industry—would fall in love with them. They simply didn't need me.

On the day of their interview, Goldfarb sent an advisory to twenty publishers, notifying them that the two detectives would appear on King's show that night, live from Washington. Any editor who wanted to see their book proposal simply had to sign a confidentiality agreement, and then Goldfarb would send the publishing house a copy.

Before the King show, Lange, Vannatter, Goldfarb, and I met at a hotel in downtown Washington. We talked briefly and signed the collaboration contract. Then, the two detectives and I went to the CNN studios for the interview. Hanging back while the production staff fawned over the cops, I saw Larry King and paid my respects. King, with whom I was acquainted, had always viewed me as a one-trick pony who only wrote about the Mafia.

"Are you writing their book, Dan?" King asked.

I smiled and nodded.

"But there's no mob angle. What are you going to do?"

I replied, "Because of what the Simpson case has done to the true-crime market in New York, this will be my revenge."

Although Lange and Vannatter occasionally appeared during the interview as Jack Webb and Harry Morgan in *Dragnet*—"just the facts"—they still cooked well together. In fact, they were a big hit, coming across as cool, competent, and professional.

After the show, King's producers took the three of us to dinner at Nathan's, a popular restaurant in the heart of Georgetown. When I walked in with the detectives, I felt like I was in the presence of two rock stars. The crowd loved them, walking up to shake their hands and to ask for their autographs.

I had no doubts that we would sell our book by the end of the week, maybe even the next day.

But that was wishful thinking. Only three of the twenty publishers requested copies of the proposal—HarperCollins, Dutton, and Doubleday—giving rise to the possibility that there might not be a book at all.

All of us were completely shocked by this disappointing response—although Goldfarb had warned that selling our book might be difficult, considering all of the other books about the Simpson case already under contract. Nearly every publishing house had already shelled out an enormous amount of money for books they now feared would not sell.

The remaining companies that had not entered the Simpson-book sweepstakes were almost defiant about it, refusing even to consider such projects as a matter of company pride and principle.

In other words, Lange and Vannatter, who had remained true to their pledges of confidentiality during the Simpson criminal trial, had simply entered the publishing market too late.

On the afternoon of March 1—after Lange and Vannatter appeared on ABC's *Good Morning America*—Goldfarb called and told me that all three publishing houses had passed.

The project appeared to be dead, and the three of us moved on with our separate lives.

103. Working with Lange and Vannatter

While I was on vacation, visiting my mom and playing golf with friends in Ohio in August 1996, I received a call from Frank Weimann, the New York literary agent who had earlier arranged the doomed collaboration between Howard Safir and me. In fact, Weimann, who had voluntarily flown down from New York, served as the key witness for us during the trial for *Moldea v. Safir*—a real act of friendship and loyalty. His testimony was decisive, and, in my opinion, led to the jury verdict in our favor.

Weimann told me that the hardback division of Pocket Books, a subsidiary of my old nemesis, Simon & Schuster, wanted to sign up Lange and Vannatter as quickly as possible—in anticipation of the upcoming civil case against O. J. Simpson, which had been filed by the families of murder victims Nicole Brown and Ron Goldman. Immediately, I placed Weimann in touch with the two detectives, who, after receiving my crash course on the economics of book publishing, agreed to reopen negotiations.

Because of my continued loyalty to Ron Goldfarb, the agent who had brought me into the collaboration with the detectives but could not sell the project earlier in the year, I asked Weimann to take his fifteen-percent commission from Lange and Vannatter's cut of all advances and royalties and to allow Goldfarb to receive a commission from the money I earned. Generously, Weimann agreed to split his commission.

According to our collaboration agreement, Lange and Vannatter equally divided seventy percent of all profits. I received the remaining thirty percent. As always, the agents' commissions came off the top. However, because of technical problems with the contract, we did not sign until November 12.

A far cry from the reported $4.5 million received by Simpson prosecutor Marcia Clark from Viking Press and the $3.5 million Ballantine Books paid to Simpson's lead defense attorney, Johnny Cochran, Pocket paid a mere $115,000 to Lange, Vannatter, and me, which we split three ways. Once again forced to justify another low advance, I believed that there was money to be made from back-end royalties.

Also, according to the November 12 signed contract with Pocket, our deadline for submitting the completed manuscript was the tightest I had ever seen: January 3, 1997, just over seven weeks away.

While I plunged into research and writing, both Lange and Vannatter became high-profile witnesses at the civil trial—heavily attacked by Simpson's defense counsel but passionately supported by the plaintiffs' attorneys. The detectives walked away from the trial, which continued with other witnesses, standing tall and looking good.

After their testimonies, I flew to Los Angeles to deliver a eulogy at a memorial service for the great Jack Tobin, "The Godfather of Mafia Reporters," who had been like a second father to me since I started work on *Dark Victory* in 1984. Warren Welsh, the former director of NFL Security, and investigative journalist Pete Noyes also gave tributes for Jack.

While in California but not with the Tobin family or my close friend and "brother," Dave Robb, I spent most of my time with Tom Lange, interviewing him, going through his day-by-day journal of the case, and collecting miscellaneous materials. (Phil Vannatter and his wife had left southern California and moved to a farm in Indiana near her family. I did all of my interviews with Vannatter by telephone.)

During a solo visit to the Robbery-Homicide Division at Parker Center, I spoke to several of my LAPD sources. One gave me the undisclosed and unedited, verbatim tape of Lange's dramatic phone conversations with Simpson during the surreal, slow-speed Bronco chase up the San Diego Freeway on June 17, 1994, which was nationally televised and had preceded Simpson's arrest.

Unknown to just about everybody in the world, Lange had literally saved Simpson's life with his heart-wrenching pleas for him to surrender. Simpson had repeatedly threatened to commit suicide during his talks with Lange, which were memorialized on these recordings. Neither the tape nor a transcript of the exchanges between Lange and Simpson had ever been made public.

Another LAPD source placed me in an interrogation room and then dropped two large manila envelopes on the table in front of me. Smiling, he left, saying that he would return in exactly twenty minutes—no more, no less—which I took as an invitation to do what I wanted with whatever was inside the packages.

When I opened them, the envelopes contained the color pictures of the autopsies of Nicole Brown and Ron Goldman, which had been shown to the jury during the criminal trial but had never been made public.

I took a particular interest in two of the photographs, which separately pictured the victims fully clothed after being removed from their body bags. In these grotesque color photos, each was lying on a metal table in the morgue, covered with blood and with many of their knife wounds clearly visible.

I pulled a small camera from my pocket and snapped several shots of these two photographs—and only these two photographs.

When my source returned to the interrogation room in exactly twenty minutes, he asked, "Did you get what you needed?"

"Got it," I replied. "Thank you."

In a memorandum to my publisher, I argued that publication of these pictures would put a "human face on these murders," adding:

> These extremely graphic photographs should absolutely silence the happy cocktail-party talk about these murders—while giving a vivid portrait of what police work is really all about.... Of course, we are all going to have to weigh whether publication of these photographs will completely cross the boundaries of good taste.

PART SEVEN: FROM RFK TO OJ

In the end, Lange and Vannatter, who were very close to the Brown and Goldman families, vetoed my suggestion, refusing to allow the two autopsy pictures to appear in our book. However, as a compromise, the detectives agreed to give me a blow-by-blow description of the autopsy of each victim, which I did feature in the manuscript.

How could anyone joke about these murders again after reading these horrific descriptions?

Meantime, daunted by the options of how to organize the book, I decided to take the safest route—a straight chronology, divided into two parts. In the first part, I concentrated on the initial five days of the investigation, starting at the moment Lange and Vannatter received their assignments to report to the crime scene and ending with the arrest of Simpson, featuring the detectives' controversial taped interview with Simpson at Parker Center on the day after the murders and Lange's dramatic telephone conversations with Simpson during the Bronco chase on the I-405 freeway.

In the second part of the manuscript, I decided to write a history of the "trial of the century," focusing on the detectives' ongoing role in that melodrama and their disputes with the prosecutors over potential trial evidence.

Once again, kicking into my Bat-mode, I worked day and night, catnapping for twenty minutes at a time and then getting back to the computer. But now 46 and clearly not in the kind of shape I was in when I published *The Hoffa Wars* eighteen years earlier, I went through periods of pressure and stress where I feared that I was on the verge of a stroke.

But, strokeless, I finished the first draft of the book on December 8 and took it to New York the following day. Our editor, Sue Carswell, and the staff at Pocket couldn't have been more pleased with the results, even though I still had an enormous amount of work to do and only three more weeks to do it.

Regardless of the intensity of this effort, I still found time to do some pre-publication promotion work. Two weeks before I submitted the draft manuscript, I played a hunch and leaked the tape of Lange's desperate conversation with Simpson during the Bronco chase to several friends in the television-news business.

Matching up this audio tape with the videotape of the actual chase, the networks ran this dramatic scene throughout the Thanksgiving-holiday weekend, demonstrating Lange's humanity in his determined effort to save Simpson's life.

Just as I had hoped, the tape completely annihilated the theory of a police conspiracy against Simpson—and set the stage for the release of our book.

104. Mark Fuhrman's lies and delusions

While working feverishly to meet the tight deadline for my book with Lange and Vannatter, I followed, with some concern, the attempts by the media to rehabilitate the reputation of the racist junior detective Mark Fuhrman. A one-time high-school dropout, Fuhrman was in the midst of three-years' probation for perjury after his "no-contest" plea in early October 1996 for making false statements during his sworn testimony at O. J. Simpson's criminal trial.

Diane Sawyer of ABC's *Prime Time Live* had softballed Fuhrman during an interview broadcast on October 8. That was followed by an announcement in the October 28 edition of *Publishers Weekly* that Regnery Publishing, a conservative, Washington-based publishing house, had purchased Fuhrman's book, which would be released shortly after ours.

Predicting that Lange and Vannatter were going to be the villains in Fuhrman's book, I advised the detectives to launch a full-scale preemptive strike against Fuhrman in our book. However, even though they were extremely critical of Fuhrman's behavior during the Simpson trial, they rejected my suggestion, still harboring a basic loyalty towards this fellow cop. In fact, our book already contained a qualified defense of Fuhrman, who had been accused by Simpson's attorneys of planting evidence at the murder scene and at Simpson's residence.

Despite all of his negatives, Fuhrman was completely innocent of that allegation. And all charges to the contrary were completely wrong and unfair. In short, because of the timing of his appearance at the crime scene, Fuhrman could not have planted this evidence, which had already been identified. It was simply impossible. And his perjury plea was limited to his repeated denials of using the racist N-word while under cross-examination by defense counsel F. Lee Bailey during the criminal trial.

Then, just before I completed our manuscript, a friend faxed me the galleys to an upcoming story about Fuhrman in *Vanity Fair*. Journalist H.G. Bissinger, the author of this shameless valentine to Fuhrman, had allowed him to charge that Lange and Vannatter had missed, among other items of evidence, a "bloody fingerprint" on the back gate of Nicole Brown's residence on South Bundy, the scene of the murders. Apparently, Bissinger, a Pulitzer Prize winner, never bothered to check this and Fuhrman's other mistaken observations at the crime scene, allowing his attacks on Lange and Vannatter to go unchallenged.

After reading Bissinger's story, I went through my files and found a copy of Fuhrman's three pages of crime-scene notes, which provided clearly erroneous information, which, along with the nonexistent "bloody fingerprint," included that:

> * a simple watchman's cap that Fuhrman wrongly claimed was a ski mask;
>
> * a delivery menu from the Thai Flavor restaurant that Fuhrman wrongly claimed was from a local pizzeria;
>
> * the killer had been bitten by a dog; and
>
> * Brown and Goldman, who had been slashed and stabbed, had died from "gunshot wounds."

In fact, other than the false and misleading statements Fuhrman had made, nothing contained in his notes added any new information beyond what had been already reported by the patrol officers who had arrived at the scene two hours before Fuhrman.

After faxing the *Vanity Fair* story to Lange and Vannatter and speaking with them on a conference call, they agreed that Fuhrman's book was going to be his last desperate attempt to rehabilitate himself—at the expense of everyone else in the case, especially them. As a result, they authorized me to add an endnote to our book, stating:

> Fuhrman claimed in his notes that he had also observed a bloody fingerprint on the locking mechanism of the rear gate at the South Bundy crime scene. However, no such fingerprint was seen by anyone else. Also in his notes, Fuhrman speculated that the victims died from gunshot wounds, and that the killer had possibly been bitten by Brown's dog.

On January 2, 1997, I completed our manuscript, submitting it at 4:26 A.M.—one day before my deadline—to our editor, Sue Carswell, who had checked into the Georgetown Inn to await my final draft. After

Carswell's last-minute editing, Pocket Books delivered the final proofs of the book to me on January 14. I spent the night reading them and personally delivered the finished product in New York the following day.

Then, shattering any schedule I had ever seen or heard of for a hardback book, *Evidence Dismissed: The Inside Story of the Police Investigation of O. J. Simpson*, was bound and finished ten days later, as 200,000 copies of the first printing began to appear in bookstores throughout the country on January 28—just twenty-six days after I had submitted our manuscript.

Remarkably, that same day, the Simpson civil case went to the jury. In other words, our timing just could not have been better.

Demands for Lange and Vannatter's appearances on a variety of radio and television shows flooded in, including those from NBC's *Today Show* and *Dateline NBC*, ABC's *Good Morning America* and *Prime Time Live*, CNN's *Larry King Live* and *Burden of Proof*, and even Howard Stern's morning radio program, among many others.

On February 4, Pocket flew me to Los Angeles, first-class, to be with the detectives when the jury returned with its verdict. When I arrived at LAX, I called Lange, who asked me to have dinner at his home that night with him and his wife, Linda, as well as Phil and Rita Vannatter.

En route to Lange's house in my rented Thunderbird, I stopped at a liquor store to buy a bottle of Cordon Rouge champagne. As I was paying the cashier, a news bulletin appeared on the television behind the counter, announcing that the jury had reached a verdict in the Simpson civil case, which would be given to the court later that night.

Although it only took me fifteen minutes to get to Lange's home from the store, two television news crews had already arrived to interview the detectives—and then the press people kept coming.

We did not even have time for dinner.

At the exact moment that the verdict was read, Lange and Vannatter were in the back seat of a Lincoln Continental while I was in the front seat with the chauffeur. We were speeding along on the Ronald Reagan Freeway, en route to an appearance on ABC's *Nightline*, which had just booked Lange and Vannatter an hour earlier. Program executives had sent the limousine to guarantee the detectives' on-time delivery. Lange and Vannatter watched the report of the jury's decision on a color television with a three-inch screen and a fuzzy picture that I had brought along.

After hearing the unanimous verdict against Simpson, neither Lange nor Vannatter cheered or gloated. There were no high fives, no gleeful back-slapping. They simply looked at each other momentarily with considerable relief, smiled, and shook hands.

For the rest of the night and early into the morning, as we hopped from one interview to the next, Lange and Vannatter were, once again, treated like major celebrities. And, even though I instinctively hung back, they always grabbed me and pulled me into the action, introducing me as their co-author and allowing me to share their experience.

The most frequently asked question in nearly every interview was: "Do you feel vindicated?"

Lange replied on one program, "I don't know that we have to say we've been vindicated. We didn't do anything wrong. What we did was our job." Then, reflecting for a moment, he added, "Our only real mistake was not sending Mark Fuhrman home that night."

On the evening of February 6, I hosted a dinner party in Lange and Vannatter's honor at Musso & Frank's on Hollywood Boulevard. Forty-six writers and law-enforcement officials attended. To my great surprise, our publisher called the restaurant in the midst of the dinner and, using a company credit card, picked up the entire check.

Why the celebration? Just the day before, the detectives and I were together between shows when we heard that *Evidence Dismissed* would enter the *New York Times* Best Sellers List at number six the following week—just twenty-one months after Christopher Lehmann-Haupt and the *New York Times* had resurrected me from the dead.

105. Back on the defensive

On February 10, 1997, while at a bookstore in Hollywood, I saw Mark Fuhrman's book, *Murder in Brentwood*, stacked by the front desk next to our work, *Evidence Dismissed*. I immediately bought three copies, keeping one and giving the other two to my co-authors.

Devouring the book in a matter of hours while seething at Fuhrman's false and misleading statements about my partners, I drafted a fifteen-page, single-spaced response to the most objectionable passages in his book. Also, I added a preface to this statement, which began:

> Psychiatrist Dr. John Hochman filed a report, quoting Fuhrman as saying: "I have this urge to kill people that upset me." Hochman speculated that this and Fuhrman's similar statements were a "conscious attempt to look bad and an exaggeration of problems which could be a cry for help and/or [an]

overdramatization by a narcissistic, self-indulgent, emotionally unstable person who expects immediate attention and pity."[167]

I shared my fifteen-page document with Lange and Vannatter, who gave me their additions and corrections, which I incorporated into the final draft.

On February 12, while our book was still on all of the national best-sellers lists, I flew back to Washington, fearing that the party was over. The television networks, which had graced Lange and Vannatter as beneficiaries of their awesome market power during the previous two weeks, were now a daunting problem. Simply put, press people were falling in love with Fuhrman—smooth, handsome, and well spoken—and redefining him.

Inexplicably, the media simply accepted the mere appearances of his story—such as his claim that Lange and Vannatter had missed the phantom "bloody fingerprint" at the murder scene—and portrayed them as realities.

Fuhrman's publisher, Regnery Publishing, and his outside publicist, Lori Ames—a real pro who, by coincidence, had supervised the publicity for my fourth book, *Interference*, eight years earlier—were principally responsible for engineering his remarkable comeback.

Meantime, Lange and Vannatter, despite all of their excellent police work during the Simpson case, were forced to return to their defensive postures as their performances, once again, were grossly misrepresented by a lazy and uninformed media, just as had occurred during Simpson's criminal trial.

Diane Sawyer of *Prime Time Live*, who had interviewed Fuhrman the previous October, promoted her scheduled February 19 segment about him with great enthusiasm. On the afternoon of her broadcast, Sawyer made her first appearance ever on *The Oprah Winfrey Show* for the sole purpose of touting Fuhrman on *Prime Time Live* that night. She appeared absolutely determined to rehabilitate Fuhrman's reputation.

On her news-magazine show, Sawyer, once again, asked Fuhrman what appeared to be tough but completely predictable questions about his racism and perjury conviction—for which he already had stock answers. And then she totally yielded with regard to his claims about the crime-scene evidence supposedly missed by Lange and Vannatter, who appeared on the show—but only in brief and heavily-edited film clips. Sawyer made no mention of Fuhrman's erroneous crime-scene notes or our detailed point-by-point refutation of Fuhrman's charges, which I had faxed to a top producer at *Prime Time Live* the day before her broadcast.

PART SEVEN: FROM RFK TO OJ

The day after Diane Sawyer's puff piece on Fuhrman—which yielded *Prime Time Live's* biggest rating of the season—Oprah Winfrey hosted Fuhrman as the only guest on her afternoon show. And, without challenge, she accepted Fuhrman's claims about Lange and Vannatter's alleged mistakes.

On Friday, February 21, in the midst of Fuhrman's extraordinary media blitzkrieg, Geraldo Rivera became the only journalist to challenge Fuhrman during his *Rivera Live* program on CNBC. Rivera specifically disputed Fuhrman's statements about the crime scene and quoted extensively from our fifteen-page statement. However, after repeatedly pinning Fuhrman against the ropes during the interview, Rivera never went in for the kill, allowing Fuhrman to escape and to resume what we considered his disinformation campaign with other talk-show hosts who knew far less about the case than Rivera.

The following week, *Larry King Live* featured Lange and then Vannatter on separate nights to respond to Fuhrman. Although the detectives were repeatedly invited to debate Fuhrman, the two detectives refused, deciding instead to ignore him.

To say the least, our publisher and I believed that the detectives' strategy was flawed, because they appeared to be hiding something, which we knew they were not. We pleaded with them to go on the attack and confront Fuhrman, but the detectives, always gentlemen, refused, insisting that they wanted to remain dignified and to stay above the fray.

But, unlike my partners in matters like this, I was no gentleman. To me, this was just another street fight.

Because I knew the crime-scene issues of the Simpson case as well as any journalist, I decided to take the offensive and defend my partners, who knew the crime-scene issues better than anybody. Even though I begged for, but never received, the opportunity to face off against Fuhrman, I took any opportunity I could—during speeches, on numerous secondary television and radio programs, and in print—to level my own attacks against him and his false claims.

During an appearance on a radio-news program, an interviewer asked me why Fuhrman had used Lange and Vannatter as his scapegoats. I replied:

> This is a situation where Mark Fuhrman had applied for a transfer to the Robbery/Homicide Division at the LAPD. The transfer was rejected by the LAPD. And this was just before the murders. He was very upset about that. He was upset when this case was taken away from him on the night of the

murders. Then, after his disgraceful performance during Simpson's criminal trial and his subsequent conviction for perjury, he became desperate.

Consequently, in his effort to seek redemption, he has written a cynical and blaming book with regard to my partners, Tom Lange and Phil Vannatter, who can refute every single one of Fuhrman's false charges, point-by-point.

And I'm amazed that this guy is being given a pass and being rehabilitated, as he is, by people, like Diane Sawyer, Oprah Winfrey, and Larry King.

On Sunday, March 23, the *New York Times Book Review* published a lengthy review of Fuhrman's book, written by Craig Wolff, a professor at Columbia University's Graduate School of Journalism. Instead of reviewing our book in tandem with Fuhrman's, a routine procedure when two conflicting books about the same subject are published simultaneously, the *Times* had earlier run a neutral "Nonfiction in Brief" review of our book.

Along with nearly everyone else in the media, Wolff, without any challenge, accepted Fuhrman's alleged discovery of the "bloody fingerprint"—and accused Lange and Vannatter of missing this evidence. "Thus," Wolff wrote, "the bloody fingerprint . . . was never pursued, and was ultimately lost."

Essentially, Wolff, who knew virtually nothing about this matter and even less about the overall case, felt comfortable blaming Lange and Vannatter for blowing the entire murder investigation. And he did it in, of all places, the powerful *New York Times*.

Considering my history with the *Times*, there was absolutely no way that I was going to allow this to go unchallenged, and I moved ahead with Lange and Vannatter's blessing and support. In my letter to Charles "Chip" McGrath, the new editor of the *New York Times Book Review*, I wrote, in part:

> To reviewer Wolff, the culprit is not Fuhrman. Instead, he blames Lange and Vannatter, two honest detectives with a combined 56 years of spotless service to the LAPD. . . .

> Yet, according to the official report of the LAPD's Latent Print Section, none of the four fingerprint technicians at the Brown-Goldman crime scene, who made seventeen lifts, found a bloody fingerprint on or near the knob area of the rear gate—where Fuhrman claimed to have discovered it. . . .
>
> Also, on page 17 of his book, Fuhrman describes this alleged bloody fingerprint as "identifiable, comparable, and high in quality," and, on page 218, Fuhrman continues, "The print was no doubt Simpson's, and it would have irrefutably connected him to the scene with his own blood, and possibly that of the two victims."
>
> Yet, during his sworn trial testimony in 1995, Fuhrman was nowhere near as sure, simply saying: "I saw a partial, possible fingerprint that was on that knob area."
>
> How did a "partial, possible fingerprint" suddenly become "identifiable, comparable, and high in quality" that "irrefutably" connected Simpson to the crime scene? Didn't Wolff find this clear discrepancy rather odd? Wasn't it, at the very least, worth noting in his review? . . .
>
> The success of Fuhrman's book—as well as his own remarkable rehabilitation with the help of an uncritical media—is a classic victory of style over substance. But his newfound public acceptance—now with the help of the *New York Times Book Review*—has done nothing more than add to the confusion, disinformation, and circus atmosphere revolving around this bizarre murder case.[168]

As I had come to expect, McGrath and the *Times* refused to make any corrections and did not publish my response, allowing Fuhrman's false and misleading record of the case to stand without challenge.

Soon after, the Fuhrman/Regnery book shot to number one on the *New York Times* Best Sellers List, as our book fell off after five weeks, never rising above #5.

Thanks to Diane Sawyer, Oprah Winfrey, Larry King, and the *New York Times Book Review*—as well as Lange and Vannatter's fateful decision not to confront their accuser in person—Fuhrman's remarkable public rehabilitation was now complete.[169]

PART EIGHT:
The road to impeachment

106. From Fuhrman to Foster

In the midst of our ongoing battle with Mark Fuhrman, attorney Ron Goldfarb, one of our two agents for *Evidence Dismissed,* called and told me that the publisher of Fuhrman's book, Alfred S. Regnery of Regnery Publishing, had invited me to lunch. Assuming that Regnery, a life-long conservative Republican whom I had never met, wanted to give me some grief about my damning public statements about Fuhrman, I agreed to the meeting, hoping to give a little back.

Regnery Publishing had earlier released former FBI special agent Gary Aldrich's controversial anti-President Bill Clinton book, *Unlimited Access: An FBI Agent Inside the Clinton White House,* as well as *Boy Clinton: The Political Biography* by R. Emmett Tyrrell, Jr., the editor of the right-wing *American Spectator; God and Man at Yale* by William F. Buckley, the publisher of the *National Review;* and Russell Kirk's *The Conservative Mind;* along with other works by Whittaker Chambers, James J. Kilpatrick, and James Burnham.

On Tuesday, March 25, 1997, at the University Club in Washington, Goldfarb and I met Regnery, who was accompanied by his executive editor, Harry Crocker, and legal counsel, Richard Vigilante.

Looking for a fight, I showed up for this lunch like a guy with a broken beer bottle in his hand. Even before I sat down at the table, I was already going off about Fuhrman, insisting that, if his book was a sworn statement, he would be indicted again for perjury.

In lieu of being goaded into an argument, Regnery—who, properly but politely, told me to shut up and sit down—said firmly, "We're here to talk about Vincent Foster, not Mark Fuhrman. What do you think happened to Vincent Foster?"

"Suicide," I shrugged as I sat down, surprised by the question but remembering the similarities between Foster's suicide and the suicide of Greg Stone six years earlier, in which Stone had shot himself in the mouth with a .38 revolver in a public park.

The former deputy counsel for the Clinton White House, Foster had been found dead on July 20, 1993, at Fort Marcy Park in northern Virginia with a gunshot wound through his head. A .38 revolver was still in his hand when the authorities arrived to document the death scene. After accumulating and analyzing this and other evidence, the FBI and the U.S. Park Police, which had jurisdiction in the case, concluded that the wound was self-inflicted.

Shortly thereafter, a variety of right-wing groups, political figures, citizen-activists, and journalists claimed that the crime-scene evidence indicated that Foster had been murdered, and that a cover up by the Clinton White House was still in progress.

After admitting that I knew very little about the specifics of the Foster case, Regnery replied, "Everyone knows that you have great sources in the law-enforcement community. Why don't you do your own investigation about Foster's death, and write a book about it? We'll publish it."

That left me speechless. Here was a distinguished, politically-conservative publisher, offering a book deal to an unabashed political lefty about the controversial death of a major player in Washington politics.

Simultaneously, though, Regnery owned the rights to the book, *The Secret Life of Bill Clinton*, by right-wing British journalist Ambrose Evans-Pritchard. A third of his manuscript, which Regnery planned to release in the fall, argued that Foster had been murdered. And to complicate matters even more, one of Regnery's closest friends since their younger days together at the Reagan Justice Department was Kenneth Starr, the independent counsel who was reinvestigating the Foster case. Already, press leaks from Starr's office indicated that he would conclude in an upcoming report that Foster had, indeed, committed suicide.

Considering his conflicting interests, I asked Regnery what he thought had happened to Foster. He simply replied, "I don't know, but I'd like to find out. And that's why we're talking to you."

Actually, neither the Evans-Pritchard book nor Regnery's approach to me were the only situations in which Regnery had considered publishing a book about Foster's death.

In October 1996, Regnery had received a pitch from literary agent Lucianne Goldberg on behalf of her client, Linda Tripp, a secretary in Foster's office and one of the last known people see him alive. Tripp had met Goldberg through her friend, Tony Snow, a conservative columnist, who encouraged her to write a book, tentatively entitled, *Behind Closed Doors: What I Saw at the Clinton White House*. Supposedly, Tripp planned to reveal, among other things, untold details about certain events that had preceded Foster's death.

However, after Richard Vigilante, on behalf of Regnery, met with Tripp and Goldberg to discuss the project, he determined that Tripp was not prepared to tell the "full story" about the Clinton White House—which included her knowledge of the President's alleged sexual liaisons with unnamed women. According to Vigilante, she feared that, in the wake of publishing such a book, she might lose her job at the Pentagon, where she had been transferred after Foster's death.

Soon after rejecting Tripp's book, Regnery introduced Mark Fuhrman to Goldberg, who became his agent. Then, Fuhrman, via Goldberg, pitched his own seven-page proposal for a book about the Foster case, *Death in Fort Marcy Park: Who Killed Vince Foster*, which Regnery also rejected.

Thus, the question in my mind was: After shooting down the Tripp and Fuhrman proposals—and with Evans-Pritchard's conspiracy book and his friend Ken Starr's pending anti-conspiracy report in the chute—why did Regnery want me? After all, in addition to being Lange and Vannatter's co-author and Fuhrman's avowed critic, I was a former associate of the left-wing Institute for Policy Studies and the author of a 1986 book that revealed the corruption of Regnery's hero, Ronald Reagan.

Furthermore, although I had never done any reporting about the Clinton Administration, I personally believed that President Clinton and First Lady Hillary Clinton, Foster's former law partner, were extremely intelligent people, who were filled with good intentions and had assembled the agenda and the personnel to deliver on their promises.

Even though I had never contributed any money to, or participated in, any of his campaigns, I had enthusiastically supported Bill Clinton in both 1992 and 1996. Also, in private settings, I had been quite vocal in my criticism of the extreme right of the Republican Party, which was refusing to cut the President any slack.

To all intents and purposes, this project would be unlike any Regnery or I had ever tackled. In effect, I had to gauge whether, through the Foster case, I could be objective about a President I genuinely admired while Regnery had to decide whether he could break with his tradition and publish a potentially positive book about a President he didn't particularly like.

Finally, in the wake of several additional conversations, Regnery and I agreed that the circumstances of Foster's death made for a unique crime story because of the political complications, which, we also agreed, were part of the story. Thus, we determined that the success or failure of this project would depend on our abilities—mine as the author and his as the publisher—to remain open-minded in the midst of the supercharged political atmosphere hovering over this case.

Consequently, we decided that, ultimately, we needed to know whether: a) Foster really committed suicide; b) the official investigators of the Foster case had erred in their crime-scene evaluations and, thus, unintentionally created controversies that should have never existed, as was the situation in the Robert Kennedy murder case; c) the investigators had done their jobs well but had been misrepresented by those with political and/or other ulterior motives, as was the predicament for Lange and Vannatter in the O. J. Simpson case, or d) there was some combination of b and c.

For me, this was a time for objective investigative journalism, not guerrilla writing.

Despite our political differences, I had already grown to like and respect Regnery, as well as his feisty guerrilla approach towards book publishing. Certainly no match made in heaven, we, nonetheless, believed that we could make our deal work. As a result, regardless of the still-unexplained reasons why he had selected me to write this book, Regnery offered me $100,000 for this project—which, he told me, was the largest advance he had ever paid to any author.

Also, it was the largest advance I had ever received.

107. The odd couple

On April 7, 1997, agreeing to accept the assignment, I sent Regnery a memorandum, based upon my preliminary investigation of the Foster case, saying:

> I appreciate the fact that you have come to me with this project without a political agenda. Knowing my background of reporting on crime and murder investigations—as well as my numerous loyal sources in the law-enforcement community—you have asked me to do this project for the sole purpose of getting to the bottom of this matter.

Two weeks later, Regnery and I signed our book contract, and I went to work on the Foster case, as well as on the seemingly endless scandals, real and contrived, revolving around the Clinton White House. Regnery designated Harry Crocker as my editor. Crocker was also the editor for Ambrose Evans-Pritchard's pro-conspiracy book. However, I also liked and respected Crocker, so his relationship with Evans-Pritchard did not concern me.

My deadline was December 31, which was pretty tight, considering all of the research and interviews I had to do.

No doubt, Regnery's friends and colleagues, like mine, were scratching their heads, trying to figure out how this *Odd Couple* arrangement would eventually play out. Some predicted that we would wind up exchanging gunfire or, at the very least, in court.

In addition to all of this, I was now supposedly competing with the newly rehabilitated and now wildly successful Mark Fuhrman who was still trying to sell his own book about the Foster case. Consequently, before I plunged full-time into this project, I was determined to get to the bottom of the history of Fuhrman's relationship with Regnery, believing that therein lay the real reason why Regnery had asked me to write this book.

In mid-June, after executing the contract and receiving $50,000, half of my advance, I took a top staffer at Regnery Publishing to lunch and asked him about the company's relationship with Fuhrman. Going over some familiar territory, the staffer explained that Al Regnery had sought out Fuhrman's book on the O. J. Simpson case. After making his deal with Fuhrman, Regnery breathed new life into the discredited former detective—who had been working in Idaho as an electrician's apprentice—by publishing and heavily promoting his work. In other words, Regnery was principally responsible for turning Fuhrman into a media star, as well as a very wealthy man.

The staffer added that, at the time that Fuhrman sold his Simpson book to Regnery, he had no agent. So, to help him negotiate a deal for his next book, Regnery introduced him to Lucianne Goldberg after Linda Tripp's book had been rejected.

All of this, I already knew.

But then, the Regnery staffer continued, Fuhrman's standard author's contract for the Simpson book contained a common, boilerplate clause, which required him to give Regnery the first right of refusal for his next project. Thus, when Regnery rejected Fuhrman's seven-page book proposal about Vincent Foster, Fuhrman and Goldberg argued that he had fulfilled his obligation to Regnery and was now free to sell his work to a bigger, more mainstream publisher in New York.

Consequently—to the chagrin of Al Regnery, who had been completely supportive of Fuhrman and sincerely wanted to publish his future works—Fuhrman abandoned Regnery Publishing, as Goldberg made plans to sell his newly updated and completely rewritten, twenty-seven-page proposal about the Foster case to one of the New York publishing houses.

Arguably, Regnery should have been permitted to exercise his option on the basis of Fuhrman's latest and more detailed proposal. But Regnery probably would have been forced to litigate if he wanted to press the issue. And, in the end, he chose not to.

Suddenly, after my lunch with the staffer, I began to view Regnery's selection of me as the author of the Foster book, at least in part, as a blatant act of disrespect towards, perhaps even revenge against Fuhrman, whom Regnery had supposedly come to view as disloyal and greedy.

Of course, considering my ongoing disdain for Fuhrman, I had no problem with any of this. As far as I was concerned, I had a legitimate deal to write an important book. And I believed that, regardless of Regnery's motives, he had picked the right guy for the job.

Still, the subsequent media coverage about the publishing dispute between Fuhrman and me appeared to confirm my suspicions about the reasons behind my selection.

On June 19, Internet gossip columnist Matt Drudge published a story on his popular website, the *Drudge Report*, "OJ's Fuhrman to do book on Vince Foster!" He reported: "Fuhrman is due in New York next week to visit publishers to convince them to take a closer look at his second book than they did at his first."

At the time, I simply assumed that Fuhrman's agent, Lucianne Goldberg—whom I had once met at a 1981 book party for her then-client, author Kitty Kelley—had given the story to Drudge. After all, Goldberg was just trying to get the best deal she could for her client.

Six days later, reporter Mike Shain of the *New York Post* wrote an article, "Foster death book duel," saying:

> O. J. detective Mark Fuhrman suddenly has competition in his search for the "killer" of Vince Foster.
>
> Veteran mob reporter Dan Moldea, who has written a detailed and scathing attack on Fuhrman's portrayal of the Simpson case, has been hired to do a rival investigation into the death of President Clinton's former aide and friend.
>
> "I don't consider Fuhrman competition," Moldea told the *Post* yesterday. "I've investigated more homicides than he has." . . .
>
> So who hired Moldea to go up against Fuhrman? Regnery Publishing, publisher of Fuhrman's No. 1 best-seller, *Murder in Brentwood*.
>
> Publisher Alfred Regnery says he approached Moldea to write a Foster book two months ago after turning down Fuhrman's book proposal. . . .

"They deliberately sought out a man who has attacked Fuhrman", says Lucianne Goldberg, Fuhrman's literary agent. "This is high school stuff."[170]

But, the following month, in its July 7 issue, *Publishers Weekly* columnist Judy Quinn wrote a story, "Fuhrman Withdraws Vince Foster Proposal," which detailed Fuhrman's surrender. Quinn stated:

> Regnery told *PW* he had been thinking about doing a book on the Foster case for some time, but felt that Fuhrman lacked the political-insider access needed to write it, so he rejected the proposal. Regnery didn't negotiate the deal with Moldea's agent, Ron Goldfarb, however, until after Fuhrman had submitted his proposal. . . . [Regnery] said he would still like to publish another book by Fuhrman, a suggestion Goldberg scoffed at.[171]

Frankly, I was disappointed that Fuhrman's book had not sold, because I really wanted to go head-to-head with him without my two good friends, Tom Lange and Phil Vannatter, getting in the way with their insistence on being dignified with this guy.

Interestingly, a year later—in the midst of the Monica Lewinsky scandal, in which President Clinton had allegedly lied about sex—Goldberg appeared on *Larry King Live* and was asked, "What do you say, Lucianne, to those who say, 'It's about sex, who cares?'"

Conveniently forgetting that her client, Mark Fuhrman, was still on probation for his 1996 perjury conviction, Goldberg replied, "Well, I'm getting a little tired of that one, too. . . . This is [about] swearing falsely, which is, to me, the worst crime in the world."[172]

108. Help from an unexpected source

Reed Irvine—the overlord of the right-wing watchdog group, Accuracy in Media (AIM)—had probably spent more time than anyone investigating the alleged dark side of the Foster case. In fact, Irvine was among those who believed—or claimed to believe—that Foster had been murdered.

After agreeing to write the Foster book, I made an appointment with Irvine to discuss the case. He was extremely cordial and wanted to help me—especially after hearing that I was under contract with Regnery, his publishing soulmate.

During our meeting about Foster, Irvine pulled a couple of files out of large box, filled with thousands of pages of documents.

"What's that?" I asked Irvine, pointing at the box.

"Believe it or not," he replied, "this is where we keep our files on the Foster case."

Irvine then invited me to come back the following day to look through the box.

The next day, I returned to Irvine's office, but he had not yet arrived. I went to his secretary who remembered me from the day before. When I asked her for the box Irvine had shown me, she led me to it and offered to seat me in a room where I could go through the files. She even offered to photocopy a file or two.

I hoisted the box on my left shoulder and followed her into a small room. I sat on the couch, placing the box on a small table in front of me. The secretary smiled and left me alone.

As I leafed through the files, I discovered not only public documents but correspondences between and among Irvine and others in the right-wing community who were involved in their own Foster investigations, as well as a stack of transcripts of taped conversations Irvine had recorded with several journalists, including Arthur Sulzberger of the *New York Times* and *Sixty Minutes* correspondent Mike Wallace.

This, I immediately knew, was another gold mine.

A few minutes later, when Irvine's secretary returned to check on me, she asked if I wanted her to photocopy anything. I laughed and said, "I want the whole box and everything in it. In fact, I'll go to Kinko's right now and Xerox everything myself. I can get it all back to you tomorrow. Is that okay?"

She thought for a moment and simply replied, "Yes, I think that'll be all right. Just . . ."

Before she even finished speaking, I had the box back on my shoulder and was on a dead sprint for the exit. Seeing Irvine, who had just entered his office, I quickly shook hands with him and then told him that his secretary had given me permission to take and photocopy the entire box of documents, as long as I returned them the following day.

Irvine smiled and nodded, adding that he hoped they would be useful.

That day, I spent nearly four hours copying Reed Irvine's personal files about Vincent Foster and his death. Then, after returning the box of documents to Irvine's office, I organized these and other files, logging each onto a database I had created on my computer.

Reading through only a handful of these records, I quickly realized that Irvine and others in the "Foster-was-murdered" crowd were basing their entire case on a series of alleged police mistakes and omissions.

"Now," I thought, "they're in my territory."

The U.S. Park Police had retained jurisdiction in the Foster case and handled the crime-scene investigation. That was my next stop.

But, at first, no one wanted to talk.

The Park Police had been hammered by everyone from right-wing congressmen and senators to a variety of conspiracy theorists, like Reed Irvine, who were trying to prove that Foster had been murdered. In short, the Foster case had brought this small but respected law-enforcement agency nothing but trouble.

But through a local police source and friend, I was introduced to and interviewed Kevin Fornshill of the U.S. Park Police. He was the police officer who had received permission to leave his security post at the CIA on July 20, 1993, and to respond to a dead-body call at Fort Marcy Park, just off the George Washington Parkway in northern Virginia.

Fornshill, who had found Foster's body in a hidden grove, personally gave me a tour of the area, which I videotaped, as well as a detailed account of what he saw and did.

After that, I was introduced to and interviewed the three USPP investigators at the crime scene—Cheryl Braun, John Rolla, and Renee Abt. I also had meetings with Pete Simonello, the criminalist assigned to the case, as well as Sergeant Pete Markland, who took over the case as its lead detective, and Captain Charles Hume, who headed the overall investigation.

Over the next few months, I interviewed every Park Police officer and official who had played any role in this case, including Robert Langston, the USPP chief. Through all of the official and unofficial investigations of Foster's death, no one else could make that claim.

Early during my research—after, among other things, conducting my interviews and reviewing all of the investigative reports in the case, as well as the photographs taken at the crime scene and during the autopsy—I found the evidence to be overwhelming: Foster had, indeed, committed suicide. It was a no-brainer.

I quickly realized that, after writing four conspiracy books, I was about to publish my third book in a row, telling the American people what they already knew. First, Sirhan acted alone. Then, O.J. acted alone. And, now, Foster acted alone.

My close friend, journalist Jeff Stein, had already begun to describe these three books as my "never-mind series."

On December 16, I had dinner with Al Regnery at the University Club. In the midst of our conversation, I pulled a computer disk from my suit jacket and handed it to my publisher. Attached was my cover letter, which read:

> [T]he purpose of showing you this draft [of my manuscript] is two-fold: one, to give you a heads-up about the book and its contents; and, two, to give us a little time to resolve any potential editorial and/or political problems that this manuscript might cause. Specifically, I don't want either one of us to be blindsided by anything after the others have seen it; i.e. I know how loyal Harry Crocker, whom I also respect and admire, is to Ambrose Evans-Pritchard.
>
> As you will see, this book is a dramatic contrast to those by Evans-Pritchard and Christopher Ruddy.

Actually, Ruddy, a former reporter for the *New York Post*, had done well with his book, greatly helped by a surprisingly favorable review in the *New York Times Book Review*, which praised his questionable research and legitimized his dubious conclusions about Foster's death that cast suspicion on the President and Hillary Clinton.[173] The *Times* had assigned Richard Brookhiser, a senior editor at William Buckley's conservative publication, *National Review*, to write the review. Brookhiser concluded:

> You don't have to believe in murder in high places to be unhappy with the way the Foster case has been handled.... [S]o many loose ends suggest that the initial Park Police investigation was sloppy and that all subsequent ones—which essentially began by accepting its conclusions—have been lazy. Zealous colleagues may have rifled Foster office; why not his body?[174]

PART EIGHT: THE ROAD TO IMPEACHMENT

On December 22—nine days before my deadline—Regnery called me and said that he liked the manuscript very much and did not suggest any changes other than routine editing.

109. The Foster crime scene

On December 31, 1997, I submitted my completed manuscript to my editor, Harry Crocker. While I was in his office, making my delivery on deadline, Crocker asked if I was willing to summarize the conclusions in my book for Regnery's staff. When I agreed, he went from office to office, inviting several people into the conference room.

Quickly pulling together some notes, I opened with my version of the circumstances of Foster's death, which served as the basis for the first chapter of my manuscript.

Leaving the White House at a little after 1:00 P.M. on July 20, 1993, Foster drove his 1989 gray Honda Accord to Fort Marcy Park. He parked his car next to a trail that led to a large open grove.

Taking off his blue pin-striped suit coat and tie, he placed them on the front passenger seat of his car, along with his White House pass and his wallet, which contained, among other things, a list of three local psychiatrists.

After loosening the top button of his white shirt, Foster opened the glove compartment and reached for an oven mitt in which he had concealed an antique, black-colored .38-Colt revolver. Inside the cylinder were two live rounds of round-nose lead ammunition.

He placed the gun in his left-front pocket, unknowingly transferring a portion of a sunflower-seed husk from the oven mitt. Leaving his car unlocked and the oven mitt in the glove compartment, Foster walked through the park, passing a Civil War cannon in a large grove, and into a smaller grove nearly 250 yards from his car. Upon entering this heavily-wooded area, he saw a second cannon.

He switched off his White House pager, sat in front of the cannon's barrel, and removed the gun from his left pocket. Bracketed by dense foliage, he was facing downhill.

— 391 —

He cocked the hammer of the revolver. Placing his right thumb on the trigger and steadying the weapon with his left hand, he put the gun in his mouth and fired a single shot.

The bullet perforated his brain and crashed out the back of his skull, killing him instantly. The backlash caused his eyeglasses to fall from his face and tumble down the hill. His hands fell limply downhill at his sides with the gun still in his right hand—his thumb trapped in the trigger guard. A stream of blood trickled from his mouth and nose, soaking the right shoulder of his shirt.

More blood from a small exit wound in the back of his head flowed down the hill and soaked the ground beneath him, as well as the back of his shirt.

Plain and simple, Foster, who left no suicide note, had taken his own life. But no one had seen him do it, and no one had heard the shot. In fact, no known person had even seen him alive in the park.

A mystery man in a white van, who had stopped in the park to urinate in the woods, stumbled upon the body at about 6:00 P.M. Quickly leaving the area, the mystery man—who was later identified—went to a nearby maintenance station for the National Park Service and told an employee what he had found, asking him to call the police. Then, the mystery man vanished into the rush-hour traffic.

The park-service employee dutifully called the local rescue squad and then the U.S. Park Police, which had jurisdiction. Within minutes, two rescue teams and a lone Park Police officer, who had been stationed nearby, arrived at the scene. The officer, Kevin Fornshill, joined two of the rescue workers in their frantic search for the reported dead body, splitting off from them in the main grove and finding his way into a shady grove. There, Fornshill located the unidentified body and called for the paramedics.

Within minutes, police investigators arrived at the crime scene and began a routine investigation, which found no evidence of a struggle and no reason to believe that Foster, who was identified after a search of his car, had been murdered.

However, during that probe, some police mistakes were made. Evidence was left unchecked, and questions remained unanswered.

Also, in the midst of the Park Police probe, the White House Counsel's Office, which did not order Foster's office sealed until the day after his death, initially stalled police investigators, preventing them from conducting interviews and searching the office. When the police were finally permitted to speak with four of the last known White House staffers to have seen Foster alive, the interviews were monitored and, in one case, disrupted by members of the Counsel's Office.

Earlier, the police had agreed to the Counsel's Office request to allow attorneys from the Department of Justice to serve as intermediaries during a review of the documents in Foster's office. As the police understood the arrangement: If the White House declared a privilege on a particular document and did not want to show it to the police, then the attorneys from Justice would view the material and decide on the merits of the claim.

But, instead, White House Counsel Bernard Nussbaum—aggressively protecting the rights of his client—conducted the search unilaterally two days after Foster's death, refusing to allow either the Park Police or the attorneys from the Justice Department to participate in the search or to see any documents. Consequently, the police investigators and the Justice Department lawyers suspected that the White House was hiding something.

Immediately, the media went into its predictable frenzy. They detailed the close friendship that Foster had enjoyed with the President and especially the First Lady—with whom Foster, her one-time law partner, was rumored to have had an affair.

Although there was little initial speculation that any foul play had occurred, journalists quickly discovered that Foster had been involved in a handful of controversies, including a recent mini-scandal involving the White House Travel Office. As a result of this and other problems, the *Wall Street Journal* had written several editorials critical of Foster prior to his death.

During the week after Foster's suicide, the White House continued to maintain that he had not been depressed. But, after an attorney in the Counsel's Office discovered a torn-up note—that bitterly derided enemies of the President, as well as the "sport" of personal destruction in official Washington—the White House's position changed.

Suddenly, Foster's family and colleagues began to reveal details of the growing depression that had led to his suicide. His sister had given him the list of three psychiatrists found in his wallet, urging him to make an appointment with one of them. Her husband had given Foster a list of six attorneys in case he faced a legal battle over the Travel Office matter. Later, Foster's wife told police investigators that her husband—the day before his death—had contacted their family doctor who prescribed a mild anti-depressant.

The torn-up note was kept from police investigators for nearly thirty hours. It had been found in Foster's briefcase, which had been supposedly emptied by Nussbaum during the search of Foster's office several days earlier. The U.S. Capitol Police eventually confirmed that the note was in Foster's handwriting.

Although the note contained no fingerprints, the Park Police, in concert with the Department of Justice and the FBI, concluded that Foster had written it just before he committed suicide—although it was not considered to be an actual suicide note.

110. Creating a political firestorm

During my briefing at Regnery, I told Crocker and the other staffers that the circumstances of Foster's death were only part of my story, and I continued with my findings.

The New York Times, in the midst of the 1992 campaign, had touted a series of questionable stories about the Whitewater real-estate project in Arkansas, sourced, in part, to Bill Clinton's most partisan and vicious enemies in Arkansas. However, the *Times*, which broke the Whitewater story just prior to the 1992 Super Tuesday primaries, refused to relent or correct its mistakes, despite clear evidence that conflicted with their news accounts. Regardless of its errors, the newspaper continued to suggest that this land deal provided a watershed of data indicative of Clinton's corruption and lack of character.

Nevertheless, Clinton won Super Tuesday and became the Democratic front-runner.

By the time of Clinton's election victory over Republican President George H. W. Bush and Reform Party candidate Ross Perot the following November, Whitewater had come to nothing. Refusing to admit it, the *New York Times* had been embarrassed by its own reporting, which, according to many experts, had been sloppy and unprofessional.[175]

Consequently, as Clinton took the oath of office in January 1993, the conservative Clinton-haters and heat-seeking media muckrakers were forced to regroup and refocus their attack. It was clear from the outset that Clinton would be held to standards of behavior that had never been applied to any other President while his enemies seemed prepared to blame him for anything and everything.

Yet, Clinton had already established a record of frustrating his political foes because of their own inability to ask the right questions. Consequently—whether the issue was the President's personal sex life, the draft, or smoking marijuana—the Clinton haters always tried to place him in a perpetual no-win situation, accusing him of not telling the full truth in response to their imprecise questions, earmarked for Clinton to self-destruct when he tried to answer them.

But, simply speaking, Clinton refused to commit political suicide and mostly remained technically truthful when confronted with personal questions, which always infuriated his political detractors.

Frankly, after *Moldea v. New York Times*, I could attest that media lawyers routinely did the same thing, twisting and torturing the English language in order to allow their clients' to evade responsibility for their mistakes.

Even though the press did not give the Clinton Administration the traditional honeymoon enjoyed by most new administrations, the only reporting that actually drew some blood resulted from the questionable firings of seven employees in the White House Travel Office during the spring of 1993. But, because the Democrats controlled both houses of Congress, no one anticipated any formal investigation.

Then, after Vincent Foster's suicide in late-July 1993, interest in the already-discredited Whitewater case was renewed by journalists who believed that more reporting needed to be done.

Even though Foster's role in Whitewater was minor, the implications from the news stories led to editorials, essays, and opinion pieces—particularly in the *Wall Street Journal*, as well as the *New York Times* and the *Washington Times*—openly suggesting a White House cover up. Speculation ran rampant that a truly depressed Foster might have killed himself in order to avoid prosecution or to protect some dark secret about the Clintons revolving around Whitewater.

During my investigation, I discovered that immediately after the Foster case was closed by the Park Police and the FBI, reporters had alleged—based on several erroneous statements by Major Robert Hines, a top official in the Park Police—that Whitewater documents had been removed from Foster's office after an official search.

In reality, the four Park Police officers who had actually seen these documents admitted to me that, at the time of Foster's suicide, they didn't even know what Whitewater was. One laughed, "We couldn't have made a distinction between Whitewater land records and whitewater rafting records."

According to my investigation, Hines had based his false statements on nothing more than bad rumors, which he then made worse by stating them as facts to the media. Hines's role in this investigation was not insignificant because his comments to the press wound up giving Whitewater a new life.

Consequently, even though no wrongdoing had been shown, the Washington press corps demanded that the White House, which had made several missteps of its own, release the missing Whitewater documents from Foster's office.

These errors and misrepresentations by the media brought the then-Republican minority in Congress to life as they began demanding the appointment of an independent counsel to investigate Whitewater.

Even though the grounds for this action were dubious at best, Attorney General Janet Reno bowed to these demands in January 1994 and appointed attorney Robert Fiske, a respected Republican and a former U.S. Attorney in Manhattan, to probe Whitewater and Foster's death.

After a six-month investigation and the release of his interim report, Fiske, in cooperation with the FBI, was able to explain most of the controversies in the Foster case—including those surrounding the mystery man in the white van, who was identified—and corroborated the conclusion by the Park Police and the FBI that Foster had committed suicide.

Fiske declared that Foster had been depressed over his role in the Travel Office scandal, as well as the bad press he had received, especially on the rabidly anti-Clinton editorial page of the *Wall Street Journal*.

To no one's surprise, disappointed right-wing extremists loudly criticized the work of Bob Fiske, their fellow Republican. Senator Lauch Faircloth (R-North Carolina) and Congressman Dan Burton (R-Indiana) angrily demanded Fiske's immediate dismissal. Faircloth was Fiske's most vocal critic during the U.S. Senate Banking Committee's oversight hearings in July that scrutinized the independent counsel's interim report.

As Fiske continued to investigate the White House's handling of the files found in Foster's office, President Clinton signed a new Independent Counsel Act into law. However, the procedure called for the appointment of independent counsels, not by the Attorney General but, by a panel of three appellate judges, who were appointed by the Chief Justice of the U.S. Supreme Court—just as the act had originally been written in 1978.

In a surprise move on August 5, 1994, the three-judge panel replaced Fiske with Kenneth Starr, who, by the way, was the author of *The World Amicus* in *Moldea v. New York Times*.

The following week, President Clinton appointed Abner Mikva—who was one of the three appellate judges and the original lone dissenter in my case—as his new White House counsel.

PART EIGHT: THE ROAD TO IMPEACHMENT

During my presentation to the Regnery editorial board, someone asked, "So how did the Foster-was-murdered conspiracy theories get started?"

"Just like the Robert Kennedy murder case," I replied, "police errors had served as fodder for the people who were looking for a conspiracy."

Embracing other erroneous statements by Major Hines, a cabal of right-wing groups and individuals—financed by notorious Clinton-hater Richard Scaife, the heir to the Mellon banking fortune—tried to make the argument that Foster had been murdered, even after Hines had forthrightly retracted and corrected his remarks.

Never accused of allowing the facts to interfere with a good conspiracy theory, many in the Scaife crowd still used Hines's false information as a means to undermine the authority of the Clinton White House.

Scaife, who employed former *New York Post* reporter Christopher Ruddy at his wholly-owned *Pittsburgh Tribune Review*, also helped to fund, among other anti-Clinton activists, Reed Irvine's Accuracy in Media, Joseph Farah's Western Journalism Center, *Strategic Investment* publisher Jim Davidson's National Taxpayers Union, Emmett Tyrrell's *American Spectator*, Barbara Ledeen's Independent Women's Forum, attorney Larry Klayman's Judicial Watch, and attorney Mark Levin's Landmark Legal Foundation.

And, from the evidence I had obtained from Reed Irvine's personal files, I could prove that some of these groups and individuals had not only received their funding from the same source, but that they also shared information, covered up each other's mistakes, and were punished by Scaife if they strayed from the cause.[176]

Upon discovering all of this during my research, which was aided by Irvine's own files, I realized what President Clinton and his wife had been up against since his first inauguration in 1993. As I wrote in my book about Foster's suicide: "[T]he forces against the Clinton Administration are, as they have been all along, formidable, well financed, and out for blood—just as others were against President Nixon, who resigned while facing impeachment."

111. Regnery's pro-Clinton book

When I completed my presentation to Regnery's people, I looked around the conference room and saw the disappointment, even anger, on everyone's faces. Almost without exception, the members of the editorial staff of Regnery Publishing were unabashed Clinton critics, and they were not at all thrilled about my conclusions. However, my editor, Harry Crocker, speaking for everyone, said that they wanted to hold their fire until they had actually read the manuscript.

A few days later, after they digested what I had written, the situation only became worse.

Battlelines drawn, several major fights broke out during the editing process, especially when someone unilaterally attempted to delete materials critical of Regnery's political allies and even placed what appeared to be false material into my manuscript. For instance, in one location in the galleys, that unknown person had altered an accurate reference to the *Fiske Report* and intentionally changed it to the *Starr Report*, which, left undiscovered, would have been extremely embarrassing. Also, I found properly spelled names in the manuscript suddenly misspelled in the galleys.

After I caught these and numerous other unauthorized changes, which I viewed as nothing less than intentional mistakes—all of which I documented—I went to Al Regnery and Harry Crocker and presented my evidence. Without hesitation, both men, clearly shocked by what was going on, came to my defense and guaranteed that the book would be published as I had written it. Like it or not, after a slew of anti-Clinton books, Regnery was about to publish a pro-Clinton book and, in the process, further expose the right-wing conspiracy against the White House.

Ironically, the outside counsel and vetting attorney for Regnery Publishing was Bruce Sanford of Baker & Hostetler, our nemesis during *Moldea v. New York Times*. Unfortunately, for reasons unknown, my anticipated vetting session with Sanford never occurred. Frankly, for all of the obvious reasons, I wanted that moment with Sanford to demonstrate how well I supported my work.

Meantime, in the March 14, 1998, edition of the *National Journal*, reporter Louis Jacobson published an article about Regnery Publishing. In a sidebar to the main story, "Dan Moldea Battles for His Book," Jacobson wrote:

> Regnery Publishing Inc. has put itself into something of a box by commissioning . . . a book written by investigative reporter Dan Moldea and scheduled for release in April.
>
> . . .
>
> Publisher Alfred S. Regnery said the company intends to publish Moldea's book. "What we told him to do is find out what

he can, and then go write it," Regnery said, adding that Moldea accomplished what he had set out to do.

Also, *Capital Style* contained another article about my upcoming book. The story, written by a friend of mine, Bill Thomas, and appropriately titled, "Dead on Arrival", stated:

> Unfortunately for Regnery, the facts surrounding Foster's death led not to a White House murder plot, but to a right-wing plot to portray it that way. . . .
>
> Al Regnery insists he's not disappointed with what Moldea produced. "It's a good investigative report done by a good, honest writer," he says, adding that he plans to promote the book on talk radio and TV.
>
> Moldea, however, is so worried that the book will be buried that he's considering hiring his own publicist.
>
> Nevertheless, he says he remains on good terms with Regnery and his executive editor Harry Crocker.[177]

In late April, my book, *A Washington Tragedy: How the Death of Vincent Foster Ignited a Political Firestorm*, was released. However, Regnery and his staff lacked any enthusiasm for promoting this pro-Clinton book. And just to drive that point home, my publishing company hired a former aide to right-wing presidential candidate Pat Buchanan, who believed that Foster had been murdered, as my publicist.

In the end, he only booked me for a religious show on a little radio station in Alabama, two other small-town right-wing radio programs, and another little-known conservative radio show in Washington State. Everything else, including several television appearances, I arranged through my own friends and colleagues.

In addition, most of those on my media list didn't even receive their review copies of my book. Yet, the few reviews that did appear in mainstream publications were quite good—although the *New York Times* did not review it, leaving its favorable review of Christopher Ruddy's pro-conspiracy work to stand unchallenged.

The Washington Post Book World, with which I previously had two bitter battles over bogus reviews, featured one on my Foster work by well-known investigative journalist Robert Sherrill—who described the book as "a smart, chronological appraisal [in which] Moldea identifies . . . 'a coalition of right-wing special-interest groups, as well as a handful of politically conservative journalists,' all subsidized by Richard Scaife, heir to the Mellon banking fortune."

Sherrill added:

> Although Moldea, a crime reporter of considerable repute and experience, uses his own investigations to clear up some of the troublesome questions about Foster's death, for the most part he is simply a neutral narrator, a levelheaded guide through the five years of sleuthing by others. His pages of notes at the end, by the way, are essential reading.[178]

Also, Steve Weinberg, a widely respected journalist's journalist, stated in the *Legal Times* that my book was "superbly reported . . . published during an era in which shoddily documented conspiracy theories tracts gain wide audiences." And then Weinberg added:

> The book opens like this: "Vincent Foster committed suicide, and he acted alone." If Regnery wanted to sell a lot of copies of Moldea's book, that sentence must have set off alarms. . . Readers who want to reward responsible rather than sensational reporting ought to buy Moldea's books.[179]

Of course, the Scaife crowd, particularly the Western Journalism Center and Accuracy in Media, went ballistic and then for my throat. Joseph Farah, a long-time recipient of Scaife's money and one of the targets in my book, published a review on his *WorldNetDaily* website in which his subtitle gave the flavor of his critique: "Moldea's dishonest, deceitful con job on Foster case."[180]

Reed Irvine, another Scaife beneficiary who had unwittingly provided so much of my ammunition against the President's enemies, lamented bitterly: "Regnery, a conservative house, had been conned into publishing Moldea's whitewash of the Foster investigations, and we had been conned into helping him."[181]

Actually, Al Regnery, who couldn't have been more of a gentleman through all of this, had earlier tried to bring me into the right-wing fold. The previous fall, I was his guest at the 30th anniversary dinner of the conservative *American Spectator*—where I sat between Regnery and *Human Events* editor Terry Jeffrey and was introduced to such right-wing superstars as Emmitt Tyrrell, Robert Bork, Ted Olson, Rush Limbaugh, Gordon Liddy, Terry Eastland, and David Brock.

And then, dressed in black tie, I attended the gala 50th anniversary celebration of Regnery Publishing at the Omni-Carlton Hotel in downtown Washington on April 15—which wound up as a pep rally against the Clinton White House. At this event—even though I was now viewed as a fox in a chicken house—I met other established and budding conservative icons, such as author William F. Buckley and political commentator Robert Novak, as well as John Fund of the *Wall Street Journal's* editorial page and Ann Coulter, a new fire-breathing right-wing pundit.

After all, this was Washington—a mecca for ex-student body presidents, of which I was one—where people could fight during the day and have dinner together at night and where political enemies could not only be friendly, but actually be friends. . . .

But that's not quite what happened in my case.

112. The Lewinsky scandal

In or about October 1996, the same month that Linda Tripp, Vincent Foster's former secretary, had tried to pitch her book about the Clinton White House to Regnery Publishing—via her agent, Lucianne Goldberg—Kenneth Starr, Al Regnery's close friend, secretly launched an investigation of President Clinton's sex life.

Tony Kornheiser, a columnist for the *Washington Post*, the newspaper that revealed Starr's sex investigation, summed up the consensus about the independent counsel's latest line of inquiry: "I thought Whitewater was about banking, not boinking. . . . Starr's tactics are so cheesy that next to him, Clinton looks like Gandhi."[182]

Finding no criminal behavior in Clinton's sex life, Starr ended this probe in February 1997—the same month that he announced that he was leaving the Office of the Independent Counsel (OIC) and accepting a top position at Pepperdine University in Malibu.

Immediately, Republicans criticized Starr for quitting before finishing what he had started. Democrats complained that the Pepperdine assignment had been made possible by a grant from Richard Scaife.

But, after the smoke cleared, Starr reversed his decision and remained as independent counsel, even though he was coming up with nothing in his efforts to indict either Bill or Hillary Clinton in the OIC's Whitewater, Travel Office, and Filegate investigations.

Meantime, while writing my manuscript about Foster's suicide, I had developed sources within the OIC. I hoped to get a heads up about an anticipated report about Foster and Whitewater, which would be released *after* the publication of my book. In pursuit of this information, I had on-the-record interviews over the phone with Starr's two top deputies, Hickman Ewing and Jackie Bennett, both respected federal prosecutors.

Neither Ewing nor Bennett ever provided me with any inside information about the OIC's specific investigations. However, they both gave me procedures for obtaining information. And Bennett kindly introduced me to another OIC attorney who could provide me with "substantive information."

On January 19, 1998, I had lunch with that attorney at the Old Ebbitt Grill near the White House. Our interview was off the record. I promised not to identify him.

During our conversation, I noted in passing that there was nothing to the rumors of the widely suspected affair between Foster and Hillary Clinton, his close friend and former law partner.

"I can't comment on that," the prosecutor replied.

Surprised by what he had just said, I responded, "I didn't ask you a question."

He continued, "I would be violating a statutory responsibility if I said something about that."

I repeated, "But I didn't ask you a question. What are you telling me here?"

He responded, "Let's just say that it's in play."

I walked away from that interview, believing that the OIC was actively investigating the alleged one-time affair between the First Lady and Foster, which apparently some members of the OIC team believed to be true.

But that issue quickly became by the way.

Two days later, on January 21, the *Washington Post* shocked the world by publishing allegations of an affair between President Clinton and Monica Lewinsky, a former White House intern. And now, the *Post* continued, Kenneth Starr and the OIC were actively investigating this relationship, as well as allegations that the President had lied about this

PART EIGHT: THE ROAD TO IMPEACHMENT

liaison during his deposition just four days earlier in the Paula Jones sexual-harassment civil suit.

Later, on the same day as the President's January 17 sworn statement, Matt Drudge had published a bare-bones version of the Clinton-Lewinsky story on his Internet website—after *Newsweek*, which had been leading the mainstream media's Clinton sex patrol, held off publishing its own article at the request of the OIC.

The source for these allegations was Linda Tripp. Since leaving the Clinton White House in August 1994, Tripp had worked in the Pentagon's press office where Lewinsky had been reassigned in April 1996. The two women became friends, and Lewinsky told Tripp of her relationship with the President.

In early-October 1997, Lucianne Goldberg, the literary agent for Tripp who later leaked the initial story to Matt Drudge, convinced Tripp to tape record Lewinsky discussing her relationship with the President. The tapes, according to press reports, were supposedly devastating.

Later, after Tripp had memorialized her conversations with Lewinsky, Goldberg privately called Al Regnery and asked him for his advice as to how use the evidentiary dynamite Tripp had in her possession. Regnery placed Goldberg and Tripp on a course of action that would lead them to Kenneth Starr—who then went with the only real investigation he had left . . . that the President had lied about sex.

Even though I was in fairly regular contact with Regnery during this period, he did not violate Goldberg's trust. I knew nothing about any of this while I was writing my book about Foster. However, I did manage to add a final endnote to my book just before it went to the printer, summarizing the evidence in the Lewinsky case.

In the first paragraph of that endnote, I wrote:

> As this book was going to press, President Clinton was in the midst of the greatest crisis of his presidency, battling for his political survival in the wake of revelations of his alleged affair with Monica Lewinsky. . . .
>
> In the midst of an unprecedented media assault, as well as calls for his resignation or impeachment, the President denied both the alleged affair and any efforts to silence Lewinsky.

In effect, I argued, the suicide of Vincent Foster had become the epicenter of President Clinton's political problems, insisting:

Foster's death beget a series of false statements from a top law-enforcement official about Whitewater, which beget the renewed bad journalism about Whitewater, which beget the entry of the President's most vicious enemies into the Whitewater frenzy, which beget the appointment of Robert Fiske as the independent counsel, which beget Fiske's interim report absolving the President from any criminal behavior during Whitewater, which beget an investigation of Fiske's work by the Senate Banking Committee (and later the Senate's Special Committee on Whitewater, as well as an assortment of U.S. House committee investigations), which beget the firing of Fiske, which beget the appointment of Kenneth Starr, which beget Starr's failure to find evidence of criminal intent during the Whitewater matter by the President, which beget a desperate effort by Starr to get the President on anything, which beget a national soap opera that now threatened to destroy the Clinton Presidency.

On January 27, First Lady Hillary Clinton appeared on NBC's *Today Show*, telling interviewer Matt Lauer:

> So having seen so many of these accusations come and go, having seen people profit, you know, like Jerry Falwell with videos accusing my husband of murder, of drug-running, seeing some of the things that are written and said about him, my attitude is, you know, we've been there before. We have seen this before. . . .
>
> It's just a very unfortunate turn of events that we are using the criminal justice system to try to achieve political ends in this country.
>
> And, you know, when I'm here today, I'm not only here because I love and believe my husband. I'm also here because I love and believe in my country. And if I were just a citizen out there, maybe because I know about the law and I have some idea of some of the motivations here, I would be very disturbed by this turn of events. . . .

PART EIGHT: THE ROAD TO IMPEACHMENT

I do believe that this is a battle. I mean, look at the very people who are involved in this. They have popped up in other settings.

The great story here for anybody willing to find it and write about it and explain it, is this vast right-wing conspiracy that has been conspiring against my husband since the day he announced for President. A few journalists have kind of caught on to it and explained it, but it has not yet been fully revealed to the American public. And actually, you know, in a bizarre sort of way, this may do it. [Emphasis added.]

When I heard her say that, I startled my sleeping dog, Noodles, by yelling at the television set, "Lady, I have just written that story!"

At that moment, instead of still hoping that Regnery would accept my book so that I could get the second half of my $100,000 advance, I now wanted them to reject my book—so that I could sell it to a mainstream publisher in New York who could appreciate what I had just done and would actually try to promote it.

113. The OIC leaks

Immediately after the *Washington Post's* earth-shaking story about the President's relationship with Monica Lewinsky ran on January 21, 1998, additional details of Kenneth Starr's secret investigation of the President's private life began appearing on the front pages of America's newspapers and on television news programs.

In response, the President's attorneys, led by David Kendall of Williams & Connolly, filed a complaint with U.S. District Judge Norma Holloway Johnson, the presiding judge in the OIC's grand-jury investigation, on February 6, charging Starr and the OIC with leaking nonpublic information to reporters—possibly in violation of federal law. However, Starr insisted that neither he nor any member of his staff had ever provided journalists with any improper materials.

Two days later, I spoke to my attorney and trusted friend, Roger Simmons, about these conflicting statements. I told Simmons, who had earlier debated Starr about *Moldea v. New York Times* on Court TV, that—based upon my on-the-record discussions with Starr's two chief deputies, Hickman Ewing and Jackie Bennett—I believed that Kendall's charges were essentially accurate, and that the OIC had been systematically leaking information damaging to President Clinton to a small stable of reporters.

Certainly, neither Ewing nor Bennett had ever given me any forbidden materials. However, they both explained to me the process by which the OIC did provide information to certain journalists.

In the wake of Kendall's charges, Simmons and I agreed that this strategy was patently unfair to the White House, because these selective leaks appeared to be applying pressure on future witnesses to slant their testimonies, as well as to influence the public opinion that was being shaped by the same reporters who were the beneficiaries of the allegedly illegal OIC leaks.

Three weeks later, in late February, Bill Thomas—a good friend of mine and the editor of *Capital Style*, where I served as a contributing editor—asked me if I wanted to write an article about the events surrounding the publication of my Foster book. I submitted a proposal to Thomas, which included details of my conversations with Ewing and Bennett, as well as what I believed to be corroboration for David Kendall's allegations. However, failing to see the significance of this information about the OIC leaks, Thomas passed on this story.

Then, just over two months later, on May 1, the *Washington Post* published an article about the upcoming release of Steven Brill's new media magazine, *Brill's Content*. In this story, the *Post* reported that Brill, my former adversary during the Hoffa investigation, was planning to reveal his own evidence about the OIC leaks in his premier issue.

According to the *Post* article, Brill had spoken to Starr about the leaks coming from his office, adding:

> Starr obligingly told [Brill] which reporters he'd spoken with and which he had not. Among Brill's questions [were]: Have you ever provided original information to a reporter? Starr said no, he hadn't. Did he ever confirm a story? No again. Had he ever leaked information? No again.[183]

I immediately realized that Brill's story, which would be released in mid-June, might be very important because it could shed new light on the OIC's strategy of leaking information, a process that, I believed, had been explained to me by Starr's top deputies, Ewing and Bennett. As a result, I started to consider beating Brill to the punch and to reveal my information first.

PART EIGHT: THE ROAD TO IMPEACHMENT

Further reinforcing my decision to step forward, Clinton attorney David Kendall filed another complaint on May 6 with Judge Johnson. Kendall requested that she order Starr and the OIC to appear at a "show-cause" hearing to determine why they should not be held in contempt for allegedly leaking grand-jury information.

Jackie Bennett immediately responded to Kendall on behalf of the OIC, threatening to file counter charges against the President's attorneys if Kendall did not withdraw the request for the show-cause hearing.

Kendall's motion to the court was followed by a letter to Kendall from journalist and Starr-defender Stuart Taylor, who wrote that Bennett had told him that the leaks were originating from the White House, not the OIC.

After all of this, Roger Simmons and I agreed that the time was right for me to become an uninvited bit player in the growing jihad between the supporters of President Clinton and Kenneth Starr.

114. Openly taking sides

On May 19, I delivered a speech at the Martin Luther King Library in downtown Washington. During the talk, I recounted that one OIC official, who spoke on the record, had explained the OIC's process of leaking to the press. I told the audience:

> According to Hickman Ewing, Kenneth Starr's chief deputy, the OIC freely provides non-public information on an off-the-record basis to reporters and book reviewers who are personally approved by Kenneth Starr and whose work is in sync with the OIC's position on key issues.
>
> This runs contrary to the OIC's public statements about its relationship with the media and is further proof that the OIC's investigation of the Clinton White House—regardless of merit—is political, partisan, and punitive. [The Starr inquiry] is built upon a series of well-timed leaks which have turned gossip into gasoline and some of these approved journalists into lapdogs who are dependent upon their sources' access and goodwill.

I also charged that some of these selected reporters, who were the beneficiaries of the OIC leaks, were covertly providing the prosecution with confidential information about the President from their own sources. To me, this was whorehouse journalism—on par with the performances of many sportswriters who covered the NFL.

In fact, I had cooperated with prosecutors twice during my career. The first time was after a target of a grand-jury investigation had threatened my father's life. The second time was after a confessed accomplice in a murder conspiracy indicated that he was willing to testify in support of another member of the conspiracy at his trial, falsely absolving him of any guilt.

In both cases, I cooperated with the prosecution openly—not as a confidential informant. As a result, in the first case in 1976, a murder contract was placed on my life. In the second in 1983, the defense was immediately notified of my cooperation, which caused a chain of events that nearly led to my imprisonment just before my father's death.

Also, I had participated in probes about murder and specific acts of violence—not specific acts of sex between two consenting adults who had allegedly lied about their relationship.

CNN, which was present at the library event, filmed my speech and aired its story on May 25—after both Starr and Ewing refused comment. However, OIC spokesman Charles Bakaly insisted that Ewing and I simply had different versions of what we had discussed during our conversation.

Nevertheless, Jim Kennedy, a spokesman for the Clinton White House, told the Reuters news service that my allegations needed to be investigated.[184]

After CNN's broadcast and the Reuters wire story, Gene Lyons, a pro-Clinton columnist for the *Arkansas Democrat-Gazette*, wrote: "It appears Ewing's normally inerrant judgment about which are the independent counsel's trusted pet reporters may have been thrown off by the fact that Moldea was under contract to Regnery, a publishing house owned by a close friend and political ally of Starr's."[185]

Also, unknown to everyone but Roger Simmons, I had limited my remarks to my one conversation with Ewing. I did not even mention my subsequent discussion with Jackie Bennett.

In the wake of my speech, I appeared on several of radio and television programs. During one of these interviews, the host charged that I was using the leaks issue to seek revenge on Starr, who, prior to his appointment as independent counsel, had filed an amicus brief for the defense in *Moldea v. New York Times*.

PART EIGHT: THE ROAD TO IMPEACHMENT

In response, I admitted, "Well, it's legitimate, I guess, to ask whether I have an ulterior motive for questioning Starr's tactics. But when I had the means and opportunity to do so between the covers of my book about Foster's suicide, I stayed fair and impartial. In fact, I praised Starr and his staff for their work on the Foster case. And, I believe that my sense of fairness in that particular matter has also been applied to this issue about the OIC leaks."

On May 28, I appeared on Keith Olbermann's nightly program, *The White House in Crisis*, on MSNBC, in which I went after the reporters covering the OIC, as well as the Starr investigation of the President's sex life.

> **Olbermann** (asking about the specifics of my conversation with Ewing): What does "not on the public record" mean, Dan? Is this grand jury information, or is it a catch-all? What does it mean?
>
> **Moldea:** I can't go further than what Ewing has said, but I think it's important that the journalists who are covering this go back and ask Ewing what he meant by that. Both Ewing and Starr have decided to make no comment on this matter, and they're allowing their flack to speak for them. And everyone seems to be allowing that to be the final word on this matter. I mean, when the President doesn't want to comment about something, the press continues to ask the question over and over again. Why is Ken Starr getting a pass on this? . . . Hey, if you're going to have an investigation, have a fair investigation. But I insist that this is not a fair investigation. And I believe that many reporters are becoming complicit in this particular situation.

In other words, I made it clear on national television that I believed that President Clinton was getting a raw deal, and that I was now openly taking the President's side.

In its June 6 issue, the *National Journal* reported that White House press secretary Mike McCurry quoted President Clinton, saying, "Why do the *Washington Post* and the *New York Times* cover up Dan Moldea and not write about that?"[186]

In his defense of what I had done, the President specifically accused the *Post* and the *Times*, neither of which had mentioned my charges against the OIC, of covering up the OIC's allegedly illegal activities.

Still, through all of this, I promised anyone who asked that, if subpoenaed, I would cooperate with any investigation of the leaks, including the OIC's own reported internal review.

Not surprisingly, the OIC never contacted me.

On June 14—twenty-six days after my speech—the *New York Times* published an article about Steven Brill's interview with Starr in his magazine, *Brill's Content*, which would be released the following day. According to the *Times*:

> [Starr] has acknowledged . . . that he and his aides have given information on the Monica Lewinsky matter to reporters. But he also insisted that these leaks were neither illegal, because they did not involve testimony before a grand jury, nor a violation of Justice Department ethics barring leaks of ***"substantive information"*** about a prosecution. . . .
>
> "I have talked with reporters on background on some occasions," Mr. Starr said in the interview. Mr. Starr also identified three reporters . . . as journalists to whom his deputy, Jackie Bennett, had talked "extensively" about the case. . . . But Mr. Bennett told Mr. Brill he was in no way a source."[187] [Emphasis added.]

After reading the story, I reviewed the notes of my on-the-record conversation with Jackie Bennett who had specifically and repeatedly offered me "substantive information." However, I decided to hold this information, just in case Brill later needed corroboration for his charges.

Responding directly to Brill's allegations, Starr issued a statement on June 13, insisting:

> Steven Brill has recklessly and irresponsibly charged the Office of Independent Counsel with improper contacts with the media. The charges are false.
>
> The Office of the Independent Counsel does not release grand jury material directly or indirectly, on the record or off the record. Nor do we violate Dept. of Justice policy or applicable ethical guidelines. . . . The contacts between the Office of the

Independent Counsel and journalists have been legal, appropriate and consistent with Dept. of Justice policy.

Also, on June 16, Starr released a formal nineteen-page response to Brill, adding:

> Your reputation suffers grave damage with the publication of 'Pressgate' in your inaugural issue. Your reporting rests on a fundamental misunderstanding of the law and a misrepresentation of the facts—errors that I will detail at length below.
>
> More disappointing, however, is that your reckless and irresponsible attack borders on the libelous. For this reason, I am compelled to respond publicly.

But, contrary to Starr's denials in his condemnation of Brill, I believed from my own conversations with Ewing and Bennett that Brill was telling the truth: The OIC had engaged in a pattern of cooperation with selected reporters, which included allegedly well-timed leaks from the OIC.

Ironically, after my bitter war with Brill twenty years earlier, I was now cheering him on and prepared to back him up.

Other than a misspelled name and failing to reveal his financial contributions to the Clinton-Gore campaigns, I was aware of only one other mistake admitted by Brill in his article. According to the June 19 edition of the *Washington Post*, Brill had become embroiled in a controversy with the *Wall Street Journal* over one of its reports about the Lewinsky matter. The *Post* continued: "Brill conceded [the] error after learning that *Journal* reporter Glenn Simpson had [secretly] tape-recorded the interview."

Reporter Simpson received no public criticism from the media for secretly taping Brill, who had justifiably attacked several journalists for their sweetheart relationships with Starr and the OIC.

115. The secret tapes

The day after my May 19 speech about Hickman Ewing and the OIC leaks, Max Stier of Williams & Connolly, one of the President's attorneys, called and asked me if I would cooperate with their probe. I replied that I would cooperate with anyone—but only after receiving a subpoena, just as I had promised from the outset. Then, I gave him Roger Simmons's telephone number. However, I never received the subpoena.

After Brill ran out of gas with his story, Stier called Simmons and again asked for a meeting with me. When Simmons called and told me about Stier's second request, I still insisted that I needed a subpoena.

Simmons speculated that the President's legal team did not have subpoena power yet but were trying to get it from the court and wanted my information to help them.

Hearing that, I agreed to the meeting with Stier and one of his aides, which took place on June 26 at 9:00 A.M. at the offices of Williams & Connolly. During this conversation, Simmons and I revealed that I had not only spoken with Hickman Ewing but with Jackie Bennett, as well.

Later that same day, Judge Norma Holloway Johnson ruled that the evidence of illegal leaking by the OIC was persuasive and again ordered Starr and his deputies to appear at a "show-cause" hearing—where the burden of proof would be on Starr and his prosecutorial team to show that they did not leak.

Also, as part of this process, Judge Johnson cited twenty-four specific examples of allegedly illegal leaks and named the reporters from the *New York Times*, the *Washington Post*, *Newsweek*, ABC, CBS, CNN, and NBC, among others, who had allegedly received them.[188]

According to Starr's own attorney in a brief filed with the court, the OIC had identified the reporters who were the beneficiaries of the leaks as confidential informants—just as I had predicted during my May 19 speech. In other words, these reporters were feeding information to the OIC from their own private sources about the President.

Like me, these journalists had taken sides in the dispute. But, unlike me, they did not announce their biases publicly, continuing instead to report for their news organizations under the false guise of objectivity.

Now under heavy fire from the court, Starr, who quickly appealed Judge Johnson's decision, suddenly kicked his investigation of President Clinton into high gear, immediately negotiating an immunity deal with Monica Lewinsky.

On July 26, after hearing the first news reports that Starr had also subpoenaed President Clinton to appear before the grand jury, I told a radio interviewer:

> You know, what upsets me most is that all reasonable people recognize that any investigation should be fair. Through

> fairness, we determine truth. And, after learning the truth, we await justice. But, if we are only interested in truth, then we might as well just arm the police with rubber hoses and allow them to beat confessions out of suspects.
>
> And that's what Kenneth Starr is doing. By forcing the President to testify before a grand jury in which the President is the target, Starr is beating a confession out of him with a political rubber hose. Ordinarily, a target refuses to testify, but, in this particular situation, he cannot.

After the interview, I called Roger Simmons and asked if I could meet with him. When I arrived at his home, I told him that I had no choice but to "jump on another hand grenade."

The next day, I called Keith Olbermann at MSNBC and revealed that I had secretly tape recorded my telephone conversations with both Hickman Ewing and Jackie Bennett and, thus, memorialized their statements about the process of OIC's leaks to the press.

However, my revelation was in direct competition with the bigger news of the day—the Lewinsky immunity deal and the President's subpoena.

Nevertheless, that night, Olbermann, without either the tapes or their transcripts in his possession, led his program by trumpeting the news of the existence of my recordings.

With NBC's attorneys' imprint throughout the script, Olbermann reported:

> On a dramatic day, . . . news is breaking at this hour about Mr. Starr's operation, news that could compromise the investigation, news that—see if this sounds familiar—a claim that there are troublesome audio tapes floating around with bad news on them for Mr. Starr. . . .
>
> Investigative reporter Dan Moldea has sent a nine-page document to MSNBC in which he asserts he has audio tapes of conversations with Kenneth Starr's deputies in which they offered "substantive information" about their investigations. He has previously made these charges without making any reference to audio tapes. Starr has been quoted as saying that releasing "substantive information" to reporters would be a violation of Justice Department standards and a firing offense.

Yet, Moldea says, in a January 12 conversation, according to him, with Deputy Independent Counsel Jackie Bennett, Moldea says his tapes show Bennett using that exact phrase—"substantive information," offering that information to Moldea. . . .

We have sought reaction from Mr. Bennett, but have been, thus far, unable to reach him. Our efforts in that regard will continue.

Moldea also claims he recorded a conversation on December 10 with Starr's chief deputy Hickman Ewing in which Ewing outlines how reporters qualify as sympathetic to Starr's point of view; that the Office of the Independent Counsel talked freely to them, "especially when we hear where they're coming from."

We have also sought the reaction of Mr. Ewing to this story and have been, thus far, unable to reach him. And our efforts will continue in that regard.

Ewing, according to Moldea, also told Moldea that Starr, personally, would have to approve Ewing's cooperation with Moldea. That's Moldea's claim.

Moldea's remarks to MSNBC included that he had no intention of ever making public the existence of these tapes or their contents, but that, upon learning that Starr had subpoenaed the President, he decided to do so.

To quote Moldea's statement to us: "Believing that the President should not be required to testify until the probe of the Office of the Independent Counsel had concluded, I decided to reveal the existence of my tape-recorded conversations with Ewing and Bennett to encourage a legitimate and expedited inquiry into the OIC leaks."

Later that evening, Olbermann called me at home. After a brief but very friendly conversation, I played portions of both the Ewing and Bennett tapes for him over the phone so that he could sleep without worry. What he had said on his program was completely accurate.

PART EIGHT: THE ROAD TO IMPEACHMENT

The following night, Geraldo Rivera invited me to appear on CNBC's *Rivera Live*. Rivera declared:

> Now comes apparent proof of what Steven Brill alleged in his explosive article that Starr's prosecutors have been willing, illegally, to provide certain kinds of information, especially to sympathetic journalists. The evidence to support that allegation is provided by my next guest, Dan Moldea. . . .
>
> I begged, borrowed, and stole to get Dan Moldea to bring just a piece of this tape. I want to prove to Ken Starr, to Jackie Bennett Jr., to Hickman Ewing, the principal deputies, that Dan Moldea speaks the truth when he says he has secretly recorded you fellows and I think you better listen up to what he has now to tell us.

In response to one of Rivera's early questions, I replied:

> I think one of the biggest stories in Washington right now is what's happening in this leaks investigation involving Starr and his two deputies. I think this is where the real story lies, because I think this explains the great haste that Starr has had since the June 26th decision by Judge Johnson—to get this case rolling and get this case rolling fast. I think the independent counsel's on the verge of having his legs cut out from under him, and he knows it.

Then, Rivera played the short excerpt of the Bennett tape I had given him, which consisted of the following exchange:

> **Moldea:** And I wanted to come and pay my respects to the independent counsel—and spend, maybe, twenty minutes with him, asking him a few questions.
>
> **Bennett:** Okay. That's really why I was calling. I talked to Judge Starr about this. And the question I had was, sort of, the ground rules: that this is just, you know, coming by as a courtesy. It's . . .
>
> **Moldea:** It's to pay—It's a respect call.

— 415 —

Bennett: It's not looking for substantive information?—

Moldea: No.

Bennett: —Because if you are, then there are other people who really are better to talk to.

Howard Kurtz, the media critic for the *Washington Post*, was not impressed with the tape, apparently believing that this brief excerpt was all I had. Kurtz wrote:

> *Rivera Live* also gave a big buildup to author Dan Moldea and (shades of Linda Tripp) yet another secret tape, this one involving alleged prosecutorial leaks. While researching a book, Moldea recorded a conversation with Starr's deputy, Jackie Bennett, in which Moldea asked to pay a courtesy call on Starr.
>
> If Moldea wanted "substantive information," Bennett said, "then there are other people who are really better to talk to." End of exclusive.[189]

What I did not play—and, thus, what Kurtz missed—was Bennett's statement later in the conversation in which he had said:

> Okay, here is my thinking: If you make this request to really get access to *substantive information* contingent on meeting with [Starr] first, it'll make it more difficult, because his schedule is more difficult. He travels a lot. What we can do is make the *substantive person* or people available to you earlier. [Emphasis added.]

In fact, Bennett had arranged my meeting with that "substantive person" with the "substantive information" with whom I had lunch on January 19 at the Old Ebbitt Grill—two days before the Lewinsky scandal exploded on January 21.

Later, in a 2007 profile that Kurtz wrote about me for the *Washington Post*, he revisited this matter in which he properly allowed Bennett to defend himself, stating:

> Moldea asked to speak to Starr, and Bennett told him, according to the transcript, that if he was looking for "substantive

PART EIGHT: THE ROAD TO IMPEACHMENT

> information . . . then there are other people who really are better to talk to." Bennett says he was just trying to accommodate a journalist's request.
>
> Several months later—after the Monica Lewinsky scandal broke—Moldea went public with his tape. Moldea might have been seeking confidential information himself, but now, in light of the attacks on Clinton, he accused the Starr team of improper leaking.
>
> "I remember being agitated at the time," Bennett says. "It was a dishonest thing to do. . . . He misled us."[190]

In my own defense, all Bennett really knew about me was that I was under contract with the conservative Regnery Publishing. Just like Reed Irvine while I was writing the Foster book, Bennett drew whatever he wanted from that simple truth. I was not about to volunteer the conclusions in my book, which had still not been released.

On Monday, August 17, the President testified before the grand jury, questioned by Bennett, Kenneth Starr, and two other OIC attorneys.

During his four hours of sworn testimony, the President admitted an "inappropriate" relationship with Lewinsky but denied ever perjuring himself during his deposition in the Paula Jones case, insisting that he had walked through the "minefield" via his technically truthful responses to Jones's attorneys' imprecise questions.

In response to a line of accusatory questions by Jackie Bennett, the President replied:

> In the face of their repeated illegal leaking, it was not my responsibility to volunteer a lot of information. . . . I was doing my best to be truthful. I was not trying to be particularly helpful to them—when I knew that there was no evidence here of sexual harassment, and I knew what they wanted to do was to leak this, even though it was unlawful to do so.

During his speech to the nation after his testimony, the President, as he had said during his grand-jury appearance, admitted an inappropriate relationship with Lewinsky while denying any violation of law. Midway through his talk, the President, appearing apologetic but still tough and defiant, attacked the OIC, adding his own complaint about the OIC leaks: "The independent counsel investigation moved on to my staff and friends, [and] then into my private life. And now the investigation itself is under investigation."

Like everyone else in Washington, I knew that the President's grand-jury testimony would either be leaked to the media or would suddenly be made public under some bizarre circumstance. And then, the President would be, once again, placed in the now-familiar no-win situation.

The President's supporters would inevitably complain about the violation of grand-jury secrecy while the President enemies would insist on the public's right to know about his private behavior.

But, when the President's supporters would then argue that the public also had a right to know about the relationship between the OIC and its selected stable of reporters, the President's enemies would insist that Starr and the OIC had a right to protect their confidential sources.

116. Heresy

On August 24, 1998—the week after the President's August 17 appearance before the grand jury and his lowest point yet during the crisis—I filed a forty-page-sworn affidavit with Judge Johnson, attaching the transcripts of my taped conversations with Starr's two deputies. I sent copies to Kenneth Starr at the OIC and Max Stier at Williams & Connolly, agreeing to release the entire Bennett tape and an edited version of the Ewing tape—edited to protect the identities of two of my OIC sources who, unlike Bennett and Ewing, had spoken off the record—upon receipt of a subpoena.

At the end of my sworn statement, I wrote: "Regardless of the President's fate, I will always view the symbiotic relationship between the OIC and its stable of selected reporters as one of the most dangerous and sinister alliances in contemporary American history."[191]

In his wire story on August 29 about my affidavit, investigative journalist Frank Greve of Knight-Ridder wrote:

> When writer Dan Moldea wanted help from independent counsel Kenneth Starr's office last winter, one call from his publisher yielded an offer of what Starr's top deputy termed "substantive information."

> True, Moldea's publisher is well-connected. He's Alfred Regnery, one of America's top vendors of anti-Clinton titles and a friend of Starr's since they served together in President Reagan's Justice Department. . . . His story of easy access to prosecutors raises questions anew about how Starr works with reporters. Among those most interested in the answers is Starr's judicial overseer, Chief U.S. District Judge Norma Holloway Johnson. . . ."
>
> [OIC spokesman Charles] Bakaly took note of what Moldea acknowledges in his affidavit: that Moldea's a "liberal Democrat" and that he's played the tapes for Clinton's defense team. . . . The tapes were edited, Moldea said, to remove the names of two sources in Starr's office to whom Moldea had promised anonymity. Bakaly is skeptical. "We suspect material that has been edited out will reveal that our discussions were entirely appropriate," he said. If need be, Moldea said, he'll let Judge Johnson hear the original tapes so long as the sources are protected.[192]

Gene Lyons of the *Arkansas Democrat-Gazette* added in his September 2 column:

> For his part, Jackie Bennett repeatedly offered to put Moldea in touch with OIC staffers who could supply "substantive information," a phrase he volunteered five times in a brief talk. Are perjurers accusing the president of perjury? The answer is up to Judge Johnson.[193]

In his best-selling book, *And the Horse He Rode In On*, Clinton defender James Carville, who, while writing his manuscript, was then unaware of my tapes of Ewing and Bennett but had been citing excerpts from my May 19 speech during television appearances on the *Today Show* and *Larry King Live*, among others, wrote:

> One journalist finally had the temerity to step forward and explain how all this sensitive information had been coming out into the light of day. Dan Moldea, a respected crime reporter with more than seven exhaustively investigated books under his belt, heard one of Starr's emphatic denials and was so disgusted that he told his tale. . . .

And if the word of Mr. Moldea wasn't proof enough, only a few weeks later an even more damning witness came forward to testify about the independent counsel's embarrassing leakage: Ken Starr. . . . In an interview with reporter Steven Brill for the premiere issue of *Brill's Content* magazine, the independent counsel announced that he and his chief partner-in-crime, Jackie Bennett, "have talked with reporters on background on some occasions," yet claimed there was "nothing improper" about discussing what witnesses tell FBI agents and other investigators before they testify in front of the grand jury.[194]

To many journalists, my revelations about the OIC leaks and my assault on the reporters who received them were ultimate acts of journalistic heresy—even after my long history of testifying against Simon & Schuster at a U.S. Senate hearing about corporate concentrations in the publishing industry, my decision to testify against the *Wall Street Journal* and a fellow reporter in a contentious libel suit, my attacks in *Dark Victory* on political writers who covered Ronald Reagan and in *Interference* on sportswriters who shilled for the NFL, my battle with the *Washington Post* for hiring an FBI informant to review one of my books, and, most of all, my libel suit against the *New York Times*, including everything that was said and done during that conflict.

Now assuming that I was a total dead man in the world of journalism because all of my alleged sins—even when they were committed in self-defense—this 48-year-old heretic decided to sin once again.

PART NINE:
The Flynt Project

117. Exposing hypocrisy

On September 11, 1998, the U.S. House released the latest *Starr Report*, which had been given to Congress by the OIC two days earlier. The House Republican leadership refused to provide anyone, including the President's attorneys, an opportunity to review it, choosing instead to release it, unabridged, over the Internet.

The report documented the Clinton-Lewinsky relationship, which had consisted exclusively of oral sex, in graphic detail. The couple apparently never had intercourse, which the President stated during his sworn testimony was the necessary threshold for a "sexual relationship." Also, when the President was asked under oath about his relationship with Lewinsky, the question was phrased in the present tense. Because the liaison had long ceased, the President responded to the question as asked—in the present tense—and gave his denial.

Indeed, the President was parsing the language, but, legally, he was being truthful—once again refusing to help his enemies rephrase their imprecise questions.

Meantime, while *Newsweek* and other national mainstream publications continued their obsession with the President's sex life, other publications were busy investigating the private lives of conservative politicians who were actively criticizing the President for his allegedly immoral behavior. For instance:

> * On September 4, as *Vanity Fair* was hot on his trail, Representative Dan Burton, the right-wing Indiana Republican who spent most of his time making wild charges against the President, publicly admitted that while married to his wife he had fathered a child with another woman. Notably, Burton had earlier described the President as a "scumbag" because of his relationship with Lewinsky.
>
> * On September 10, Representative Helen Chenoweth, an Idaho Republican, who had also been extremely critical of President Clinton's relationship with Lewinsky, suddenly admitted to the *Idaho Statesman* that she recently had an affair with a married man.
>
> * On September 11, *Salon*, the popular Internet magazine, exposed Representative Henry Hyde, an Illinois Republican, for

his earlier five-year "sexual relationship" with a woman whose marriage was destroyed by her relationship with the congressman. In the same edition that revealed this affair—which Hyde reluctantly admitted, calling it a "youthful indiscretion," even though he was 51 at the time—*Salon* published an on-point editorial, stating:

> Aren't we fighting fire with fire, descending to the gutter tactics of those we deplore? Frankly, yes. But ugly times call for ugly tactics. When a pack of sanctimonious thugs beats you and your country upside the head with a tire-iron, you can withdraw to the sideline and mediate, or you can grab it out of their hands and fight back.[195]

In response to the sudden outings of Republican hypocrites, House Majority Whip Tom DeLay insisted: "This is not politics as usual. This is an assault on the very foundations of our democracy, and we believe it warrants an investigation by the FBI. I have no doubt in my mind that [the President] has an operation in the White House that is trying to destroy members of Congress in order to intimidate them from doing their duty as members of the House of Representatives under the Constitution of the United States."[196]

As the powerful chairman of the U.S. House Judiciary Committee, Henry Hyde, who remained absolutely livid after his sexual indiscretion was exposed by *Salon*, agreed with DeLay, believing that the White House had inspired the expose about his infidelity.

Consequently, Hyde's resolve to bring the President to justice stiffened.

After the release of the *Starr Report*, porn-king Larry Flynt, the controversial publisher of *Hustler* and over thirty other publications of both sexual and non-sexual content, sent a letter to Kenneth Starr on September 22 and offered him a job.

Flynt wrote, tongue-in-cheek:

> Let me take this opportunity to thank you on behalf of all the employees at *Hustler* magazine and LFP, Inc. for your tireless work in producing the *Starr Report*. I have been impressed by the salacious and voyeuristic materials in your work. The

PART NINE: THE FLYNT PROJECT

> quality and quantity of material you have assembled in your report contains more pornographic references than those provided by *Hustler* Online services this month. I have included a chart in this letter that confirms this fact.
>
> Given your exemplary work, I would like to enter into negotiations with you regarding full-time employment for Hustler magazine and related services offered by LFP, Inc. [a.k.a. Larry Flynt Publications], when you conclude your work at the Office of Independent Counsel.

Accepting the letter as a joke, few in politics or the media ever expected to hear from Flynt again on this matter.

But, then, on October 4, 1998—just four days before the House voted 258-176 for an open-ended impeachment inquiry against President Clinton—Flynt purchased a full-page ad in the *Washington Post*, costing $85,000 and asking readers:

> Have you had an adulterous sexual encounter with a current member of the United States Congress or a high-ranking government official?
>
> Can you provide documentary evidence of illicit sexual relations with a Congressman, Senator or other prominent officeholder? Larry Flynt and *Hustler* magazine will pay you up to $1 million if we choose to publish your verified story and use your material.

The ad contained a toll-free telephone number, as well as an e-mail address, noting, "All calls and correspondence will be kept strictly confidential."

Was this just another joke? Or was Flynt really serious?

Columnist Maureen Dowd of the *New York Times* had fun with Flynt's ad, writing on October 7: "Larry Flynt is clearly looking for a deliciously high duplicity level. . . . [C]onfessed philanderer Henry Hyde didn't pose enough of a challenge. We needed a real shocker."

118. Trying to remove the President

The Republicans' high confidence in their effort to remove President Clinton from office was not without foundation. With the mid-term elections approaching in early November, the pollsters and media pundits were universally predicting that the Republicans would greatly increase their majorities in both the House and the Senate.

But the Republicans and the press underestimated the President's continued strength in the polls. According to the American public, the President was still performing effectively, even in the face of an impeachment-obsessed Republican majority in Congress.

While the President appeared to be battling for the American people, the Republicans continued trying to destroy him. U.S. House Speaker Newt Gingrich made the President's personal behavior "Issue Number One" during the mid-term campaign, encouraging the GOP to run television ads that ripped at the President for his allegedly immoral acts. Attacking the President's sexual relationship with a young woman, Gingrich even called Clinton "a misogynist."[197]

But, on November 3, the Democrats stunned the Republicans and the political pundits by picking up five seats in the House while maintaining the status quo in the Senate. In addition, two of the Republicans biggest Clinton haters, Senator Lauch Faircloth and Senator Alfonse D'Amato, who headed the Senate's Whitewater investigation, went down in huge defeats.

Three days later, after the Democrats' remarkable performance, Gingrich—whom Republicans principally blamed for their poor showing at the polls—announced his resignation as both Speaker and a member of the House.

On November 18, 55-year-old U.S. Representative Bob Livingston of Louisiana, another ultra-conservative Republican, was selected by the Republican majority to succeed Gingrich as House Speaker. Notably, Livingston had allowed his office to be one of the site locations during the filming of a 1994 anti-Clinton video promoted by Reverend Jerry Falwell, *The Clinton Chronicles*, which accused the President of drug trafficking and murder, among other preposterous charges.

The House anticipated formally electing Livingston on January 6, 1999, when the new 106th Congress arrived in Washington. Until then, he accepted the role as the "designated" House Speaker.

With Gingrich out, Tom DeLay and Henry Hyde—now in concert with Speaker-designate Bob Livingston—were more determined than ever to impeach the President, forcing a trial in the Senate that could end his Presidency.

On November 19, the members of the House Judiciary Committee, chaired by Hyde, opened their hearings in consideration of the President's impeachment, calling Kenneth Starr as their first witness. After his thirteen-hour appearance—reading from his prepared statement, followed by softball questions from the Republicans and knuckleballs from the Democrats and Clinton attorney David Kendall—Hyde led the Republicans and their supporters in the audience in a standing ovation for Starr. To the President's enemies, Starr's case was enough to justify the President's removal from office.

The Republicans' prospects were further buoyed by the President's attorneys' high-handed and legalistic responses on November 27 to a set of 81 interrogatories earlier sent to the President by the committee. As a result, the President began receiving some unexpected public criticism for what was viewed as his refusal to accept real responsibility for his role in the Lewinsky scandal.

Three Democratic U.S. Senators—Robert Byrd of West Virginia, Dianne Feinstein of California, and Joe Lieberman of Connecticut—along with several Democratic members of the U.S. House were already speaking out against the President.

Consequently, the President was in serious trouble which only escalated after his attorneys, led by special counsel Gregory Craig, were given two days to present their defense before the committee. They appeared overshadowed by the committee's majority counsel, David Schippers—a former U.S. Strike Force attorney in Chicago.[198]

In his own presentation to the members of the committee, Schippers made Starr's performance seem almost docile, taking the case against the President even further than the OIC.

To no one's surprise, on December 11 and 12, the House Judiciary Committee voted to recommend the President's impeachment to the full U.S. House, charging him with two counts of perjury, one count of obstruction of justice, and a fourth count for abuse of power.

In 1974, after the House Judiciary Committee had voted articles of impeachment but before the case went to the full House, President Nixon resigned from office.

Already, dozens of newspapers had called for President Clinton's resignation, including the *Atlanta Journal-Constitution*, the *Chicago Tribune*, the *Cincinnati Enquirer*, the *Daily Oklahoman*, the *Denver Post*, the *Des Moines Register*, the *Indianapolis Star*, the *Orange County Register*, the *Orlando Sentinel*, the *Philadelphia Inquirer*, the *Reno Gazette-Journal*, the

San Jose Mercury News, the *Seattle Times*, the *Tampa Tribune*, *USA Today*, and the *Washington Times*, among many others.

Under this extraordinary pressure, many wondered if and when the President would resign from office.

119. I become Larry Flynt's investigator

After Larry Flynt's ad in the *Washington Post*, six members of *Hustler's* staff began responding to the calls from those who had dialed his 800-number. The project was directed by Allan MacDonell, the magazine's executive editor. Over 2,000 calls were logged—although most were from well-wishers who supported the project but had no information.

About 40 of the callers, reaching for the "up to" million-dollar reward, claimed to have information either about their own experiences or about those of someone they knew. MacDonell instructed those conducting the preliminary interviews to assign a rating number to each informant, based upon the credibility of the source and the potential news value of his or her information. The final list consisted of twenty targets.

Via a trusted friend in Washington, Flynt was introduced to the politically-conservative head of a private-investigations firm.

During the late morning of November 23, the private investigator called and asked me to come to his home immediately. When I arrived, he simply asked me with a straight face, "How would you like the opportunity to help save the President of the United States and, possibly, American democracy?"

After we stopped laughing, he explained that he had been contacted by Larry Flynt's office and asked to participate in the project which stemmed from the porn king's full-page ad in the *Washington Post* the previous month.

"They need a lead investigator, a point man," he said.

When I replied that I was interested, the private investigator called Allan MacDonell and put me on the telephone with him. During my conversation with MacDonell, who was familiar with my books about the Mafia, I explained that, indirectly, Flynt and I had crossed paths before.

In 1978, after the release of my first book, *The Hoffa Wars*, Jim Heinisch—the guy who brought me to the podium to speak to the angry crowd of students on the night of the Kent State shootings in 1970

PART NINE: THE FLYNT PROJECT

and who later became the managing editor of *Hustler*—called and offered me $10,000 to write an article about the murder of John Kennedy. But, after a long discussion about our days at the University of Akron, I politely turned down the offer, pointing out the obvious differences between writing for *Playboy*, which I had done, and writing for the already notorious *Hustler*, which I would not do.

Although Heinisch had died in April 1989, MacDonell still remembered him fondly. And our mutual connection to Heinisch seemed to bring about a sense of goodwill between us.

During our friendly exchange, I also told MacDonell that Reverend Jerry Falwell's landmark libel case against Flynt, which was decided in Flynt's favor by the U.S. Supreme Court, was a key precedent cited against me during my libel case against the *New York Times*. In short, Flynt wanted opinion writers to have the right to express themselves freely and without any restrictions while I wanted opinion writers held accountable for what they publish, just as news reporters are.

MacDonell laughed when I said that—among the First Amendment crowd—Flynt had become a saint while I was viewed as a sinner.

Discussing Flynt's current project, we agreed that public officials should be entitled to private lives—unless they judged other public officials by their private lives. And, even though we opposed what had already become known as "the politics of personal destruction," we were extremely concerned about the methods that were being used to remove President Clinton from office, which we viewed as unfair, unprincipled, and unrestricted.

I volunteered that I viewed the entire movement to remove the President from office as nothing less than a right-wing effort to overthrow the Executive Branch of the United States Government. I even quoted from *Salon's* September 11 editorial, saying: "Ugly times call for ugly tactics."

When MacDonell asked if I was willing to "get ugly," I replied that—although I would always be proactive and go beyond the call of duty—I would never agree to break the law or to participate in any bedroom dramas. Also, I would never misrepresent myself. Anyone I spoke to would know that I was on assignment for Larry Flynt.

I added that—sooner or later, especially if I did a good job—I might be called to testify in deposition or in a court of law. I told MacDonell that, if subpoenaed and placed under oath, I would always tell the truth.

MacDonell agreed with all of that, assuring me that no one would ever ask me to do anything illegal. To the contrary, my orders would be to err on the side of caution.

Finally, after this lengthy conversation, MacDonell formally offered me the job as Flynt's lead investigator. Although I fully recognized this as a potentially life-altering decision, I immediately accepted the assignment—even though there were a slew of problems I had not completely thought through yet, not the least of which would be the issue of checkbook journalism.

My initial reaction was that the big media condemns the concept of checkbook journalism—because it is checkbook journalism that levels the playing field between the big media and the smaller media operations. With checkbook journalism, someone like Flynt can compete with the big media for the big stories. To be sure, there were numerous examples of big media organizations paying big money for big stories. And MacDonell assured me that Flynt would not use anything he could not prove whether he paid for it or not.

Another problem I had not given much thought to was my own standing in Washington. More to the point, near the end of my book about Vincent Foster's suicide, I had written:

> [W]hen Foster ended the bitter note found in his briefcase with, "Here ruining people is considered sport," he spoke a final truth before committing his last desperate act. However, in doing so, he failed to recognize that, in Washington, the sport is best played with toleration, as well as dignity and finesse. In this town, the real survivors are the bridge and chess players, not the brawlers who skate on the thin ice upon which the game of politics has always been played.

But to try to justify to myself or to anyone else that Flynt's project was playing the sport "with toleration, as well as dignity and finesse" was pointless. To the contrary, what we would be doing was a no-holds-barred assault on official Washington. And, from the outset, I recognized it.

When I contacted Mrs. Nolte, she admonished me, writing:

> I do think you need to consider your self-respect. If you feel you will lose or are losing it, you probably shouldn't work with [Flynt]. But, if you are comfortable with yourself, no matter what other people think, you should be okay. I am assuming everything is legal and minimally deceptive. . . .
>
> As far as reputation goes, in this culture, being notorious is as good as being heroic if you want attention, fame, celebrity, and

PART NINE: THE FLYNT PROJECT

maybe money. [The] problem with working with Flynt is he gets all the publicity. However, in time, perhaps an interesting book would come out of it.

During our second conversation, MacDonell wanted to structure a deal whereby I would be hired as an investigative consultant, which was how I wanted to identify myself to those I interviewed. But, instead of my usual $150-$200 an hour, I accepted the lesser offer of $125 without complaint, knowing that I could get more money if I needed it. Upset with the President's treatment by the Republicans and many in the press, I was prepared to sell apples on a street corner, if necessary, to finance a fight against the President's enemies.

Significantly, I never had a written contract with Flynt. We sealed our entire business relationship on the strength of each other's verbal agreements over the telephone, as well as a simple handshake when we later met for the first time.

120. Targeting Clinton's critics

Verbal agreements made, MacDonell provided me with his final list of the twenty most credible tipsters who had responded to Flynt's full-page ad. Immediately, I divided them into geographical regions and assigned each source my own rating number, based on the numbers given to each informant by MacDonell's staff for news value and overall credibility. I simply added the two results. The higher numbers had the highest priority.

Of the original twenty names, I immediately cut three from the list—because the telephone numbers the callers had provided did not exist or they had given false names. I also cut four more people because their information had already been published.

Immediately, I began working the phone, talking to every remaining source I could reach prior to the Thanksgiving holiday weekend. If someone had given MacDonell's staff only a first name, I was usually able to identify them on my Caller ID when they called me back. Sometimes, if they only gave a phone number and no name or a false name, I was able to identify them via a reverse telephone-number search on the Internet.

The first woman I reached admitted to being a hooker who had been receiving money for several years from one of the top Republicans in

Congress—married with children, Moral Majority, Christian Right, and a very vocal critic of President Clinton's alleged immorality. She even claimed to have photographs, memorializing moments during their trysts, taken by a second woman who had occasionally joined in their sexual exploits. The target had supposedly paid for these services with a credit card, and she claimed to have all the receipts. And, to add to her credibility, she had no interest in receiving any reward money, saying that she was only interested in exposing the hypocrisy of her long-time client.

We agreed to meet the following week at an airport near her home.

As I made the arrangements for my interviews with this informant and others, I was always wary of a possible setup through which someone would attempt to discredit Flynt by discrediting me. Consequently, while traveling alone, I insisted that our individual informants meet me at public places, usually at airport restaurants.

MacDonell sent me several confidentiality agreements he had signed, drawn up by the attorneys for Flynt's corporation, Larry Flynt's Productions (LFP). Upon meeting potential sources, I gave each an agreement for his or her signature. A signed agreement guaranteed that the informant's information would not be used without his or her permission.

I spent most of the next two weeks, hopping from one airport to the next, coast-to-coast, and meeting with those who wanted to talk. Also, during my whirlwind trip, I tried repeatedly to meet the hooker who had claimed to have the photographs and credit-card receipts of her politician-client. However, despite her promises and claims, she simply did not deliver the goods—and I had no choice but to remove her name from the list, even though she had never asked for any money.

From the beginning, I was always extremely loyal to our sources. For whatever reason, they wanted or needed the reward money. I made no judgments about that. Instead I just wanted to help them get it. Larry Flynt, a very wealthy man, was offering the money, and I wanted to put as much of it as possible in our informants' pockets, as long as they were honest with me.

But, in order to get to the point of paying reward money, I needed their evidence. During each of my interviews with our sources, my mantra was, "Help me help you."

Even though Flynt and his team had placed a baseball bat in my hands and told me to swing away, they still demanded a high degree of proof for anything I brought to them—an even higher standard than any newspaper, magazine, television network, or publishing house had ever required from me in the past. A mere claim of a relationship with

PART NINE: THE FLYNT PROJECT

a political figure—even the execution of a sworn statement—was not good enough. Knowing that he could be lured into a fatal mistake by his enemies, Flynt demanded hard evidence—legal documents, correspondences, videotapes, audio tapes, still photographs, or whatever was available—to support anything he would consider making public.

Actually, Flynt wanted to raise the bar on our efforts. He instructed me, whenever possible, to go beyond uncovering the sordid details about sex and try to find possible instances of perjury and obstruction of justice, which were more consistent with the most serious charges leveled against the President.

121. The Flynt team's first meeting

On December 6, the day before my first scheduled meeting with Flynt and MacDonell, I wrote and faxed a memo, saying:

> On or about December 1, Geraldo Rivera told his television audience on CNBC's *Rivera Live* that, through a reliable source, he learned that Larry Flynt had obtained evidence that no fewer than a dozen women have been having affairs with Republican congressmen. I assure you that I was not the source for this story.
>
> But, now that this is out, I have some concerns about this investigation, which should be considered:
>
> * When I am interviewing sources, what are the guidelines I may use about the reward money? Because the initial offer claimed "up to a million dollars" for information, they are all assuming that they are in line for the big score—and are disappointed when they don't receive it.
>
> * To what degree can we protect the women and our other sources? I am assuming that once the targets are confronted with the evidence against them, they will call press conferences and admit their infidelities, trying to minimize the damage.
>
> * What will be the timing of the release of this material?

* Will the early release of our material have any impact on the impeachment vote?

* Will this material be used as a preemptive strike or as a means of retaliation for a hypocritical vote for impeachment?

* At what point does this story become cold coffee and viewed as a mean-spirited attack?

* What is the possibility that one of our callers is setting us up, trying to get inside the investigation in an effort to sabotage it?

—⚏—

On December 7, I flew to Los Angeles, rented a Thunderbird at LAX, and drove to Flynt's corporate headquarters on the corner of Wilshire and La Cienega in Beverly Hills. My meeting with Flynt, MacDonell, and Alan Isaacman—Flynt's trusted attorney who had won *Falwell v. Hustler* before the U.S. Supreme Court—was strictly business. There was no joking or kidding around. Everyone was deadly serious.

A few days earlier, I had watched the 1996 Milos Foreman film, *The People vs. Larry Flynt*. I did not meet the bizarre man depicted in that movie. I met a cool and determined businessman, well dressed and completely in control.

At our meeting, I gave each man a bound copy of my first status report, which was over 300 pages. In addition, I had prepared biographical materials on each of our prospective targets, concentrating on the six I had investigated since I joined Flynt's team fourteen days earlier.

Then, as I read the list of our targets and informants, Flynt gave me the amount of money he was willing to spend on each. The rewards ranged from $50,000 to $500,000.

No one would be offered anywhere near a million dollars.

Among other discoveries, we had obtained information linking Newt Gingrich—who was in the midst of his second marriage—to a young congressional staffer.[199] This was the same Gingrich who, two months earlier, had the audacity to describe President Clinton as "a misogynist."

Specifically, in my status report to Flynt on December 7, I wrote: "[A source] alleged that Newt Gingrich had an affair with [Wisconsin Republican Representative Steve] Gunderson's secretary, who now works as a scheduler for the House Agriculture Committee." Through my research, I identified the woman as Callista Bisek, who was a $36,000-a-year assistant hearing clerk and scheduler for the committee.

Remarkably, because Gingrich had already announced his resignation from the U.S. House earlier in the month, Flynt decided not to expose his relationship with her.

Flynt was more interested in Gingrich's successor, Bob Livingston, the new speaker-designate.

122. Going after the House Speaker

Representative Bob Livingston, the Speaker-designate, was one of my earliest targets—with information about his activities provided by a Republican source in Louisiana who was not involved with him but knew somebody who was. However, because of this Republican source's connections to the Louisiana gambling community—which I had discovered in my own personal files—I had difficulty, at first, trusting the information provided, even though the source was not asking for any reward money.

Also, because of Livingston's new high-profile role in the U.S. House, I was particularly concerned about the fallout that could result simply from investigating him. Could we be accused of blackmail or obstruction?

On the other hand, if a trap had been laid for us, this Republican source with the gambling connections, I feared, could be the trap setter. Consequently, I had initially balked on an aggressive investigation of Livingston's alleged activities.

Then, on December 12, Livingston announced that he would vote for the President's impeachment and use his influence to block the Democrats from voting on censure, a punishment Flynt said he could accept.

After Livingston's announcement that he was going for the gold, Flynt called and instructed me to move on the next House Speaker immediately—regardless of my reservations about the informant's gambling connections. In effect, Flynt made Livingston our top priority.

I contacted the source in Louisiana—but the source did not know where Livingston's mistress was.

That same night—after receiving a still-untold lucky break—I located the woman, a lobbyist involved in Deep South politics, and cold called her. After our conversation, I wrote and faxed a memorandum to Flynt:

> I spoke with [the woman] tonight. She is very sharp.
>
> As I gave her my intro, she complained that I had called her with a Caller ID block. I apologized and offered to call her back without using the block. She invited me to do that, and I did.
>
> She asked me every conceivable question about who I worked for. I explained that I was an independent contractor who had been hired by . . . Larry Flynt Productions.
>
> I asked her no questions but told her that we had received an anonymous call, telling us that she had been Rep. Livingston's lover. She neither flinched nor scoffed at that—but wanted to know more. . . .
>
> I told her that I wanted to send her a confidentiality agreement, which I invited her to show to her attorney. I told her that I was willing to come and meet with her, assuming that she would tell me her basic story before I made the trip.
>
> She gave me her fax number, and I faxed the confidentiality agreement at the conclusion of our call.
>
> During our conversation, she volunteered that she was very upset with what was happening in Washington—especially with the hypocrisy among the President's critics, even though she is a Republican.
>
> Either she is setting me up or she is thinking about cooperating.

During my second conversation with the woman on the morning of Wednesday, December 16, I confronted her again about her alleged relationship with Livingston. To my surprise, almost matter-of-factly, she admitted it. Although her admission was good, it was not good

PART NINE: THE FLYNT PROJECT

enough. I still needed evidence of the relationship in order to satisfy Flynt's high standards of proof.

Meantime, she never asked for any reward money or even ballpark figures—only for more information about me and Flynt's project. However, she still refused to sign our confidentiality agreement, making me wonder, once again, whether I had walked into a trap.

But, to keep everything honest and provable, I invited her to tape record our conversations. And, of course, I recorded them, as well.

On the night of December 16—after I had faxed my daily report to Flynt, which included a statement about my conversation with the woman earlier that morning—she called me. Like the other two conversations, I taped this one as well, assuming that she was taping me as I had invited her to do.

When I answered the telephone, we immediately began discussing the President's bombing of Iraq earlier in the evening.

> **Moldea:** I think it's so dramatic on the backdrop of impeachment. I mean just remarkable. If you sent a proposal for a book up to New York, talking about how, the day before the impeachment vote, the President invaded another country, they would say, "Oh, this is too unbelievable."
>
> **The woman:** The problem with that is that there will probably be too many [books] published. You know?
>
> **Moldea:** Yeah, probably true.
>
> **The woman:** And that's why I called you.

Before she detailed the reason for her call, I stopped her and read the memorandum I had sent to Flynt just an hour earlier. In that report, I had quoted the woman, asking: "How can a lamb walk through a forest filled with wolves and come out alive?"

> **Moldea:** So talk to me little lamb.
>
> **The woman:** I thought about something that was an option in discussion but might not be for reality.... You've talked a lot about history being made. What if history was to be changed and the impeachment was delayed? Another way to phrase it would be: What if the impeachment failed by one vote as a

result of someone's leadership? That would make a good story, wouldn't it?

Moldea: That's a fact. But, at the same time, I don't want to be the person who makes the decision to try to change votes. I just..."

The woman: That's not in your hands or mine. I'm only ...

Moldea: Well, if we released this material early, it could have an impact on that. And there could be a reaction.

The woman: What if nothing got revealed? This is a scenario: What if a lot of faces were saved, and it failed by one vote because of leadership, quiet leadership. ...

Moldea: Well, I know a lot about what's going on right now over in the House. And this is a runaway train. And there is nobody who could step in and say, "This stops now." Not Livingston. Not Gingrich. Not Tom DeLay. Nobody. . . . I don't want to affect the history of what's going on. After the vote is cast, then let the chips fall where they may. But, like I said, I don't think anything can stop what's going on. Nothing can stop it.

The woman: That's interesting, because you're certainly closer to it than I am.

Moldea: I'm real close to it. Nothing can stop this. I'm watching the news right now. . . .

The woman: It [the impeachment vote] will be delayed, you know [because of the bombing of Iraq].

As I reported to her what I was seeing on television, it seemed clear that she was right: The U.S. House was going to postpone its vote. After a brief discussion about the delay, she asked again whether I was interested in "changing the course of history."

PART NINE: THE FLYNT PROJECT

Moldea: Well, let me tell you how I would interpret what you just said. It sounds to me as though there is somebody who would go to somebody in power and say, "Listen, I want you to stop this," or "I want you to influence enough votes so that this doesn't happen." And, I'm telling you, if that happened, the messenger would be handled in a situation like that. That's the reason why I won't go to anybody right now, because I'm afraid of influencing this vote in any way. I think that we have to allow this vote to happen. [Someone I knew] asked me to go to [a specific] congressman and say before the [impeachment] vote, "Hey, I've got you, and [we're] going to call a press conference in six hours," or whatever.

The woman: Well, I don't think that's how it would be handled. To me, the message would simply be, "This is scorched earth. This is going to hurt everyone. There are some folks who are looking for a life raft. Certainly, Mr. Speaker, do whatever you think you need to do, but all of this will go away if it fails by one vote."

Moldea: Like I said, I don't know that that's true. I would kind of hope that it was true. But I think we have to allow things to develop. . . .

The woman: They're going to ruin the Republican Party is what they're going to do.

Moldea: I think that's exactly right. *[New York Times* columnist] Maureen Dowd wrote that this was tantamount to the Republicans getting ready to drink their "Kool-Aid in Paula Jonestown." And that's exactly what's going on. This is Jonestown 1978.

The woman: They're walking over each other to get there first.

Moldea: What you have are a bunch of congressmen from conservative districts who have constituencies that want the President out, who have safe seats, and aren't really concerned about much—who are just taking this hard line. And these right-wingers, they bedevil not just the liberal Democrats but the moderate, responsible Republicans who want an end to this madness and want a proper punishment for the President.

The woman: You're probably right about the runaway train. Instinctively, I don't agree with you, but I have nothing to base that on. I happen to think that a quiet consultation would [end the matter].

Moldea: No, no. Anyone who comes in right now and tries to be reasonable will receive the full wrath of the hard right. That's a fact.

The woman: No, I'm not talking about the high road where they declare themselves. They could easily vote "yes" to it. I'm saying that that's not where this conversation takes place anyway. . . .

Moldea: This is what I interpret you saying; you tell me if I'm wrong: "I will pick up the phone. I will call Bob Livingston. And I will tell him, 'Listen, I don't want this [impeachment] to happen. And, subtly, through diplomacy and negotiation, I sure want to see this thing fail. And, if this thing fails, a lot of things that were going to happen probably won't happen. And then all will be right with the world. And we will have peace in our time.'" That's essentially what it sounds like to me.

The woman: I wouldn't say that to him, but I'm certain that there are people who would.

Moldea: Right. That's why I'm saying: I don't think you want to do that, because you will have your head handed to you if you do that. All the things you are afraid might happen to you could happen to you after that scenario. . . . These guys are going to do what they're going to do now. That decision is made. They have declared themselves. You're going to see a vote; I betcha it could be as many as 228 votes for impeachment. And that's a lot. Everyone is thinking it's going to be close. I don't think it's going to be close at all. . . . [But] even if the President is impeached, it's still not checkmate. I mean, it's damn close, but it's still not checkmate. And, so, what we're doing is we're just trying to be as responsible as we can in this thing. I know

PART NINE: THE FLYNT PROJECT

I am. I'm not going to be part of any irresponsibility, because I know that my name is going to get dragged into this thing, sooner or later. And I want to make sure that I have a clear conscience about what I've done and how I've handled this.

The woman: I want to make sure that my name doesn't get dragged into this.

Moldea: And that is one of my considerations. I'm not just protecting you; I'm protecting a lot of people. And that's one of the reasons why I might want to write [the *Flynt Report*], because, if I do, then I know that all of the sources are protected—because I will never give up their names.

After listening to my pitch for her complete cooperation with us, the woman informed me that she had already talked to her attorney about my offer—but was still inclined not to cooperate. "My attorney was very uncomfortable," she said.

Moldea: So you've talked to your attorney then?

The woman: Yeah.

Moldea: Oh, okay, I didn't hear that. Okay, fine. You've talked to an attorney. Great. And you trust this man, right?

The woman: Oh, yeah.

Moldea: Okay, fine. He's not going to pick up the phone and call his old friend, Bob [Livingston], and say, "Hey, Bob, guess what?"

The woman: Oh, no. I have leverage there. He wouldn't do that.

Still, by the end of the conversation, the woman was not interested in accepting any reward money. However, she genuinely appeared to be interested in correcting the direction in which the country was moving.

When I spoke with Flynt that night and expressed my admiration for this woman, he asked me if there was any chance that she was simply a mercenary who was playing me.

"No," I replied, "I think she views herself as a patriot. And I'm not going to disagree with that."[200]

123. The bombshell

Early the following morning, December 17, Livingston's mistress called to inform me that she had made a telephone call the previous night and told an unnamed person about her conversations with me and what she had learned about the Flynt project. And then she hung up.

I was stunned by this news but could not manage to keep her on the telephone long enough to find out exactly what she had done. Had she just double-crossed me or carried out her ill-fated plan to try to stop the impeachment, single-handedly?[201]

Regardless, after hearing that she had made her move, I immediately decided to make one of my own. Acting unilaterally, without talking to Flynt or MacDonell, I made a call, too. (I will never give up whom I called—although I will say that it was not to anyone connected with the White House or anyone who played a role in the impeachment proceedings.)

About an hour after that conversation—which would set in motion everything that followed—I took the Amtrak Metroliner to New York to deliver a eulogy at the memorial service for my old friend, Jon Kwitny of the *Wall Street Journal*, who had died of cancer on Thanksgiving Day.

On the train, I picked up the op-ed page of the *Boston Globe*, which was on an empty seat, and read a column by John Ellis, a first cousin of Texas Governor George W. Bush, who wrote in his first paragraph what many people were already saying:

> Iraq will not save him. The U.S. House of Representatives will impeach President William Clinton. The vote will break down more or less on party lines. As time passes, Clinton's support in the U.S. Senate will evaporate, leading inexorably to his resignation.

I tossed the newspaper where I had found it, already realizing that the President's condition was grave. In fact, on the morning of December 17, 1998, many people in authority believed, like Ellis, that the President was finished. He would be impeached within the next few days, and

PART NINE: THE FLYNT PROJECT

then he would either resign or be removed from office after the Senate trial—even though the votes were not yet there to convict him.

Because I was busy seeing so many friends and colleagues who had come to New York for Kwitny's memorial service, I did not get around to checking my answering machine until 1:30 A.M. on Friday, December 18. When I did, I received the shocking news—from MacDonell and a couple of close friends who knew of my secret involvement with Flynt—about what had happened since I had left Washington the previous morning after making my secret call.

Journalist Jim VandeHei of *Roll Call*, an important newspaper covering events on Capitol Hill, reported that Bob Livingston was about to be outed by Larry Flynt. Interviewed by VandeHei—whom I do not know and have never spoken with—Livingston, who called the reporter at 6:00 P.M., said:

> I have decided to inform my colleagues and constituents that during my 33-year marriage to my wife, Bonnie, I have on occasion strayed from my marriage and doing so nearly cost me my marriage and my family.
>
> I want to assure everyone that these indiscretions were not with employees on my staff and I have never been asked to testify under oath about them.

Earlier that afternoon, Livingston had admitted his indiscretions to the House Republican Caucus, saying that he had been *"Larry Flynt-ed."* Reportedly, the gasps from the closed-door caucus were audible down the hall.

In his prepared statement, Livingston said: "To those who are investigating me or others of my colleagues, please understand that I will not be intimidated by these efforts. These efforts will not deter me from performing my sworn duty under the Constitution as a member of Congress."

Concluding his remarks, Livingston told his Republican colleagues, "My fate is in your hands."

Livingston's Republican colleagues rose to give him a standing ovation.

While I was up in New York, totally oblivious to what my secret call that morning had started, the reaction to Livingston's admission was swift and severe. Many in Congress refused to believe that Flynt did not have White House help in his pursuit of Livingston. Like his Republican colleagues—Representatives Gerald Weller of Illinois and J.D. Hayworth of Arizona—Representative John Linder of Georgia told reporters, "This is what the White House calls a 'scorched earth' policy."

Another right-wing congressman, Dana Rohrabacher (R-California), added that the President's supporters "have done everything they could to try to intimidate people. . . . Every time you turn around they're trying to find any little thing to dig up on everybody. This is the worst God-awful tactic that I've ever seen by anybody on the planet."

In other words, the Republicans' tactics during their six-year offensive against the President and the First Lady had boomeranged. And, now, they were whining about it.

White House press secretary Joe Lockhart insisted:

> There is no evidence that anyone at the White House had anything to do with this story. Any suggestion to the contrary, without evidence, might be irresponsible.
>
> It doesn't surprise me the Republicans are doing this. What is surprising is that the media will roll over as easily as they do and assume the burden is on us to prove we had no involvement.

Flynt issued a public statement of his own, saying:

> I don't take my marching orders from the White House. I did this on my own to expose the hypocrisy in Washington. If they're going to be passing judgment on the President, they shouldn't have any skeletons in their own closets. . . . When our report comes out, Clinton's going to look like Mary Poppins compared to the rest of these guys.

In short, everyone was caught completely off guard by the Flynt project, as well as the revelation about Livingston.

PART NINE: THE FLYNT PROJECT

After I returned to Washington on December 18, the day after Livingston's confession, Jim VandeHei of *Roll Call*, the reporter who broke the Livingston story, was interviewed by Katie Couric on the *Today Show*.

> **Couric**: So, tell me how you first learned about Bob Livingston's indiscretions, if you will.
>
> **VandeHei**: We had learned yesterday afternoon that Speaker-to-be Bob Livingston was going to inform the Republican conference that, in fact, he had had extramarital affairs, fearing that they were going to be disclosed in a publication such as *Hustler*. . . . [H]e wanted to let them know and he wanted to be the one that informed his colleagues.
>
> **Couric**: Was *Roll Call* itself working on a story as well?
>
> **VandeHei**: No. I want to stress that we do not report on the sex lives of members of Congress. We only became interested when I learned that Speaker-to-be Livingston would possibly resign his post if members were disgusted by his revelation. . . .
>
> **Couric**: Do you think we're going to hear more revelations of this nature in the next few days and weeks?
>
> **VandeHei**: My understanding is we are going to hear several more revelations. Larry Flynt has hinted that there are many more to come. And I know there are a lot of members of Congress that are probably shaking in their boots right now.

Tim Russert, the Washington bureau chief of NBC News, also appeared on *Today* and was asked for his assessment of the political atmosphere in the wake of Livingston's admission.

> **Russert**: The biggest fear here is "scorched earth." People are looking over their shoulders, wondering what is coming next and what are politicians doing to themselves. It is almost a season for cannibals. The entire foundation of the system seems to be shaken. People are very nervous in Washington as the impeachment debate begins.

Couric: You talk about scorched earth. People are wondering, Tim, when does it end? We heard about Henry Hyde's "youthful indiscretion" in recent months. Now we're hearing about Bob Livingston. Larry Flynt, apparently, says he has dirt on ten more Republicans, so, I mean, this whole atmosphere must be so strange.

Russert: Katie, it is a policy called M. A. D.: Mutually Assured Destruction. And unless people call a truce, they realize there are going to be more victims for the next several months and years.

Early on Saturday morning, December 19, the *Washington Post* placed a story on its website, "GOP Support for Livingston Appears Solid." Reporter Eric Pianin predicted that Livingston, who appeared quiet during the impeachment debate the day before, "continued to maintain solid support among most GOP members and appears headed for easy election next month to succeed Rep. Newt Gingrich as speaker. An aide said Republicans have been 'incredibly supportive' and that many are saying: 'Let's get back to business.'"

But Pianin's reporting was hardly prophetic.

In contrast, Alan Fram of the Associated Press, which published its assessment, wrote:

> Some conservatives are beginning to question whether Rep. Bob Livingston should become the next House speaker, even as many other Republicans are rallying behind him following his admission of marital infidelity . . . Livingston's problem is intensified by the narrow GOP margin in the next House: just 223-211, plus one independent who usually votes with Democrats. If just six Republicans refuse to support him for speaker, he would lack the 218 votes needed to be elected—assuming the Democrats and independents vote against him.[202]

PART NINE: THE FLYNT PROJECT

124. Livingston resigns

Exhausted after the pressure and excitement of the past two days, I stayed in bed as my telephone began ringing during the late morning of Saturday, December 19, 1998. I was too tired to answer it, so I just let it ring, call after call.

"Who is doing this to me?" I shouted at the phone, placing a pillow over my head. "Obviously, I'm not here!"

But after a half dozen more calls came in, I finally surrendered and picked up the receiver.

"For heaven's sake," I muttered at the person on the other end, "I'm trying to get some sleep here."

"I can't believe you're not watching this!" My good friend and poker buddy, Jeff Goldberg, shouted at me. "Turn on your TV! Turn to any channel!"

I grabbed the remote control and switched on the television, as well as the record button for the VCR, realizing that something important was happening.

Goldberg, who was still on the phone, yelled out, "Do you see what's going on?"

After only seconds of watching the incredible scene on the thirteen-inch Sony in my bedroom, all I could do was say to myself, "Oh my God! . . . Oh my God!"

"Thanks for getting me up for this," I told Goldberg as I hung up the phone.

Speaker-designate Bob Livingston had just taken the floor of the U.S. House to announce his vote to impeach President Clinton, declaring:

> To the President, I would say: "Sir, you have done great damage to this nation over this past year. And while your defenders are contending that further impeachment proceedings would only protract and exacerbate the damage to this country, I would say that you have the power to terminate that damage and heal the wounds that you have created. You, sir, may resign your post."

As he was being booed, jeered, and told "You resign!" by House Democrats, Livingston raised his hand slowly and dramatically asked for quiet. Then he continued:

> And I can only challenge you in such fashion if I am willing to heed my own words. . . . So I must set the example that I hope President Clinton will follow. I will not stand for Speaker of the House on January 6th, but rather I shall remain as a back-bencher in this Congress that I so dearly love for approximately six months into the 106th Congress. Whereupon, I shall vacate my seat and ask my Governor to call a special election to take my place.

As mouths dropped all over the country, this moment represented the motherlode of the politics of personal destruction. . . . The Speaker-designate of the U.S. House of Representatives—second in the line of succession to the U.S. Presidency—had just announced his resignation.

Realizing that low comedy had just evolved into high tragedy, I shouted at myself, "This is *not* what was supposed to happen!"

I ran into the shower. En route, I turned on my two other televisions full blast while ignoring the telephone, which continued to ring.

After I stepped out of the shower, grabbed a towel, and threw on a robe, I walked quickly into my office where the phone was still ringing. Looking at my Caller ID screen, I saw that the call was coming from Allan MacDonell.

"Allan!" I exclaimed as I answered the phone, not waiting for him to identify himself. "What have we just done?"

He replied nearly out of breath, "I have no idea how this is going to play out! What do you think?"

"The guy wasn't supposed to resign! Whether he wanted to or not, he was supposed to join our team! He was supposed to rail against the politics of personal destruction and demand that even public officials are entitled to private lives! He wasn't supposed to quit and try to take Clinton down with him!"

"I think you better jump on the next plane and get out here! Larry's going to want to see us!"

"I'm on my way! I'll call you when I arrive!"

Shortly after Livingston's resignation, the House of Representatives voted to impeach the President of the United States, setting the stage for the upcoming trial in the United States Senate.

During my flight to Los Angeles, I was manic, trying to calculate the damage we had just done to the country and to America's body politic. And, even though the media had not yet linked me to Flynt or his investigation, I also began to worry about how quickly I would be destroyed after my role in all of this inevitably became known.

But the more I thought about Livingston's resignation and the President's preordained impeachment, the more I became convinced that we had done something extremely important, perhaps monumental—maybe even something really historic.

By the time I arrived at LAX, I was convinced that Livingston's resignation might just diffuse the entire post-impeachment, pre-Senate-trial process by bringing this entire situation to critical mass.

"That," I thought, "I can live with."

I also believed that we had just helped to destroy the Woodward-and-Bernstein dreams of a handful of arrogant and biased Washington journalists who had become shills, stalking horses, and confidential informants for Independent Counsel Kenneth Starr. They desperately needed the President's removal from office in order to justify their abuses and excesses.

All in all, it didn't turn out to be such a bad day after all. And I was as proud as I could be to have played the role I did.

Jonathan Alter—a columnist for *Newsweek*, which had led the Washington sex patrol against President Clinton—disagreed, writing: "Saturday, Dec. 19, 1998—a day that will live in inanity—felt like the set of a bad Peter Sellers movie. In the morning, Speaker-to-be Bob Livingston quit, a de facto admission that pornographer Larry Flynt was running the country."[203]

On Sunday, December 20, Maureen Dowd of the *New York Times* wrote:

> Ordinarily one would feel sorry for Mr. Livingston. But the Republicans have brought this sexual doomsday machine [of Larry Flynt] on themselves by focusing so single-mindedly on Mr. Clinton's sex life.

Weeks later, the *New York Times* revealed a remarkable but terrifying reality:

> The shock waves of the Livingston resignation spread far beyond the West Wing of the White House, and had a sobering effect on members of Congress of both parties who might have been contemplating calling for Clinton to step down in the aftermath of the impeachment vote.
>
> Fearful of the entire Government unraveling, very few members of Congress joined a clamor for Clinton's resignation.[204]

125. At play in the fields of scandal

After I arrived in Los Angeles, rented a car, and checked into my hotel, the desk clerk gave me a message, telling me to meet Flynt at the Four Seasons Hotel in Beverly Hills.

Instead of the strictly business-like atmosphere of our first meeting on December 7, this meeting was much more comfortable and familiar. Truth be told, we were absolutely jubilant.

When I saw MacDonell, we grabbed each other. Then, I went to Flynt, bent down to him in his gold-plated wheelchair, and hugged him, too.

Even though we were still deadly serious about our overall project, we could not help but be thrilled by what had just happened.... The iron will to force the President's resignation or for the U.S. Senate to convict and to remove him from office already appeared to be dissipating.

In effect, we believed that Livingston's resignation—and our role in that decision—had stopped a runaway train.

Flynt raised my hourly fee an extra $100 to $225 and gave me a $25,000 bonus and another $10,000 advance for my future work.

Frankly, I needed the money and gratefully accepted it. But that evening, alone in my hotel suite, I did not feel much like a journalist. I didn't even feel like a guerrilla writer who was on a crusade to advance a particular cause. Instead, I felt like a freelance hit man who had just taken sides in a local mob war.

But, as the long night wore on, I kept reminding myself, over and over again, why I had joined this battle in the first place.

And then, I remembered the Washington journalists who had taken the side of Kenneth Starr and the OIC, accepting their questionable leaks while covertly shilling for the prosecution—in the midst of pretending to be objective reporters while being identified as confidential informants by the OIC. All the while, they were being well paid by their employers and receiving six-figure book contracts for the inside stories about their investigations of the President's sex life.

To me—a hard-bitten crime reporter, who had spent his career probing far more dangerous crimes and was now off on a temporary political tangent—this situation suddenly became laughable. My libel case against the *New York Times*—in which I was nearly destroyed by a sportswriter who misrepresented my work in a book review and was then protected by the First Amendment crowd—proved to me that even those who made the rules of our profession were capable of tremendous hypocrisy, too.

PART NINE: THE FLYNT PROJECT

Now, at least for the moment, I was working for pornographer Larry Flynt—perhaps the king of the First Amendment. To me, Flynt's cause was righteous and worth everything I was risking.

By the next morning, I had overcome any lingering doubts about my mission and went back to work.

Meantime, the public-opinion polls told the tale. The CNN/Gallup/*USA Today* polling group discovered that on December 21, two days after impeachment and Livingston's resignation, the President's approval rating had skyrocketed to 73 percent—while the Republicans' favorability rating had dropped to 31 percent.[205]

On December 21, I obtained evidence—not from someone on our original list—of Republican Senator Tim Hutchinson's affair with a young law student who had also worked as his legislative director in Arkansas. Supposedly, Hutchinson's wife of twenty-nine years had confronted the young woman in public.

I wrote a memorandum to Flynt and MacDonell, saying:

> Tim Hutchinson has allegedly been having a long-term affair with [the woman]. He is the brother of Rep. Asa Hutchinson, a [U.S. House] manager in the Senate trial, who has been taking the legal and moral high ground against the President. . . . Allegedly, Hutchinson's wife became aware of the affair and created a scene in the office, causing [the woman] to quit. However, according to the source, Hutchinson, despite his pledges to the contrary, allegedly can't stay away from her. . . .
>
> For the record, no one has signed a confidentiality agreement on this matter. . . .[206]

However, we were faced with the dilemma about what to do with information about a juror/judge in the upcoming Senate trial of President Clinton. If we pulled the trigger, could we be legitimately accused of tampering with the jury?

Meantime, on December 22, Flynt received a telephone call from Bonnie Livingston who pleaded with him not to go further with his investigation of her husband. Mrs. Livingston had been widely identified in press reports as the person who convinced him to resign from Congress.

Moved by her call, Flynt—struck by the human cost of his project, which had started out as a whimsical gimmick but had now become a lethal weapon—ordered me to back off on my continuing probe of Livingston.

Because Livingston had threatened Flynt in that day's *New York Times*—saying that Flynt "would eventually get his 'just rewards'"[207]—I protested and wanted to continue. But, seeing that Flynt was showing compassion for Mrs. Livingston and her family, I relented and agreed to end my investigation of Livingston.

In a December 27 article by reporter Steve Profitt of the *Los Angeles Times* who had interviewed Flynt, the journalist wrote:

> Would it be at all ironic, then, if it turns out the white knight in this current round of sexual McCarthyism is the pornographer Larry Flynt, the publisher of *Hustler* magazine, the anti-Christ of family values....
>
> Flynt, a Democrat, says he has evidence of sexual misconduct by a number of other Republicans, and he threatens to publish the details sometime after the new year.
>
> Yet, if you believe him, Flynt would rather not publish the dirt he bought with his million-dollar reward. In fact, he says, his intent is to stop the prying and probing into private sex lives altogether by applying his own brand of mutually assured destruction....
>
> [Flynt concluded,] "Pundits and politicians can talk until they're blue in the face about perjury and obstruction of justice by Bill Clinton, but it all comes down to sex. The man had an affair, and he lied about it."[208]

126. "The rule of law"

One of the callers on Flynt's original list of tipsters was an anonymous person who claimed but could not prove that Gail Barr—the second of the three wives of Representative Bob Barr, the congressman who had filed the original articles of impeachment against the President long before Monica Lewinsky became public property—had an abortion while married to Barr who also had an alleged history of philandering.

Significantly, Barr had actively portrayed himself as an anti-abortion, pro-family advocate, widely supported by the religious right. In fact, Barr, a member of the Pro-Life Caucus, had stated in a speech on August 4, 1992, "I would do absolutely everything in my power to stop" a family member from having an abortion.

Flynt sent me to Marietta, Georgia, on December 3, 1998, to investigate Barr. During that trip, I could not find any evidence of the alleged abortion, but I did discover that Gail Barr had filed three separate legal complaints against Bob Barr between 1985 and 1995—all stemming from their decision to divorce, which became final in 1986.

However, after collecting and reading everything available in Marietta's hall of records, I realized that the sworn depositions of Bob and Gail Barr were not part of the public record.

Also, I learned that Bob Barr had married his third wife within days of his final divorce decree, raising suspicions that Barr had been seeing this woman while he was still married to Gail who had been in the midst of a potentially deadly bout with cancer.

Furthermore, I was surprised to learn that adultery was illegal in Georgia. For anyone else, I could not have cared less. But for Barr—whose mantra on the U.S. House Judiciary Committee, which recommended the President's impeachment, were the words "the rule of law"—I wanted to press the issue. And, more importantly, I knew that Flynt would want to drive that point home.

I photocopied everything available on *Barr v. Barr*, sending the certified originals to Flynt and keeping copies for my files.

But, knowing that I would probably have only one shot at Gail Barr, I decided not to contact her while I was in Georgia. Before doing anything, I wanted to talk strategy with Flynt and MacDonell, both of whom I was scheduled to meet for the first time in Los Angeles on December 7. And, in a memorandum to them before our meeting, I addressed the issue of how to handle Gail Barr, as well as several other women who had been named by other informants, saying: "I would like an approved plan as to how to approach these women—with the understanding that when we approach them and if they reject us, our [work] ... will become public."

At our first face-to-face meeting, Flynt was particularly interested in Gail Barr's story. We agreed that the key to the investigation of her ex-husband was obtaining the sealed depositions in their divorce case, so

Flynt instructed me to use my best judgment and to move on her when I returned to Washington.

Back in Washington, I reached Gail Barr on Saturday afternoon, December 12. Following our very brief conversation, I wrote a memorandum to Flynt and MacDonell, saying:

> I spoke to Gail Barr, who listened and then abruptly ended the conversation. A young man had answered the telephone, so she had at least one person at her home. I didn't get to the home-run question before she cut me off. Also, she said that she was in the midst of mowing her lawn.
>
> However—even though she said that she didn't want to discuss her ex-husband—I did sense that if approached in a more comfortable way, she might talk.

Two days later, I called her back. After that conversation, I sent another memo to Flynt and MacDonell, saying:

> This was my second call to Gail Barr, and, this time, she was alone. After I reminded her who I am, she tried to get rid of me. Then, I mentioned that I was in a position to offer her a great deal of money if she had the information we have been looking for, specifically evidence of her ex-husband's alleged public hypocrisy in light of his alleged private deeds. I did not mention the story about the abortion. . . .
>
> At that point, she told me that she said that she had worked for her ex-husband and helped him get elected to Congress. I replied that, from everything I had heard, she had been a loyal and devoted wife, adding that I had obtained the entire case history of their 1986 divorce, her 1988 contempt charge against him, and her 1995 litigation to modify their previous agreements.
>
> She asked me if Bob Barr was the only politician we were going after. I told her that he was one among many whom we were investigating and about whom we were receiving cooperation.
>
> Clearly fearing the fallout, she said that her two boys loved their father very much.

PART NINE: THE FLYNT PROJECT

> I told her that we could arrange for her to have cover, but that I couldn't do anything until I talked to her. I offered to meet her in person and to give her a confidentiality agreement, inviting her to bring her attorney or anyone else she trusted, adding that I would be happy to meet her and her representative in a public place or anywhere else where they would feel comfortable.
>
> When she asked who was putting up the money, I told her Larry Flynt Publications. She didn't react to that. . . . She still seemed to be against the idea, but I gave her my name and telephone number, telling her to think about the offer and inviting her—or her attorney—to call me back.

Soon after, I received a call from Gail Barr's attorney who was tough but appeared willing to open negotiations. At the conclusion of our first conversation, I sent him a confidentiality agreement for his client's signature.

On December 21—while I was back in California, two days after Bob Livingston's resignation and the President's impeachment by the full House—I arranged for Gail Barr's attorney to fly to Los Angeles the next day to meet with Flynt, MacDonell, Isaacman, and me in Flynt's office. Because I was acquainted with Mrs. Barr's attorney through our telephone conversations over the past few days, I volunteered to pick him up at the airport, in lieu of a chauffeur whom Flynt wanted to send. I wanted to get a feel for what the attorney would be willing to say and offer before the meeting began.

During our trip from LAX to Beverly Hills, the attorney made it clear that he was ready to drive a hard bargain for something that Gail Barr really did not want to do.

As the meeting opened, the attorney showed us the sealed depositions in *Barr v. Barr*. These sworn statements indicated that Bob Barr in 1986, the year he became U.S. Attorney in Atlanta, had allegedly been having an affair with the woman who became his third wife. But, when confronted about this subject by Gail's attorney during his sworn deposition, Bob Barr had allegedly balked in his deposition and then gave the Georgia state-law equivalent of the Fifth Amendment.

Also, Gail Barr's attorney—who confirmed that she did have an abortion—brought along the receipt from the abortion clinic, which we would also receive as part of his proposed deal.

After hearing the attorney's offer, Isaacman proposed that the value of the depositions would be greatly enhanced if Gail executed a sworn affidavit, detailing, among other matters, the episode about the abortion.

127. Abortion and aftermath

After nearly two weeks of negotiations with Alan Isaacman, Gail Barr and her attorney agreed to Flynt's offer—for an undisclosed amount of money. This would be the only payment Flynt made to any source—at least to my knowledge—during our entire project.

On January 8—the day after the Senate trial of the President officially began—MacDonell flew to Atlanta with the check for Mrs. Barr. In return, he received the sealed depositions, along with her sworn affidavit, and the receipt from the abortion clinic.

Mrs. Barr's sworn statement placed everything into perspective, especially in view of the fact that, regarding his wife's abortion, Bob Barr had stated under oath: "It was against my wishes."

When an attorney asked him, "And you opposed this?," Barr replied, "Yes."

Gail Barr's affidavit, which challenged all of this, was heart wrenching and even infuriating to read—a classic story of an older woman, suffering from cancer, who was abandoned by her husband for a younger and healthier woman. Specifically speaking of her abortion, Mrs. Barr stated:

> In March of 1983, . . . when I became pregnant the third time, our two sons were three years old and a year-and-a-half. I was 38 years old, concerned with health complications the pregnancy might present, and Bob's [law] practice was slow, and he was not home much. We did not have any health insurance. I asked Bob what we should do; whether I should have an abortion. He said it was entirely my decision and that I should do whatever I wanted to do. This was an extremely difficult choice, but Bob did not want to help in making the decision, even though he was the father. If Bob had said, "No, don't have an abortion," I never would have had it done.

PART NINE: THE FLYNT PROJECT

Bob never told me not to have the abortion, or that he was in any way against my having the abortion. Any statement he made that he expressed his opposition to the abortion is simply not true.

On the Saturday of the Memorial Day weekend in 1983, Bob drove me to the clinic to have an abortion. He watched our boys at home while this procedure was done. He then came to the clinic to get me. He paid for the procedure. . . .

In 1984, Bob was running for a state representative seat in Georgia against an incumbent. I asked him to stop campaigning after my cancer surgery and while going through chemotherapy, but he refused. He told me that the campaign would take my mind off my health problems. He never went to the chemotherapy treatments with me. He never tried to understand what I was going through. He was not there for me when I needed him. . . .

On a Saturday night about two weeks before Thanksgiving of 1985, Bob announced to me in our garage, "I don't love you anymore," and that he was moving out. Our boys were five-and-a-half and four. I asked him to stay at least through Thanksgiving, but he refused and left immediately. . . .

A few months after Bob left home, he moved into an apartment building where Jeri resided. Our children would visit him there. They would come home and tell me about "Dad's water bed" and how they were spending time with "Jeri". While Bob and I were separated and before our divorce, Bob and our boys also would spend the night at Jeri's. . . .

In May and June of 1986, Bob and Jeri, Bob's current wife, were deposed. Both refused under oath to answer questions about their relationship either as it existed prior to [the] time Bob left us or during the time Bob and I were separated. Specifically, each refused to answer whether they were having an affair during my marriage to Bob. . . .

In September of 1985, I was helping out as a secretary in Bob's law office. He had me call to make luncheon arrangements

— 457 —

with the woman he later married. Obviously, at the time, I did not realize Bob was having a romantic relationship with this woman. Friends would tell me that they saw Bob and Jeri holding hands at the mall or in restaurants. . . .

Our divorce was finalized on November 3, 1986. A month before, in October of 1986, Bob was named United States Attorney. Bob married Jeri in December of 1986. I was given custody of our children. I have not remarried.

And, just for the record, Gail Barr added in her sworn statement: "I did not approach LFP, Inc., or Larry Flynt. They contacted me regarding Bob."

Flynt arranged to release his findings about Bob Barr, which were designed to be a surprise, at a press conference in Los Angeles on January 11, 1999, at 7:00 P.M.—10:00 P.M., Eastern time.

Throughout the day, speculation ran wild about what Flynt was going to reveal, raising expectations into the stratosphere. For instance, the *New York Post* reported that morning:

> According to the rumor mill, Flynt is ready to reveal that one powerful Republican likes to cross the Mexican border and hire teen-age prostitutes; a second forced his lover to have an abortion; a third was caught having phone sex on his car phone; a fourth . . . had an affair last year at the height of the intern scandal; and a fifth will be outed as gay.

128. Geraldo sandbags Flynt

Before Flynt's widely anticipated media event, he agreed to appear on CNBC's *Rivera Live*, hosted by Geraldo Rivera, to reveal a portion of his evidence against Barr.

However, on his highest-rated program since the October 1995 verdict in the O. J. Simpson trial, Rivera chose to sandbag Flynt, refusing to allow him to discuss Gail Barr's abortion or Bob Barr's questionable statements under oath about the abortion.

"Give us the headline, Larry," Rivera said.

"Well, the individual we're talking about is Bob Barr," Flynt replied. "He was the first member of Congress to ask for President Clinton's resignation. We have established that he did not tell the truth under oath, and we have depositions to back this up."

After getting that out, Flynt then unwittingly entered Rivera's forbidden territory, saying, "I find even more troubling than that is the fact this man consented to his wife having an abortion."

"Wait, wait, wait, wait, wait," Rivera interrupted. "I don't want to go into abortions."

Simply trying to explain what we had uncovered, Flynt continued, "I only want to make one statement about that. It's very important."

Rivera—whose staff had known well in advance that the abortion issue was going to come up and in what specific context—interrupted again, saying, "Why is that? It is a legal right in this country."

"Because he stood [in] the House of Congress and said abortion was equivalent to murder," Flynt argued, still hoping to get his information into the interview. "But he still had permitted it [with his wife]."

"Larry," Rivera said with great condescension, "you undermine your case by going there."

Only allowing Flynt to discuss Barr's alleged affair with his soon-to-be third wife and his alleged taking of the Georgia equivalent of the Fifth when asked about it, Rivera said sarcastically, "Is that the smoking gun about Robert L. Barr?"

"Yeah," Flynt replied, "that alone is enough. But I know you don't want me to go to the other direction."

"Please," Rivera chided him. "Please, do me . . ."

"But . . ."

"Honor me that," Rivera pleaded. "Honor me."

"All right. To me, the other is more egregious than this."

Then, after a commercial, Rivera went to his other two guests, Jerry Falwell and Alan Dershowitz, who knew only what they had heard in the earlier segment. Predictably, both trashed the significance of what Flynt had to say about Barr.

After a year of reveling in gossip about knee pads, cigars, and stained dresses, Geraldo Rivera was obviously trying to regain his journalistic footing by silencing Larry Flynt.

The interview was such a disaster that East Coast news organizations, facing a late deadline, watched Rivera's program and, for the most part, dismissed Flynt's charges against Barr. The *New York Times*, for instance, completely ignored Flynt's findings in the following day's newspaper.

Even Matt Drudge, certainly no supporter of President Clinton, was baffled by Rivera's behavior, writing the next day in the *Drudge Report*: "It was not clear if Geraldo was just not fully briefed on the nature of what Flynt was going to unload; if Geraldo, a lawyer himself, really believes that lying under oath is not a crime; or if Flynt was just salt and peppering his Barr discoveries."

Immediately after Rivera's interview with Flynt, C-SPAN, which had earlier announced that it would cover Flynt's press conference live, suddenly changed its programming schedule. A C-SPAN spokesman, blaming Flynt's appearance on *Rivera Live*, told his television audience that C-SPAN would consider broadcasting the Flynt press conference on prerecorded tape—but only after reviewing its content.

Sitting in my home in Washington, seething with anger after watching *Rivera Live* and then C-SPAN cancel its live coverage of the press conference, I called Flynt on his private line just moments before he met with the media. I strongly advised him to launch an all-out attack on Rivera because the talk-show host had double-crossed him and jeopardized our work on Representative Barr.[209]

Despite the *Rivera Live* debacle, the press conference went off on schedule, packed with 200 reporters. Along with his prepared statement, Flynt provided reporters with Gail Barr's affidavit, her receipt from the abortion clinic, and excerpts from the sworn depositions of Bob Barr and the woman who became his third wife.

129. Barr overplays his hand

Even though Flynt and our team had clearly nailed Barr for hypocrisy, Barr appeared to have survived the evening and even watched as Flynt went on the defensive. At that point, all the congressman really had to do was refer his critics to Rivera's interview with Flynt and the C-SPAN cancellation, and then issue a public statement, taking the high ground.

Indeed, the congressman did issue another kind of statement, saying:

> I am deeply saddened that Larry Flynt's money has been used in an attempt to drive a wedge between the mother and father of two wonderful boys who deserve better than to become

PART NINE: THE FLYNT PROJECT

involved in the politics of personal destruction. I will not add to his efforts to attack me, my children or the wonderful woman to whom I have been married for over twelve years, by discussing our personal lives in any way, shape or form with the news media.

That being said, it is important to set the record straight on two accusations relating to issues on which I have taken a public stand. First, as an officer of the court for over twenty years, I have never perjured myself. Secondly, as a public official who has cast dozens of pro-life votes in Congress, and a strong opponent of abortion, I have never suggested, urged, forced or encouraged anyone, including my ex-wife, to have an abortion.

The only thing worse than Larry Flynt's conduct is the scarcely concealed glee this White House has displayed toward it. By refusing to condemn the actions of Larry Flynt and others like him, the White House has proven that its lofty statements against the politics of personal destruction are no more than empty words.

But, then, overplaying what could have been his winning hand, Barr felt the need to say more. He agreed to an interview the following day with CNN's Wolf Blitzer, who confronted him with questions about Flynt's revelations—some of which Barr badly bobbled.

Then, Barr appeared on CNN's *Crossfire*, where co-host Bill Press bludgeoned him with more questions, confronting him about his alleged adultery and hypocrisy.

Even Larry King became unusually aggressive with Barr who appeared on CNN's *Larry King Live* that same night:

> **King:** Let's discuss one of the things [Gail Barr] said in her [affidavit]. She said that you didn't say you were having an affair with someone else, but you didn't answer the question. Is that correct? You didn't answer the question?"
>
> **Barr:** Under Georgia law, that's the procedure. I mean, when you go into a deposition in Georgia, the same as when Bill Clinton goes into a deposition, he has three choices. He can just tell the truth. He can afford himself of whatever privilege there might be that he wants to assert under the law, the

federal law in his case, or he can lie. One of the differences between the two of us is he chose the last one. . . .

King: Why didn't you tell the truth? Why didn't you answer?

Barr: Everything that we have said, Larry, on this was in our statement. It's well documented. It's no surprise that all of this came out today. It was, I think, well orchestrated. It's no coincidence that this came out. This is very clearly an effort to take old documents, old matters, twelve years old, and try and derail to some extent or divert attention to some extent from the trial in the Senate beginning Thursday of William Jefferson Clinton for perjury and obstruction.

King: Is it unfair, though, if the person making the charge believes that you committed perjury and therefore how could you judge a perjurer as a perjurer?

Barr: Larry Flynt doesn't have anything nor should he have anything to do with the trial of William Jefferson Clinton—although it's interesting that they have a circle of friends that overlap rather substantially, apparently. And even when Mr. Flynt was leveling these charges last evening, he could not, would not, and did not make a flat-out statement that there was no communication, no discussions, no interfacing between his investigators and people at the White House. And I think that tells us something
. . . .

King: Had Clinton, then, done the same as you and taken the privilege, would you have not been for his impeachment?

Barr: The only way you can either convict in a criminal sense or impeach for perjury is if somebody lies under oath. . . . .

King: And what is the story on the abortion question?

Barr: That is something that I will not go into beyond what I have said in our statement today, Larry. It's unfortunate that people go into these things, but I will not other than to say I

PART NINE: THE FLYNT PROJECT

have never, ever encouraged or forced anybody to get an abortion. I would never do that.

King: How about the printing of a check, though, your signature for the abortion?

Barr: Well, here again . . .

King: I mean, that seems *prima facie*, as they might say in legal terms.

Barr: Some people may go into these things—when you're married to somebody, Larry, you have joint accounts. You have insurance plans and so forth. But I have never encouraged, condoned or forced somebody to have an abortion. Those sorts of things should play no role in any sort of dialogue in any of the substantive matters we're involved in. It has not the remotest connection to the perjury and obstruction by William Jefferson Clinton.

Earlier, on ABC's *Good Morning America*, host Elizabeth Vargas asked Flynt, "How many people do you plan to target in this campaign of yours?"

Flynt replied, "We have eight other investigations that I feel very strongly about. And if any of them materialize, the Republican Party will be in shambles, because they're all right-wing conservative Republicans."

Later in the program, Bill Kristol, editor of the conservative *Weekly Standard*, revealed, "I've talked to a bunch of Republicans this weekend. And I have to say the issue of Larry Flynt and what he was going to reveal and how that will be treated by the media was the number-one topic of conversation. . . . It's personally somewhat sickening to me that Larry Flynt is now driving the nation's political agenda."[210]

Senator Frank Lautenberg (D-New Jersey), during an appearance on MSNBC, had a different opinion about our project, saying, "Larry Flynt says his mission is against hypocrisy and, boy, I think that's a pretty good mission!"

Meantime, the one person seemingly lost in the shuffle was Gail Barr. In a moving defense of her recent action, columnist Marie Cocco of *Newsday* also summarized her ex-husband's hypocrisy, writing:

> Barr votes to ban any and all abortions, no matter what. To prohibit federal workers from getting a health-insurance policy that covers it. He voted against protecting abortion clinics from violence. Against allowing military women to use their own money to get abortions at American hospitals abroad. Against letting the District of Columbia use its own taxpayers' funds to provide Medicaid abortions for poor women. Against even covering birth control for federal employees.
>
> He's a four-star general in the war to take abortion back to the back alleys.[211]

Not surprisingly, on January 13, the day after CNN had placed Barr back on defense, U.S. House Majority Whip Tom DeLay selected Barr—who had already been chosen as one of the President's prosecutors during the Senate trial—as the Assistant Majority Whip.

130. "Who got Bob Livingston?"

In the aftermath of Speaker-designate Bob Livingston's startling admission to the Republican caucus on December 17, 1998, and his announced resignation two days later—two events which took the Congress, the White House, and the media completely by surprise—the search intensified for Larry Flynt's still-anonymous investigator.[212] Underscoring the mystery, reporter Mary Leonard of the *Boston Globe* asked: "Who got Bob Livingston? It has become a hot question since the speaker-designate shocked the House on Saturday with his decision to decline the leadership post and resign from Congress."[213]

Through everything that had happened, I remained silent, quietly continuing my work.

Early on, the only person to call and ask me the big question was Karen Foerstel, a reporter for *Congressional Quarterly*. While I was in Los Angeles on December 20, she had left a message on my answering machine in Washington, giving me her home and work numbers. I assumed that she had heard my name from someone close to Livingston, who could have known as early as December 12 that I had been interviewing sources in New Orleans.

PART NINE: THE FLYNT PROJECT

I telephoned Foerstel two days later at her home during work hours, trying to avoid speaking to her but still wanting to return the call so as not to raise more suspicions. Without specifically denying my role with Flynt, I left a non-denial denial—something like, "Where could you have possibly heard something like that?"—on her answering machine and invited her to call me after the holidays. Mercifully, she never did.

I still had high hopes for the successful completion of my work for Flynt and then a quick ride out of Dodge without ever being identified. Even though I was proud of what I had done and why I had done it, the intense warfare between President Clinton's enemies and his supporters threatened to annihilate anyone who entered—or got dragged into—the fray. I already had a taste of that through the chain of events which began with the publication of my book about Vincent Foster's suicide in April 1998 that led to my affidavit on the alleged leaks from Kenneth Starr's office, which I submitted to Judge Norma Holloway Johnson the previous August.

In his effort to provide cover for me, Flynt was intentionally coy about the identity of his investigator. Consequently, knee-jerk speculation reflexively pointed to Terry Lenzner, the president of the Washington-based Investigative Group International, who was also a friend of President Clinton.

On the MSNBC program, *News Chat*, on December 21, host John Gibson asked Flynt, "Can you tell me it is not Terry Lenzner, the P.I. firm that has done the investigation for the White House and the President's defense team?"

"I'm not answering that question," Flynt replied curtly.

Another guest, GOP consultant Craig Shirley, snapped back, "You can put that down as a yes, John."

Flynt responded, "You can't put that down as a yes or a no, either one. I'm not going to answer it."

"Larry," Gibson continued, "do you understand how this looks? It now appears that the President has given a wink and a nudge to Larry Flynt and said, 'Go get him,' and that Larry Flynt is."

"No. That's not true at all," Flynt insisted.

That same day, Mark Levin, the head of the Landmark Legal Foundation—another right-wing, Richard Scaife-funded operation—issued a statement, claiming:

> Last Friday, *Hustler* magazine publisher Larry Flynt, who is paying $1 million for embarrassing information on Republican officials—and helped end the political career of would-be

> House Speaker Bob Livingston . . . would not deny that Terry Lenzner, the private detective hired by the president to trash his adversaries, is working for him. Flynt promises more disclosures.

On December 28, Lenzner released his own formal denial to MSNBC, saying in a written statement:

> The Investigative Group categorically denies ever having been retained by *Hustler* magazine to conduct any investigation or inquiry at any time. We have never spoken to Larry Flynt or any agent or representative of Mr. Flynt. Furthermore, Investigative Group has never conducted an investigation of Speaker Livingston nor were we asked to do so.

Flynt and I felt horribly about placing Lenzner, whom we both respected, in such an awkward position.[214] However, at that time, Flynt and Allan MacDonell were still in the midst of sensitive final negotiations with Representative Bob Barr's ex-wife while I was still working alone and juggling over twenty separate investigations.

On the same day as Lenzner's official denial, Representative Bob Barr sent Flynt a letter, stating:

> I have been informed you are publishing an article in your magazine, *Hustler*, suggesting that I have lied under oath. Such an allegation is outrageous and absolutely untrue. As a lawyer and officer of the court for over 20 years, and a former United States Attorney sworn to uphold the laws of the United States, I have never lied under sworn oath.
>
> Consider yourself on notice this entirely unfounded and salacious accusation is false, and uttering it through your magazine would demonstrate an utter and malicious disregard for the truth.

In response, Flynt drafted a letter on January 5, 1999—three days before MacDonell flew to Atlanta to pick up the evidence against the congressman—saying:

> I do want to advise you that we are investigating various allegations involving your moral and ethical conduct in relation to subjects upon which you have taken a public position.
>
> If you would like to comment on these allegations, please call my investigator, Dan Moldea.

Flynt then gave Barr my telephone number in Washington.

Before sending this letter, Flynt's executive assistant telephoned and read it to me, asking for my thoughts. I told her that I still had a great deal to do and didn't want to be recognized or hassled while doing it, adding that there was no way that Barr would keep the name of Flynt's mystery investigator a secret. She responded that she understood my concerns and said that she would have Flynt talk to me.

A few minutes later, Flynt, who sounded very ill, called and said that he had given this matter a great deal of thought and decided that we had to give Barr an opportunity to respond. Yielding to Flynt's sense of fairness, I consented to the letter, as written. However, I predicted that when I was publicly identified as his investigator, the news would be a total anticlimax—inasmuch as the President's enemies were hoping that someone close to the White House had been doing all of these investigations.

Regardless, Flynt and I agreed that the time had come for us to take the White House—as well as Terry Lenzner and even James Carville—off the hook.[215] They never had anything to do with us or what we were doing.

Knowing that it would be just a matter of days before my role in Flynt's investigation became public—and that the right-wing media was going to try to tear my head off—I asked a trusted friend, Pam Braden, the president of Gryphon Technologies in Washington, to design a website for me, *www.moldea.com*. It would give me an opportunity to respond to what I knew would be an immediate onslaught of false accusations and disinformation.

Among other things, I posted my August 24 affidavit on OIC leaks, which I believed would clarify much of what I had done since the publication of my book about Foster's suicide.

131. *Newsweek* outs me

On January 8, 1999, Mark Hosenball of *Newsweek*, with whom I had been acquainted for several years, called and asked me to confirm or deny that I was Flynt's mystery investigator. Deciding that I would get a fair shake from this one-time poker buddy, I admitted that I had handled the probes of Livingston and Flynt's other targets while reminding him about the sworn affidavit on my website about the OIC leaks and denying any White House involvement in our investigation. However, I refused to go into any further detail about my ongoing work for Flynt.

Hosenball's story, written with Andrew Murr—"Who's on Larry List?", which identified me for the first time as Flynt's mystery investigator—ran in *Newsweek's* January 18 issue, released on January 11, the same day that Flynt revealed our information about Bob Barr.

Hosenball and Murr reported:

> Flynt had a tough time finding respectable journalists or gumshoes willing to take on the job. But at least one, *Newsweek* has learned, eagerly accepted: Dan Moldea. An investigative crime reporter and author of controversial books about pro football and the O. J. Simpson case, Moldea is a Clinton sympathizer. *Last year he approached the president's private lawyers with a tantalizing story: in phone calls Moldea secretly recorded, two of Kenneth Starr's top deputies admitted that their office routinely briefed sympathetic reporters.* Moldea later repeated the leak charge in a sworn statement to the judge overseeing the Starr probe. Moldea investigated the allegations against Livingston. He confirmed to *Newsweek* that he is continuing to investigate other Clinton critics. (Moldea and the president's attorneys deny there is any connection between the White House and Flynt.) [Emphasis added.]

However, the fact remained: I did not approach the President's attorneys; rather, they had approached me. Hosenball—who apparently was trying to dismiss me as some sort of sycophant—had specifically asked me about this and even had a copy of my sworn affidavit to Judge Johnson in which I explained my contacts with Williams & Connolly. Still, he got the story wrong, and his error would start another chain of events that would cause me huge problems.[216]

PART NINE: THE FLYNT PROJECT

On January 13, 1999—the eve of the opening arguments in the Senate's impeachment trial against President Clinton—the *Washington Post*, *Newsweek's* parent company, published its own article by reporter Howard Kurtz, repeating that I was Flynt's investigator. Authorized by Flynt to comment in the wake of the erroneous *Newsweek* article, I told Kurtz that, indeed, Flynt had several "big fish" on his plate. However, I added that some of them would not be made public, saying:

> Some Republicans on Capitol Hill should be sending us flowers and thank-you cards. They weren't going on TV talk shows shooting off their mouths [about Clinton], or going to the floor of Congress to seize the moral high ground. We've thrown them back in the river. We're not going to interfere with their lives.[217]

Actually, I had meant these remarks to be conciliatory.

That same day, Bill Sammon of the *Washington Times*, another right-wing Clinton critic with whom I had also agreed to speak, published a front-page story, "Flynt sleuth dished dirt for White House," cynically using my role in the OIC leaks investigation as evidence of my—and, thereby, Flynt's—connection to the White House.[218]

Sammon wrote in his lead paragraph: "The investigator who dug up dirt on Republican Reps. Bob Barr and Robert L. Livingston for pornographer Larry Flynt is a Clinton sympathizer who has supplied the president's attorneys with evidence against independent counsel Kenneth W. Starr."

Although Sammon portrayed this as a major expose, he failed to mention that I had detailed all of this and more in my sworn affidavit, which was already posted for all to see on my public website.

Continuing his story, Sammon then quoted me about the Flynt investigation, saying: "I don't think there's anybody on our team who's getting much joy out of this. When you start hurting families, that's something that makes you pause and think about what's going on. But at the same time, I just haven't seen any mercy shown towards Clinton—I mean, none, zero."

Using a version of the quote I had given to the *Post* about throwing non-hypocritical Republicans "back in the river," Sammon gave this statement a nefarious twist, writing: "[Moldea] made it clear he has uncovered salacious material on more Republicans whose identities will remain secret as long as they refrain from speaking out against Mr. Clinton."

As spun by Sammon, I appeared to be threatening or even blackmailing unnamed members of Congress! Although this allegation was nonsense, it quickly took on a life of its own.[219]

As the Senate trial of President Clinton began, Flynt and I were widely accused of political terrorism with our campaign. Along with other members of Congress, Senator Larry Craig (R-Idaho), who would later have his own personal problems, insisted, "Intimidation is something we have to resist. You don't negotiate with terrorists. This is almost a terrorist-like tactic being used here."[220]

Senator James M. Jeffords (R-Vermont) told reporters, "I'm deeply concerned. I think any effort to blackmail a person . . . That's very serious."[221]

Meantime, Senator Orrin Hatch (R-Utah) continued to suggest a link between Flynt and the White House, using me as his foil on NBC's *Meet the Press*: "I don't know anybody who's hiring these tough, mean investigators like has been done for the President."[222]

On January 14, Senator Jon Kyl (R-Arizona) was asked by a reporter, "Any backlash about the Larry Flynt stuff in the Senate you heard today in the cafeteria or in the gym or anything, Senator?"

"Sure," Kyl replied, "there was a lot of backlash."

"What did you hear?"

"Well, the usual. This is not helpful to the process."

"Are the senators angry about it?"

"I might characterize some of them as pretty upset about it, yes."

"Was this going to influence the trial one way or the other in any way?"

Kyl then said, "Well, you know what? I don't even want to talk about it because it simply gives [Flynt] credibility that I don't want to give him."[223]

The following day, responding to a question about Flynt's alleged threats against Republican senators, GOP consultant Heather Nauert said during a television appearance on Fox News, "I think the problem with that is that these members are keeping quiet—members that would normally be out front denouncing the President are now remaining silent because they're so afraid of this campaign that they've—that . . ."

"You really think so?" The host asked. "You really think they're intimidated by it?"

"I absolutely do."[224]

Reporter Peter Baker of the *Washington Post* told Terry Gross, the host of NPR's *Fresh Air*:

PART NINE: THE FLYNT PROJECT

Well, there was a real atmosphere of fear among congressmen, particularly Republicans. Just the fact of Larry Flynt out there was terrifying to them. . . . [A] number of the managers, the people who would prosecute the president in the Senate trial, were convinced that they were the next target.

One congressman got phone calls to his office threatening to out him as gay, even though he says he, of course, is not. But the fact that he's conservative and from a Southern district, just the whisper of that would be damaging. Another congressman feared that he was on the list and so he had sort of a cleansing conversation with his wife in which he sort of admitted all, all of the things that maybe she wouldn't have liked to have known, just so she wouldn't hear about them from anybody else. And, of course, it turned out he wasn't actually on Larry Flynt's list. So there was a real atmosphere of fear that these people were living through at the time.[225]

At the daily White House briefing on January 13, press secretary Joe Lockhart fielded a question from a reporter who asked, "Larry Flynt's investigator, Dan Moldea, says that he has uncovered information on additional Republicans, but is going to withhold it as long as they don't criticize the President. Does this strike you as blackmail and will the White House call for him to cease and desist?"

Lockhart simply replied, "Listen, the President has been as clear as possible that he thinks the politics of personal destruction should cease and desist, and should have ceased and desisted a long time ago. I don't know anything about this gentleman you're talking about. I believe, as the President agrees, that all of this kind of sleazy politics ought to stop and it ought to stop from the right, from the left, and from the people who create the market in this stuff. And it's our hope that it does."

Regardless of anything the White House said, the false claims that Flynt and I were linked to the President and his operatives continued and escalated.

132. The right-wing media reacts

High noon had come for the President's enemies as the Senate trial got underway on January 7, 1999, the culmination of years of vicious allegations, wild conspiracy theories, and wholly partisan investigations—all of which had gone nowhere. Now reduced to criminalizing the President's personal life by alleging that he had lied about sex, the Clinton haters were finally at center stage. The time had come for them to put up or shut up.

However, their earlier high confidence for the President's removal from office had dissipated considerably after the circumstances of Livingston's resignation on December 19—and was further diminished by Flynt's continuing crusade to expose hypocrisy in the wake of his revelations about Bob Barr.

In fact, other than the unmasking of Kenneth Starr as an alleged partisan sexual witch hunter after the release of the *Starr Report* in September 1998 and the excellent legal work performed by the President's attorneys before and during the Senate trial, there was no single factor which had a greater impact on the impeachment process than Larry Flynt.

Had Flynt never emerged in this drama, Bob Livingston would have become Speaker of the House and the impeachment of the President would have shifted from the House to the Senate with a tremendous, even a devastating momentum. At the very least, the pressure on President Clinton to resign from office would have been overwhelming.

Instead, with Livingston's stunning resignation and the hypocrisy of the President's enemies clear and present to the American public—who then, in response, kept the President's approval ratings high—the case limped to trial.

Consequently, the right-wing media, which had invested so much time and energy to bring about the downfall of the President, turned their guns on Flynt and anyone close to him, especially me. And, as with their other dead-end investigations of the President—involving the circumstances revolving around the Foster suicide, Whitewater, Travelgate, and Filegate, among others—they did not allow the facts to get in their way of a good story.

Here is a sampling of what Flynt and I were up against:

* Syndicated columnist Tony Snow, the right-wing journalist who introduced Linda Tripp to Lucianne Goldberg, declared: "Larry Flynt, abetted by investigative reporter Dan Moldea,

has attempted to blackmail Republicans into cutting Clinton free."[226]

* Jamie Dettmer, in his article for *Insight*, a magazine owned by the *Washington Times*, wrote:

Right and left the battle rages and good men act out of character, such as author-turned-hired-gun Dan Moldea, who has swapped his reputation for free thinking and independence to become Flynt's blackmailer in chief. . . . [M]oral equivalence or truth-seeking apparently doesn't matter to Moldea. The point again is media terrorism, scandal, intimidation—he makes no bones about it, saying publicly he'll hold back on outing Republicans who keep their mouths shut about the president. Isn't that a possible contempt-of-Congress offense and a potential breach of the federal statutes concerning obstruction of justice?[227]

* Matt Labash of the conservative *Weekly Standard* added:

Flynt has repeatedly asserted that he hired a Washington private investigative firm chock full of ex-FBI and CIA operatives, but he declines to name it. Inquiring minds assumed he'd hired Terry Lenzner, the Clinton camp's usual private eye. But when I talked to Moldea, he denied knowing anything about this, adding, "Personally, I don't believe there is a detective firm. If there is, where's their work? I don't see their work. Who did Barr? I did Barr. Who did Livingston? I did Livingston." Moldea also denies any White House connection.[228]

* On January 14, Mark Levin of the Scaife-funded Landmark Legal Foundation filed a formal complaint with the Criminal Division of the U.S. Department of Justice, charging Flynt and me with attempting "to influence and impede" the Senate's impeachment trial and adding:

Messrs. Flynt and Moldea are not free to corruptly "endeavor to influence" a congressional inquiry, such as an impeachment inquiry or an impeachment trial inquiry, by threatening, intimidating or coercing Republican members of Congress to keep silent about Mr. Clinton's conduct lest potentially embarrassing personal information involving the members and/or their families—which was either purchased by Mr. Flynt or otherwise gathered by Mr. Moldea—be made public.

* The following day, Republican National Committee chairman James Nicholson issued a press release, stating that he had "joined in the non-partisan Landmark Legal Foundation's demand for a criminal probe of pornographer Larry Flynt and his investigator, Dan Moldea, for the felony of Obstructing Congress. Besides assisting Flynt, Moldea assisted Clinton's defense team, Nicholson noted. . . 'The Flynt-Carville-Moldea tactics of intimidation and blackmail aren't just wrong, they're illegal, and our Attorney General ought to take off her blindfold and begin criminal prosecutions.'"

* On January 16, the *Washington Post* reported on all of this nonsense, stating:

In a letter addressed to officials of the department's criminal division, the foundation said Flynt's efforts and those of his investigator, author Dan Moldea, could constitute obstruction of a congressional investigation. Flynt may have violated federal law by allegedly "threatening, intimidating or coercing Republican members of Congress" to remain silent about Clinton's conduct or face embarrassing disclosures about their personal lives, the letter said, adding that obstructing Congress is "a felony punishable by five years imprisonment and a fine of $250,000." . . . Justice Department spokeswoman Chris Watney said the request for an investigation "is under review." Flynt's attorney, Alan Isaacman, called the demand for an investigation "absurd."[229]

* Then, playing off the initial erroneous *Newsweek* story, televangelist Jerry Falwell, who had lost a landmark U.S. Supreme Court defamation case to Flynt, wrote a column on January 15 that was totally false, alleging:

Dan Moldea, the lead investigator for Larry Flynt's ongoing quest to uncover sexual indiscretions of Republican congressional members, has now admitted he was hired by the law firm defending President Clinton. Moldea affirmed that the firm of Williams & Connolly initially contacted him to uncover evidence that Kenneth Starr, Whitewater independent counsel, had violated rules against leaking grand jury information to the press."[230]

* Robert J. Caldwell, an editor for the *San Diego Union-Tribune*, published an article on January 17, repeating Falwell's false charge that I had actually admitted working for Williams & Connolly. Caldwell wrote:

> Moldea's former employment was with the Washington law firm of Williams and Connolly, whose lawyers are defending President Clinton in the impeachment proceedings. Moldea says his job at Williams and Connolly included investigating special prosecutor Ken Starr's investigation of the president.[231]

* On January 18, the *Wall Street Journal* ran an editorial, entitled, "Abetting Blackmail," once again falsely charging that I had "worked for" Williams & Connolly, just as Falwell and Caldwell had claimed. Further, the *Journal* charged that Flynt and I were actively involved in a pattern of threats and blackmail against Congress. Joining the calls for the Criminal Division of the Department of Justice to investigate us, the *Journal* continued:

> [The Department of] Justice says the complaint is under review, and surely the criminal issue needs official study. Also, of course, there is the further issue of whether Mr. Moldea dug up all this dirt himself, or whether he is being aided and abetted by agents of the President. *He has, as it happens, previously worked for the President's law firm, Williams & Connolly.* [Emphasis added.]

From the outset, I realized that I was going to take a ton of grief for my role in the Flynt project and already decided to turn the other cheek to almost all of it. But, after seeing this editorial in the *Wall Street Journal*, I was mortified, as well as angry, and wrote harsh letters to Robert Bartley, the executive editor of the *Journal's* editorial page, as well as to Falwell and Caldwell, demanding retractions, threatening litigation, and insisting that I had never "worked for" or received any money from the President's lawyers or Williams & Connolly.

I also added: "I have had no contact, directly or indirectly, with anyone from the White House or any of the President's attorneys or operatives during my investigation for Mr. Larry Flynt."

Responding to my demands in a second editorial two days later, the *Wall Street Journal*, which referred to my earlier libel case against the *New York Times*, published perhaps the most disingenuous retraction in the history of journalism, writing:

> Dan E. Moldea, official mud-miner for scatology king Larry Flynt, says we have done him wrong. . . . What is in question is the phrase "worked for." If we wanted to play Clintonesque word games, we could ask, what is "for" for? Does it not mean "on behalf of" and isn't that what happened? But we desist, because many readers would indeed take "worked for" to mean he got paid, which the public record does not currently support. So as requested, we hereby retract the word "for." Substitute the word "with." . . . Here we see in all their splendor the current point men in the Clinton defense movement. Is this how the Senate and the Democratic Party want to be represented, or will they separate themselves from the gutter inhabited by Mr. Flynt and Mr. Moldea?[232]

I allowed this version of the *Journal's* retraction to stand without further comment.[233]

But, regardless of whatever the right-wingers charged, Flynt and I had done nothing illegal.

I did have my defenders in the mainstream media, and their comments appeared in, among others, articles published by *Newsday* and the *New York Observer*. Journalist Steve Love, a long-time friend at the *Akron Beacon Journal*, my hometown newspaper, wrote an op-ed piece about my growing dilemma. Critical of my recent actions but concerned for my personal and professional safety and welfare, Love wrote:

> [B]y becoming what Republican National Committee Chairman Jim Nicholson refers to as a "goon" for "the president's favorite pornographer," Moldea is walking a thinner line between acceptable investigative journalism and salaciousness. Nicholson and the nonpartisan Landmark Legal Foundation

> are demanding that the Justice Department investigate Flynt and Moldea for obstructing Congress, a felony. . . .
>
> Moldea, who is single, is no candidate for sainthood. He also knows the harm he is doing to others' lives. This bothers him, but not as much as the sexual McCarthyism he sees plaguing America.
>
> I don't know Flynt. But I do know Moldea. To him this is a holy war. He would wage it for nothing. Scorch enough beds and maybe Americans will be repulsed enough to stop this. It is the sexual equivalent of a nuclear deterrent.
>
> I hope it works, but I doubt it will.
>
> Escalation remains the order of the day. No one is sheathing his weapon.[234]

Remarkably, I never received a single death threat either over the telephone or in person during my work for Flynt. However, a steady stream of cars and vans, sometimes three at a time, parked daily in front of my home, as well as up and down the street.

Through some of my long-time friends and sources who were able to check licenses and auto registrations, I learned that no fewer than eight of these vehicles were linked to the same private-detective firm in Virginia. Another journalist who lived in my neighborhood even became friendly with one of these surveillance people who did identify me as their target. The journalist executed a sworn statement about this conversation and gave it to me.

At one point, out of sheer frustration, I approached one of the drivers and complained about the intrusion. He replied, "Fuck you, Moldea! I am in a private car on a public street."

Knowing there was nothing I could do about this situation and fearing a possible home invasion—especially after my surveillance guy found a tracking device in the wheel well of my car—I simply had the doors to my apartment alarmed, among other internal precautions.

Realizing that I was working alone in Washington and half expecting FBI agents to come crashing into my apartment at any second to make an arrest, Flynt brought me back to Los Angeles and placed me in a suite at a Beverly Hills hotel under an assumed name until we thought it was safe for me to return home.

133. Flynt nearly dies

On the afternoon of January 14—as oral arguments began in the Senate trial—Flynt was rushed to the Cedars-Sinai Medical Center in Los Angeles after experiencing severe breathing problems. The medical staff at the hospital concluded that Flynt, who had clearly been ailing over the past couple of weeks, had double pneumonia.

In fact, Flynt nearly died. He had actually stopped breathing while with his wife, Elizabeth Berrios-Flynt, a nurse who had cared for him for several years before they were married in June 1998.

Liz, one of the finest people I had ever met, wound up reviving him and saving his life.

Later that week, as Flynt was recovering, Frank Rich, a columnist for the *New York Times*, wrote approvingly:

> It is almost too delicious to watch Mr. Flynt throw his high-minded colleagues in the news business into conniptions. . . .
>
> Mr. Flynt's antics have similarly prompted many mainstream TV news outlets—CNBC, ABC's *20/20*, CNN, *CBS This Morning*—to demonstrate yet again that, for all their pious declarations to the contrary, the scandals they care most about are those with sex. . . .
>
> Larry Flynt is a bull in the china shop of false pieties, empty pretensions and sexual sermonizing that have brought us to this low moment in American history. On Thursday, alas, he checked into a Los Angeles hospital with pneumonia. The networks that have been broadcasting soap operas rather than the Senate trial . . . can only pray that Mr. Flynt, who has it in his power to make impeachment must-see TV again, gets well soon.[235]

Although MacDonell and I went on with our work, we had no idea how Flynt's ill health would impact on our overall project. To us, his condition could not have come at a worse time.

PART NINE: THE FLYNT PROJECT

Regardless of our situation, informants continued to call Flynt's headquarters, claiming to have information about the President's enemies. But, after *Newsweek* revealed my role in the investigation, I told both Flynt and MacDonell that I did not trust any of the new tips we were receiving, because the tipsters knew that they were going to get a call from me. And I simply refused to walk into a potential ambush. Consequently, I continued my work, concentrating only on those investigations initiated before I was identified.

Interestingly, while Flynt was recovering, the President's enemies tried to use the Flynt project as a means of discrediting political rivals and suspected mutineers within the Republican Party. For instance, Rush Limbaugh alleged on his radio show that Senator Richard Shelby (R-Alabama), who had announced that he would not vote to convict the President of perjury, "may have a Larry Flynt problem."[236]

In fact, Shelby was never under investigation by our team. We had never even received any rumors about him.

Then, after the President's State of the Union address on January 19, televangelist Pat Robertson shocked his conservative colleagues by saying of the President's speech on his syndicated *700 Club* program, "It was a boffo performance. You couldn't have staged anything any better. And as far as I'm concerned, the impeachment hearings are over. There's no way that the Senate is gonna vote to convict him and remove him from office, regardless of what he's done."

Robertson's comments were viewed by many among the religious right as nothing short of a public betrayal. In fact, reporter Noah Adams of National Public Radio spotlighted *The Eric Hogue Show*, a syndicated right-wing religious radio program, and those who called the show about Robertson's statement.

After one caller expressed his opinion about the pastor's remarks, Hogue replied, "Somebody emailed me and said maybe Larry Flynt has something on [Robertson]. I sure hope not."[237]

However, as with Shelby, we had nothing on Pat Robertson—not even a rumor.

134. The Byrd resolution

As the Senate trial got underway, a friend of mine called me at home, extremely upset. She sobbed that someone she knew well believed that he was next on Flynt's list and was planning to kill himself after being publicly named. According to my friend, he had brought a gun to work and was keeping it in a desk drawer. Even though I had refused to confirm or deny that he really was a target, she pleaded with me to convince Flynt to exhibit some mercy towards this man who was prepared to take his own life.

Immediately after this call, I talked to MacDonell and faxed a memorandum to Flynt, who had been released from the hospital and was recovering at home.

Clearly, the threat of a suicide chilled all of us. How could we live with ourselves if we outed this family man, and then he made good on his threat?

In the end, Flynt gave the guy a pass. And I admired him for making that decision.

Similarly, another top political figure received a reprieve after one of our sources had been careless with the documents I had given her, and he discovered them in her possession. Fearing that the source could be harmed, Flynt personally made the final decision to let him go, too.

Actually, throughout the Senate trial of President Clinton, Flynt intentionally balked, because he did not want to inflame the situation more than it already was.

If Flynt had really started this project for nothing more than headlines and money, as many had claimed, he would have pulled the trigger on the dead-bang information I had collected on Senator Tim Hutchinson (R-Arkansas), a judge/juror during the Senate trial—whose brother, Representative Asa Hutchinson (R-Arkansas), was a House manager/prosecutor, as well as a harsh and vocal critic of the President. Frankly, MacDonell and I both wanted to reveal what we had on Hutchinson, but Flynt ordered us to hold our fire until we saw how the trial unfolded.

Later, Senator Hutchinson, who voted to convict the President, shocked his colleagues and constituents by filing for divorce from his wife of twenty-nine years—in the midst of his long-term affair with the same woman whom I had identified: a young law student who had worked in his office.

Had the Senator ever lied to anyone about his relationship with this woman, who was not much older than Monica Lewinsky? Had he ever obstructed anyone from finding out about it?

And what did his brother, Asa, know—and when did he know it?

The silence about the Hutchinsons within the Republican majority in Congress was deafening.

PART NINE: THE FLYNT PROJECT

On January 22, after I had returned to Los Angeles, Allan MacDonell confirmed a news report that Senator Robert Byrd, perhaps the President's sternest critic among Democratic senators, had just announced that he would propose a motion to dismiss the entire impeachment case. Byrd's resolution had no chance of passage in the Republican-controlled Senate. However, the senator had placed the entire situation in context, saying, "I am convinced that the necessary two thirds for conviction are not there and that they are not likely to develop."

MacDonell gave the news to Flynt's trusted attorney, Alan Isaacman, and me. The three of us then called Flynt at home and put him on the speakerphone in Isaacman's conference room.

Undaunted, MacDonell wanted to move forward with more outings, insisting that we had to make good on our promise to finish what we had started, including the publication of the *Flynt Report*, which, at first, had been planned but, in recent weeks, had been placed on hold.

Isaacman, who also spoke for me, told Flynt that Byrd's proposed resolution, regardless of whether it passed or failed, guaranteed that the Democrats would remain firmly behind the President and not vote to remove him from office. The votes were simply not there. And we had already helped to derail any calls for his resignation.

Flynt agreed and, at that moment, declared an official cease-fire. "The politics of personal destruction have to end now," Flynt told us. "The least we can do is show some good faith and make the first move."

Later that day, I voluntarily left Flynt's payroll and returned to my life in Washington. But, before doing so, I advised Flynt to make a public announcement of his decision to end the project—even though there were still some tense moments ahead before the end of the Senate trial.

Soon after, the February 8 issue of *Newsweek*—which reported that Larry Flynt's public approval ratings were higher than those of both Kenneth Starr and Congress—quoted Flynt, saying: "My idea was to expose hypocrisy, but now if I released any more, it would just be to embarrass people."[238]

Even though many of our supporters were disappointed that we didn't reveal all of the information we had collected, Flynt's finest hour in this project, other than his handling of the Bob Livingston matter, came when he finally said, "That's it. No more."

In the end, we no longer had the stomach to go for the throat—unless the President was suddenly convicted and removed from office.

135. Light my fire

After I was identified by *Newsweek* as Flynt's investigator on January 11, 1999, friends and acquaintances, particularly from the world of journalism, began feeding me information about the personal and professional indiscretions of dozens of right-wing political figures, as well as some of the President's top critics in the mainstream media—including many of those who had become regulars on the television talk-show circuit.

For instance, one well-known and respected journalist—married with children and a relentless critic of what he repeatedly described as, "President Clinton's reprehensible behavior"—made the mistake of giving a credit card to the female-escort service he had retained during a recent trip to New York. A copy of the receipt, as well as a statement from the woman, wound up in my possession.

Also, I had received information about another brazen anti-Clinton reporter and his secret long-term affair with the wife of a colleague within his own media organization.

In addition, I learned that a third nationally known reporter, another high-handed critic of the President's alleged immorality, had recently and quietly settled a sexual-harassment complaint filed by a co-worker. Lying and obstruction accompanied each of these alleged activities.

As in the world of politics, hypocrisy was in ample supply within the tight-knit community of political journalists, especially among those who had recently enhanced their careers by attacking the President's morality.

On Friday, February 12, even though the President's survival was assured, some drama was still clear and present as the Senate, which had spent the past three days in closed session, voted on the reduced counts of perjury and obstruction of justice.

The President's enemies failed to receive a simple majority for either remaining count—let alone the two thirds required to remove him from office. On Article One, the perjury count, 45 senators voted guilty, and 55 voted not guilty. On Article Two, the obstruction of justice count, 50 senators voted guilty, and 50 voted not guilty.

At 12:39 P.M., Chief Justice William Rehnquist, who had presided over the trial, announced that the President had been acquitted.

After the Senate's verdict, President Clinton spoke to the nation, saying, "Now that the Senate has fulfilled its constitutional responsibility, bringing this process to a conclusion, I want to say again to the American public how profoundly sorry I am for what I said and did to trigger these events and the great burden they have imposed on the

PART NINE: THE FLYNT PROJECT

Congress and the American people.... This can be and this must be a time of reconciliation and renewal for America."

As the President walked away from the podium, a reporter shouted out, "In your heart, sir, can you forgive and forget?"

Clinton stopped and returned to the microphone, replying, "I believe any person who asks for forgiveness has to be prepared to give it."

After watching the President's speech on television, I just sat on the couch in the living room of my apartment for a few moments, thinking about everything that had happened over the past thirteen months, as well as what the President had just said during his brief address.

I really did not believe that this mess was finally over, but I truly wanted it to be.

As I started to think how I could end this matter as far as I was concerned, I looked back at my desk in an adjacent room and the file cabinet next to it. Then, I stood up, went to the cabinet, and opened the top drawer.

I pulled out my "J. Edgar Hoover file," which contained all of the leads and materials that had been fed to me by people inside and outside the Flynt operation.

Putting all of this material in three large boxes, I carried them to my car and drove to the Virginia home of Danny Wexler, one of my best friends. Upon arriving, I went into his den where he and his wife, Arlene, already had a small fire in their fireplace.

While my friends watched in disbelief, I took every document, one-by-one, and placed them on the fire.

When I completed my task about forty-five minutes later, I looked back at my friends and smiled, saying with considerable satisfaction, "Now, as far as I'm concerned, it's finally over."

The President's critics had demanded a public showdown on the issue of morality—and we had given it to them.

PART TEN:

Intermezzo

136. Buried alive by the Jello Left

One thing I will say for most conservatives is that after political combat they return to the battlefield, pick up their wounded, and nurse them back to health—so that they'll be ready for the next big fight.

No matter how many times right-wing blowhards—like Rush Limbaugh (alleged drug abuse), Bill Bennett (alleged gambling addiction), and Bill O'Reilly (alleged unrequited sexual advances towards an employee)—screw up, they always return to the front lines with the enthusiastic support of their rabid fans and the implicit support of the conservative wing of the Republican Party. They forgive these media stars for their lack of accountability, even though they demand it from everyone else.

The left, on the other hand, has a long history of leaving its wounded bleeding on the field of battle—or simply burying them alive. There is little loyalty among liberals for other liberals, especially for independent operators, like me, who work outside the mainstream.

In 1999, there was particular reason for my concern. On March 3, Congressman Bob Barr sent a letter to the U.S. Department of Justice, which stated:

> This request for an investigation focuses on attacks, and threats of attacks on members of Congress before and during the [Senate impeachment] trial; specifically the House Managers. These attacks came from Larry Flynt, James Carville, Dan Moldea, and other individuals, and represent what appeared to be a deliberate and concentrated effort to impede the House of Representatives from fulfilling its duties under the United States Constitution to conduct matters relating to the impeachment of the President, first in the House of Representatives and then in the Senate.

Barr's letter followed similar complaints and requests to the Justice Department's Criminal Division from the Republican National Committee, the Landmark Legal Foundation, and a variety of private citizens. They charged Flynt and me with blackmail, jury tampering, and obstructing the Senate impeachment trial, among other allegations.

Worried about an unjust indictment, I maintained a low profile during the Department of Justice's continuing probe into our activities.

On March 23, Jo Ann Farrington, Deputy Chief of the Criminal Division's Public Integrity Section, responded to a January 18 letter from community-activist Jane Spillane of South Carolina, the wife of mystery writer Mickey Spillane. She had insisted that Flynt and I be prosecuted. A Knight Ridder wire story on April 9 stated:

> According to Spillane, Flynt and his investigator, Dan E. Moldea, violated a federal criminal statute against individuals who "corruptly, or by threats or force, or by any threatening letter or communications, influences, obstructs or impedes . . . under which any inquiry or investigation is being had by either House, or any committee of either House." Conviction carries a maximum five-year penalty or $5,000 fine, or both.

Replying to the letter from Spillane, Farrington at the Justice Department wrote:

> I write in response to your January 18, 1999 letter requesting that the Department of Justice open an official investigation into whether Larry Flynt and Dan Moldea sought to obstruct the congressional impeachment inquiry and trial, in violation of 18 U.S.C. 1505. This matter is currently under review by the Criminal Division.[239]

White-knuckled, I had to wait and see whether I would be prosecuted.

Meantime, against my advice, Flynt released *The Flynt Report* on April 6, 1999. Although some of the information I received during my investigation was contained in this report, specifically about Livingston and Barr, I did not directly participate in its preparation because I believed it was overkill. In my opinion, we had done our jobs well by helping to save the Clinton Presidency. And I thought we should have simply left our silver bullet and rode into the sunset.

In the report, Flynt and his staff did not violate any confidentiality agreements signed by our sources. Consequently, much of the meat of our project went unreported—and would never be revealed. In other words, out of conscience, Flynt chose not to unleash the arsenal he had in his possession. His critics, as well as the unnamed targets of our investigation, should have been grateful that he was not the monster they believed him to be.

However, the media's reaction to the report was almost universally hostile. But, out of sheer loyalty, I felt compelled to defend Flynt wherever I could.

In her critical review of *The Flynt Report,* Carol Lloyd of *Salon* wrote:

> Dan Moldea defends Flynt, even though Flynt ignored his advice not to publish the report. [Moldea said,] "Since the beginning of his project, Larry has demonstrated restraint and compassion. He demanded the highest standards of documentation and responsibility. I believe that he was effective. History will cite the resignation of Bob Livingston—as well as Larry's role in that decision—as the critical moment that diffused the entire impeachment process, and I'm proud to have been associated with him."[240]

On June 25, apparently because we had not yet been indicted, Representative Barr filed suit against the Executive Office of the President (EOP) and the U.S. Department of Justice in the U.S. District Court for the District of Columbia. In this civil litigation, Barr, represented by the Scaife-funded Judicial Watch, suggested that the President had authorized James Carville to provide me with FBI files, which I then used as the basis of my investigation for Flynt. Both Carville, whom I had never met or spoken to, and Flynt were also named as defendants.

For reasons unknown, Barr did not name me with the others, even though Barr's complaint specifically stated:

> Defendant EOP's willful and intentional release of records and information concerning Plaintiff to persons such as Flynt, Carville, Moldea and/or others, without prior written consent or knowledge of Plaintiff, or any lawful justification violates . . . relevant provisions of the Privacy Act.

The court soon dismissed the case. Later, Barr, whose congressional district was reorganized, was defeated when he ran for reelection.

Still, in the wake of the war to save President Clinton, I had virtually no public defenders. Buried alive, I became a cautionary tale among my colleagues in journalism while liberal organizations, like the People for the American Way, expressed sheer terror at the prospect of any association with me.

Simultaneously, some on the right appeared to admire the precision and effectiveness of what Flynt and I had done. Eric Dezenhall of

Dezenhall Resources in Washington, D.C., a respected conservative and a successful crisis manager for corporations under siege, wrote:

> The Republicans' worst nightmare came when Flynt retained investigative reporter Dan E. Moldea, who had been standing up to Mafia kingpins, assassins, and corrupt union bosses for decades. Moldea, who made no bones about sympathizing with President Clinton's struggle, proceeded to systematically expose the sex lives of Republican congressional leaders on the grounds that they were not qualified to judge Clinton's morality. Regardless of where one stands on the political spectrum and the techniques employed on both sides of the Clinton wars, one thing soon became clear: The strategy worked.[241]

And, while attending a book party, my good friend, Janet Donovan, introduced me to one of the President's attorneys who was holding court at that moment with several guests. Initially, he dismissed me. But after his wife tugged on his jacket and repeated my name, he stopped in mid-sentence, turned and bowed, shaking my hand and saying, "Sir, you were a godsend."[242]

Also, in his controversial best-selling book, *American Rhapsody*, author Joe Eszterhas published a chapter, "Larry Flynt Saves the Day," in which he wrote:

> The pornographer saved the president by threatening to reveal other acts of pornography committed by—this time Republican—politicians. Larry Flynt was a hero, a self-appointed, self-financed Kenneth W. Starr. . . . He'd brought in a crack investigative reporter, Dan Moldea, who'd exposed Ronald Reagan's questionably close ties to Hollywood mogul Lew Wasserman and Teamster money, to run his million-dollar project.[243]

Because the spin on the entire Flynt project was so diverse—and because *The Flynt Report* had done so little to clear things up—I shifted gears and asked Flynt to allow me to publish an entire book about our experience. After receiving permission, I sent him a 400-page draft manuscript, a first-person account of my role. I invited him to give me his own personal story, hoping that Allan MacDonell and Allen Isaacman would follow suit.

PART TEN: INTERMEZZO

Generously, Flynt gave me full rights to the book project, even though we both recognized that he could claim complete ownership.

However, after I asked literary agent Frank Weimann to shop the manuscript in New York, we failed to get a single bid. In fact, the publishing houses appeared totally hostile towards this proposed book project, seemingly disgusted with both sides of the impeachment battle.

Meantime, inasmuch as I had voluntarily taken myself off Flynt's payroll on January 22, 1999, I simply tried to make enough money to clean up my remaining debt.

My lecture business—directed by my booking agent, Jodi Solomon—helped pay some of the bills. But at one university in Virginia, a right-wing professor tried to organize a boycott against me because of my work with Flynt. In the end, his tactic backfired, and I wound up pulling my biggest crowd of the year.

However, an attempt to award me with a one-year distinguished professorship at a university in Florida was literally blocked when another professor successfully organized against the appointment.

Also, as a result of the fallout from the Flynt project, I felt compelled to resign from the board of directors of a private-security firm, which was operated by two close but very conservative friends, one of whom was absolutely furious with me for my role during the impeachment process.

But others still remembered me for my work against the mob. I was invited to be the keynote speaker at the annual dinner of the Citizens League of Greater Youngstown, an Ohio community that had been plagued for years by organized-crime corruption. In its coverage of my speech the following day, the *Youngstown Vindicator* wrote in its lead paragraph: "Author Dan E. Moldea took the check for his speaking engagement, ripped it up and told the [citizens' league] to use it for a crime commission."[244]

Also, the Project On Government Oversight (POGO), via the Fund for Constitutional Government (FCG), retained me to investigate the circumstances behind the effort to charge POGO's leaders with criminal contempt of Congress in the aftermath of a serious dust-up this wonderful public-interest group had with six pro-oil-company members of Congress, including Senators Frank Murkowski (R-Alaska) and Kay Bailey Hutchison (R-Texas), as well as congressmen Don Young (R-Alaska), W.J. "Billy" Tauzin (R-Louisiana), Barbara Cubin (R-Wyoming), and Kevin Brady (R-Texas).

In the aftermath of my investigation, the charges against POGO were dropped—just as quietly as the manner in which I had conducted my probe. I had targeted the American Petroleum Institute, which I alleged had hired an outside firm to "dig for dirt" on POGO.

However, a disgruntled member of the FCG's board ratted out POGO, leaking details of my work to the right-wing *Washington Times*. Reporters Jerry Seper and Audrey Hudson, who attacked the FCG's decision to hire me on POGO's behalf, stated:

> During the Monica Lewinsky scandal in the Clinton administration, Mr. Moldea dug up dirt on Republicans for pornographer Larry Flynt.
>
> While on Mr. Flynt's [1998] payroll, he uncovered adultery by Rep. Robert L. Livingston, forcing the Louisiana Republican to quit Congress.[245]

Both FCG and POGO allowed me to comment for the story:

> Mr. Moldea, who last week confirmed the investigation for POGO, said he was "an advocate" and "a friend" of [POGO]. "Some bullies in Congress were trying to beat them up and they came to someone who could do something about it."

Machismo aside, I was absolutely defiant about the manner I had approached and handled the POGO caper.

During a bout with the flu, which kept me at home for nearly two weeks, I posted an open letter to the ultra-conservative *FreeRepublic.com*—one of the largest and, in my opinion, most dangerous political forums on the web. During the four-day period prior to my letter, these Freeper-sharks had posted no fewer than a half-dozen defamatory threads about me, including, "Moldea Blackmailed Congress During Clinton's Impeachment," "The Curious Case of Dan Moldea," and "The Evil of Dan Moldea Exposed." All of these threads wound up on search engines throughout the Internet.

In part, I wrote:

> Over the past several months, friends and colleagues of mine have expressed their concerns about the numerous, baseless accusations of criminal activity that have been leveled against me at the Free Republic.... As a tribute to your effectiveness, I have admittedly been harmed by the lynch-mob atmosphere revolving around many of these posts, particularly those which

have been not only false and misleading but reckless and malicious.

In short, many of you have drawn ridiculous and irresponsible conclusions about people, subjects, and events you know nothing about. And most of you have done so under false names, which is very frustrating to people, like me, who have to live with these charges without any means of making those responsible accountable for what they write.

Although I have no objection to those who use cyberspace handles for benign purposes, it is simply unfair that someone may state false facts and even allege criminal behavior anonymously. And I believe that making such statements without giving one's name is not only irresponsible but cowardly. The perennial argument that anonymity protects against retribution is lame and disingenuous.

The fact is that many of you post anonymously under your [Internet] handles (i.e. moneyrunner, sourcery, Doctor Raoul) to evade responsibility for your mindless speculations, half-baked opinions, and poorly-sourced facts. When people have no responsibility for what they say, they are apt to say anything. And the posts from the recent threads against me serve as a testament to that. . . .

With the publication of my letter, I made the decision to take the time to challenge any and all such defamations with my own public responses—which would hopefully appear on those same search engines.

137. Collateral damage

While I waited for a final decision from the Department of Justice on whether or not I would be indicted, I experienced renewed difficulties selling my book projects—after publishing three books in the four years since losing my libel suit against the *New York Times*, which included a national bestseller.

Prospective publishers look to the performance of an author's most recent book. So, before anything else was discussed during a pitch, I always had to explain how my last one wound up with Regnery, a notoriously right-wing publisher, which appeared to lack any enthusiasm to promote it because of my conclusions—even after giving me a $100,000 advance.

Regarding specific projects, I had proposed without success the inside story of the Las Vegas murder of casino owner Ted Binion for which I had the full cooperation of the two lead prosecutors in the case, as well as the memoir of a top leader of the Hell's Angels motorcycle gang and a book about on-the-lam Irish gangster Whitey Bulger in Boston with the assistance of one of the key witnesses against him.

In addition, I had to sideline a project in which I had exclusive access to a major Indian-gambling operation. Also, I had even tried but failed to sell the personal story about Dr. Jack Kevorkian, the very controversial physician whose assisted suicides had created a national debate, which I proposed to write with his attorney.

For a while, it seemed that all I was doing was writing book proposals.

Simultaneously, I watched in amazement as right-wing zealots—like Bill O'Reilly, Ann Coulter, and Barbara Olson—published huge bestsellers, demonizing Bill and Hillary Clinton, as well as American liberalism.

Meantime, as my career as an author went on the rocks, my college-lecture business for "The Mafia in America"—which had gotten me through previous hard times—went south. With no new books, I had fewer and fewer lectures.

Also, I had some new competition on the circuit. Michael Franzese, a Brooklyn mobster who had somehow managed to "retire" from the underworld after a supposed religious awakening, published his memoir and then gone on the national lecture tour. Also a right-wing conservative, Franzese, who had spent 43 months in prison after a federal racketeering conviction and then did additional time for a probation violation, was the son of the infamous John "Sonny" Franzese, the feared long-time underboss of the Colombo crime family in Brooklyn.[246]

In the midst of all of this bad news, I tried to get some good karma by continuing my Authors Dinner Group at The Old Europe restaurant and by helping writers in need. The problems of two of them—television producer April Oliver and author Jan Pottker—led to major litigations.

Oliver, a producer for CNN, had co-produced a program on Operation Tailwind, which claimed that the U.S. military had launched a lethal Sarin-gas attack on a Laotian village in September 1970 where a group of American soldiers had defected and then lived. The story

PART TEN: INTERMEZZO

received widespread criticism, so much so that CNN disavowed the program and fired both Oliver and her respected co-producer, Jack Smith.

In the aftermath of her dismissal, Oliver called and asked me to lunch to discuss her situation. During our conversation, I advised her to do what I would do: Fight back.

I introduced Oliver to my trusted attorney, Roger Simmons, who immediately took her case, along with Jack Smith's. Skillfully as usual, Simmons negotiated undisclosed settlements with CNN for both producers, who continued to stand by their reporting and never backed down from their work.

I also introduced Jan Pottker to Simmons. However, Pottker's problems were far more complicated. Several years earlier, Pottker had written a story for *Regardie's* about the Ringling Brothers and Barnum & Bailey Circus, which was owned by Kenneth Feld. The article was extremely critical of Feld and some members of his family.

After publishing the story, Pottker decided to write a book about Feld and the circus. Shortly after making that decision—unknown to Pottker—she became the target of a massive dirty-tricks campaign that lasted for several years. Running this operation was Clair George, the former chief of covert operations for the CIA, who had executed a sworn affidavit in a separate case, admitting his role in an ongoing effort to sabotage Pottker's life.

In an outstanding article in *Salon* about the Pottker case, investigative journalist Jeff Stein picked up the story:

> After Pottker read George's affidavit, she faxed it to her friend Dan Moldea, a well-known investigative reporter and author of several books. . . . Moldea's beat is cops, the Mob and corruption, but even he was shocked.
>
> "Jesus Christ," he said when he called Jan back. It was one of the most amazing documents he'd ever seen.
>
> "I was completely stunned," Moldea says. "Every investigative journalist I know has moments of paranoia—where we believe that higher powers are actively but covertly attempting to sabotage our work. But after reviewing the George affidavit, I had never seen such overwhelming evidence that just flat-out proved it."[247]

Roger Simmons filed the suit on her behalf in 1999. The principals settled the case nine years later—with the terms undisclosed.

In the midst of all this, Simmons—whose law partner, Ralph Gordon, had recently died after a sudden heart attack—had a triple-bypass heart procedure. His successful surgery followed the deaths of six of my closest friends and mentors during the past few years: Walter Sheridan, Mae Churchill, Carl Shoffler, Jack Tobin, Jon Kwitny, and Barbara Raskin.

With the exception of Roger Simmons in D.C., George Farris in Ohio, and John Sikorski in Massachusetts, all of my most loyal protectors were now gone.

Back in Los Angeles, Larry Flynt claimed to have developed information that Republican Presidential candidate George W. Bush, an anti-abortion advocate who promised a new morality in the White House, had allegedly committed adultery with an unidentified woman, which resulted in an allegedly unwanted pregnancy that was ended by an alleged abortion. After I turned down the assignment, Flynt hired two Los Angeles-based freelance writers to handle the job.

But, in the wake of a lengthy investigation, they failed to prove this allegation to the satisfaction of the national media.

After Bush's dark victory in the 2000 South Carolina GOP presidential primary—in which he fortified his status among hard-core right wingers with his trashy campaign against his chief opponent, Senator John McCain—I decided to return to journalism and see how I would be received.

Along with David Corn, the Washington editor of *The Nation*, I co-authored a major article about the Bush family's influence-peddling operations in China and Southeast Asia, as well as a second story about John Ashcroft's cronyism while he served as governor of Missouri.[248] Ashcroft later became Bush's attorney general.

But, despite the importance of these works, I simply could not afford to continue. The influence-peddling article took three months to research, write, and fact-check—for which I only received $2,000. And I earned even less for the Ashcroft story.

Consequently, what I posted on my website and my limited work for *The Nation* was the extent of my contribution during the 2000 Presidential campaign. As much as I wanted to get into the action and make a difference, I simply could not find a legitimate home inside the world of journalism. I was still too radioactive.

PART TEN: INTERMEZZO

Somehow, I had managed to survive in the wake of my libel case against the *New York Times*, but I did not appear to be surviving very well in the aftermath of my work for Larry Flynt. I started to feel a degree of solidarity with Tsutomu Yamaguchi, a Japanese businessman who had survived the nuclear attack at Hiroshima on August 6, 1945, and then took a train to Nagasaki where he barely survived the second blast three days later.

Still, remembering all that Flynt and I had accomplished, I had no regrets—although I started to wish that I had done more to protect myself with the media, which had redefined me.

The 2000 election of George Bush by the U.S. Supreme Court in the wake of Al Gore winning the nationwide popular vote annihilated any residual belief I still had in the judiciary in the aftermath of my 1994 loss to the *New York Times* and the Clinton impeachment debacle. With the Supremes' decision, the right-wing takeover of all three branches of the United States Government was now complete.

With a new crop of conservative attorneys expected to man the Schedule-C political jobs throughout the government, I fully expected to be indicted for my role in the Flynt investigation within a year. Because I felt so incredibly vulnerable, I sought protection wherever I could find it.

In early January 2001, just two weeks before Bush's inauguration, I accepted a consulting assignment with a conservative investigative firm.

Actually, I enjoyed the routine of going to an office, the closest thing I had to an actual job since my short stay at ACTION/Peace Corps in 1979-1980. In fact, since I worked on my own schedule, I started arriving at 6:00 A.M. to open the office. And then I'd usually be home by 3:00 in the afternoon—with the rest of the day to do whatever I wanted.

Throughout the six months that I did this consultancy, I worked on a single project—in which I was an advocate for a liberal cause—for which I signed a non-disclosure agreement.

Continuing my independent consulting work, I participated in several television documentaries about the Mafia, as well as the Jimmy Hoffa, Robert Kennedy, and even the Dean Milo murder cases that were aired on cable television.

Also, I received an assignment from CBS News, investigating the disappearance and presumed murdered of Chandra Levy, the young woman who had worked for the U.S. Bureau of Prisons when she vanished from her apartment near Dupont Circle in May 2001.

As the media's attention centered on Levy's affair with Representative Gary Condit, a California congressman—who, in fact, played no role in her disappearance—we focused our probe on one of her closest friends. Although he was never named publicly as a suspect, he was on the FBI's short list of persons of interest. We interviewed him in the midst of the media frenzy. We walked away from that interview even more suspicious of his possible involvement.

In the end, he agreed to take a polygraph examination, which he passed. However, when I spoke with him after the test, he replied, "You know, it could've gone either way."[249]

More than anything else, I now played the role of an investigative consultant. Hired by private parties, usually law firms, I entered battleground situations and advised clients, based upon my independent research, how to resolve their disputes. Their fights become my fights.

To be sure, while working as a consultant, I did not misrepresent myself as a journalist who was innocently and objectively working on a story. I scrupulously told all sources of information, up front, which hat I was wearing: journalist or consultant. And I did not identify my clients without authorization.

Consistent with my personal politics, I refused to work for people whom—or on matters that—I opposed on principle. And, of course, I had never and would never participate in any illegal operation.

During the early morning of September 11, 2001, I rushed around my apartment, getting ready for a routine appointment with my doctor in downtown Washington.

I stopped for a few moments to watch ABC's *Good Morning America* which presented a report that federal agents had alleged that DNA testing showed that a strand of Jimmy Hoffa's hair had been found in the backseat of the car that Chuck O'Brien had driven on the day of the ex-Teamsters boss's disappearance.

Just before leaving, I heard host Charles Gibson say that something had happened at the World Trade Center in New York City. The next camera shot showed one of the twin towers on fire. I immediately called Mimi, as well as a couple of friends in New York. All of us assumed that some terrible accident had just occurred.

While in the midst of a conference call, we watched in horror as a passenger jet crashed into the second tower.

PART TEN: INTERMEZZO

Having no idea what was happening, I drove downtown to my doctor's appointment on Pennsylvania Avenue. While putting quarters in the meter where I had parked, I saw a police officer. When I advised him to be careful in light of what was happening in New York, he replied that he was en route to the White House, which was just a few blocks away.

"The White House?" I asked.

"Haven't you heard about the Pentagon?" He replied.

"No, I've heard nothing."

He pointed to the south.

When I turned around and looked down the street, I saw billowing black smoke in the distance.

"That's the Pentagon?" I said.

"Yeah, a plane hit it just a little while ago. And another plane destroyed the Washington Monument and crashed on the Ellipse," which is just south of the White House.

Of course, this "news" about the Washington Monument was among the many false rumors that wildly circulated throughout Washington, which was nearly paralyzed by traffic jams.

Horrified by all this, I arrived at my appointment at 10:00 and was the last patient taken by my doctor that day. I was back on the crowded street, which was now nothing more than a parking lot, twenty minutes later.

I tried to call Mimi several times, but my cell phone, like just about everyone else's, only received a perpetual busy signal. When I finally got through to her momentarily, she told me that the twin towers of the World Trade Center had both collapsed.

Unable to go anywhere in my car, I spent the rest of the morning and much of the afternoon walking around the White House and down to the Ellipse. Nearly everyone I saw, like me, had the look of alarm or just plain fear on their faces.

No one had any idea what was going to happen next.

Later, the country started to learn the details about the brave passengers on United 93, who fought terrorists for control of a fourth hijacked plane which crashed into an open field in Somerset County, Pennsylvania. The terrorists' target appeared to be the U.S. Capitol, which would have completed a devastating blow against key symbols of America's financial, military, and political institutions.

A few days later, I received a call from an old friend, Amtrak attorney and former D.C. police officer Hamilton Peterson, who gave me the sad news that his father, Donald, and Donald's wife, Jean, were among those passengers killed on United 93.

In the aftermath of the 9/11 attacks, I started routinely carrying my digital camera, along with my cell phone—before they were part of the same device. With a camera in my hand, I thought that I would be more inclined to run into a situation unfolding in front of me—instead of running away.

In addition to the camera and phone, I packed other gadgets, such as a mini-digital tape recorder, a Swiss army knife, a flashlight, a thumb drive on my keychain for my important computer files, an antenna-like device that I could stretch for an additional three feet of reach, a small container of pepper spray, and a rosary or a Scapular—or both. With all of this in my pockets, I felt ready for anything.

138. Caucus of One

When it became obvious that the Bush Justice Department was not going to indict Flynt and me, I looked for another book project while continuing to do my independent consulting work. Later, on the advice of several friends who were private investigators, I decided to "get legal" and take the necessary course work, as well as the state-required test in Virginia. Shortly thereafter, I officially registered as a private investigator.

To be sure, I had zero interest in hanging a shingle and opening my own licensed agency. Even though I was having difficulties getting another book deal, I still viewed myself as a writer and an author, not a private eye. I saw my investigative consulting work as nothing more than a means of paying the bills until I finally received another publishing contract.

On the home front, Mimi was upset with me, demanding that I forget about publishing books and reinvent myself. She wanted me to open my own private-investigations business or, if necessary, get a job working for someone else.

As part of my sincere attempt to accommodate her, I accepted an invitation from Jonathan Tasini, the president of the National Writers Union, to run for a seat as one of his delegates to the union's annual convention during the summer of 2002. Prompted by Tasini, whom I viewed as a very committed and effective advocate of writers' rights, I also recruited three close friends—Washington authors Jim Bamford, John Dinges and Jeff Stein—to run, as well. Dinges, Stein and I were among the scores of founding members of the NWU in 1981. Dinges was widely known as the union's James Madison in that he had drafted its first constitution.

During the convention, the split between the forces supporting Tasini and his active opposition appeared to be heading for a contentious election of the new board of directors. In an eleventh-hour agreement, both warring sides agreed to a compromise coalition slate that would be supported by all. The accord determined that the eleven-member board would be composed of six supporters of Tasini, four members of the opposition, and one independent member, ideally trusted by everyone.

Because I had long-time friends in both camps, I was the "lucky" person selected as the neutral member. If I agreed to accept this position—which actually was quite an honor—I would become one of the three National Vice Presidents of the union.

Even though my painful experience as WIW president twenty years earlier was still vivid in my mind, my vanity trumped all, and I accepted the job as the nonaligned member of the board.

Predictably, the tentative peace quickly collapsed as the board—and thereby the union—was victimized by loose talk, wild charges, and escalating hostilities, foreshadowing a continuation of the unpleasantness within the organization. Between the two groups, little was stipulated and even less forgiven. Consequently, I immediately discovered that navigating safely between the two warring groups was impossible. And I quickly became a Caucus of One.

Meantime, the Bush Administration and its Republican brethren in the U.S. House and the Senate had taken the non-partisan goodwill that they had enjoyed since 9-11 and cynically used it to advance their right-wing domestic agenda. The Republican-controlled Congress passed controversial legislation, like the Patriot Act, which had an adverse affect on the state of writers, among others.

Hoping that these issues could reunite our membership, a colleague in the union and I proposed an idea for the creation of a Writers Rights Project, which would give us a common adversary.

In our pitch, we co-authored a story for the *American Writer,* the official voice of the NWU, saying:

> Writers in America are under attack—not just by terrorists, but also by their own government.
>
> The opening shot was fired by the Department of Justice just one month after the September 11 tragedy when Attorney General John Ashcroft partially suspended the Freedom of

Information Act (FOIA) in an internal memorandum to various Federal agencies. "When you carefully consider FOIA requests and decide to withhold records, in whole or in part, you can be assured that the Department of Justice will defend your decisions unless they lack a sound legal basis or present an unwarranted risk of adverse impact on the ability of other agencies to protect other important records," Ashcroft wrote.

To be sure, the creation of the Department of Homeland Security has blown another enormous hole in the FOIA. Under a controversial section of this newly approved legislation, virtually any document submitted to the new department becomes exempt from FOIA requests. Authors and investigative journalists, working to expose corporate crime, environmental abuses, or questionable government actions, have already seen their FOIA requests denied or held up indefinitely—with documents hidden behind the cloak of national security.

Not surprisingly, government surveillance under the Patriot Act and domestic programs like "Total Information Awareness" continue to receive the favor of the Bush Administration. Writers and activists defending civil liberties or labor rights—such as journalist Roger Calero, the associate editor of *Perspectives Mundial*, a Spanish-language news magazine published in New York—have already been targeted.

Also, as of this writing, the United States appears to be heading for war—with all of the tough rhetoric, chronic cheerleading, and brutal consequences that traditionally accompany a war campaign. As we all know, the first casualty of war is Truth, and, no doubt, the Truthtellers are next on the list.

Even though no one can predict how bad this situation could get, no crystal ball is required to recognize the dangerous period we are about to enter. As during the witch-hunting period after World War II, dissenting freelance writers and independent journalists may be attacked and blacklisted by the right-wing's sophisticated disinformation and personal-destruction machinery. In the worst-case scenario, writers will be prosecuted and imprisoned by the law-enforcement community.

And, just [as in] the bad-old-days, the mainstream media, which has no love and very little respect for freelancers, will allow all this to happen. The only difference between now and then is that the crusading mom-and-pop newspapers are gone, eclipsed by corporate concentrations in the publishing industry—which some still disingenuously claim has a liberal bias.[250]

However, as President Bush pushed for a war against Iraq, citing Saddam Hussein's alleged weapons of mass destruction, the writers' union pushed for a declaration against it. In fact, the group's board of directors passed a resolution unanimously with only one abstention—mine. In my defense, I wrote:

> In short, I have nothing but disdain for the right-wing coup and its war machine. However, I've learned from experience—as president of Washington Independent Writers during the first year of the Reagan Administration—that politicizing a writers' organization outside the arena of writers' rights only serves to divide the membership. Such stands also hurt the organization's credibility with the outside world.

The enormous amount of criticism I took for my neutral position on the Iraq war forced me to write another statement to all of the union's delegates, in which I stated:

> If "silence is betrayal" with regard to America's anticipated war against Iraq, then we better hurry up and make sure that the National Writers Union also takes a stand on the explosive situation between India and Pakistan—and let's not forget North Korea and its newfound weapons of mass destruction. Hey, do we have an opinion about what percentage of the Gaza Strip should be controlled by the Palestinian Authority? If so, let's get the delegates to pass a resolution. To be sure, there are moral imperatives all around us.
>
> Closer to home, how about a stand on abortion? What about capital punishment? Shouldn't we say something publicly on behalf of the union about the effects of second-hand smoke? The speed limit on interstate highways? The construction of nuclear power plants? Or the need to spade and neuter dogs and cats?

> We have it in our power to alienate every single member of this writers' union with non-writers' rights issues. So why be silent?
>
> Once again, for the good of the union—which has suffered from a long history of self-destructive behavior—I respectfully appeal to each of you to vote on the . . . anti-war resolution with your head, not with your heart.

Even Mimi and I argued over the war. She absolutely insisted that President Bush had no evidence of Hussein's weapons of mass destruction, his principal justification for the invasion.

I kept saying, "Bill Clinton was impeached for supposedly lying about sex. Do you think that George W. Bush is going to lie about the rationale for getting the United States into a war?"

In hindsight, I now know that Mimi was right, and I was wrong. To this day, I still don't know how President Bush survived this massive blunder, just as I will never understand how President Reagan survived all of his lies and deceptions during the Iran-Contra scandal. And, yet, it was President Clinton who was impeached.

In my final written report to the NWU membership before leaving my one-year term as a National Vice President, I wrote:

> I believe that the NWU is in the midst of a long-term identity crisis. In 1981, at an organizing meeting for the American Writers Congress, I predicted, in writing, that the organizers of the newly created writers' union would be frustrated by their inability to organize independent contractors. And, twenty-two years later, we still haven't been able crack the legal barrier for unionizing independent-contractors, which now seems even less likely while right-wing Republicans control all three branches of government. Consequently, since 1981, we have negotiated only a handful of sweetheart contracts with friendly publications, all of which are probably unenforceable if push ever comes to shove.
>
> Thus, the question remains: Are we really a union without the power to bargain collectively—or are we simply another trade association which walks and talks like a union. At the American Writers Congress, along with supporting the writers' union, many of us also endorsed the creation of a lean-and-mean fighting writers' organization, which would protect

writers with the same zealous resolve as the National Rifle Association defends gun owners.

Summing up my heresy, if we're not really a union and have no hope of ever becoming one, then perhaps we should redefine our role in the writers' community. Until we know who we really are, collectively, and what we can really do, legally, I believe that the acrimony and dissension within the union will continue.

I could not have been more relieved when my first and only term ended. I had no desire to seek a second—or to redefine myself as a union activist, even though I was proud to be a union member. I will always believe that unions have been and continue to be the social conscience of all great societies. However, after my experiences with independent truckers and independent writers, I just don't believe that a real union of independent contractors can work.

With my brief stint as a union leader now behind me and through my independent consulting work which resulted in a timely windfall for a job well done on a single caper, I was able to clean up all of my debt. For the first time since 1986, I did not owe anything to anyone.

139. When I'm 64

On Friday, September 10, 2004, I went to see my doctor at Kaiser Permanente for my annual physical after completing the required lab work a few days earlier.

Looking at his computer screen in the examination room, the doctor told me that everything looked fine. "You're now fifty-four years old. Are you having any problems?" He asked.

"Well, I've been having the same headache for quite a while."

"How long?"

"Maybe six weeks."

"You've had a headache for six weeks?"

"It's nothing that's been bringing me to my knees—but, yes."

"Well, I don't like that. I'm going to arrange for you to have a CT scan."

The following Friday, I drove to Fairfax, Virginia, for the test during which a technician placed my head in a machine shaped like a big donut.

After the scan, the tech man said I was probably fine. And I felt fine. So, when I left the building, I forgot about the test.

On Tuesday, September 28, my doctor called, saying immediately when I answered the phone, "Dan, I can't tell you how sorry I am."

Taken aback by that remark, I replied, "What are you talking about?"

He proceeded to tell me that the CT scan had revealed a serious problem. When his explanation became too complicated, I asked him to fax the report to me, which he did.

I ran the wording of the report through Google.

Stunned by the news of a suspected lesion on the left front lobe of my brain, I asked the doctor how he wanted to proceed.

He replied that he wanted a more sophisticated MRI image and quickly arranged for that test to be conducted the following day in Largo, Maryland.

On my calendar entry for that day, I simply noted, "Beginning of the end?"

I was well aware of the fact that my dad and my great-grandfather, Vasile Moldea, had both died at 64. And my grandfather, Danila Moldea, had died just one month into his 65th year. Although I certainly had no idea how death would take me, I did accept the fact that I had an early expiration date, just like the other Moldea men.

I always assumed that on my 64th birthday on February 27, 2014, I would either be hiding under my bed or throwing a wild farewell party.

On Wednesday, the MRI technicians put me in a torpedo tube and ran their tests for nearly forty-five minutes. They would not give me the results right then but assured me that my doctor would talk to me on Thursday.

When my doctor did call, he appeared somewhat puzzled. The MRI had been inconclusive.

On October 11, I went to see a specialist who also seemed confused by my condition. However, that didn't stop him from scaring the hell out of me. He didn't know whether I had a brain tumor or suffered a stroke.

Consequently, I tried to scale down—without telling anyone what I was in the midst of.

I really didn't think that whatever was going on would be life-ending in the short term, but I did believe that it would probably be dramatically life-altering.

I started by going through my files and removing over 3,000 pounds of documents, all of which I had shredded at a recycling operation by the

Navy Yard near Capitol Hill. In addition, I went through my personal library, which contained nearly 3,000 books, pulling about two-thirds of the titles. Then I boxed up these volumes, gave them to several friends and contributed the rest to the Bryn Mawr Bookshop in Georgetown.

Also, I made out a will, and generally put my affairs in order. I left everything to Mimi and my sister, Marsha. But I didn't even tell Mimi, who was going to Washington State to work with friends on Senator John Kerry's campaign for the President, about my medical condition.

If I needed surgery, I was going to schedule it while Mimi was away—and then tell her and everyone else that I had been in a car accident when they saw the scar on the left side of my bald head.

Later that month, I took a second MRI. This time, I was strapped down with a plastic helmet on my head while lying in the torpedo tube for nearly ninety minutes.

Smiling, my doctor handed me the second MRI report on November 1. Cutting through the medical jargon, everything was completely normal. Apparently, something had gone wrong during the original CT scan, causing a blur, which was erroneously interpreted as some sort of lesion.

Of course, I was overjoyed.

A final battery of tests, including a sonogram on November 22, confirmed the second MRI test, leaving the doctors, even the specialist, scratching their heads. They could not figure out what was going on—and what was causing my headaches—even after all of these expensive tests.

Then, in the midst of a casual conversation with my personal doctor, he asked me if I grind my teeth while sleeping. When I replied that I did, he instructed me to get fitted for a mouthguard, which I would wear at night.

After using the $60 mouth guard for just two days, my headaches, which had started all of this in the first place, were gone.

PART ELEVEN:
The D.C. Madam

140. Cowboy and Lightfoot

On February 20, 2007, Larry Flynt called my home, saying that he wanted me to put together a surveillance operation as part of his latest anti-hypocrisy campaign. The targets for this caper were two U.S. Senators whom Flynt suspected as being gay—but who opposed pro-gay rights and were real pricks about it.

Needing to get back into the game—somewhere, somehow—I accepted this assignment. By then, I had resigned myself to a basic tenet: "If you can't get out of it, then get into it."

Flynt knew that, except in emergency situations, I do not do surveillance. During President Clinton's 1999 impeachment trial, I had hired a Virginia team of professionals to perform those duties. That team was responsible for videotaping a congressman, one of President Clinton's prosecutors, with his mistress in the midst of a weekend break during the Senate trial. Despite our clear documentation of the congressman's blatant hypocrisy, Flynt decided not to pull the trigger and use the evidence accumulated by my surveillance team—because we feared that the woman, our principal source, could be at risk after our target discovered some of our materials in her possession.

Thus, because of their previous good work, Flynt suggested that I contact that team to handle this matter in 2007.

Actually, Larry did not need me for this assignment. A few years after Clinton's acquittal, Allan MacDonell, then still the editor of *Hustler*, had called and asked me how he could reach the surveillance team's leader, so that he could hire him for a project on behalf of Flynt. I never knew what that project was, but I did make the introduction.

For this 2007 operation, Flynt literally wanted 24-hour coverage. But, after I contacted the Virginia team, it was clear that such a job would cost a fortune. To me, that money would not be well spent. So I asked the team leader to give me an estimate for a more streamlined approach. In addition, I was concerned that Flynt, a very successful blackjack and poker player, had no evidence of anything. He was willing to make this very expensive gamble on nothing more than a hunch.

After I provided him with background reports for each Senator, the team leader gave me a total price of $11,640 for a 56-hour surveillance job for both targets, whom he code-named "Cowboy" and "Lightfoot."

Based on our previous experiences, we agreed to take six precautions:

1) Do not discuss specific business on home or office landline phones.

2) Be very careful when discussing these matters on cell phones. Talk briefly and in shorthand.

3) Correspond by fax and overnight mail, rather than email.

4) Use different people for different projects, with no communication among these various work groups.

5) Document everything.

6) Always be wary of a set-up.

Further, everyone on our team had been conditioned to assume that, sooner or later, we might be required to defend our actions in a court of law. As always, if and when we took the oath, we would always tell the truth.

In my opinion, Larry Flynt had repeatedly demonstrated compassion and restraint during his previous crusades against political hypocrisy. In other words, he knew when to step on the gas, and he knew when to apply the brakes. For that reason, I still trusted and remained loyal to him.

Delusional or not, we always viewed ourselves as the good guys in a very complicated drama—especially after my work on Speaker-designate Bob Livingston, who resigned from Congress when our probe of his activities went public. And we still had no interest in interfering with the lives of those on the public stage who had not engaged in blatant acts of hypocrisy. As I said during the impeachment drama, "We let 'em go. Right or wrong, we throw 'em back in the river," almost always without them even knowing that they had been caught.

Actually, on this new caper, other than preparing dossiers on the two Senators, my role was really nothing more than supervisory. Flynt paid me $150 an hour, providing $5,000 up front with the understanding that I would receive more when I used up the advance. Through all of this on a day-to-day basis, I reported to Bruce David, Allan MacDonell's successor as the editor of *Hustler*.

Meantime, while the surveillance team prepared to begin its job on March 30, I read about the upcoming prosecution of a woman who had directed an escort service in the Washington metropolitan area. In my memo to Flynt, I wrote: "You should be aware of this woman, Deborah

PART ELEVEN: THE D.C. MADAM

Jeane Palfrey. . . . She operated as a madam in D.C. from 1993 to 2006 and might be looking to reveal her client list—for a price."

To make a very long story short, in 2006, federal agents had raided Palfrey's home in a San Francisco suburb from which she ran the D.C. escort service and seized all of her assets with the exception of 46 pounds of telephone records, which included the phone numbers—but not the names—of both her escorts and her clients. Even though Palfrey and her attorney had possession of these phone lists, prosecuting attorneys had requested and received a protective order from a federal judge, forbidding her to sell or otherwise release these records.

After I obtained a copy of the protective order and sent it to Flynt's shop in Los Angeles, I received authorization from Bruce David to pursue Palfrey on behalf of Flynt.

On March 12, I called Palfrey's attorney, Montgomery Blair Sibley, who specialized on financial seizures in civil court, and asked to meet with him to pay my respects. At that point, he was extremely busy, fielding dozens of requests for information while aggressively defending his client.

Sibley did tell me that, prior to the judge's execution of the protective order, he had made a deal with ABC News, giving the network 80 percent of Palfrey's phone records from 2002-2004. ABC News reporter Brian Ross was scheduled to broadcast his findings during the evening of May 4 on ABC's *20/20*.

When Sibley asked me what phone records I wanted, I replied that I would like to run checks of those numbers between October 1998 and February 1999—in the midst of the impeachment drama. In addition, I wanted to examine the phone records after the disputed November 2000 Presidential election and through the January 2001 inauguration of President George W. Bush. These were the two periods during which I believed that the Republicans would have celebrated most.

On April 12, after a personal meeting with Sibley, I wrote a memorandum to Flynt and David, referring to Sibley as "The Lawyer" and saying:

> When I asked what we can do for [Palfrey], "The Lawyer" replied that she desperately needs a criminal lawyer. All of her cash and assets, worth no less than $1.5 million, have been seized by the government. And she is currently arguing before U.S. District Judge Gladys Kessler that she wants to drop her court-appointed public defender. "The Lawyer" doesn't have the legal standing to represent her in this matter. But he has

revealed to the court that he has helped Ms. Palfrey with her *pro se* filings.

She doesn't have the money to retain a real professional. And the attorneys she has interviewed—none of whom she trusts to keep her secrets—are demanding as much as $300,000 to get her through the criminal-trial process.

In other words, she wants Larry to enter the fray by either 1) providing her with an attorney, or 2) throwing a fund-raiser for her through which he could raise the money for her to retain a top-flight criminal lawyer. Needless to say, the publicity on this is going to be huge.

During a court hearing that same day, the name of Harlan Ullman, one of the Bush Administration's principal architects of the Iraq war and a columnist for the *Washington Times*, was revealed as one of Palfrey's clients. His telephone number appeared on several occasions in her phone records.

On April 19, Bruce David called and complained that he wanted the names of the people on Palfrey's phone lists—not just their telephone numbers. I explained to David that phone numbers were all that ABC News had—and all that we would get. Like ABC News, we would have to go through the grueling process of running the numbers via reverse-phone-number databases in order to find the names of their owners, assuming that they were available.

Soon after, I arranged a face-to-face meeting between Larry Flynt and Jeane Palfrey for April 25 while she was traveling in California. But, when Palfrey appeared at his office in Beverly Hills as scheduled, Flynt was not there. I was very upset with Flynt for standing up Palfrey—but not nearly as angry as Jeane who was absolutely livid.

In the aftermath of this debacle on the West Coast, I feared that Palfrey and Sibley would not have anything further to do with me. But, instead, I received a call from Sibley the following day. He told me that Palfrey wanted to meet me, adding that they were "inclined" to give me the specific sections of the phone records that I had requested—after the judge lifted the protective order.

On April 28, the Associated Press named U.S. Deputy Secretary of State Randall Tobias as another client of the D.C. Madam. He resigned after receiving a call from ABC News, asking him why his name was in Palfrey's phone records.

PART ELEVEN: THE D.C. MADAM

That same day, I sent Flynt a memorandum about Tobias, adding:

> I must ask: Do I have your permission to continue representing you in this matter—or have you decided to distance LFP [a.k.a. Larry Flynt Publications] from this caper? If you want out, I won't bother you anymore with this. But my advice is for you to remain involved and let me try to work things out. The restraining order should be lifted soon.

Before receiving an answer to that question, I also sent them a brief report about the surveillance operation, writing:

> I just spoke to our "man on the ground." He reported that his team is moving slowly and deliberately in a cost-effective manner. They are firing rifle shots, not shotgun blasts. He didn't give me any details—and I didn't ask for any over the phone—but he said that they are making steady progress. Meantime, they have everything they need, and they are determined to win for us.
>
> Because I trust the guy from experience, I'm not pressing him.

On April 30, Sibley and I arranged to pick up Jeane Palfrey for dinner at the J.W. Marriott Hotel on 14th Street, next to the National Press Building. It was my first meeting with her.

Feminine and impeccably dressed, Palfrey—who had an undergraduate degree in criminal justice and had spent a year in law school—initially came across as a very tough woman. She put out a "don't-even-think-of-messing-with-me" vibe.

Palfrey and Sibley felt like walking, so we strolled up 15th Street to Bobby Van's Steakhouse and had a great time. After being with her for just a few minutes, anyone could see how scared and vulnerable she really was. She loved to laugh and have fun, but she appeared to have self-imposed limitations. It was as though she didn't want to laugh too much or be too happy—which was understandable considering that she was under federal indictment and facing a long prison sentence if convicted.

During dinner, she and Sibley promised to give me those portions of the phone list that I had requested. In addition, they asked me to find a literary agent for Palfrey who wanted to write a book about her life and times. We agreed that she needed a woman to represent her.

When I arrived at home that night, I called Alice Martell, the attorney-agent who had done such a great job handling my book about the Robert Kennedy murder—but with whom I had an unfortunate separation during the dueling-agents scenario in the midst of the negotiations for my O. J. Simpson book with the two lead detectives in that murder case.

It was the first time I had talked to Martell in several years, and I fully expected her to be cold towards me. To my surprise, both she and her husband, who answered the phone, could not have been nicer. I told Martell that Palfrey needed and deserved the best agent in New York, and I immediately thought of her. Martell agreed to speak with Palfrey.

Also that night, I sent another memorandum to Flynt and David, asking for their decision as to whether they wanted me to pursue the Palfrey matter on their behalf.

According to David, Flynt had deferred the matter to him. However, David admitted that he was having difficulty making a decision.

Still upset over Flynt's shabby treatment of Palfrey, I took the initiative and resigned from the Flynt project on May 3, saying in writing:

> Thank you for considering my ideas for LFP 2008. Apparently, you didn't think that this was the right time to go to war—at least with me and the [Palfrey] project. But, let me assure you, I have always been loyal to you, and I have always tried to protect what I believed were your best interests.

I still had a couple of hundred dollars on account from the original $5,000 that I received from Flynt, which I applied towards my continuing supervisory role with the surveillance team.

141. "Are you two working together?"

On May 4, Brian Ross's program on ABC's *20/20* aired. Although it contained a fairly positive portrait of Jeane Palfrey, Ross released no new names, despite all the pre-show hype, claiming that ABC News had uncovered "hot stuff."[251]

Of course, Palfrey was disappointed that more names were not revealed, but she was philosophical, writing to me:

PART ELEVEN: THE D.C. MADAM

> ABC News certainly didn't hurt me. In fact, my public relation's image went from about a 1–3 to a solid 10 after last night's 20/20 broadcast (my opinion). For this—if nothing else—I am grateful. In addition, considering a general public which functions on far too many levels in our society on a junior to senior high school level, ABC was able to get the general message of hypocrisy out there. And frankly, this was no small feat all the while making me look a bit like the heroine. With this said, it was not great investigative journalism.

In the days that followed, Ross's staff told other reporters that ABC's attorneys had subjected them to nothing less than a legal mugging, refusing to allow them to air the names they had collected.

Adding to this, Palfrey's meeting in New York with literary agent Alice Martell had not gone well. From what I could piece together, Martell had asked Palfrey some very tough but totally legitimate questions about what she wanted in her book. Trying to bring the best out of Palfrey's story, Martell pressed her hard for details. Palfrey, whom I already knew did not take criticism well, was offended and decided not to do business with Martell—despite my admonition that she was making a huge mistake.

Regardless of my reservations about Palfrey's thin-skinned demeanor, I had grown to like and respect her. Legal and moral considerations aside, I viewed her as a good person.

I still had not introduced Palfrey to Mimi, but Mimi remained open minded about all of this. More than anything else, Mimi just wanted to see me get back into the game—even at this or any other level.

On May 22, during my dinner with Palfrey and Sibley in the back room at Morty's, a popular local delicatessen where I was a regular among the lunchtime crowd, Palfrey asked me to be her co-author. Frankly, I was thrilled to be asked and accepted immediately—even though I had no clue what she knew and how much damage she could actually inflict on official Washington.

The following day, in an exchange of emails with Palfrey, I wrote:

> My inclination is to keep this collaboration as quiet as possible—for as long as possible. I don't want to deal with the attention that you and Blair have been receiving until I finish my job. So, whenever you feel comfortable, let's get to work.

On May 25, Palfrey and I arranged to have lunch in downtown Washington. When I arrived at the Capital Hilton on the corner of 16th and K, I suggested that we eat at the hotel restaurant—where we likely would not be noticed. She turned down that suggestion, saying that she wanted to go out. Specifically, she said that she wanted to go to McCormick & Schmick's, a popular seafood restaurant near the hotel on K Street.

After we were seated, I could see the eyes of nearly everyone in the place staring at Palfrey who had already become a local celebrity. Mel Krupin, the restaurant's maître d', even came up to the table after we were seated, looking for an introduction. Like just about everyone else in Washington, I had been acquainted with Krupin for years—since his days as the maître d' at Duke Zeibert's. Also, his brother, Morty Krupin, was the manager of Morty's Deli.

After lunch, I took Palfrey back to her hotel and then drove home.

While walking up the steps to my apartment, I heard someone recording a message on my answering machine. Too late to get it, I played my messages. The last one—the one I had just missed—was from the *Washington Post's* Reliable Source gossip column. The reporter said, "One of our eagle-eyed readers spotted you lunching with Deborah Jeane Palfrey today. Are you two working together for a book? If so, can you tell me more?"

In lieu of calling, I sent back an email, saying:

> You're good. You're very good.
>
> Like many other journalists in Washington, I'm interested in interviewing the fascinating Jeane Palfrey and pursuing her remarkable story. . . .
>
> I'm just a grunt crime reporter—an independent writer without an assignment—who is always looking for an interesting story.
>
> As far as I'm concerned, all options are open.

Predictably, the *Post* did not buy any of this, writing the following day:

> Looks like Deborah Jeane Palfrey is trying to strike while the iron's hot.

PART ELEVEN: THE D.C. MADAM

Palfrey, a.k.a. the D.C. Madam, was spotted power-lunching with local author Dan Moldea at McCormick & Schmick's on K Street yesterday. Moldea, an "independent crime reporter since October 1974," according to his Web site, tends to stick with subjects like organized crime and American politics in his books. Hmm . . .

Our source says Palfrey looked "very together" in a conservative white top with a black cardigan while she dined on crab cakes and sipped a Diet Coke.

When she read the story, Palfrey laughed, writing to me:

No question whatsoever, it was the overly solicitous waiter. Diet Coke? No one other than the waiter/wait staff would have known such a detail. I now comprehend the wisdom of Morty's backroom. –PS: I thought you looked rather dapper at lunch. Yet, no comments about your appearance. The pressure we women are under.

On June 5, I signed my collaboration contract with Palfrey, who then returned to California.

Over the next month, Palfrey and I had eight two-hour interviews over the telephone, which would serve as the basis for the book proposal we hoped to send to New York.

On May 23, my surveillance-team leader finally gave me his first report about Operations Cowboy and Lightfoot. In effect, he had discovered a location in Arlington, Virginia, as well as a four-story Capitol Hill townhouse on C Street SE—which were tantamount to private clubhouses mostly for right-wing Republicans. There, some of these politicians congregated and prayed, as well as allegedly engaged in sexual fantasies, both gay and straight, outside of their marriages.[252]

Our team leader had developed a source close to one of these sanctuaries. And, to my delight, our team did not have to stake out the house and wait for something to happen. Instead, our team leader's source promised to call him when something was about to happen. Thus, my surveillance team had logged in fewer than a dozen hours since March

30, leaving plenty of money on account for the main event if and when it finally came.

After I sent my report to Flynt's office, I quickly received a call from Bruce David, authorizing me to instruct my Virginia team to continue with their work.

"Strike when you think the time is right," I wrote to the team leader. "You have everyone's full confidence. . . . Stay in touch."

Then, on Sunday morning, June 3, I opened the *Washington Post* and was shocked to see that Flynt had placed a full-page ad, resembling the one he had published in October 1998 in the midst of the impeachment battle. Once again, Flynt was offering "up to $1 million" for "documented evidence of illicit sexual or intimate relations with a Congressperson, Senator or other prominent officeholder." As before, Flynt put up an 800-number hotline for those with information to call.

I immediately sent a note to Flynt, saying: "I just saw the full-page ad in today's *Washington Post*. Respectfully, may I ask what's going on?"

Neither Flynt nor anyone from LFP responded.

That same day, the leader of our surveillance team called, screaming at me into the phone, "What the hell are you guys doing? We've been setting up our sting for weeks! Now, the targets know that they are at risk! They know that someone might rat them out in an effort to claim the reward! Now, they are less likely to walk into the trap we've set!"

I assured him that I didn't know anything about the ad, saying that, other than serving as the liaison between him and Flynt, I had no other role.[253]

On Tuesday, June 5, *Radar Online*, a web-based gossip site, published a story based on a conversation I had with one of its reporters earlier in the day. The article stated:

> Larry Flynt is taking aim at hypocrisy again, but it seems he won't be using his secret weapon. Dan Moldea, the private investigator who worked with Flynt to expose the marital infidelities of Bill Clinton antagonist Bob Livingston, says he hasn't been contacted by the *Hustler* publisher. . . . Claims Moldea: "I haven't talked to Larry in a long time. I opened the paper on Sunday and was surprised like everybody else."

Later that afternoon, I turned on MSNBC where someone had told me that Flynt was scheduled to appear on *Hardball with Chris Matthews*. Boston journalist Mike Barnicle filled in for Matthews who was on vacation. In the midst of the interview, Barnicle asked, "Larry, you indicated

PART ELEVEN: THE D.C. MADAM

in the last segment that you already had a hundred or a couple hundred tips after this ad was posted. How do you check them out?

Flynt replied, "Well, we go through each one very meticulously. And we say documented evidence. What we need is . . . we need photographs. We need hotel or motel lodgings. There are a variety of different things that can link the two together. . . . I've got one of the best detectives in Washington. His name is Dan Moldea. He is very good."

As I sat at my desk, aghast that Flynt—whom I continued to like and respect even after our recent dispute over Jeane Palfrey—had just placed a target on my back. I immediately called his office and left a message, registering my complaint.

Later that day, Flynt returned my call, making light of what he had said on *Hardball*. "I'm coming to Washington this weekend," he said. "Let's have lunch on Saturday."

Flynt had purchased an entire table at the annual Larry King Cardiac Foundation on Saturday night. He also asked me to be one of his guests at the dinner. "Come onnnnnn . . . ," he said in a mocking tone.

Still upset, I tried not to laugh and told him I wanted to think about it.

The following day, June 6, *Radar Online*, after interviewing me again, filed a second story, "Larry Flynt Outs Fibbing Gumshoe on TV," which stated:

> It seems that all the time he's spent around dirty politicians has taught Dan Moldea a thing or two about skirting the truth. Yesterday, the D.C.-based private investigator assured us he had not been hired by Larry Flynt to help out in his new $1 million quest to nail a cheating government official. "I haven't talked to Larry in a long time," he said.
>
> Not two hours later, the *Hustler* publisher dropped by MSNBC's *Hardball* to talk about his mission. "I have got one of the best detectives in Washington," he bragged. "His name is Dan Moldea. He is very good."
>
> "Yeah, that was a problem, wasn't it?" laughed Moldea when we called him this morning. "I just probably shouldn't comment about anything right now. I stand by what I said. I have made no deal to participate in this."

I sent the article to Flynt and Bruce David, adding:

> Judging by the article below, I think this situation is getting too complicated. Now, these screwballs are calling me a liar. The simple facts are: 1) I am very loyal to you guys; 2) [Prior to yesterday,] I have not talked to Larry in a long time—to my chagrin; 3) The full-page ad in the *Washington Post* on Sunday came as a complete surprise to me; and 4) I currently have no deal with you about your project.
>
> I would really enjoy seeing and talking to Larry when he comes to Washington this weekend. Although I sincerely appreciate the invitation to the Larry King event, I don't think it's wise for us to be together at such a public event. Remember, the last time we did this, I sometimes had as many as three cars parked in front of my place with the drivers monitoring my movements and God knows what else. [A surveillance expert] detected a tracking device in the wheel-well of my car. And I received nothing but bad press.
>
> I'm hoping to play these things a little smarter this time around—if we decide to do something together.

Although I did not attend the Larry King function with Flynt, I did agree to the lunch at the Ritz-Carlton at 22nd Street and M on Saturday, June 9. Also, I came armed with a written statement, which outlined my thoughts about another possible working relationship. In this memorandum, I wrote:

> Because of what we did during the impeachment process, my name is always going to be associated with yours. I will be remembered as the investigator who, on your behalf, nailed the U.S. House Speaker-designate on the day of Bill Clinton's impeachment. And I am as proud of that distinction as I am proud of my association with you—and, for that matter, anything I have ever done during my career, including any of my seven books. I honestly believe that we derailed a right-wing coup.
>
> In matters like this, I know how you operate. I know how much you value and demand full documentation. And I have a track record of responsible work and success with you. In addition, I am completely accountable to you. And my actions have never

PART ELEVEN: THE D.C. MADAM

gotten you into trouble. When there has been trouble, I have always been willing to take the hit so that you didn't have to. You trust me, and I trust you.

Unfortunately, when I came to you with Jeane Palfrey, you blew her off. With respect, I believe that was a mistake. But, because of what both of you are now in the midst of, that mistake can be reversed.

I have now signed a collaboration contract to write her book. I am currently writing our proposal and structuring the manuscript. I have exclusive access to her and her secrets. She trusts me, and I trust her. And I believe that she could be very valuable during your investigation.

To be clear, you and Jeane can make history in the coming weeks and months. And the two of you are natural allies who can only help each other from behind the scenes, using me as your bridge.

Please understand that if we work together again, I am going to be pulling huge exposure. As before but with more intensity, I am going to be tracked and harassed. I'm going to be judged harshly by my friends and colleagues for re-entering this world with you in what will be viewed as the motherlode of checkbook journalism.

In addition, I will receive more bad press than I have ever received before, trumping even the trouncing I took the last time—from the *Washington Post* to the *Wall Street Journal*, not to mention from all of those right-wing publications and organizations. As you recall, you and I were targeted by the Public Integrity Section of the Department of Justice after being formally accused by the National Republican Committee and the Landmark Legal Foundation with obstructing the impeachment trial, as well as blackmail and extortion. Although these allegations were groundless, we could've easily been indicted and prosecuted.

Nevertheless, the idea of working with you again on another major project is very appealing to me. If you want me as your lead investigator, I am more than happy to consider the assignment. But we need to be very careful and deliberate in our approach, keeping in mind your goals along with the well-being of Jeane Palfrey.

I am in a very unique position to help both of you.

All of this said in the midst of our very pleasant lunch, I agreed to return to the fold.

On June 20, we settled the money issues in my role as an investigative consultant. My fee was raised to $175 an hour, which was the price I gave him.

Simultaneously, I accepted a consulting assignment with French-TV, which was putting together a five-part documentary on the 100th anniversary of the FBI. There would be no authors, journalists, or academics serving as talking heads on this program. Producers Fabrizio Calvi, a French journalist, and David Carr-Brown, a British journalist, wanted this story told exclusively by FBI agents and officials—and only by past and present FBI personnel. Calvi and Carr-Brown asked me to help them arrange interviews with FBI people I knew, both active and retired.

142. "So tell me about David Vitter"

On Thursday, July 5, Jeane Palfrey and I completed our book proposal and sent it to the agent she had selected to represent her. In the preface to the proposal, I wrote:

> A sensitive girl from a good family in Charleroi, Pennsylvania, goes to college in Florida, receives her degree in criminal justice and then attends law school in California, dropping out in the midst of her first year. After a man she wanted to marry breaks her heart, she winds up opening an escort service, entertaining businessmen in San Diego.
>
> Betrayed by an employee, then arrested and prosecuted, she returns to the escort-service business after her release from prison, relocating to Washington, D.C. She operates from 1993 to 2006 virtually undetected by the law-enforcement community,

running the business from a suburb of San Francisco. But, weary of the daily grind, she closes down the service and makes plans to start a new life in Europe.

While buying a home in Germany, she learns that her house in the United States has been raided by federal agents and that all of her money and property have been seized. Shortly after her return to the U.S., she is indicted in a major federal-conspiracy case, marking the beginning of her desperate fight for survival.

In the midst of her legal battle, she reveals publicly that she has kept possession of the telephone records which can help to identify those on her 10,000-plus client list, whom the trial judge in her case describes as "unindicted coconspirators."

Suddenly, that sensitive girl from Charleroi becomes one of the most dangerous people in American politics.

Actually, other than Ullman and Tobias, we had no other big-name clients in the proposal. Jeane and I knew that this would probably hurt our chances to sell the book for a legitimate price. As Jeane explained it, most of her clients had code names. She never knew who most of them really were.

Also, twice in the final version of the proposal, I quoted Palfrey discussing suicide as an alternative to prison. Specifically, she said, "I considered suicide after my arrests. Every girl in similar situations who emailed me in sympathy—the Vegas Madam, the High-Tech Madam—have all considered suicide. No one knows what it's like to be in this position. This is like being in a Kafka novel."

In fact, Palfrey had told me on no fewer than three occasions that she would kill herself in lieu of returning to jail. She constantly referred to Brandy Britton, a Baltimore escort with a PhD in sociology who occasionally worked for her. Britton hanged herself the week before her scheduled trial for prostitution.[254]

Convinced that she was serious about the suicide option, I reported this to her civil attorney, Blair Sibley, who replied, "I know. I know. I know. It's a *real* problem."[255]

Also on July 5, the judge in Palfrey's criminal trial lifted the protective order, allowing Palfrey and Sibley to distribute the phone list, which included 300,000 numbers of her 10,000 to 15,000 clients. In anticipation of this action, Sibley had already addressed and stamped envelopes to 50 reporters. He wanted to get them in the mail before the prosecution's attempt to convince the U.S. Court of Appeals for the D.C. Circuit to reverse the lower-court decision.

Trying to preempt the other journalists—who probably would not receive their copies until the following Monday—I called Sibley and invited him to dinner, adding, "And, yes—oh, by the way—maybe you could bring my CD with Palfrey's telephone numbers along with you. I'll get started on it tonight."

Sibley—who, at my request, also promised to send a copy to Flynt—laughed and agreed to meet me at Morty's.[256]

After dinner, I drove home and downloaded the thousands of pages of phone numbers onto my computer. And, as I began the arduous task of going through these numbers, I focused on the same two periods of time that I had originally asked for—the 1998-1999 impeachment battle and the aftermath of the 2000-contested Presidential election.

I started with the impeachment period. The first number I ran was on December 12, 1998, the day that the Republican-controlled U.S. House Judiciary Committee voted its fourth and final article of impeachment against President Clinton.

Here was the process: I would look at a typical page with dozens of telephone numbers listed. Then, I would copy each number and paste it in a reverse-phone database. If I received a hit, I would print out the page. Then, using either a search engine or Nexis-Lexis, I would research the name.

Working through the night as my eyes grew weary, I accumulated the names of hundreds of men who lived in the Washington, D.C. metropolitan area. However, I could not find anyone with a public persona who had also engaged in acts of political hypocrisy, such as Bob Livingston, Newt Gingrich, Bob Barr, and Tim Hutchinson, among many others that I had investigated during the impeachment crisis.

Of the hundreds of other names I came up with—men who were not public figures—I took all of my research about them and fed it into my shredder. I had no interest in interfering with any of their lives.

A little after 6:00 P.M. on Friday, July 6—while I was in the midst of going through the D.C. Madam's phone records during the Clinton-Bush transition period—I was trying to figure out where to finish. Seeing that I was in February 2001, I decided to stop looking on February 27, which was my 51st birthday, a totally random date.

On that day at the logged-in time of 3:06 P.M., I came across a telephone number for Washington, D.C. that I had not seen before. When I ran it through the directory, the name, "David Vitter," appeared.

Stunned, I ran the number again—and received the same result: David Vitter, then the U.S. congressman from Louisiana who, ironically enough, had succeeded Bob Livingston in 1999.

Now, in 2007, Vitter was a powerful conservative United States Senator, elected in 2004.

I also subscribed to two other reverse-phone databases, and I ran the number through both, receiving confirmations from each. In addition, I ran a cursory background check on him.

I took a deep breath and called Jeane Palfrey. When she answered, I said, "So tell me about David Vitter."

"Who?" She replied.

"David Vitter."

"Who's that?"

"He's the junior Senator from Louisiana. I just found his number in your telephone records."

Palfrey took a moment and then told me, "I knew a Dave on C Street. But I never knew his real name. In fact, I really didn't want to know. I never wanted to know."[257]

I instructed Palfrey to sit tight and not to speak with anybody about anything—especially about this.

Then, I called Flynt, saying, "Larry, I got one."

"Who'd you get?"

"United States Senator David Vitter of Louisiana. He was the guy who won Livingston's congressional seat after we forced his resignation on the day of Clinton's impeachment. He has since been elected to the U.S. Senate."

"That's great!" Flynt replied. "Is he a hypocrite?"

"Just wait until you see this guy, Larry."

I spent about forty-five minutes putting together a more-detailed dossier about the 46-year-old Vitter, a married Harvard graduate and Rhodes Scholar with four children who had built his reputation as a "family values" Roman Catholic. During his 2004 run for the U.S. Senate, he campaigned to protect the sanctity of traditional marriage and to stop same-sex marriage. He was also a co-author of the "Federal Marriage Act." Pro-war, anti-choice, and pro-gun, he was a classic right-wing politician.

Among other things, I found a specific quote from Vitter during his Senate campaign on the subject of "Protecting the Sanctity of Marriage." Vitter remarked, "The Hollywood left is redefining the most basic institution in human history. . . . We need a U.S. Senator who will stand up for Louisiana values, not Massachusetts values."

During a conference call with Flynt and Bruce David, we tried to figure out how to proceed. Flynt asked me if I wanted to make the call and confront Senator Vitter.

"Can you imagine Vitter's reaction if he gets a call from us?" I asked. "We could get accused of blackmail—just like the last time. We could wind up with an indictment hanging over our heads again. . . .

"We need to feed this material to someone in the mainstream media. We should give him everything we have and let him publish whatever he wants—with the proviso that he credits us for the discovery. Then, Larry, you can go out, call a press conference, and do your thing."

After a few minutes of conversation, we agreed to this approach. But the question remained: Who would we give the story to?

In the midst of a discussion about journalists, I suggested Adam Zagorin, a respected reporter for *Time* magazine. I knew Adam to be very professional, as well as honest and completely trustworthy. It would be impossible for us or anyone else to manipulate him. He would play it straight. And Flynt agreed with my suggestion.

After our conference call, I called Zagorin on his cell phone and asked to meet with him immediately. He was just returning from Dulles airport and replied that he could meet me in an hour.

At 11:00 P.M., Zagorin and I met at the Chevy Chase Lounge on Connecticut Avenue. We grabbed a table at The Parthenon, the Greek restaurant attached to the bar, and got down to business.

I gave Zagorin a package of information, documenting everything that had happened during the past few hours, including the key page from Palfrey's phone records and the corroborating identifications of Senator Vitter on the other reverse-phone-number directories.

Clearly, Zagorin was floored by this information, saying immediately that he wanted the story and adding that he had no problem giving us credit for the discovery.

Taking him at his word, I replied, "The story is now yours. If you need anything from me, please call. But, apart from that, I don't expect to hear from you until after your story is published. Just do your usual good work."

On Saturday morning, I sent Flynt and his team a memorandum, saying:

PART ELEVEN: THE D.C. MADAM

> The meeting went very well with the trusted reporter last night. He is a completely ethical and honest guy, who will be doing things by the book. Even though I am an investigative journalist and author, I am nothing more than his source on this matter. And, in that role, I gave him a package of information, impressing upon him that we are in a "use it or lose it" situation. Of course, he will still corroborate everything before he proceeds.
>
> Presumably, he will work on the material over the weekend and then make the pitch to his high command on Monday—after they return from the long weekend in the wake of July 4th.
>
> Fasten your seat belts. This could be a bumpy ride. Even if all goes well, the reaction is going to be ferocious.

Nothing happened over the weekend. And all of us were getting nervous, knowing that 49 other reporters were going to be receiving their packages of Palfrey's telephone records from Blair Sibley in the mail on Monday, July 9.

Seeing that nothing had been published by lunchtime on Monday, I sent another memo to Flynt and David, asking them to remain patient at least to the close of business. I assumed that Zagorin was dealing with his editors at *Time* who were, no doubt, demanding absolute documentation—confirmed and reconfirmed.

At 5:00 P.M., when Zagorin and *Time* still had not broken the story, Flynt told me that if *Time* did not move, he would.

Departing from my strategy, I called Zagorin and said, "With respect, Adam, I don't want to interfere with your work. But I need to give you a heads up. If you don't call Vitter and confront him, Flynt's people are going to make the call."

Just as I ended my call with Zagorin, I received a call from Bruce David's assistant, Mark Johnson. He told me that David had instructed him to call Vitter's office and ask to speak with the Senator. When Vitter's secretary said that he was not in, Johnson told her that he was from *Hustler* without explaining why he was calling.

Then, as my call with Johnson ended, I received one from Zagorin, who said that he had just gotten off the phone with one of Vitter's aides. Unlike Johnson, he did ask why Vitter's phone number was in the D.C. Madam's records.

While we were talking, Zagorin received a call from Vitter's press secretary. He put me on hold and took the call. When he returned to me, he refused to say what he had discussed with Vitter's flak, and I didn't press him to tell me. However, he did say that he was waiting for an email with an official statement from Senator Vitter.

During this conversation, I was struck by the thought that Vitter's office had received back-to-back calls from *Hustler* and then *Time*. "Their office must be in turmoil," I thought.

While everything played out, I went to dinner at Morty's with my producer at French TV. When I returned home, I checked my messages and then the news online.

I stumbled across an Associated Press story, which just came off the wire, in which Vitter had confessed. But instead of confessing to Zagorin and *Time*, he had gone to an AP reporter in Louisiana in an obvious effort to get ahead of the story. Vitter admitted:

> This was a very serious sin in my past for which I am, of course, completely responsible. Several years ago, I asked for and received forgiveness from God and my wife in confession and marriage counseling. Out of respect for my family, I will keep my discussion of the matter there—with God and them. But I certainly offer my deep and sincere apologies to all I have disappointed and let down in any way.

After notifying Flynt, who was jubilant, I spent the next several hours on the phone, making courtesy calls and trying to make sure that we received credit for the events leading to Vitter's confession.

That same night, the online publication, *Politico*, revealed that, during the Clinton-Lewinsky scandal, Vitter's wife, Wendy, was specifically asked how she would handle an unfaithful husband—and whether she would stand by him, like Hillary Clinton.

"I'm a lot more like Lorena Bobbitt than Hillary," Mrs. Vitter replied back then. "If he does something like that, I'm walking away with one thing, and it's not alimony, trust me. . . . I think fear is a very good motivating factor in a marriage. Don't put fear down."[258]

Politico also suggested that Flynt might have had something to do with Vitter's outing.

Early Tuesday morning, I received an email from Geoff Earle at the *New York Post*, who asked if I was doing a book with Jeane Palfrey. In addition, he asked whether I was behind the disclosure about Senator Vitter. In my reply, I wrote:

PART ELEVEN: THE D.C. MADAM

Thank you for your message. With regard to Jeane's book, I'm going to yield to her on this matter.

With regard to Jeane's telephone logs—yes, I found Senator Vitter's number. The full story will come out soon. But make no mistake that this was a Larry Flynt operation—a team effort.

With respect, I cannot comment any further, except to say that Larry and I are very weary of listening to moral hypocrites, like Senator Vitter. . . .

At the same time, I can assure you that we are experiencing no joy from the trauma that this is, no doubt, causing the Senator's family.

Shortly after that, Zagorin and *Time* released their article, stating:

> Members of a team assembled by pornographer and self-described free speech advocate Larry Flynt, publisher of *Hustler*, are understood to have identified Vitter's name through their own analysis of Palfrey's phone records. Flynt has a long record of exposing what he regards as "hypocrisy" on the part of politicians who tout family or religious values, while falling short in their own lives. Flynt recently placed a full page advertisement in the *Washington Post*. . . . On Tuesday afternoon, Flynt's *Hustler* magazine issued a press release claiming responsibility for Vitter's decision to confess.
>
> Could Palfrey and Flynt be working together? One of Flynt's lead investigators, crime reporter Dan E. Moldea, was recently reported by the *Washington Post* to be having lunch with Palfrey. *TIME* has confirmed that he is helping her write a book currently being shopped to New York publishers which details her exploits as the "DC Madam". But both she and Flynt have said they have never met and are not coordinating their efforts.[259]

By the end of the day, Flynt, who was very generous in his praise for my work, received universal credit for launching the Vitter scandal, which surprisingly gained widespread approval within the mainstream media. The general tenor, emphasized at Flynt's press conference on July 11, was that Vitter—whose telephone number wound up appearing in Palfrey's phone records no fewer than five times—was a complete hypocrite who got his due.[260]

Also, Howard Kurtz of the *Washington Post* put out an important message, echoing what I had said nearly a decade earlier. Kurtz wrote:

> "When you go through the list, there are a lot of normal men who were patronizing this escort service," said Moldea, who specializes in covering organized crime. "I can assure you, we have no intention of hurting these people, no intention of interfering with their lives. This is about hypocrisy."
>
> Moldea cited Vitter's conservative record on family issues"[261]

Even the right-wing *Pittsburgh Tribune-Review*, which is owned by Richard Scaife, published a letter to the editor in which the writer wrote: "It pains me to acknowledge it, but America is in the debt of Larry Flynt today. His mission to unmask the fakers in public life is just and right."[262]

143. Morals of a Muckraker

Remarkably enough, unlike my fate after our battle during the impeachment drama, I came out of this most recent episode with Flynt in one piece. This time, I did not shy away from print interviews, which gave me the opportunity to defend myself—although I did refuse to do any television programs. "I think it would be in bad taste, which is probably an ironic term to use under these circumstances," I told the producers for news programs of all three television networks, as well as for CNN, MSNBC and Fox.

I was determined not to make the same mistakes that I made during the impeachment fight—when I mostly remained quiet while the print media ran over me.

Newsweek reported the frenzy over Palfrey's phone list, which was now available online, stating:

> The question is who will be next, now that the numbers are so accessible. Vitter's number was unearthed by Dan Moldea,

PART ELEVEN: THE D.C. MADAM

> a D.C. reporter who is helping Palfrey write her memoir and who also moonlights for Flynt. Palfrey's list of almost 200,000 numbers is a gold mine for Flynt, who already has a team of investigators trying to dig up dirt on the sexual indiscretions of lawmakers and has placed ads in The *Washington Post* offering rewards for info. "But the bloggers and the techies are really doing the greatest job," says Moldea. "And they are all obsessed with numbers starting with 202-224 . . . numbers coming from the Hill." A new Web site, dcphonelist.com, allows anyone to punch in a number and it will cross-reference it to "madam's" list.[263]

Also, I appeared on National Public Radio's *Talk of the Nation*. During the program, the host, Rebecca Roberts, asked me why I, whom some still viewed as a legitimate journalist and author, would work with Flynt, "Why do you do it?"[264]

I replied:

> I was radicalized, I think, by the Clinton impeachment effort. I thought it was so incredibly unfair what was happening to Bill Clinton. As I say, he was shown absolutely no mercy whatsoever. I had written a book on the Vince Foster suicide, the White House counsel who went out to Fort Marcy Park and who sat on the side of a hill and put a .38 in his mouth and pulled the trigger.
>
> And I saw how the coverage of that case by certain right-wing journalists who were sharing information, receiving funding from the same source, was a cynical attempt to try to undermine the Clintons and their authority in the White House by claiming that they had murdered Vince Foster, by claiming that they are somehow involved in the cover-up of his death, when I found that there really was nothing more than a right-wing conspiracy, let's say, to make it look that way. When Hillary Clinton was talking about the right-wing conspiracy against the Clinton White House, she was telling the truth. . . .

Reporter Jonathan Tilove published a story about me for the Newhouse newspaper chain—dubiously entitled "Noir Character/Nice Guy at Center of D.C. Sex Scandal"—in which he wrote:

Moldea . . . thinks Flynt has been on the side of the angels in his campaign to expose the sexual hypocrites of the Republican right.

"I'd sell apples on a street corner to go after these guys," says Moldea. "That's the thing, I've started to view right-wing Republicans as the new organized crime."

"Dan reminds me of Gary Cooper in 'High Noon' –the quiet, tough-as-nails professional who believes he should uphold the honor and law of the badge he swore to wear," says James Grady, author of the book on which the film *Three Days of the Condor* was based, who has known Moldea since Grady worked as an investigator for columnist Jack Anderson. "For Dan, the badge is investigative reporting, muckraking at its best, and the oath is the idea that if you dig up the truth, people in a democracy will care and good things can happen."

Grady believes that next to Seymour Hersh, Moldea is the top investigative reporter of his time. "He should be one of those name-brand journalists, but he's not very comfortable in that role."[265]

In its first official full-blast, front-page Style-section profile of me, the *Washington Post* began its story, "Morals of a Muckraker," saying: "Dan Moldea has been beaten up by thugs, trashed in the press, accused of chilling free speech and threatened with prosecution."

Later in the story, reporter Howard Kurtz allowed the person who really started all of this to give me a compliment: "Palfrey, who is under indictment on prostitution-related charges, considers him an ideal partner. 'I didn't want a writer of sensational Hollywood works,' she says. 'I really need a hard-core investigative journalist here. I thought, this is the man to do it. He's a good and decent man, and very upfront and straightforward.'"

Also, Kurtz asked me to comment about my motivation to work with Flynt during the impeachment drama, quoting me saying, "There was a right-wing attempt to overthrow the executive branch of government, and I thought I could be sacrificed. This was important enough for me to risk being destroyed."[266]

Sadly, all of the publishers to whom we pitched our book proposal complained that Palfrey did not know any other big names or "really juicy stuff," which was really all they wanted. Consequently, our proposal had made Palfrey "look like Rebecca of Sunnybrook Farm," according to one editor.

When we could not sell Palfrey's book, I backed away immediately—instead of continuing to write the manuscript on spec and hope for the best down the road. I told Palfrey, to whom Flynt finally gave $10,000 for her legal defense, that I wanted her to have a big payday. I asked for nothing in return.

Soon after, she teamed up with a woman reporter at *Vanity Fair*.

144. "Are you okay?"

On July 30, 2007, Jeane Palfrey, with whom I remained a friend, sent me a letter that she had received from her court-appointed trial attorney, Preston Burton, who had given her a cold dose of reality.[267] In this extraordinarily candid and somber correspondence, Burton wrote:

> As to raising issues with Judge [Gladys] Kessler, I have raised all issues I deemed to have merit and will not raise those I deem to lack merit. Candidly, I do not believe she will grant any of the pretrial motions to dismiss and, having now analyzed the suppression issues more closely, I also doubt she will grant the motion to suppress the evidence—in other words, I believe this case will be resolved by a trial or guilty plea and you would be better served by focusing on how to defend the case and to provide insight on how to discredit the numerous witnesses against you than betting on this case to collapse before trial.
>
> You are facing serious jail time and I will devote as much time defending this case as necessary to prevent that or minimize your incarceration but, based on my understanding of the government's case, I believe you will be ultimately be convicted of at least one of the charges against you.[268]

After Palfrey sent me this letter, she called, sobbing, and asked for my opinion, adding that she just had a very harsh conversation with Burton.

Expressing no appreciation for Burton's straight talk, Palfrey, who was hoping to bombard the court with a slew of motions, was extremely upset and wanted to fire him immediately.

Respectfully, I told her that I believed that Burton was right—that she had to start preparing for trial and abandon all of the conspiracy theories that she had concocted. In my opinion, none of them had any basis in reality.[269]

Terrified of returning to prison and finding her legal options waning, she asked me to communicate with Burton and try to smooth things out with him on her behalf.

I then sent Burton an email, saying:

> Last night, I had a very long talk with Jeane—who sometimes drives me crazy. I know you're hip.
>
> As you probably know, she was very upset at the letter you wrote to her. Frankly, I thought that it was a great letter, and I told her so. In effect, you were telling her, at long last, to help you to help her. You were trying to get her to recognize that she is fighting for her life and her freedom.
>
> Of course, she didn't take it that way at first, but Jeane, as you know, has been running scared for a long time. I don't know exactly how she responded to your letter initially, but I am sure that it was inappropriate.
>
> I sense that, after our conversation last night, she is looking for the right way to come back to you with her hat in her hand and to apologize for her cataclysmic, knee-jerk reaction to your tough but honest and on-point letter.
>
> I'm asking you to make it easy for her to make peace with you. She knows that you're a fabulous lawyer, and she just wants your respect.

However, Palfrey's desire to keep Burton was short-lived. During a hearing on August 28, Jeane formally asked the judge to replace Burton with Blair Sibley, whom I viewed as Palfrey's best and most loyal friend.

But, even though I liked and respected Sibley, I told Palfrey, in front of both him and Burton, that she was making a huge mistake.

After the hearing, Sibley, who harbored no hard feelings towards me, invited Palfrey and me to join him and a close friend of his for lunch. But, for reasons unknown, Sibley was mysterious about the restaurant.

As we followed Sibley from the federal courthouse, across The Mall in front of the U.S. Capitol and towards Independence Avenue, the mystery continued.

After a short walk, Sibley stopped at 300 First Street SE, the National Republican Club of Capitol Hill. "Here's where we're having lunch. We'll meet my friend inside."

Palfrey and I couldn't stop laughing. "We're gonna have to fight our way out of there!" I exclaimed only half-joking. I genuinely believed that this could turn into a really ugly situation—even though Sibley's friend was a member of the club.

The maître d' seated us at a table for four with Palfrey facing the entire room of well-informed Republicans. But we never saw any indication that anyone even recognized her, concluding that the entire room was probably in a state of mass disbelief.

That lunch was the last time that I had fun with Palfrey and Sibley. After that, everything became deadly serious.

On December 4, Judge Kessler—who had earlier identified the male clients of Palfrey's escort service, like Senator Vitter, as "unindicted coconspirators"—voluntarily removed herself from the case, yielding to U.S. District Judge James Robertson, who would now preside over Palfrey's trial.

My long-time friend, author Jim Grady, wanted to meet and interview Palfrey—as he had fashioned a fictitious character based on her in his upcoming novel. I arranged for the three of us to have lunch together on December 13 at Café Mozart in downtown Washington. Seeing that Palfrey and Grady were hitting it off and talking freely, I left immediately after finishing my Wiener Schnitzel and red cabbage, leaving them alone at the table to discuss business.

On January 16, 2008, Palfrey had a complete meltdown—when she fired Blair Sibley and asked the court to allow her to handle her case, *pro se*. In other words, she decided to represent herself in her criminal case.

Knowing my reaction to this moronic decision, she wrote to me the following day: "NOT ONE NAYSAYER REMARK FROM YOU. Now is not the time for second guessing. I have 81 days to trial and I have to spend every possible hour judiciously preparing for the fight of my life. So, calm down." (Palfrey's emphasis)

Also, in the aftermath of the failure of her new co-author, the *Vanity Fair* reporter, to sell her book, Palfrey came back and re-offered the project to me, saying:

> I think it is obvious we REALLY have a salable story here. After all, CNN and the BBC, along with the Arab world news networks will be sitting front and center noting every word and every move the Government and I make during trial, as a real life David and Goliath battle takes place in—of all years—a presidential election year. Any thoughts? Want to do it yourself? If so, I am game. You have been intimately involved in my story from the onset. In many ways, you would be perfect. (Jeane's emphasis)

I immediately turned down her offer to return as her co-author, saying:

> I just can't tell you how shocked I am by the recent turn of events in your case. But, obedient to your wishes, I'm not going to say anything more. Clearly, you have enough on your plate right now.
>
> To business, there is nothing to indicate that a book can be sold at this moment. Without additional revelations about big-name clients, the publishers will still want to know how this ongoing drama is going to end before they commit big money to the project. Your best chance is to stick with the *Vanity Fair* reporter, who will hopefully run her long-awaited (and, hopefully, widely-read) story about you—and then use that article as the proposal for your book. The success of that story could get you what you're looking for.
>
> Meantime, I'm going to continue with my plan and cheer for you from the sidelines.

Two days later, Palfrey sent me another note, saying that Judge Robertson had insisted that she have a real attorney assist her during

PART ELEVEN: THE D.C. MADAM

her *pro se* defense. Pushed against the wall, Palfrey returned to Preston Burton.

In my reply to that, I wrote: "I'm very relieved that Preston is returning to your corner. In fact, I wish you would drop this *pro se* business and just let him handle your defense."

Then, a few weeks before Palfrey's day of legal reckoning, she contacted me, saying that she did not have any money and needed a free place to stay for the duration of her trial.

A close friend of mine, Mike Pilgrim, an airport-security expert and the latest host of our then thirty-year-old poker game, had a beautiful home in McLean, Virginia. In an incredible gesture of friendship, he told me that Palfrey could have his entire house while he was traveling on business.

However, Palfrey decided to bring her mother, Blanche Palfrey, to the trial for support. So, instead of flying to D.C. and residing at my friend's home, they chose to stay at an inexpensive motel in Bowie, Maryland.

On Monday, April 7—the same day that the *Idaho Statesman* was named as runner-up for a Pulitzer Prize for its investigation of Republican Senator Larry Craig's arrest in an airport bathroom in Minneapolis—Palfrey's trial began with Preston Burton serving as her defense attorney. The jury was picked quickly and opening arguments commenced during the afternoon.

The Legal Times published an article that day with the headline, "Courtroom Fireworks Predicted as D.C. Madam Trial Opens."[270]

My colleagues with French television were in the midst of interviewing FBI agents, many of whom I had introduced them to, for their documentary on the 100th anniversary of the bureau. Consequently, I was wrapped up with that project for much of the week.

On Tuesday morning, after my meeting with an FBI source at Morty's, I jumped on the subway and went downtown to the federal courthouse to watch the first federal conspiracy case I had ever seen with only one defendant—in effect, a conspiracy of one.

In the courtroom, I saw two witnesses questioned on direct by the prosecution and then ripped apart on cross by Preston Burton, whom I believed was doing a great job.

At the lunch break, I asked Burton for permission to take Palfrey to lunch. Clearly, he and Palfrey were not getting along very well, so he was more than happy to cut her loose for an hour. I wanted to take Palfrey's mother, too, but she was not feeling well and had stayed at the motel.

During our lunch in the cafeteria at the courthouse, Palfrey appeared very upbeat, miffed at Burton for not listening to her amateur legal advice but still pleased with his performance on cross-examination. She seemed very excited about the prospect of presenting her own case, which was slated to begin early the following week.

On Thursday, I emailed Palfrey, asking if Jim Grady and I could take her to lunch on Friday. A sushi lover, she was up for that idea. With the courtroom dark that day, we agreed to meet at the Uptown Cathay, an Asian restaurant up Connecticut Avenue with an all-you-can-eat-sushi menu.

Earlier in the day, the *Washington Post* had published a couple of stories about Palfrey's trial—including a column by Dana Milbank who criticized the prosecution's conduct of this criminal case, saying:

> Sen. David Vitter of Louisiana and other powerful men appear likely to get a pass. Less lucky: the 15 terrified women being hauled by prosecutors into court to recount in graphic detail their past work as prostitutes—and more than 100 other former prostitutes whose names prosecutors are trying to make public.
>
> Wednesday, prosecutors forced a 63-year-old retired PhD—her name, like those of other witnesses, now a matter of public record—to testify about inducing orgasms in her client; the government's lawyers had similar questions for a mother of three who worked briefly for the escort service nearly 15 years ago.
>
> Yesterday, it was the turn of a young naval officer to take the stand; the case will almost certainly end her career.[271]

Also, a fashion article appeared in the Style section about Palfrey's clothes and makeup in the midst of the trial. She had not seen the newspaper that day, so I ran across the street to a drug store to buy a copy, leaving Palfrey and Grady to talk privately.

When I returned to the restaurant, Palfrey took Grady and me into her confidence, telling us that she and Burton had decided to rest immediately after the prosecution completed its case. In other words, after all of her bravada and promises to take on the government with her supposedly overwhelming evidence of its abuses, she had decided to roll the dice, gambling that the jury would reject the government's case, which she hoped had not proven her guilty beyond a reasonable doubt.

Despite all of the anticipation and hype, there would be no fireworks, only a total anticlimax.

Completely confident of acquittal, Palfrey did not discuss her future, but she certainly gave us no indication that she felt she had no future if she lost her case—although I did warn Grady, just as I had with her attorneys, that she had thrice threatened to commit suicide in lieu of returning to prison.

On Sunday, I drove to Annapolis to visit with Bob and Nancy, two close friends from Ohio, and spent the night in their guest bedroom. The following day, I drove to Salisbury State University on the Eastern Shore where I was scheduled to lecture about the Mafia on Monday night. When I arrived at the university, I checked the news and read that Palfrey and Burton had indeed rested their case, which had been given to the jury.

On Tuesday morning, April 15, as I was preparing to leave Salisbury, I sent an email to Burton, which I cc'd to Palfrey, in which I wrote: "You did a great job. And, before the jury returns, I wanted you to know that I believe you made all the right decisions. Good luck to you and Jeane!"

While I was driving back to Washington late Tuesday morning, I received the news on the radio that the federal jury had convicted Palfrey on all counts of racketeering and money laundering.

When I arrived home, I wrote to both Palfrey and Burton, saying, "I am so shocked, and I am so sorry that this has happened."

I called Palfrey and left a message on her cell phone that evening. She did not call me back.

When eight days had passed without hearing from her, I emailed a note—with "From a concerned friend" on the subject line—which simply asked, "Are you okay?"

I knew that the danger of suicide was clear and present. However, at the time of her conviction, the judge said that she would not be sentenced until July 24—nearly three months away.

I really didn't think that she would even consider ending her life until her complete loss of freedom was at hand later in the summer.

145. Suicide before prison

At 1:18 P.M. on Thursday, May 1—while sitting at my desk at home—I received a message from a friend, a partial news report from MSNBC. All I could read on the page was: "BREAKING NEWS: Fla. Police believe apparent suicide victim m . . ."

That's all it said. And I didn't need to see anything more to know what had happened.

Minutes later, I received a call from Adam Zagorin at *Time* magazine to whom I had leaked the David Vitter story the previous July. Zagorin, whom I had also introduced to Palfrey, told me what little he knew about her death and then interviewed me.

Poor Jeane, 52, had hanged herself in a small storage shed attached to her mother's trailer in Florida. Most tragically, her mother found her body.

In the story that Zagorin immediately broke on *Time's* website, he wrote:

> Deborah Jeane Palfrey, known as the "D.C. Madam," once implied that suicide was cowardice but, in the end, she seems to have chosen that same path herself. "She wasn't going to jail, she told me that very clearly. She told me she would commit suicide," author Dan Moldea told *Time* soon after news broke of her body being found in Tarpon Springs, Florida, an apparent suicide. Palfrey's body, along with a handwritten suicide note, was discovered by police in a storage area attached to her mother's mobile home. Palfrey contacted Moldea last year to provide her help writing a book. "She had done time once before [for prostitution]," Moldea recalls. "And it damn near killed her. She said there was enormous stress — it made her sick, she couldn't take it, and she wasn't going to let that happen to her again." Palfrey had been free pending her scheduled July 24 sentencing on a series of racketeering and money laundering charges as part of running a prostitution ring that had as clients many prominent Washingtonians, including Senator David Vitter of Louisiana. She faced as many as 55 years behind bars (though sentencing guidelines could well have limited her prison time to a maximum of 71 months.)
>
> According to Moldea, who last year examined Palfrey's phone records and discovered the name of Vitter, a Republican, as a client of Palfrey's escort service — Pamela Martin & Associates — the last time he saw Palfrey in person was less than week before her conviction on prostitution charges on April 15. "A friend and I met with Jeanne and we had a sushi lunch near the courtroom," he said. "She was upbeat and hopeful. She felt the prosecution had not made the case and that she was

going to walk. She was hopeful to the end." But, when the jury came in with her conviction, she reportedly was taken aback. "When I heard that I knew that, for her, it was all over. There is no question in my mind that she took her own life."

Vitter remains a Senator and has not been censured, despite coming under intense public criticism. Of Palfrey, Moldea said, "I liked her. She was a good person, she was kind, funny, she had a sense of humor, and what she may have done in business, I bring no judgment to that. You have to remember that all those who worked for her service and those who used it — none of them were held to account, or punished. And now, she is dead."[272]

The story on the front page of the *Washington Post* the following day was similar:

> Dubbed "the D.C. Madam" after a grand jury in Washington indicted her 14 months ago on prostitution-related racketeering charges, Palfrey, 52, repeatedly told journalist Dan Moldea last year that she would rather die than live behind bars, Moldea said.
>
> He said Palfrey—who was incarcerated for 18 months in California in the early 1990s after being convicted of running a prostitution ring—told him on three occasions: "I'm not going back to jail. I'll kill myself first. I'll commit suicide first."
>
> "Those were her exact words," said Moldea, who interviewed Palfrey last spring and summer for a possible book. . . .
>
> Moldea said Palfrey's 18-month California prison term was a terrible memory for her.
>
> "The first time she did time, it damn near killed her, she told me," he said. "She wound up in a fairly tough prison, and the stress caused some sort of an illness that affected her eyesight. It was just a horrible, horrible period for her."
>
> After Palfrey was released, Moldea said, "she began looking forward to what she was going to do with her future. Although

she had a college degree, she viewed herself as a convicted felon who couldn't do anything else. So she came to Washington and got back into the business again."[273]

These and other articles wound up as an unmitigated disaster, because they launched an array of conspiracy theories aimed at me.

A nutty talk-show host in Austin, Texas, named Alex Jones, had interviewed Palfrey the previous March—during which he asked her if she planned to commit suicide. She replied on tape, "No I'm not planning to commit suicide. I'm planning on going into court and defending myself vigorously and exposing the government."

The simple fact was that circumstances had changed for Palfrey. She did not wind up "vigorously" defending herself in court, and, since she never presented a defense, she certainly never exposed the government.

However, Jones—who believed that Palfrey had been murdered in some bizarre connection to the 9/11 terrorist attacks—had a piece of news and appeared willing to exploit it in a cynical effort to sell his books, videotapes and "infogear" on his website. He fired up his flock of sheep to ratchet up the conspiracy theories, using my statements in Adam Zagorin's *Time* magazine piece as evidence of my complicity in her murder.

On one of his sites, *Prison Planet,* Jones used his stooges to attack my quotes in *Time* by simply linking my previous conclusions that there were no conspiracies in either the Robert Kennedy murder case or the Vincent Foster's suicide.

In addition, Geraldo Rivera, now of Fox News, presented a program about Palfrey's death—with Alex Jones as his principal guest—during which Rivera, who specifically cast suspicion on me and showed my photograph on full-screen, concluded, "It does not appear likely that she committed suicide."[274]

Another radio talk-show host, Dr. Katherine Albrecht, also tried to implicate me in Jeane's supposed murder, adding that I wrote "cover-up books." Inexplicably, she also accused me of protecting and cooperating with Vice President Dick Cheney while serving as "the mouthpiece of the power elite" and claiming that I was "thick as thieves with Washington insiders."[275]

Under normal circumstances, I would have laughed at such allegations.

However, along with Albrecht, nearly seventy blogs and websites picked up Alex Jones's defamations against me and repeated them. The situation became so bad that I wound up creating a webpage on my own website specifically to address Jones's charges, as well as to list those who were repeating them in print, on radio and television, and on the Internet.

To my surprise, Larry Flynt, to whom I had not spoken in nearly nine months, was among the first to jump onto the Jeane-was-murdered bandwagon. He told Fox News: "I think the media should be very cautious in treating this as a suicide. . . . I personally believe that [she was murdered], but I have no proof. . . .

"She did not have the demeanor of the type of person that would carry certain signs of suicide, like being withdrawn or depressed. You know, those are the kinds of signs that you look for. She didn't display any of those traits."[276]

And, just for good measure, the *New York Times* weighed in, placing me at the epicenter of the conspiracy theories by stating:

> Most controversially, Dan Moldea, who tried to develop a book proposal for a Palfrey biography, is quoted by *Time* magazine saying that Ms. Palfrey told him she would sooner kill herself than go to prison again (she served a sentence for prostitution in California in the 1990's).
>
> That claim is being called a part of a cover-up by many of those disinclined to believe that Ms. Palfrey's death was suicide, because she had often said the opposite—that she was *not* the kind to kill herself. . . .[277]

In Washington, I was besieged with calls. In addition, camera crews from three of the four principal local television stations showed up in front of my apartment building in what amounted to ambush interviews. Two of the reporters who interviewed me actually had the gall to ask for my whereabouts at the time of Palfrey's death in Florida. . . . They wanted my alibi.

The CBS-television affiliate in Washington, WUSA-9, stated:

> Moldea's claim [that Palfrey told him that she would commit suicide in lieu of returning to prison] has the web abuzz. "Murder!" says the conspiracy theorists. They accuse Moldea of participating in a cover up. . . .
>
> Moldea does wonder why prosecutors went after Palfrey so hard, especially when the newspapers and the yellow pages are

rife with listings for other escort services. "There are more escort services in Washington, D.C. than there are McDonald's restaurants," says Moldea.[278]

Much of the pressure on me abated when the police released two lengthy suicide notes that Palfrey had written—one to her mother and the other to her sister—in which she explained, in considerable detail, her tragic decision. In fact, these were not simply "goodbye-cruel-world" typed messages. They were long and detailed handwritten statements of a distressed woman who was about to take her own life.

In part, Palfrey wrote to her mother:

> Mom, I want you to know how very much I love and appreciate you. I sincerely apologize for any pain which I have caused you in this lifetime. Additionally, I can't sufficiently express to you how badly I feel for this burden I am leaving you with here.
>
> However, I cannot live the next 6-8 years behind bars for what both you and I have come to regard as this "modern day lynching," only to come out of prison in my late 50s a broken, penniless and very much alone woman.

It was impossible to dismiss these emotional handwritten letters as forgeries.

On May 6—the day after the Tarpon Springs medical examiner officially declared that Palfrey had committed suicide—the chief investigating detective for the Tarpon Springs Police Department contacted me for additional material which he wanted for his formal report. I gave him a copy of my book proposal with Palfrey—in which she twice discussed the possibility of suicide, as well as copies of my final emails to her. Also, I arranged a conference call among the detective and me with Jim Grady, who was at the April 11 lunch where Palfrey and I last saw each other.

After speaking with the police, I called Blanche Palfrey to express my sympathy and to discuss her daughter's death. At the outset, I told her how upset I was with Jeane for placing her mother in the position to find her body hanging at the end of a rope.

Blanche, who couldn't have been happier to hear from me, said that Jeane "was so upset about going back to prison that she couldn't stop crying."

PART ELEVEN: THE D.C. MADAM

During our continuing conversation, she spoke of Jeane's recent overdose in Orlando. When I said that I didn't know what she was talking about, she explained that on April 25, Jeane had gone to her condominium in Orlando and taken an intentional overdose of pills. She was unconscious for nearly thirty hours.

Failing to end her life in that manner, Jeane then returned home and hanged herself.

I asked Blanche if she had told the police this story. She replied that she had not, adding that she didn't want to cause any more trouble.

I told her that she had to tell the police. I gave her the lead detective's name and telephone number. She assured me that she would make the call.

I called Blanche again on May 9 and asked her if she had provided the information about Jeane's earlier unsuccessful attempt to kill herself to the police. She replied that she had not.

I then asked for her permission to represent her with the police and disclose this information. Blanche agreed, and I immediately called the lead detective in the case and told him what Blanche had told me about Jeane's attempted suicide in Orlando.

The detective knew nothing about this. I invited him to call Blanche who would give him all the details.

On Saturday, May 10, I appeared on CNN to respond to the ludicrous but nagging accusations against me.

> **RICK SANCHEZ:** All right, joining us now and Josh mentioned this while we're talking is one of the last people to see Palfrey alive. Dan Moldea has been planning to write a book about the D.C. Madam. He's good enough to join us now.
>
> Dan, I understand that you had lunch with her just a few days before she died. How do you find her?
>
> **MOLDEA:** Well, actually, I had lunch with her and a friend of mine, Jim Grady, a few days before her conviction here in Washington. She was fine. She was very upbeat. She confided in Jim and I that she and her attorney had decided that they were going to claim that the prosecution had not made its case, and they were going to rest. And she was onboard with that. She was very upbeat and was convinced that she was going to be acquitted.

SANCHEZ: Given that, do you think she killed herself?

MOLDEA: There's no doubt in my mind that she committed suicide. She told me on no fewer than three occasions that in lieu of going back to prison where she had spent 18 months back in the early 90s, she would commit suicide. As soon as I heard that, I immediately went to her attorney, who was probably her best friend and most loyal friend.

I said, "Listen, I think we've got a problem. . ." He said, "I know, I know, I know. It's a *real* problem."

I was not the only person she told that to.

SANCHEZ: What do you make of all these conspiracies then? I mean, the blogosphere is absolutely jam packed with them as I'm sure you've notice.

MOLDEA: I'm not calling it the Internet. I'm calling it the Defamation Zone. Because I'm being accused of either participating in the murder of Jeane or at the very least participating in an act of cover up of the circumstances of my friend's death.

Let me say, first of all, that I liked Jeane. She was a kind person. She was very smart. She was a funny person. Legal or moral considerations aside, she was a good person.

With regard to the conspiracy theories, let me break a little news for you right now.

SANCHEZ: Okay.

MOLDEA: I received information from a very reliable source in this matter. And I gave this information to the police yesterday morning—That Jeane had tried to kill herself prior to this after her conviction. She had gone to Orlando shortly after she returned to Florida. She had taken an intentional overdose, and it failed. In the wake of the failure of her overdose to end her life, she went back to Tarpon Springs, and she [hanged] herself.

PART ELEVEN: THE D.C. MADAM

SANCHEZ: Dan Moldea making news for us here, or should we say sharing it with us. We thank you for your insight into this story. Thanks again, Dan.

Four days later, Blair Sibley and I had lunch at Morty's. Of course, our primary topic of conversation was Palfrey's death. Sibley told me that I should go ahead and publish a book about her. I replied that he should be the one to write and publish it, which he later did.[279]

On October 30, 2008, the Tarpon Springs Police Department released a 48-page investigative report, declaring, once and for all, that Jeane Palfrey had committed suicide.

146. Opposition research

My behind-the-scenes work as an investigative consultant required that I lead a life of virtual anonymity, enforced by the non-disclosure agreements I routinely signed as I moved from client to client and caper to caper. Over the years—apart from hundreds of general due-diligence background checks—I investigated, among others, corporate mergers, mortgage-fraud cases, state lotteries, foreign banks, Indian-gambling operations, a municipal-fraud scheme, a drug company, corrupt car dealers, corrupt attorneys, several defamation cases (for both plaintiffs and defendants), a copyright case, a mobbed-up music company, and an attempted hostile takeover of a small software company by a major corporation—which I helped to foil.

However, most of my work revolved around opposition research because of my personal politics and admitted partisanship, both of which I now wore on my sleeve.

I had come to view the right wing of the Republican Party as an emerging organized-crime group. And, since the impeachment drama, I had gone after targeted Republicans with the same zeal that I went after mobsters and labor racketeers at the beginning of my career. But, back then, during the mid-1970s, the leaders of the Republican Party included reasonable people, like U.S. Senators Howard Baker, Edward Brooke, Robert Griffin, Mark Hatfield, Jacob Javits, Charles Mathias, Bob Packwood, Charles Percy, William Saxbe, and Lowell Weicker.

In 21st Century America, none of those great leaders could get past a GOP primary.

Ronald Reagan's presidential campaign and subsequent victory in 1980 had brought knuckle draggers into the political process—who managed to obtain real power in Congress during the Clinton years and then used that power in a relentless effort to remove him from office. Actually given the opportunity to govern during the George W. Bush presidency, they managed to lock the country into two bloody wars of attrition and nearly busted out the American economy with their wild military spending, as well as their lax enforcement and regulation of the business community.

To me, right-wing demagogues were screwing up the country just as much as the Mafia.

Working with two different clients against GOP candidates during the 2008 general-election campaign, I played key behind-the-scenes roles in two U.S. Senate races—finishing with one win and one loss. In the winning race, my team and I played a decisive role in what was an extremely close election, which helped increase the Democrats' majority in the Senate.

To this day, I doubt that the senator has any idea of what my team and I did for him.

Although I had no assignment in the Presidential race—Senator Barack Obama v. Senator John McCain—I did play a minor role in the aftermath of Obama's November 4 election when I discovered the telephone number of one of the President-elect's soon-to-be-nominated Cabinet appointees on Jeane Palfrey's phone list. In lieu of allowing the appointment to be made and then breaking the story, I quietly worked through a well-placed friend who communicated with a key member of Obama's inner circle to help the President-elect avoid a major early embarrassment.

Although I do not know all the specific details, the appointment was not made. I neither asked for nor did I receive any compensation or favors of any kind in return. I simply moved on and continued my work on another front.

From 2009 to 2011, I worked for a wonderful public-interest group, which used me to conduct over twenty investigations. Although the group made the results of several of these probes public, I never received a single public acknowledgment for any of my contributions. And the fee for my work was half of what I normally charged.

But, considering my great respect for this client, I was fine with that, too.

I felt honored when its leadership invited me to their annual holiday party in December 2010. During the dinner, the executive director asked everyone in the room to make predictions for the coming year. When my turn came, I replied, "During 2011, Fox News will be declared as a criminal enterprise."

Amidst the laughter that followed, the general counsel shouted out, "And be the subject of a federal RICO case?"

Laughing, too, I pleaded, "Please, Lord, let me be part of it!"

We didn't do that job, but the British government did. In November 2011, James Murdoch—the son of media tycoon Rupert Murdoch and the chairman of News International, a subsidiary of News Corporation, which is also the parent company of Fox News in the United States—testified before a parliamentary committee. In the midst of Murdoch's testimony, Tom Watson, a Member of Parliament, compared News International to organized crime, saying to Murdoch, "You must be the first Mafia boss in history who didn't know he was running a criminal enterprise."[280]

PART TWELVE:
Hoffa redux

147. Frank Sheeran's conflicting confessions

Weary of the dark and treacherous world of probing American politics, I decided to take a hiatus and return to the serenity and tranquility of investigating the Mafia.

In 1997, the *Detroit Sunday Journal*, a newspaper created by striking journalists from both the *Detroit Free Press* and the *Detroit News*, published a series of articles about the Hoffa case. The centerpiece of these fascinating reports was a cache of 1,704 official FBI documents that had been discovered in an abandoned file cabinet at a local recreational facility. No one, including the FBI, could explain how these records got there.

To all intents and purposes, the documents were part of the old *Hoffex* file upon which the *Hoffex Memo*, the compendium of information that summarized the FBI's early knowledge of the case, was based. Written by staff reporter Michael Betzold, the series, entitled "The Hoffa Files," buttressed with specific documents that had previously been reported by author Steven Brill and me in our 1978 books and added many new details about the investigation.[281]

Betzold's series reenergized the efforts of Hoffa's daughter, Barbara Crancer, a circuit-court judge in St. Louis, to force the FBI to release its entire case file of her father's murder investigation.

Filing a lawsuit against the FBI, the *Detroit Free Press*, led by two-time Pulitzer Prize winning reporter David Ashenfelter, also tried to get the secret files. Working in concert with Judge Crancer, the *Free Press* eventually prevailed and later obtained the entire *Hoffex* file, which was nearly 17,000 pages. About 5,000 of those pages were unredacted.[282]

On September 30, 2002, Ashenfelter sent me a complete copy of the *Hoffex Memo*. It was the first time I had seen this document after first hearing about it from Brill in 1977.

Regarding the information provided by Ralph Picardo, the government's key witness in the case, the *Hoffex Memo* stated:

> [O]n November 5, 1975, Ralph Picardo . . . began to furnish information to Bureau Agents regarding criminal activities of Tony Pro, Salvatore and Gabriel Briguglio and Thomas and Stephen Andretta, all New Jersey Teamsters associated with Local 560. Picardo contended that he had personal knowledge of two other aborted attempts by Tony Pro on JRH's life. These purportedly occurred in November of 1973, and

December of 1974. However, source did not know the reasons that these plans were not carried out.

> Picardo alleges that in August, 1975, a few days after the disappearance of JRH, he was visited at the New Jersey State Penitentiary (where he is serving a sentence for Second Degree Murder) by Stephen and Thomas Andretta and [accountant] Martin Shindler to transact business regarding Lift Van, Incorporated, a business owned by Picardo. When Thomas Andretta and Shindler were out of the room, [Steve] Andretta asked Picardo if Federal Agents had been to see him and then made admission and references that Provenzano's group was involved in the JRH disappearance and stated that the body was . . . [transported] by Gateway Transportation Company. Stephen Andretta stated that he was not present in Detroit, but had stayed in New Jersey to provide an alibi for Tony Pro. Investigation at Newark showed that Picardo was visited by Andretta and Shindler during the pertinent time period. During interview of Tony Pro on August 4, 1975, Provenzano claimed he was with Stephen Andretta the day of JRH's disappearance. . . .
>
> It is believed that if Picardo's information is correct, Tony Pro was responsible for JRH's disappearance and used his continued attempts to have a meeting with JRH as an excuse for the set-up on July 30, 1975. Details of the abduction, if any, are unknown; however, Tommy Andretta and the Briguglios figure to have had a part in it.[283]

In a separate FBI document, which focused specifically on Picardo and his allegation of the two previous plans to kill Hoffa, Special Agent Robert J. Garrity wrote:

> In regard to Hoffex investigation, Picardo alleges that in mid November, 1973, he and Stephen Andretta traveled to Miami, Florida, to consult Tony Provenzano on another matter. All three met at the Americana Hotel, Miami, and registered in true names. Picardo witnessed an argument between Provenzano and Hoffa, and that on the following day, Provenzano ordered . . . Andretta to kill Hoffa. On the same day, Gabriel Briguglio was called to Florida by Provenzano to

be advised regarding his intention to kill Hoffa, and that the message was to be delivered to Salvatore Briguglio, who at that time was incarcerated [in] Lewisburg, Pennsylvania, prison. . . .

Picardo further alleges that two weeks subsequent to above incident, he met with Tony Provenzano in a North Bergen, New Jersey restaurant regarding another matter, and that Provenzano reported to Picardo that JRH was destined to be killed, and that Provenzano was awaiting the right time.

Picardo further states that on [December 16 or 17, 1974], he was ordered by Gabriel Briguglio to insure that a station wagon in his possession was in good running condition, and that his citizens' band radio [was] working. He was told to drive the vehicle by [sic] both Briguglio and Tony Provenzano the following day to [a Provenzano associate's] office in New York City. Picardo advised the he delivered the above station wagon. . . . While at [Provenzano's associate's] office, Picardo overheard arrangements between Hoffa and Provenzano to have dinner at Ponte's Restaurant, New York City. Provenzano was to meet later that day with Salvatore Briguglio and Stephen Andretta. Picardo alleged Provenzano told him on this occasion that Hoffa would be killed that day.[284]

In 2001, prior to obtaining all of this information from Ashenfelter, I received a call from a producer at NBC News who asked how important I thought Frank Sheeran was to the Hoffa case.

"On a scale of one to ten," I replied, "he's a ten."

With regard to Sheeran, the 1976 *Hoffex Memo* stated:

FRANCIS JOSEPH "FRANK" SHEERAN, age 43, president Local 326, Wilmington, Delaware. Resides in Philadelphia and is known associate of [Russell] Bufalino, La Cosa Nostra Chief, Eastern Pennsylvania. [Sheeran's] vehicle seen at meeting of La Cosa Nostra figures in Wilkes Barre, Pennsylvania, August 29, 1975, and also in Detroit December 4, 1975, during [federal grand jury] appearance of New Jersey teamsters. Known to be in Detroit area at the time of JRH disappearance, and is considered to be close friend of JRH.[285]

In my book on Hoffa, I had implicated Sheeran—with whom I had tape recorded a brief interview on March 28, 1978—in the murder conspiracy and identified him as an eyewitness to the killing. This provoked Sheeran, via his attorney, to threaten legal action against me.

Specifically, the attorney, F. Emmett Fitzpatrick, wrote:

> Mr. Sheeran wishes me to inform you that he emphatically denies the allegations about his involvement in Mr. Hoffa's alleged death and to state specifically that your allegation that he was present in Detroit on the last day that Mr. Hoffa was seen is false, unfounded and has been specifically contradicted by evidence supplied by Mr. Sheeran to the Federal Government.
>
> On Mr. Sheeran's behalf, I demand a retraction and a public apology for all of your many allegations of his activities surrounding and contributing to the alleged disappearance or death of Mr. Hoffa.

The NBC producer then told me that Sheeran, who was still alive, was writing a book in which he would reveal the details of his involvement in Hoffa's murder. He added that NBC was trying to gain Sheeran's cooperation for a television-news program.

Specifically, the producer told me that Sheeran was claiming that he and Sal Briguglio were in the car that Chuck O'Brien was driving when they allegedly picked up Hoffa. Then, they drove to a private residence where Briguglio committed the murder, shooting Hoffa in the head—with the assistance of Tom Andretta and, possibly, his brother, Steve Andretta. After that, according to Sheeran, Hoffa's body was taken to an incinerator where it was destroyed.

The producer asked for my cooperation with his project, and I enthusiastically agreed to give it. "This could be huge," I told him.

I heard nothing more until the producer called several weeks later and told me that NBC had interviewed Sheeran—but quickly backed away from their original plans to air the program. In short, for reasons not fully explained to me, they did not believe what he had said.

In late July 2003, I had another exchange with a different producer at *Dateline NBC*, who had also been offered Sheeran's story. When he asked me in a July 23 email what I thought about Sheeran, I replied in writing, "I've been hearing about Sheeran's book for nearly two years.

Take him very, very seriously. From what I understand, he has been sick, and this could be tantamount to a death-bed confession."

During the early evening, the NBC producer wrote back, saying that the network was moving forward with the Sheeran story. He wanted to bring me on as a consultant.

However, internal problems developed at NBC six days later. The producer wrote that his boss was extremely skeptical of Sheeran's version of events and, simply speaking, believed that he was lying. Meantime, the producer and others were trying to turn their boss around.

In my written reply, I recounted what I had learned from the previous NBC producer.

This new producer corrected me on one very key point: Sheeran was now saying that he, not Sal Briguglio, had committed the murder.

"Tell me," he continued in his email, "what would sell more books? A book by someone who was there? Or the triggerman himself? I think Sheeran has made his bed with all his lies over the years. If nobody will touch his book he has only himself to blame."

Shocked, I wrote back: "Sheeran's claiming that he did the job, personally???!!! That's a new one on me."

Three weeks later, on August 18, the producer gave me NBC News's final word on Sheeran: "My bosses decided that Sheeran has made too many claims proven false over the years to be believed now. So we are passing on the story."

A few days before the end of 2003, I received the news that the 83-year-old Sheeran had died on December 14 at a nursing home in a suburb of Philadelphia. His passing went virtually unnoticed.

On March 13, 2004, three months after Sheeran's death, David Ashenfelter broke a major story in the *Free Press*, revealing Sheeran's undated three-page statement, on which his signature appeared on each page, confessing to his role in the murder.

However, Ashenfelter also reported that Sheeran's daughter, Dolores Miller, had claimed that the "confession" was a forgery, insisting that the signature was not her father's. Specifically, she accused Omaha writer John Zeitts of creating the document in an effort to "upstage a book to be published in June by another Sheeran biographer, Charles Brandt, a former Delaware chief deputy state attorney general."[286]

Zeitts denied to both Ashenfelter and me that he had fabricated the document, explaining that Sheeran had executed this declaration in

November 2003—just a month before his death. In early March 2004, Zeitts forwarded it to Barbara Crancer who then gave it to Ashenfelter.

A combat veteran in Vietnam who was captured and then escaped, Zeitts had been convicted of sending pornography through the mail after he returned from Southeast Asia. He met Sheeran while the two men were in a federal prison during the mid-1980s. Sheeran was doing time for labor racketeering.

After their separate releases, they got together and began a series of conversations about Sheeran's life and times, many of which Zeitts videotaped.[287] During their talks, they concocted a couple of different scenarios—both of which proclaimed Sheeran's complete innocence and lack of involvement in the Hoffa murder.[288] However, while denying any personal role in the crime, Sheeran did finger Sal Briguglio as Hoffa's actual killer.

In his 2004 article, Ashenfelter reported the specifics of the signed statement and described what Sheeran now allegedly confessed to:

> Hoffa called Sheeran on July 27, 1975, to set up a meeting between Hoffa and Pennsylvania crime boss Russell Bufalino to resolve Hoffa's conflict with [Anthony] Provenzano. Hoffa called back the next day to say that he had set up a meeting with Provenzano for July 30 and that Hoffa wanted Sheeran there to "watch his back."
>
> That night, Bufalino hinted to Sheeran that Hoffa would be killed so there was no reason for Sheeran to attend the meeting.
>
> On July 30, Sheeran, Bufalino, their wives and Bufalino's sister-in-law headed to Detroit from Pennsylvania to attend a wedding.
>
> Along the way, Sheeran left the group, went to an airstrip, flew to Pontiac and got into a car that had an address in the glove box.
>
> Sheeran drove to the address and was met by Provenzano henchmen Salvatore Briguglio and brothers Thomas and Stephen Andretta, who were suspected but never charged in Hoffa's disappearance.

PART TWELVE: HOFFA REDUX

"The deed had already been done," the document said. . . .

> Sheeran returned to Pontiac and flew back to the airstrip to rejoin his group. [Emphasis added.]

Obviously, with Sheeran writing, "The deed had already been done," he was certainly not taking credit for the actual murder.

Sheeran's statement went on to assert that several days later he met Detroit mobsters Peter Vitale and Jimmy Quasarano, who owned a Hamtramck incinerator, at a restaurant in New York. "After lunch, while walking to our cars," Sheeran stated, "Peter Vitale told me that if I waited long enough, I could pay my respects to Hoffa in the soot surrounding his trash incinerator."

Ashenfelter called and asked me for comment. I replied with a prepared statement, which I immediately placed on my website, saying:

> As I wrote in my 1978 book, *The Hoffa Wars*, Frank Sheeran was directly involved in the murder of former Teamsters boss Jimmy Hoffa. Even though I do not believe that Sheeran, either in his alleged signed confession or [an] upcoming book, was telling the truth about his specific role at the crime scene, I do believe that he honestly revealed many important details about certain events that occurred prior to the killing.
>
> Make no mistake: This is the biggest break in the case since Hoffa disappeared on July 30, 1975. Now, in the wake of Sheeran's death in December 2003, the task will be to separate fact from fiction.

Of course, I was also skeptical about Sheeran's version of the supposed manner in which Hoffa's body had been disposed. That Hamtramck incinerator, also known as Central Sanitation, was the centerpiece of Steve Brill's theory—which the FBI had repeatedly told me was wrong. In 1978, when Brill's book was released, the FBI issued a public statement, specifically rejecting the Central Sanitation scenario.

Apparently, Sheeran, who seemed to be borrowing from the public record to fill the gaps of his own story, didn't get the memo.

148. Not a distinction without a difference

Shortly after David Ashenfelter's 2004 story, Eric Shawn, a reporter for Fox News, called and asked me to participate in a major news report that he was preparing on Charles Brandt's upcoming book, *I Heard You Paint Houses: Frank "The Irishman" Sheeran and the Inside Story of the Mafia, the Teamsters, and the Last Ride of Jimmy Hoffa*.

Because the idea of the late Frank Sheeran telling this tale—regardless of his numerous lies and contradictions in the past—was so intriguing, I agreed to participate in Shawn's report.[289] Inasmuch as I had already put Sheeran in the murder conspiracy in my 1978 book—as had Steve Brill in his own book—I really wanted Brandt to hit this one out of the ballpark in 2004.

After all of these years, I hoped that the Hoffa case would finally be solved, once and for all.

To my surprise, on the acknowledgments page of his book, Brandt, with the concurrence of Sheeran, had written: "Thanks to those writers, such as Dan Moldea, Steven Brill, Victor Riesel, and [Jonathan] Kwitny, whose skillful investigative reporting, at risk of physical harm, uncovered and preserved so much of the history of Jimmy Hoffa, his times, and his disappearance."

Also on the acknowledgements page, I could not help but notice that author Brandt's literary agent for this project was Frank Weimann, who had sold my book about the O. J. Simpson case to Pocket Books but had been unable to sell my book about the Flynt project.

Later in his text, Brandt stated that the first publisher-to-be of Sheeran's controversial story had canceled the book—because of Sheeran's credibility problems.[290]

Consequently, Brandt wrote: "My agent, Frank Weimann, told Sheeran over the phone that if he wanted to get another publisher he would have to come clean and stand behind the book"[291]

After speaking with Weimann, Sheeran had a conversation with his attorney, Emmett Fitzpatrick—the same lawyer who had threatened to sue me in 1979 because I had alleged that Sheeran was involved in the Hoffa murder conspiracy while Sheeran was claiming that he had not even been in Detroit on the day Hoffa disappeared. Fitzpatrick convinced Sheeran to be filmed, accepting the credit for killing Hoffa.

Brandt, upon turning on his video camera, noted that Sheeran "became hesitant and withdrawn." However, he soon snapped out of his

PART TWELVE: HOFFA REDUX

funk and agreed to hold up the galleys of his book while on camera, intoning what would become his mantra: "I stand behind what's written."

When Brandt tried to prod Sheeran to say something more, Sheeran replied on camera, "You have to go into questions, then one question leads to another. Let the book speak for itself."

At that point, according to Brandt, "the camera battery died, and it was awhile before I discovered it and plugged the camera in."[292]

On an earlier audio tape, however, Sheeran had told Brandt that he was the killer.

Weimann managed to sell the book to a second small publisher, Steerforth Press in Hanover, New Hampshire. The financial splits between Brandt and Sheeran's family for the book's royalties were not made public. However, it is fair to speculate that the business partnership between Brandt and Sheeran made Brandt less of a skeptical interviewer and more apt to embrace anything Sheeran said—which could help them publish this single-source manuscript, which had already been rejected by at least one other publisher.

After all, the clock was ticking. Sheeran, who was nearly broke and would be leaving little for his family, was about to die. And without Sheeran's latest version of events in the wake of a long series of lies and deceptions, there would be no book.

Regardless, Brandt allowed himself to say during an interview on CNN, "[T]here's no question that Sheeran is telling the truth. Interrogation and cross-examination . . . is my passion. I had him for five years. This was not an afternoon on the witness stand. And he was trying to unburden himself in his later years. He had returned to his Catholic faith [and] gotten absolution."[293]

Even though I knew that Sheeran had something important to say, I also believed that he changed his story about his role as Hoffa's actual killer in a cynical effort to salvage his book project so that he could leave his family some money—and for no other reason.

Frank Sheeran did not kill Jimmy Hoffa. Salvatore Briguglio did, based on everything I have seen and heard about this case since 1975.

Eric Shawn of Fox News broke the story about Brandt's book on Sheeran on May 28. Shawn had interviewed Sheeran shortly before his death. Sheeran had supposedly admitted that he had killed Hoffa—just as the *Dateline NBC* producer told me the previous year—but, inexplicably, he refused to say so on camera to Fox News. From his hospital bed, he would only say, "I stand by what's written in the book."[294]

I agreed to appear in the report, repeating with considerable enthusiasm, "I'm convinced without any question that this is the biggest break in the Hoffa case since Hoffa disappeared on July 30, 1975. There's no doubt in my mind about this." [295]

However, reporter Shawn added: "Moldea . . . believes Sheeran was involved in Hoffa's murder, but is skeptical if he actually fired the fatal shots."

To me, the question of whether Hoffa's killer was Frank Sheeran or Sal Briguglio was not a distinction without a difference. It went right to the heart of the issue of who was involved in the murder, as well as the motive behind it.

Earlier, on November 26, 1976, nearly a year *after* the *Hoffex Memo* was written, Robert C. Stewart, the head of the U.S. Strike Force in Buffalo, sent a memorandum, "Status Report – Hoffa Investigation," to Kurt W. Muellenberg, the acting chief of the Justice Department's Organized Crime and Racketeering Section. In a discussion about Provenzano's failed attempt to solicit Hoffa to help Local 560, Stewart indicated that Sal Briguglio was given "the actual assignment" to kill Hoffa, stating:

> [I]n June and July of 1975 . . . Provenzano tried again to enlist Hoffa's support through Giacalone and that Hoffa gave a final refusal with a possible threat of exposure. The sequence of calls is suggestive of the proposition that, when Hoffa conclusively told Giacalone that he would not help Provenzano (7/18/75), Giacalone and Provenzano agreed to eliminate Hoffa; . . . that Briguglio was given the actual assignment and, thereafter, he notified the interested parties of its successful completion on the evening of 7/30/75 either personally or through a third party.

What I did agree with was Sheeran's very plausible account of what had preceded the actual murder which author Brandt presented extremely well in his book.

To be sure, Brandt's version was very similar to the declaration that Sheeran had executed for John Zeitts, except that Brandt had added important new details.

PART TWELVE: HOFFA REDUX

According to Brandt, Sheeran claimed that Hoffa had earlier asked for his protection at Hoffa's anticipated meeting with Tony Provenzano and Tony Giacalone on July 30, 1975.[296]

On the day of this scheduled meeting, Sheeran and his wife, along with Russell Bufalino and his wife, were driving from Pennsylvania to Detroit to attend the wedding of William Bufalino's daughter. En route, Russell Bufalino directed Sheeran to make a stop off the Ohio Turnpike at an airport in Port Clinton, where a private plane was waiting. Leaving his wife and the Bufalinos behind at the airport, Sheeran was flown across Lake Erie to Pontiac Airport, near Detroit.

Upon his arrival, Sheeran climbed into a gray Ford and, with directions provided by Bufalino, drove to a three-story, brick-and-wood private residence at 17841 Beaverland Street in northwest Detroit.[297] There, Sheeran suggested, he met with Sal Briguglio, as well as Tom and Steve Andretta, who had placed a roll of linoleum in the house's foyer. Sheeran kept his car parked in the driveway.

Shortly after that, Chuck O'Brien allegedly drove up in a maroon automobile—unaware, according to Sheeran, of what was about to happen. Sheeran and Briguglio entered O'Brien's car. Together, the three men drove to the Red Fox.

When they arrived at the restaurant at 2:45 P.M., an angry Hoffa complained that they had kept him waiting. Even though he expressed concern that neither Tony Provenzano nor Tony Giacalone was in the car, he trusted Sheeran, who was sitting in the front passenger's seat, and stepped into the back seat behind Sheeran.

This was consistent with the statement of one of the alleged eyewitnesses interviewed by the FBI, who stated that he had seen Hoffa sitting in the back seat behind the front-seat passenger.

Briguglio sat next to Hoffa and behind O'Brien, according to Sheeran's account.

To me, despite Sheeran's past discrepancies, all of this rang true—and I was very excited when I first read it. There was no doubt in my mind: Hoffa had completely trusted Sheeran and would have gotten into the car with him.

With Sheeran's confession, Brandt had been able to accomplish in 2003 what I just couldn't do while I was writing my 1978 book: He placed Frank Sheeran in the car with Hoffa. Back then, I believed that to be true, but I had absolutely no source information to support it.

Consequently, I simply portrayed Sheeran in *The Hoffa Wars* as an eyewitness, who had possibly driven Hoffa's killers from the Pontiac

Airport to the scene of the crime. That was as far as my law-enforcement sources could speculate with their limited inside information.

However, what I did not buy into was Sheeran's tale of what happened after that.

Sheeran claimed in his book that upon their return to the house on Beaverland Street, which was eight miles from the restaurant, he and Hoffa got out of the car. Then, they walked through the front door and into the foyer where the roll of linoleum had been placed—while O'Brien and Briguglio drove away.

Significantly, Sheeran had earlier claimed that Briguglio's primary role was to make sure that he did the job on Hoffa. However, Sheeran's story had Briguglio leaving the scene before the actual crime was even committed.

Continuing his story, Sheeran told Brandt that when Hoffa entered the empty house, he immediately reacted to a suspected ambush:

> He turned fast, still thinking we were together on the thing, that I was his backup. Jimmy bumped into me hard. If he saw the piece in my hand he had to think I had it out to protect him. He took a quick step to go around me and get to the door. He reached for the knob and *Jimmy Hoffa got shot twice at a decent range*—not too close or the paint splatters back at you—in the back of the head behind his right ear. My friend didn't suffer. [298] [Emphasis added.]

I wondered: Why the weasel words? Why didn't Sheeran just flat out say, "I shot Hoffa twice," instead of distancing himself from the act by saying, "Jimmy Hoffa got shot twice at a decent range"?

Also, I could not help but notice the similarities between Sheeran's version of Hoffa's murder and the manner in which the Joe Pesci character was killed, also in the entrance to a private residence, in the classic 1990 Martin Scorsese-Robert De Niro movie, *Goodfellas*, which was based on Nicholas Pileggi's best-selling book, *Wiseguy*.[299]

After supposedly killing Hoffa, Sheeran said that he looked around to make sure that no one was there to kill him. Seeing he was safe, he climbed into the gray Ford that he had driven from the Pontiac Airport and then returned to catch his private plane back to Port Clinton, Ohio, where he rejoined his wife and the Bufalinos.

Remarkably, according to Sheeran, the whole operation had only taken an hour.

PART TWELVE: HOFFA REDUX

Then, together, the Sheerans and the Bufalinos resumed their drive to Detroit.

According to Sheeran, Bufalino later told him that Hoffa's body had been incinerated, either at a trash disposal or at a funeral home.[300]

Fox News had gained entrance to the Beaverland Street home where Hoffa had allegedly been killed, authorizing crime-scene investigators to search for any residue of blood in its foyer. Using Luminol, a chemical spray that illuminates blood, the forensics team discovered what appeared to be traces of blood, both in the foyer and in a hallway that led to the kitchen.

Everyone, including me, hoped that the subsequent DNA analysis would show that this was Hoffa's blood.

Repeating my own mantra that this "could be the biggest break in the Hoffa case," David Ashenfelter added in his latest article:

> Moldea, who wrote an authoritative book about Hoffa and who has read Sheeran's biography, said he still thinks Hoffa was killed by Sal Briguglio, not Sheeran. But Moldea said he believes Sheeran witnessed the crime because of the details he provided for the book. He said the book provides important new information that he thinks could help investigators.[301]

In his remarkably uncritical analysis of Brandt's book, Bryan Burrough of the *New York Times Book Review* actually celebrated Sheeran's restraint in his tale of killing Jimmy Hoffa, saying:

> [Sheeran's] version of the murder involved a quick plane flight, an empty house, two well-placed bullets and a roll of linoleum. Sheeran was plainly conflicted about his task, but his retelling steers clear of the maudlin. "My friend didn't suffer" is all he adds to the grisly details. Sheeran's veracity is actually enhanced by his inability to say exactly what happened to Hoffa's corpse, though he is confident that it did not end up at Giants Stadium.[302]

On February 14, 2005, the Bloomfield Police Department issued a press release about the results of the DNA test of the blood residue found in the foyer of the home on Beaverland Street where Sheeran had supposedly killed Jimmy Hoffa. The release stated:

> In late December 2004, the FBI contacted our department with an oral report on the findings. We were advised that blood was found in some of the wood floor samples but they did not believe that it matches Hoffa's. They then indicated that the flooring submitted for examination, as well as a detailed written report would be forthcoming.
>
> This morning, we received a written report submitted by the FBI that concludes that human blood was found on wood flooring but the blood was not Hoffa's. As a result, the lead supplied by Fox News in New York has been determined to be unfounded.

Trying to give support to Brandt and Eric Shawn at Fox News, both of whom were extremely disappointed, I issued a statement, asserting:

> As I have been saying all along, Frank Sheeran was involved in Jimmy Hoffa's murder—and, despite today's news, the FBI believes this, as well. However, like the FBI, I have never believed Sheeran's story about his role at the crime scene. Nevertheless, I continue to insist that Sheeran's information about the events that preceded the actual murder—as reported in Charles Brandt's book, as well as by Fox News and the *Detroit Free Press*—are extremely important to understanding what really happened to Hoffa on July 30, 1975.

149. "They're digging at a farm in Wixom"

Apart from the information about the mechanics of Jimmy Hoffa's actual murder, I still believed, as I had written in *The Hoffa Wars*, that Rolland McMaster and his zombie/stooges were involved in the disposal of Hoffa's body—and that they did it right there in the Detroit area.

PART TWELVE: HOFFA REDUX

Referring to McMaster, the *Hoffex Memo* stated:

> McMaster served as an officer in Detroit Teamsters Local 299 from 1955 to 1967, and since 1970 as a General Organizer for the Teamsters in Chicago and Detroit. Numerous acts of violence have occurred over the years at Local 299; and the month [preceding] the Hoffa disappearance there was a beating of a Local 299 business agent and the bombing of Richard Fitzsimmons' teamster automobile on July 10, 1975. In 1970, McMaster was transferred from Local 299 to Chicago after one of his associates had beaten another Teamsters official in an argument about expenses. Since that time almost every act of violence has somehow been traced to a present or former associate of McMaster. Because of this and because it is known that McMaster has always wanted to exercise control over Local 299, he almost immediately became a suspect.
>
> Source information was received that the Fitzsimmons' car bombing was used as a means of covering the JRH disappearance by making the disappearance look like a Local 299 problem and in retaliation for the car bombing. The car bombing investigation is being handled separately by the Detroit Division; however, in view of this information the investigation was intensified. Two of the chief suspects developed in the case are Jim Shaw and Lawrence McHenry . . . [who] are closely associated with McMaster. . . .
>
> Obviously, numerous pieces of unrelated information tend to imply that McMaster may be involved in the JRH disappearance. . . . Based on all information there is no concrete evidence to indicate McMaster's involvement; however, there is enough independent testimony that he be retained as a suspect. Investigation will continue regarding McMaster.[303]

In addition, I learned that at 8:00 A.M. on Thursday morning, July 31, the day after Hoffa disappeared, McMaster had met with Vincent Meli, a top Detroit Mafia figure closely associated with Tony Giacalone, in the coffee shop at the Ramada Inn near McMaster's Southfield home at Twelve-Mile and Telegraph Roads.

On May 17, 2006, I received a telephone call from David Ashenfelter at the *Detroit Free Press*. He asked if I had heard the latest on the Hoffa case.

"What's happened?" I replied.

"They're digging at a farm in Wixom."

Hearing that, I joyfully sprang out of the chair at my desk and did a quadruple fist pump, hoping that it was the farm I thought it was.

I started calling some of my old FBI contacts, most of whom had already left the bureau. But, at that point, none of them had heard the news yet. Other than the failed DNA test of the blood found at the house where Frank Sheeran falsely claimed to have personally killed Hoffa, the only thing we had recently heard was yet another deathbed confession, this time from a convicted murderer named Richard Kuklinski, also known as "The Iceman," who claimed that he was paid $40,000 to kill Hoffa.

Clearly, that was just another phony story, ranking right up there with the conjecture that Hoffa was encased in the end zone at Giants Stadium in East Rutherford, New Jersey.

Almost like clockwork, a new and well-publicized theory about Hoffa's whereabouts seemed to surface every two or three years. But this latest excavation in Oakland County had the sound of real legitimacy to it.

By late afternoon, Ashenfelter and I had pieced together what was happening at that 85-acre Wixom farm in Milford Township, about 35 miles northwest of Detroit. FBI agents, armed with a search warrant, were digging at a specific location and actually looking for the body of Jimmy Hoffa. An FBI spokesman told reporters that investigators were pursuing "evidence of criminal activity that may have occurred under previous ownership."

We were quickly able to confirm that the previous owner was, indeed, Rolland McMaster.

We also discovered that the information upon which the FBI based its search warrant had been supplied by Donovan Wells, who was serving a ten-year stretch in a Lexington, Kentucky, prison in the wake of his conviction for smuggling marijuana. After his recent falling out with McMaster, the 75-year-old Wells had decided to flip and turn state's evidence.

When I heard that Don Wells was the informant, I was thrilled—especially since I had interviewed him thirty years earlier, writing about him and his associates in *The Hoffa Wars*, saying:

> Wells lived with McMaster at his . . . Wixom farm and was a partner of McMaster's brother-in-law, Stanton Barr, in a

PART TWELVE: HOFFA REDUX

trucking company called Spot Leasing. Wells also owned a Time-D.C., Inc., terminal in suburban Detroit, and Jim Shaw worked for him [in April 1975] . . . .

Soon afterward, Shaw, through McMaster, got a job with the Detroit steel division of Gateway Transportation Company, which was headed by Stanton Barr. Shaw's former employer says he worked at Gateway "for the next several months."[304]

Along with Larry McHenry, Jim Shaw was the FBI's top suspect for the bombing of Dick Fitzsimmons's union car twenty days before Hoffa disappeared—just as the *Hoffex Memo* had declared. Stanton Barr and McMaster had driven to Gary, Indiana, early on the morning of Hoffa's disappearance and returned to Detroit later in the day.

Although McHenry and Shaw were both dead, McMaster, now 92, was alive, living on a farm on Clyde Road in Fenton, Michigan. Stan Barr, who lived on another farm on Clyde Road, was his neighbor, as well as his brother-in-law.

In an email, Ashenfelter asked me to explain how I thought that McMaster and his crew were involved. In my response, I wrote:

> With regard to McMaster and the disappearance, I believed from the outset that the people behind the violence in Local 299 also played a role in Hoffa's murder. And, as you know, I have always believed that McMaster was behind the 299 violence—using people like Larry McHenry and Jim Shaw . . . . as his weapons of mass destruction.
>
> In addition, Ralph Picardo supposedly claimed that Hoffa's body was shipped via a Gateway Transportation truck to an unknown destination. And you and I both know that McMaster's alibi for at least part of the day Hoffa disappeared was that he went to Gary with Stanton Barr, the head of Gateway's steel division—where Jim Shaw worked as a driver. That's all in *The Hoffa Wars*. (BTW: Shaw also worked as a driver for Don Wells at Time DC.)
>
> And, then, there were my taped interviews with McMaster, McHenry, and Shaw—in which they did nothing but ratchet up my suspicions with their bravado. Also, my FBI sources, who had the job of keeping me on track, always encouraged

me to remain on the McMaster train. After I interviewed the Briuglios and the Andrettas in October 1976, I was sure that they had committed the murder. But I was just as sure that McMaster and company had something to do with the final act of the drama—the disposal of Hoffa's body.

In short, I still embraced the Ralph Picardo-inspired theory that Hoffa had been placed in a 55-gallon drum, shipped via a Gateway Transportation truck to an unknown destination where my sources had indicated that Hoffa's body was crushed and smelted.

The following day, May 18, Daniel Roberts, the director of the FBI's Detroit Field Office since 2004, issued a statement about the Wixom excavation, saying, "Since I've been here, this is the best lead I've seen . . . in the Hoffa investigation."[305]

Roberts—who had brought in heavy equipment, cadaver dogs, and ground-penetrating radar, along with anthropologists and archeologists for the search—added that Wells, whom he still did not publicly identify, had passed a polygraph test.

At this point, I had heard enough—even though I still did not know exactly what Wells had told the FBI. I decided to jump into this situation with everything I had. No matter where anyone looked or studied, the only place where investigators could read about McMaster, Wells, Barr, McHenry, and Shaw, as well their associations with Gateway Transportation was in *The Hoffa Wars*.

I only had about a dozen hardback copies of my twenty-eight-year-old book on Hoffa, but I immediately mailed them to the key reporters covering this story for the wire services, the major newspapers and the television networks—most of whom were new to this case and had never heard of me or my work. Then, I bought another hundred copies of the paperback from my reprint publisher, which was in the midst of a bankruptcy but still had *The Hoffa Wars* in its inventory.

Ashenfelter of the *Free Press* was the first to reveal publicly the five-foot-nine-inch, 300-pound Wells's identity. He noted what I had written about McMaster and Wells, adding that Wells "may know what happened to Hoffa if McMaster was involved in the disappearance. . . . Moldea said he interviewed Wells in 1976 and that Wells denied any knowledge of Hoffa's disappearance."[306]

However, while Wells was denying any knowledge of Hoffa's fate to me back then, he was simultaneously attempting to strike a deal with federal prosecutors after his guilty plea to hauling stolen steel in December 1975. The Associated Press interviewed Wells's one-time attorney, Joseph J.

PART TWELVE: HOFFA REDUX

Fabrizio, who said that Wells "claimed to have some definite information [about the Hoffa case]—[but] whether it was helpful or not, I have no way of knowing."[307]

The *Free Press* interviewed another Wells attorney, James Elsman, Fabrizio's one-time law partner, who had represented Wells during his earlier criminal case. Elsman told Ashenfelter that in 1976 federal agents were not very interested in Wells's information about the Hoffa caper. "I assumed the agents would pounce on his information right away, but they only seemed interested in solving the steel-theft case."[308]

Elsman, who said he knew where Wells thought that Hoffa's body was buried, offered to come to the farm and personally show the FBI the specific location. But he said that, for reasons unknown, the FBI had rebuffed him—although Ashenfelter and I could not figure out why the FBI did not bring Wells, personally, to the site of the excavation.

On May 23—the sixth day of the dig—the *Free Press* finally revealed specifically what Don Wells had supposedly told the FBI. Elsman told reporters that "Hoffa may have been rolled up in a carpet and tossed into a hastily dug grave" at the farm where Wells and his wife, Monica, lived with McMaster and his wife. The newspaper added:

> Attorney James Elsman said a former client, Donovan Wells, whose tip has prompted the biggest FBI search for Hoffa in decades, told him he was standing in a house at the Milford Township farm in July 1975 and saw two strangers digging a large hole with a backhoe a day after Hoffa vanished. Wells saw a cylindrical object that looked like a rolled-up carpet lying next to the hole.
>
> As the men went about their business, Wells' friend and landlord—former Detroit Teamster official Rolland McMaster—snickered and remarked, "That was Jimmy going down."

Elsman added that Wells never actually saw Hoffa's body, just the cylinder, which might or might not have been a rolled-up carpet—or even a 55-gallon drum.

During one of my appearances on NBC News, I told the reporter, "Rolland McMaster is a very smart guy. Even at 92, he's a . . . very dangerous man. I can't believe that he would leave a trophy lying around that could put him in jail for the rest of his life. I'm going to be surprised if they find the body. But the FBI is taking this seriously, so I'm taking it seriously."

I emphasized that point the following day during an interview with Paul Egan of the *Detroit News*, during which I said, "The FBI doesn't want to look like Geraldo opening up an empty grave. I can't believe they are intentionally walking into a situation where they are going to be ridiculed. They believe in the credibility of their witness."[309]

On May 24, the FBI tore down a 4,700-square-foot barn on the property. Where that structure once stood, workers started placing shovels of dirt on sifting screens in what appeared to be a coordinated effort to find trace evidence of either Hoffa's body or his clothing.

To me, in lieu of a fishing expedition, this procedure seemed to indicate that the diggers were getting close to paydirt.

But, when the barn came down—with a promise to rebuild it with taxpayer dollars—the matter of money suddenly became a major public issue.

Congressman Joe Knollenberg (R-Michigan) began beating his tambourine, insisting that the FBI reveal its budget for the search and demanding that the FBI set a deadline for completing the dig.

In the midst of the public heat that the FBI was taking, I came to its defense, telling Paul Egan of the *Detroit News*, "The U.S. Government has to stand up against a situation where a guy as famous as Jimmy Hoffa can be snatched in broad daylight from a public place, killed, and his body disposed of. . . . I think this is righteous."[310]

In addition, I appeared on CNBC's *The Big Idea* with host Donny Deutsch who sided with the congressman. In response, I accused Deutsch of unwittingly carrying water for the Mafia, which also, no doubt, wanted to see this dig shut down. "This is about the war against organized crime," I argued. "This is about investigating organized crime and the nefarious actions it takes. The most prominent murder it has ever waged was the one against Jimmy Hoffa. We need to find a solution to this murder."

Then, suddenly after fourteen days, the entire operation came to a screeching halt.

Completely stunned by this decision, I called my sources in Detroit who simply told me that the revelations about the high cost of the dig had forced its shutdown. In effect, it was a political decision made in Washington, D.C.

Micheline Maynard of the *New York Times* reported in her news story—which included an extraordinary admission from the FBI:

PART TWELVE: HOFFA REDUX

> "After a thorough and comprehensive search, no remains of Mr. Hoffa have been located," Judith M. Chilen, an assistant special agent, said at a news briefing at the entrance to the farm this afternoon.
>
> **But Ms. Chilen said she was convinced that Mr. Hoffa's body had been buried on the farm, and there was "no indication that it has been moved."** Investigators said that they might return to the farm in the future and that the investigation would remain open.
>
> "There are still prosecutable defendants and they know who they are," Ms. Chilen said.[311] [Emphasis added.]

Late-night talk-show host Conan O'Brien joked, "Officials say it's the first time they've ever been to Detroit . . . and *not* found a body."

Going to the dueling authors for comment, the *Detroit News* demonstrated the range of opinions about this operation, writing:

> "It was astonishingly bad information that they acted on," said Charles Brandt of Sun Valley, Idaho, who wrote *I Heard You Paint Houses*, a 2004 book about Hoffa's disappearance. . . .
>
> "I've been saying they will find nothing. . . . This was a silly dig." . . .
>
> Dan Moldea of Washington, D.C., author of the 1978 book, *The Hoffa Wars*, said he believes the FBI is on the right track, even though he did not believe the excavations would turn up Hoffa's body.
>
> "The FBI is going to take some grief for this, and they don't deserve it," Moldea said.[312]

I continued to believe that the Hoffa murder consisted of a three-act drama with different characters in each act. And I also continued to believe—just as I had since the summer of 1975—that Rolland McMaster played the key role in that final act.

150. "It's going to be a great day tomorrow"

Federal officials ordered the release of Don Wells from a Kentucky prison shortly after the Wixom dig concluded—even though no one outside the law-enforcement community knew exactly what Wells had claimed to cause such an uproar. To this day, the search warrant which authorized the excavation at the Wixom farm has remained sealed.

That was what I wanted to discuss when I visited Wells and his wife, Monica, at their home on August 14, 2009. It was the first time I had seen him since I interviewed him in 1976.

Meantime, Rolland McMaster had died of natural causes at 93 years old on October 25, 2007, at his horse farm on Clyde Road in Michigan's Hartland Township.[313] Wells had had a falling out with him years earlier—after Wells learned that McMaster was thinking about having him killed.

My visit to Wells came during the same trip that I described in the Prologue to this book in which a con man claimed to know the site of Hoffa's final resting place—on a farm once operated by McMaster but was now owned by his brother-in-law, Stanton Barr.

Getting down to business after we enjoyed Monica's breakfast, I asked about the now-famous moment—as told by his former attorney—in which Wells was looking out of a window with McMaster on the night of Hoffa's disappearance. Watching what appeared to be a rolled-up carpet being lowered into a hole—which had just been dug by a nearby backhoe—McMaster supposedly said to Wells, "That was Jimmy going down."

Wells's response? . . . That never happened.

What he did witness—and the information about which he took and passed an FBI polygraph test—had happened the night before.

On Tuesday evening, July 29, between 8:30 and 9:00, Wells was at Carl's Chop House in downtown Detroit with McMaster and Stanton Barr, the head of the steel division of Gateway Transportation Company.[314]

Wells explained, "We usually met there to talk. We were all in business together. We owned property, along with trucking and trailer companies.

"Suddenly, Tony Provenzano comes up and starts banging on the table, 'It's going to be a great day tomorrow! A great day tomorrow! Right, Mac?' And he slapped Mac on the back. Mac says, 'Yeah, I guess so.'

"Then, Mac and Tony Pro walked back towards the bar.

PART TWELVE: HOFFA REDUX

"And I asked Stan, 'What the hell is going on? What does he mean, it's going be a great day tomorrow?'"

"And Stan said, 'Well, Provenzano and Hoffa are going to make up. They're going to bury the hatchet tomorrow.'" Wells alleged that Barr had told him that Tony Giacalone and Chuck O'Brien were making the arrangements.

Wells continued, "A few minutes later, Mac and Provenzano came back. And Provenzano stood between Mac and Stan, and he said, 'I've got my brother back there.'"

Wells looked at Provenzano's table and saw Tony Giacalone who was sitting with two people he did not recognize. Wells also alleged that O'Brien was at the table.

Wells continued, "Before Provenzano returned to his group, he said to Mac and Stan, 'Do you guys know where you're going to be tomorrow?'"

"Mac said, 'Yeah, we're all straight on that.'"

After Provenzano left the table, Wells said to Barr, "Stan, we're supposed to have a meeting with the credit company tomorrow."

Barr, who appeared completely oblivious to whatever was going on between McMaster and Provenzano, replied, "We're going to have to forget about that. I have to go to Chicago tomorrow with Mac."

Wells did not see McMaster again for a day and a half. Meantime, McMaster and Barr had changed their plans on July 30. In lieu of flying to Chicago, they drove to Gary, Indiana, which is about a four-hour drive. At the moment that Hoffa disappeared, McMaster and Barr were clearly out of town—although they returned to the Detroit area that night, according to both of their statements to the FBI.

While in prison in 2006, Wells also told the FBI about a pre-dug hole at McMaster's Wixom farm in Milford Township, which was also called "Idle Acres"—near the end of a long dirt path, which ran north off Pontiac Trail, past the main farm house, and up against the tree line at the back of the farm.

According to Wells, McMaster's had dug that hole several weeks before Hoffa vanished.

Wells drew a diagram for an FBI special agent, indicating that the hole, which could have been fifteen-feet deep, was on the side of the path and beyond a set of railroad tracks that ran east and west through McMaster's farm.

What made this story even more significant was that Wells's wife, Monica, had been alone at the farm while McMaster and Barr were out of town on business during the afternoon that Hoffa disappeared.

— 577 —

Monica, standing in the kitchen and looking out of a window towards McMaster's driveway, told me, "During the mid-afternoon, I saw three dark-colored cars coming from the east on Pontiac Trail at a high rate of speed. They turned right onto the path next to the house and drove straight back to the area where a hole had been dug. I once asked Mac what the hole was for. He said that he was going to build a barn there. But he never did."

Monica confirmed that "the hole was to the right of the path, just across some railroad tracks that ran across the back of the property."

Monica said that the cars that sped onto the property "surprised me. I was at the kitchen sink, and they came by very fast. Usually when people came there, they would make an appointment with Mac. It was very strange."

After twenty or thirty minutes, the three cars sped off the property the same way they had entered.

The farm was located exactly 15.36 miles from the Red Fox restaurant where Hoffa was last seen.

Monica added that McMaster did not come back to the farm that night, noting that he had gone to his other home on Wildbrook Drive in Southfield—which was a mere five-minute drive or just 2.74 miles from the Red Fox.

This was the house on the car tour that one of my FBI sources had arranged for me on October 31, 1975. Clearly, even then, there was a suspicion that this was the private residence where Hoffa had been taken and killed. (Stan Barr later bought this property on Wildbrook.)

During the evening of Hoffa's murder, Monica told her husband about the speeding cars when he came home. Wells simply thought that they were looking at some structures near the tree line at the back of the farm.

The early rumors about Hoffa's disappearance didn't start to break until the following day.

Monica continued, "The next time I saw McMaster, I said, 'Mac, something strange happened. Three cars went up the road very fast, and they went straight back.

"He just said that the people in the cars were looking at horses. . . . But there were no horses where the cars went. The horses were in the barn to the left of the house."

During their conversation, Monica asked, "Mac, did you know that Mr. Hoffa is missing?"

PART TWELVE: HOFFA REDUX

She said that McMaster became very quiet and then replied, "'Young-un'—which is what he called me—'our brother, Jimmy, has met his demise.'"

In the midst of our interview, Monica showed me an exhibit she had put together on a large poster board for my visit, displaying numerous photographs of McMaster's farm as it appeared during the mid-1970s. She pointed out where she was standing in the farmhouse when the three cars came roaring by on the day of Hoffa's disappearance. Also, she had a picture of the path they traveled, which led to the tree line.

Don Wells also drew a diagram for me of the property—and where the hole had been pre-dug. He agreed with his wife that it was north of the railroad tracks and just east of the road.

—⚭—

At that point of our interview, I suggested that we drive to their old farm and try to reconstruct what they had seen. Both of them were concerned about the new owner of the property who was angered by the commotion that resulted from the 2006 excavation.

Telling them not to worry, I grabbed the photo display that Monica had prepared, and we went outside to Wells's car.

When we arrived at what was once the front of McMaster's Wixom farm on Pontiac Trail, we saw that the main house was long gone. Grass and dirt now covered most of the path that the three fast cars had traveled on the afternoon of Hoffa's disappearance. Everything on the farm had been subdivided and reconfigured.

The landmark railroad tracks were on the other side of a tall fence—which was the property of the new owner of the northern portion of what was once McMaster's farm—the area that had been searched by the FBI in 2006.

At my request, Wells then drove us around the farm to the front entrance of that property, which was adorned with "No Trespassing" and "No Admittance" signs. Ignoring all of these warnings, I told Wells to drive down the winding driveway to the main house.

Just outside the garage, we saw a man in gray overalls, working on the engine of a pickup truck.

I grabbed the picture exhibit Monica had prepared and walked up to the mechanic, leaving Don and Monica in the car behind me. After I introduced myself, I asked the man where I could find the owner.

To my surprise, he said that he was the owner. His name was Ron Lusk.

At first, Lusk appeared a little annoyed that three uninvited strangers had just driven onto his property. But when I showed him Monica's exhibit, indicating how his farm had looked during the 1970s, he could not have been more accommodating.

I motioned to Don and Monica to join us. I introduced them to Lusk, saying that they had once lived on his property. Lusk immediately started asking them questions about the photographs that Monica had collected.

Don and Monica began drawing his attention to the contrasts between what had been and what was now on the property. And Lusk expressed fascination to learn how his farm was once configured.

I asked Lusk if we could see the site where the FBI had torn down and then rebuilt the barn in its effort to look for Jimmy Hoffa.

"Sure," Lusk replied, telling us to drive to another parking area and adding, "The government really did build us a nice new barn. . . . It was like a carnival around here."

Returning to the car with his wife and me, Wells drove down the narrow road alongside the new red barn which loomed large on the right. We pulled into the parking lot at the end of this structure, which was perpendicular to two older red barns where farmhands were attending to several horses.

As we stepped out of the car, we saw a tall man in a cowboy hat and a red shirt. I went up to him, introduced the three of us, and asked, "Where are the railroad tracks that ran along this property?"

The man named Doug, who turned out to be the farm's manager, pointed to the area near a tall fence—the same fence that we had earlier seen from the other side.

As I walked towards the fence, I stepped onto a dirt road. I looked back at Don and Monica, asking, "Is this the path that started on Pontiac Trail, the one on which Monica saw the three fast cars that day?"

Don and Monica came over to where I was standing and looked around the area. Then, for a further perspective, we walked towards the tall fence.

They confirmed that we were on the dirt road that once ran north and south off Pontiac Trail, alongside McMaster's farmhouse.

About ten yards from our side of the fence was another long path that stretched east and west and was littered with discarded railroad ties.

"Jesus, Don," I said, now standing where the two paths intersected. "Is this where the railroad tracks were?"

Both Don and Monica came over, along with Doug—and now Ron Lusk who had also joined us.

PART TWELVE: HOFFA REDUX

All four of them agreed that we were standing at the location of the now abandoned railroad tracks, as well as the road that had once run from Pontiac Trail to the back of the farm near the tree line.

Pulling Don and Monica off to the side, I asked privately, "Okay now, where was that pre-dug hole?"

Both Don and Monica agreed that it was in a field north of the railroad tracks and *east of the road*.

When we walked just a few yards to that location, it was nothing more than a fenced-in pasture, occupied at that moment by two horses, which appeared as interested in us as we were in the land they were occupying.

However, the site of the 2006 FBI dig was north of the railroad tracks and about twenty to thirty yards *west of the road*—the site of the new red barn built by the FBI.

I am not even going to try to hazard a guess as to why the FBI chose to dig west of the road instead of east—and, of course, the FBI is not talking.[315] Actually, Wells never made any claim about this hole—at least to me—beyond the fact that it once existed.

Regardless, the big untold story here is that Don Wells—who passed an FBI polygraph test—witnessed Rolland McMaster and Tony Provenzano together at a restaurant in Detroit on July 29, 1975, the night before Hoffa disappeared. Wells also heard a portion of their conversation which was clearly about Provenzano's scheduled 2:00 P.M. sitdown with Hoffa on July 30, as well as the need for McMaster and his brother-in-law, Stanton Barr, who headed the steel division of Gateway Transportation, to have established alibis for that same afternoon when Hoffa was last seen.

After my interview with Wells and returning to the East Coast, I visited my best underworld-connected source who was in a position to know the specific details about the Hoffa murder—but discloses information with the same frequency as a kosher butcher sells pork chops. To my surprise, in response to my latest appeal, he confirmed Wells's contention that Tony Provenzano was in Detroit the night before Hoffa vanished—an allegation that Provenzano had always denied.

Then, my source permitted himself to add that there is much more to the story about the Hoffa murder than is known—although he conceded that Ralph Picardo basically had it right. Even though the source refused to confirm that Salvatore Briguglio was Hoffa's killer, he did dismiss any and all speculation that Frank Sheeran committed the murder.

"I'm not going to talk about Sal," he told me, "but I can assure you that Sheeran had no role in the actual killing of Jimmy Hoffa."

151. Brother Moscato and the Jersey City landfill

His family and friends called him "Brother." His true name was Phillip Bernard Moscato. In recent years, although extremely cagey in his dealings with me, Brother Moscato had been my best East Coast underworld-connected source on the Jimmy Hoffa murder case. I thought highly of him, and I respected him.

Two days after Valentine's Day 2014, Brother died after a long illness. He was 79 years old. With Moscato now gone, I can speak of my conversations and interviews with him since 2007, many of which were recorded.

On background, on or about November 5, 1975, a little over three months after Jimmy Hoffa disappeared, prison inmate Ralph Picardo told federal agents, among other things, that Hoffa's body, which had been supposedly placed in a fifty-five gallon barrel, was transported to New Jersey via a Gateway Transportation truck. He also suggested that the barrel holding Hoffa's body might have been buried at Brother Moscato's landfill in Hackensack.

As noted earlier, Picardo, then an insider with Tony Provenzano's illegal operations at Local 560 in Union City, based his information on the "confession" he had received from Steve Andretta, a top Provenzano lieutenant, during a prison visitation in August 1975, just a few days after Hoffa's disappearance.

In FBI Special Agent Robert Garrity's memorandum about Picardo on December 22, 1975, Garrity memorialized this information, saying:

> STEPHEN ANDRETTA asked PICARDO if Federal Agents had been to see him and made admissions and references that PROVENZANO'S group [was] involved in HOFFA disappearance and stated that [the] body was brought back to New Jersey by Gateway Transportation Company. (Garrity's emphasis)

Later in that same memorandum, Garrity reported that another FBI source from Albany, New York, had "advised that he had learned that HOFFA'S body is allegedly located in a 34 acre tract of land containing a dump owned by a friend of Teamsters Local 560. According to source, body was allegedly transported by a Gateway truck from Detroit, and that Teamsters officials are worried about the 'barrel.'" (Garrity's emphasis)

During my exclusive October 1976, interview with Steve Andretta, Salvatore Briguglio, and the others named by Picardo as being involved in Hoffa's murder, Briguglio, Hoffa's alleged killer, told me, "They said we took Hoffa from Detroit, put him on a truck, brought him all the way down here in a fifty-five gallon drum—and we put him in Brother Moscato's dump."

Once again, that was all based on Picardo's information—although the part about Moscato's dump was nothing more than Picardo's educated guess, pure speculation based on his knowledge of how the Provenzano crew operated. Andretta had never specifically told him that.

Just to be clear, Briguglio, Provenzano's right-hand man, was speaking about the same Brother Moscato whom I would later meet.

During the spring of 2007, I received a grant from The Nation Institute's Investigative Fund to probe the background of a former federal judge with fellow journalist David Corn, then the Washington editor of *The Nation*. During our research in connection with the judge, I discovered Moscato's name in several official FBI and Strike Force documents. These records revolved around a complicated scam engineered by Tony Provenzano, Sal Briguglio, and Steve Andretta to bilk their Local 560 pension fund by diverting as much as $6.4 million in loans.

The recipients of the loans were two brothers, Thomas and Frank Romano, who had become the targets of a federal grand jury investigation in February 1976—the month after the creation of the secret January 1976 *Hoffex Memo*—as part of an aggressive attempt by federal prosecutors to get one or both of the brothers to flip and to turn state's evidence against Provenzano, Briguglio, and/or Andretta. However, despite the federal prosecutors' best efforts, the Romano brothers were not indicted on RICO conspiracy charges until November 1978, eight months after Briguglio was murdered on a New York street in broad daylight.

They were convicted two years later.

The judge in the Romanos' case made a bizarre and fatal procedural error during the trial, causing the convictions of both brothers to be overturned on appeal. Subsequently, the judge was accused of accepting a payoff from the Romanos.

Although the judge was acquitted on federal bribery charges, he was later impeached by the U.S. House of Representatives and convicted by the U.S. Senate, which considered additional evidence against him.

By sheer coincidence, the trial judge in the Romanos' case, who was ultimately removed from the bench, was the same former federal judge whom David Corn and I were investigating.

According to evidence presented, the alleged middleman for the attempted payoff from the Romanos to the judge was Phillip "Brother" Moscato.

A confidential Department of Justice document that I had obtained stated, "Investigation of this offense stemmed from a larger scale investigation by the Federal Bureau of Investigation which was being conducted following the disappearance of former labor official Jimmy Hoffa."

Indeed, a secret DOJ timeline of the key events leading to Hoffa's disappearance featured nearly every single transaction involving the Local 560 loans to the Romanos. As a result of the fraud, the pension fund was badly depleted.

Getting more specific, a top federal prosecutor who was directly involved in the Hoffa case told me, "We always had the impression that these loans may have been granted to help fund the assassination of Jimmy Hoffa."

Further, another confidential FBI report highlighted Hoffa's refusal to help Provenzano replenish the Local 560 pension fund with money from the Central States Pension Fund where Hoffa still had considerable influence in mid-1975. The report indicated that the loans to the Romanos were the pre-arranged topic of conversation between Hoffa and Provenzano on the day Hoffa vanished, adding that Sal Briguglio had been specifically designated to kill Hoffa.

The FBI report, which I discovered buried in the 17,000-page FOIA release of the Hoffex files, specifically stated:

> [Provenzano] made another abortive effort in December of 1974 to enlist Hoffa's assistance ... so that the Local 560 Fund would not be depleted to the extent which has in fact occurred, that in June and July of 1975 (when the first signs of instability had become manifest and the Romanos were fraudulently converting the Fund's construction payments at a rapid rate), Provenzano tried again to enlist Hoffa's support through [Tony] Giacalone and that Hoffa gave a final refusal with a possible threat of exposure. The sequence of calls is suggestive of the proposition that, when Hoffa conclusively told Giacalone that he would not help Provenzano (7/18/75), Giacalone and Provenzano agreed to eliminate Hoffa; ... that Briguglio was given the actual assignment and, thereafter, he notified the interested parties of its successful completion on the evening of 7/30/75 either personally or through a third party.

PART TWELVE: HOFFA REDUX

After collecting all of this information, I located Moscato and called him at his residence in New Jersey on April 28, 2007. He was very cordial and agreed to the interview.

I told Moscato that the first time I had heard his name was in early December 1975 after the Briguglio brothers and the Andretta brothers—along with Rolland McMaster and his brother-in-law Stanton Barr of Gateway Transportation—had appeared before the federal grand jury investigating Hoffa's murder in Detroit.

Saying that he had also been called before that grand jury and taken The Fifth, Moscato told me that he had known Sal Briguglio and Steve Andretta "since we were kids," adding, "Sally, as far as I was concerned, was one of the greatest guys. We hung out together. We had a little business together. Super guy."

I asked, "They were talking about the FBI doing a search at Brother Moscato's Dump . . . underneath the Pulaski Skyway along the [Hackensack] River. And it turns out, they were never looking for Hoffa. Right? They were looking for Armand Faugno or somebody like that?"

(Faugno was a murdered New Jersey loan shark associated with Sal Briguglio and Phil Moscato, among others. Picardo claimed to the FBI that Briguglio told him that he had buried Faugno's body—wrapped in a rolled-up carpet and delivered in a brown station wagon—at Moscato's dump.)

In response to my question, Moscato replied, "No, they were looking for Hoffa."

Surprised, I asked, "They were looking for Hoffa there? Tell me what happened? What was the story with that?"

"Well, they said that me and Sally Briguglio buried Hoffa in my dump."

I laughed, "They thought you were part of this?"

"Yeah. Well, I was close with all them guys. And there was a rat by the name of Ralphie Picardo . . . "

"Ralph Picardo. He was in Trenton State Penitentiary."

"You've been doing your homework, huh?" Moscato laughed.

"Hey, I've been around for a while, too," I quipped.

"Okay. Ralphie Picardo shot a guy in the back of the head. . . ."

I replied, "But he got nailed for manslaughter, didn't he?"

"Yeah. Now he was in jail. Ralphie, I knew for years. I helped him out in business, in the trucking business. I helped him. Faugno helped him. Sally [Briguglio] helped him to get him started in his trucking business. He was around us a lot. And after he shot this guy, he wanted to get out of jail. So, he goes and tells the FBI that he knows where

Hoffa's buried. That he was with me and Sally when we buried Hoffa in my dump."

"Picardo said that he was with you and Sally?"

"Yeah. So, he took them [the FBI] down there. They dug the dump up for three months."

"I remember that," I said. "I thought they were looking for Faugno."

"No," Moscato replied.

I asked, "In a fifty-five-gallon drum? They were looking for Hoffa himself?"

Moscato continued, "*That was Hoffa in the fifty-five-gallon drum. He said a pick-up truck brought [the body]. . . .*"

"Gateway truck," I corrected him.

"*Yeah, brought the truck in and Hoffa was in it, and we buried him.*"

"I never heard that story that you were part of it. I never heard that one before."

"That's what it was all about." (Emphasis added)

Although Moscato seemed cool, I was completely stunned.

The information Moscato had just given me—that "Hoffa was in the fifty-five-gallon drum," that they "brought the [Gateway] truck in and Hoffa was in it," and that Moscato and Briguglio buried Hoffa at Moscato's dump—was never provided to federal agents by Picardo.

Moscato was telling me something new. But I didn't want to overplay my hand with an important figure whom I knew I could interview again. So, for the moment, I didn't press him.

One obvious problem with Moscato's story was that Picardo—who had been sent to jail in May 1975—was in prison at the time Hoffa disappeared two months later. Consequently, there was no way that he could have made a claim to have been present when Moscato and Briguglio buried Hoffa at the landfill.

So what was Moscato telling me, wittingly or unwittingly? Was he actually admitting that he and Sal Briguglio, the likely killer of Jimmy Hoffa, had buried Hoffa's body at Moscato's dump?

Later, on May 8, 2007, when Moscato and I met face-to-face at his home in Ocean, New Jersey, we continued our tape-recorded conversation about the Hoffa case. A tall and handsome man who was suffering from a variety of health issues, Moscato, a U.S. Army paratrooper during the Korean War and a demolition expert, had also owned more than forty restaurants during his career, along with an auto-repair shop and a stable of racehorses. And, at one time, he was a scratch golfer.

PART TWELVE: HOFFA REDUX

"Let me ask you," I said, "when I interviewed you over the phone—again this is in my notes—did you say that Picardo said he was with you and Sal when you guys buried the body at the dump?"

"Yeah."

"So he wasn't in jail then—in July '75?"

"The government took him out."

"No, no. In July '75. Was he in jail for manslaughter then?"

"I don't know. I don't know. But he took them down there. 'Oh, here's where he is.' And they dug and dug. 'No, it was over there. . . . No, it was over here.'"

I then asked, "He said he knew?"

"Yeah."

Clearly, if Picardo ever did accompany federal agents to Moscato's dump to search for Hoffa's body, it was after he flipped and turned evidence in November 1975.

I told Moscato, "We never thought that Hoffa was any place but Detroit. I mean, why would you move him? I mean, Detroit's capable. There are plenty of places in Detroit to take care of a body for heaven's sake."

At that point, I told Moscato what was then known about the circumstances revolving around the May 2006 dig at McMaster's farm in Wixom, Michigan, which included the FBI's public statement that the bureau believed that Hoffa's body was buried on the farm and that there was "no indication that it has been moved."

In response, Moscato replied with absolute certainty in his voice, "Put that to rest."

"That McMaster . . . that the farm?" I stammered.

Moscato, who said that he had known and respected McMaster for years, shook his head.

I continued, "So you don't think he's at the farm?"

Again, Moscato shook his head.

"Do you think he was taken care of right there in Detroit? I mean, why not, right?"

Yet again, Moscato shook his head.

As I completely lost whatever poker face I had maintained during the interview, I replied somewhat sheepishly, "What are you telling me? He was at Moscato's dump?"

Moscato barked, "I ain't telling you nothing. But I'm telling you that he ain't [at McMaster's farm]."

152. "Picardo basically had it right"

For reasons never completely clear to me, the story that David Corn and I wrote about the former federal judge was never published and that raised Moscato's suspicions about my intentions and motives. He appeared to sense—and rightfully so—that I was more interested in what he knew about the Hoffa case than in what he knew about the Romano brothers and the federal judge.

When I spoke with Moscato again on September 24, 2009, after I returned from my meeting in Detroit about the 2006 dig at McMaster's farm with FBI informant Donovan Wells, Moscato appeared cold and distant. Once again, I chose not to press him, hoping for a better time to continue our discussion.

Then, three years later, Moscato called me and said that he wanted to talk. Now refusing to do so over the phone—suddenly wary of recorded conversations—he invited me to his new home in New Jersey on July 18, 2012, three days before his 77th birthday. Of course, I jumped at the offer and immediately made an appointment to see him.

I arrived at his beautiful apartment-condominium early in the morning and stayed until nearly 10:00 that night. But, during our thirteen-hour visit, we spoke very little about the Hoffa case. Finally, during our pasta dinner with a delicious tomato and prosciutto sauce prepared by his devoted wife, Angela, at their home, I said to him with considerable exasperation, "Phil. I'm here at your invitation. Please tell me what you can."

When he still balked, I added, "I'm even willing not to report anything until after you're gone—unless I have your permission."

I had a small video camera in my pocket and wanted to film Moscato. However, Moscato not only refused to allow me to videotape the interview, he also insisted that I not turn on my audio recorder. He told me, "There are no statute of limitations on these things."

When I reluctantly agreed not to turn on any recording device, here is what was revealed:

* Moscato said, "Ralph Picardo basically had it right."

* Moscato, confirming a portion of Don Wells's story, told me that Tony Provenzano was in Detroit on the night before Hoffa's murder. However, Moscato would not confirm whether or not Provenzano was an actual witness to the killing.

PART TWELVE: HOFFA REDUX

* Although he made it clear that Frank Sheeran had nothing to do with Hoffa's actual murder, he refused to confirm that Sal Briguglio did the job—although he strongly implied it and allowed me to accept it as a fact without correction.

* Tom Andretta was in Detroit on the day of the murder—but Moscato also refused to confirm his involvement. (However, it is unclear whether Steve Andretta was there. Picardo told federal investigators that Steve was in New Jersey on the day of the killing, serving as Provenzano's alibi witness. Frank Sheeran claimed in his 2004 book that Steve Andretta was at the crime scene. But Sheeran had also claimed that Andretta was dead, which was also not true.)

* Moscato added, "There is a lot more to the story than is known." For instance, he said, Vito Giacalone had played a much more important role than was previously known. Moscato suggested that Giacalone, not Chuckie O'Brien, had driven the car that picked up Hoffa and delivered him to the scene of his murder.

* Moscato said that Chuck O'Brien was a frequent houseguest at his home in Florida. However, he also refused to implicate O'Brien in any phase of the murder conspiracy.

* Moscato confirmed that the Hoffa murder was financed by the Local 560 pension-fund scam involving the Romano brothers, just as a federal prosecutor had told me.

On June 18, 2013, in the midst of a new FBI search for Hoffa's body and my appearances on national television to discuss the case, I called Moscato and asked him how seriously I should be taking this effort.

Moscato laughed and confidently told me that this latest excavation of a field in Oakland Township, just north of Detroit, would also amount to nothing. He added, "I think I've already told you what happened."

When I asked him what he meant by that, he laughed again and refused to say anything more, except to repeat that the current dig was "a wild-goose chase."

I did not tape record this conversation either.

Then on July 28, 2013—the day before I sent the first edition of this book to the printer—I called Moscato and asked for his permission to use the following statement from him about the Hoffa case. I did memorialize this conversation:

> Just before I submitted this book for publication . . . I called my best source who was in a position to know the details about the [Hoffa] case but discloses information with the same frequency that a kosher butcher sells pork chops. Responding to my appeal, he confirmed that Tony Provenzano was in Detroit the night before the disappearance. He permitted himself to add that there is a lot more to the story than is known—although he conceded that Ralph Picardo basically had it right. The source refused to confirm that Sal Briguglio was the killer, but he did dismiss any and all speculation that Frank Sheeran played any role at all in the actual murder.

After Moscato confirmed this, including the statement that "Picardo basically had it right," I asked Moscato, "Hoffa: Detroit or New Jersey? Did he wind up in Detroit or New Jersey?"

With no hesitation, Moscato replied, "I would venture to say New Jersey."

A few minutes after this conversation, Moscato called back to ask me for my home address, which I gave him. I tried to use his call as an opportunity to get more information out of him about the murder of Hoffa. But all he would do was repeat, "I'm not going to talk about Sal, but I can assure you that Sheeran had no role in the actual killing of Jimmy Hoffa."

I decided not to push Moscato any further—at least for the moment. I still wanted to wait until he was completely comfortable with me and my work.

During the late summer of 2013, I sent Moscato the first edition of this book which proved that I had not betrayed his trust. At the end of Chapter 150, he saw that I had not quoted him by name but, instead, referred to him as "my best underworld-connected source *who was in a position to know the specific details about the Hoffa murder*—but discloses information with the same frequency as a kosher butcher sells pork chops." With Moscato approving that description, I hoped that he and I would have a final interview during which he would give me the entire story about Hoffa's murder and the disposal of his body.

But my patience was not rewarded. Shortly after receiving this book in September, Moscato started having extremely serious health problems, including what would be a fatal bout with liver cancer.

My final conversation with Moscato, who was bedridden and could barely speak, was by telephone on January 6, 2014. Although I attempted to get him to tell me what he already knew I needed to know, he repeated in his weak and raspy voice that when he recovered, I could return to his home, and we could pick up where we had left off.

We both knew that would never happen. He died the following month.

PART THIRTEEN:
Intermezzo II

153. "Remember where you heard it first"

In my 1989 book, *Interference: How Organized Crime Influences Professional Football*, I predicted that the time would come when the NFL owners would offer a wholly-owned process for gambling on NFL games, even going as far as to host gambling operations in their stadiums.

One of my top law-enforcement sources, Ralph Salerno, the former supervisor of detectives for the New York Police Department, favored legalizing sports gambling and told me, "[Former NFL Commissioner] Pete Rozelle [had] always been violently against sports betting. That is going to continue until the owners decide that they want some of the income and will take the bets at the stadium or elsewhere. The TV money isn't going to pay for everything forever. They're going to be looking for additional revenue."

Speaking about legalizing sports gambling and how the NFL, one day, would embrace it, Gene Klein, the former owner of the San Diego Chargers, remarked during our 1988 interview: "People are going to gamble. One day, you will go to a baseball game or a football game, and there will be betting booths. You'll have all kinds of exotic bets. You'll pay your money, you'll get a receipt, and you'll win or lose. . . .

"Why should the Mafia get all the profits."

During my September 11, 1989, appearance on ABC's *Nightline* to discuss the NFL and the Mafia, the final moments of the program focused on the prospect of legalized gambling. The segment wound up in a contentious dispute, pitting me against the two other guests, NFL Security Director Warren Welsh and the prominent Las Vegas oddsmaker, Roxy Roxborough, about the future.

Jeff Greenfield hosted and opened up the debate:

> **Greenfield**: Dan Moldea, your principal concern is organized crim's influence. Wouldn't legalized gambling diminish the influence of organized crime?
>
> **Moldea**: No, I don't think so. I think it's going to enhance it.
> . . . *I think what's happening in the NFL is that the NFL owners want to control the gambling themselves. I think they want to have it right in the stadium, just as you would at a horseracing track, where you could go to a pari-mutuel window and make a bet on . . . any game that's going on. . . .*

Roxborough: That's too bizarre, Dan. Too bizarre.

Welsh: It'll never happen.

Moldea: I think that's coming, because I think that's why Jim Finks is being caught up for NFL commissioner, because they want a commissioner who's going to be a little more sensitive to the problem of gambling in the NFL.

Roxborough: Totally outrageous. Totally outrageous.

Moldea: We'll see.

Roxborough: Okay.

Moldea: Remember where you heard it first.

Greenfield: Mr. Welsh, you have any sense that Mr. Moldea is predicting the future?

Welsh: Absolutely not. I think he's 100 percent incorrect.

Moldea: Talk to Gene Klein, former owner of the San Diego Chargers. He agrees with that.[316] The NFL owners want ot control the gambling. They want to control the vigorish.

Welsh: He's a former owner.

Moldea: He's a former owner who wishes he could have controlled the gambling and the vigorish.

Roxborough: (laughing)

Moldea: You have to understand that these new owners, the eleven owners who are stopping Pete Rozelle from finally retiring—after a fine job that he did—are putting themselves in a position where they're holding a lot of paper, holding a lot of debt. They're spending $100 million for their teams. Television revenues aren't going to carry the day for these NFL owners for long. They need the gambling. They need the vigoish.

PART THIRTEEN: INTERMEZZO II

Welsh: Absolutely incorrect. [Emphasis added]

Four years later, on May 19, 1993, I testified before the appropriations committee of the New Jersey General Assembly on behalf of the New Jersey Thoroughbred Horseman's Benevolent Association, speaking against legislation that would legalize sports gambling in Atlantic City.

During my testimony, I insisted:

> On the surface, the NFL's opposition to legalized sports gambling appears to be sheer hypocrisy, particularly since its fortunes have been so enhanced by any form of gambling, legal or illegal. It is not. The NFL has a proprietary interest here and does not want someone else profiting from the sale of its product. As television revenues decline and NFL owners continue paying over $100 million for their franchises, other forms of income will become necessary in order for these franchises to remain viable. I believe that the NFL team owners want those new revenues to come from the gambling operations that they, themselves, will control. But that is another discussion for another time.

In the end, the state assembly voted twice to reject placing a proposed state constitutional amendment on the ballot which, if approved, would permit sports gambling.

On November 5, 2012, Lawrence P. Ferazani, the general counsel of the NFL Management Council, testified in a sworn deposition in a federal civil case in New Jersey, *National Collegiate Athletic Association, et al v. Christopher Christie, et al.*

Ferazani declared: "The NFL is a revenue-generating business. If the NFL believed that sports gambling would allow it to increase its revenue, the NFL would engage in that activity."

On October 18, 2017, *Gambling Compliance*, a respected trade publication that tracks gambling on a global scale, published a story, saying:

> Money from mammoth television contracts has fueled the NFL's prosperity, but [Dan] Moldea remains convinced additional revenue sources will be necessary for the league's future growth, and one of those sources will be gambling.
>
> The NFL did not respond to a request for comment.

"The amount of money required to buy NFL teams when I wrote *Interference* is nothing compared to what owners have to pay today," Moldea told *Gambling Compliance* during a recent interview in Washington, D.C.

"Television revenues are not going to carry the day for these guys for long," he said. "They need the money from sports betting. They need the vigorish (the percentage deducted from a gambler's winnings by the organizers of a game)."

Moldea, 67, said virtually the same thing in 1989 when he appeared on the ABC news program, *Nightline*.

The *Nightline* segment is posted on his website and shows famed Las Vegas oddsmaker Michael Roxborough and Warren Welsh, then director of NFL security, scoffing at Moldea's comments.[317]

On May 14, 2018—twenty-nine years after the publication of my book about the NFL and the Mafia, as well as my appearance on *Nightline*—the U.S. Supreme Court in *NCAA v. Christie* struck down the federal law prohibiting states from legalizing sports betting, a ruling that opened the door to legalizing sports betting in states across the country.

Two days later, Thom Loverro, a widely read and respected sports reporter for the *Washington Times*, discussed the high court's decision, stating: "[The NFL] will likely be in the sports betting business, along with perhaps other professional leagues. Don't be surprised to see sports betting opportunities in NFL stadiums perhaps right in your seats from winners and point spreads to all sorts of prop bets.

"Much of this was predicted by investigative reporter Dan Moldea's landmark 1989 book, *Interference: How Organized Crime Influences Professional Football*."[318]

Making the first move in February 2020 was Dan Snyder, the owner of the Washington Redskins, who publicly declared that he wanted sports-gambling operations in a proposed new stadium.

The Washington Post reported: "The Washington Redskins have deepened a multistate effort to secure a spot in the burgeoning sports betting industry, dangling to both Maryland and Virginia the prospect of building a stadium within their borders—so long as the team can offer wagering. . . .

PART THIRTEEN: INTERMEZZO II

"Neither state has a legal sports betting industry. Snyder's effort to get in on the ground floor is the most publicly known advocacy for a sports betting license by an NFL owner, noteworthy in a league that actively lobbied against the proliferation of wagering out of concern it would threaten the 'integrity' of the game."[319]

Welcome to what will soon be The New Normal in professional sports.

154. RFK Jr. calls to discuss his father's murder

During the early evening of December 27, 2017—forty years to the day after my last face-to-face interview with Jimmy Hoffa, Jr., about the circumstances of the murder of his father—I received a surprise call at my home from Robert Kennedy, Jr., who wanted to speak with me about the circumstances of the murder of his father.

Kennedy told me, "My whole life has been about trying to figure out the truth."

He and I spoke for about forty-five minutes during which it was clear that Kennedy was woefully uninformed about the details of his father's murder case. For instance, he thought that security guard Gene Cesar, in whom Kennedy expressed a special interest, was of Mexican decent. In fact, Cesar's family is a mixture of English, French, and German.

Notably, along with discussing his father's assassination, I told Kennedy that I had dedicated my book about that horrible crime to both my writing coach and to Walter Sheridan, the head of Attorney General Kennedy's "Get-Hoffa Squad," whom I considered a personal mentor while I was a young crime reporter, investigating Hoffa, the Teamsters, and the Mafia.

Kennedy noted that Sheridan was "like a brother to my father."

Because of my career-long admiration for RFK Sr., there was nothing I wanted more than to get along with RFK Jr.

Shortly after that conversation, I received a note from a documentary producer in Hollywood, saying that he was working with Kennedy, who wanted me to arrange an interview between Kennedy and Gene Cesar, saying:

> I'm just getting started so I don't have a main thesis or any interviews filmed. I have a network client that commissioned

my company to do a bio on RFK, and I need a fresh angle. Through a mutual friend I reached out to Bobby Kennedy Jr. to ask if he would do an interview about his father. In our conversations he mentioned that he would like to meet with Gene Cesar as a cathartic experience for him, and I thought that would make for an impactful segment within my film. We have an open mind right now about the assassination and I think it would be amazing for Bobby Jr. and Cesar to speak eye to eye.

In response, I wrote:

I'm still confused as to your intentions. Would the role of Thane Eugene Cesar be anything more than him discussing the tragedy with RFK Jr? If so, it appears that he would be walking into an ambush in which he would be accused of murdering Senator Kennedy. Once again, he is an innocent man, wrongly accused.

In his reply, the filmmaker assured me:

You expressed concern about the possibility of a "trap" or "ambush" somehow awaiting Gene. Bobby is approaching this with an open mind. He wants to hear Gene's story. I believe this would be a cathartic experience for Bobby (maybe for Gene, too?) So let's give Gene this chance of a lifetime to personally tell Bobby whatever it is Gene may want to tell him directly.

Gene can pick the location where he's most comfortable. Please ask him where he would like to meet Bobby.

The film will not accuse anyone. It will raise questions, explore theories and provide information so viewers can draw their own conclusions.

I contacted Cesar at his home in the Philippines and asked if he wanted to participate, encouraging him to do so. When Cesar said that he was interested—as long as I was with him during the filming—I wrote back to the producer, saying:

Gene Cesar has agreed in principle to participating in the event. Of course, he has a handful of conditions.

PART THIRTEEN: INTERMEZZO II

> I am waiting to hear from someone. After that conversation, I will get back to you.
>
> However, before our next step, I will need to know who else you have interviewed or are planning to interview for your program. With that information, I will have a better understanding of your intentions.
>
> I still believe that you are setting an ambush for Cesar—once again, an innocent man, wrongly accused—but he is willing to walk into it . . . under the right conditions.

On April 2, 2018, RFK Jr. called me for a second time. During this conversation, he revealed that he had recently visited Sirhan Sirhan in prison and spent a few hours with him.

I was shocked by that disclosure. Significantly, two years earlier, Kennedy had stated publicly that he believed that Sirhan was not his father's murderer.

Upon hearing this news—which Kennedy asked me to keep quiet for the moment—I simply replied to him, solemnly, "Bobby, this is the guy who killed your dad."

He added, as his producer had requested, that he wanted me to arrange a face-to-face interview between him and Gene Cesar.

Kennedy knew that I was the only person in the world, living or dead, who had interviewed both Sirhan and Cesar.

After speaking with Kennedy, I again contacted Cesar, who told me, "If they want to waste my time, it will cost them $10,000."

With Cesar's request in hand—and asking nothing for myself—I wrote to the producer, saying:

> Bob asked me to participate in your program—as you had earlier suggested—and I agreed to do so, specifically to make the case that Sirhan Sirhan committed the murder and acted alone. *Other than any required expenses—out of respect for Bob and his family, as well as for my late mentor, Walter Sheridan—I will not ask for either a consulting fee or an honorarium for your proposed interview with me or for my help in arranging Bob's interview with Gene Cesar.*
>
> Notably, however, Bob made it clear to me that he does not believe that Sirhan killed his father.

> Although he did not explicitly say so, it is also clear to me—by a simple process of elimination—that he believes that Cesar is the killer . . . although he was careful to note that he did not want to falsely accuse anyone of murder, either Sirhan or Cesar.
>
> Consequently, with regard to Cesar, who is 76 and ailing, he wants $10,000 for his participation. He wants $5,000 paid two weeks before the interview. He wants the balance paid just before the interview starts. In short, he doesn't want you to withdraw payment in the midst of the interview after you quickly discover that he is an innocent man, wrongly accused. [Emphasis added.]

Also, Cesar, a college dropout, wanted his attorney and me to be present during the interview while Kennedy, a graduate of Harvard and the University of Virginia School of Law, interrogated him. And he wanted to do the interview on Skype, not in person.

Two days later, RFK Jr. sent me the following:

> I completely understand Gene's reticence and I don't object to the payment; I know he has been through Hell and I imagine that the suspicions and accusations have injured his capacity to support himself.
>
> But I don't think the arrangements Gene is proposing serve his best interests. I think most people would feel that an innocent man would be anxious to clear his name in a direct and very personal conversation with the son of the man he has been falsely accused of murdering.
>
> I'm enclosing copies of my best-selling book *Framed* for both you and Gene. I think if you take a look at this, you will feel confident that I have an allergy against false accusations against innocent men. My cousin Michael Skakel was falsely accused of committing a murder that he had absolutely nothing to do with. Those accusations destroyed his life. I would never do to another human being what his accusers did to Michael.
>
> Dan, I want to learn what happened to my father. I do not believe that Sirhan fired the bullet that killed him. By his own

PART THIRTEEN: INTERMEZZO II

admission, Gene was standing immediately behind my father when he was shot in the back of the head. Some have raised doubts about Gene's innocence. Others speculate that he might have panicked over Sirhan's gunshots and shot Daddy by accident. I want to ask him, face to face and man to man, what he said and did that night.

I think that people viewing Gene's proposed arrangement will be skeptical of Cesar. An innocent man with nothing to hide would jump at the opportunity to sit down in the same room with Robert Kennedy's son to tell him, eye to eye and from his heart" mind and soul that he is not only innocent of this crime but is outraged over the accusations he's had to endure for decades. He would want the murdered man's son and the world to know that he is innocent.

The Skype proposal from Cesar makes Cesar look more guilty because it feels like there would be a bail-out option for him if the conversation went poorly from his point of view.

Please let me know what assurances Gene Cesar might be needing from me. such as perhaps keeping confidential the location of our meeting and where he currently resides, or making it clear there will be no attempt made to arrest or follow him (that he'll be a free man walking into our meeting and a free man walking out).

Shortly after I received Kennedy's letter, the film producer insisted that the Kennedy-Cesar interview be face-to-face in Manila on June 1—four days before the 50th anniversary of Senator Kennedy's murder.

To sweeten the deal, the Kennedy production team—unilaterally, without any prodding from me—bumped up Cesar's honorarium from $10,000 to $25,000 if he agreed to their terms, even though they continued to insist that they had drawn no conclusions about Cesar's guilt or innocence. After Cesar agreed to the latest proposed arrangement, I wrote to the Kennedy production team: "I will do everything I can to help this go smoothly."

And I meant it. I really wanted to see this happen, because I knew that this debate over the circumstances of the murder of Senator Kennedy would wind up as a verbal confrontation between Kennedy and me about who killed his father: Sirhan or Cesar. And I knew that, by claiming Sirhan was innocent, Kennedy was playing a very weak hand.

But Cesar, who was ailing from multiple health issues, did not share my enthusiasm.

Convinced that he was walking into a trap, Cesar decided that, among other things, he was not well enough physically to deal with this. Further, he had been through years of tolerating false accusations, and he didn't want to participate in another situation that would bring more unnecessary and unfair grief to him and his family.

Clinging to the illusion that they were still impartial about Cesar's role, the Kennedy production team sent me an email on May 6 about what they were now calling "the historic meeting" between Kennedy and Cesar.

In my reply that same day, I wrote:

> "[T]he historic meeting?" . . . What's so historic about Robert Kennedy Jr. meeting with just another eyewitness to his father's tragic murder, one of 77 people in the kitchen pantry that night?
>
> By you framing the proposed Kennedy-Cesar confrontation that way—along with Bob's long-standing, on-the-record belief that Sirhan is innocent and the fact that you are willing to pay Cesar a whopping $25,000 for that face-to-face interview—indicates to me and certainly to Cesar that you are, indeed, going to make the case that he is the actual killer.
>
> And, thus, Cesar believes that he will be walking into an ambush—and will be forced to address whatever old or new evidence, real or imagined, you believed you have. And he will have to do so during a filmed interview with Kennedy, a skilled, world-class attorney. . . . Then, you, as the producer, will conveniently "allow the viewer to be the judge" when your program finally airs.
>
> Further, I am still upset that Bob did not disclose to me that he has a memoir coming out between May 15 and May 22, which, I assume, will play some role in your documentary. And Cesar is now upset with that, too. . . .

PART THIRTEEN: INTERMEZZO II

> Just to be clear, although I will not sign a nondisclosure agreement, I have no intention to write anything about you and/or your documentary prior to its release, if ever—unless I read articles or promotional material, indicating that your program will be suggesting that Cesar, an innocent man, committed the murder.
>
> Please note that my decision not to write about you and your documentary does not extend to what I might or might not write about Bob Kennedy, Jr.—who, once again, is already on the public record for his belief that Sirhan is innocent of the crime for which he was convicted.
>
> As I said before, with respect, I believe that Bob is wrong—and misguided. And I reserve the right to express my expert opinion, fully and freely in writing, about this.
>
> With regard to Cesar's participation in your documentary, the simple fact is that Cesar doesn't trust this situation, and neither do I. . . .
>
> *Consequently, Cesar and I are out. We're done with this.*
>
> If there is something Cesar needs to respond to down the road, then he'll surely respond—either through me or in person, if necessary. [Emphasis added]

After I sent that letter, I received a response from Kennedy's personal assistant, who wrote, in part, on May 9:

> When we spoke on the phone, I tried to emphasize the fact that Bobby is only searching for the truth. He approaches this with an open mind and he isn't pre-judging Gene Cesar's guilt or innocence. Gene, after enduring decades of accusations in the public arena, would have a chance to tell Bobby his side of the story, face to face. . . .
>
> The filmmakers were planning to interview you separately but, during the filmed conversation between Bobby and Gene, it's my understanding that you would be present in the room. If Gene would feel more comfortable with you sitting next to him

on-camera, we could require the producers to agree to this arrangement.

You've expressed your respect for Bobby and his father, and I'm sure that as a well-known author and researcher, yourself, you can empathize with his 50-year quest for answers surrounding his father's murder. I've spent countless hours witnessing his tireless search for the truth and it's my duty as Bobby's deputy to facilitate an arrangement that is comfortable for everyone involved. . . .

I sincerely ask that you and Gene reconsider the meeting in Manila and I hope you won't hesitate to reply with any thoughts or concerns.

The following day, I replied, in part:

I see Cesar being used in [the] documentary as nothing more than a punching bag for Bob, the hero of this staged drama, who would, Perry Mason-like, point out the inconsistencies in Cesar's story and then "allow viewers to draw their own conclusions." . . .

If Bob has new evidence that someone else at the crime scene was holding a gun near his father, I would certainly like to hear about it. Barring that, then Cesar is the only game in town as the second gunman. Regardless of how open Bob's mind is. . . . If it wasn't Sirhan, then it had to be Cesar.

I remember a time many years ago when I believed that false premise, too.

On May 20, I blogged about the anticipated activity revolving around the upcoming 50th anniversary of Senator Kennedy's killing, writing:

Get ready for the 50th anniversary of the tragic murder of Senator Robert Kennedy on June 5-6. We will soon know which side of the rainbow the "Sirhan-didn't-do-it crowd" will land this time. Much of their work has been embargoed, cynically concocting dramatic releases. . . . Be prepared for big celebrities to come out publicly, proclaiming poor Sirhan's

PART THIRTEEN: INTERMEZZO II

innocence and insisting that he was "hypno-programmed" to kill and then programmed to forget about it.

You will marvel at so-called experts, spewing what appears to be impressive minutia and factoids about the case while railing about muzzle-distance discrepancies, extra bullets in the walls and door frames at the crime scene, and bullet slugs that don't match Sirhan's eight-shot gun—not to mention promoting a new crop of eyewitnesses, polka-dot-dress girls, and a tape recording that, some say, indicates that thirteen shots were fired. . . . It will all be bullshit and easily explained away. . . .

Once again—like it or not—Sirhan did it, and he did it alone.

Of course, I did not betray Kennedy's secret about having met with Sirhan.

—m—

On Sunday, May 27, Tom Jackman, a respected Pulitzer Prize-winning reporter for the *Washington Post*, published a front-page story about the upcoming 50th anniversary of the murder of Senator Kennedy, inexplicably legitimizing the claims of Kennedy's son and namesake that the confessed and convicted assassin who killed Senator Kennedy was an innocent man, wrongly accused.

For weeks prior to publication, Jackman and I had met for lunch and spoke frequently on the phone. Indeed, I knew that he was troubled by some of the facts of the case. At one point, he called and pleaded only half-jokingly, "Dan, talk me off the ledge."

Jackman, who revealed RFK Jr's secret meeting with Sirhan Sirhan, followed up that outrageous story with a disgraceful multi-part series which essentially cleared Sirhan of the role as assassin.

The reporter celebrated the conspiracy crowd, giving new life to old and long-discredited controversies in the case. Consequently, with the *Post* leading the way, other media organizations—including ABC, CBS, and NBC, as well as CNN, MSNBC, and Fox—also promoted the conspiracy theorists, along with their new champion, RFK Jr.[320]

As part of his reckless work, Jackman published stories with such headlines as:

* "Was Sirhan Sirhan hypnotized to be the fall guy?"

* "The Bobby Kennedy assassination tape: Were 13 shots fired or only 8?"

* "CIA may have used contractor who inspired Mission: Impossible to kill RFK, new book alleges,"

These were articles published in the *Washington Post*, one of the most honored and respected newspapers in the world.

In response, I asked on my blog and elsewhere on social media: "When will the *New York Times* clean up the mess that the *Washington Post* is making on the RFK murder case?"³²¹

Shortly after publication of Jackman's first story, the *Boston Globe* called me for comment about the *Washington Post* putting its credibility on the line with its tacit endorsement of Jackman's irresponsible journalism.

On June 2 at 12:25 A.M., RFK Jr. sent me an email which contained nothing more than the link to the *Globe* story, written by reporter Nik DeCosta-Klipa and titled, "Bobby Kennedy's son thinks he was killed by a second shooter. Is there anything to it?"

DeCosta-Klipa wrote, in part:

> Moldea says the second-shooter theory persists because authoritatively making the case that Sirhan was the sole shooter isn't a clean and easy task. The 68-year-old journalist says he talked to RFK Jr. earlier in the year after he visited Sirhan and tried to explain that Sirhan's team was promoting the theory to increase the odds he might get released from prison.
>
> "I would not want to take the blame for this crime as long as there is exculpatory evidence that I didn't do the crime," Sirhan admitted to Moldea in 1993.
>
> Moldea said he is "livid" with how the *Post* treated the recent story and imagines Sirhan is "in his jail cell right now spiking the football." Quoting from his book, he reiterated his point that nearly every murder can be made to look like a conspiracy if "occasional official mistakes and incompetence" are not taken into account.

PART THIRTEEN: INTERMEZZO II

"I think [RFK Jr.] has been misled, conned, and corrupted by the conspiracy crowd to believe this garbage that the man that murdered his father is innocent," Moldea said.

In response to Kennedy's late-night email to me, I replied to him:

And what? . . . I told you on the phone and in writing that I would not be silent if you decided to go public with your Sirhan-didn't-do-it fantasy.

BTW: Tom Jackman's piece in the *Washington Post* last Sunday, which celebrated your proclamation that Sirhan Sirhan was innocent, was a disgrace. And I told that to Jackman when he called me on Thursday.

That confessed, convicted, and cowardly assassin, whom you have now chosen to defend, murdered your father.

On the anniversary of Senator Kennedy's murder, I published a story, saying:

I was hoping that the controversies would finally be put to rest today on this sad 50th anniversary of RFK's death. Instead, reporter Tom Jackman of the *Washington Post* continues to make a fool of himself with the latest installment of his uncritical series of articles, celebrating, without challenge, the conspiracy theories revolving around the RFK murder. . . .

I am assuming that Jackman and the *Washington Post* will move heaven and earth to get an interview with the poor and misunderstood Sirhan Sirhan, the confessed and convicted killer of Senator Kennedy—whom I interviewed three times for a total of fourteen hours. At the end of those interviews, there was no doubt in my mind that Sirhan did it and did it alone. . . .

Meantime, I am waiting for the *New York Times* to enter this fray—and clean up the mess that the *Washington Post* is leaving in Jackman's wake.

On September 11, 2019, I published a copyrighted, spur-of-the-moment story on my blog, revealing:

> 12:30 PM. . . . Thane Eugene Cesar—the security guard still falsely accused of killing Senator Robert Kennedy in June 1968—died an hour ago at a Manila hospital in the Philippines after a long illness. He was 77 years old. . . . When I first entered the RFK murder investigation in 1987, I, too, believed that Cesar—who was standing next to Senator Kennedy with a gun in his hand and powder burns on his face—was a possible second gunman. However, I continued to investigate and was able to find and repeatedly interview Gene, whom the Los Angeles District Attorney's Office believed to be dead.
>
> After spending over forty hours with him, I wanted some test or measurement to determine how much time and money I needed to continue pursuing him. Marvin Rudnick, a trusted friend who was a former federal prosecutor in LA, suggested that I arrange for Cesar to take a polygraph test. . . . Thus, if he failed, I would never stop coming after him. If he passed, I would treat him as another eyewitness to the killing.
>
> Cesar agreed to take the lie-detector test—personally conducted by Edward Gelb, then the president of the American Polygraph Association. Cesar passed with flying colors and no room for doubt.
>
> In short, Gene Cesar was an innocent man, wrongly accused of murdering one of the greatest crimefighters in American history. And I was proud to proclaim his innocence in my 1995 book about the murder of Senator Kennedy. Four years later, Cesar invited me to be the godfather of his newborn son, and he asked me to handle all media inquiries for him, giving me his legal power of attorney, which I still retain.
>
> Attached is a 1:28-minute excerpt of my twelfth and final recorded interview with Cesar which took place on June 4, 1994, the day before my third and final face-to-face interview with Sirhan Sirhan, whom I concluded in my 1995 book committed the murder and acted alone. . . .

PART THIRTEEN: INTERMEZZO II

God bless Gene Cesar, a tragic character in a footnote of American history, who will sadly continue to be defamed long after his death.

Within minutes after my announcement about Cesar's death, RFK Jr. came out on Instagram, suggesting that Gene Cesar, not Sirhan Sirhan, had murdered his father, adding:

Thane Eugene Cesar died today in the Philippines. Compelling evidence suggests that Cesar murdered my father. . . . I had plans to meet Thane Eugene Cesar in the Philippines last June until he demanded a payment of $25,000 through his agent Dan Moldea. Ironically, Moldea penned a meticulous and compelling indictment of Cesar in a 1995 book and then suddenly exculpated him by fiat in a bizarre and nonsensical final chapter. Police have never seriously investigated Cesar's role in my father's killing.

Of course, that was hardly what happened. Cesar asked for a $10,000 honorarium for an interview on Skype. But it was Kennedy's production team that kicked up the sum to $25,000, hoping to convince Cesar to do the interview with Kennedy, face-to-face, in Manila. And, indeed, Cesar agreed to do the interview for the price offered. And I did everything I could to make the arrangements—asking nothing for myself—until Cesar and I determined that Kennedy and his team were operating in bad faith.

After Kennedy's public statement about Cesar's death, Tom Jackman of the *Washington Post* sent me an email, saying:

Hi Dan – Would like to hear your thoughts on the passing of Mr. Cesar, if that is confirmed, and also your response to Bobby Kennedy Jr.'s statement about Mr. Cesar. . . . I have appreciated your previous help. . . . (Which reminds me, can we use your video of Mr. Cesar denying involvement?) . . . Thanks much.

In response, I wrote to Jackman:

RFK Jr. inexplicably believes that Sirhan Sirhan is an innocent man, wrongly accused. When he called to give me that news in 2018, I admonished him, saying: "Bobby, this is the guy who killed your dad."

RFK Jr, has been manipulated, misled, and conned by the conspiracy crowd—as you, Tom Jackman, have been. Just as you have been a total disgrace to the *Washington Post* with your sloppy reporting about the RFK case, as well as your warm embrace of loony conspiracy theorists, RFK Jr. is a disgrace to his father's memory with his mindless speculations, his half-baked opinions, and his poorly sourced facts. . . .   Among many other exculpatory facts contained in my 1995 book about the RFK murder, RFK Jr. fails to note that Cesar passed a polygraph test that I arranged. He also did not mention that my three interviews with Sirhan, totaling fourteen hours, provided persuasive evidence that Sirhan did it and did it alone.

I am still waiting for the *New York Times* to clean up the mess that you and the *Washington Post* have created.

No, you may not use my videotape of Gene Cesar.

To his credit, Jackman did not publish a story about RFK Jr's lame accusations against the now-deceased Gene Cesar. However, along with some of the British tabloids, the *National Enquirer* did—front page with bold print, "RFK Jr. Finds Dad's Real Killer."

155. Working to save an ex-KGB officer

In October 2018, because of the pending release of a new book, I had to brace for the possibility of some potentially unwanted attention and even harsh criticism for something I had done thirteen years earlier.

On background, on October 2, 1994, I was introduced to former CIA officer Jack Platt, retired since 1987, by our mutual friend, Carl Shoffler, a former detective in the intelligence division of the Metropolitan Police Department of Washington, D.C. At that time, Shoffler was the chief intelligence investigator for the Prince George's County Fire Department.

Shoffler, who was like a big brother to me, was well known as the arresting officer of the Watergate burglars in June 1972.

PART THIRTEEN: INTERMEZZO II

Also in attendance was Phil Manuel, a former long-time congressional investigator who owned and operated a successful private-investigations business in Virginia.

The purpose of the meeting was for me to introduce former mob bookmaker William J. Jahoda, who was then in the Federal Witness Protection Program, to Shoffler and Platt. Jahoda, whom I had earlier introduced to Manuel, was looking for people he could trust while living in Washington. Jahoda, who had been an associate of the Chicago Outfit, served as the key witness in a federal RICO prosecution against top Mafia figures and associates in Chicago.

The result? Twenty convictions.

In retaliation, Chicago mobsters placed a contract on Jahoda's life.

This first meeting led to a series of Sunday brunches, usually twice a year, that included Manuel, Platt, Shoffler, Jahoda, and me, along with several other former FBI and CIA agents, as well as past and present law-enforcement officials, congressional investigators, private investigators, and journalists. It was agreed that everything discussed was off the record unless specifically stipulated to the contrary.

After Shoffler died on July 13, 1996, we began calling this event, "The Shoffler Brunch." I was with Shoffler and his family at Johns Hopkins University Hospital in Baltimore at the moment of his death. And, at his family's request, Jahoda, Platt, and I did eulogies at Carl's memorial service.

In February 1997, my book about the O.J. Simpson case, *Evidence Dismissed*—which I had co-authored with Tom Lange and Philip Vannatter, the two lead detectives of the Simpson murder case—appeared on every major bestsellers' list in the country, including the *New York Times*.

Because of the success of that book, Jack Platt was interested in having me write a book about the relationship between him and former KGB agent Gennady Vasilenko, Platt's long-time nemesis during the Cold War.

But, since the official end of U.S.-Russian hostilities, Platt and Vasilenko had gone from mortal enemies to the best of friends, as well as business partners.

At the time, though, I was working on a book proposal, hoping to get a publishing contract to write about the life and times of Bill Jahoda. But that book never materialized.[322]

On February 8 and 22, 1997, Platt sent emails, inviting me to lunch with a group of visiting former KGB officers, including Vasilenko, who were doing business legally in the United States.

Also, on February 22, Platt—along with his U.S. partner, Ben Wickham—invited me to serve on the board of directors of his company, Hamilton Trading Group, which was based in McLean, Virginia. I accepted the invitation the following day, February 23.

I neither asked for nor received any compensation for this volunteer position.[323]

On March 7, 1997, Platt, Manuel, and I had lunch with the former KGB officers at Stella's restaurant in Alexandria, a short distance from Manuel's office. Along with Vasilenko, the three other ex-KGB agents in attendance were Victor Cherkashin, Alexander Pavlovskij, and Victor Popov. This was the first time I had met Vasilenko, along with his three KGB colleagues. A photograph was taken of the seven of us outside the restaurant.

All of these former KGB people were doing business with both Hamilton Trading Group and Manuel's company, MDB International. The objective was to provide investigative and due-diligence capabilities for American companies that wanted to do business in post-Soviet Russia.

Other than Vasilenko, I neither saw nor communicated with any of these ex-KGB agents ever again. Further, I did no work and received no money at any time for anything associated with any of these KGB agents, including Vasilenko.

On September 21, 1997, Platt brought Vasilenko to our Shoffler Brunch at the Sequoia restaurant at the Washington Harbour. Another photograph was taken of some of those in attendance, including Manuel, Platt, Vasilenko, and me. The Watergate complex appears in the background of the picture.

―――ɷ―――

In or about 2005, specific date unknown, Platt told me that Vasilenko was in a Russian jail, saying that he had run afoul of Russian President Vladimir Putin and adding that Vasilenko had been accused and convicted on a trumped-up weapons charge.

Platt asked me to come up with an idea about how to get Vasilenko out of prison.

Significantly, he revealed that Vasilenko had helped the U.S. intelligence community expose the treason of FBI Special Agent Robert Hanssen, who had pleaded guilty to espionage in July 2001 and had been sentenced to fifteen life sentences in May 2002.

I had never before heard of Vasilenko's role in the Hanssen matter. It was a closely guarded secret. And I was stunned by this news.

In effect, because he had exposed a traitor in the FBI, I considered it my patriotic duty to help free Vasilenko.

Getting to work, I contacted my long-time friend, Ronald Fino, whose father was the late-Joseph Fino, a one-time interim boss of the Buffalo Mafia. As a young man, young Ronnie was being groomed by his father and his associates as a Mafia prince and a possible rising star in the underworld.

However, Ron's mother guided her son away from the dark side and into the light. So, simply speaking, instead of becoming a bad guy, he became a good guy.

A former officer in a mobbed-up union in Buffalo, Ron Fino had secretly worked as an undercover consultant for the FBI for many years and helped put scores of major Mafia figures in prison. Years later, Fino worked in Russia, importing vodka into the United States while developing information about Russian mobsters, among many others, for U.S. intelligence and law-enforcement agencies.

During our meeting, Fino and I discussed the Vasilenko situation. I asked him what we could do to free him from prison. Fino suggested that we raise money and make a payoff to a Russian government official who might be able to help.

Because of the sensitive and even dangerous nature of this operation, I neither recorded conversations nor kept any notes of anything that transpired. In addition, I have no recollection of anything specifically discussed during any of the meetings I attended about this matter. To all intents and purposes, I willingly served in the following roles: arranger, messenger, and peacemaker.

Although there were complications with our mission, I later learned that the payoff to the Russian official was made and that Vasilenko received a significantly reduced prison sentence.

Notably, I neither asked for nor received any money or compensation of any kind for my role in this caper. This was strictly a favor for a friend.

Later, on July 8, 2010, the American and Russian governments engaged in a historic fourteen-person spy swap—ten were sent by the United States to Russia and four were sent by Russia to the U.S. Among the four from Russia was Gennady Vasilenko.

On October 17, 2010, I saw Vasilenko at the Shoffler Brunch at Chadwick's in Georgetown for the first time since his release from the Russian prison and the prisoner swap three months earlier. Vasilenko was Platt's guest at the brunch. He physically embraced me and expressed his gratitude for the roles that Fino and I had played on his behalf.

On January 15, 2015, during a meeting at the Woodside Deli in Silver Spring, Maryland, Platt asked me to give my full cooperation to the co-authors of a book about his relationship with Vasilenko: Gus Russo and Eric Dezenhall, both of whom had been good and trusted friends of mine for many years. Vasilenko, Russo, and Dezenhall were also present for this meeting.

Platt died on January 4, 2017, and did not see their finished work. I saw Vasilenko again at a final family-and-close-friends celebration of Platt's life at The Old Brogue restaurant in Great Falls, Virginia.

The Russo-Dezenhall book, *Best of Enemies: The Last Great Spy Story of the Cold War*, was published on October 2, 2018.

In their book, Russo and Dezenhall wrote, in part:

> "After Gennady disappeared again, Jack called me," Moldea says, remembering that Jack's usual jovial voice sounded uncharacteristically somber. Moldea had met Gennady twice before at Shoffler Brunches in 1997, when Gennady and his ex-KGB pals like Cherkashin had been visiting Jack on HTG business.
>
> "Meet me ASAP," Jack said. The next day, at the Marriott Hotel restaurant in Rosslyn, he pleaded with Moldea. "Can you help Gennady?" He told Dan that Gennady's situation stemmed from how Gennady had assisted the FBI with a huge security problem. "Without even knowing it, he led the FBI to [Robert] Hanssen," Jack whispered.
>
> "I had never heard of Vasilenko's role in this matter before," Moldea says. "In effect, I considered it my patriotic duty to help free him." After a nanosecond of consideration, Moldea replied, "I think I got a guy."
>
> Moldea's recommendation was his longtime friend and source Ron Fino, a former officer in a mobbed-up union in Buffalo, New York, who had secretly worked as an undercover consultant for the FBI and the CIA for many years, helping put scores of major mafia figures in prison. Fino would eventually work in Russia, importing vodka into the United States while

developing information about Russian mobsters, among many others, for US intelligence and law-enforcement agencies.

The next day, Moldea approached Fino, "During this meeting, Fino and I discussed the Vasilenko situation," says Moldea. "He suggested that we raise the necessary money to bribe a Russian government official who might be able to get Vasilenko out of prison. Jack remembered Fino from years earlier, but only by his code name, GORKY, from when the two of them had helped legendary CIA officer Dick Stolz on arms-smuggling investigations. Jack recalled the reintroduction years later: "Moldea introduced me to Fino because his wife's family, which owns a meat-packing factory in Belarus, are in contact with Russian mobsters who might be able to help."[324]

156. On reversions, wiretappers and whistleblowers

Tired of being accused by friends and colleagues of suffering from a severe case of "non-rewarding repetitive behavior" because of my long and unhappy relationship with the mainstream-publishing industry, I began the task of regaining the rights to my previously published books, hoping to self-publish and rerelease them. I now wanted control over all of my works, starting with this one, which I self-published in 2013, along with its second edition two years later.

Notably, I had spent years trying to get the rights to my second book, *The Hunting of Cain*, reverted back to me. But through the corporate-takeover process from its first incarnation with Atheneum to Macmillain Publishers and two paperback editions published by its subsidiary, St. Martin's Press, the book somehow wound up with a subsidiary of Simon & Schuster, which defiantly refused to revert the rights back to me.

This ridiculous situation about this 1983 book, detailing a murder in my beloved hometown, Akron, Ohio, convinced me to go my own way. I no longer wanted to be at the mercy of these major publishers.

In 2015, I also self-published an updated version of my 1998 book, *A Washington Tragedy*, focusing on the suicide of Vincent Foster. In 2016, former LAPD Detective Tom Lange and I updated and self-published the reprint of our 1997 book about the O.J. Simpson murder case, *Evidence Dismissed*. And, in 2018, I self-published my 1995 book, *The Killing of Robert F. Kennedy*, to commemorate the 50th anniversary of the murder.[325]

Also, as part of this effort, I made a three-book deal with Open Road Media, which had started The Forbidden Bookshelf series, featuring books that were the targets of attempted suppression.

According to Open Road's promotional literature:

> For more than half a century, America's vast literary culture has been disparately policed, and imperceptibly contained, by state and corporate entities well placed and perfectly equipped to wipe out wayward writings. As America does not ban books, other means—less obvious, and so less controversial—have been deployed to vaporize them. The purpose of Forbidden Bookshelf is to bring such disappeared books back to life so that readers may finally learn what those in power did not want anyone to know.

The editor of this twenty-seven-eBook series, Mark Crispin Miller, selected three of my books for the project. The first published was *Interference*, my 1989 book about the NFL and the Mafia, which was re-released on June 10, 2014. The second, *The Hoffa Wars*, came out on March 3, 2015, along with a new afterword that featured the controversy over Frank Sheeran, the subject of the highly anticipated Martin Scorsese-Robert De Niro motion picture, *The Irishman*. And my third book for Open Road, *Dark Victory: Ronald Reagan, MCA, and the Mob*, originally released in 1986, was republished on April 18, 2017.

In May 2003, I became involved in a doomed book project, revolving around the federal investigations and criminal indictments of Los Angeles private detective Anthony Pellicano, the so-called "Sleuth to the Stars." Directly or indirectly, usually working through a group of prominent Los Angeles attorneys, Pellicano had represented a wide variety of Hollywood celebrities, including actresses Rosanne Barr, Farrah Fawcett, and Elizabeth Taylor; actors Kevin Costner, Tom Cruise, and James Woods; corporate executives Brad Grey, Kirk Kerkorian, Michael Nathanson, Michael Ovitz, and Don Simpson, as well as Michael Jackson, George Harrison of The Beatles, and television personality Jerry Springer, among many others.

PART THIRTEEN: INTERMEZZO II

My two years of free work on this matter served as a testament to the old adage, "No good deed goes unpunished." In fact, the fallout from this period continues to this day—even after Pellicano's conviction in 2008 for conspiracy and racketeering.

I have described this situation to friends and colleagues as "The Book Project from Hell," which, among other major consequences, led to the tragic destruction of my long friendship with my once-great friend and "brother," Dave Robb. As of this writing, we have not spoken since 2006.

Trusted friends admonished me not to discuss this very complicated case in this book, preferring that I tell that story—if I must—in a subsequent stand-alone book.

In January 2018, unable to resist the urge to make my side of that story available, I self-published, *Hollywood Confidential: A True Story of Wiretapping, Friendship, and Betrayal*.

I never expected to write a book about blatant corruption in higher education, but I was simply blown away by the whistleblower accounts I first learned about on the front pages of the *New York Times*.

Following up, I met Dr. Jon Oberg, featured in one such story in the *Times*, page one and above the fold. His brilliant and courageous work fighting student-loan fraud among lenders led to my interest in whistleblowers at for-profit colleges and, inevitably, to investigative journalist and public-interest attorney David Halperin, along with his detailed exposés of predatory schools that ruin students' lives.

Meantime, I also learned about Rod Lipscomb, who, at great personal sacrifice, blew the whistle on ITT Tech, a for-profit college.

Then, I saw another front-page article in the *New York Times* about the whistleblower, Dr. James Keen, a respected professor and veterinarian, who became the object of frightening retaliation at the hands of a land-grant university and a federal agency.

Further, I could not even consider writing about whistleblowers without asking for the participation of one of the greatest protectors of America's whistleblowers, Louis Clark, the executive director and CEO of the Government Accountability Project (GAP), whom I asked to write the Introduction to my new book project. I had known, admired, and respected Louis for nearly forty years.

These whistleblowing stories, all from the world of higher education, provided the trail to my book about corruption in the federal bureaucracy. I never would have imagined that there was such waste, fraud, and violations of basic humanity in its institutions. But there was and still is.

I was able to gain the full cooperation of these three whistleblowers and two of their greatest champions and to put their stories into one volume as a clarion call to all who believe that the world of higher education is exempt from bad behavior and even flat-out corruption.

In May 2020, I released my tenth book, *Money, Politics, and Corruption in U.S. Higher Education: The Stories of Whistleblowers*.

In his Introduction to the book, Louis Clark of GAP wrote:

> Author Dan Moldea focuses on three whistleblowers: Dr. Jon Oberg, Rod Lipscomb, and Dr. Jim Keen, as well as attorney David Halperin, a well-known and respected advocate of whistleblowers. Moldea traces the origins of the complex scandals that these whistleblowers exposed, identifies the allies and enemies they attracted, and illuminates the retaliation they have courageously endured. From these case studies, a powerful narrative emerges: Moldea shows his readers what happens when good people decide not to remain silent when confronted with rampant corruption in higher education.

PART FOURTEEN:
Hoffa redux II

157. Three-act drama, different characters in each act

As a prelude to what I hope will be big news, here is a brief summary, highlighting the key details of my probe of the murder of Jimmy Hoffa.

Early work
I began my investigation of Jimmy Hoffa and the Teamsters Union in December 1974 while I was a twenty-four-year-old graduate student at Kent State University and writing a column for *The Reporter*, a small Akron-based newspaper that served the African-American community in northeastern Ohio. During the late-winter and early-spring of 1975, I published an eight-part series, "The Teamsters, Their Pension Fund, and the Mafia."

Shortly after I completed that work, I received a phone call from Jonathan Kwitny, a veteran investigative journalist for the *Wall Street Journal*. He said that he was doing his own three-part series about the corruption of the union's pension fund and asked for my help, which I was happy to provide. Kwitny's series, with my assistance, ran in the *Journal* from July 22-24, 1975.

The following week, Jimmy Hoffa disappeared on July 30, 1975.

Shortly after the news broke, Kwitny called, and we concocted a wild theory that Hoffa was alive and hiding at a mob-owned lodge in Eagle River, Wisconsin. We met in Chicago and flew to Rhinelander, Wisconsin, where we rented a car and drove to Eagle River.

Although we had an amazing adventure—which included me getting bitten by a German shepherd while trespassing on the grounds of the lodge—our search for Hoffa was nothing more than a wild-goose chase.

After Kwitny returned to New York, I flew to Detroit and immediately went to the Machus Red Fox restaurant in Bloomfield Hills, a northern suburb, where Hoffa was last seen. While I was at the restaurant, I met the legendary NBC News correspondent, Irving R. Levine, who was covering the Hoffa case for the network. He immediately hired me as a researcher after he called Kwitny who enthusiastically vouched for me.

The Hoffa murder
The murder of Jimmy Hoffa was a three-act drama with different characters in each act.

In Act One, Hoffa went to the Red Fox restaurant, expecting to meet two Mafia figures: labor racketeer Anthony Provenzano of New

Jersey, a capo in the Vito Genovese crime family, and Anthony Giacalone, a top mobster in the Detroit Mafia who was related, by marriage, to Provenzano.

Within days of Hoffa's disappearance, dozens of theories surfaced as to who was in the car that picked up Hoffa and drove him into Act Two where he was murdered. And there were just as many theories as to the location of the scene of the crime and who actually executed the killing.

In Act Three, the co-conspirators disposed of Hoffa's dead body, launching hundreds of theories as to what happened to Hoffa's remains.

Rolland McMaster

On August 5, my first full day on the job with NBC News, I received an introduction to an associate of Rolland McMaster, a Teamsters official who had stood shoulder-to-shoulder with Hoffa since their earliest days in the union. However, in recent years, Hoffa and McMaster had a huge falling out over control of Teamsters Local 299 in Detroit, Hoffa's home local. Consequently, they became mortal enemies.

In fact, my new source alleged that McMaster had played a key role in the disposal of Hoffa's body six days earlier—but he could not prove it. NBC authorized me to pursue the McMaster lead but put me on a short leash, giving me a limited amount of time to get results.

With the help of my friends and sources in the rank-and-file reform movement within the Teamsters, I received introductions to several key players in the Hoffa drama. I quickly learned that since 1971, McMaster, an international organizer, had directed a 32-member Teamsters organizing unit which was traveling around the country, shaking down trucking companies in return for labor peace.

In addition, I obtained interviews and documents, showing that McMaster and his goon squad were behind a series of unsolved acts of violence in Local 299. They included bombings, beatings, shootings, and sabotage, almost exclusively directed against Hoffa's supporters. And I was able to produce evidence showing that three of McMaster's men—Larry McHenry, Jack Robison, and Jim Shaw—were responsible for many of these incidents.

Still, the high command at NBC News was not convinced. So, after accepting and completing a short-term assignment in New York to help with the production of a major NBC special on Hoffa, I returned to my career as a scuffling independent investigative journalist.

Contacting the FBI and Hoffa Jr.

Back in Ohio in early September 1975—a little over a month after the murder—I prepared a fifteen-page theory about what had happened to Hoffa and submitted it to the FBI's field office in Detroit. On September 24, an FBI special agent interviewed me.

Based on our conversation, he wrote a report, stating:

> Specifically, Moldea advances the theory that Hoffa's disappearance and other incidents of Teamster related violence have been the work of Rolland McMaster and other former Teamster International organizers who worked for McMaster in the Teamster Central States Division for Steel and Special Commodities in the early 1970s. In his theory, Moldea sets forth sufficient factual info, which indicates he has good sources close to McMaster and knowledgeable of his union activities.

Two more FBI special agents interviewed me again at my home in Akron for two days, October 15-16, 1975. Although I refused to give them the name of my principal source without his permission, the agents, who encouraged me to come back to Detroit to continue my independent investigation, wrote in another official report:

> Moldea provided a great deal of information from a source who claims to have worked for Rolland McMaster in "task force" comprised of about 15 men whose overt purpose was to organize non-union truckers; but whose actual purpose was to instigate labor violence and unrest. Allegedly, McMaster would then extort money from trucking firms for a guarantee of labor peace.
>
> Moldea and his source feel that McMaster and his "task force," acting on orders from above, are responsible for various instances of labor violence, including Hoffa's disappearance. Moldea appears sincere, resourceful, cooperative, and is attempting to convince his primary source to cooperate with the FBI.

Two weeks later, on October 28, I returned to Detroit, where I received an introduction to Jimmy Hoffa, Jr., the attorney/son of the murdered Teamsters boss, at his downtown law office. During our first meeting, I explained my theory about McMaster to Hoffa, who immediately called the local FBI headquarters and asked an agent with whom he was on a first-name basis to come to his office to meet me.

Within a half hour, two FBI special agents walked into Hoffa's office. As instructed by Hoffa, I repeated my information about McMaster. The agents, who said they were already familiar with my work, confirmed to Hoffa that my information was solid and that my investigation of McMaster was both important and trustworthy.

Declaring that he believed that I had solved the violence in his father's local before he disappeared, Hoffa gave me $2,100 in reward money from the "Hoffa Reward Fund," a bankroll put up by local unions and private individuals, among others, who wanted to solve the Hoffa case. Hoffa Jr. served as the administrator of the fund.

In addition, Hoffa helped to arrange a free-lance assignment with the *Detroit Free Press* where I was tasked to focus on a single story: the McMaster goon squad and its shakedown of trucking companies around the country.

Ralph Picardo and the federal grand jury

On November 5, 1975, the same day that I started my work for the newspaper, a new federal witness in the Hoffa case secretly flipped and turned state's evidence: Ralph Picardo, a long-time associate of Tony Provenzano and his crew. Picardo, Provenzano's former driver, was serving twenty years for manslaughter at Trenton State Penitentiary in New Jersey.

According to federal law-enforcement officials, Picardo had a visitor a few days after Hoffa vanished: Stephen Andretta, who allegedly confessed to Picardo his own role and that of his brother, Thomas, in the Hoffa murder conspiracy—as well as those of two other brothers, Salvatore and Gabriel Briguglio. All four men were also closely associated with Provenzano.

In short, Picardo alleged that Andretta told him that Hoffa had been a) murdered in Detroit, b) stuffed into a 55-gallon oil drum, c) loaded onto a Gateway Transportation truck, and then d) shipped to New Jersey.

When the FBI asked Picardo whether Andretta had revealed the identity of Hoffa's killer, Picardo replied that he had not. However, Picardo knew from his work with the Provenzano operation that Provenzano had personally put a contract on Hoffa in either late 1973 or early 1974 which was specifically given to Sal Briguglio.

When the FBI asked Picardo whether Andretta revealed the location of Hoffa's remains after it was shipped to New Jersey, Picardo, once again, replied that he had not.

However, Picardo knew from personal experience that when Provenzano ordered someone murdered, their bodies often wound up in 55-gallon oil drums, buried at a landfill in Jersey City called "Brother Moscato's Dump," which was owned by Phillip "Brother" Moscato, a reputed soldier in the Vito Genovese crime family. Specifically, Picardo named one of Provenzano's victims as Armand Faugno, a local loan shark who wound up in a grave at the dumpsite.

Later, using Picardo's information as probable cause, the FBI obtained a search warrant for Moscato's landfill, ostensibly looking for Faugno when, in fact, they were looking for Jimmy Hoffa. However, the size of the area and its toxic conditions, along with the wintery weather and the lack of a known specific location, caused agents to abort their search.

On December 4, 1975, the Andrettas and the Briguglios appeared before a federal grand jury in Detroit, investigating the Hoffa case. All four, who had been identified in press reports the previous day, took The Fifth against self-incrimination.

A fifth suspect was not previously identified by the news media: Rolland McMaster, whom, after several phone interviews, I met, face-to-face, for the first time at the federal courthouse as he waited his turn to appear before the grand jury. He told me later that same day that, like the Andrettas and the Briguglios, he had taken The Fifth.

Significantly, on the day Hoffa disappeared, McMaster's alibi was that he was with his brother-in-law, Stanton Barr, the head of the steel division for Gateway Transportation, at a meeting of Gateway officials in Gary, Indiana—the same Gateway company that Picardo had referred to in his statement to the FBI, the same one that had allegedly carried Hoffa's body to New Jersey.

My story about McMaster's goon squad was published in the *Detroit Free Press* on June 20, 1976. However, my bosses at the *Free Press* would not allow me to print details about McMaster's alleged roles in either the Local 299 violence or Hoffa's disappearance.

My interviews with the Andrettas and the Briguglios

In early July 1976, I began my next free-lance assignment with Washington columnist Jack Anderson, addressing the two issues about Rolland McMaster that the *Free Press* refused to publish. Marc Smolonsky, one of the top reporters in Anderson's office who became a life-long friend, introduced me to the well-known columnist.

During my research, I interviewed McMaster and Stan Barr of Gateway, as well as McMaster's top henchmen: Larry McHenry, Jack

Robison, and Jim Shaw, about whom I had collected new evidence that they were behind the violence in Local 299.

Notably, Shaw, at the time of Hoffa's murder, was a long-haul driver for Gateway Transportation.

In addition, on October 25, 1976, I conducted an exclusive three-and-a-half-hour recorded interview with Steve Andretta and Salvatore Briguglio, who were accompanied by their attorney, William Bufalino, the cousin of Mafia boss, Russell Bufalino, and Provenzano's younger brother, Salvatore Provenzano, a former president of Local 560 and a member of the general executive board of the international union. Also, that same day, I had interviews with Tom Andretta over the phone and Gabe Briguglio in person, which were not recorded.

Among several other subjects, I received new details about Andretta's prison visitation with Ralph Picardo and Briguglio's relationship with both Jimmy Hoffa and Phillip Moscato, the co-owner of "Brother Moscato's Dump." Both Briguglio and Moscato were reputed soldiers in the Vito Genovese crime family.

158. Murder, oil drum, Gateway truck, Jersey City

The Hoffa Wars

In late-August 1978, my first book, *The Hoffa Wars*, which chronicled Jimmy Hoffa's rise and fall, was released. Earlier, a blatant attempt to suppress my work by the publishing house of a rival author was detailed in a June 29, 1978, article in the *New York Times* by the newspaper's chief literary critic, Herbert Mitgang, who wrote: "Publishing lawyers said that the attempted delay of the Moldea book was one of the first examples of [a] possible loss of independence—with implicit censorship—where there is a conflict on a controversial nonfiction book."

After the attempted sabotage of *The Hoffa Wars* was revealed by Mitgang and the *Times*, my book was supercharged. *Playboy* bought a long excerpt of the book. *The Observer* of London acquired worldwide rights, and the *New York Times* purchased the U.S. rights. It was also a Book of the Month selection.

My work was widely viewed as the most revealing account of the battles revolving around Detroit's Local 299 which had spiraled into a

PART FOURTEEN: HOFFA REDUX II

war zone when Hoffa tried to retain his power after he was sent to prison in 1967 in the aftermath of his convictions for jury tampering and pension fraud. I chronicled the specific acts of violence against pro-Hoffa supporters, directed by Rolland McMaster and carried out by his goon squad, climaxed by Hoffa's murder in July 1975.

I concluded that Hoffa's murder was engineered by Tony Provenzano and carried out by Sal Briguglio—with his brother, Gabe, along with Steve and Tom Andretta, playing supporting roles. I also alleged that, although Sal Briguglio was the actual killer, Frank Sheeran, a Teamsters thug from Philadelphia who was close to Hoffa, was also part of the overall murder conspiracy.

Based on information from my sources in the law-enforcement community, I alleged that Charles "Chuckie" O'Brien, Hoffa's "foster son," had driven the car that picked up Hoffa and driven him to the scene of his murder. In later years, I backed away from that description of O'Brien's role after he passed a polygraph test in 1999. Then, in 2007, Phillip Moscato, Sr., alleged that the real identity of the person who drove Hoffa to his death was Vito Giacalone, the bother of Tony Giacalone.

Notably, even though I had viewed Ralph Picardo's information as the firewall of the Hoffa case and admonished other investigators when they diverged from his version of events—that Hoffa was murdered in Detroit, stuffed into a 55-gallon oil drum, loaded onto a Gateway Transportation truck, and shipped to New Jersey—I failed to follow my own warning when I published my book.

During my interview with Charles Crimaldi, a Chicago mobster-turned-federal-witness, he convinced me that the Mafia would not have taken the risk of transporting Hoffa from Detroit to New Jersey, adding that his information was that Hoffa was disposed of in a car compactor in or near Detroit. Consequently, after I learned that Gateway's steel division—which was headed by McMaster's brother-in-law—was near the Ford River Rouge Plant in Dearborn, Michigan, I wrote that, after Hoffa was murdered and stuffed into the oil drum, the Gateway truck likely took him to the Ford location where he was "crushed and smelted."

Nearly thirty years later, in 2007, Moscato convinced me that I was wrong about that, too.

Remarkably, there were no serious threats of litigation against *The Hoffa Wars*—with one exception. On March 22, 1979, attorney Frank Fitzpatrick, who represented Frank Sheeran, sent me a letter, saying, in part:

> Mr. Sheeran has recently become familiar with the book authored by you entitled *The Hoffa Wars*.
>
> Mr. Sheeran wishes me to inform you that he emphatically denies the allegations about his involvement in Mr. Hoffa's alleged death and to state specifically that your allegation that he was present in Detroit on the last day that Mr. Hoffa was seen is false, unfounded and has been specifically contradicted by evidence supplied by Mr. Sheeran to the Federal Government.[326]

Frank Sheeran and I Heard You Paint Houses

In the spring of 2001, broadcast correspondent Eric Shawn of Fox News interviewed Frank Sheeran, who, over the years, had developed a reputation for telling conflicting versions about his knowledge of the circumstances of Hoffa's death. During their meeting, Sheeran falsely admitted to Shawn that he had personally killed Hoffa.

At the time, Sheeran was working on a book project with Charles Brandt, a respected former Delaware prosecutor. Their book, *I Heard You Paint Houses*, was a one-source story about Sheeran's life and times which was slated for release in the spring of 2004.

Shawn embraced Brandt's book, along with Sheeran's version of the Hoffa murder, and skillfully used his platform at Fox News to help launch the Brandt-Sheeran project.

Shawn asked me, among others, to sign a non-disclosure agreement, read the embargoed book, and then, upon its release, provide my comments on camera about its conclusions.

In my pre-NDA evaluation to reporter David Ashenfelter of the *Detroit Free Press*—which became the basis for my post-NDA comments—I stated that Sheeran had lied about his role in the case, adding: "Make no mistake: This is the biggest break in the case since Hoffa disappeared on July 30, 1975. Now, in the wake of Sheeran's death in December 2003, the task will be to separate fact from fiction."

In other words, I knew that Sheeran—whom I had interviewed in March 1978—had fabricated his role in the killing of Hoffa, along with those of other infamous criminals he falsely claimed to have killed in Brandt's 2004 book, including but not limited to mobster Joey Gallo and Sal Briguglio, Hoffa's actual killer.

Soon after, Shawn and his team at Fox discovered traces of blood at the exact location in the same house that Sheeran had specified as the scene of Hoffa's murder. However, DNA testing refuted claims that this blood was Hoffa's.

Don Wells and McMaster's farm in Wixom

In 2006, the FBI served a search warrant at a farm in Wixom, Michigan, which, in 1975, was owned by Rolland McMaster and his wife, Marilyn. Living on the farm with the McMaster family back then were a business partner, Donovan Wells, and his wife, Monica.

While in a federal prison, Wells provided evidence to federal agents which served, at least in part, as the necessary probable cause for obtaining their court-authorized search warrant on the property. Importantly, Wells took and passed a polygraph test arranged by the FBI.

Although the search did not yield Hoffa's body, the FBI still believed that Hoffa had been on that farm on the day of his murder. According to an article in the *New York Times*:

> "After a thorough and comprehensive search, no remains of Mr. Hoffa have been located," Judith M. Chilen, an assistant special agent, said at a news briefing at the farm entrance.
>
> Ms. Chilen added that she was convinced that his body had been buried on the farm and that there was "no indication that it has been moved.[327]

I had first interviewed Wells in 1976 while he was still doing business with McMaster. Subsequent to the failed FBI excavation thirty years later, I interviewed Wells once again after his release from prison. I also interviewed his wife.

During this 2009 interview, Don and Monica Wells told me the following:

> * McMaster had dug a large hole in the back of his farm a few weeks before Hoffa disappeared.
>
> * On the night before Hoffa's murder, Wells was having dinner with Rolland McMaster and his brother-in-law, Stanton Barr of Gateway Transportation, at a Detroit restaurant when Tony Provenzano came up to their table and said, "It's going to be a great day tomorrow! A great day tomorrow! Right Mac?" He then asked McMaster to join him at the bar for a private conversation.

When Wells asked Barr what Provenzano was talking about, he replied that Provenzano planned to meet Hoffa the following day.

When Provenzano and McMaster returned, Provenzano pointed to McMaster and Barr and asked, "Do you guys know where you're going to be tomorrow?"

McMaster replied, "Yeah, we're all straight on that."

* During the mid-afternoon on the day of the murder, Monica Wells, who had blonde hair, was looking out the window at the McMaster farmhouse when she saw two or three dark-colored cars turning onto a dirt road at the farm, speeding towards the pre-dug hole in the back of the property. After about twenty-to-thirty minutes, the same cars left the way they came.

When she saw McMaster the following day, Monica told him what she had witnessed. He replied, "Blondes who talk too much don't get old."

Also, during my visit with Wells, I suggested that we go to the farm, which was no longer owned by McMaster, who died in 2007. When we arrived, with the new owner's permission, Wells gave me a tour of the property, as well as a copy of the diagram that he had given to the FBI upon which federal agents based their search.

It quickly became clear during my 2009 visit that the FBI had misread Wells's hand-drawn map—and dug in the wrong place three years earlier.

However, I believed, as both Wells and the FBI special agent believed, that persons unknown had taken Hoffa, alive or dead, to McMaster's property on the day he disappeared.

Journalist and author Scott Burnstein, arguably the top expert on the Detroit Mafia, later published an exclusive story, revealing that one of his sources alleged that Lenny Schultz, a mob-connected businessman who was close to Tony and Vito Giacalone, had given him a remarkable confession that included a startling revelation about McMaster.

Burnstein reported:

PART FOURTEEN: HOFFA REDUX II

One of Schultz's former associates, who declined to be named, says Schultz told him in the 1990s that Hoffa was murdered at his home in Franklin, Michigan, a short drive from the Machus Red Fox restaurant where Hoffa was last seen getting into the passenger's seat of a maroon-colored Mercury Marquis and driving away.

"Lenny and I were driving and he just said it, Tony Jack had the house keys, they choked him out in the living room and gave the body to Rolland McMaster to get rid of," said the associate. "It seemed like he just wanted to get it off his chest and he never said another word about it to me."[328]

After Burnstein's important story, I began to ask: Was Hoffa taken to the McMaster-Wells farm after he was killed at Lenny Schultz's home?

Phillip Moscato Sr.

During my investigation of a corrupt former federal judge in Florida with investigative journalist David Corn, then the Washington editor of *The Nation*, I discovered documentation, showing that a New Jersey Mafia figure had allegedly made cash payoffs to the judge: Phillip Moscato, Sr., the co-owner of "Brother Moscato's Dump" in Jersey City. Remembering him from the Hoffa case and Ralph Picardo's statement to the FBI, I called Moscato at his home in Ocean, New Jersey.

Between 2007 and 2014, I conducted a series of interviews, many of which were recorded, with Moscato. During our talks, which went way beyond his relationship with the judge, he told me that—although the murder conspiracy against Hoffa was more complicated than publicly known—"Picardo basically had it right." Moscato also confirmed Don Wells's claim that Tony Provenzano was in Detroit on the night before the murder.

In addition, Moscato essentially revealed to me that in Act One, Vito Giacalone, the brother of Tony Giacalone—not Chuck O'Brien—had driven the car that picked up Hoffa at the Red Fox and took him to the scene of his murder. In Act Two, Sal Briguglio killed Hoffa. And, in Act Three, Hoffa's body was, indeed, buried at his dump in New Jersey—which was the target of a subsequent EPA Superfund cleanup during the late 1970s and 1980s.

Further, Moscato told me that Frank Sheeran played no role in Hoffa's actual murder.

However, despite my best efforts, Moscato refused to give me the entire story of Hoffa's murder by the time of his death on February 16, 2014.

I did not publish what Moscato did tell me until July 30, 2015—the 40th anniversary of Hoffa's murder. Moscato's story, which I excerpted in several publications, appeared in the second edition of my memoir, *Confessions of a Guerrilla Writer*, in which I had earlier debunked Sheeran's claim that he was Hoffa's killer in the 2013 first edition of my book.

Also, in *Confessions*, I detailed my interviews with John Zeitts, who—before Charles Brandt and *I Heard You Paint Houses* came along in or about 1999—had written an unpublished manuscript about Frank Sheeran with Sheeran's full cooperation. The Zeitts-Sheeran book was titled, *Stand-Up Guy: Frank "Big Irish" Sheeran*.

Before his death in 2011, Zeitts gave me full access to, among other materials, his many hours of audio-and-video-recorded interviews with Sheeran, as well as their draft manuscripts—which contradicted key events in the Brandt-Sheeran book and would likely conflict with the much anticipated Martin Scorsese-Robert De Niro film, *The Irishman*.

159. Great cinema, bad history

Phillip Moscato Jr.
At my request, a few months after Phillip Moscato's death in 2014, I received an introduction to Phillip Moscato Jr., who—I was told by a member of his family—knew something about the Hoffa case. The family member would only say that a New Jersey gangster with a long criminal history, named Vincent Ravo, was somehow involved in Hoffa's disposal which took place on a piece of land by "a miniature golf course," just off Route 3 which runs through the Meadowlands.

During my five years of interviews with young Moscato from 2014 to 2019—following seven years of interviews with his father—Moscato Jr. told me that Ravo, a once-close friend of Moscato, Sr., had taken him to a specific location. At this place, Ravo, who moored his boat there, allegedly pointed to a spot in a parking lot, which Ravo described to young Moscato as "sacred ground."

For reasons unknown, Ravo never mentioned Hoffa's name.

PART FOURTEEN: HOFFA REDUX II

From the outset, Moscato Jr. made it clear to me that he was looking for a deal with a production company or a media-news organization before disclosing the actual location—despite my constant admonition that he should not ask for a financial reward before "The Trophy," my code name for Hoffa's body, was found.

Adding to the mystery, Moscato Jr. told me that ten days before his father died, Moscato Sr. gave him critical details about Hoffa's murder and the location of his body, instructing young Moscato to "trust and work with Dan Moldea."

But other than saying that the elder Moscato confirmed that Sal Briguglio had killed Hoffa, young Moscato kept his cards close to his chest—even from me—about the details of what his father had told him before he died. And I simply could not figure out the connection between what Vinnie Ravo and Moscato Sr. had separately told Moscato Jr.

Thus, what young Moscato appeared to be suggesting was that—after the Provenzano crew discovered in 1975 that Steve Andretta had confessed to Ralph Picardo and that Picardo was cooperating with federal law-enforcement officials—Moscato Sr. was directed to move Hoffa's body from the dump and to relocate it, possibly with the help of Vinnie Ravo.

With the random minutiae provided to me by young Moscato, I was able to piece together information that led me to the actual location of "the sacred ground," which was somewhere at or near a parking lot at 200 Outwater Lane in Carlstadt, New Jersey, which was part of a golf club—that included a miniature golf course—owned by an attorney, Alfred Porro, who had represented both Vinnie Ravo and Phillip Moscato, Sr., among other underworld figures.

The golf club and its clubhouse had a different address from its adjacent parking lot: 56 Patterson Plank Road.

In May 1988, local police fished the murdered body of New Jersey mobster John DiGilio out of the Hackensack River, just a few yards offshore from the parking lot at 200 Outwater Lane. Missing for three weeks, DiGilio was a long-time associate of both Vinnie Ravo and Phillip Moscato, Sr.

Between 2017 and 2018, Moscato Jr. and I were still at odds over his relentless attempts to profit before Hoffa's body was found and identified. Thus, because I felt that I was in danger of losing Moscato as a source, I decided to buy some insurance.

Without fanfare, I posted an item on my Twitter page, which was nothing more than an old ad for the sports site: "Lawrence Taylor's Golf Center and Marina," noting the Patterson Plank Road address.

Also, I added the following statement to my photograph of the ad: "LT, Renaissance Man: Football, golf, boating, . . . and mob guys, like Vincent Ravo, aka Vinnie Ravo."[329] I posted this tweet on July 30, 2018, the 43rd anniversary of Hoffa's murder. Also, a few days earlier, I had published an online profile of Ravo.[330]

Moscato Jr. was furious with me after I sent him aerial photographs of the Outwater Lane and Patterson Plank Road locations in Carlstadt. Even though I did not print or broadcast any of this, my reporter-source relationship with young Moscato continued to deteriorate, as he resumed his efforts to search for deals which would pay him before he proved anything.

A contentious meeting with Robert De Niro

Since 2008, when Robert De Niro publicly announced his intention to produce a major motion picture based on the life and death of Jimmy Hoffa, attempts were made by mutual friends—specifically former CIA case officer Jack Platt and the respected crime reporter and author, Gus Russo, among others—to arrange a meeting between De Niro and me. Because De Niro was so incredibly busy, I didn't think the meeting would ever happen.

Then, on December 2, 2014, Russo called, telling me that De Niro would be his last-minute guest that night at a twice-a-year dinner that I hosted since 1989 for published authors at The Old Europe restaurant in the Glover Park section of Washington, D.C.

I didn't tell anyone about our special visitor.

Eighty unsuspecting authors attended the dinner that evening where they were shocked to see De Niro, who couldn't have been friendlier, nicer, or a better sport. He posed for hundreds of photographs and treated all who approached him with respect.

Then, as the crowd thinned out, Russo invited De Niro and me to a table in a corner of the restaurant where the three of us could talk privately. A photograph was taken of the meeting.

Still proud of his purchase of the rights to *I Heard You Paint Houses* six years earlier, De Niro—who had hired Oscar-winner Steven Zaillian to write the screenplay for his movie, *The Irishman*—told Gus and me: "This is the book. This is the real story about the murder of Jimmy Hoffa."

Taken aback, I replied: "With all due respect, you don't know what you're talking about. . . . Bob, you're being conned if you believe that."

"I'm not getting conned," he replied.

The conversation deteriorated from there. De Niro and I did not part as friends.

PART FOURTEEN: HOFFA REDUX II

Eric Shawn of Fox News and Frank Sheeran

Over the years, Eric Shawn of Fox News, to his great credit in light of our differing views about the Hoffa murder, continued to ask me to appear on camera during his filmed reports about Hoffa, essentially allowing me to play the role as the principal naysayer of his "Sheeran-did-it" theory.

Actually, along with author Charles Brandt, Shawn had remained at the epicenter of the Hoffa investigation, keeping the case alive since 2004 with his unwavering support of Brandt's book and the upcoming movie he unofficially helped to develop, *The Irishman*.

Without Eric Shawn, Charles Brandt's book would have received very little attention, and the movie, *The Irishman*, probably never would have been made.

On November 27, 2018, Shawn broadcast a hour-long special on Fox Nation, a new subscription streaming service of the Fox News empire: *Riddle: The Search for Jimmy Hoffa*, his latest installment about the Hoffa murder case during which he continued to embrace the badly flawed theory that Frank Sheeran had murdered Jimmy Hoffa.

Once again, Shawn, showing his objectivity and sense of fairness, featured my reporting on his program, even though it directly contradicted his own work.[331]

On December 16, Shawn, as part of the promotion of his special report, interviewed me on his Sunday afternoon news program on Fox. In addition to my criticism of his claim that Sheeran killed Hoffa, Shawn also permitted me to give him some good-natured grief, because he had repeatedly reported that Steve Andretta was dead, as Frank Sheeran had claimed in his 2004 book.

In fact, Andretta was alive and well and still living in New Jersey.

On February 3, 2019, Shawn again asked me to appear on his program, this time to discuss the recent death of Tom Andretta, Steve Andretta's younger brother and an alleged co-conspirator in the Hoffa case.

Between my December and February appearances on Fox News with Shawn, I suggested to Phillip Moscato, Jr., that—with the Scorsese-De Niro false-fact-filled film fantasy, *The Irishman*, slated for a fall release—we might want to consider working with Shawn, whom I considered to be a friend.

Actually, whether I liked it or not, Fox News was the only game in town. ABC, CBS, NBC, CNN, and MSNBC, along with the other cable networks, did not appear to be doing anything in conjunction with the movie's release.

However, Moscato still refused to relent on his "no money, no show" demand which continued to cause considerable friction between us. Consequently, Moscato and I went for several months with no communications between us.

Working with Fox for free

On July 16, 2019—two days after I had announced on my blog that I had new information about the Hoffa caper—Eric Shawn called and left a message on my answering machine, saying that he and his bosses at Fox wanted to offer me a paid-consulting agreement to work with them on their Hoffa investigation. Before calling Shawn back, I decided to speak first with Moscato Jr. who told me that he was working with a Florida production company. He added that the producers wanted me to write his book.

I repeated, as I had for the past several years, that without Hoffa's body confirmed, there was no book. However, I volunteered to do a nine-hour-recorded interview with Moscato, which I personally paid to have transcribed. Then, I used it as the basis for a book proposal I wrote for Moscato, gratis, about his life as the son of a Mafia soldier. I gave it to Moscato for any purpose he chose—even if I was not the author—as long as he kept me "in the loop."

During my subsequent conversation with Eric Shawn, he revealed that he and Moscato had met through the producers with the Florida production company, adding that he had interviewed him during the past few weeks.

That news really shocked me. Still, Shawn insisted that we should all work together, repeating the offer from Fox News to hire me as a consultant.

Because Shawn had developed his own reporter-source relationship with Moscato, I had no grounds to complain to Shawn for using Moscato Jr. as a source and taking credit for what he told him. But I did feel somewhat betrayed by Moscato with whom I had invested five years of my time.

Regardless, I liked and respected both Moscato and Shawn, and I wanted to work with both of them. But I offered to do so for free, rejecting Fox News's proposed paid-consulting arrangement. I wanted to remain independent so that I could speak to and write for any media organization in the aftermath of the release of *The Irishman*.

Our handshake agreement made, Shawn and I, with the help of Moscato, were determined to solve Act Three of the Hoffa case: The disposal of his body.

PART FOURTEEN: HOFFA REDUX II

Moscato accompanied Shawn and me to the parking lot at 200 Outwater Lane in Carlstadt, New Jersey, where Vinnie Ravo supposedly showed him the location of Hoffa's burial site—without ever mentioning Hoffa's name. Independent of me, Shawn had already learned the address of the parking lot, presumably through his interviews with Moscato Jr.

However, Moscato still refused to tell us what his father specifically said just before his death about the location of Hoffa's body, something inexplicably consistent with what Ravo had told Moscato Jr.

Significantly, Moscato did say that his father declared with no equivocation that Salvatore Briguglio was Hoffa's killer.

Meantime, Moscato refused to pledge his full cooperation with the law-enforcement community. He balked at executing a sworn statement about what he knew. And he refused to take a polygraph test.

Consequently, in the midst of all this, I started to distance myself from Moscato while Shawn embraced him. And, to be clear, I was not a party to whatever deal they made with Fox News and each other.

In short, I had simply lost confidence in Moscato's story—unless we could prove that Hoffa's body had been moved from his father's landfill.

The Irishman

What was even more unexpected was that Eric Shawn was reconsidering his then eighteen-year position that Sheeran had killed Hoffa. In fact, Shawn was preparing to do a very public about-face, saying that Sal Briguglio, not Frank Sheeran, had killed Hoffa, based, in part, on what Moscato Sr., had told Moscato Jr.

Also leading to his amazing turnabout, Shawn had heard of and asked me about an internal Department of Justice memo dated November 26, 1976, from federal prosecutor Robert C. Stewart to DOJ official Kurt W. Muellenberg which had named Briguglio as Hoffa's killer. I had a copy of this document and was more than happy to share it with Shawn, which he used to reinforce his new "Sheeran-didn't-do-it" position.[332]

Shawn's brave adjustment was strengthened by the pending releases of a slew of accompanying investigative articles that disputed the facts in *The Irishman*.

The most influential of these stories were published by Larry Henry for The Mob Museum, Bill Tonelli in *Slate*, Nick Vadala in the *Philadelphia Inquirer*, Scott Burnstein in the *Gangster Report*, George Anastasia of the *Philly Voice*, Vince Wade in the *Daily Beast*, Julie Miller of *Vanity Fair*, John Wisely and Julie Hinds of the *Detroit Free Press*, Allan Lengel of *Deadline Detroit*, Michael Wilson of the *New York Times*, Mark Dawidziak of the

Cleveland Plain Dealer, Amanda Darrach of the *Columbia Journalism Review,* Leo Sisti of *L'Espresso,* and Manuel Roig-Franzia in the *Washington Post.*

Arguably, the biggest negative impact on the false facts and fabrications in *The Irishman* came from Harvard law professor Jack Goldsmith, the author of the newly released, *In Hoffa's Shadow,* the story of Goldsmith's relationship with his stepfather, Chuck O'Brien. Along with his book, Goldsmith published devastating essays about the motion picture's inaccuracies and examples of sheer irresponsibility in the *New York Review of Books, Lawfare,* and as an op-ed in the *New York Times.*

In his book, Goldsmith noted one of my own turnabouts, writing:

> The dean of Hoffa journalists, Dan Moldea, has been gripped by the disappearance since literally the day after it occurred, when he was twenty-five years old. Like so many longtime observers, he no longer believes, as he claimed in his 1978 book *The Hoffa Wars,* that Chuckie was involved in the disappearance. Moldea interviewed many of the leading suspects and players in the case, including Sal Briguglio, the Andretta brothers, and Brother Moscato, a Provenzano protégé. Moldea knew more details about the Hoffa case than anyone I met outside the government, has offered many theories of the disappearance over the years, and is always close by with analysis when a new rumor or ostensible piece of evidence pops up. "Even though the FBI hasn't located Hoffa's body," Moldea told me in August 2018, at the start of his forty-fourth year on the case, "I still hope to find it."[333]

Seeing his film under siege, Martin Scorsese cynically but wisely embraced what I called "an artistic-license dodge," simply claiming that his people had bought the rights to *I Heard You Paint Houses* and then turned its major character, Frank Sheeran, into their own character whom they essentially recreated.

However, Robert De Niro continued to defend the film as the true and accurate version of what really happened to Jimmy Hoffa.

Simultaneously, news about my warning to De Niro in December 2014 that he was "being conned" by Sheeran's story, generated much attention, too. And De Niro was specifically asked about our meeting:

> During a recent interview with IndieWire Executive Editor Eric Kohn, De Niro addressed Moldea's accusation and did not seem phased by claims *The Irishman* depicts an untrue story.

PART FOURTEEN: HOFFA REDUX II

"Dan is a well-respected writer. I met him in D.C. for a writers thing where they get together every year. He said that we were getting conned. I wasn't getting conned," De Niro said. "I have no problem with people disagreeing. He of course is an authority on Hoffa and everything else. As Marty says, we're not saying we're telling the actual story, we're telling our story. I believed it."

De Niro continued, "I know one thing — I know all the stuff that Frank said, the descriptions of the places he was at, the way he talked, that's all real. The way he describes what happened to Hoffa is a very plausible thing to me. I'd love to hear what actually happened to him. But this made a lot of sense to me."[334]

After momentarily suspending all disbelief and seeing *The Irishman*, I issued a statement, saying, "It is a stunning work of filmmaking by Martin Scorsese—although it appears to be his homage to Oliver Stone's own film fantasy, *JFK*, with its great cinema but bad history."

160. "This is where my dad buried Jimmy Hoffa"

Frank Cappola, son of Paul Cappola, Moscato's partner at PJP
On February 3, 2019, I received a call from a Florida businessman, Paul Cappola, Jr., the youngest son of the late Paul Cappola, Sr., the partner of Phillip Moscato, Sr., at Brother Moscato's Dump in Jersey City, aka the PJP Landfill. Young Cappola told me that he believed that his older brother, Frank Cappola, might have specific information about the location of Jimmy Hoffa's remains at the dump.

I asked for an introduction to Frank Cappola but, for whatever reason, I did not receive it at that time. Several months later, on September 6, 2019, I contacted Cappola Jr., and appealed to him to arrange an introduction for me to his brother.

Through my research since the previous February, I learned that Frank Cappola, who had a criminal record, worked for many years as a top lieutenant for New Jersey gangster Vincent Ravo—the same

Vinnie Ravo who had supposedly shown Phillip Moscato, Jr., the location of Hoffa's body, aka "sacred ground," buried in a parking lot at 200 Outwater Lane in Carlstadt.

In the small-world category, the owner of the property had tasked Ravo years earlier to arrange for a major clean up and overhaul of that same parking lot. And the person to whom Ravo gave this assignment was Frank Cappola.

Under the circumstances, I just had to talk to this guy. There was no stopping me.

On September 7, 2019, I received a call from Frank Cappola. During this interview, he told me that Jimmy Hoffa was, indeed, buried at the PJP Landfill.

And he added that he knew the exact location of Hoffa's unmarked grave.

Cappola had never even heard the theory that Hoffa was moved from the dump and taken to the parking lot in Carlstadt.

After that first conversation, we had six additional interviews, all by phone.

On September 26, Fox News, for reasons unknown, balked at bringing Cappola onto our team, refusing to pay for his airfare from Florida to New Jersey after initially agreeing to do so several days earlier. Cappola had planned to fly to Newark the following day to meet with me, but he had no ticket. And he was so angry about it that he threatened to cancel his trip.

After Fox News dropped the ball, I recovered it and personally paid for Cappola's round-trip ticket, which caused considerable tension among Fox News, Cappola, and me—with Eric Shawn insisting that he was caught in the middle.

I was not under contract with Fox, so, inasmuch as I found Cappola and paid for his expenses, I told Shawn to tell his bosses, with respect, that Frank Cappola was now my source, exclusively.

Cappola arrived in New Jersey on Friday, September 27, the same day as *The Irishman* premiered at the New York Film Festival.

During our dinner the following night, September 28, Cappola—who felt disrespected by Fox News and refused to speak with Shawn—told me that he was going to drive to PJP the following day.

I replied, smiling, "Motherfucker, you are taking me with you."

On Sunday morning, September 29, Cappola picked me up at my hotel in Secaucus, and we drove to the remnants of the former PJP Landfill in Jersey City, aka "Brother Moscato's Dump."

PART FOURTEEN: HOFFA REDUX II

When we arrived, Cappola gave me a tour of the area which he had not visited in nearly twenty years. But his memories seemed to sharpen just by being there, and he went on to repeat what he had told me during our numerous phone interviews over the past three weeks—with few, if any, changes to or variations on his original story.

The tour culminated with his identification of the exact spot where, according to Cappola, Hoffa was buried in the unmarked grave dug by his father, Paul Cappola, Sr.

"This is it," Cappola told me. "This is where my dad buried Jimmy Hoffa."

The site was the approximate size of a little-league baseball diamond, 60-feet-times-four.

I filmed the entire tour and interviewed Cappola on videotape that same afternoon.

—⁂—

Since Hoffa disappeared on July 30, 1975, I had been involved in no fewer than a half-dozen previous searches—all of which wound up as intriguing adventures but cruel disappointments.

But, after closely scrutinizing Cappola's story, his version of events was something very special and unique. In fact, during my many years of investigating Hoffa's fate since 1975, Cappola's information provided me with the best lead I had ever seen or heard with regard to a possible site of the unmarked grave of the ex-Teamsters boss.

On the basis of the information I collected from the tour and the recorded interview, I drafted a proposed sworn declaration for Cappola to sign, which he corrected, amended, and executed under the penalty of perjury on October 7.

Meantime, I asked Cappola—as a favor to me and out of respect for a friend and colleague—to agree to an interview with Eric Shawn on October 11, adding that I would be sitting at the table with them and protecting his information. Cappola agreed and the interview went well.

On or about November 21, 2019—three days after Shawn and I revealed our information about Moscato Jr., on Shawn's next installment about Hoffa for Fox Nation—I published my article about Cappola's breathtaking revelations at *FoxNews.com*. Shawn broadcast portions of his brief interview with Cappola as part of his Sunday, December 1, prime-time special on Fox News.

In my article about Cappola and his father, I wrote:

"This is it," Frank Cappola said to me in a hushed voice on a sunny Sunday afternoon, September 29, as he compared the foreboding area where we were standing with aerial photographs of this same scene. "This is where my dad buried Jimmy Hoffa." . . .

The location—widely thought to be operated by mobsters—was a familiar one to the FBI and those who had studied the Hoffa-murder case: "Brother Moscato's Dump" in Jersey City, New Jersey—once a sprawling . . . toxic-waste site bordered by the Hackensack River and directly beneath the Pulaski Skyway which stretched between Jersey City and Newark. The dumpsite was targeted for cleanup by the EPA during the late 1970s and 1980s. Most of the land was now a public park and a wildlife refuge.

"Brother Moscato's Dump" was also known as the PJP Landfill: "P" for Phillip "Brother" Moscato; "J" for local political figure John Hanley; and "P" for Paul Cappola, Frank Cappola's father. Moscato, according to federal and state law-enforcement officials, was a reputed soldier in the Vito Genovese crime family. He worked under Anthony Provenzano of New Jersey, one of two mobsters Hoffa's expected to meet on the day he disappeared. Moscato died in 2014.

The late Paul Cappola was a respected businessman who owned a waste-management company in Jersey City and was Moscato's partner at the PJP Landfill. Cappola was certainly connected to the underworld but, unlike Brother Moscato, was not a "made" member of the Mafia. Still, like Moscato, he was obedient to the powers that controlled the waste-management industry in New Jersey and New York during the 1970s.

The alleged specific location of Jimmy Hoffa's remains

Frank Cappola, who was seventeen and working part-time at the dump when Hoffa disappeared during the summer of 1975, recalled: "While I was talking to my dad, a black limousine drove onto our lot in the mud. My dad said to Moscato, something like, 'They're here.'

"Moscato went to the limousine and spoke with its occupants, none of whom were known to me. During their conversation, Moscato turned and pointed to a specific area in the northeast section of the landfill. At the time, I didn't know why.

"After Moscato made this hand gesture, my father threw his hands up in the air and exclaimed, 'Now, the whole fucking world will know!' I didn't know what my dad was talking about then.

"When the limousine left, Moscato told my father that he had to be somewhere that night, adding, 'You have to handle it, Paul.' They walked into the PJP office for a closed-door meeting. At that time, I didn't know what they discussed.

"Shortly before I left work that day, I saw that a large hole had been dug with an excavator. At the time, I had no idea why."

In 1989, Frank Cappola was working on a waste site adjacent to the long-defunct PJP Landfill. During a visit from his father, the two men walked onto what was once PJP. When they came to the location of the hole Frank saw that night in 1975, Paul Cappola told his son, "This is where Jimmy Hoffa is buried."

Frank recalled, "This was the first time that my dad admitted that Hoffa was buried at PJP although he had referred to Hoffa in unspecific terms in our previous conversations."

In or about March 2008, while Paul Cappola was dying, he provided his son with the specific details about what had happened to Hoffa's body, adding that he wanted his son "to help Hoffa return home to his family."

Cappola's sworn statement

In his affidavit, executed at my request, Frank Cappola listed what his father told him:

> a. A person or persons he did not name instructed my father and Mr. Moscato to bury Jimmy Hoffa's body. My father led me to believe that they were the people in the limousine with whom Mr. Moscato met that muddy day during the summer of 1975.
>
> b. Mr. Moscato told my dad that he had something to do that night and asked my father to take care of it.
>
> c. Mr. Moscato had a burial location for Hoffa on the landfill site. While he was talking to the people in the limousine, both my father and I witnessed him pointing in the direction of this location.

d. My father was upset with Mr. Moscato for pointing to that area at the landfill, because the dump was constantly under police scrutiny, and Mr. Moscato's gesture could have given away the location of Hoffa's body.

e. After Mr. Moscato left PJP, my father, who didn't trust anybody, decided to dig a second hole with a company excavator and to place Hoffa at that location—unknown to Mr. Moscato. My dad never told him.

f. Unidentified people brought Hoffa's dead body to PJP. Because of the awkward position of Hoffa's corpse after they removed him from whatever container he was in before, they were unable to place him, feet first, in a 55-gallon steel drum retrieved at PJP. So, they put him in the drum headfirst. Then, they sealed the container. My father saw but never handled Hoffa's dead body.

g. After those people left, my father likely placed the steel drum containing Hoffa's body on a front loader. Then, he positioned the drum at the bottom of the large hole my father dug, which was eight-to-fifteen feet deep.

h. I will reveal the exact location of that hole to law enforcement, along with two additional and provable details about that site.

i. My father then placed as many as fifteen to thirty chemical drums in the hole where Hoffa's body was encased, along with chunks of brick and dirt.

j. Notably, as a common practice, the chemical drums would be marked. The steel drum that contained Hoffa's body was likely not marked.

k. Then, my father covered the grave with a bulldozer, which completed his task. The site was his secret.

l. My father also placed something detectable just under the surface of the gravesite, which I am willing to disclose to law enforcement.

PART FOURTEEN: HOFFA REDUX II

Along with executing his sworn statement, Cappola told me that he was prepared to cooperate fully with the law-enforcement community, and he was also willing to take a polygraph test.

According to a statement from the FBI's field office in Detroit about the information Eric Shawn and I had developed about Phillip Moscato, Jr., and Frank Cappola:

> Over the years, our office has followed all credible leads we received from the public. We are aware of the recent reports of two individuals, who claim to have knowledge about the whereabouts of Mr. Hoffa. Just as we would with anyone who purports to have information relevant to this—or any—ongoing investigation, the FBI welcomes the opportunity to speak to those individuals.[335]

161. "Frank, are you okay?"

In early January 2020, Frank Cappola was in New Jersey, visiting his longtime girlfriend, Joy DiBiaso, a legal assistant for a law firm in New York City. Joy, whom I had met during my first visit with Cappola, adored him and was very protective of him. Tough-guy Frank and sweet Joy, both in their early sixties, looked like a couple of carefree school kids when they were together. They were in love.

With Joy's upcoming retirement, she and Cappola were making plans to live together in Florida.

Before he returned to his home from this trip, I called and invited Cappola and Joy to dinner on Friday, January 10. I took the train to Secaucus and checked into a hotel which was near a sushi buffet that Frank and Joy liked, a place we had been to before.

I was first to arrive at the restaurant. While I was in the lobby, Frank slowly walked through the front door with a breathing tube in his nostrils and a small tank of oxygen slung over his shoulder. Joy was outside parking the car. I knew that Frank was still ailing after a serious bout with pneumonia the previous year.

Shortly after the maître 'd seated us, Frank became very weak—so much so that he couldn't even get up to go to the buffet table. I knew that he enjoyed oysters on the half shell and shrimp cocktail. So, while he rested, I went to the seafood bar and fixed him a small plate of food. He ate three of the six oysters and three of the six shrimp before pushing his plate away.

When I looked at him, he had a glassy gaze. I reached across the table and patted him on the shoulder, asking, "Frank, are you okay?" Moments later, Cappola, breathing irregularly, went headfirst into the table, clearly suffering from some sort of a respiratory event.

Joy immediately sprang out of her chair and adjusted his breathing equipment so that he could get more oxygen.

"Jesus, Frank," I exclaimed, "let me call an ambulance!" Joy, almost on the verge of tears, agreed.

Cappola shook his head, saying that he just needed to get to Joy's home and go to bed. He added that he was extremely tired.

We had only spent about fifteen minutes together.

Joy ran out to get the car. While Cappola and I sat together in the lobby, I snapped a photograph of him, looking almost peaceful.

I helped Cappola to Joy's car, repeating that we should go to the hospital. But he refused again, saying that he just needed to get some sleep.

That was the last time I saw Frank.

In the days that followed, Joy took him to a local hospital which was not equipped to deal with Cappola's condition. Consequently, medical personnel moved him to the Hackensack University Medical Center where he was fitted with a ventilator and placed in a drug-induced coma.

Although he briefly opened his eyes from time to time, he never fully regained consciousness, and he never spoke another word.

On March 16, 2020, Frank Cappola died before the FBI arranged for the polygraph test he had offered to take, a missed opportunity.

I blogged out the news, adding that if Frank was right, then I was now probably the only person in the world—with one possible exception—who knew where Hoffa was buried.

I immediately found a safe place for the videotapes of my September 29, 2019, "tour" with Cappola at the PJP Landfill, aka "Brother Moscato's Dump," as well as for the films of our interviews.

Determined to discover whether Frank was right or wrong, I mapped out a strategy with trusted friends which we hoped to execute immediately. However, when the worldwide pandemic struck with its full force shortly after Frank's death, everything was frozen and put on hold.

As of this writing, we are waiting for an opportunity to strike.

PART FOURTEEN: HOFFA REDUX II

I started investigating Jimmy Hoffa and the Teamsters while I was a graduate student at Kent State, eight months before Hoffa disappeared on July 30, 1975. And I have been involved in the investigation of his killing since Day One.

After all of these years, I am still Ahab, and the Hoffa murder case is still my white whale.[336]

EPILOGUE:
So far . . .

After the Kent State shootings in 1970, I made a youthful pledge in the midst of the unfolding history to become an independent man and to live "a committed life." Staying faithful to that promise—after some early twists and turns in the road—I succeeded at achieving those two goals. To be sure, though, I am allowed to be a judge of my own independence and my own history of commitments.

But I had also vowed to become a "society-serving" person, which was a little more ambitious and a lot more difficult to attain. And, in the end, society has the right to determine how well I have served it. But I do have my own opinion about this, too.

Frankly, although I did some good work and helped a lot of people along the way, I admittedly have fallen short of that objective—certainly not for lack of intent but rather for an inability to execute. In short, I couldn't stay out of trouble and was usually ill-prepared to deal with the inevitable fallout brought about by the problems caused by my stubborn determination to remain independent.

To this day, I still don't know how I survived some of the controversies and situations in which I became embroiled. But I am very grateful that I somehow managed to survive, even though I became more and more isolated with each new battle in which I was forced to fight for my independence.

Consequently, my ambition to become "society serving" was too often eclipsed by my basic need for self-survival—which, by definition, made me the "self-serving" person I had always dreaded.

Sad but true, even though I succeeded at becoming an independent man, I failed to become the "society-serving" person I really wanted to be.

But I am going to keep trying during the time I have left—with the recognition that the world needs more journalists who remain impartial and fewer guerrilla writers who take sides.

Endnotes

Part One

1 On February 12, 2016, I ran into Dick Gregory in a parking lot behind our dry cleaners in Washington, D.C., saying: "Excuse me, sir. I bet you get told all the time how much you look like Dick Gregory." He replied with some impatience, "That's because I AM Dick Gregory."

Extending my hand, I continued, "I gotta tell you, sir, you changed my life with a speech you gave at the University of Akron after the Kent State shootings."

Shaking my hand, he responded, "I hear that a lot from white people."

After we talked for a few minutes about some mutual friends and our specific interests, he asked me to have coffee with him.

Alternatively, I invited him to The Clubhouse, our local hangout for journalists and investigators, where Jeff Stein of *Newsweek* and I spent an interesting couple of hours with this funny and very intelligent, but extremely intense man who was still a crusader. At 80-plus, he was still looking good and standing tall.

After Gregory died on August 19, 2017, Stein published a story for *Newsweek* on August 21 about our fascinating afternoon with this great man.

2 No byline, *Akron Beacon Journal*, "Quick Truck Driver Averts Serious Blast," July 9, 1971.

3 Editorial, *Buchtelite*, "*Buchtelite* Endorses Botzum," May 16, 1972.

4 Brian Williams, *Buchtelite*, "Power Politics Invade ASG," November 21, 1972.

5 No byline, *Buchtelite*, "Meeting with Dean Leads to Sit-in," January 12, 1973.

6 Bliss had been a member of the board of trustees at the University of Akron during my tenure as student body president and bitterly remembered my battles with the board, especially the one over the proposed creation of the Black Cultural Center, which culminated when I led fifty long-haired, blue-jeans-clad students into the room where the trustees were holding their monthly meeting in April 1973. A photograph taken at the scene showed Bliss smoking a cigarette and looking more than a little agitated by the disturbance. One of the trustees later told me that Bliss had angrily broken a glass after we left.

7 No byline, *Cleveland Plain Dealer*, "Figetakis hits indictment of 8," April 9, 1974.

8 The co-counsel for the Kent 25 was Bill Whitaker who had represented me after my arrest in the midst of a protest while I was student body president at the University of Akron.

9 Mickey Porter, *Akron Beacon Journal*, "Mickey Porter," April 12, 1974.

10 Editorial, *Akron Beacon Journal*, "For the Ohio House: 39th District," May 2, 1974.

11 Letter from Nancy Nolte to Moldea, July 10, 1974.

12 Department of the Army, Award of the Silver Star to Robert N. Davis, February 7, 1970.

13 Just around the corner from Jim Switzer's home on Elmore Avenue is 855 Ardmore Avenue, the birthplace of Alcoholics Anonymous, which is now a National Historical Landmark. Also, living at the end of the block on Elmore was the widely renowned American sculptor and master craftsman, Don Drumm.

14 Editorial, *Akron Beacon Journal*, "Fighting the good fight," October 13, 1975.

15 Dan E. Moldea, *The Hoffa Wars: The Rise and Fall of Jimmy Hoffa* (Shapolsky Publishers, 1992), pp. xiii-xvi, an introduction by Jonathan Kwitny.

Part Two

16 On October 8, 1975, an FBI teletype out of Cleveland, addressed to the Detroit field office—which I obtained through the Freedom of Information Act—reported: "Moldea . . . did extensive research and developed valuable sources close to the Teamsters Union and plans to put this info into book form.

"Moldea provided [an FBI special agent] with a 15 page written theory on the disappearance of Jimmy Hoffa. This theory was forwarded to the Detroit office for evaluation prior to initiating further investigation. In this theory, Moldea appears to be quite knowledgeable of local Teamster politics and individuals associated with the disappearance of Hoffa. Specifically, Moldea advances the theory that Hoffa's disappearance and other incidents of Teamster related violence have been the work of Rolland McMaster and other former Teamster international organizers who worked for McMaster. . . . In his theory, Moldea sets forth sufficient factual info, which indicates he has good sources close to McMaster and knowledgeable of his union activities."

17 Lester Velie's 1977 book, *Desperate Bargain: Why Jimmy Hoffa Had to Die*, discussed Jo Thomas's relationship with O'Brien, stating:

> On the third night after Hoffa's disappearance, Chuckie O'Brien showed up, unannounced, at the home of *Detroit Free Press* reporter Jo Thomas.
>
> "Jo is the kind of a girl who takes in strays," a fellow reporter said of her. "She had dated Chuckie several times before he remarried, and he seemed to fascinate her."
>
> This time, however, Jo Thomas found little to be fascinated about. She knew O'Brien was wanted for questioning in the Hoffa disappearance. She was scared.
>
> Overcoming her fears, Jo let Chuckie in . . . [page 22]

In the 1981 movie, *Absence of Malice*, an aggressive woman reporter, portrayed by Sally Field, has a relationship with the son of a local gangster, played by Paul Newman, during her investigation of the disappearance of a powerful labor leader.

The screenplay was written by Kurt Luedtke, the former executive editor of the *Detroit Free Press* and Jo Thomas's ex-boss. The general similarities between fact and Luedtke's fiction are striking.

By the time of the film's release, Jo Thomas had left the *Detroit Free Press* and become a staff reporter for the *New York Times*.

18 Drinkhall forthrightly addressed this alleged $6,000 payment in an October 1973 article he published in *Overdrive*, "Eck Miller President Finally Admits Knowledge of Teamsters Bugging."

Drinkhall wrote that Jeffries had called and told him, "We had just had a call [the day before Drinkhall's arrival in Owensboro] from a source our law firm won't even reveal to me that there was going to be some kind of stranger in town ... and we were in fact not even supposed to have any interviews with anybody."

Drinkhall continued that ten minutes after he spoke with Jeffries, he received a call from Jeffries' wife: "Mrs. Jeffries said that their source had told them that the Sunday night before the *Overdrive* reporter arrived, the Teamsters had received $6,000 cash at their Holiday Inn headquarters in Owensboro, and that this money was to be used to pay off the 'stranger' Paul Jeffries mentioned. Frankly, *Overdrive* had nothing to say to this increasingly-ridiculous story except to say goodbye.... If people like Paul Jeffries think they can fool owner-operators into thinking we 'sold out' to the Teamsters Union, or that we are influenced by anyone there, he is a fool himself...."

19 Deposition of Michael Louis Boano, *United States Steel Division Corporation v. Fraternal Association of Steel Haulers, a.k.a. Fraternal Association of Special Haulers*, United States District Court, Western District of Pennsylvania, Civil Action No. 70-418, April 30, 1971, page 49.

20 Mike Hoyt later became the executive editor of the *Columbia Journalism Review*.

21 In 1946, Paul Brown became the head coach for the Cleveland Browns of the new All-American Conference, which merged with the National Football League in 1950. Later, in 1968, Brown founded, owned, and coached the Cincinnati Bengals.

22 Michael MacCambridge (editor), *ESPN College Football Encyclopedia: The Complete History of the Game* (Bristol, Connecticut: ESPN Publishing, 2005), pp. 122-125.

23 Letter from Daniel F. Reeves to Emil Moldea, December 5, 1947.

Part Three

24 Three fascinating books that advanced the state of evidence were Pulitzer Prize-winner Ed Reid's 1969 book, *The Grim Reapers: The Anatomy of Organized Crime in America*; Los Angeles television producer Peter Noyes's 1973 book, *Legacy of Doubt*; and Berkeley professor Peter Dale Scott's 1977 book, *Crime and Cover-Up: The CIA, the Mafia, and the Dallas-Watergate Connection*. The books by Noyes and Scott were released only in paperback editions; thus, they did not receive as much attention as they should have.

In Reid's book, the author stated that, in 1962, New Orleans Mafia boss Carlos Marcello had blurted out that he was planning to kill President Kennedy in front of three associates.

The principal target of Noyes's book was Jim Braden, a mystery man who was picked up by local law-enforcement officials in Dealey Plaza immediately after the shooting. Braden, whom I later interviewed for my book, *The Hoffa Wars*, had alleged ties to Hoffa, as well as to Marcello and other mobsters.

The subtitle of Scott's book pretty much described what he believed, but he did a good job of including some of mob material amidst his army of alleged conspirators.

Also, in the *Washington Post's* Outlook section on May 16, 1976, journalist George Crile III had written an article, "The Mafia, The CIA, and Castro." For this story, Crile had interviewed a successful Cuban-exile businessman, Jose Aleman, who revealed that Tampa Mafia boss Santo Trafficante had told him that President Kennedy was going to be murdered—over a year before the murder. Crile also referred to a recently released CIA document, stating that an American "gangster-gambler named Santos [who was in a Cuban prison in 1959] . . . was visited by an American gangster type named Ruby."

25 For details about the relationship between the mobbed-up Irv Davidson and Jack Anderson, a great man with a bad conflict of interest, see Mark Feldstein's excellent book, *Poisoning the Press: Richard Nixon, Jack Anderson, and the Rise of Washington's Scandal Culture* (New York: Farrar, Straus & Giroux, 2010).

26 On the nationally syndicated television program, *The Maury Povich Show*, Chuck O'Brien took and passed a polygraph test in January 1993, during which he claimed that he played no role in the disappearance of Jimmy Hoffa. The test was administered by Natale Laurendi who was the New York Police Department's top lie-detector expert until 1975 when he went into private practice. Laurendi died in 1999.

27 Notably, in its February 8, 1994, obituary for Richard M. Bissell, the former chief of CIA covert operations, the *New York Times* stated that Bissell was the agency's point man in the CIA-Mafia plots against Castro, adding that they had come "at [President] Kennedy's request after the Bay of Pigs." However, on March 23, the *Times* ran an Editors' Note, which included the following statement: "There exists no proof of involvement by President Kennedy" in any assassination plot against Castro, including those jointly engineered by the CIA and the Mafia.

And, as of this writing, there is still no proof—because, in my opinion, the Kennedys were never involved in these plots. To me, there is just no way in the world that the Kennedy brothers, especially Robert, would have worked in concert with the Mafia.

28 On February 8, 1981, I wrote a review of Ovid Demaris's new book—*The Last Mafioso: The Treacherous World of Jimmy Fratianno*, which appeared on the front page of the *Washington Post Book World*—I summed up my belief about this ongoing controversy:

> [W]hen Fratianno told Demaris that Operation MONGOOSE—which directly involved both President Kennedy and Attorney General Robert Kennedy—was really the code name for the CIA-Mafia plots to assassinate Fidel Castro that was damaging to historical truth and nothing less than irresponsible journalism when printed. Demaris should have known better. The Church Committee clearly stated that Operation MONGOOSE was designed in 1962 to infiltrate and organize the Cuban population to incite a counterrevolution; it had nothing to do with the CIA-Mafia plots against Castro—which began in 1960 under President Eisenhower.
>
> Neither John nor Robert Kennedy was aware of these plots. . . . Upon hearing this, Robert Kennedy was particularly

outraged by the underworld's involvement. But he was assured by the CIA that the plots had ceased with the failure of the Bay of Pigs invasion in April 1961—when in fact they were being escalated.

Incredibly enough, Demaris acknowledged this in his book. Yet, he leaves the reader with the clear impression—based on hearsay passed from Rosselli to Fratianno—that the Kennedys had not only authorized the plots but also approved of the mob's participation.

29 FBI-302 report from "A. Rosen" to "Mr. DeLoach," Subject: Ed Reid, Information concerning, May 15, 1969. Edward Becker is identified as Reid's source.

30 Curt Anderson, a reporter for the Associated Press, published a story on May 29, 2006, about his interview with Chuck O'Brien. Anderson wrote: "O'Brien said it was also known that Hoffa intended to testify before the special U.S. Senate investigative panel, known as the Church Committee, about the Mafia's involvement in the U.S.-backed plots to assassinate Cuban President Fidel Castro."

31 After my initial face-to-face interview with Sal Briguglio and his alleged coconspirators on October 25, 1976, I spoke with Briguglio three more times on the telephone. The dates of those interviews were October 13, 1977; January 11, 1978; and February 20, 1978. I also did a second interview with Stephen Andretta on February 12, 1978.

32 In the September 11, 1978, issue of *Newsweek*, the magazine's Periscope section threw a bouquet to *The Hoffa Wars*, saying: "A mystery man who reportedly took part in a CIA plot to assassinate Cuban Prime Minister Fidel Castro in 1961 is identified in a forthcoming *Playboy* excerpt from *The Hoffa Wars*. According to author Dan E. Moldea, the mystery figure was a Cuban counterrevolutionary named Antonio de Varona, a pre-Castro president of the Cuban Senate. Moldea's book says that 'the CIA passed a set of poison pills earmarked for Castro' to mobster John [Rosselli], and that the pills were then delivered to de Varona, but 'de Varona's attempts to murder Castro failed.' De Varona is said to be alive and in hiding; [Rosselli's] body turned up in an oil drum found floating off the Florida coast in 1976, a year after he told a U.S. Senate committee that he had participated in plots to kill Castro."

33 Herbert Mitgang, *New York Times*, "2 Hoffa Books Pose Publishing Problem," June 29, 1978.

34 Dan E. Moldea, *Playboy*, "The Hoffa Wars," November 1978.

35 No byline, *Village Voice*, "This Much Can Be Told: The Singer Is Innocent," September 4, 1978.

36 Bill Wallace, *Berkeley Barb*, "Reviews: The Hoffa Wars & The Teamsters," May 23, 1979; Mike Friedman, *Convoy*, "A Review: The Hoffa Wars," October 1978.

37 Ralph Orr, *Detroit Free Press*, "Hoffa slain by 2 N.J. men, author says," September 10, 1978.

38 No byline, *Detroit Free Press*, "FBI disputes tale of Hoffa slaying," September 11, 1978.

39 Earl Golz, *Dallas Morning News*, "Search for James Hoffa leads to two new books," October 22, 1978.

40 Michael Novak, *New York*, "The Highwaymen," November 6, 1978.

41 Ralph Orr, *Detroit Free Press*, "Moldea's book draws fire from several quarters," October 15, 1978.

42 When asked by committee investigators what his father thought about the JFK assassination, Hoffa replied that his father believed that "the CIA may have been involved in some way."

43 Dan La Botz, *In These Times*, "Teamster Davids plan to bury Goliath," November 1, 1978.

44 Jack Barbash, *Christian Science Monitor*, "Teamsters and the mob: slingshots at Goliath," December 13, 1978.

45 Notably, Vincent Canby, the *New York Times's* top film critic, published a column on March 18, 1978, about "movies that express some interest in the shape and direction of society
... It was because of this that last year I responded to *F.I.S.T.*, Norman Jewison's attempt to deal with big unionism. The movie romanticizes its characters and simplifies its subject, and nothing in it comes close to the

impact of almost any chapter in *The Hoffa Wars*, Dan Moldea's book about the International Brotherhood of Teamsters."

46 Sidney Lens, *Chicago Tribune*, "Review: The Hoffa Wars," October 8, 1978.

47 Robert Merry, *Wall Street Journal*, "Review: The Hoffa Wars," November 3, 1978. (Years later, Bob Merry, who became a highly respected editor for a variety of publications, joined my semi-annual Authors Dinner Group and became a friend.)

48 Kenneth Crowe, *Newsday*, "Review: The Hoffa Wars," October 8, 1978.

49 Murray Kempton, *New York Review of Books*, "The Pessimist," February 22, 1979.

50 Dan E. Moldea, *New York Review of Books*, "Letters: Hoffa and JFK," May 3, 1979. Also—on November 22, 1993, the 30th anniversary of President Kennedy's murder—the Associated Press published a timeline of the "key developments" since the murder. The only notation for 1978 read: "Dan Moldea publishes *The Hoffa Wars*, the first book to lay out the theory that Teamsters boss Jimmy Hoffa recruited mobsters Carlos Marcello and Santos Trafficante to arrange the assassination."

51 Jan Schaffer, *Philadelphia Inquirer*, "Sheeran: U.S. pushing him to talk of Hoffa," October 25, 1979.

52 Carl Oglesby and Jeff Goldberg, *Washington Post*, "Did the Mob Kill Kennedy?" February 25, 1979. Also, I published my own prediction on the HSCA's final report: Dan E. Moldea, *Montreal Star*, "Hoffa Linked to Kennedy Killing: Report Connects Oswald, Ruby with Organized Crime," April 11, 1979.

53 Our poker game ended in 2012 after a 34-year run. Along with me and those mentioned in the text of this book—Jeff Goldberg, Scott Malone, Phil Manuel, Carl Oglesby, Mark Perry, Mike Pilgrim, Carl Shoffler, Marc Smolonsky, Jeff Stein, Tom von Stein, and Danny Wexler—other players over the years included authors Dick Billings and Jim Hougan, Tom O'Neill of the *National Geographic*, CNN war correspondent Cal Perry (Mark's son), businessman David Wexler (Danny's brother), and ace political strategist David Williams.

54 No byline, AP via *New York Times*, "Assassination Panel's Final Report Backs Theory of Plot on Kennedy," June 3, 1979.

55 Jack Anderson was not so reticent about giving me some credit, writing in his column on January 3, 1979: "During the three months before the assassination, Jack Ruby made phone calls to shadowy figures who were close to Hoffa or Marcello. These included Hoffa associate . . . Robert Baker, also Marcello aide Nofio Pecora. Some of the people reached by Rudy had weak or changing explanations, investigators say. [The committee] got the tipoff from Dan Moldea's *The Hoffa Wars*."

While working with Anderson on this story about the committee's findings, I very respectfully chided him about his relationship with Irving Davidson who had worked for both Hoffa and Marcello.

On August 10, 1980, Anderson published a cover story in *Parade* magazine, "The Life and Trials of Carlos Marcello."

56 Aljean Harmetz, *New York Times*, "History Catches Up to Hoffa-Kennedy Book," June 11, 1979.

57 On June 10, 1979, the day before Harmetz's article, Martin Levin, a syndicated columnist for the Associated Press, wrote a review of *Blood Feud* in the *New York Times Book Review*. Levin criticized the book for its lack of documentation. In addition, he stated: "A book of nonfiction, such as Dan Moldea's *The Hoffa Wars*, which suggests how Hoffa's life may have ended, is fascinating because it bases conjecture on the freshest information."

Nevertheless, a truly excellent television mini-series, based on *Blood Feud*, was later released. Actor Robert Blake played a feisty Jimmy Hoffa; newcomer Kotter Smith portrayed Robert Kennedy; with Ernest Borgnine as J. Edgar Hoover; and José Ferrer as Hoffa's attorney Edward Bennett Williams.

58 Later, Brill and Windrem had a falling out. In the September/October 1990 issue of the *Columbia Journalism Review*, Windrem said of his former boss, "If faced with the choice of spending one minute with Steve Brill or spending all eternity with demons tearing my flesh, I might go with the demons." After leaving Brill, Windrem became a producer for NBC News.

59 "The living saint," John Lewis, the great civil-rights leader and future legendary U.S. congressman, was ACTION's Associate Director for Domestic Operations while I was at the agency. He asked me to write a few speeches

for him the year before he ran for Atlanta City Council. It is one of the great honors of my life to have served him.

One thing that John taught me was that there is a time to step on the gas, and there is a time to apply the brakes. I have never forgotten that.

Part Four

60 In late 1980, two conservative journalists—Arnaud de Borchgrave, a former senior editor for *Newsweek*, and Robert Moss, a columnist for the *London Daily Telegraph*—published a best-selling novel, *The Spike*. The authors portrayed a fictional conspiracy to overthrow the United States Government. At the center of the plot was the "Institute for Progressive Reform," a thinly disguised facsimile of the Institute for Policy Studies. The book's publisher, Stein & Day, appeared to promote *The Spike*, which was a novel, as a nonfiction book, causing IPS enormous grief.

But, on April 26, 1981, an even bigger blow came to IPS.

The New York Times Magazine inexplicably published a scathing article—in my opinion, a complete hatchet job—about IPS by Joshua Muravchik, a controversial neo-conservative writer.

Muravchik, who mercilessly attacked IPS, wrote: "With Ronald Reagan in the White House and Republicans controlling the Senate, the political climate in Washington is likely to become less hospitable to I.P.S. than at any time since its founding."

61 Kenneth C. Crowe, *Newsday*, "Williams Seen as Teamster Chief," May 7, 1981.

62 Cliff Kincaid, *Human Events*, "Left Launches New Line of Attack Against Reagan," June 13, 1981.

63 Jack Anderson, *Washington Post*, July 18, 1981.

64 Others testifying before the Senate subcommittee included author Barbara Tuchman; author E.L. Doctorow, the vice president of Poets Editors and Novelists (PEN); author John Brooks, the president of the Authors Guild, and Irwin Karp, its general council; Townsend Hopes and Alexander Hoffman, president and chairman, respectively, of the Association of American Publishers; Maxwell Lillienstein, general counsel of the American Booksellers Association; and William Jovanovich, the chairman of Harcourt Brace Jovanovich, a New York publishing house.

65 On the same day as Steve Love's story, Ned Whelan of *Cleveland* magazine and I sent a proposal to my agent, Philip Spitzer, for a book about the colorful life and brutal murder in 1977 of Irish gangster Danny Greene of Cleveland, who was killed in a sloppy car-bombing attack by rival Sicilian mobsters. The subsequent federal investigation and brilliant prosecution—by Strike Force prosecutors Abe Poretz and John Sopko—led to the downfall of the Cleveland Mafia.

We were never offered a legitimate bid for this book project and eventually dropped it.

In 2004, author Rick Porrello, the chief of police of a Cleveland suburb, published *To Kill the Irishman* (Next Hat Press), which was later adapted as a motion picture.

66 Dan E. Moldea, *The Nation*, "More Than Just Good Friends: Reagan and the Teamsters," June 11, 1983.

67 Dennis McEaneney, *Akron Beacon Journal*, "*Hunting of Cain*: 'God's eye view' of Milo case," July 31, 1983.

68 Jim Quinlan, *Chicago Sun-Times*, "Facts of the matter is Moldea's forte," August 7, 1983.

69 Jonathan Yardley, *Washington Post*, "Murder Dissected: A Well-Told Tale of Greed and Envy," July 27, 1983.

70 Actually, Korshak's name had already come up once before in connection with one of Reagan's top appointees. On December 12, 1980, Frank Sinatra hosted a party for his 65th birthday at his home in Rancho Mirage, California, near Palm Springs. The 200 guests included media-mogul Walter Annenberg and other members of Reagan's Kitchen Cabinet, as well as an array of Hollywood luminaries. Although Reagan and his wife could not attend, his attorney general-designate, William French Smith, did. *New York Times* columnist William Safire created a flap over Smith's attendance at the Sinatra party, writing: "[T]he involvement of the designee for attorney general in the rehabilitation of the reputation of a man obviously proud to be close to notorious hoodlums is the first deliberate affront to propriety of the Reagan Administration."

In response to Safire, Smith claimed that he was "totally unaware" of Sinatra's long association with underworld figures.

Washington Post columnist Maxine Cheshire revealed the presence of another prominent guest at the Sinatra party: Sidney Korshak, who had been described by reporter Seymour Hersh of the *New York Times* in 1976 as the link between the legitimate business world and organized crime. Like Smith, Korshak was a well-known attorney in Los Angeles. When Cheshire asked whether Smith had talked to Korshak, one of Smith's aides replied that if he did "it was purely accidental."

71 In late August 1984, I went to the Los Angeles County Hall of Records and then the county record's section in Riverside, California. Performing public-records searches on Reagan's real-estate properties, I received certified copies of everything on file.

On December 13, 1966, the month after Reagan's election as governor of California, Jules Stein and Taft Schreiber of MCA, along with Reagan's personal attorney, the future Attorney General William French Smith, sold 236 acres of Reagan's 290 acres in Malibu Canyon to Twentieth Century-Fox. The motion picture company paid $1.93 million for the property, or $8,178 an acre, although Fox's experts had appraised the land at only $944,000 or $4,000 an acre.

In July 1968, Reagan had used his remaining 54 acres in Malibu Canyon, which were said to be worth $165,000, as a down payment on a $346,950 property in Riverside. He bought the property from the Kaiser Aluminum Company. However, Kaiser insisted on a proviso in the contract that said that if Kaiser couldn't sell the 54 acres within a year, Reagan would have to buy them back.

By July 1969, Kaiser still had not sold the land. To bail out Governor Reagan, MCA's Jules Stein created the 57th Madison Corporation, chartered in Delaware, and purchased the property himself under the guise of his new Delaware corporation.

The first reporters to break this story were Lowell Bergman and Howard Kohn in an article for *Rolling Stone*, "Reagan's Millions: Inside the Candidate's Closet Cabinet," August 26, 1976.

72 In June 1983, I was contacted by literary agent Sterling Lord and Oscar-winning screenwriter Abby Mann. Both were fans of my 1978 book, *The Hoffa Wars*, in which I had alleged that Carlos Marcello, Santo Trafficante, and Jimmy Hoffa had arranged and executed the 1963 murder of the President. During our conference call, they asked me if I was interested in co-authoring the autobiography of Joseph Hauser, the FBI's sting man during its BRILAB probe which targeted Marcello. As Lord and Mann explained the situation to me, Hauser had allegedly induced Marcello to discuss the murder—during a covertly tape-recorded conversation. And,

according to Lord and Mann, Hauser had supposedly extracted some sort of "thinly-veiled" confession, which they assured me had been memorialized.

In the end, supposedly because Hauser was demanding so much up-front money, the entire deal collapsed.

73 One of the reasons why I had moved so fast on my manuscript was that I was supposedly in competition with another writer doing a book about MCA, Wendell Rawls, a Pulitzer Prize-winning reporter for the *New York Times*.

74 Also, I interviewed Roy Brewer, the Hollywood representative of IATSE and one of most notorious redbaiters and blacklisters in Hollywood. Brewer told me that he believed, like Reagan, that the biggest threat to the film industry came from communism, not organized crime.

75 In the January 3, 1987, issue of *The Nation*, the magazine's "editors and friends" picked their favorite books of 1986. Katrina Vanden Heuval wrote: "Few books this year can match the tales of the Reagan Administration for sheer corrupt fantasy. But Dan Moldea's *Dark Victory* provides a dark and timely look at Reagan in his first incarnation as a president—of the Screen Actors Guild."

The significance of Vanden Heuval's choice? She was Jean Stein's daughter and Jules Stein's granddaughter.

To the credit of Bob Borosage, Marc Raskin, and Roger Wilkins, they each noted Katrina's recommendation when I next saw them. Borosage told me that Jean Stein had decided not to give IPS any money from her foundation that year, and that Lew Wasserman never threw the Hollywood fundraiser.

But, because I had reluctantly resigned from IPS over this matter, I found no consolation in its bad fortune. I continue to have great respect for what IPS stood for, as well as for everyone who worked there.

76 Thomas Pryor, *Daily Variety*, "*Dark Victory* Doesn't Back Up Claims Re MCA, Reagan, Mob," September 24, 1986.

77 David Pecchia, *Los Angeles Times*, "*Dark Victory*," October 12, 1986.

78 Pisello later sued me and several other reporters for libel for our 1988 articles about him. It was the only time in my career that I have been sued for any reason. However, the suit filed by Pisello, who had just been convicted for criminal-tax fraud for a second time, was frivolous. None of us named

in the case—including *Regardie's*, the magazine in which I had published my story—were even required by the court to file a response.

After Pisello went to prison, the case was dropped.

Notably, after his release from prison, Pisello contacted me. We got together for dinner at Emilio's at Melrose and Highland in Hollywood and had a pleasant evening.

79 Kim Masters, *Los Angeles Daily News*, "MCA finds itself in the spotlight," October 27, 1986.

80 In his fascinating 1993 book, *Stiffed*, (HarperCollins, p. 269), Bill Knoedelseder wrote about U.S. Strike Force prosecutor Marvin Rudnick questioning a grand-jury witness, Milton Malden, the partner of Joe Robinson of Sugar Hill Records, before a federal grand jury.

> Malden, however, seemed more concerned about MCA. In the midst of his questioning before the grand jury, he blurted out to Rudnick, "You're never going to find out the truth, you know."
>
> "Why is that?" Rudnick asked reflexively.
>
> "Because of this," Malden said. He reached down into a shopping bag he'd placed on the floor between his feet and pulled out a book, which he held up for the grand jurors to see—*Dark Victory: Ronald Reagan, MCA and the Mob*. Written by investigative reporter Dan E. Moldea and published just a few months earlier, *Dark Victory* was the hottest read in Hollywood at the time. It traced Reagan's connections to MCA and MCA's connections to organized crime going back many years. The gist of the book—and Malden's reference to it—was that MCA was a corporation so powerful that it literally owned the president of the United States.

81 Ron Curran, *L.A. Weekly*, "Reagan, MCA and the Mob," October 3–9, 1986.

82 John McClintock, *Peninsula Times Tribune*, "Ronald Reagan is an invention of MCA," October 19, 1986.

83 Nicholas von Hoffman, *Grand Street*, "Functional Criminals," Winter 1987.

84 In early November 1986, a small magazine in Beirut revealed that the United States had engaged in a secret deal to sell weapons to Iran in return for American hostages held in Lebanon. The arrangement violated, among many other things, the expressed Reagan policy against making concessions to terrorists. The revelation by the Beirut publication, a story missed by every American news organization, caused a public outcry against the Reagan Administration in the United States.

On Monday, November 17, Reagan made false statements during a press conference about the extent of his knowledge of this very serious matter, saying, among other things, that no third country had been involved in the arms deal. When it became obvious that Reagan was lying, his aides scrambled to provide clarification and cover. His lies were portrayed as innocent misstatements.

Then, on Tuesday, November 25, Attorney General Ed Meese announced that as much as $30 million in profits from weapons shipped to Israel and sold to Iran were deposited in Swiss bank accounts—laundered through a network of dummy corporations—and "made available to the forces in Central America" at war with the Sandinista government in Nicaragua. In other words, the money from the Iranian arms sale had been diverted to the Contra rebels, in violation of congressional legislation, prohibiting such actions. The Iran-Contra scandal was also called "Contragate," among many other names.

On Monday, December 29, I appeared on CNN's *Take Two*, my first national television program since my book tour for *Dark Victory* began.

During the interview, co-host Dave Walker asked, "So you maintain that [Reagan] is still sort of in the pocket of MCA and some of the people he helped back then?"

"No," I replied. "I'm saying that he was an invention of MCA. I'm further saying that MCA has dealt with organized crime throughout its history. That Reagan, himself, has been influenced by people associated with organized crime throughout his career. And that some of his appointments and policies while in the White House have been influenced by these associations."

"In spite of his well-known, well-publicized stand against organized crime?"

"I believe that his war against organized crime, his war against drugs has been nothing more than a charade and a public-relations campaign. And I think that the evidence is clear on that. I think that this entire Contragate situation, when it bottoms out, will bottom out into drugs. . . . That there were people who were selling drugs to purchase weapons for the Contras as part of their eleemosynary activity. And then there were those who were more mercenary about it, selling drugs for profit, using the Contras as a cover for their operations. I think that the entire scenario—where you talk about missing millions of dollars, laundered money, Swiss bank accounts—is going to bottomline at drugs."

85 Al Delugach, *Los Angeles Times Book Review*, "Reagan's America," January 11, 1987.

Delugach later gave a quote for the trade-paperback edition of *Dark Victory*, saying: "Moldea's book is a hardnosed, fascinating study of Reagan in his formative Hollywood years. *Dark Victory* gives valuable insight into the powerbrokers of the movie industry, convincingly and clearly laying out the pervasive influence of organized crime and its 'respectable' allies upon this business and upon high public officials."

86 Following up on what I had learned from literary agent Sterling Lord and Oscar-winning screenwriter Abby Mann in June 1983, I contacted federally protected witness Joseph Hauser, indirectly, via a respected federal investigator. According to my trusted source, Hauser corroborated what Lord and Mann had told me.

In my 1986 book, *Dark Victory: Ronald Reagan, MCA and the Mob*, I wrote about Hauser on pages 338-339, saying: "Hauser had allowed himself to be used as the hub of several FBI sting operations during the Carter administration that yielded a pending indictment against [Santo] Trafficante of Florida and the bribery conviction of Carlos Marcello of Louisiana. Hauser had also received thinly veiled admissions on tape from Marcello during the FBI's BRILAB sting operation that he had been directly involved in the assassination of John Kennedy twenty years earlier."

87 Jeff Gerth, *New York Times Book Review*, "In Short—Nonfiction: *Dark Victory*," October 30, 1986.

88 Michiko Kakutani, *New York Times*, "Books of *The Times*: *Reagan's America*," December 31, 1986.

Part Five

89 Charles Trueheart, *Washington Post*, "The Magazine Reader: A Fan's Notes," February 2, 1988.

90 No byline, *Extra!* "Pro Football, the Media & the Mob," March/April 1988.

91 Earlier, my prized agent at the William Morris Agency was supposedly forced to drop me as a client after I had a knock-down-drag-out argument on a Denver radio program with a former but still-powerful vice president of the agency who claimed that the Mafia never had any real influence in Hollywood. After the show, he complained loudly to Norman Brokaw, the agency's CEO, who, despite his respect for *Dark Victory*, made the agency's decision to dump me. . . . Or, at least, that's the story I was told.

92 During my investigation, I received a copy of an FBI-302 report, which detailed the FBI's investigation of NFL referees and game officials. The report stated that "two or three referees" had allegedly been paid $100,000 by a New York Mafia figure for their participation in each of eight allegedly fixed games—which I listed on page 308 of *Interference*. The referees' alleged job was to ensure that the unnamed mob figure covered the spread and, thus, won his bets. The referees' names were not mentioned in the FBI report.

As I stated in my book, the FBI eventually dropped its probe, because the evidence of game fixing was, supposedly, inconclusive. In addition, the bureau's principal informant was caught trying to sell the same information to the IRS.

During my own interview with the informant, who had passed a polygraph test, he identified the two referees.

Even though I had the FBI report, the results of the informant's polygraph examination, and the names of the two game officials, I decided not to publish this material without further corroboration. My FBI sources, who had provided a considerable amount of help to me during my research for *Interference*, refused to comment about this particular game-fixing investigation for my book. I never fully understood why.

Subsequently, I contacted nationally known oddsmaker, Bobby Martin, who said that he had similar game-fixing suspicions about at least one NFL game official, whom he named. This referee was one of the two identified by the informant. Martin told me that he had also shared this information with Las Vegas gambler Lem Banker, who confirmed to me both Martin's personal investigation of the referee, as well as his name. Both Martin and Banker told me that they could prove that unnatural money had shown up on the referee's games—but they could not prove that any of the games had been actually fixed.

I then contacted IRS agent Leo Halper, who was involved in Project Layoff, which included the IRS's investigation of game fixing in the NFL. He told me that the FBI informant, who had also sold his information to the IRS, had given him the outcomes of the eight fixed games, along with the names of the two referees, *in advance* of the games being played.

Halper added that the referees had made their own bets on the eight fixed games through beards in Las Vegas. The initial IRS probe included surveillance on one of the beards, who reportedly bet so much money on these games that the betting line actually moved in response to the vast amount of money wagered. According to Halper, this wagering activity occurred at the Barbary Coast's sports book on the Las Vegas Strip.

Also, during my research, I received a correspondence from one of the beards involved with the two NFL referees. He confirmed, in writing, the fixes and named the same two referees.

But the IRS probe, according to Halper, collapsed when agency executives—despite the reliability of the informant's information—refused to authorize a full-scale federal investigation, even though the IRS had concluded that the games had, indeed, been fixed. Unconfirmed rumors circulated that government agents—who had received the outcomes of NFL games in advance of the contests—were scoring their own betting coups.

On the basis of the overwhelming evidence—the FBI report, my interviews with Martin and Banker, statements made to me by the IRS agent in charge of the investigation, the letter from the beard allegedly involved with the officials, and the statements made by the FBI/IRS informant, who had passed a polygraph examination—I published the material about the eight fixed games in *Interference*, hoping that a subsequent official investigation would answer the lingering questions about this matter.

However, upon the advice of my personal attorney, I decided not to publish the names of the two referees.

In 1992, Halper of the IRS sat down for a sworn deposition during a separate investigation of game fixing in the NFL, which had developed in the midst of a civil litigation. Halper was specifically questioned about the accuracy of what I had written in my book.

Question: So you say you knew Dan. That is Dan Moldea?

Halper: Yes.

Question: Where did you know him from?

Halper: He had contacted me when he was doing research for his book. That's how I knew him. . . .

Question: Did you read his book?

Halper: I have read most of it.

Question: What did you think of his book from a professional point of view?

Halper: I thought it was well done. . . .

Question: Does he mention in the book the 1979 football season, the games that were fixed?

Halper: Yes.

Question: Did you read that particular component in the book?

Halper: Yes.

Question: Is the book accurate in its detailing or referring to the events of the 1979 football season?

Halper: Yes.

93 Dave Anderson, *New York Times*, "49er Owner Is a 35er," January 18, 1982.

94 Neil Amdur, *The Fifth Down: Democracy and the Football Revolution* (Coward, McCann & Geoghegan, Inc. 1971), pp. 139-140.

95 Bernie Parrish, *They Call It A Game* (Dial Press, 1971), pp. 108-109.

96 Standing his ground, Welsh retaliated by criticizing me for my assault on NFL Security for its handling of, among other situations, the Stanley Wilson case. I told Welsh that until I started seeing some good faith from the NFL I would continue to use the Wilson incident as evidence of how the league handled messy situations.

The facts of the Wilson case were simple: On the night before Super Bowl XXIII between the Cincinnati Bengals and the seven-point-favorite San Francisco 49ers on January 22, 1989, Bengals running back Stanley Wilson, who had already been suspended twice for cocaine use and was being tested three times a week, was found in the bathroom of his hotel room in a "disoriented state" by a team official. Cocaine was reportedly found in his possession. While arrangements were being made to take Wilson to a hospital, he bolted, running down a fire escape and into the night. Wilson, who missed the Super Bowl, did not resurface until the following Tuesday.

After the Wilson situation became public, questions were raised as to the whereabouts of the proof of drug use found in Wilson's hotel room. Soon after, it was discovered that all of the evidence at the scene had been confiscated by Cincinnati's chief of police, who also headed the Bengals' security unit during the week of the Super Bowl. However, instead of turning the evidence over to a law-enforcement agency, the Cincinnati lawman gave it to NFL Security, which then went into its damage-control mode.

97 Keith Olbermann, *L.A. Style*, "Sacked by the NFL?" January 1992.

98 Desiree Ward, *Milwaukee Journal*, "Don't let this interfere," August 31, 1989.

99 I had misspelled thoroughbred-racing breeder Wayne Lukas, "Lucas"; NFL star Howard Cassady, "Cassidy"; and New York Jets' president Steve Gutman, "Guttman." *The Los Angeles Times* had misspelled the names of Cassady and Lukas in its December 7, 1986, and January 3, 1988, editions, respectively. *The Washington Post*--which had the audacity to attack me in its August 26, 1990, editorial, specifically for the misspellings--misspelled the names of both Gutman and Lukas on October 14, 1982, and October 6, 1983, respectively.

100 At that time, John Dowd, then a Washington attorney, represented Major League Baseball and had headed the investigation of Pete Rose and his ties to gambling and gamblers.

Part Six

101 The other panelists included First Amendment attorney Leonard Marks, the former head of USIA; Jane Kirtley, the executive director of the Reporters Committee for Freedom of the Press; Barbara Cohen, the chief of

CBS's Washington bureau; Clark Hoyt, Washington bureau chief of Knight-Ridder Newspapers; and James Vicini, who covered the courts for Reuters.

102 In 1988, the Reporters Committee for Freedom of the Press arranged for attorney Warren W. Faulk of Westmont, New Jersey, to represent me after I was subpoenaed—along with Bill Knoedelseder of the *Los Angeles Times*—in *U.S. v. Vastola*, a federal RICO trial in Camden, New Jersey. Attorneys for Gaetano Vastola, a notorious New Jersey Mafia figure, had demanded that we reveal our law-enforcement sources regarding an incident revolving around the MCA case. Of course, both of us refused to cooperate. In the end, our attorneys convinced the trial judge to quash the subpoenas.

103 Jack Miles, *Los Angeles Times Book Review*, Endpapers: Sticks and Stones: Can a Review Be So Bad It Is Libelous?" April 3, 1994.

104 I pitched similar proposed investigations to Professor Robert D. Richards, executive director of the Pennsylvania Center for the First Amendment at Penn State University and Henry R. Kaufman, executive director of the Libel Defense Resource Center. Richards refused to conduct any investigation of the case in a letter dated September 9, 1992; Kaufman refused to conduct any investigation of the case during a telephone conversation with me on September 16, 1992.

105 Jack Newfield, *New York Post*, "Hoffa Had JFK Killed," January 14, 1992.

106 Carlos Marcello died on March 2, 1993, at his home near New Orleans.

107 Eloise Salholz, *Newsweek*, "Did the Mob Kill JFK? January 27, 1992. In 1988, author, David E. Scheim, wrote an excellent book, *Contract on America: The Mafia Murder of President John F. Kennedy* (Shapolsky Publishers), which built upon my work, as well as that of the U.S. House Select Committee on Assassinations.

108 Charles Stuart, PBS *Frontline*, "JFK, Hoffa and the Mob," November 17, 1992.

109 Dan E. Moldea. *Washington Post*, "Tales of Hoffa: Why Does Hollywood Make Thugs Into Heroes?" December 27, 1992.

110 Ragano published his autobiography, *Mob Lawyer* (Charles Scribner's Sons, 1994), which he wrote with Selwyn Raab, a respected crime reporter

with the *New York Times*. A controversy erupted over the date of an alleged final confession that Trafficante had given to Ragano on March 13, 1987—four days before Trafficante's death. Supposedly, Trafficante had said during a car ride in Tampa, "Carlos screwed up. We shouldn't have killed John. We should have killed Bobby." Hospital records showed that Trafficante had spent that particular day receiving dialysis in North Miami Beach. Ragano told me that he was simply mistaken on the exact date.

Ragano died on May 13, 1998, at his home in Tampa after serving ten months in prison in 1993 for income-tax evasion.

111 In 2006, the Authors Dinner Group became co-ed once again.

112 A good friend of mine, author Gus Russo, published a fascinating and remarkably detailed biography about Sidney Korshak: *Supermob: How Sidney Korshak and His Criminal Associates Became America's Hidden Power Brokers* (Bloomsbury, 2006).

113 David Streitfeld, *Washington Post*, "Suit Over Book Review Reinstated," February 19, 1994.

114 David G. Savage, *Los Angeles Times*, "Libel Suit Is Reinstated for Book Review in *N.Y. Times*," February 19, 1994.

115 Paul M. Barrett, *Wall Street Journal*, "Author Who Sued Over Scornful Review Is Now Scorned by the Publishing World," April 7, 1994.

116 Edwin Diamond, *New York*, "Can You *Prove* the Hollandaise Was Curdled? – The Legal Uproar Over a *Times* Critic," April 18, 1994.

117 Debra Gersh Hernandez, *Editor & Publisher*, "$10 million lawsuit against *N.Y. Times* revived on appeal," March 19, 1994.

118 Roger C. Simmons, *Washington Post*, "Beyond a 'Bad Review,'" March 23, 1994.

119 The Association of American Publishers and the PEN American Center filed a second amicus. Poorly researched and presented, this brief—which even got the title of my book wrong, along with numerous other mistakes—paled in comparison to Starr's brief.

120 Christopher Hanson, *Columbia Journalism Review*, "Capital Letter: Playing 'Chicken' With the First Amendment," May/June 1994.

121 D.T. Max, *New York Observer*, "*Moldea* Reversal Delights *The Times*," May 16, 1994.

122 Allen Barra, *New York Observer*, "Some Reviewers Predisposed to Throw the Book at Authors," May 9, 1994.

123 John Leonard, *The Nation*, "Revenge of the Fettuccini," July 11, 1994.

124 Steve Love, *Akron Beacon Journal*, "It's ironic, but writer's suit could harm right to criticize," April 19, 1994.

125 Tamar Lewin, *New York Times*, "In Reversal, Appeals Court Dismisses Libel Suit Against *Times*," May 4, 1994.

126 Paul M. Barrett, *Wall Street Journal*, "In Rare Reversal, Court Blocks Libel Suit Over Book Review," May 4, 1994.

127 David Streitfeld, *Washington Post*, "Judges Switch Sides in Libel Suit," May 4, 1994.

128 Joan Biskupic, *Washington Post*, "In Libel U-Turn, Judge Admits Starting In the Wrong Direction," May 5, 1994.

129 Abner J. Mikva, *Legal Times*, "Oh, Never Mind," June 14, 1999.

130 Dan E. Moldea, *Los Angeles Times*, "Can a Bad Book Review Ruin a Writing Career?" May 29, 1994.

131 Carlin Romano, *The Nation*, "Paper Chase – I," June 6, 1994; and Carlin Roman, *The Nation*, "Paper Chase – II," June 20, 1994.

Romano's two-part series infuriated many in *The World Amicus* crowd, because he had placed his prestige as NBCC president on the line. In lieu of blindly accepting the *New York Times's* spin on the unfolding events, Romano courageously had done his own investigation, interviewing the principals on both sides of the dispute. And the results of his independent probe, which supported our point of view, were startling.

132 Bruce W. Sanford, *Don't Shoot the Messenger*" (Free Press, 1999), pp. 186-189.

133 Linda Greenhouse, *New York Times*, "High Court Opens Its Fall Session By Refusing Cases: All Appeals Are Denied," October 4, 1994.

134 Editorial, *Los Angeles Times*, "Libel in Reviews: The Book Is Still Open," October 10, 1994.

135 David Streitfeld, *Washington Post*, "Moldea Appeal Rejected: Justices Refuse to Hear Book Review Case," October 4, 1994.

136 David Streitfeld went to work for the *New York Times* in December 2007.

137 David Traxel, *New York Times Book Review*, "J. Edgar Hoover, Literary Critic – Alien Ink," April 12, 1992.

138 Natalie Robins, *Alien Ink: The FBI's War on Freedom of Expression* (William Morrow and Company, 1992), pp. 373-374,

139 Letter from SA Scott Nelson to Mr. Ahlerich, "Re: Book Review, *Interference*, by Dan E. Moldea," September 1, 1989.

140 Sanford J. Ungar, *FBI* (Atlantic Monthly Press; Little, Brown and Company, 1976), pp. 284-285.

141 William F. Roemer Jr., *Roemer: Man Against The Mob* (Donald I. Fine, 1989), pp. 46-49.

142 In Chapter 51 of *Interference*, pages 415-417, I discussed Hundley's role in the killing of a recent federal investigation of MCA, which he represented as a private attorney. I concluded this section about Hundley—which was also based on my book, *Dark Victory: Ronald Reagan, MCA, and the Mob*, as well as a June 1988 article, "MCA and the Mob," in *Regardie's*—charging:

> "The evidence is clear that there has been a cabal among some past and present officials of the Justice Department's Organized Crime and Racketeering Section and some of its Strike Force offices. And the NFL, through its long-term sweetheart relationship with a variety of law-enforcement agencies, particularly the OCRS has been a direct

beneficiary of this situation—which raises serious questions about possible conflicts of interest, as well as activities that border on sheer political corruption."

Hundley, whom I had interviewed twice, denied my charges about the MCA case, which have since been corroborated by, among other publications, the *Los Angeles Times* and the *Sacramento Bee*, as well as the *American Lawyer*. In addition, Hundley directly attacked me in the June 4, 1988, issue of *Billboard*, over a year before his client, Sandy Smith, reviewed my book.

Hundley died on June 11, 2006.

Part Seven

143 Charles Trueheart, *Washington Post*, "Did Sirhan Act Alone?" May 26, 1987.

144 Bill Steigerwald, *Los Angeles Times*, "The Mystery Persists in R.F.K. Killing," June 12, 1987.

145 Chuck Conconi, *Washington Post*, "Personalities: RFK Files to Be Released," June 26, 1987.

146 Kevin McManus, *Insight*, "RFK Assassination Conspiracy Theory," August 3, 1987.

147 Dan E. Moldea, *Washington Post Outlook*, "RFK's Murder: A Second Gun?" May 13, 1990.

148 Actually, I had two truth tests conducted—with the most recent in June 1994. The second test, a voice stress analysis, corroborated Gelb's polygraph results.

149 During my second interview with Sirhan on October 10, 1993, I looked across the visitation room and noticed Charles Manson sitting at a table. Sirhan confirmed that it was him.

At the beginning of our third and final interview on June 5, 1994, Sirhan said to me: "Charlie and I were having lunch the other day, and he asked, 'Who was that guy you were with?' And I said a reporter from Washington named Moldea."

Sirhan explained that Manson had told him to "ask that Moldea guy if he could get me a deal for $25,000 for a TV interview," because he needed to pay a lawyer.

Sirhan saw me shaking my head and asked what was wrong. I replied, "I'm trying to picture this scene of you and Charles Manson having lunch together."

Seeing Sirhan smile, I continued, "Sirhan, do me a favor, and don't mention my name to Charlie anymore. I didn't want my name to be part of his conscious thought."

150 Mary Sirhan died on February 7, 2005. Adel Sirhan had passed away nearly four years earlier on May 21, 2001.

151 Memorandum from Dan Moldea to Michael McCowan, "McCowan's conversation with Sirhan," signed by McCowan, February 25, 1995.

152 Six weeks before the publication of my book, I decided to break the news of my conclusions to other critics of the RFK case, sending them a letter, saying: "I am writing out of respect to notify you that in my upcoming book about the murder of Senator Robert Kennedy, I will be concluding that Sirhan Sirhan knowingly committed the crime and acted alone.

"Obviously, I have a lot of explaining to do, and I am prepared to do just that."

153 Regarding the question of muzzle distance: All twelve of the eyewitnesses to the shooting claimed that they did not see Sirhan fire a point-blank shot at Senator Kennedy—who was hit three times at point-blank range. (A fourth shot, also fired at point-blank range, passed through his clothing without touching his body.)

The fact is that none of these twelve eyewitnesses ever saw Kennedy get shot. All twelve of the eyewitnesses' statements about muzzle distance were based on—and only on—their view of Sirhan's first shot. After the first shot, their eyes were diverted as panic swept through the densely populated kitchen pantry. The seventy-seven people in the crowd began to run, duck for cover, and crash into each other.

Simply speaking, I believe that the kinetic movement of the crowd trapped Kennedy against a steam table, which was bolted to the floor, as Sirhan, just inches away on the side of that same steam table, fired his weapon at him. Consistent with this, the last person to shake Kennedy's hand remembered seeing the senator lose his balance—while another eyewitness remembered seeing him "jerk a little bit, like backwards and then forwards."

Kennedy had recoiled from the sound of Sirhan's first shot, which didn't strike him, but then was accidentally pushed forward by the panic-stricken crowd into the steam table and Sirhan's weapon—where he was struck three times at point-blank range.

And who was hit with the first shot? Paul Schrade—standing a few feet behind Kennedy and one of the five others wounded—told me that he was looking at Kennedy when he lost consciousness. Before Schrade was shot in the head, the last thing he saw was the senator smiling and just beginning to turn towards the steam table. Consistent with this, another eyewitness testified, "I saw the fellow behind the Senator fall, then the Senator fell."

Contrary to the LAPD's official report, I believe that Sirhan's first shot missed Kennedy and hit Paul Schrade—and that was the only shot from Sirhan's gun that the twelve eyewitnesses saw.

No one knows for sure what Senator Kennedy saw before he was gunned down. However, his last known words, while lying on the floor of the kitchen pantry, were: "Is Paul all right?"

I believe that Kennedy—who, while pinned against the steam table, had reacted defensively by turning his back on his assailant—saw his close friend get hit with the first shot—just before Sirhan shot him, at point-blank range.

154 When I received my contract from Norton in 1993, I decided to reexamine everything in the RFK case like a government bureaucrat approaches "zero-based budgeting." I took nothing for granted; everything was open for review. So, in the wake of my third and final interview with Sirhan, I returned to a basic question: Why did police officials and FBI agents believe they had seen bullet holes in the walls and door frames in Sirhan's line of fire?

The key pieces of evidence about these extra bullets were contained in a little-known FBI report in which a special agent had identified four bullet holes, which appeared in photographs attached to this report. Each of the four pictured bullet holes was circled. In each circle, someone had scribbled the number "723" and two sets of letters, one of which was "LASO." At first, I was unable to decipher the other set of scribbled letters.

While researching my story for the *Washington Post* in 1990, I speculated that the person who had circled these holes was someone from the Los Angeles Sheriff's Office—and that "723" was his badge number. After telephoning one of my sources at the LASO, he identified the holder of badge 723 as deputy patrolman Walter Tew who had died eighteen months earlier.

After identifying Tew, I took another look at the photographs and easily deciphered "W Tew" as the second set of scribbled letters in each circle. Then, I re-interviewed the commander of the LASO contingent, which was the first group of law-enforcement personnel to arrive in the kitchen pantry after the shooting. He clearly remembered Tew among his team of men that night, even though Tew's name didn't appear in any of the police records at the California State Archives.

At the time of my discovery in 1990 that Tew had circled the alleged bullet holes, I was jubilant and portrayed Tew as an example of a conscientious police officer who had innocently marked evidence of bullet holes at a crime scene—even though Tew wasn't a firearms-identification expert.

However, during my re-review of this material in 1994, I was suddenly struck by the fact that, regardless of his good intentions, *Tew wasn't a firearms-identification expert.* He simply was not qualified to make such identifications.

Nevertheless, in the aftermath of the shooting, his evidence remained as he had marked it—as scores of police officers and FBI agents walked through the crime scene and saw the holes in the walls and the door frames that Tew had circled.

No wonder so many law-enforcement officials had told me that they had seen bullet holes in the kitchen pantry. They had simply seen what Tew had marked as evidence and assumed that they were bullet holes, identified by a competent firearms expert.

Even the special agent, who had written the controversial FBI report with the four attached photographs of identified bullet holes, had been fooled. Like Tew, this agent, Alfred Greiner, was not a firearms-identification expert. He was from the bureau's photography lab and had been assigned to the kitchen pantry to obtain orientation shots of the crime scene.

Soon after, I learned that the person who had given Greiner and his photographer their tour of the crime scene also was not a firearms expert—rather he was a desk clerk from the Ambassador Hotel. During this tour—which is chronicled in an official police report—Greiner saw the holes that Tew had circled, had them photographed, and then, without any supporting evidence, identified them as "bullet holes" in his report.

In short, what Tew had identified as bullet holes were not bullet holes at all. There were no extra bullets at the crime scene.

155 In 1999, Thane Eugene Cesar—who had married a woman from the Philippines and left the United States shortly after the publication of my book—asked me to be the godfather to his newborn son. I accepted this honor.

156 Dan E. Moldea, *Washington Post,* "For the Last Time: Who Killed RFK?: My Ten-Year Journey to The Mind of the Assassin." June 4, 1995.

Unfortunately, *Regardie's* magazine, in which I had published my first story about the RFK case in 1987, had folded in 1992.

157 No byline, *Kirkus Reviews*, "The Killing of Robert F. Kennedy," April 1, 1995.

158 Gilbert Taylor, *Booklist*, "The Killing of Robert F. Kennedy," May 15, 1995.

159 Godfrey Hodgson, *Washington Post Book World*, "Who Really Shot RFK?" June 25, 1995.

160 Dan E. Moldea, *Washington Post Book World*, "The RFK File," July 16, 1995. In his published reply to my letter, Hodgson continued to insist: "I was 'in that crowd' and 'a few feet away from the senator.' . . . I did not state or imply that I was an eyewitness or in the pantry when Kennedy was killed."
 The reader can judge what Hodgson really said on three different occasions—and what he was trying to get away with in his review of my book.

161 Christopher Lehmann-Haupt, *New York Times*, "Open Door to Conspiracy Theories." May 25, 1995.

162 Alex Kuczynski, *New York Observer*, "Off the Record," June 5, 1995.

163 John Diamond, Associated Press, "New book concludes no plot in RFK murder," June 9, 1995.

164 Steve Waldman, *Newsweek*, "Closing the Case on RFK," June 12, 1995.

165 Robert Gearty, *New York Daily News*, "Writer's suit scorches commish," December 13, 1995.

166 A friend of mine, Larry Gurwin, had written an excellent book, *The Calvi Affair: Death of a Banker*, which was published by Macmillan in 1983. In addition, while in Milan, Italy, Mimi and I met Italian journalist Leo Sisti of *L'Espresso*. Sisti is one of the top experts on the international Mafia who has written not one but two books that featured the Roberto Calvi scandal: *Il Banco paga* (*The Bank pays*, with Gianfranco Modolo, 1982) and *Il caso Marcinkus* (*The Marcinkus Case*, with Leonardo Coen, 1991).

167 Jeffrey Toobin, *The Run of His Life: The People v. O. J. Simpson* (Random House, 1996), p.149.

168 Letter from Dan E. Moldea to Charles McGrath, Editor, *New York Times Book Review*, March 25, 1997.

169 Stricken with cancer, Philip Vannatter died on January 20, 2012. He was 70 years old.

Part Eight

170 Mike Shain, *New York Post*, "Foster death book duel," June 25, 1997.

171 Judy Quinn, *Publishers Weekly*, "Fuhrman Withdraws Vince Foster Proposal." July 7, 1997.

172 CNN, *Larry King Live*, "Transcript: Lucianne Goldberg," July 30, 1998.

173 Interestingly, Ruddy admitted to *Washington Post* columnist Howard Kurtz in a September 28, 2009, story "that he was 'overzealous' and 'over the top' when publisher Richard Mellon Scaife was financing his Clinton investigations.... 'I think he was a much better president than I thought,' Ruddy says. 'I think he was a great president.'"

174 Richard Brookhiser, *New York Times Book Review*, "Body Politics," September 28, 1997.

175 The most important book about the Whitewater case—*Fools for Scandal: How the Media Invented Whitewater*, written by journalist Gene Lyons of the *Arkansas Democrat-Gazette*—predictably received rough treatment in the *New York Times Book Review* in August 1996. Reviewer Phil Gailey, an ex-*Times* reporter, wrote that Lyons's book "accuses the *Times* . . . of lies, distortions and the suppression of exculpatory information, among other things. . . . This is a nasty book, not because it challenges the reporting of the Whitewater story but because it assaults the integrity of the journalists who did the reporting."

In an attempt to mediate the dispute between Lyons and Gailey, reporter Jim Naurecleas in a story for *Extra!*—the voice of the media watchdog group, Fairness and Accuracy in Reporting—enthusiastically sided with Lyons, adding, "the *Times* repeated the same errors in subsequent stories, and defends them to this day."

On April 13, 2000, President Clinton told 500 people at the American Society of Newspaper Editors, "I would like just once to see someone acknowledge the fact that this Whitewater thing was a lie and a fraud from the beginning."

176 Regarding the issue of punishment, in my book on Foster's suicide, I wrote in my manuscript:

> [A]fter R. Emmett Tyrrell, the editor of the *American Spectator*, which is heavily backed by Richard Scaife, fired Ronald Burr, the *Spectator's* publisher, who, according to an October 20 article by Howard Kurtz of the *Washington Post*, "objected to spending the bulk of the Scaife funds on reporters poking around Arkansas and hiring investigators to examine Clinton's past."
>
> This flap over Burr's firing is followed by another when the *Spectator*, which had earlier run a major story about the Foster case by Ambrose Evans-Pritchard, published its own opinion of Ruddy's book by senior correspondent John Corry, who renews the Ruddy-bashing with a remarkably bad review in the December issue.
>
> Soon after publication of Corry's scathing attack, Scaife informs Emmett Tyrrell that he is not renewing his annual six-figure grants to the publication, which have totaled over $2 million over the past seven years.
>
> Commenting on all this, Reed Irvine of AIM, who has always openly and honestly acknowledged the money he has received from Scaife, issued a press release, criticizing the Spectator for its act of conscience and insisting: 'Ruddy has been a highly-valued employee of Scaife's paper since 1994. Since Scaife believes that his work on the Foster case has been very important, the *Spectator's* attack on Ruddy was an attack on Scaife as well.'
>
> But, more than anything else, that innocent comment speaks volumes about the dilemma of those who are dependent on Richard Scaife's money.
>
> They cannot back down without his permission.

177 Bill Thomas, *Capital Style*, "Dead on Arrival?" May 1998.

178 Robert Sherrill, *Washington Post*, "Anatomy of a Suicide," June 21, 1998.

179 Steve Weinberg, *Legal Times*, "Conspiracies: Real and Invented," August 10, 1998.

180 Joseph Farah, *WorldNetDaily*, "A tragedy of a book," May 14, 1998.

181 Reed Irvine, *AIM Report*, "The Tragedy of *A Washington Tragedy*," May-B, 1998.

182 Tony Kornheiser, *Washington Post*, "Shooting Starr," June 29, 1997.

183 Lloyd Grove, *Washington Post*, "The Watchdogs' Watchdog: Steve Brill Grills Ken Starr About Other Reporters," May 1, 1998.

184 No byline, Reuters, "Author accuses Starr of anti-Clinton leaks," May 26, 1998.

185 Gene Lyons, *Arkansas Democrat-Gazette*, "Double standard for Starr coverage," June 3, 1998.

186 Alexis Simendinger, *National Journal*, "Look Who Suspects a Cover-Up," June 6, 1998.

187 Adam Clymer, *New York Times*, "Starr Admits Role in Leaks to Press," June 14, 1998.

188 On October 30, Judge Norma Holloway Johnson made documents public, showing that in September she had appointed a "special master," Judge John Kern 3rd, a senior D.C. judge, to investigate, among other matters, the source of twenty-four illegal grand-jury leaks. Once again, she had found "a *prima facie* violation" of secrecy rules and demanded that "a complete and thorough review of these allegations must be undertaken."

In her ruling, Judge Johnson "ordered that the OIC and individual members therein must "show cause" why they should not be held in contempt for violating Rule 6(e) through disclosures contained in the 24 news reports found by the Court to constitute *prima facie* violations of Rule 6(e)."

Those reporters named for allegedly receiving the illegal leaks from the OIC were: Jackie Judd at ABC; Phil Jones and Scott Pelley at CBS; John

King at CNN; David Bloom, Lisa Myers, and Claire Shipman at NBC; Susan Schmidt and Peter Baker at the *Washington Post*; James Bennet, John Broder, Francis X. Clines, Jeff Gerth, and Don Van Natta at the *New York Times*; Thomas Galvin at the *New York Daily News*; John Ellis at the *Boston Globe*; and Karen Breslau, Howard Fineman, and Michael Isikoff at *Newsweek*.

Baker, Bloom, Broder, Clines, Myers, Schmidt, Shipman, Van Natta were all cited for two violations. Scott Pelley at CBS led the pack with three. Steve Brill was also named, but he used the leak he received as the impetus to expose the other reporters.

Not surprisingly, the U.S. Court of Appeals for the D.C. Circuit, upon which Starr had once sat, reversed Judge Johnson's ruling on September 14, 1999, claiming that these twenty-four leaks from Starr's office were *not* illegal. However, as the *Washington Post* noted in an editorial the following day, "The ruling does not clear Mr. Starr on all allegations of grand jury leaks."

79-year-old Judge Johnson died on September 18, 2011.

189 Howard Kurtz, *Washington Post*, "Media Revel in Another Starr Turn," July 30, 1998.

190 Howard Kurtz, *Washington Post*, "Morals of a Muckraker," August 8, 2007.

191 Brett Kavanaugh worked as a young attorney for the OIC during Kenneth Starr's investigation of Bill and Hillary Clinton. On July 9, 2018, Donald Trump nominated Kavanaugh as an associate justice of the U.S. Supreme Court. As the U.S. Senate Judiciary Committee's confirmation hearings approached, my August 24, 1998, affidavit about OIC leaks became an issue. Senate staffers and reporters contacted me, asking if the person I identified in my declaration as "OIC #2" was Kavanaugh.

In response, I executed a second sworn affidavit on September 3, 2018. In addition, I published an essay about the controversy, "Brett Kavanaugh exposed as Ken Starr's designated leaker," which was published in the *National Memo* on September 11.

192 Frank Greve, Knight-Ridder, "Writer Raises New Questions About How Starr Works With Reporters," August 29, 1998.

193 Gene Lyons, *Arkansas Democrat-Gazette*, "Can we live with these standards?" September 2, 1998.

194 James Carville, *And the Horse He Road In On* (Simon & Schuster, 1998), pp. 104-105.

Part Nine

195 Editorial, *Salon*, "Why we ran the Henry Hyde story," September 16, 1998.

196 PBS transcript: *NewsHour*, "The Tape Debate," September 17, 1998.

197 David Espo, Associated Press, "Gingrich: Clinton's account makes him 'misogynist,'" September 16, 1998.

198 David Schippers had earlier represented former Chicago mob associate Bill Jahoda whom I had met while he was in the Federal Witness Protection Program. While Jahoda and I were considering writing a book together, I spoke with Schippers twice on the telephone. But I had no discussions with him during the impeachment inquiry.

199 Three years earlier, *Vanity Fair* had published an article which was widely discussed in 1998, indicating that U.S. House Speaker Newt Gingrich, while married to his first wife, had an affair with Anne Manning, one of his married campaign workers. Manning told reporter Gail Sheehy that she never had intercourse with him, adding that he preferred her to perform oral sex. At the time of the magazine's publication, Gingrich was on tour, promoting his new pro-family book, *To Renew America*, in which he condemned sex outside of marriage.

200 MacDonell published a book in 2006 in which he provided an error-ridden account of our work together during the impeachment drama. The most egregious mistake was MacDonell's statement: "Bob Livingston, if you're out there, know that some people did their best to cover up for you. When Moldea finally called in to report his progress, I was sure that Livingston had slipped away. At my insistence, Dan contacted the alleged other woman. She told him to fuck himself and clicked the phone down, refusing to answer again. . . . The truth is that we [had] nothing on Livingston. We bluffed; he folded."

This account—which was also featured without my name by Charles "Chip" McGrath in his article about MacDonell in the *New York Times* on April 29, 2006—is completely false. Not only did I speak to the woman on several occasions—during which she confessed her relationship with Livingston—I tape recorded all but one of those conversations. I wrote and gave reports of each of these encounters to Flynt who apparently did not share them with MacDonell.

In short, MacDonell, who was an important member of our team in 1998-1999, went over the top in his book as part of his apparent effort to seek revenge on Flynt, the man who had fired him from his job.

201 During an exclusive interview, which was published on January 12, 2000, in *The Hill*, Livingston told journalists Albert Eisele, Robert Schlesinger, and Mary Lynn F. Jones: "About midnight that night, I got a call [from his district representative], saying that I had a problem at home, [about] a person I used to know. . . . I mean, look, there were ads taken out offering $1 million [by *Hustler* magazine for information about sexual misbehavior by members of Congress]. Who was responsible for those ads? I don't know, but I sure can guess. I mean when James Carville months earlier says, 'We're declaring war,' all I can say is war got pretty dirty. By the way, I surmise I'm a product of that ad."

On September 19, 2000, Livingston appeared on *The O'Reilly Factor*, saying: "They put out an ad. . . . And I think the White House was directly involved in that. I personally believe that. Carville was involved in that. And it had its impact with respect to me."

In short, Livingston, understandably bitter, was totally wrong. Carville had nothing to do with our project, directly or indirectly—on the record or off the record.

202 Alan Fram, Associated Press, "Gaps Appear in Livingston Support," December 19, 1998.

203 Jonathan Alter, *Newsweek*, "The Era of Bad Feeling," December 28 – January 4, 1999.

204 Alvarez, Lizette, John M. Broder, and Katharine Q. Seelye, *New York Times*, "Drawn-Out Impeachment Battle Dealt Its Meager Spoils to All Sides," February 14, 1999.

205 CNN, *Inside Politics*, "President Buoyed by Highest-Ever Approval Numbers; Livingston's Resignation Sends Scarlet Letter to Congress," December 21, 1998.

206 In the end, Flynt decided not to break this story first. Later, Senator Hutchinson, an ordained minister, divorced his wife of twenty-nine years and married his young mistress. In 2002, he lost his bid for reelection.

207 Katharine Q. Seelye, *New York Times*, "Resignation Was Prompted by Desire to Make a Point," December 22, 1998.

208 Steve Proffitt, *Los Angeles Times*, "*Los Angeles Times* Interview: Larry Flynt," December 27, 1998.

209 On January 12, Flynt told CNN, "I had talked to Geraldo a month ago, and he had asked for an exclusive. But after the way I was treated on Geraldo last night, I can't see that happening again. I didn't feel I was given an opportunity to make my case. My information is important."
   That same night, Rivera told his television audience: "The reason I didn't let Larry get into the abortion issue last night—and there was some friction between us—is that [Bob Barr] hasn't accused the President of sneaking out and having an abortion. He's accused the President of cheating on his wife and then lying about it, and he believes that perjury is impeachable. I think it was appropriate when Larry Flynt says, 'Hey, wait a second, you did the same thing, in essence, and if the President had invoked his privilege the way you invoked your privilege in that lawsuit, we wouldn't be where we are now.'"
   Later in the same program, Rivera, still backpedaling from his shoddy performance the night before, revisited the abortion issue as it related to Bob Barr—and defended Flynt for raising it.

210 ABC, *Good Morning America*, "Impeachment Trial Moves into High Gear," January 11, 1999.

211 Marie Cocco, *Newsday*, "Bob Barr: Poster boy for the politics of abortion," January 14, 1999.

212 Speaking of Livingston's resignation on CNN's *Capital Gang* on December 19, reporter Margaret Carlson of *Time* summed up the moment earlier that morning for her colleagues in the Washington press corps, saying, "Well, in the chaotic world we're now living in, it would be foolish to predict that A is going to have any effect on B. This morning at the office, [the news of Livingston's resignation] hit like a thunderclap, so much so that no one even pretended to be in the know. We admitted we were completely surprised."

During a CNN special on the impeachment the following day, correspondent Jeff Greenfield stated, "The most surprising, the most dramatic news of the day wasn't impeachment; it was the resignation of Livingston, because nobody expected it. . . . Livingston did something that, in a way, hadn't been done since Lyndon Johnson renounced the presidency in March of '68. He did something nobody expected."

213 Mary Leonard, *Boston Globe*, "Livingston exit deepens partisan rancor," December 24, 1998.

214 Flynt told me that he had never met Terry Lenzner. I had only met Lenzner once—at a book party in Washington for agent/author David Obst, nearly two months before I accepted the assignment with Flynt. During the party, Lenzner and I shook hands and spoke to each other—with mutual friends present. We have never had a private conversation. And, as of this writing, I have not seen or talked with him since.

215 Although Flynt had never met President Clinton, to whom he had contributed money and voted for in 1992 and 1996, James Carville, the President's most loyal defender, had played the role as Flynt's prosecutor in Milos Foreman's highly praised 1996 motion picture, *The People vs. Larry Flynt*.

However, according to the public statements of both parties, Carville had no connection to the Flynt project. Certainly, I had no contact with Carville.

216 In short, this is what had happened: After I revealed my information about the OIC leaks during a speech in May 1998, Max Stier, one of the President's lawyers called me and asked for a meeting—which was a perfectly proper and legitimate request. I replied that I wanted a subpoena before cooperating and gave him my attorney's telephone number.

The following month, after Steven Brill's controversial "Pressgate" article was released, my attorney, Roger Simmons, called me, saying that Stier had telephoned again and repeated his request for a meeting. When I said that I still wanted a subpoena, Simmons replied that the President's lawyers apparently did not have subpoena power and wanted to use my information to help them get it.

At that point, I agreed to the meeting—my first and only meeting with anyone from Williams & Connolly—which took place on June 26, 1998. Just to be clear, I was never on the law firm's payroll, and I never, directly or indirectly, received any money or favors from the firm or anyone associated with it.

217 Howard Kurtz, *Washington Post*, "Airing on the Side of Caution; C-SPAN Delays Broadcast of Larry Flynt's Revelation," January 13, 1999.

218 Bill Sammon, *Washington Times*, "Flynt Sleuth dished dirt for White House," January 13, 1999.

219 On January 24, Bill Sammon of the *Washington Times* appeared on the Fox News Channel's *O'Reilly Factor*, hosted by Bill O'Reilly—who is to the news business as Dr. Frank Burns is to *M*A*S*H*. During the previous month, the hypocritical Clinton-bashing O'Reilly had promised "new revelations linking Flynt to those close to the White House." Using Sammon's January 13 story, I was as close as O'Reilly got to delivering on his promise.

220 CNBC, *The Tim Russert Show*, "Senators Larry Craig and Robert Torricelli Discuss the Impeachment Trial of President Clinton," January 16, 1998. Four days earlier, Bill O'Reilly interviewed Senator Craig about Flynt's efforts to expose Republican hypocrisy, which O'Reilly described as "deplorable." Craig replied, "I am angered by that kind of sleaze and the perpetuation of that kind of sleaze. I say to Larry Flynt: 'Shame on you!'"

Notably, in June 2007, Senator Craig was arrested for lewd behavior, a felony, after allegedly making a pass at another man in an adjacent stall in a bathroom at the Minneapolis-St. Paul International Airport. Two months later, he pleaded guilty to a lesser charge of disorderly conduct, a misdemeanor. He did not seek reelection in 2008.

221 Sean Scully, *Washington Times*, "White House tacitly backs Flynt 'blackmail,' GOP says."

222 NBC News, "*Meet the Press*, "Senators Christopher Dodd, Orrin Hatch, [et al] Discuss the Impeachment Trial of President Clinton," January 17, 1999.

223 Fox News, *The O'Reilly Factor*, "Interview with John Kyl," January 13, 1999.

224 Fox News, *The O'Reilly Factor*, "Back of the Book: Women's view on Senate trial," January 14, 1999.

225 NPR transcript, *Fresh Air*, "Peter Baker . . . Discusses the Politics of the Clinton Impeachment Trial," September 28, 2000.

226 Tony Snow, syndicated column, "Don't be fooled, folks," January 17, 1999.

227 Jamie Dettmer, *Insight*, "Comity in Freefall as Trial Begins," February 8, 1999.

228 Matt Labash, *Weekly Standard*, "Clinton's Hustler," January 25, 1999.

229 No byline, *Washington Post*, "GOP Leader Seeks Investigation of Flynt; Focus on Affairs Is Called Bid to 'Intimidate,' Silence Congress.," January 16, 1999.

230 Dr. Jerry Falwell, *Falwell Confidential*, "The Bizarre Flynt-Clinton Connection," January 15, 1999.

231 Robert J. Caldwell, *San Diego Union-Tribune*, "Scorched Earth: Clinton's allies trigger 'Doomsday Machine' against his enemies," January 17, 1999.

232 Editorial, *Wall Street Journal*, "What is 'for' for?" January 21, 1999.

233 On February 5, 1999, Falwell, in response to my threat to sue, published a statement in his newsletter, retracting his charge that I had worked for Williams & Connolly. (See: Dr. Jerry Falwell, *Falwell Confidential*, "Correction," February 5, 1999.)

234 Steve Love, *Akron Beacon Journal*, "Moldea risks respect to end hypocrisy," January 19, 1999.

235 Frank Rich, *New York Times*, "Larry Flynt Stoned," January 16, 1999.

236 Richard Johnson, et al., *New York Post*, "Page Six," January 27, 1999.

237 Noah Adams, NPR, *All Things Considered*, January 22, 1999.

238 On February 1, America's self-appointed moral conscience, Bill Bennett, author of *The Death of Outrage* and a member of the board of directors for one of Richard Scaife's foundations, was clearly livid about Flynt's high poll ratings during his appearance on *Larry King Live*. "Ken Starr has

got the dignity, decorum, not to get out and give press conferences, which he's not supposed to do," Bennett insisted. "He's not been able to defend himself while he's been under a full-scale attack—a 'war,' as James Carville called it, a 'war' against the independent counsel. And, as a result, the American people—in their wisdom, thanks to White House spin and other things—regard Larry Flynt more favorably than they regard Ken Starr. So much for the wisdom of the American people."

Seemingly stunned that Bennett had the audacity to make such a high-handed statement, King asked, "You're saying [the public is] dumb?"

With seemingly no remorse for he had just said, Bennett replied, "Well, they're wrong. They've been spun, and they're wrong about this. I mean, you know, four or five out of ten Americans approve of what Larry Flynt did. This is what Clinton has wrought."

Part Ten

239 Stephen Van Drake, *Costal Observer*, "Janes [sic] Spillane asks Justice to investigate obstruction of Congress," April 8, 1999.

240 Carol Lloyd, *Salon*, "Finally, the Flynt Report," March 26, 1999.

241 Eric Dezenhall, *Damage Control: Why Everything You Know About Crisis Management Is Wrong* (Portfolio, 2007), p. 84.

242 In late June 2004, the documentary—*The Hunting of the President: The Ten-Year Campaign to Destroy Bill Clinton*—premiered in Washington, D.C. and opened at theatres around the country. I had a small role in the film, which was written and directed by Harry Thomason and Nickolas Perry—and based on the best-selling book by Joe Conason and Gene Lyons.

With considerable passion, I discussed the right-wing fabrications about the circumstances of the suicide of White House attorney Vincent Foster, who some still insisted had been murdered. In addition, I resurrected my criticisms of the stable of Washington journalists who had served as cheerleaders and stalking horses for Kenneth Starr's witch hunt against the President and the First Lady in return for allegedly illegal leaks.

243 Joe Eszterhas, *American Rhapsody* (Alfred A. Knopf, 2000), pp. 305, 312.

244 No byline, *Youngstown Vindicator*, "Author suggests creating a crime commission," April 18, 1998.

245 Jerry Seper and Audrey Hudson, *Washington Times*, "POGO used grant to probe GOP lawmakers," April 11, 2001.

246 Sonny Franzese is widely known to have a daughter and two sons, Michael and John, Jr. In August 2006, I received a call from a hidden and protected third son, a small-time film producer with whom I had been acquainted for several years. He told me that his father, who was then nearly 90 years old, wanted his autobiography written. Considering Franzese's extraordinary role in mob history, I replied that I was very interested in the assignment—with the understanding that I could pull my name from the project if I felt that his story was evolving into a fairy tale.

In the midst of our negotiations, I was contacted by one of Franzese's top lieutenants who tried to shake me down, asking me for money to ensure that the deal proceeded smoothly. I rejected that offer and immediately withdrew from the book project.

247 Jeff Stein, *Salon*, "The Greatest Vendetta on Earth: Why would the head of Ringling Bros.-Barnum & Bailey hire a former top CIA honcho to torment a hapless freelance writer for eight years?" August 30, 2001.

248 Dan E. Moldea and David Corn, *The Nation*, "Influence Peddling, Bush Style," October 23, 2000; and David Corn and Dan Moldea, *The Nation*, "Did Ashcroft Take the Low Road on the Highroad?" January 15, 2001

Also, soon after Bush announced his candidacy for the Republican presidential nomination, I began a separate page on my website, called "Bushology Interactive," which contained links about the Bush family. In addition, I had turned a portion of the main page of my website into an information service for investigators, which could also be accessed at *www.FreedomOfInformationAct.com.*

249 In 2009, federal prosecutors indicted Ingmar Guandique—a laborer from El Salvador who was already doing ten years for two assaults in Rock Creek Park—for the murder of Chandra Levy. He pleaded not guilty but was convicted on November 22, 2010. Law-enforcement officials believe that Levy was a random victim of Guandique.

Frankly, I still believe that the person responsible was someone close to her.

250 Christopher Berg and Dan E. Moldea, *American Writer*, "The Writers Right Project," Spring 2003.

Part Eleven

251 Brian Ross appeared on Fox News's *O'Reilly Factor* on the evening of May 3, 2007. Here's a portion of their exchange:

> **O'Reilly:** And you are going to name some people, right?
>
> **Ross:** We are. We've been going through these phone records. Now we have 4 years of the 13 years that she operated. And because she actually ran the business from her home in California every phone call she made was a long distance call and therefore there's a record. So we've been going through the numbers and sometimes the numbers don't pan out. Sometimes she dialed the wrong number. There have been a couple of very prominent people who it turns out got wrong numbers called and they ended up on the list. So we're not going to put out the whole list because that wouldn't be right.
>
> **O'Reilly:** Are you going to have a headline on Saturday, Sunday?
>
> **Ross:** I hope so.

252 In 2008, author Jeff Sharlet published a remarkable book called, *The Family: The Secret Fundamentalism at the Heart of American Power.* Sharlet discussed the house on C Street, which was operated by the C Street Foundation, saying that it "is registered as a church, which allows it to avoid taxes."

253 Never able to recover from Flynt's surprise reward offer in the midst of his own delicate operation, my surveillance man later returned $10,642 of the $11,640 he had received from Flynt for Operations Cowboy and Lightfoot.

254 On February 1, 2007—without the knowledge of her attorneys—Palfrey sent a letter to her prosecutor, William Cowden, appealing to him to back away from a public trial. Attaching a news story from the *Baltimore Sun* about Brandy Britton's suicide, Palfrey wrote, almost prophetically:

> I realize the anomalous nature of writing to you. And
> I apologize for any discomfort this may cause you.
> Regardless, I simply cannot emphasize to you the terrible
> and quite unnecessary ramifications this case (civil and/
> or criminal) will set off, if permitted to advance for both
> sides. The press will have a field day at each of our expense.
> Despite my aforementioned disclaimer not to comment
> upon my case, let me say this: The attached item rings more
> true than false when juxtaposed to my situation. Unlike Ms.
> Britton, however, I am [a] ferocious fighter when need be.

255 Sibley had already placed a memo in his file, which he shared with Palfrey's other attorneys, about her frequent threats, including to him, to commit suicide.

256 When Jeane Palfrey learned that I had requested that Blair Sibley send a copy of the CD to Flynt and his staff, she was furious, writing to both of us: "[A]bsoutely not! [Flynt] hasn't any interest in me. If he does, then he can apply for the records just like everyone else."

Later, as a favor to me, Jeane soften and allowed Blair to send Flynt a copy.

257 Palfrey confirmed to CNN that she didn't know Senator Vitter personally, saying, "I had no idea who he was prior to then—although I'm sure he was a client and he's stated accordingly, but I don't remember this man."

258 Carrie Budoff Brown, *Politico*, "GOP senator admits link to escort service," July 9, 2007.

259 Adam Zagorin, *Time*, "Did Senator Vitter Get Hustled?" July 10, 2007.

260 Later, Wendy Yow Ellis, also known as Wendy Cortez, a New Orleans prostitute, alleged that Vitter had paid her to have sex during the year he was elected to Congress in 1999. Flynt asked me to arrange a polygraph test for her, which I did via Edward Gelb, the former president of the American Polygraph Association. (Earlier, I had personally retained Gelb to give Gene Cesar a lie-detector test, which he passed.) According to Gelb, Cortez showed "no deception" during her polygraph test.

261 Howard Kurtz, *Washington Post*, "Hustler's 'Moral Hypocrites' Hit List," July 11, 2007.

262 Owen M. Spiegler, Letter to the editor, *Pittsburgh Tribune-Review*, "We owe Larry Flynt," July 15, 2007.

263 Eve Conant, et al., *Newsweek*, "Scandal: Follow the numbers," August 15, 2007.

264 Transcript, National Public Radio, *Talk of the Nation*, "Private Errors, Public Lives," August 2, 2007. (Guests: Eric Dezenhall and Dan Moldea)

265 Jonathan Tilove, Newhouse News Service, "Noir Character/Nice Guy at Center of D.C. Sex Scandal," July 26, 2007.

266 Howard Kurtz, *Washington Post*, "Morals of a Muckraker," August 8, 2007. Notably, Kurtz never seemed to have much regard for me, so I was quite nervous about his upcoming article. When he sent me a note on August 7, saying that it would appear the following day, I sent him back an email, asking, "One question: Come tomorrow, will I be dead or alive?"
 Kurtz replied, "Very much alive, I believe."
 Although the story was certainly no valentine, reporter Kurtz, who had the power to kill me, allowed me to live.

267 Burton had served on the legal teams for former CIA intelligence agent Aldrich H. Ames, former FBI Special Agent Robert Hanssen, and Monica Lewinsky during Kenneth Starr's pursuit of President Clinton.

268 Letter from Preston Burton to Deborah Jeane Palfrey, "Re: *United States v. Palfrey*," July 30, 2007.

269 Palfrey sent an email on January 7, 2008, to Blair Sibley, finally conceding that there was "no massive government conspiracy by [the government] to get me. . . . [T]here is no monumental effort to destroy me, as much as there is one hell of a mess which someone must find an exit strategy, for the sake of all involved."

270 Joe Palazzolo, *Legal Times*, "Courtroom Fireworks Predicted as D.C. Madam Trial Opens," April 7, 2008.

271 Dana Milbank, *Washington Post*, "The D.C. Madam Case, All Sordid Out," April 11, 2008.

272 Adam Zagorin, *Time*, "D.C. Madam: Suicide Before Prison," May 1, 2008.

273 Paul Duggan and Amy Shipley, *Washington Post*, "Operator of D.C. Call-Girl Ring Is Dead in Apparent Suicide," May 2, 2008.

274 Geraldo Rivera, Fox News, *Geraldo*, "Alex Jones on D.C. Madam," May 3, 2008.

275 Albrecht's broadcasted this radio show on the We the People Network via WTPRN.com on May 2, 2008.

276 Greg Simmons, Fox News, "Death of D.C. Madam Becomes Rich Ground for Conspiracy Theory," May 1, 2008.

In addition, on December 22, 2008, Flynt's staff published a story, "The D.C. Madam Was Murdered!" on his personal website, *LarryFlynt.com*, based upon an interview with Jeanette Maier, a.k.a. "The Canal Street Madam," who insisted—with absolutely no evidence—that Jeane Palfrey had been the victim of foul play.

277 Patrick J. Lyons, *New York Times*, "Skepticism and Sadness After Death of D.C. Madam," May 2, 2008.

278 Bruce Leshan, WUSA-9, "Despite her apparent suicide, lawyers for the DC madam tell 9News Now that her legal case will continue," May 3, 2008.

279 Montgomery Sibley, *Why Just Her: The Judicial Lynching of the D.C. Madam, Deborah Jeane Palfrey*. (Full Court Press, 2009).

280 No byline, *BBC News*, "James Murdoch denies 'code of silence' over hacking," November 10, 2011.

Part Twelve

281 The 1997 series ran in the July 27-August 2 and August 3-9 editions of the *Detroit Sunday Journal*. Among other things, Betzold publicly revealed the name of the eyewitness who had identified Salvatore Briguglio as one of the people sitting in the car that Jimmy Hoffa entered at the Red Fox on the day of his disappearance. However, during a police lineup, this witness could not positively identify Briguglio, who most law-enforcement officials

and reporters involved in the investigation continued to believe had actually killed Hoffa.

Betzold also named the person who saw Hoffa in the passenger-side rear seat as the car traveled south on Telegraph Road. According to this man, Hoffa was yelling at the driver, who he believed but could not confirm was Chuck O'Brien.

On September 7, 2001, reporters Norman Sinclair and David Shepardson of the *Detroit News* broke a story revealing that a DNA test confirmed that a strand of Hoffa's hair had been found in the back of the car that Chuck O'Brien was driving on the day Hoffa disappeared. However, no charges have ever been filed against O'Brien or anyone else specifically for Hoffa's murder.

282 In March 2005, Ashenfelter shipped me several large boxes, which contained his extra copy of the Hoffex case file—all of the nearly 17,000 pages.

283 *Hoffex Memo*, pp. 35-37.

284 FBI report from Special Agent Robert J. Garrity to the Detroit Field Office, December 22, 1975, pp. D-F.

285 *Hoffex Memo*, pp. 3-4.

286 David Ashenfelter, *Detroit Free Press*, "Hoffa mystery gets deeper in new tale," March 13, 2004.

287 In Sheeran and Zeitts's collaboration agreement—which they signed on August 10, 1994—the two men agreed to split all royalties evenly. However, Sheeran allowed Zeitts to take 75 percent of any publisher's advance they might receive. Also, on February 23, 1995, Sheeran wrote a letter to Hoffa's daughter, Barbara Crancer, introducing her to Zeitts and asking her to "answer any questions that Mr. Zeitts" might have. Sheeran identified Zeitts as his "biographer." (Zeitts, who gave me all of his videotapes of Sheeran in 2009, died on December 28, 2011.)

288 Harry Jay Katz, a publicist who was a third party to a 1995 collaboration contract between Sheeran and Zeitts, told reporter Kitty Caparella that Sheeran had "blamed the late Attorney General John Mitchell and the late ex-President Richard Nixon, who gave Hoffa a pardon with restrictions, with arranging the contract with Bufalino in the early 1970s." In an earlier

scenario, also while working with Zeitts, Sheeran had credited Vietnam mercenaries with Hoffa's murder.

Katz also told Caparella that he had arranged for Sheeran to be interviewed with NBC-TV's Washington Bureau by his friend Maria Shriver. Katz said Sheeran was interviewed for "seven or eight hours" in Katz's home, but Shriver's report was never broadcast. (See: Kitty Caparella, *Philadelphia Daily News*, "Harry Katz: Sheeran said he killed Hoffa," March 17, 2004.)

Notably, Sheeran wrote a letter to Barbara Crancer on or about March 13, 1993, in which he denied any role in her father's murder. However, Caparella reported that Sheeran had supposedly told Katz in 1996 that he "shot Hoffa in the car and took him to an undisclosed location" in Detroit.

289 Sheeran further suggested in the book that Hoffa and his friends in the Mafia were behind the assassination of President Kennedy in 1963. Specifically, Sheeran claimed that he had delivered "a duffel bag with three rifles in it" to Carlos Marcello's personal pilot, David Ferrie "a few days to a week before" the President's murder (See: Brandt, pp. 163, 241-242.)

290 Both Brandt and Sheeran had signed a publishing contract with Running Press Book Publishers, a subsidiary of Perseus Books, on May 8, 2003. The completed manuscript was due on June 1. Brandt and Sheeran received $20,000 upon signing the contract and were to receive another $20,000 upon publication. The copyright was in Brandt's name alone.

291 Charles Brandt, *I Heard You Paint Houses: Frank "The Irishman" Sheeran & The Inside Story of the Mafia, the Teamsters, and the Last Ride of Jimmy Hoffa* (Steerforth Press: Hanover, New Hampshire, 2004), p. 284.

292 Brandt, p. 286.

293 Transcript, *CNN Live Saturday*, "Charles Brandt, Author," July 31, 2004.

294 Eric Shawn, Fox News, "Detroit House Searched for Clues in Hoffa Case," June 13, 2004. In addition, Sheeran confessed to twenty-five murders, including those of mobster Joey Gallo in 1972 and Salvatore Briguglio in 1978. Notably, along with the Hoffa hit, Sheeran's self-proclaimed roles in these killings are in dispute.

295 Eric Shawn, Fox News, "Detroit House Searched for Clues in Hoffa Case," May 28, 2004.

ENDNOTES

296 In yet another discrepancy, Sheeran sent a letter on March 15, 1993, to Hoffa's daughter, Barbara Crancer, in which he included a handwritten note, saying: "On July 28 or July 29, 1975, I had a conversation with your Father on the phone. We set [an] appointment to meet Saturday, August 2, 1975 at his residence at Lake Orion, Michigan, as he was not going to attend Bill Bufalino's daughter's wedding [on] Aug 1, 1975, that was Friday evening."

Sheeran made no mention of Hoffa asking him for protection at the meeting with Giacalone and Provenzano.

297 In 1975, the house was owned by an unmarried, retired school teacher, 79-year-old Martha Sellers, who had died in 1995. According to several sources, Sellers had an unnamed boarder, who rented an upstairs bedroom and had access to the entire house.

298 Brandt, p. 257.

299 As of this writing, Robert De Niro has purchased the rights to the Sheeran-Brandt book and is reportedly in the process of working with Martin Scorsese, Al Pacino, and Joe Pesci to produce a motion picture based on that work. Oscar-winning screenwriter Steven Zaillian has been commissioned to write the screenplay.

Brandt told reporter Harry F. Themal of the *News Journal* of Wilmington, Delaware, in a story published on March 19, 2011, that he received a $40,000 option, along with the promise of an additional $80,000 when the film actually goes into production. It is not clear how much of the money Brandt will share with Sheeran's heirs.

Dolores Miller, one of Sheeran's three daughters, told reporter Annette Witheridge of the U.K.'s *Daily Mail* that her father had given her his power of attorney before he died.

300 Brandt, p. 261. Inspired by Brandt's work, Jeffry Scott Hansen, a police officer, published his own book in 2009, *Digging for the Truth: The Final Resting Place of Jimmy Hoffa* (Spectre Publishing), in which he claimed that Hoffa's body was cremated at Evergreen Cemetery in Detroit.

301 David Ashenfelter, *Detroit Free Press*, "Was Hoffa killed inside this home?" May 29, 2004. After hearing about all this, a former top FBI official in Detroit sent me an email, simply saying, "I still think [Hoffa] was killed by Sal Briguglio, that Chuckie O'Brien was driving, and that he ended up in a mulching machine in Inkster."

302 Bryan Burrough, *New York Times Book Review*, "Killing Him Sofly," June 20, 2004.

303 *Hoffex Memo*, pp. 46-47, 48.

304 Moldea, *The Hoffa Wars*, p. 375.

305 David Ashenfelter and Joe Swickard, *Detroit Free Press*, "FBI director calls Hoffa tip credible," May 18, 2006.

306 David Ashenfelter and Joe Swickard, *Detroit Free Press*, "Inmate's tip leads FBI to dig for Hoffa at farm," May 18, 2006.

307 Sarah Karush and Pete Yost, Associated Press via the *New York Times*, "FBI told in 1976 of possible Hoffa site," May 20, 2006.

308 David Ashenfelter, *Detroit Free Press*, "Lawyer: FBI knew Hoffa tip years ago," May 21, 2006.

309 David Shepardson and Paul Egan, *Detroit News*, "Dig for Hoffa could cost up to $500 K," May 23, 2006.

310 Paul Egan, *Detroit News*, "Hoffa hunt cost questioned," May 29, 2006.

311 Micheline Maynard, *New York Times*, "FBI Calls Off Its Latest Search for Hoffa," May 31, 2006.

312 Paul Egan and John Wisely, *Detroit News*, "Hoffa dig ends. Mystery lives on," May 31, 2006.

313 I had been personally devastated by the sudden death of 55-year-old John Sikorski, my long-time friend and "brother" since his days at PROD. John had first explained the background of Rolland McMaster to me on August 5, 1975, while I was with NBC News. On August 23, 2008, John did not feel well after a quick jog in his neighborhood in Northampton, Massachusetts. As John's physician-wife, Anne, was driving him to the hospital, he had a massive heart attack and was pronounced dead soon after. John and Anne had two children, Kim and Christy. I did one of the eulogies at his funeral.

314 Married to his third wife, the former Marilyn A. Turner, at the time of his death, Rolland McMaster was divorced from Elaine Mastaw, his second wife. (He divorced his first wife, Yvonne, in 1961.)

Stanton Barr was married to Elaine Mastaw's sister, Terry, for 54 years. Terry Barr died on November 12, 2012.

315 From June 17-19, 2013, another FBI-led search for Jimmy Hoffa captured national headlines, based on information provided by Anthony Zerilli, a former top leader of the Detroit underworld.

Tony Zerilli's father was Joseph Zerilli, the long-time boss of the Detroit Mafia, also known as "The Detroit Partnership." During the early 1970s, the elderly Zerilli handed the day-to-day operations to his son. However, Tony Zerilli, the acting boss, was indicted and convicted on federal racketeering charges and went to prison in 1974, forcing Joe Zerilli to leave his emeritus status and return to the throne. He served as the boss until his death in October 1977.

In the midst of his tenure, he appointed Jack Tocco as his underboss. (Tocco's father, William, had married Joe Zerilli's sister.)

While Joe Zerilli and Jack Tocco were running The Partnership, Jimmy Hoffa disappeared on July 30, 1975. And because Detroit mobsters—such as Tony and Vito Giacalone—were likely involved in the murder conspiracy, Zerilli and Tocco must have given their approval for this crime.

Shortly after Zerilli died in 1977, Tocco assumed control of the Detroit Mafia. And after Tony Zerilli's release from prison in 1979, Tocco appointed Zerilli as his underboss.

First cousins, Tocco and Zerilli were not thugs. They were both college educated—with degrees in finance from the University of Detroit. Also, they were both Mafia royalty in that they each had married daughters of Joseph Profaci, who headed one of New York's Five Families until his death in 1962.

Tony Zerilli had a reputation as a bad-tempered man who shot off his mouth. During the early 1960s, he was caught on an FBI recording device, plotting to kidnap Jimmy Hoffa. Apparently, that talk never went passed the discussion stage.

Reporter Scott Burnstein, who specializes on investigations of the Detroit underworld, told me that Tocco and other Detroit gangsters had held Zerilli responsible for unwittingly providing information to federal law-enforcement officials about The Partnership's illegal activities, including its hidden ownership of a major casino in Las Vegas. The federal investigation led to the 1996 RICO indictments and subsequent convictions of nearly the entire hierarchy of the Detroit Mafia, including Jack Tocco and Tony Zerilli, both of whom went to prison.

When Zerilli was released in 2008, Tocco, as punishment for his indiscretions, had already demoted him and declared him as a *persona non grata*. Out respect for Zerilli's father and father in law, Tocco allowed Zerilli to live, but he left him in the wilderness, without a family and with no real money. According to Burnstein, "Tocco took away Zerilli's stripes and put him on the shelf."

Consequently, the 85-year-old Zerilli, looking for a score, cooperated with reporters Marc Santia at WNBC in New York and Kevin Dietz of WDIV in Detroit. Hoping to sell his story, Zerilli told them that he knew where Jimmy Hoffa was buried, citing a specific property in Oakland Township, about twenty miles north of the Red Fox.

On January 13, 2013, the two reporters went wide with their exclusive story. Simultaneously, Zerilli created a website, "HoffaFound.com," saying: "Federal agents have claimed Anthony Zerilli is a main character in the infamous unsolved mystery regarding the disappearance of Jimmy Hoffa, according to NBC. Zerilli is finally breaking his silence after decades of refusing to answer any questions."

Upon the public release of this information, investigators went to the local land records office and discovered that in 1975 the property was owned by Jack Tocco.

As soon as that story broke, I issued a statement on my website, saying: "If Zerilli is doing this in a cynical effort to seek revenge on Jack Tocco, the FBI will see right through it. But, if Zerilli is giving the FBI details that are consistent with what is already known, then his story could be extremely important. We are waiting for the FBI to weigh in."

Five months later, on June 17, the FBI started an excavation of the property.

I appeared on CNN that afternoon, saying, "When the FBI takes these things seriously, I take these things seriously. I've been involved in this thing now for thirty-eight years. We would like to see this thing end once and for all. We would like to see this case solved."

The following day—Day Two of the three-day dig—I received a copy of a twenty-one-page PDF download that Zerilli was selling on his website for $4.99. His version of events for Hoffa's murder—supposedly based on what Tony Giacalone had told him—completely shocked me while simultaneously making me even more skeptical of his story. According to this account, Jack Tocco had ordered Hoffa killed and instructed Giacalone to handle the details.

ENDNOTES

Giacalone allegedly told Zerilli that he and his brother, Vito, had gone to the Red Fox, ostensibly to pick up Hoffa. However, because the backseat of their car was loaded with boxes, they told Hoffa that there was no room for him, adding that he should get in the car behind them. In that second car, according to Zerilli, were Peter Vitale and Jimmy Quasarano with Anthony Palazzolo behind the wheel.

Zerilli then claimed that these three Mafia guys took Hoffa to the Tocco property. Upon their arrival, Hoffa was pulled from of the car and tied up. Quasarano supposedly hit Hoffa in the head with a shovel after which he was thrown into a pre-dug hole. Zerilli said that he was still alive when they buried him and placed a "cement slab" over his grave.

Meantime, Zerilli absolved Tony Provenzano and his supporting cast in New Jersey of any role in the abduction and murder. There was no mention of Chuck O'Brien, Frank Sheeran, or Rolland McMaster.

The simplicity of Zerilli's story was impressive—inasmuch as the same characters, all Detroit mobsters, were allegedly responsible for Hoffa's pickup, murder, and disposal. But I just could not imagine Hoffa getting into a car alone with these three hard-core Mafia figures, especially Vitale and Quasarano whom he had known and done business with years earlier. He was well aware of how dangerous they were.

Contacting me for comment after I had read Zerilli's statement, the *Detroit Free Press* reported:

> Dan Moldea, author of *The Hoffa Wars* who has been following Hoffa's disappearance for decades, said he's not sure he buys Zerilli's story and sees some holes in it.
>
> "Why would they keep the trophy buried in the backyard?" Moldea said, referring to Hoffa's body. "You chop up a body. You burn a body. You don't leave it laying around for it to be found. I'm just kind of surprised that they would allow the body to remain intact."

But, to me, there was an even bigger problem, which NBC News explained:

> Zerilli's overall account also differs in several ways from the accumulated evidence regarding Hoffa's disappearance, according to Moldea.

"This is very problematic for a lot of people, myself included, if the body is found out there," Moldea said. "The scenario that Zerilli is putting out there is basically saying, 'Forget everything you've ever heard about the Hoffa case, here's the whole new scenario.' It would be dismissing 38 years of intelligence."

On Day Three of the dig, ABC's *Good Morning America* allowed me to repeat my admonition in a filmed report, saying:

> Still, others are skeptical about Zerilli's claims, arguing it's a ploy to push his new book.
>
> Moldea (on screen): "It's a complete departure from all the intelligence we have heard about this case over the past 38 years."

Later that morning, the FBI called off the search, declaring that nothing relevant to the Hoffa investigation had been found.

When the Associated Press called and asked me why solving the Hoffa case still mattered, I replied: "An American citizen vanished in broad daylight from a public street in an American city without a trace. There are countries where that is a daily occurrence—but that cannot be tolerated in America. . . . It's legitimate for the FBI to keep investigating and searching when the evidence, the timelines, and the cast of characters are right."

Part Thirteen

316 I interviewed Gene Klein the owner of the San Diego Chargers, at his Del Rayo Racing Stables in Rancho Santa Fe, California, on September 9, 1988.

317 Tony Batt, *Gambling Compliance*, "Author Says National Football League Wants Its Own Sportsbooks," October 18, 2017.

318 Thom Loverro, *Washington Times*, "NFL catches life preserver from Supreme Court with legalized sports gambling ruling," May 16, 2018.

319 Erin Cox and Ovetta Wiggins, *Washington Post*, "Redskins seek sports betting license in Virginia even as they lobby for one in Maryland," February 9, 2020.

320 The best and most responsible critic of the conspiracy crowd in the RFK murder case is the British researcher and author, Mel Ayton. Along with his 2007 book, *The Forgotten Terrorist: Sirhan Sirhan and the Assassination of Robert F. Kennedy* (Potomac Books)—which was reprinted in a second edition in 2019—Ayton is also the author of *Plotting to Kill the President: Assassination Attempts from Washington to Hoover* (Potomac Books, 2017) and *Hunting the President: Threats, Plots, and Assassination Attempts—From FDR to Obama*. In addition, he has been a history consultant for the BBC, the National Geographic Channel, and the Discovery Channel.

321 Zac Stuart-Pontier—an Emmy and Peabody Award-winning journalist who is also the co-host and senior producer of the *Crimetown* podcast—broadcast a multi-part audio series about the murder of Senator Kennedy during the summer of 2018. The first seven parts appeared to make the case for conspiracy. However, part eight, which featured an interview with me, started to deflect the storyline that Sirhan was an innocent man wrongly accused. The deflection was complete on August 14, 2018, in part nine, which was pretty much all about my work. In the end, Stuart-Pontier, who produced an excellent and courageous piece of broadcast journalism, agreed with me that Sirhan did it and did alone.

322 Jahoda died of liver disease on May 7, 2004.

323 Because of a personal falling out I had with conservative-Republican Jack Platt—over my work with Larry Flynt in support of President Clinton during the impeachment drama in 1998-99—I did not stand for retention on the HTG board after two years. However, long term, Platt and I patched things up and still remained friends.

324 Gus Russo and Eric Dezenhall, *Best of Enemies: The Last Great Spy Story of the Cold War* (New York: Twelve, 2018).

325 I added an appendix to the 2018 reprint of my RFK book, "Did Jimmy Hoffa, Carlos Marcello, and Santo Trafficante Kill President John Kennedy?" It was the text of an address I delivered to The Mob Museum in Las Vegas on October 24, 2017. See: https://www.moldea.com/MobMuseum10242017.pdf

Part Fourteen

326 For a copy of the 1979 Sheeran letter to me, see: https://www.moldea.com/Sheeran-threatens-to-sue-Moldea.pdf

327 Micheline Maynard, *New York Times*, "F.B.I. Calls Off Its Latest Search for Hoffa," May 31, 2006.

328 Scott Burnstein, *Gangster Report*, "Detroit Mafia Associate Says Jimmy Hoffa Had His Last Stand at Lenny Schultz's House," January 4, 2020.

329 See: https://twitter.com/DanMoldea/status/1024141935307567104

330 Dan E. Moldea, *Moldea.com*, "Who is Vinnie Ravo? After 42 years, a possible new cast member emerges in the mystery of the disposal of Jimmy Hoffa," July 20, 2017. See: https://www.moldea.com/HOFFA-RAVO.pdf

331 Via Fox Nation, Eric Shawn released the second part of *Riddle: The Search for Jimmy Hoffa*, on November 18, 2019. Part Three was broadcast on March 17, 2020.

332 Also, I gave Eric Shawn a letter that the late former FBI Special Agent Ken Walton of Detroit, a long-time friend of mine, had sent to me on July 11, 2004, shortly after the release of *I Heard You Paint Houses*. Walton, who spent many years investigating the Hoffa murder, wrote: "Regarding Jimmy and the latest [revelations] by Frank Sheeran, I don't buy it, and when I spoke to Eric Shawn, . . . I told him the same thing. . . . I still [think] he was killed by Sal Briguglio."

On September 25, 2019, I blogged about a videotape in the Zeitts archive in which Sheeran had claimed on film that another reporter and I were misled by the FBI to believe that the Teamsters and the Mafia were behind Hoffa's murder when, according to Sheeran in this recording, the person who engineered the killing was former U.S. Attorney General John Mitchell, which, of course, was ridiculous.

333 Jack Goldsmith, *In Hoffa's Shadow: A Stepfather, a Disappearance in Detroit, and My Search for the Truth* (New York: Farrar, Straus and Giroux. 2019) p. 294.

334 Zack Sharf, *IndieWire*, "Robert De Niro Defends *The Irishman* Against Claims It's Based on an Untrue Story," November 13, 2019.

335 Eric Shawn, Fox Nation, "Exclusive: FBI wants to talk to subjects of Fox Nation's Jimmy Hoffa investigation," January 15, 2020.

336 Dates of deaths of persons of interest in the Hoffa-murder case (*) interviewed by Dan Moldea:
* Thomas Andretta: January 25, 2018
* Stanton Barr: November 13, 2019
* Salvatore Briguglio: March 21, 1978
Russell Bufalino: February 25, 1994
* William Bufalino: May 12, 1990
* Frank Cappola: March 16, 2020
Paul Cappola, Sr.: March 8, 2008
Anthony Giacalone: February 23, 2001
Vito Giacalone: February 19, 2012
* Lawrence McHenry: January 17, 1994
* Rolland McMaster: October 25, 2007
* Phillip Moscato, Sr.: February 16, 2014
* Charles O'Brien, February 13, 2020
Ralph Picardo (federal witness): January 26, 2004
Anthony Provenzano: December 12, 1988
* Salvatore Provenzano: May 27, 2013
* Jack Robison: July 27, 2003
* Leonard Schultz: September 6, 2013
* Jim Shaw: March 31, 1987
* Frank Sheeran: December 13, 2003
* Donovan Wells (federal witness): August 5, 2019

Still alive, as of this writing (May 15, 2020):
* Gabriel Briguglio, living in New Jersey
* Stephen Andretta, living in New Jersey

The author in 1975.

Photo by Michael deBlois

www.ingramcontent.com/pod-product-compliance
Lightning Source LLC
Chambersburg PA
CBHW021147230426
43667CB00006B/280